Advance Praise for *Anthropology: Asking Questions About Human Origins, Diversity, and Culture*

" Again and again, these authors jettison tired old concepts from mid-twentieth-century anthropology and present a current synthesis of key concepts, cutting-edge examples, and backing theories and explanations in a very accessible way. "
—Ramie A. Gougeon, *University of West Florida*

" I was really drawn in by each chapter introduction, followed by the questions to engage critical thinking. I would definitely use this in my course. I also love that there is a chapter on sustainability. "
—Jaclyn McWhorter, *Agnes Scott College*

" Chapter 10 has an excellent opening story. The text I currently use does not address the biocultural implications, especially for health and disease, of human variation. "
—Molly Zuckerman, *Mississippi State University*

" This book would be an ideal fit for my course. It offers students a comprehensive guide to the broader relevancy of anthropology and focuses their attention on the ways that their lives are shaped by culture. "
—Megan D. Parker, *Georgia Perimeter College*

" The approach of this book meets and exceeds my expectations. It's organized in a student-friendly way that will hold the attention of the modern college student. "
—Katie Binetti, *Baylor University*

Anthropology: Asking Questions About Human Origins, Diversity, and Culture provides students with a cutting-edge and integrative vision of Anthropology

Although my graduate training was as a cultural anthropologist, the holistic approach that embraced linguistic anthropology, archaeology and prehistory, and biological anthropology has been part of my professional life as an anthropologist from the moment I began my dissertation research. These concerns were heightened during my years studying museum collections, where comparative analysis often drew holistically on collections in the zoology, botany, or geology departments. The holistic approach, as we present it in this book, is merely an expansion on what most anthropologists already do, without necessarily realizing the diverse evidence they have implicitly linked together to draw some conclusion. If you don't believe me, consider your own research or one of your lectures, and then compare it with an introduction to psychology, economics, or political science textbook.

Robert L. Welsch

Because I was an undergraduate religion major—and then a graduate student at Princeton, which is focused solely on cultural anthropology—I have to admit that four-field anthropology does not run deep in my intellectual veins. But in recent years that has been changing for me. Some of it comes from the opportunity to teach in a four-field department, but even more so, it has come from the process of writing this book with two great colleagues who do approach matters holistically. Working through rich issues, like the biocultural synthesis and materiality, has really proved to me the power that holistic anthropology has to explain complex issues, and I see it as more necessary than ever.

Luis A. Vivanco

Trying to relate what anthropology is and does is no easy task. Writing an engaging, informative, and holistic textbook gives students the opportunity to experience how anthropologists study and think about what it means to be human. The final product you hold in your hands is not just a textbook for classes, but an invitation to glimpse into the world of anthropology—the world that all three of us love.

Agustín Fuentes

On the following pages, take a look at three chapters that offer a fresh, contemporary, and holistic view of Anthropology . . .

Human Biocultural Evolution

9 CHAPTER

Emergence of the Biocultural Animal

Sleeping is one of the most important aspects of human life. We spend about a third of our lives doing it, and our daily well-being is shaped by how much of it we get. Over time, regular sleep deprivation can lead to more serious maladies like memory loss, depression, chronic illness, and even death. Because our bodies need it, it is common to think of sleeping in terms of its biological functions. This view is supported by research that shows the critical role of sleeping in human cognitive development, hormonal regulation, long-term memory and learning, energy conservation, and physical restoration.

But sleep also has complex cultural and behavioral dimensions. How, when, where, and with whom people sleep are patterned by collective social expectations, moralities, and available paraphernalia such as bedding, head rests, and so on (Mauss 1973; Glaskin and Chenhall 2013). Because they are learned, sleep practices are a key site of enculturation in every society. Although North Americans tend to think of sleep as something to do in private, many people around the world view it as a social activity and sleep in groups. The cross-cultural diversity surrounding how people think about and engage in sleep argues against viewing it as a solely biological phenomenon.

For all of these reasons, sleep is, from a holistic anthropological perspective, a complex **biocultural** phenomenon that intertwines

---

Sleeping as a Biocultural Phenomenon The human behavior of sleeping is variable and plastic across our species. Because sleeping involves the complex intertwining of biological, evolutionary, and cultural processes, it is useful to approach it as a biocultural phenomenon.

IN THIS CHAPTER

How Do Biocultural Patterns Affect Evolution?
- Inheritance Involves Multiple Systems
- Evolutionary Processes Are Developmentally Open-Ended
- Niche Construction and Ecological Inheritance
- The Importance of Constructivist Evolutionary Approaches for Biocultural Anthropology

How Does Behavior Evolve?
- Prominent Approaches
- Why These Approaches Oversimplify Matters
- A Contemporary Biocultural Approach to the Evolution of Human Behavior

Are Modern Humans Evolving?
- The Impact of Disease on Evolution
- Culture, Morphology, and Evolution

Where Are Biocultural Evolutionary Patterns Taking Us?
- Global Population and Human Density
- Genetic Manipulation
- Adaptive Behavioral Patterns

237

Chapter 9: Human Biocultural Evolution explores how biocultural patterns affect evolution, how behavior evolves, if modern humans are evolving, and where biocultural evolutionary patterns are taking us. The *Anthropologist as Problem Solver* feature on **pages 253 and 254** discusses the **biocultural and evolutionary dimensions of obesity.** This holistic example shows that, from a biocultural perspective, obesity is a complex metabolic syndrome—or combination of medical conditions—that has some genetic dimensions, but also non-genetic ones. We now understand that it's a mix of biological and cultural factors that contributes to weight gain.

Anthropologist as Problem Solver
Clarifying the Biocultural and Evolutionary Dimensions of Obesity

Obese Morphology.

The past sixty years have seen a dramatic global rise in obesity, which is the creation of excess body fat to the point of impairing bodily health and function, and of people being overweight, or having abnormal fat accumulation. There are now more overweight and obese people in the world than undernourished people, and several dozen countries have obesity rates exceeding 10% of their populations. Because these conditions can cause chronic diseases—diabetes and heart disease among them—health officials and researchers consider them to be among the most serious public health crises facing our world today. Because of our detailed knowledge of human relationships with food, morphology, and socioeconomic patterns, holistic anthropology has important contributions to make to address this crisis.

The ability to become obese is a universal human trait. But it was essentially non-existent until about 10,000 years ago (Brown 1991). Although historically obesity is associated with the wealthy, the situation is reversed in industrialized nations like the United States, where rates of obesity among the poor have far surpassed those of the wealthy. This fact has led to two explanations that have captured the public imagination and shaped national dialogue about the matter. One is that cheap, processed fast foods cause obesity and that some people simply cannot resist the temptations of food that is bad for them. In these terms, obesity is a problem of simply not having the individual willpower to control oneself in the face of tempting and inexpensive foods.

The other explanation is some version of the "thrifty gene hypothesis," which holds that certain groups of people evolved to metabolize energy efficiently, which helps them when food is scarce. But in times of abundance, these same

people are predisposed to gain weight quickly because their bodies are ill-equipped to handle the extra calories (Neel 1962). Both of these explanations assume that eating "bad" foods that diverge from the normal human diet causes obesity (Leonard 2002). As appealing as these explanations may sound, however, they wrongly assume that humans have a "normal" diet, which is not the case. As omnivores, our dietary physiology evolved to be open-ended, leaving our needs to be met within the natural environments and socioeconomic and cultural contexts in which we live.

Deep in our evolutionary past, hominins evolved traits that promote the accumulation and storage of energy as adipose tissue, or fat. These traits likely developed for lean times when food was less available, but they are also linked to the demands of our developing brains, and, among females, to fertility. As a result, there are genetic dimensions to obesity (Choquet and Meyre 2011), but there is no single gene (thrifty gene) that causes individuals to gain a lot of weight, and obesity is definitely not genetically determined anyway.

From a biocultural perspective, obesity is a complex metabolic syndrome, or combination of medical conditions, that has some genetic dimensions but also non-genetic ones. Factors like maternal health and diet during pregnancy as well as local environmental conditions can influence an individual's predisposition. For example, smoking, insufficient nutrition during pregnancy, socioeconomic class, high temperatures in the natural environment, and certain environmental toxins all appear to be linked to a higher likelihood of developing obesity later in life. Cultural factors also shape access to food and how much is consumed at a meal. Furthermore, obesity is not inevitable. Although individuals may be predisposed to gain weight more easily than others, it can only develop if a person eats a lot of food while expending little energy (Ulijaszek and Lofink 2006). We now understand that it is a mix of biological and cultural factors that contributes to weight gain.

What contributions do biocultural insights have on public efforts to tackle obesity? One major point is that obesity cannot be successfully addressed as a public health issue by reducing it to a matter of an individual's willpower, "thrifty genes," and/or genetic predispositions, all of which have often led to failed diets or inappropriate medical solutions. Obesity is a complex emergent phenomenon that

(continued)

The Body

Biocultural Perspectives on Health and Illness

In April 2009, breaking news headlines flashed across Americans' TV screens and newspapers, announcing that a deadly new strain of influenza, identified as swine flu, had killed more than 100 people in Mexico City. Influenza virus spreads rapidly through direct contact between individuals, especially hand to hand. But the response to this outbreak demonstrates that disease, even when the biological agent is clear, is about more than viruses and human biology. People in Mexico, the United States, China, and Egypt responded differently to the same outbreak.

In Mexico the epidemic produced a rapid and vigorous response. The government closed schools and universities. The busy streets of Mexico City were practically empty as Mexicans hunkered down in their homes. People wore surgical masks if they went out into the streets.

Soon a few cases were confirmed in several American cities among people who had recently visited Mexico. Intense TV and radio coverage prompted the White House and the Centers for Disease Control (CDC) to issue daily reports. But they seemed to heighten rather than calm public anxiety. Several prominent anti-immigration politicians called for sealing the border with Mexico. Even after six months there had been many fewer deaths in the United States than the more than 20,000 deaths each winter from ordinary seasonal flu.

Swine Flu and Cultural Differences   In Mexico City, many people responded to the threat of swine flu by wearing surgical masks in public spaces, such as the subway pictured here. In other countries, where ideas about contagion and illness differ, people responded differently.

IN THIS CHAPTER

How Should We Make Sense of the Biological and Cultural Factors That Jointly Shape Our Bodily Experiences?
- Uniting Mind and Matter: A Biocultural Perspective
- Culture and Mental Illness

What Do We Mean by Health and Illness?
- The Individual Subjectivity of Illness
- The "Sick Role": Social Expectations of Illness

How and Why Do Doctors and Other Health Practitioners Gain Social Authority?
- The Disease–Illness Distinction: Professional and Popular Views of Sickness
- The Medicalization of the Non-medical

How Does Healing Happen?
- Clinical Therapeutic Processes
- Symbolic Therapeutic Processes
- Social Support
- Persuasion: The Placebo Effect

What Can Anthropology Contribute to Addressing Global Health Problems?
- Understanding Global Health Problems
- Anthropological Contributions to Tackling the International HIV/AIDS Crisis

Chapter 11: The Body discusses the linkages between **biology, culture, health and illness, and how healing happens.** On **pages 298 and 299,** coauthor Rob Welsch shares his experience of suffering from malaria while conducting fieldwork among the Ningerum in Papua New Guinea. He examines the vast cultural difference between his expectations of what would make him feel better, and those of the Ningerum. **This holistic example shows that while culture shapes communities' expectations of the sick role, medical schools and hospitals have created a culture of medicine that often leads to tensions between the views of professionals and those of laypeople.**

This statement demonstrates both the subjectivity of illness and how health and illness are inherently linked to social behavior and expectations, especially when our symptoms impair us so much that we cannot perform the normal social and economic duties expected of us—jobs, school, and, in this case, caring for her family.

To understand when a particular symptom is considered significant enough to provoke someone to seek medical care, we have to understand people's ordinary expectations. In the United States, these expectations are linked to issues like social class, gender, age, the kind of work people perform, and their routine lifestyles. The poor and working class routinely work more physically, eat less healthy food, and pay less attention to their health concerns than do wealthier people. It is not that lower class people do not care about their health, of course. They simply have less time for doctors visits, work in jobs they could lose if they miss a day, and eat the least expensive foods, which as we will discuss in Chapter 15, are the processed foods made available by the industrial food system. And they often have less adequate health insurance or no health insurance at all.

A number of cross-cultural anthropological studies confirm that cultural background also shapes the subjectivity of illness. For example, anthropologist Katherine Dettwyler (2013) conducted research in Mali, a West African nation at the southern edge of the Sahara. There she observed high infection rates of schistosomiasis, a liver and bladder problem caused by a parasitic worm that lives in water. This worm enters the human body through the feet and legs, causing sores on the skin and releasing blood into the urine. Dettwyler found this condition so common in Mali that by puberty nearly all rural men had blood in their urine. Instead of viewing red urine as a shocking symptom, as Americans would, Malian men understood it as a normal condition typical of the transition to adulthood. For these adolescents it meant they were becoming men, not that they were diseased (Figure 11.3).

Americans might interpret Malian understandings as ignorance, and perhaps there is some lack of biomedical knowledge among youth in Mali. But the important point is that people rarely worry about conditions that are common. Just as manual laborers rarely worry about lower back pain, Malian youth never worry about dark urine but see it as normal and even desirable.

The "Sick Role": The Social Expectations of Illness

In all societies around the world, when a person is ill there are expectations of how that person, as well as friends and family, should behave. For Americans this typically means the sick person should skip school or work, stay in bed and rest, be given chicken soup, and so on. But these patterns vary cross-culturally. One of this book's authors, Robert Welsch, experienced this kind of cultural difference while conducting field research in Papua New Guinea among the Ningerum people.

One day Welsch noticed that his body ached all over and his forehead burned with a high fever. It was malaria. At first he retired to his bed to rest, but the fever turned into chills, followed by sweats and an even worse body ache. He took antimalarial pills and aspirin, but the headache became so bad it was unbearable to lay his head on a pillow. Like most Americans he wanted to be by himself and endure this agony alone.

But Ningerum villagers did not sit idly by. As Welsch's condition worsened, more and more of his friends in the village came by the house to sit and chat and smoke. He later realized that most people in the village attributed his sudden symptoms to sorcery: someone

Figure 11.3 Undernourished Adolescent in Mali. This condition is caused by a heavy disease load as much as poor nutrition in the diet.

in the area had used magic to hurt him, and people expected him to die. If it were sorcery, there was nothing anyone in the village could really do for him, but nobody wanted to be accused of having caused his death. The only sure way to avoid suspicion of being a sorcerer was to demonstrate concern. Fortunately for everybody, by the eighth day, the fever broke, and the headache and body aches subsided. The villagers who had been keeping vigil for several days went back to their normal activities.

Welsch and the villagers clearly had very different ideas of how they expect patients and caregivers to behave. Anthropologists and sociologists refer to these unwritten rules as the sick role, or the responsibilities and expected behaviors of sick people by their caregivers (Parsons 1951). To be considered legitimately sick—rather than as malingering, or faking sickness—one must accept specific responsibilities and a new social role, which exempts one from his or her ordinary daily roles and responsibilities such as school or work. Two key aspects of the sick role are to want to get well and to cooperate with medical experts.

A great example of this phenomenon comes from our own childhoods. During cold and flu season in the winter, many schoolchildren feel under the weather and want to stay home. When a parent agrees to it, many kids may decide later in the day that it would be fun to go out and play in the snow. But "Dr. Mom" steps in with her authoritative zeal to explain that if you are sick enough to stay home, you are too sick to go outside to play. Playing outside does not demonstrate that you want to get well—which is a key aspect of American ideas of the sick role—and slipping out of the house in defiance of Dr. Mom's explicit orders to stay in bed is not compliance with her medical expertise.

Welsch found that Ningerum people had a different sick role model, believing that if patients still enjoy a minimum of physical strength, they should themselves deal with the illness. For the Ningerum patient to get help with his or her care and treatment, the patient is obliged to display to family and friends precisely how sick and disabled he or she is. Patients convey this information through their actions or visible physical signs of illness rather than through their words. Startling symptoms such as fainting, bleeding, vomiting, shrieking, and sudden weight loss call family members to action. Patients can also display the severity of their condition by using props like a walking stick to limp cautiously across the village plaza, shedding clothing, refusing to eat, or smearing their chests and legs with mud and dirt. All these actions communicate to family and friends that the patient is sick and (silently) demand that family members show their sincere concern for the patient. Not to do so would suggest that one was not sensitive to a relative's needs—an indifference that, to the Ningerum, whose culture prescribes very close kinship ties, would suggest not being fully human.

While culture shapes a community's expectations of the sick role, our medical schools and hospitals have created a culture of medicine that often leads to tensions between the views of professionals and those of laypeople. These tensions often have to do with the social authority given to doctors that makes the relationship asymmetric, a topic we consider next.

THINKING CRITICALLY ABOUT THE BODY

The "sick role" concept works well for acute diseases like measles, bad colds, and chicken pox. But how might the sick role from an acute infection compare with a chronic condition like diabetes, chronic shortness of breath, or severe arthritis?

Chapter 19: Materiality examines why ownership of artifacts from other cultures can be contentious, how we should look at objects anthropologically, why and how the meanings of things change over time, and the role that material culture plays in constructing the meaning of a community's past. **Page 508** discusses how **Indian activists demanded repatriation** when their cemeteries were desecrated by pot hunters. **Repatriation legislations have created new relationships between native communities and museums, as discussed in the *Anthropologist as Problem Solver* feature on page 511. This holistic example suggests that repatriation is not the inevitable consequence of these changing relationships between indigenous communities and the museums who own traditional objects, because objects help people in all cultures construct meaning.**

Materiality

Constructing Social Relationships and Meanings with Things

Along old U.S. Highway 77 about eight miles south of the town of Brookings, South Dakota, near the intersection with 220th Road is a roadside historical marker that reads:

You Are About to Enter
BROOKINGS COUNTY
home of roving Indians until 1862. The exploring party of Nicollet, scientist, and Fremont, "Pathfinder of the West," visited Oakwood Lakes,
July 1838, leaving the first reliable record.

This marker further explains that the Santee Sioux—the "roving Indians"—"ceded" the eastern part of the county to the U.S. government in 1858 and offers highlights of early white settlement in the years following.

Most people would simply drive by, vaguely registering the marker's presence. But for someone interested in the real history of this place, this marker likely raises more questions than it answers. Just who were these "roving Indians"? Had they always been "roving" or had something happened to make them so? How and why did they "cede" this territory to whites? Here's what we know. Originally, the Santee Sioux had lived in the region around Mille Lacs Lake in what is now east central Minnesota. There they were a sedentary tribe raising corn, squash, and other woodland crops. By 1700 the expansion of British settlers in New York, southern Canada, and New England displaced

Sioux Indians Performing in a Modern Pow Wow.

---

in Colorado; and the Moai statues on Rapa Nui (Easter Island), all of which are typical of what we often think of as ancient historic and prehistoric sites. UNESCO cannot force countries to protect these sites, but it can formally delist a site if the host country fails to protect it from destruction (UNESCO 2015c). Internationally, there is agreement that such archaeological and historical sites belong to all peoples, not just to the governments that happen to control them at any particular moment.

Indian Reactions to Archaeological Excavations of Human Remains

In the United States, "The Tragedy of Slack Farm" aggravated long-brewing tension over who has a moral right to examine, study, and possess the artifacts and bones recovered from archaeological sites. On the one hand, many archaeologists felt that as scientists they had the moral right to excavate, while pot hunters had no rights because they were simply out to make money. Where they excavated, archaeologists also felt that they and their institutions owned the bones because of their labor and research grants. But the laws governing excavations of human remains were highly discriminatory, treating Native Americans differently than Euro-Americans.

A notorious example of this took place in Glenwood, Iowa, in 1971, where archaeologists excavated twenty-seven skeletal remains. Of these skeletons, twenty-six belonged to Euro-American pioneers, and one was that of an Indian woman. Reflecting the same sort of dismissive attitudes that we saw in the Brookings, South Dakota, historical marker, existing Iowa state policy required the Euro-American remains to be reburied, while the Indian skeleton was sent to a local museum for "study." Local Indians protested this disrespectful treatment, and eventually the Indian remains were also reburied (Ubelaker and Grant 1989:253).

The Road to NAGPRA

• **AIM (American Indian movement).** The most prominent and one of the earliest Native American activist groups, founded in 1968.

• **Repatriation.** The return of human remains or cultural artifacts to the communities of descendants of the people to whom they originally belonged.

During the 1970s, activists associated with the **American Indian movement (AIM)**, a prominent Native American rights group founded in 1968, began to protest how national, state, and local officials treated Indian remains. AIM activists asserted that the treatment of Indian remains was an element of a larger pattern of disrespect for Indian cultures. They pointed to histories of forced settlement on reservations; punishment for speaking their native languages in government schools; and pressures on reservations after the Dawes Act of 1887, which allowed reservations to be broken up into individually owned lots that could be sold to white Americans. Calls for **repatriation**, or the return of human remains and artifacts to the communities of descendants of the people to whom they originally belonged, came to stand for something much more important than the objects themselves. Repatriating artifacts became a material symbol of Indian identity itself.

These concerns grew throughout the 1980s. Archaeologists have always held a range of views on whether prehistoric bones should be studied scientifically, reburied after examination, reburied without being studied, or never excavated at all. A number of Indian groups took more radical positions, asserting their right to rebury all Indian bones found in any museum, regardless of whether the bones had a connection to their own tribe (Council for Museum Anthropology 1983). The professor of American Indian Studies James Riding In, who is Pawnee, succinctly expressed his opposition to "scientific grave looting" arguing that excavation of burial sites is and always has been a sacrilege, and all Indian remains should be reburied (Riding In 1996).

The Anthropologist as Problem Solver

John Terrell, Repatriation, and the Maori Meeting House at the Field Museum

At the heart of any Maori community in New Zealand is a meeting house where rituals, business, and other important community processes take place. Meeting houses have elaborately carved images in the posts and ridge poles, which not only symbolize a Maori family's ancestry but embody the spirits of these ancestors as well.

In 1905 The Field Museum of Chicago purchased a nearly complete meeting house named Ruatepapake [roo-ah-tay-pah-**poo**-kay] that originally came from Tokomaru Bay, New Zealand. The museum bought it from a European curio dealer who had convinced one member of the family to sell this house. The structure had been quietly and quickly dismantled and shipped overseas. For the Maori family, this was a shameful act that amounted to selling off their ancestors carved in the boards.

When archaeologist John Terrell became The Field Museum's Curator of Oceanic Archaeology and Ethnology in 1971, he began researching this Maori meeting house. He brought specialists to the museum to examine the carvings, including Hirini (Sidney) Moko Mead, one of the leading Maori anthropologists. Terrell also visited Tokomaru Bay to confirm what he and other specialists had suspected—that this was indeed their meeting house that had been sold and packed off around 1900.

Terrell began working with elders at Tokomaru Bay, discussing the future of the structure. Some of the young people wanted their house and their ancestors to come back to the community. But after talking over the matter with Terrell, the elders agreed to keep the house in Chicago, so long as The Field Museum would work with the community to restore the structure. Terrell, in collaboration with Tokomaru elders, chose Maori curators, conservators, and artists to help with the restoration (Hakiwai and Terrell 1994).

The house went on display for the public in 1986 as part of an exhibition called Te Maori, and Maori elders were invited to help with the opening. Later, more than twenty elders, both men and women, came to Chicago to perform the rituals that would bring their ancestral spirits from the museum's lower level, where the house had been for many decades, to the second floor, where the house would be reassembled. Elders have been involved with planning and executing all important decisions about Ruatepapake ever since. They selected their own Maori curator and conservator, as well as a Maori artist who was tasked with carving new pieces missing from the front of the structure. Maori carver Arapata Hakiwai discovered several boards from this meeting house in Te Papa, the National Museum of New Zealand, and Tokomaru elders requested that these carved boards join the house in Chicago where they belonged, and the museum complied with the request. One carved house board was found in the collections of the Peabody-Essex Museum in Salem, Massachusetts. It too has been reunited with the other boards from Te Papa in Chicago. The people of Tokomaru Bay are now well known by Maori across New Zealand because their meeting house is so prominently displayed overseas. By working with Terrell and The Field Museum, the people of Tokomaru Bay

(continued)

John Terrell at the Maori Meeting House at The Field Museum in Chicago. John Terrell speaking at a workshop held in the meeting house. #GN91326_119d by John Weinstein. (below) The restored meeting house. #A112518c by Diane Alexander White and Linda Dorman. Both courtesy of The Field Museum.

Instructor and Student Support and Alternative Formats

For Students

➢ **Companion Website (www.oup.com/us/welsch):** This free and open-access Companion Website offers chapter outlines, interactive exercises, a glossary of key terms, flashcards, additional links, additional recommended readings, and self-grading review questions.

For Instructors

➢ **Ancillary Resource Center (ARC):** The ARC is a convenient, instructor-focused single destination for resources to accompany *Anthropology: Asking Questions About Human Origins, Diversity, and Culture.* This online resource center, available to adopters of the text, includes:
  ○ An **Instructor's Manual** featuring a comprehensive introduction written by the authors, chapter outlines, learning objectives, key controversies, key terms and definitions and summaries, lecture outlines, PowerPoint slides, web links and blogroll, in-class activities and project assignments, suggestions for class discussion, and an image bank
  ○ A **Computerized Test Bank** written by the authors, offering multiple-choice, true/false, fill-in-the-blank, and essay questions
➢ A selection of **ethnographic video clips** and a complete **Course Management Cartridge** are available to qualified adopters.

Choices

Oxford University Press offers cost-saving alternatives (30% discount for loose-leaf format; 50% discount for eBook format) to meet the needs of all students. You may also customize textbooks to create the course material that you want for your class.

➢ **loose-leaf:** 978-0-19-064781-0
➢ **eBook:** 978-0-19-994762-1

For more information, please contact your Oxford University Press representative or call 800.280.0280.

Package and Save!

Package *Anthropology: Asking Questions About Human Origins, Diversity, and Culture* with an ethnography from the *Issues in Globalization* series for **FREE!**

➢ Martin, *Haunted*
➢ Tassi, *The Native World-System*
➢ Mannon, *City of Flowers*
➢ Davidson, *Sacred Rice*
➢ Hewlett, *Listen, Here is a Story*
➢ Ward, *Gangsters Without Borders*
➢ Gomberg-Muñoz, *Labor and Legality*
➢ Roland, *Cuban Color in Tourism and La Lucha*

Package one of Oxford's *Very Short Introductions* with this text for FREE!

➢ Monaghan/Just, *Social and Cultural Anthropology*
➢ Steger, *Globalization*, Third Edition

Package this text with Vivanco's *Field Notes: A Guided Journal for Doing Anthropology* or Brown's *Writing in Anthropology: A Brief Guide* for **only $5 more!** Or pair with Wagley's *Amazon Town: A Study of Human Life in the Tropics*, Anniversary Edition, **for only $10 more!**

For more information, please contact your Oxford University Press representative or call 800.280.0280.

Anthropology

ASKING QUESTIONS ABOUT HUMAN
ORIGINS, DIVERSITY, AND CULTURE

Robert L. Welsch
FRANKLIN PIERCE UNIVERSITY

Luis A. Vivanco
UNIVERSITY OF VERMONT

Agustín Fuentes
UNIVERSITY OF NOTRE DAME

NEW YORK   OXFORD
OXFORD UNIVERSITY PRESS

Oxford University Press is a department of the University of Oxford. It furthers
the University's objective of excellence in research, scholarship, and education
by publishing worldwide. Oxford is a registered trade mark of Oxford University
Press in the UK and certain other countries.

Published in the United States of America by Oxford University Press
198 Madison Avenue, New York, NY 10016, United States of America.

© 2017 by Oxford University Press

CIP data is on file at the Library of Congress
ISBN 978-0-19-994759-1

9 8 7 6 5 4 3 2 1

Printed by LSC Communications, United States of America

Robert L. Welsch:

To Sarah for her love and support, and to my students, who have nudged me toward a broader and more complex view of the human condition and humanity's remarkable diversity.

Luis Vivanco:

To Peggy, Isabel, Felipe, and Camila for their love and support, and to my students, who have taught me much about the importance of inspired teaching and learning.

Agustín Fuentes:

To all the students in my classes, who listened, learned, spoke up, and pushed me to be a better teacher and a more effective scholar.

Brief Contents

v

Contents

PART I: Key Concepts and Methods in Anthropology 1

1 Anthropology: Asking Questions About Humanity 3

PART III: Human Social Relations 315

12 Early Agriculture and the Neolithic Revolution: Modifying the Environment to Satisfy Human Demands 317

19 Materiality: Constructing Social Relationships and Meanings with Things 503

Letter from the Authors

Dear Reader,

Humans are fascinating and complex beings. With our large brains, flexible diets, and ability to get around on two feet, evolutionary history has made us different from other primates and facilitated our adaptation to practically any environment on the planet. At the same time, we are more than our biology, and there is nothing we do that does not involve culture, which encompasses our capacities for symbolic communication, intensive social cooperation, intergenerational learning, and metaphysical thinking.

These points raise some interesting questions. What is it about our humanity that distinguishes us from other species? What is culture and how does it shape our origins, prehistoric pasts, and present? How do we as humans construct meaningful social worlds? What are the reasons for human biological and cultural diversity? Such questions are at the core of the study of anthropology.

The goal of our textbook is to help students develop the ability to pose good anthropological questions and begin answering them; our inspiration comes from the expression "99% of a good answer is a good question." We present problems and questions that students will find provocative and contemporary, and then use theories, archaeological and ethnographic case studies, and applied perspectives as ways of explaining how anthropologists have looked at these topics over time. Our approach emphasizes what is currently known within the study of anthropology and issues that continue to challenge.

Central to the plan of this book are four underlying principles that guide our approach to anthropology:

- A holistic view of anthropology, emphasizing the complementarity and integration of its subfields.
- Respecting tradition, with a contemporary perspective.
- An emphasis on learning how to ask important and interesting anthropological questions.
- Applying anthropology to understand and solve human problems.

Every chapter and every feature of the book have been written with these principles in mind. We have written a book about anthropology that draws on insights anthropologists have learned during the twentieth century. At the same time, with its cutting-edge content and pedagogy, this is a textbook that provides what students need for the twenty-first century.

For most students, an introductory course in anthropology is the only educational exposure they will have to anthropological thinking. Most readers are unlikely to see anthropological thinking as relevant to their own lives unless we find a way to make it so. This book represents our endeavor to do just that.

Here's wishing you greater appreciation of our discipline and a lifetime of anthropological revelations to come.

Sincerely,

Robert L. Welsch

Luis A. Vivanco

Agustín Fuentes

About the Authors

Robert L. Welsch currently teaches cultural anthropology at Franklin Pierce University and previously taught for many years at Dartmouth College. He was affiliated with the Field Museum in Chicago for more than two decades. Trained in the 1970s at the University of Washington, at a time when anthropologists still focused mainly on non-Western village-level societies, and when cultural materialist, Marxist, structuralist, and interpretive theories dominated the discipline, Welsch's research has focused on medical anthropology, religion, exchange, art, museum studies in the classic anthropological settings of Papua New Guinea and Indonesia, and the history of anthropology as a professional discipline. He is Associate Professor of Anthropology at Franklin Pierce University.

Luis A. Vivanco teaches cultural anthropology and global studies at the University of Vermont, where he has won several of the university's top teaching awards. He was trained in the 1990s at Princeton when poststructuralist perspectives and "studying up" (studying powerful institutions and bureaucracies, often in Western contexts) was becoming commonplace. Vivanco has worked in Costa Rica, Mexico, Colombia, and the United States, studying the culture and politics of environmentalist social movements, the media, science, ecotourism, and urban mobility with bicycles. He is Professor of Anthropology and Co-Director of the Humanities Center at the University of Vermont.

Agustín Fuentes teaches biological anthropology and primatology at the University of Notre Dame. Trained at U.C. Berkeley during the 1990s, his work has focused on cooperation and bonding in human evolution, evolutionary theory, public ideas about human nature, and ethnoprimatology and multispecies anthropology. His work on primates has taken him to Gibraltar, Bali, and Singapore. A prolific writer in the public sphere, he is also a *National Geographic* "Explorer." He is Professor of Anthropology and Chair of the Anthropology Department at Notre Dame.

Preface

What is anthropology, and how is it relevant in today's world? Answering these core questions is the underlying goal of this book.

Anthropology is the most panoramic of the social sciences, focusing on the study of human origins, diversity, and culture, past and present. It provides a powerful framework to organize the intertwined complexities of human biology and evolution, social organization and experience, and symbolic communication and beliefs. It helps us comprehend how our species spread globally, as well as what globalization means for us in the contemporary world. The practice of anthropology also provides knowledge that helps solve some of our most pressing human problems today.

Thinking Like an Anthropologist

Unlike textbooks that emphasize the memorization of facts, *Anthropology: Asking Questions About Human Origins, Diversity, and Culture* teaches students how to think anthropologically. This approach helps students view cultural issues as an anthropologist might. In this way, anthropological thinking is regarded as a tool for deciphering everyday experience and what it means to be human.

A Cutting-Edge and Integrative Vision of Anthropology

The demands of disciplinary specialization mean that very few—if any—anthropologists can claim to be truly "four-field." Yet many of anthropology's biggest questions require a holistic perspective. Cutting-edge research areas like the biocultural synthesis and materiality—both of which are examined in detail in this book—are meeting the challenges of integration. The structuring of the book into four parts, each with its own introduction that frames the connections between the chapters, is intended to bring subfields together around common concerns.

Organized Around Key Questions

Inspired by the expression "99% percent of a good answer is a good question," each chapter opens with a contemporary story and introduces key questions that can be answered by anthropology. Each main section of a chapter is built around these questions. Through these unique chapter-opening and follow-up questions, students will see how classic anthropological concerns relate to contemporary situations.

The Past Through a Contemporary Perspective

Anthropology: Asking Questions About Human Origins, Diversity, and Culture represents our effort to close the gap between the realities of the discipline today and traditional views that are also taught at the introductory level. We believe that there is much to be gained, for ourselves and our students, by strengthening the dialogue between generations and subfields of anthropologists. We endeavor to bring classic anthropological examples, cases, and analyses to bear on contemporary questions.

Solving Human Problems

At the heart of *Anthropology: Asking Questions About Human Origins, Diversity, and Culture* is the belief that anthropology can make a difference in the world. We explain how anthropologists have looked at a wide range of human issues over time—mediating conflict, alleviating social problems, contributing to new social policies—exploring examples but also explaining challenges that still remain.

Why We Wrote This Book

In view of how most academic work and life is organized and practiced today, our coauthorship is a somewhat unlikely collaboration. We come from different generations of anthropological training, teach at different kinds of institutions, do our research in opposite corners of the world, and work on different topics in different subfields. Given the pressures and realities of regional and topical specialization within the discipline, we might not even run into each other at conferences, much less have reason to work together.

But as teachers concerned with sharing the excitement of anthropological findings and thinking with our undergraduate students, we share a lot in common. For one, we believe that there is strength in diversity, and we think our different backgrounds are more representative of the breadth of the discipline and who actually teaches introductory courses in anthropology. Because the three of us feel that anthropological thinking is for everyone, we wrote this textbook to appeal to instructors who blend traditional and contemporary views of anthropology and teach students of many cultural backgrounds. We do this by treating the learning experience as a process of actively asking questions about real-world problems and applying theoretical insights to understand them, as nearly all anthropologists actually do.

Guiding You Through the Book

Anthropology is distinguished by four underlying principles:

- A holistic view of anthropology, emphasizing the complementarity and integration of its subfields.
- Respecting tradition, with a contemporary perspective.

- An emphasis on learning how to ask important and interesting anthropological questions.
- Applying anthropology to understand and solve human problems.

Each of these principles informs the scholarship, narrative, and features of the book.

Chapter Introductions

1. Each chapter opens with a real-life story introducing the theme of the chapter.

2. The chapter-opening narrative concludes with the core questions at the heart of the chapter.

3. The core questions posed at the beginning of the chapter are reflected in the titles of each major section in the chapter.

How Does Language Actually Work?

Over the past century, linguists and linguistic anthropologists have studied the majority of the world's languages have found that each is highly structured. Moreover, most people, even those who speak unwritten languages, are largely unaware of the structure of their language until someone makes a mistake. Even then, they do not always know what is wrong, they just know the sentence sounded wrong.

To explain such reactions, the French linguist Ferdinand de Saussure (1916; 1986) suggested a distinction between the structure, or formal rules, of a language (*langue*) and how people actually speak it (*parole*). Distinguishing *langue* (language) and *parole* (speech) allows linguists to separate the rules and expected usage of language from what people actually say. The distinction is useful because it helps us realize that the rules we use to produce the sounds, word formation, and grammar as native speakers of a language can differ from how we actually speak, which is as much a social and cultural phenomenon as it is a function of language's structure. Here we explore how language is formally structured, which is the field of descriptive linguistics, and then sociolinguistics, the field that studies the social contexts of language use.

Descriptive Linguistics

The study of *langue*, or the formal structure of language, is called **descriptive linguistics**, which refers to the systematic analysis and description of a language's sound system and grammar. Linguists distinguish three types of structure in language: (1) **phonology**, the structure of speech sounds; (2) **morphology**, how words are formed into meaningful units; and (3) **syntax**, how words are strung together to form sentences and more complex utterances, such as paragraphs. (High school grammar classes mostly focus on morphology and syntax). All languages have predictable phonological, morphological, and syntactic structures.

Phonology: Sounds of Language

The sounds of language are organized by marking systematic contrasts between pairs or groups of sounds. The majority of both these sounds and the contrasts appear in many of the world's languages, and yet each language has its own unique pattern of sounds. When linguists listen to natural language, such as when people talk unselfconsciously in ordinary conversations, they identify minimal pairs, which are pairs of words that differ only in a single sound contrast.

Sound Contrasts: Pan, Ban, and Man

Consider, for example, the initial sounds in the English words "pan," "ban," and "man." Three sounds, [p], [b], and [m], distinguish these three words, while the other sounds in these words are the same. The consonants *p*, *b*, and *m* are formed at the front of the mouth at the lips. The differences among three consonants parallel differences among the initial sounds in the words "tab," "dab," and "nab," or the final sounds in the words "pig," "pick," and "ping."

These nine contrasts distinguish three series of what linguists call **stops**, sounds that are made by an occlusion, or stopping, of the airstream though the oral cavity or mouth. But in addition, [b], [d], and [g] differ from [p], [t], and [k] in that the first group are voiced, formed by the vibration of the vocal cords (glottis), at the Adam's apple. The triplet of nasal consonants, [m], [n], and [ng], are also voiced

- **Descriptive linguistics.** The systematic analysis and description of a language's sound system and grammar.
- **Phonology.** The systematic pattern of sounds in a language, also known as the language's sound system.
- **Morphology.** The structure of words and word formation in a language.
- **Syntax.** Pattern of word order used to form sentences and longer utterances in a language.
- **Stops.** Sounds that are formed by closing off and reopening the oral cavity so that it stops the flow of air through the mouth, such as the consonants p, b, t, d, k, and g.

4. The end of each section is capped with a thought-provoking question.

• •

THINKING CRITICALLY ABOUT ANTHROPOLOGY

How might you use a comparative perspective even if you only visit just one country while on vacation? Consider the other cultural contexts you have experienced and how these might provide a comparative framework for experiencing a novel society and culture.

• •

Thematic Boxes

Four types of thematic boxes are used throughout to highlight key themes and principles of the book.

5. Classic Contributions considers the history of anthropological thought on a particular topic, presenting a classic passage from an important historical figure in the discipline. It is followed up with questions to promote anthropological problem-solving.

6. Thinking Like an Anthropologist invites the student to exercise his or her own anthropological IQ. This is a two-part box. The first presents students with a concrete ethnographic situation and several proposed questions for further inquiry. The questions serve as a model for thinking anthropologically about the scenario. The second part introduces another scenario and prompts students to formulate questions of their own about this new but related subject matter.

CLASSIC CONTRIBUTIONS

E. B. Tylor and the Culture Concept

LIKE OTHER ANTHROPOLOGISTS of the latter half of the nineteenth century, Edward B. Tylor believed that the social and cultural differences of humanity could be explained as the product of evolutionary forces. Tylor's primary intellectual concern throughout his career was developing an evolutionary sequence that would explain how people evolved from a state of what he called "primitive savagery" to more "advanced" levels of civilization. In his book *Primitive Culture*, published in 1871, he advanced his argument that humans are subject to evolutionary forces in all aspects of their lives, including what he called "culture," offering the now classic definition presented here. Although contemporary uses of the term *culture* have changed since Tylor's definition—mainly because anthropologists today reject Tylor's evolutionary perspective—Tylor's definition is important because it provided a basis for the scientific study of culture that has been central to the discipline ever since.

E. B. Tylor

Culture or Civilization, taken in its wide ethnographic sense, is that complex whole which includes knowledge, belief, art, morals, law, custom, and any other capabilities and habits acquired by man as a member of society. The condition of culture among the various societies of mankind, in so far as it is capable of being *investigated on general principles, is a subject apt for the study of laws of human thought and action. . . . [I]ts various grades may be regarded as stages of development or evolution, each the outcome of previous history, and about to do its proper part in shaping the history of the future. (Tylor 1871:1)*

Questions for Reflection

1. How is this definition different from or similar to the notion of culture you had before taking an anthropology course?

2. Tylor believed that people acquire culture as members of a society. But how specifically might someone acquire his or her culture?

culture. In Chapter 2 we explore the concept of culture more deeply, but here it is important to know that when anthropologists use the term *culture* they are nearly always referring to ideas about the world and ways of interacting in society or in the environment in predictable and expected ways.

Cultural Relativism

All humans participate in culture. Anthropologists, of course, also carry with them basic assumption
typically becom
different assum
comes with bein

• **Ethnocentrism.** The

Thinking Like an Anthropologist

Making Sense of Genetic Relationships

ANTHROPOLOGISTS BEGIN THEIR research by asking questions. In this box, we want you to learn how to ask questions as an anthropological researcher. Part 1 describes a situation and follows up with questions we would ask. Part 2 asks you to do the same thing with a different situation.

PART ONE: WHAT DOES IT MEAN TO BE 98% CHIMPANZEE?

One frequently cited comparison between humans and chimpanzees is that the two species share 98% identical DNA. This statement is generally taken to mean that chimpanzees share 98% of our genetic sequences, and by extension 98% of our genes. But this interpretation is not quite true. Humans and chimpanzees belong to the same family (Hominidae), and we are both a kind of ape, but we differ at many levels. The current trend of comparing sequences of DNA between species, or even between groups of humans, and expecting it to have functional significance, has the potential for serious misuse of already common misconceptions about DNA. University of North Carolina-Charlotte anthropologist Jonathan Marks has tackled this issue and its potentially dangerous genetic implications. In his books *What It Means to Be 98% Chimpanzee* (2002) and *Human Biodiversity: Genes, Race, and History* (1995), Marks reveals misconceptions and a few problematic generalizations that threaten an accurate understanding of genes, behavior, and evolution.

Marks approached this problem on three fronts. First, he has long questioned the notion that humans and chimpanzees are more closely related than humans and gorillas (or chimpanzees and gorillas). While many studies of proteins and DNA show humans and chimpanzees as having a slightly closer phylogenetic relationship, a few studies do show gorillas and chimpanzees or even humans and gorillas as being closer in molecular terms.

Second, Marks applies a theoretical perspective to the problem, demonstrating how we tend to forget some very basic aspects of DNA. For example, there are only four nucleotide bases in all DNA, so that *any* two randomly selected, very large DNA sequences will differ, on average, by no more than 25%. Of course, more closely related organisms share more sequences in common, as they have been separate species for less time and thus the forces of evolution have had fewer chances to shuffle existing sequences or allow mutations to occur. Because humans and chimpanzees have only about seven to nine million years of separate evolution, we are quite similar at the level of the DNA sequence.

Third, Marks points out that 98% similarity is a statement about the chemical structures of the DNA, not necessarily the actual function of the genes. Overall, only about 5% of the human DNA is actively coding for proteins.

Marks's work forces researchers to be very careful about making assertions about genetic differences or similarities between groups of people. All humans share 100% of the same DNA, but there are a huge number of variations in the frequencies and even the presence of certain alleles across the different human populations. What questions does this situation raise for anthropological researchers?

1. Are the same 5% of active human genes also active in chimpanzees?
2. If we accept the simplistic idea that all human–chimpanzee differences arise from 2% of our DNA, what are we to make of the differences in allele frequencies between human populations?
3. What do these similarities mean about changes in behavior and morphology relative to changes at the level of the DNA?
4. What do we gain and lose when we primarily construct our understanding of human and primate behavior through the analysis of DNA?

How Closely Are We Related?

Doing Fieldwork

Conducting Holistic Research with Stanley Ulijaszek

STANLEY ULIJASZEK IS a British anthropologist who has been conducting research for several decades in the swamplands of coastal Papua New Guinea, an island state in the Southwest Pacific. In recent years, he has turned his attention to an interesting question: In this difficult landscape that is unsuited to agriculture, how do people acquire a sufficient, safe, and nutritious food supply? To answer this question properly requires substantial knowledge of the human biology, prehistory, and culture of coastal New Guinea.

At the center of this story is the sago palm, a palm tree that grows abundantly in swamps. Its stem contains starch, a staple food for the people who cultivate it. People cook sago in long sticks resembling dense French bread, eating it with a bit of fish. Sago is not a great staple food, because it is 99.5 % starch, making it an excellent energy food, but it has few other nutrients. Worse, perhaps, is that sago is toxic when eaten uncooked or improperly prepared. Its toxicity threatens people with a specific genetic mutation that does not allow the red blood cells to carry the toxins out of the body, a mutation common among coastal New Guinea populations. Thus, because of this toxicity, eating sago presented a risk to these coastal people (Ulijaszek 2007).

It turns out, however, that this same genetic mutation confers some resistance to malaria, a mosquito-borne infectious disease common in the tropics. The key to protecting the people while releasing the nutritional energy of sago is to separate the starch from the pith at the center of the sago palm by washing and straining it, then cooking the starch, all of which reduces its toxicity to safe levels. Archaeological evidence indicates that people in this region figured out this process at least 6,000 years ago, which is when they began leaving behind their hunting-and-gathering way of life to take up agriculture. Ulijaszek concludes that they adapted sago for human consumption by detoxifying it, which in turn allowed people's genetic mutation to survive, thus providing some resistance to malaria in this difficult environment. People then continued to pass on the genetic trait of malarial resistance.

Ulijaszek's research addresses an interesting puzzle about how humans can successfully adapt to a challenging natural environment, and how those changes are intertwined with genetic factors like the resistance to malaria. To achieve this,

Cultivating Nutrition from the Sago Palm. Transforming the pith of the sago palm into food is a complex process. First the pith must be chopped out of the trunk and pulverized using simple cutting and pounding tools, and then the starch must be leached from the dense mass of fiber using a frame made from the base of the leaf stalk in which the starch is pounded with water to release and strain the edible starch, leaving the inedible fiber behind in the frame. Later the sago flour is collected from a basin where it has settled.

he drew on the evidence of cultural and linguistic anthropology, gained by observing how people cultivate, process, consume, and talk about sago. He also drew on archaeological evidence of sago production that goes back thousands of years, not necessarily by conducting the excavations himself, but by relying heavily on the evidence archaeologists working in that area had produced. He also drew on evidence about the genetic makeup of local populations drawn from blood samples and genetic analyses.

Questions for Reflection

1. How do you think Ulijaszek's findings would have differed if he relied only on the evidence of cultural anthropology? Archaeology? Biological anthropology?

2. Do you think Ulijaszek's approach would be applicable to a study of lowfat diets in the United States? How would you apply it?

Anthropologist as Problem Solver

Kim Hopper, Homelessness, and the Mentally Ill in New York City

HOMELESSNESS DID NOT become a recognized social problem in the United States until the late 1970s. Before then, of course, there were people who had nowhere to live, but homelessness was commonly understood as an extension of their poverty, the result of alcoholism, or lifestyle choices (Beriss 2005). Few researchers tried to understand how and why some people were homeless or what Americans thought about people without homes. One exception was anthropologist Kim Hopper of the City University of New York.

Since the 1970s, Hopper has lived among, studied, and worked as an advocate for homeless people in New York City. He has spent most of his professional life outside academia, working in non-profit agencies, advocacy organizations, and government (Hopper 2002). He helped draft legislation and legal briefs, submitted affidavits, served as a court-appointed monitor, testified as an expert witness, and served as a board member of the National Coalition for the Homeless.

According to Hopper, anthropology's strength in this arena is its ability to focus attention on the cultural concepts that shape our thinking about homelessness, the social and policy conditions that prevent adequate solutions, and the social control that service institutions exert on homeless people.

One area where these concerns come together is in the connection between homelessness and mental health. In the 1970s, the closing of mental hospitals, asylums, and psychiatric clinics led to an explosion of homelessness in large cities, leading many people to believe that most homeless people are mentally ill. Social service institutions were built on the assumption that people become homeless because of psychiatric problems. Their model suggests that the best way to approach homeless people is to treat them as mental patients.

Hopper has been highly critical of this model. Not only is there little evidence to prove its assumptions, there is no way of knowing if a perceived disorder is a *cause* or a *consequence* of homelessness. In other words, are the homeless people's patterns of behavior "symptoms" of mental illness or caused by, if not adaptations to, the homeless way of life (Hopper 1988, 158)? According to Hopper, homelessness typically has its roots in larger developments, like housing crises, increases in unemployment, changes in household composition, and the reduction of government assistance programs. Defining all homeless people as deviant mental patients is an exercise in social control and leads to coercive policies of hospitalization. These actions preempt questions

Kim Hopper

both about the quality of immediate assistance offered such people and about the long-term subsistence alternatives to the hospital (Hopper 1988).

From Hopper's point of view, the issue is not whether the problem of homelessness will be solved, because it will not. One reason, Hopper argues, is that industrialized societies produce "surplus people," which means that there are more people than positions in technology-driven industrial economies, so there will always be people on the margins of the economy and out of work. One key issue is to recognize that the opposite of homelessness is not a homeless shelter. Rather, it is a home, which is currently lacking in treatments of homeless people.

Hopper insists that ethnographic research offers useful on-the-ground insights into these matters, because policymakers, judges, and social service bureaucrats are unlikely to find these things out for themselves. But, he argues, fieldwork is not enough: anthropologists also need to familiarize themselves with clinical knowledge and the government's legal, regulatory, and procedural constraints to be able to evaluate proposed interventions.

Questions for Reflection

1. How and why do you think homeless people might develop traits of mental illness?

2. Why would social institutions want to define people as mentally ill if they are not?

3. What might you say to officials in your hometown to explain American cultural attitudes toward homelessness?

7. Doing Fieldwork draws upon an actual field project to explore the special methods used by anthropologists to address specific questions and problems.

8. Anthropologist as Problem Solver describes how a particular anthropologist has applied disciplinary insights and methods to help alleviate a social problem, mediate a conflict, or (re)define a policy debate related to the central problem of the chapter. These cases also provide insight into careers that take advantage of an anthropology background.

9. Visual Program

A rich ensemble of relevant photographs, maps, and figures underscore the key points of each chapter.

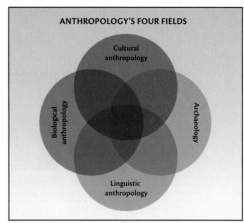

10. Each chapter closes with key terms, recommended readings, and a unique table recapping the main points of each section and unresolved matters that anthropology is still exploring.

Reviewing the Chapter

Chapter Section	What We Know	To Be Resolved
How did anthropology begin?	During the nineteenth century, the rise of industrialization, the influence of evolutionary theory, and colonial contact with less industrialized cultures led to the discipline of understanding how cultures operate and interact.	Anthropologists are still fascinated—and challenged—by the contrasts and changes in culture worldwide as a result of globalization.
What are the four subfields of anthropology, and what do they share in common?	Anthropologists in all subfields share certain fundamental approaches and concepts including culture, cultural relativism, diversity, change, and holism.	Some anthropologists continue to debate the idea that the subfields, with their distinct methods and specialized research interests, belong together in the same discipline.
How do anthropologists know what they know?	Anthropology has a strong relationship with the scientific method; all anthropologists use theories, collect data, and analyze that data.	While most cultural anthropologists reject the possibility of a completely objective analysis of human culture, other subfields of anthropology, such as archaeology and biological anthropology, are thoroughly committed to the scientific method.
How is anthropology put to work in the world?	All four subfields have both theoretical and applied aspects. Applied research uses the insights of anthropological theory to solve problems.	Most anthropologists see an anthropological approach as providing a better way of understanding people from different backgrounds than any other discipline, but anthropologists continue to disagree among themselves about how to apply that understanding to address human problems.
What ethical issues does anthropology raise?	Issues of ethics—moral questions about right and wrong and standards of appropriate behavior—are at the heart of anthropology.	Certain ethical issues have no easy resolution, such as the ideal that anthropologists should do no harm, or how to resolve conflicting responsibilities anthropologists have to different communities and publics.

Ensuring Student Success

Oxford University Press offers students and instructors a comprehensive ancillary package for *Anthropology*.

For Students

Companion Website

Anthropology: Asking Questions About Human Origins, Diversity, and Culture is also accompanied by an extensive **companion website (www.oup.com/us/welsch)**, which includes materials to help students with every aspect of the course. For each chapter, you will find:

- **Chapter outlines**
- **Interactive exercises**
- **Glossary of key terms**
- **Flashcards** to assist students in studying and reviewing key terms
- **Additional links** to websites providing supplemental information on the topics and ideas covered in the chapter
- **Additional recommended readings** that delve more deeply into the topics discussed in the chapter
- **Self-grading review questions** to help students review the material and assess their comprehension

For Instructors

Oxford University Press is proud to offer a complete and authoritative supplements package for both instructors and students. When you adopt *Anthropology: Asking Questions About Humanity,* you will have access to a truly exemplary set of ancillary materials to enhance teaching and support students' learning.

Ancillary Resource Center (ARC) at **www.oup-arc.com** is a convenient, instructor-focused single destination for resources to accompany *Anthropology: Asking Questions About Human Origins, Diversity, and Culture.* Accessed online through individual user accounts, ARC provides instructors with access to up-to-date ancillaries at any time while guaranteeing the security of grade-significant resources. In addition, it allows OUP to keep instructors informed when new content becomes available.

The ARC for *Anthropology: Asking Questions About Human Origins, Diversity, and Culture* includes:

- Digital copy of **Instructor's Manual**, which includes:
  * A comprehensive introduction written by the authors describing their pedagogical vision, the question-centered pedagogy, and advice on how to promote active learning in the classroom
  * Chapter outlines
  * Learning objectives
  * Key controversies: Expanded discussion of What We Know/To Be Resolved
  * Key terms and definitions and summaries
  * Lecture outlines
  * PowerPoint slides
  * Web links and blogroll

* In-class activities and project assignments
* Suggestions for class discussion
* Image bank
- **Test Bank** written by the authors and organized around principles from Bloom's Taxonomy for cognitive learning including:
    * Multiple-choice questions
    * True/false questions
    * Fill-in-the-blank questions
    * Essay prompts

In addition, a selection of ethnographic video clips drawn from the Documentary Educational Resources (DER) catalogue is available to qualified adopters, as well as a complete **Course Management Cartridge**. Contact your Oxford University Press sales representative for more information.

Acknowledgments

The authors thank the many individuals who have supported this project from its inception to the final stages of production. The impetus for this book lies with Kevin Witt, who had an inspired vision for a new kind of anthropology textbook and the foresight to identify and support the team to write it. In its early stages while this project was with McGraw-Hill, development editors Pam Gordon, Nanette Giles, Susan Messer, and Phil Herbst each played an important role in shaping the manuscript.

At Oxford University Press, Sherith Pankratz, our acquisitions editor, and Thom Holmes, our development editor, have managed this project and helped us further refine our vision with exceptional care and expertise. We would also like to thank assistant editor Meredith Keffer, development assistant Alexandra Boehmke, and photo researcher and permission-seeker Cailen Swain. In production, we would like to thank art director Michele Laseau, project manager Christian Holdener, production editor Keith Faivre, copy editor India Gray, and proofreader Leslie Anglin. And last, but by no means least, we acknowledge and thank the hardworking men and women who are marketing this book and getting it into the hands of the students for whom we wrote it. Although the sales and marketing team often go unsung and unacknowledged by many authors, we know their work is critical to the success of a project like this one.

We are grateful to Franklin Pierce University, the University of Vermont, University of Notre Dame, Dartmouth College, University of California Berkeley, Central Washington University, the Hood Museum of Art, the Field Museum, the U.S. National Museum of Natural History, a branch of the Smithsonian Institution, and the American Museum of Natural History in New York, all of whom have provided support in diverse ways. In particular, we appreciate the support and encouragement of Kim Mooney, President of Franklin Pierce University; Andrew Card, former Franklin Pierce University President; Kerry McKeever and Paul Kotila, Academic Deans at Franklin Pierce; and Jean Dawson and John Villemaire, Division Chairs of the Social and Behavioral Sciences at Franklin Pierce. At the University of Vermont the Provost's Office and the Office of the Dean of the College of Arts and Sciences have provided important institutional support for this project. The Department of Anthropology at the University of Notre Dame and Mark Roche, the former Dean of the College of Arts and Letters, provided support and encouragement.

Numerous librarians aided the development of this project at various stages, including Paul Campbell, Eric Shannon, Leslie Inglis, Melissa Stearns, Jill Wixom, Gladys

Nielson, Wendy O'Brien, Lisa Wiley, and Amy Horton at Frank S. DiPietro Library at Franklin Pierce University in Rindge, New Hampshire; Laurie Kutner at Bailey-Howe Library at the University of Vermont; Amy Witzel, Fran Oscadal, John Cocklin, and Ridie Gheie at Baker Library at Dartmouth College; and staff of Alden Library at Ohio University in Athens, Ohio.

We especially thank our colleagues Kirk M. and Karen Endicott, Robert G. Goodby, Debra S. Picchi, Douglas Challenger, John E. Terrell, and Robert J. Gordon, all of whom have offered support, encouragement, and insights throughout the various phases of writing this book. Patrick Fazioli, Brad Lepper, Bob Goodby, Michael Surrett, and Scott Van Keuren were especially helpful with framing some of the archaeological issues. Many other colleagues have contributed to this project in direct and indirect ways, including shaping our thinking about various anthropological topics, sparking ideas and being a sounding board about matters of content and pedagogy, and reading and responding to draft chapters. These colleagues include at Dartmouth College, Hoyt Alverson, Sienna R. Craig, Brian Didier, Nathaniel Dominy, Seth Dobson, Dale F. Eickelman, Kathy Hart, Sergei Kan, Brian Kennedy, Kenneth Korey, Joel Levine, Deborah Nichols, and John Watanabe; and at the University of Vermont Ben Eastman, Scott Van Keuren, Cameron Wesson, Brian Gilley, Jennifer Dickinson, Teresa Mares, Amy Trubek, Scott Matter, Deborah Blom, and the late Jim Petersen. And we extend our thanks to colleagues Thad Bartlett, Carola Borries, Greg Downey, Hope Hollocher, Lee Gettler, Andrewa Koenig, Kelly Lane, Daniel Lende, James Loudon, Nick Malone, Katherine C. MacKinnon, Thom McDade, Jim McKenna, Rahul Oka, Catherine Panter-Brick, Michael Park, Elsworth Ray, Emily Schulz, Karen Strier, Carel van Schaik, Bob Sussman, Richard Wrangham, Matthew A. Wyczalkowski, and many others for conversations that helped think through the biological anthropology chapters. Special thanks to Phyllis Dolhinow and David Wake.

Several students at Franklin Pierce, University of Vermont, and Dartmouth College have helped with research during the various stages of writing and rewriting. These include D. Wes Beattie, Justyn Christophers, Brian Dunleavy, Keenan Phillips, Brian Kirn, Cooper Leatherwood, Adam Levine, Rebecca Nystrom, Adam Slutsky, Nathan Hedges, Michael Surrett, Scott Spolidoro, Kevin Mooiman, Matthew Dee, Kelsey Keegan, Kyle Brooks, Cory Atkinson, Taber Morrell, Saige Kemelis, Shannon Perry, Catherine Durickas, and Kristin Amato. We also thank Jonathan Jimanez, an undergraduate at Whittier College, for his reactions and insights to the archaeological chapters of the book.

We want to thank our students at Franklin Pierce University and the University of Vermont who have test driven various earlier drafts of this book. Their feedback and insights have been invaluable. But in particular we want to thank Courtney Cummings, Kimberly Dupuis, John M. Gass, Kendra Lajoie, Holly Martz, Scott M. McDonald, Lindsay Mullen, and Nick Rodriguez, all of whom were students in AN400 at Franklin Pierce during the Fall Semester of 2012. Having used drafts of part of this text in one of their courses, they reviewed many of the chapters in the book in focus-group fashion and offered useful insights about examples and writing in each chapter.

Last but certainly not least, we would like to thank our families for all the critical emotional and logistical support they have provided over the years to ensure the success of this project. Luis's children, Isabel, Felipe, and Camila, have aided us in various ways, from prodding questions about the book and anthropology to, at times, comic relief when we needed it. Rob's wife, Sarah Welsch; Luis's wife, Peggy O'Neill-Vivanco; and Agustín's partner, Devi Snively, deserve our deepest gratitude for all their wise counsel at many junctures in the development of this book; their behind-the-scenes support to enable us to research, write, and revise it; and their (long-suffering) patience until finally seeing it finished.

Manuscript Reviewers

We have greatly benefited from the perceptive comments and suggestion of the many talented scholars and instructors who reviewed the manuscript of *Anthropology*. Their insight and suggestions contributed immensely to the published work.

Anita Barrow
William Paterson University

Chase W. Beck
Texas A&M University

Katie M. Binetti
Baylor University

Renée M. Bonzani
University of Kentucky

Marni Finkelstein
John Jay College of Criminal Justice

Kanya Godde
University of La Verne

Ramie A. Gougeon
University of West Florida

Renee Gralewicz
University of Wisconsin-Fox Valley

Adam S. Green
Georgia State University

Katie Green
Rappahannock Community College

Christine E. Haney
University of Nebraska-Lincoln

Diane Hardgrave
College of Southern Nevada

Jayne Howell
California State University, Long Beach

Ludomir Lozny
Hunter College, CUNY

Dave Matsuda
California State University, East Bay

Jaclyn McWhorter
University of Florida

Kathryn T. Molohon
Laurentian University

Megan D. Parker
Georgia Perimeter College

Mirjana Roksandic
University of Winnipeg

Vicki Root-Wajda
College of DuPage

Larry Ross
Lincoln University, Missouri

James Sewastynowicz
Jacksonville State University

B. Katherine Smith
The University of Southern Mississippi

Jesse Todd
Brookhaven College

Janel Tortorice
Lone Star College, CyFair

Amy Rector Verrelli
Virginia Commonwealth University

Melissa Vogel
Clemson University

LuAnn Wandsnider
University of Nebraska-Lincoln

Donald A. Whatley
Blinn College

Max E. White
Piedmont College

Benjamin Wilreker
College of Southern Nevada

Walter R. T. Witschey
Longwood University

Catherine S. Wright
Jefferson State Community College

Brita Wynn
Sacramento City College

Lauren A. Wynne
Utica College

Molly Zuckerman
Mississippi State University

And three anonymous reviewers

Ancillary Co-Authors

Our sincere thanks to the scholars and instructors who aided in the creation of the ancillary materials. Along with the textbook co-authors, they helped create high-quality additional resources specifically for this text.

Jason Fancher
Mt. Hood Community College
(Parts of the Instructors Manual,
PowerPoint slides, web links in cultural
chapters)

Meghan Ference
Brooklyn College, CUNY (Test Bank,
interactive exercises, self-quizzes,
additional readings in cultural chapters)

K. Patrick Fazioli
Medaille College
(Web links, interactive exercises,
additional readings in cultural chapters)

Lola D. Houston
Burlington, Vermont
(Updates of Instructor's Manual, Power
Point slides, Test bank, student
materials)

Part I

Key Concepts and Methods in Anthropology

As a discipline, anthropology is concerned with the origins and diversity of human life on the planet, as well as the conditions under which human bodies, technologies, societies, and beliefs change. These concerns bring anthropologists in touch with numerous other disciplines that share similar concerns across the natural sciences, social sciences, and humanities, which is one reason it is often said that anthropology is the most interdisciplinary of academic disciplines. But all anthropologists agree that there are certain key concepts, methods, and theoretical orientations that count more than others. These key concepts and methods encompass our holistic aspirations and at the same time define the distinctive anthropological perspective.

We begin this part with two chapters that introduce two especially important concepts—culture and evolution—that provide basic theoretical foundations for the discipline as a whole. Culture clarifies why groups of people around the world think and act in the distinctive ways they do, while evolution provides an explanation for how and why species, including our own, have emerged and changed over time. The next chapter describes the specific methods that anthropologists use to study the stories of human origins and biological variation, our prehistoric pasts, and our contemporary lives and languages. Recognizing that symbolic thinking lies at the heart of what makes us human, we then turn to a chapter that explores the fundamental linkages between culture and language. We end this section with a chapter on globalization and culture, which helps us understand how and why the cross-border inter-connections of migration, global media, economic globalization, and other dynamics of our contemporary world have made the concepts and approaches of anthropology more relevant than ever.

Anthropology
Asking Questions About Humanity

Human beings are one of the world's most adaptable animals. Evolutionary history has endowed our species with certain common physical characteristics, instincts, and practices that have helped us survive, even thrive, in every conceivable terrestrial environment. Yet no group of people is exactly like another, and as a species we exhibit tremendous variations across groups, variations in our adaptations to the environment, physical appearance, language, beliefs, and social organization.

Humans have always encountered groups of people who look different, speak peculiar languages, and behave in unexpected or unpredictable ways. Although sometimes hostility and wars break out between groups because of such differences, usually people have found ways to get along, often through trade and alliances. To be effective at establishing strong social and political bonds in spite of human differences has always required that people have a practical understanding of human variation.

Some of history's great travelers and explorers developed that practical understanding, among them the Venetian Marco Polo (1254–1324), the Norman cleric Gerald of Wales (1146–1223), the Franciscan missionary William of Rubruck (1220–1292), the North African Muslim Ibn Batuta (1304–1433), and the Chinese admiral Zheng He (1371–1433). These individuals were all deeply interested in

☙ **Intercultural Interactions.** In 1767 Captain Samuel Wallis and his crew were the first Westerners to reach Tahiti. Their first interactions were peaceful and included an exchange of gifts between Wallis and Queen Oberea. The cultural differences between Tahitians and the English raised many important questions about human differences and similarities, for both parties—the kinds of dynamics that interest anthropologists today.

other peoples, and their writings express sophisticated understandings of how and why the groups they encountered looked, acted, worshiped, and spoke as they did (Bartlett 1982; Larner 1999; Menzies 2002; Dreyer 2007; Harvey 2007; Khanmohamadi 2008; Fazioli 2014). Similarly, there is a rich historical legacy of intellectual thought about human variation. The great Chinese philosopher Confucius (551–479 BCE) wrote in two of his *Analects* some principles for establishing relationships with *yi* [yee], meaning cultural and ethnic outsiders. A generation later, the Greek historian Herodotus (484–425 BCE), in his seven-volume *Histories*, described the diverse peoples and societies he encountered during his travels in Africa, Southwestern Asia, and India, offering a number of possible explanations for the variations he observed across groups.

While all of these individuals were curious about other peoples and at times quite rigorous in their ways of thinking about human variation, they were not anthropologists as we think of anthropology today. They were not researchers asking systematic questions about humanity, and anthropology as a discipline did not emerge from their writings. Still, their various studies show that getting along with peoples from different cultures has always been important, a point that is sometimes lost on us in the United States, where our international prominence and our preoccupation with American exceptionalism may lead us to think that we don't need to understand people and cultures from other countries. But if we Americans want to be most successful in dealing with people internationally in politics, trade, treaties, and global environmental or health policies, we need to understand in systematic ways the people from other countries and the cultures that guide and motivate them.

These points lead us to our first question, the question at the heart of this chapter: *What is anthropology, and how is it relevant in today's world?* Embedded in this broader question are the following problems, around which this chapter is organized:

How did anthropology begin?

What are the four subfields of anthropology, and what do they share in common?

How do anthropologists know what they know?

How is anthropology put to work in the world?

What ethical issues does anthropology raise?

Anthropology is the study of human beings, their biology, their prehistory and histories, and their changing languages, cultures, and social institutions. Anthropology provides a framework for asking questions about and grasping the complexity of human experience, both past and present. Anthropology is about where humans have been, but it also provides knowledge that helps solve human problems today.

How Did Anthropology Begin?

During the nineteenth century, **anthropology** emerged in Europe and North America as an academic discipline devoted to the systematic observation and analysis of human variation. It was made possible once intellectuals and scholars had developed rigorous ways of comparing different species and people with different cultures. The Enlightenment or Age of Reason, which began in the early 1700s with the rise of modern science, demonstrated that careful observation and analysis could lead to understanding the natural world. Sir Isaac Newton explained the principles of physics and gravity; geologists demonstrated that many species of animals, like the dinosaurs and (later) enormous elephant-like creatures such as wooly mammoths and mastodons, had once lived on earth; and biologists began to describe different species of plants, insects, birds, and mammals, grouping them into families and larger level groupings. But while scholars acknowledged differences among peoples living on the different continents, they did not attempt to explain these variations until their own societies had begun to change as a result of industrialization. Previously, cultural differences were assumed to be a given; cultural variation in the 1800s was thought to be essentially as it always had been. But as intellectuals began to notice that their own societies were changing because of the rise of factories, they realized that other societies around the world had also been changing.

Three key concerns began to emerge by the 1850s that would shape professional anthropology. These were (1) the disruptions of industrialization in Europe and America, (2) the rise of evolutionary theories, and (3) the growing importance of Europe's far-flung colonies with large indigenous populations whose land, mineral wealth, and labor Europeans and Americans wanted to control.

- **Anthropology.** The study of human beings, their biology, their prehistory and histories, and their changing languages, cultures, and social institutions.

The Disruptions of Industrialization

Industrialization refers to the economic process of shifting from an agricultural economy to a factory-based one. Industrialization disrupted American and European societies by bringing large numbers of rural people into towns and cities to work in factories. The rise of industrial towns and cities raised questions about how society was changing, including how a factory-based economy and the attendant growth of cities shaped society, government, residential patterns, and culture. These were the questions that motivated great social thinkers, in particular German political economists Karl Marx (1818–1883) and Max Weber (1864–1920) and the French anthropologist-sociologist Émile Durkheim (1858–1917), each of whom influenced the rise of anthropology as a social scientific discipline.

At the beginning of the nineteenth century, most people in Western countries were rural and were usually engaged in farming. Industrial inventions like the cotton gin, the steam engine, and factory machinery made it possible to quickly produce goods in large numbers that used to be made slowly by hand. In the factories, workers did repetitive tasks for long hours to mass-produce goods. Factory economies affected basic aspects of life such as who individuals would marry, what activities they would spend their days doing, and the role of religion in their lives.

In the midst of these social and economic upheavals, anthropology developed as a discipline that sought to understand and explain how people in rural and urban settings organize their communities and how they change. It also led these scholars to consider how industrialization affected peoples in European colonies in Africa, Asia, Latin America, and the Pacific Islands. Important, new questions were posed: Why did these diverse societies organize their lives in the ways they did? Why had Native

- **Industrialization.** The economic process of shifting from an agricultural economy to a factory-based one.

Americans and Africans not developed industrial societies as European societies had? Why had the civilizations of China, India, and the Arab world developed social, political, and economic patterns distinct from those of Europeans? And why had these other civilizations not experienced industrialization as Europeans had? Asking about how European villages and cities were structured and how they perpetuated their cultures ultimately led to questions about how all sorts of non-Western societies worked as well.

The Theory of Evolution

- **Evolution.** The adaptive changes in populations of organisms across generations.

A second key influence on the development of anthropology was the rise of evolutionary theory to explain biological variation between and within species. **Evolution** refers to the adaptive changes in populations of organisms across generations. English naturalist Charles Darwin (1809–1882) developed a theory of how different species of plants and animals had evolved from earlier forms. He based his ideas on personal observations made during his travels with the British survey ship HMS *Beagle,* as well as his own backyard experiments raising pigeons, among other things. The key mechanism of his evolutionary theory was what he called "natural selection," a process through which certain inheritable traits are passed along to offspring because they are better suited to the environment. Thus, in Darwin's view, in subtle ways nature was sorting out, or selecting, those forms best adapted for their environment.

Darwin had developed his theory of evolution in the late 1830s but delayed publishing his findings. He knew that his theory would be controversial, and he feared a backlash from the conservative religious community and from more established scientists. The idea of biological evolution was a remarkable notion for people used to thinking of species as fixed and stable. Religious scholars interpreted the book of Genesis in the Old Testament to suggest that God had created all the natural species once at the time of creation and that no new species had been created since then. For Darwin, however, the question of the origin of species was not a religious one but an **empirical** one. It was a question that could be answered by observing whether species had changed and whether new species had emerged over time. From the findings of contemporary geologists, Darwin knew that many early species, such as the dinosaurs, had arisen and died out. For him, such changes were evidence that the natural environment had selected some species for survival and that extinction was the outcome for those not well suited to changing environments.

- **Empirical.** Verifiable through observation rather than through logic or theory.

When Darwin published his groundbreaking work, *On the Origin of Species,* in 1859, he experienced the backlash he feared, and few scientists accepted Darwin's ideas immediately. Indeed, as late as the 1920s some biologists continued to be uncomfortable with the idea that species might change over time. But as the older generation left the scene, younger scientists recognized how easily this simple theory explained most kinds of biological variation both within and between species. Today, biologists and anthropologists no longer view biological evolution as controversial, and nearly all anthropologists and biologists accept evolution as the only way to explain the relationship among animal and plant species and the only way to explain why humans have the biological abilities and characteristics we can observe today.

Since Darwin's time, the broader scientific community has borrowed from his theory to produce a wave of new ideas involving evolution. Evolution seemed to provide a framework for studying both the biological and cultural development of humans and their societies. Among biological anthropologists, the inheritance of physiological traits allowed science to understand the history of human origins and our relationship to other primates. Among early cultural anthropologists, evolutionary models seemed ideal for explaining how different societies had come to be as they were when Europeans encountered them for the first time. The notion of evolution allowed early anthropologists to rank societies along an evolutionary scale, which they assumed showed which societies were more "advanced" because they had passed through more "primitive" forms of society with simpler technologies by adapting to their environments with more complex tools. Anthropologists today challenge such models of cultural evolution because this model does not fit the observed facts, but these early models motivated anthropologists to collect data from these so-called primitive societies before industrialization caused them to change or die out.

Colonial Origins of Cultural Anthropology

A third driving force behind anthropology was **colonialism,** the historical practice of more powerful countries claiming possession of less powerful ones. We can think of American domination over Indian lands as a form of colonialism, particularly when government policies moved Native Americans from the southeastern states to what is now Oklahoma, largely because white settlers wanted their land. Overseas, the colonial period flourished from the 1870s until the 1970s, and whites established mines, fisheries, plantations, and other enterprises using local peoples as inexpensive labor. Colonies enriched the mother countries, often impoverishing the indigenous inhabitants.

Colonial peoples everywhere had different cultures and customs, and their actions often seemed baffling to white administrators, a fact that these officials chalked up to their seemingly primitive or savage nature. To understand how to govern such radically different peoples, Europeans and Americans began developing methods for studying those societies.

Most Europeans and Americans expected their colonial subjects to die out, leading to the urgent collection of information about tribal societies before it was too late. Well into the 1920s, anthropologists pursued an approach known as the **salvage paradigm,** which held that it was important to observe indigenous ways of life, interview elders, and assemble collections of objects made and used by indigenous peoples because this knowledge of traditional languages and customs would soon disappear (Figure 1.1). Of course, today we know that while some Indian tribes, especially along the East Coast, largely died out, many other groups have survived and grown in population. But these Native American cultures have had to adjust and adapt to the changing American landscape and all the changes that Americans of different national origins have brought to the continent.

Anthropology as a Global Discipline

By the end of the nineteenth century, anthropology was already an international discipline, whose practitioners were mainly based in Western Europe and the United States. Although they had some shared concerns, anthropologists in particular countries developed specific national traditions, studying distinct problems, and developing their own styles of thought. Throughout the twentieth century, anthropology began to emerge in many other non-European countries as well. Many students in colonial territories had gone to European and American universities where they learned anthropology and, in many cases, brought anthropology back home.

- **Colonialism.** The historical practice of more powerful countries claiming possession of less powerful ones.

- **Salvage paradigm.** The paradigm which held that it was important to observe indigenous ways of life, interview elders, and assemble collections of objects made and used by indigenous peoples.

Figure 1.1 The Salvage Paradigm. Efforts to document indigenous cultures "before they disappeared" motivated anthropologists and others to record the ways of traditional people, including well-known Western photographer William S. Prettyman, who took this picture of an Otoe family in Kansas in the 1880s.

In these countries, anthropology often focuses on practical problems of national development and on documenting the minority societies found within the country's borders. Today, anthropology is a truly global discipline with practitioners in dozens of countries asking many different kinds of questions about humanity.

THINKING CRITICALLY ABOUT ANTHROPOLOGY

Can you think of something you do at your college or university that feels "natural" but is probably done somewhat differently at another college? Consider, for example, how your experiences in high school classes may have led you to expect something different from your college classes.

What Are the Four Subfields of Anthropology and What Do They Share in Common?

Anthropology has traditionally been divided into four subfields: cultural anthropology, archaeology, biological anthropology, and linguistic anthropology (Figure 1.2).

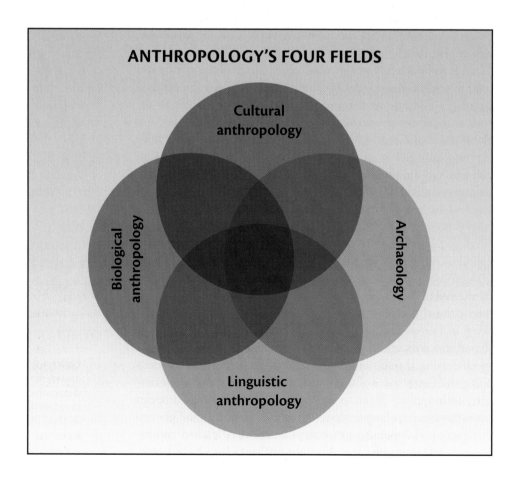

Figure 1.2   Anthropology's Four Fields.

Cultural anthropology focuses on the social lives of living communities. Until the 1970s, most cultural anthropologists conducted research in non-Western communities, spending a year or two observing social life. We call this kind of research anthropological fieldwork. These anthropologists learned the local language and studied broad aspects of the community, recording information about people's economic transactions, religious rituals, political organizations, and families, seeking to understand how these distinct domains influenced each other. In recent decades they have come to focus on more specific issues in the communities they study, such as how and why religious conflicts occur, how environmental changes affect agricultural production, and how economic interactions create social inequalities. Today, anthropologists are as likely to study modern institutions, occupational groups, ethnic minorities, and the role of computer technology or advertising in their own cultures as they are to study cultures outside their own.

Archaeology studies past cultures, by excavating sites where people lived, worked, farmed, or conducted some other activity. Some archaeologists study prehistory (life before written records), trying to understand how people lived before they had domesticated plants and animals. Or they may reconstruct the patterns of trade or warfare between ancient settlements. Two themes have been traditional concerns of prehistoric archaeology: (1) the transition from hunting and gathering to agriculture, and (2) the rise of cities and states, when complex social, political, and economic institutions arose, along with occupational specializations, social class distinctions, and the emergence of early political forms that resemble states.

Another branch of archaeology is historical archaeology, in which archaeologists excavate sites where written historical documentation about the sites also exists. The goal is to supplement what we know about a community or society from what is found in the ground with written records. Interestingly, historical archaeologists often find that few people actually lived as they described themselves in diaries and published accounts. For example, excavations on American cotton plantations have added a great deal to what we already know about the living conditions of slaves on plantations, information that does not generally appear in written records because the lives of slaves and poor white farmers were rarely documented in more than cursory ways.

Biological anthropology (also called physical anthropology) focuses on the biological and biocultural aspects of the human species, past and present, along with those of our closest relatives, the nonhuman primates (apes, monkeys, and related species). A mainstay of biological anthropology has been the attempt to uncover human fossils and reconstruct the pathways of human evolution. By the 1950s and 1960s, biological anthropologists expanded into the study of human health and disease and began to look at the nonhuman primates (especially monkeys and apes) to determine what is part of our basic primate biology and what comes with culture. Biological anthropology is currently a field of many specializations; researchers still explore human evolution, health and disease, and primate behavior, but they also study topics such as human genetics, the impact of social stress on the body, and human diet and nutrition.

Linguistic anthropology studies how people communicate with one another through language, and how language use shapes group membership and identity. Linguistic anthropologists also look at how language helps people organize their cultural beliefs and ideologies. These anthropologists have traditionally studied the categories that indigenous people use in their own languages, attempting to understand how they classify parts of their social and natural worlds differently from peoples in other societies.

Anthropology is by nature an interdisciplinary discipline. Its subfields cross into many other academic disciplines across the social and natural sciences. Cultural anthropologists, for example, often draw on sociological and psychological approaches,

- **Cultural anthropology.** The study of the social lives of living communities.

- **Archaeology.** The study of past cultures, by excavating sites where people lived, worked, farmed, or conducted some other activity.

- **Biological anthropology.** The study of the biological and biocultural aspects of the human species, past and present, along with those of our closest relatives, the nonhuman primates.

- **Linguistic anthropology.** The study of how people communicate with one another through language and how language use shapes group membership and identity.

as well as historical and economic data for some projects. Most archaeologists need to understand the principles of geology, including stratigraphy (the layers of earth in which human artifacts might be found) and techniques used to date artifacts. Many archaeologists also need to understand ecological and environmental sciences to be able to reconstruct ancient landscapes. Biological anthropology draws heavily on the biological study of morphology (which deals with the form and structure of organisms), cellular biology, and genetics.

One thing that keeps such diverse subfields together is a shared history. In the early twentieth century, anthropology became organized into the four subfields we know today, from a shared evolutionary perspective. Archaeologists and cultural anthropologists, especially in North America, generally see themselves as asking similar kinds of questions about human cultures. The major difference is that cultural anthropologists can observe cultures as they are lived, while archaeologists can only reconstruct these cultures from what they have left behind. Another reason for the persistence of the four-field approach is that anthropologists share certain fundamental approaches and concepts they agree are important for making sense of humanity's complexity. These include culture, cultural relativism, diversity, change, and holism.

Culture

Imagine how people would react if you went to the university bookstore to buy textbooks, and you haggled over the price at the cash register. Or if you caught a cold, and you explained to your friends that the sickness was caused by someone's jealousy, and this jealous person had hired a witch to cast a spell on you. In both cases most people would think you were crazy. But in many societies throughout Africa, Asia, Latin America, the Pacific, and other regions, a lot of ordinary people would think you were crazy for *not* haggling or for not explaining your misfortunes as the workings of a witch.

Every human group has particular rules of behavior and a common set of explanations about how the world works. Within the community, these behaviors and explanations feel totally natural, which is to say, self-evident and necessary. People who behave differently are strange, wrong, or maybe even evil. What feels natural to us may seem totally arbitrary to another group of people, because the rules and explanations vary from one group to another. In anthropology, the term **culture** refers to these taken-for-granted notions, rules, moralities, and behaviors within a social group that feel natural and the way things should be.

- **Culture.** The taken-for-granted notions, rules, moralities, and behaviors within a social group.

The idea of culture is one of anthropology's most important contributions to knowledge. It is also one of anthropology's oldest concepts, its first use commonly credited to British anthropologist Edward Burnett Tylor in the 1870s. In "Classic Contributions: E. B. Tylor and the Culture Concept," we examine his original definition of culture.

Anthropologists believe that people have culture in two senses: the general and the particular. Culture in the general sense refers to humans' possession of a generalized capacity, even necessity, to create, share, and pass on their understandings of things through culture. From this point of view, the development of culture is *the* defining feature of our species' evolutionary history, and thus of great relevance to the subfield of biological anthropology.

Culture in the particular sense refers to the fact that people live their lives within particular cultures, or ways of life. For example, although the "American way of life" is actually culturally diverse, with differences across regions, social classes, and ethnic groups, most Americans share very similar beliefs about such things as the value of a formal education, what kinds of clothes women and men should wear to the office, and what side of the road to drive on. Archaeologists, linguistic anthropologists, and cultural anthropologists tend to study people's lives in the context of a particular

CLASSIC CONTRIBUTIONS

E. B. Tylor and the Culture Concept

E. B. Tylor.

LIKE OTHER ANTHROPOLOGISTS of the latter half of the nineteenth century, Edward B. Tylor believed that the social and cultural differences of humanity could be explained as the product of evolutionary forces. Tylor's primary intellectual concern throughout his career was developing an evolutionary sequence that would explain how people evolved from a state of what he called "primitive savagery" to more "advanced" levels of civilization. In his book *Primitive Culture*, published in 1871, he advanced his argument that humans are subject to evolutionary forces in all aspects of their lives, including what he called "culture," offering the now classic definition presented here. Although contemporary uses of the term *culture* have changed since Tylor's definition—mainly because anthropologists today reject Tylor's evolutionary perspective—Tylor's definition is important because it provided a basis for the scientific study of culture that has been central to the discipline ever since.

Culture or Civilization, taken in its wide ethnographic sense, is that complex whole which includes knowledge, belief, art, morals, law, custom, and any other capabilities and habits acquired by man as a member of society. The condition of culture among the various societies of mankind, in so far as it is capable of being investigated on general principles, is a subject apt for the study of laws of human thought and action.... [I]ts various grades may be regarded as stages of development or evolution, each the outcome of previous history, and about to do its proper part in shaping the history of the future. [Tylor 1871:1]

Questions for Reflection

1. How is this definition different from or similar to the notion of culture you had before taking an anthropology course?

2. Tylor believed that people acquire culture as members of a society. But how specifically might someone acquire his or her culture?

culture. In Chapter 2 we explore the concept of culture more deeply, but here it is important to know that when anthropologists use the term *culture* they are nearly always referring to ideas about the world and ways of interacting in society or in the environment in predictable and expected ways.

Cultural Relativism

All humans participate in culture. Anthropologists, of course, also carry with them basic assumptions about how the world works and what is right or wrong, which typically become apparent when one is studying a culture that makes completely different assumptions. One possible response to the gap in understanding that comes with being in another culture is **ethnocentrism**, assuming our way of doing

- **Ethnocentrism.** The assumption that one's own way of doing things is correct, while dismissing other people's practices or views as wrong or ignorant.

things is correct, while simply dismissing other people's assumptions as wrong or ignorant. Such a position would render the attempt to understand other cultures meaningless and can lead to bigotry and intolerance. To avoid such misunderstandings, anthropologists have traditionally emphasized **cultural relativism**, the moral and intellectual principle that one should withhold judgment about seemingly strange or exotic beliefs and practices.

Human Diversity

Another of anthropology's major contributions to knowledge has been to describe and explain human **diversity**, the sheer variety of ways of being human around the world. When anthropologists talk about diversity, they mean something different from the popular usage of the term in the United States, which typically refers to different kinds of art, cuisine, dress, or dance, as well as to differences among various racial and ethnic groups.

Defined anthropologically, diversity refers to multiplicity and variety, which is not the same as mere difference. Within multiplicity and variety, there is both difference *and* similarity. This idea of diversity-as-multiplicity can shed light not just on racial differences but also on another important issue of our time: the cultural effects of globalization, which refers to the rapid movement of money, people, and goods across national boundaries. People now drink Coca-Cola, wear Levi's jeans, and watch CNN all over the world, leading many observers to believe that the diversity of human cultures is in decline because more and more people are participating in a global economy. Yet cultural differences do not just disappear. In fact, globalization creates many new opportunities for cultural diversity—differences *and* similarities—to thrive.

An example drawn from the southern Mexican state of Chiapas illustrates this point (Figure 1.3). In Chiapas, some indigenous people have adapted Coca-Cola for use in their religious and community ceremonies. For many generations Tztotzil Mayas [**tso**-tseel **my**-ahs] in the community of San Juan Chamula used alcoholic

- **Cultural relativism.** The moral and intellectual principle that one should withhold judgment about seemingly strange or exotic beliefs and practices.

- **Diversity.** The sheer variety of ways of being human around the world.

Figure 1.3   San Juan Chamula, Chiapas, Mexico.

Figure 1.4   San Juan Chamula, Chiapas, Mexico.

drinks, particularly fermented corn drinks and distilled sugar cane liquor, in their public and religious rites (Nash 2007) (Figure 1.4). To create these rites, traditional Mayan religious leaders blended Catholic and indigenous traditions, combining Catholicism's celebration of saints' days with the Maya belief that consuming intoxicating spirits helps individuals access sacred powers. Alcoholism, however, became a severe problem, and beginning in the 1940s many Maya began converting to Protestant sects that banned alcohol, eroding the power of traditional religious leaders. In the 1980s these leaders began substituting Coca-Cola for alcoholic drinks in ceremonies. Some leaders gained great personal wealth as distributors of Coca-Cola, deepening socioeconomic class divisions in the community (Nash 2007). But community members incorporated Coke into their ritual lives easily, accepting the notion that the soft drink's bubbles have powers once associated with alcohol, for example, the ability to help individuals belch out bad spirits residing in their bodies (Thomas 2008).

Here is a powerful example of diversity-as-multiplicity: Globalization has brought changes to San Juan Chamula that resemble conditions in many other places around the globe, but Maya have imposed their own meanings on the soft drink, using it in ways that reinforce some of their own distinctive cultural traditions.

Change

As the previous example about globalization and Coca-Cola demonstrates, our world is dynamic and constantly changing. Anthropologists in each subfield are specialists in studying human change. For example:

- In *cultural anthropology*, researchers study topics as diverse as how and why religious change happens; what happens when a dominant economic system like socialism collapses or a new one like capitalism is incorporated into a traditional economy; and how and why political violence can erupt in societies experiencing rapid social change.
- In *archaeology*, researchers study the effects of environmental change on past societies; how changes in material culture reflect ongoing social, economic, and

political changes; and the processes through which complex state societies were formed and disintegrated.

- In *biological anthropology*, researchers study the specific processes of human evolution, and how our bodies and genetic makeup change in relation to environmental changes, migration, diseases, and other dynamics.
- In *linguistic anthropology*, researchers study how new languages are formed when different languages come together; and how social changes, such as changes in gender relations, are reflected in and emerge from how people communicate with each other.

Some of these changes—particularly changes in cultural practices such as the consumption of Coca-Cola—can emerge over a few years or a generation or two. Others, like changes in human biology, can take many generations and are imperceptible to most living observers. Americans, for example, have gotten considerably taller than we were in colonial times 250 years ago, probably because of changes in diet, especially in the first few years of life. But this fact is largely unnoticed by modern Americans unless we tour fine colonial houses from the 1700s when we notice that the doors are not nearly as tall as the standard door of today.

Anthropology also mirrors the changing world in which it is practiced. As new topics, issues, and problems emerge, anthropologists study things they would not have studied several decades before. Today, for example, archaeologists may study garbage dumps and how high technologies are made in contemporary Silicon Valley computer factories to understand what people actually consume and throw away. Cultural and linguistic anthropologists explore how people create communities and identities and produce new forms of communication in cyberspace. Biological anthropologists specializing in primate behaviors design studies to aid wildlife conservation officials.

Moreover, the face of anthropology has changed dramatically in recent decades. Once a discipline dominated by white European and American men, anthropology is increasingly practiced by women and members of many ethnic and racial minority groups. In the United States today, in fact, women constitute the majority of professional anthropologists. Around the world, decolonization of former colonies has brought once excluded indigenous peoples and members of internal minority groups into universities where many studied anthropology, further expanding the kinds of backgrounds and perspectives represented in the global discipline.

Holism

- **Holism.** Efforts to synthesize distinct approaches and findings into a single comprehensive interpretation.

In bringing together the study of human biology, prehistory, language, and social life under one disciplinary roof, anthropology offers powerful conceptual tools for understanding the entire context of human experience. The effort to synthesize these distinct approaches and findings into a single comprehensive explanation is called **holism**. It is American anthropology that has strived to be the most holistic. This was a legacy of German-born Franz Boas, later known as the "Founder of American Anthropology," through his work in the American Anthropological Association and at Columbia University in the early twentieth century. His student Alfred Kroeber once described four-field anthropology as a "sacred bundle" (Segal and Yanagisako 2005).

In the discipline's early years, it was possible for individuals like Boas, Kroeber, and some of their students to work in all four subfields because the body of anthropological knowledge was so small. But within several decades, the expansion of the discipline and increasing specialization within its branches forced anthropologists to concentrate on a single subfield and topics within subfields, a continuing trend today.

In the face of specialization and calls to "unwrap the sacred bundle" (Segal and Yanagisako 2005)—that is, have the subfields go their separate ways—anthropology has struggled to retain its holistic focus.

And yet many anthropologists are deeply dedicated to holism, citing its ability to explain complex issues that no single subfield, much less any other social science, could explain as effectively (Parkin and Ulijaszek 2007). In "Doing Fieldwork: Conducting Holistic Research with Stanley Ulijaszek," we highlight how one anthropologist conducts research in a holistic fashion.

As Ulijaszek's research demonstrates, no single subfield by itself could address complex research problems. Working together, however, the subfields draw a compelling holistic picture of a complex situation. So how do anthropologists actually come to know such things? We turn to this issue in the next section.

THINKING CRITICALLY ABOUT ANTHROPOLOGY

Can you suggest ways that you may learn how people in your town or city view college students from your campus?

How Do Anthropologists Know What They Know?

Anthropology employs a wide variety of methodologies, or systematic strategies for collecting and analyzing data. As we explore in this section, some of these methodologies are similar to those found in other natural and social sciences, including methods that involve the creation of statistics and even the use of mathematical models to explain things. Other methods aimed at describing cultures very different from our own are more closely allied with the humanities.

The Scientific Method in Anthropology

Anthropology often uses the **scientific method**, the most basic pattern of scientific research. The scientific method is quite simple. It starts with the observation of a fact, a verifiable truth. Next follows the construction of a hypothesis, which is a testable explanation for the facts. Then that hypothesis is tested with experiments, further observations, or measurements. If the data (the information the tests produce) show that the hypothesis is wrong, the scientist develops a new hypothesis and then tests it. If the new tests and the data they produce seem to support the hypothesis, the scientist writes a description of what he or she did and found, and shares it with other scientists. Other scientists then attempt to reproduce those tests or devise new ones, with a goal of disproving the hypothesis (Figure 1.5).

Note that this way of doing things is a method, not the pursuit of ultimate truths. The goal of the scientific method is to devise, test, and disprove hypotheses. Life's big questions—"Why are we here?" "Why is there evil in the world?" and so on—are *not* the goal of science. At best, science can provide a reasonable degree of certainty only about more limited questions—"Do the planets revolve around the sun?"

• **Scientific method.** The standard methodology of science that begins from observable facts, generates hypotheses from these facts, and then tests these hypotheses.

Doing Fieldwork

Conducting Holistic Research with Stanley Ulijaszek

STANLEY ULIJASZEK IS a British anthropologist who has been conducting research for several decades in the swamplands of coastal Papua New Guinea, an island state in the Southwest Pacific. In recent years, he has turned his attention to an interesting question: In this difficult landscape that is unsuited to agriculture, how do people acquire a sufficient, safe, and nutritious food supply? To answer this question properly requires substantial knowledge of the human biology, prehistory, and culture of coastal New Guinea.

At the center of this story is the sago palm, a palm tree that grows abundantly in swamps. Its stem contains starch, a staple food for the people who cultivate it. People cook sago in long sticks resembling dense French bread, eating it with a bit of fish. Sago is not a great staple food, because it is 99.5% starch, making it an excellent energy food, but it has few other nutrients. Worse, perhaps, is that sago is toxic when eaten uncooked or improperly prepared. Its toxicity threatens people with a specific genetic mutation that does not allow the red blood cells to carry the toxins out of the body, a mutation common among coastal New Guinea populations. Thus, because of this toxicity, eating sago presented a risk to these coastal people (Ulijaszek 2007).

It turns out, however, that this same genetic mutation confers some resistance to malaria, a mosquito-borne infectious disease common in the tropics. The key to protecting the people while releasing the nutritional energy of sago is to separate the starch from the pith at the center of the sago palm by washing and straining it, then cooking the starch, all of which reduces its toxicity to safe levels. Archaeological evidence indicates that people in this region figured out this process at least 6,000 years ago, which is when they began leaving behind their hunting-and-gathering way of life to take up agriculture. Ulijaszek concludes that they adapted sago for human consumption by detoxifying it, which in turn allowed people's genetic mutation to survive, thus providing some resistance to malaria in this difficult environment. People then continued to pass on the genetic trait of malarial resistance.

Ulijaszek's research addresses an interesting puzzle about how humans can successfully adapt to a challenging natural environment, and how those changes are intertwined with genetic factors like the resistance to malaria. To achieve this,

Cultivating Nutrition from the Sago Palm. Transforming the pith of the sago palm into food is a complex process. First the pith must be chopped out of the trunk and pulverized using simple cutting and pounding tools, and then the starch must be leached from the dense mass of fiber using a frame made from the base of the leaf stalk in which the starch is pounded with water to release and strain the edible starch, leaving the inedible fiber behind in the frame. Later the sago flour is collected from a basin where it has settled.

he drew on the evidence of cultural and linguistic anthropology, gained by observing how people cultivate, process, consume, and talk about sago. He also drew on archaeological evidence of sago production that goes back thousands of years, not necessarily by conducting the excavations himself, but by relying heavily on the evidence archaeologists working in that area had produced. He also drew on evidence about the genetic makeup of local populations drawn from blood samples and genetic analyses.

Questions for Reflection

1. How do you think Ulijaszek's findings would have differed if he relied only on the evidence of cultural anthropology? Archaeology? Biological anthropology?

2. Do you think Ulijaszek's approach would be applicable to a study of lowfat diets in the United States? How would you apply it?

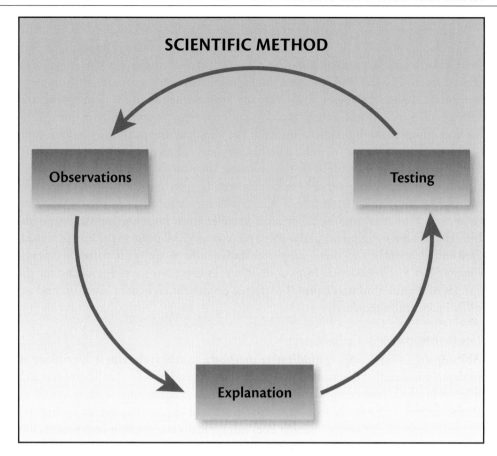

SCIENTIFIC METHOD

Observations

Testing

Explanation

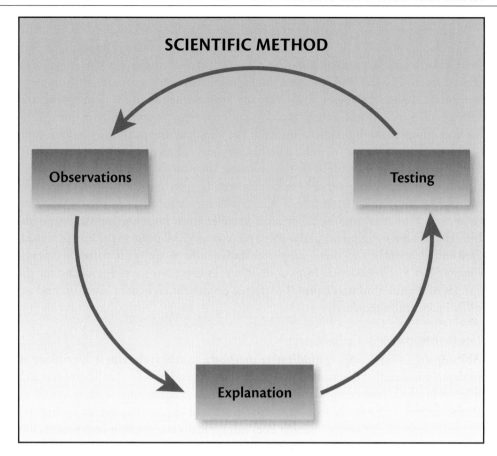 **Figure 1.5 The Scientific Method.** The process is circular, not linear.

"Do mold-encrusted bagels cause people to get sick?" "How did our species develop the traits we now have?" and so on. Scientists regularly disagree among themselves, often passionately. Researchers with different intellectual backgrounds and orientations ask different types of questions and look at data in different ways. Scientists tend to see such debates as beneficial to the practice of science because the more questions asked, the more observations made, and the more tests conducted, the more knowledge is produced.

Theories Guide Research

Theories, which are tested and repeatedly supported hypotheses, are key elements of the scientific method. A **theory** not only explains things; it also helps guide research by focusing the researcher's questions and making the findings meaningful. It is important to note that while many Americans assume that a theory is some wild hunch or guess, when scientists in the natural and social sciences use the term *theory*, they mean a carefully constructed hypothesis that has been tested and retested. There is rarely any guessing involved.

- **Theory.** A tested and repeatedly supported hypothesis.

Quantitative Data Collection

To build and test hypotheses and theories requires data. All of anthropology's subfields employ a number of techniques for gathering and processing data. Some of these techniques use **quantitative methods**, which classify features of a phenomenon, count or measure them, and construct mathematical and statistical models to explain what is observed. Most quantitative research takes place in the subfields of biological anthropology and archaeology, although some cultural and linguistic anthropologists use quantitative techniques as well.

- **Quantitative method.** A methodology that classifies features of a phenomenon, counting or measuring them, and constructing mathematical and statistical models to explain what is observed.

As an illustration of quantitative research, consider the work of one of the authors of this book, Agustín Fuentes. His research examines the nature of human–monkey interactions, and how, when, and why diseases, such as viruses, get passed between these species. Fuentes and his team (including many undergraduate anthropology students) observe monkeys and humans interacting in Bali, Singapore, and Gibraltar. In each location they record quantitative details about interactions: Who interacts, how many individuals interact, the length of interactions, whether interactions are aggressive or friendly, whether physical contact between species occurs, and whether food is involved in the contact. They interview humans at the locations, sometimes using surveys or administering questionnaires, and collect detailed physical information about the landscape inhabited by the people and monkeys. They also take blood or fecal samples from both the monkeys and the humans, analyzing them for pathogens and parasites. All these variables are considered independently and then compared statistically to see what patterns emerge. Fuentes has discovered that human–monkey interactions vary depending on the species of monkey, human cultural patterns, gender differences in humans, and sex differences in the monkeys.

Qualitative Data Collection

- **Qualitative method.** A research strategy producing an in-depth and detailed description of social activities and beliefs.

Anthropologists also employ **qualitative methods**, in which the aim is to produce an in-depth and detailed description of social behaviors and beliefs. Qualitative research usually involves interviews with people, as well as observations of their activities. Research data comes in the form of words, images, or objects. In contrast with quantitative methods, qualitative research does not typically use research instruments like surveys or questionnaires. The research instrument is the researcher him- or herself, whose subjective perceptions and impressions of the subject matter also become the basis for knowledge. The **ethnographic method**, which involves prolonged and intensive observation of and participation in the life of a community, is a qualitative methodology and is a hallmark of cultural anthropology.

- **Ethnographic method.** A prolonged and intensive observation of and participation in the life of a community.

Luis Vivanco, another one of this book's authors, is a cultural anthropologist who uses qualitative methods to ask how global environmentalism changes people's relationships with nature in Latin America. In one of his projects, he conducted more than twenty months of research in Monteverde, Costa Rica, a rural community bordering a tropical cloud forest, and renowned worldwide as a site of conservation and ecotourism. He interviewed local farmers, environmental activists, ecotourists, and scientists, usually on multiple occasions, sometimes with a tape recorder and notepad and other times in informal conversations at the local grocery store or in some other public setting (Figure 1.6). He observed these people interacting with others and participated in community events, including celebrations and public protests. Working as a volunteer in a nature preserve, he listened to how its managers and the ecotourists talk about tropical rain forests. He collected newspaper clippings and reports from local environmental groups and took pictures of people doing things. His fieldnotes, recordings, images, documents, and personal experiences with environmentalists and farmers have helped him understand environmentalism to be a complex arena of social conflict where people struggle not just over how to protect nature but also how to deal with rapid social changes caused by globalization.

The Comparative Method

- **Comparative method.** A research method that derives insights from careful comparisons of aspects of two or more cultures or societies.

Unlike other scientists, anthropologists do not conduct experiments or make predictions. Instead, anthropologists use the **comparative method** (Kaplan and Manners 1972:42–43). The comparative method allows anthropologists to derive

Figure 1.6   Monteverde Bus. In Vivanco's research on environmentalism in Costa Rica, his interest in the social dynamics of ecotourism led him to spend a lot of time among ecotourists, such as the ones shown here arriving in Monteverde by bus.

insights from careful comparisons of two or more cultures or societies. The actual "method" is nothing like a precise recipe for research, however, but a general approach, which holds that any particular detail of human behavior or particular social condition should not be seen in isolation, but should be considered against the backdrop of the full range of behaviors and conditions in their individual social settings.

Some of the research of this book's other author, cultural anthropologist Robert Welsch, illustrates how anthropologists can use the comparative method. Welsch has conducted extended ethnographic research both in Papua New Guinea and in Indonesia. One of his research projects explicitly made use of comparative research strategies to understand the social and religious meanings of masks and carved objects in three societies along the Papuan Gulf of New Guinea that are now in museum collections. To conduct his comparative study, Welsch studied the museum collections, pored over published and unpublished accounts of the people who collected the masks, and interviewed older villagers about their traditional practices (Figure 1.7). He learned that although these three societies used the same kinds of objects, their differing decorative styles suggested differences in the social purposes for which each society used the objects (2006).

When Anthropology Is Not a Science: Interpreting Other Cultures

Not all anthropologists characterize what they do as science. Prominent British anthropologist E. E. Evans-Pritchard (1902–1973) pronounced in 1961 that anthropology should be grouped with the humanities, especially history, rather than natural sciences (Evans-Pritchard 1961). Describing other people, he argued, requires an understanding of their inner lives and beliefs that no scientific methodology can grasp. His view was that the complexity of social behavior prevents any completely objective analysis of human culture.

Figure 1.7   Boards Inside Longhouse at Naharo. Welsch visited many longhouses to discuss ritual carvings and their meaning as part of his comparative analysis of art and its social contexts in traditional societies of the Papuan Gulf. This image shows boards he was discussing with elders and their families in Naharo village.

These days most cultural anthropologists agree with this position. They disregard the scientific ideal of the researcher's detachment from the subject of study: the belief that researchers are not supposed to talk about what they feel and experience, or how emotions and experiences influence what they learn and know as anthropologists (Fabian 2001). The work of American anthropologist Renato Rosaldo (b. 1941), who studied head-hunting in a Filipino society called the Ilongot [Ill-**lahn**-goht], illustrates this point of view. When Rosaldo (1989) asked the Ilongots to explain why they take heads, they explained that when a loved one dies, their grief turns to rage, and the only way to vent that rage and get on with life is to take the head of a traditional enemy. Rosaldo initially dismissed this explanation, assuming there had to be a "deeper" purpose for head-hunting, such as creating group cohesion or allowing young men to prove their worthiness for marriage by showing they could kill an enemy.

That is, until his wife Shelly, also an anthropologist, died in an accident during fieldwork in the Philippines. His own devastating loss generated a similar combination of grief and rage. While he was adjusting to Shelly's death, Rosaldo could grasp emotionally what the Ilongot were getting at. Dealing with the death opened his eyes to the force of emotions in social life, something he and most other anthropologists had never really considered. Rosaldo (1989) realized that his training as an anthropologist, which emphasized scientific detachment, accounted for his initial dismissing of Ilongot notions of head-hunting. He concluded that his other interpretations of head-hunting were not wrong, but they presented an incomplete picture of why Ilongot did it. He also concluded that ethnographic knowledge is an open-ended process; that is, as the ethnographer's own life experiences and knowledge change, so do his or her insights into other cultures.

Ethnographers know other cultures from particular points of view. Although they strive to see things from many perspectives—the perspectives of the many people they interview and observe—anthropologists' insights are always partial, indeed, only some of many possible interpretations of culture. But anthropologists do not just try to understand the world of culture and other human concerns; they also intervene in practical ways, which is an issue we explore next.

THINKING CRITICALLY ABOUT ANTHROPOLOGY

How might you use a comparative perspective even if you only visit just one country while on vacation? Consider the other cultural contexts you have experienced and how these might provide a comparative framework for experiencing a novel society and culture.

How Is Anthropology Put to Work in the World?

Anthropological research is relevant and useful for addressing many social problems. At some point in their careers, most anthropologists get involved in work with practical, real-world concerns, applying their research skills and knowledge to the creation or implementation of policies, management of social programs, conduct of legal proceedings, or even the design of consumer products.

Applied and Practicing Anthropology: "The Fifth Subfield"?

Practical applications are such an important component of anthropology that some anthropologists consider them the "fifth subfield." These practical applications include those of **applied anthropology**, anthropological research commissioned to serve an organization's needs, and those of **practicing anthropology**, the broadest category of anthropological work, in which the anthropologist not only performs research but also gets involved in the design, implementation, and management of some organization, process, or product. One reason some consider these two enterprises a fifth subfield is that the numbers of anthropologists doing these things has swelled in recent decades as university budget cuts have diminished job opportunities in academia. But the notion of a fifth subfield sets up a false dichotomy between academic (or theoretical) and practical (or applied) work, which have often been intertwined throughout the history of the discipline (Field and Fox 2007).

- **Applied anthropology.** Anthropological research commissioned to serve an organization's needs.

- **Practicing anthropology.** Anthropological work involving research as well as involvement in the design, implementation, and management of some organization, process, or product.

Putting Anthropology to Work

Putting anthropological skills and knowledge to work is a challenging enterprise, not least because of tensions it creates with some anthropologists who feel that "we should never forget that a commitment to improving the world is no substitute for understanding it" (Hastrup and Elass 1990:307). In spite of the challenges, however, anthropologists have effectively put their discipline to work addressing difficult social, health, and educational problems, as the following snapshots demonstrate.

Figure 1.8   Cultural Anthropologist Mary Amuyunzu-Nyamongo.

Mary Amuyunzu-Nyamongo: Bringing Cultural Knowledge to Health Programs in Kenya

Like many other anthropologists, Kenyan anthropologist Mary Amuyunzu-Nyamongo works on pressing social and health problems confronting her country. She is currently director and cofounder of the African Institute for Health and Development, an organization that provides research and training on the social dimensions of debilitating illnesses in Kenya, including HIV/AIDS. Amuyunzu-Nyamongo was among the first students of anthropology at the University of Nairobi. She went on to postgraduate studies in medical anthropology at Cambridge University. Some of the problems Amuyunzu-Nyamongo has studied include the lack of detailed knowledge of local communities that is necessary to make health programs work. Amuyunzu-Nyamongo collected local knowledge from insights about people's health beliefs and practices through qualitative research. For example, during a campaign to control mosquito-borne illness in a coastal village, government officials wanted to conduct blood screenings to identify levels of infection. They told school children to tell their parents to get screened, which failed. Amuyunzu-Nyamongo knew that in this culture, male heads of households control decision-making. She organized a meeting where the issue of screenings was introduced to them. Once these men became involved, the screenings became successful (Amuyunzu-Nyamongo 2006).

Davina Two Bears and Applied Archaeology on the Navajo Reservation

Figure 1.9   Archaeologist Davina Two Bears.

Because archaeologists often encounter burials when they excavate prehistoric Indian sites, American Indian communities have often found themselves at odds with archaeologists over the question of what to do with the human remains uncovered. Some Indians object to any excavation at all. But the work of Navajo archaeologist Davina Two Bears (2006) runs counter to the expectations many people may have about the inherent tensions between Indians and archaeologists. For several years now, she has worked with the Navajo Nation Archaeology Department, which emerged in 1988 from the Navajo Nation Cultural Resource Management Program. As both an archaeologist and a cultural resource management professional for the Navajo, she advises on potential damage to archaeological sites that might be caused by road construction or building projects. Two Bears uses her professional archaeological training to prevent damage to ancient sites, which many Navajo people view as deserving great respect. Two Bears identifies and records the locations and characteristics of sites. When proposed projects would damage archaeological sites, Two Bears and her colleagues try to identify alternative locations. She feels that although she has been professionally trained, her work is more an extension of what Navajos have always done in protecting their ancestors and their ancestors' special sites.

James McKenna: The Naturalness of Co-sleeping

Figure 1.10   Biological Anthropologist James McKenna.

In much of the Western world, it is considered "healthy" for an infant to sleep in a crib, alone, for long stretches during the night. When a baby wakes frequently or wants to sleep alongside the parents, many see the child as too dependent and not doing well. In our society we also have many deaths from sudden infant death syndrome (SIDS) in which infants die in the night for unknown reasons. After decades examining how humans and their infants share social and physiological space, biological anthropologist James McKenna (1996) and his colleagues developed an explanation for how and why many SIDS deaths occur in the United States.

Through intensive studies of sleeping mothers and infants around the planet, McKenna and his colleagues found that the frequent stirring of young infants, nursing, and the carbon dioxide and oxygen mix created by bodies close together are important aspects of the healthy development of human babies. The physical closeness to the parent not only fosters the healthy development of the child's body, but it also facilitates feelings of well-being in both mother and child. It appears that co-sleeping assists the infant's development and dramatically reduces the risks of SIDS (see Chapter 9).

Akira Yamamoto: Supporting Indian Language Revitalization in Arizona

A number of linguistic anthropologists now work on the revitalization of endangered languages, including professor emeritus Akira Yamamoto at the University of Kansas, who has supported language revitalization efforts among the Hualapai [**wah**-lah-pie] Indians of Northwestern Arizona. Yamamoto helped convince school officials of the value of using Hualapai language in schools, and he codesigned and implemented a bilingual school curriculum (Watahomigie and Yamamoto 1992). Yamamoto emphasizes a collaborative approach with native speakers. Recognizing that no language will survive if it relies on an outside specialist to promote it, Yamamoto supports these people with his linguistic skills in their everyday use of their language.

These snapshots offer a small sample of the range of ways anthropologists put their discipline to work. As we discuss in the next section, anthropology—whether practical or academic in its orientation—raises important ethical issues.

Figure 1.11   Linguistic Anthropologist Akira Yamamoto.

THINKING CRITICALLY ABOUT ANTHROPOLOGY

Compare how an anthropologist and an engineer might each approach a problem involving where to situate a bridge or highway in a heavily populated area.

What Ethical Issues Does Anthropology Raise?

At the heart of anthropology are issues of **ethics**—moral questions about right and wrong and standards of appropriate behavior. They come up in two ways. First, anthropologists learn about how and why people in other cultures think and act as they do by researching their moral standards. Anthropologists often find these things out in the process of adjusting themselves to that culture's rules of ethical behavior.

Second, doing anthropology itself involves ethical relationships between researchers and others, raising many important and complex issues about the ethical conduct of anthropological research and practice. Ethics in anthropology—the moral

● **Ethics.** Moral questions about right and wrong and standards of appropriate behavior.

principles that guide anthropological conduct—are not just a list of "dos and don'ts." Nor is ethics just cautionary tales of research gone awry. Ethics is organically connected to what it means to be a good anthropologist (Fluehr-Lobban 2003). Two common ethical dilemmas that face all anthropologists have to do with the effects of their research on the people, objects, or animals they study and on those to whom they are responsible, which we introduce here.

Do No Harm. But Is That Enough?

The Nuremberg trials after World War II revealed that Nazi scientists had conducted harmful experiments on people in concentration camps. Scientists responded by establishing informal ethical codes for dealing with research subjects. But in 1974 abuse of medical research subjects in the United States led Congress to pass a law preventing unethical research with human subjects (Figure 1.12). This new law required research institutes and universities where research was conducted to establish an Institutional Review Board (IRB) to monitor all human subjects–based research. Medical, scientific, and social science organizations, including anthropologists, published codes of ethics emphasizing avoiding harm for people and animals who are the subjects of research.

"Do no harm" continues to be a bedrock principle in anthropology's primary code of ethics, the American Anthropological Association's Principles of Professional Responsibility (see inside front cover). Anthropologists routinely explain to people involved in their research any risks their participation might carry and obtain their "informed consent" to participate. Anthropological publications avoid sharing confidential information and commonly disguise their informants' identities, in case those individuals could be targeted for harm because of what they say. Some anthropologists feel the principle of "do no harm" is not enough, asserting that anthropologists have a moral imperative to go further by doing good, by working for social justice and the alleviation of suffering in powerless and marginalized communities (Scheper-Hughes 1995; Fluehr-Lobban 2003).

Figure 1.12   Scandal at Tuskegee. Between 1932 and 1972, the U.S. Public Health Service studied syphilis among white and black men. When scientists learned they could treat syphilis with penicillin, they gave it to the white men but not the black men. This abuse precipitated reform in the use of humans as research subjects in the United States.

Thinking Like an Anthropologist

Anthropological Responsibilities to Informants and People in Authority

ANTHROPOLOGISTS BEGIN THEIR research by asking questions. In this box, we want you to learn how to ask questions as an anthropological researcher. Part 1 describes a situation and follows up with questions we would ask. Part 2 asks you to do the same thing with a different situation.

PART 1: ANTHROPOLOGISTS AND THE WARS IN IRAQ AND AFGHANISTAN

The U.S. government has been an influential supporter of anthropological research and researchers. For example, many anthropologists in all the discipline's subfields work in U.S. governmental service. The types of jobs anthropologists do are as wide-ranging as the discipline's interests and strengths, among them genetics research at the National Institutes of Health; working on the protection and conservation of archaeological sites for the National Park Service; and facilitating community involvement in watershed conservation programs at the Environmental Protection Agency. The U.S. government also provides substantial financial support for university-based anthropologists not directly in its employment through research funding agencies like the National Science Foundation and the Fulbright Scholar Program.

The responsibility anthropologists have to the government may be nothing more than conducting rigorous, accurate research, or research that is publishable or useful for decision-makers, which is what most private foundations that sponsor anthropological research also expect. But sometimes the sponsor's desire to know something in particular can conflict with the anthropologist's ethical obligation to protect informants.

An example of this conflict emerged in the context of the U.S. military's involvement in wars in Iraq and Afghanistan beginning in 2001. U.S. military leaders recognized that a basic lack of cultural and linguistic knowledge about local people among U.S. troops can negatively impact their abilities to identify enemy combatants and the social networks that support those combatants, as well as to build alliances with local people necessary to help U.S. troops complete their missions.

As a result, the Department of Defense established a unit called the "Human Terrain System" (HTS), composed of applied social science and humanities researchers. The program was closed in 2014 when funding ended. Some of these researchers were cultural anthropologists. Their work involved accompanying troops into villages to conduct

Human Terrain Systems Member Conducting Interviews in Afghanistan.

interviews of local people, identifying village leaders and power brokers, and advising military commanders and State Department officials about the possible social consequences of their decisions. These social scientists were not intended to be combatants themselves, although they were allowed to carry weapons for self-defense. As one member of the program said, "One anthropologist can be much more effective than a B-2 bomber—not winning a war, but creating a peace one Afghan at a time" (HTS 2010).

HTS researchers underwent training in research ethics and internal ethics reviews to help them better manage relations with the vulnerable populations with whom they work. They sometimes even found themselves at odds with the military commanders they were advising when they expressed that military action could negatively affect those populations. The American Anthropological Association nevertheless condemned this use of anthropology as an ethical violation because the primary responsibility and accountability of the anthropologists was to the military, not to their informants. Furthermore, critics argued that anthropologists are also responsible to the discipline's standards of integrity, truth, and openness. An individual anthropologist who does not follow these standards can affect the reputation of other anthropologists. One reason for rejecting military-oriented research, for example, is that the association of anthropology with military action hurts other anthropologists' abilities to gain people's trust, a key component of anthropological research.

(continued)

Thinking Like an Anthropologist (continued)

What questions does this situation raise for anthropological researchers?

1. What are the possible consequences of such research for the individual researchers and the discipline at large?
2. Is the anthropologist obliged to tell everything he or she finds out through research or can and should some information be held back?
3. Should loyalty to one's nation transcend loyalty to one's informants?
4. Would hiding the identity of the informants be enough to quell ethical concerns raised by the military's use of anthropology?

PART 2: ANTHROPOLOGY STUDENTS AND ETHICAL RESPONSIBILITIES

As a student of anthropology, you may be confronted with ethical dilemmas about your responsibilities to your informants and people in authority. For example, it is possible that you will be asked to conduct basic research, such as studying a club or fraternity on campus, or a social setting or group in the community. It is not unlikely that during the course of your research, you may witness an illegal activity—such as alcohol use by a minor, drug dealing, or some other situation in which a law is broken. What questions would you ask about this situation as an anthropological researcher? (Sample questions can be found at the end of this chapter. There is no single set of correct questions, but some questions are more insightful than others.)

To Whom Are Anthropologists Responsible?

The primary ethical responsibility of anthropologists is to the people, species, or artifacts they study. Whether it is a pottery shard, baboon, or person, anthropologists are expected to side with their subjects. It does not mean that an archaeologist is expected to throw himself or herself in front of a bulldozer to prevent an archaeological site from being destroyed or that a cultural anthropologist should take up arms in defense of informants threatened by the police or the military. It means that anthropologists should take whatever action is possible when their subjects are threatened, short of doing something illegal. Such action might include helping prepare legal paperwork necessary to stop the bulldozer and conserve the artifacts.

What complicates this principle is that anthropologists are also responsible to other parties. For example, anthropologists also have a responsibility to the public, including the obligation to disseminate the findings of their research—even when something that is published can lower public opinion about a group of people. Anthropologists also have responsibilities to their sponsors who fund their research—a theme we explore in "Thinking Like an Anthropologist: Anthropological Responsibilities to Informants and People in Authority."

THINKING CRITICALLY ABOUT ANTHROPOLOGY

If you were studying a local Head Start program with few resources and observed problems with local funding for the facility, could you suggest some "Action Anthropology" projects that might help the organization?

Conclusion

Ever since the 1850s, anthropologists have been asking questions about and developing perspectives on human societies past and present. Their expertise is on culture, diversity, how and why social change happens, the dynamics of human biology, and the ways people communicate with each other. The four subfields of anthropology—cultural anthropology, archaeology, biological anthropology, and linguistic anthropology—sometimes come together to offer powerful conceptual tools for understanding the whole context of human experience, an approach called holism. Together with the range of methodological tools represented in the discipline—sophistication with theory, quantitative methods, qualitative methods, and the comparative method—anthropology offers a highly relevant discipline for today's world.

But because anthropology deals with people, their bodies, and cultural artifacts meaningful to people, nearly everything anthropologists study invokes ethical concerns. Throughout this book we consider the ethics and application of anthropology research as we explore anthropological research in all four subfields. But let us begin our journey toward an understanding of anthropology with a fuller discussion of the concept of culture.

KEY TERMS

Reviewing the Chapter

Chapter Section	What We Know	To Be Resolved
How did anthropology begin?	During the nineteenth century, the rise of industrialization, the influence of evolutionary theory, and colonial contact with less industrialized cultures led to the discipline of understanding how cultures operate and interact.	Anthropologists are still fascinated—and challenged—by the contrasts and changes in culture worldwide as a result of globalization.
What are the four subfields of anthropology and what do they share in common?	Anthropologists in all subfields share certain fundamental approaches and concepts, including culture, cultural relativism, diversity, change, and holism.	Some anthropologists continue to debate the idea that the subfields, with their distinct methods and specialized research interests, belong together in the same discipline.
How do anthropologists know what they know?	Anthropology has a strong relationship with the scientific method; all anthropologists use theories, collect data, and analyze that data.	While most cultural anthropologists reject the possibility of a completely objective analysis of human culture, other subfields of anthropology, such as archaeology and biological anthropology, are thoroughly committed to the scientific method.
How is anthropology put to work in the world?	All four subfields have both theoretical and applied aspects. Applied research uses the insights of anthropological theory to solve problems.	Most anthropologists see an anthropological approach as providing a better way of understanding people from different backgrounds than any other discipline, but anthropologists continue to disagree among themselves about how to apply that understanding to address human problems.
What ethical issues does anthropology raise?	Issues of ethics—moral questions about right and wrong and standards of appropriate behavior—are at the heart of anthropology.	Certain ethical issues have no easy resolution, such as the ideal that anthropologists should do no harm, or how to resolve conflicting responsibilities anthropologists have to different communities and publics.

Readings

There are numerous books that examine the historical emergence and intellectual history of anthropology. One of the best is the 2007 book *A New History of Anthropology*, edited by Henrika Kuklick (Malden, MA: Wiley-Blackwell).

●●●●●●●●●●●●●●●●●●●●●●●●●

The 2005 book *Anthropology Put to Work*, edited by Les Field and Richard G. Fox (Oxford: Berg Publishers), offers an introduction to both the opportunities and the disciplinary, social, and political complexities involved in applying anthropological expertise.

●●●●●●●●●●●●●●●●●●●●●●●●●

For a detailed exploration of the primary ethical concerns and dilemmas involved in anthropological research across the subfields, see Carolyn Fluehr-Lobban's 2003 book *Ethics and the Profession of Anthropology: Dialogue for Ethically Conscious Practice* (Walnut Creek, CA: AltaMira Press).

●●●●●●●●●●●●●●●●●●●●●●●●●

The 2007 book *Holistic Anthropology: Emergence and Convergence*, edited by David Parkin and Stanley Ulijaszek (New York: Berghahn Books), provides a contemporary perspective on the development of cross-subfield collaborations dedicated to the notion of holism. For a critical perspective on that desire for holism, see the 2005 book *Unwrapping the Sacred Bundle: Reflections on the Disciplining of Anthropology* (Durham, NC: Duke University Press), edited by Daniel Segal and Sylvia Yanagisako.

• • • • • • • • • • • • • • • • • • • •

Renato Rosaldo's 1989 book *Culture & Truth: The Remaking of Social Analysis* (Boston: Beacon Press) is a classic text that reflects critically on cultural anthropology's complicated relationship with the sciences and objectivity.

• • • • • • • • • • • • • • • • • • • •

SUGGESTED ANSWERS TO "THINKING LIKE AN ANTHROPOLOGIST"

Use these examples as a guide to answering questions for other "Thinking Like an Anthropologist" boxes in the book.

1. Does withholding information about illegal activities compromise the integrity of the discipline?
2. Would you be obliged to tell your professor everything you've found out through research or can and should some information be held back?
3. Should loyalty to one's peer group transcend loyalty to one's university or the discipline of anthropology?
4. How could you protect the identity of your informants?

Culture

Giving Meaning to Human Lives

In 2005, the body that governs intercollegiate sports in the United States, the National Collegiate Athletic Association (NCAA), banned teams with American Indian names and mascots from competing in its postseason tournaments. Clarifying the ruling, an official stated, "Colleges and universities may adopt any mascot that they wish. . . . But as a national association, we believe that mascots, nicknames, or images deemed hostile or abusive in terms of race, ethnicity or national origin should not be visible at the championship events that we control" (NCAA 2005). The ruling affected a number of schools with competitive sports programs: Florida State (Seminoles), University of North Dakota (Fighting Sioux), and University of Illinois (Fighting Illini), among others.

The ruling brought to a close decades of pressure from American Indians, students, and others who have argued that these mascots stereotype and denigrate Indian traditions. As one Oneida woman expressed, "We experience it as no less than a mockery of our cultures. We see objects sacred to us—such as the drum, eagle feathers, face painting, and traditional dress—being used, not in sacred ceremony, or in any cultural setting, but in another culture's game" (Munson 1999:14). To Indians, the mascots seem to be just another attack on Indian cultures by non-Indians—attacks they have endured for several centuries.

Outraged students, alumni, and political commentators have countered that these mascots honor Indian traditions, pointing to the strength and bravery of Native Americans they hope to emulate in their teams. They also point out that the mascots are part of venerable

---

Mascot Chief Illiniwek. Chief Illiniwek performs during a University of Illinois football game. In 2007, after a long controversy, the university retired the mascot.

traditions, part of the living cultures of their universities. Abandoning their mascots is like turning their backs on a part of their own cultural heritage.

Each side in the controversy calls into play an issue of deep concern to them that divides the participants into two opposing groups, each with a radically different interpretation of the issue. It is a cultural conflict.

The concept of culture is at the heart of anthropology. *Culture* as anthropologists use the term refers to the perspectives and actions that a group of people consider natural and self-evident. These perspectives and actions are rooted in shared meanings and the ways people act in social groups. Culture is, as we will see, a human capacity that helps us confront the common problems that face all humans, such as communicating with each other, organizing ourselves to get things done, making life predictable and meaningful, and dealing with conflict and change.

The culture concept provides a powerful lens for making sense of the differences and similarities across and within societies, a point that leads to a key question: *How does the concept of culture help explain the differences and similarities in people's ways of life?* Embedded in this broader question are the following problems, around which this chapter is organized:

What is culture?

If culture is emergent and dynamic, why does it feel so stable?

How is culture expressed through social institutions?

Can anybody own culture?

In this chapter, we present an overview of how anthropologists approach culture and explain why it is so relevant to understanding human beliefs and actions. We also offer a definition of culture that informs and shapes the rest of this textbook. We start with the key elements that all anthropologists accept as central to any definition of culture.

What Is Culture?

Culture has been defined many ways by anthropologists, and there are nearly as many approaches to studying it as there are anthropologists. This lack of agreement does not frustrate or paralyze anthropologists. In fact, most anthropologists see this diversity of perspective as the sign of a vibrant discipline. We will examine the elements of culture in this section, emphasizing the different perspectives that enliven the discipline.

Elements of Culture

English scholar Sir Edward B. Tylor (1832–1917) was a founding figure of cultural anthropology. He offered the first justification for using the word *culture* to understand differences and similarities among groups of people. He defined culture as "that complex whole which includes knowledge, belief, art, morals, law, custom, and any other capabilities and habits acquired by man as a member of society" (1871:1). Two aspects of Tylor's definition, especially that culture is *acquired* (today we say *learned*) and that culture is a "complex whole," have been especially influential.

Since Tylor's time, anthropologists have developed many theories of culture, the most prominent of which are summarized in Table 2.1. We discuss many of these theories in later chapters and explore in more detail how they have changed over time.

One of the most important changes in cultural theory is that early anthropologists tended to see cultures in societies with simple technologies as more fixed and stable than anyone does today. Nevertheless, across all these theories, there are seven basic elements that anthropologists agree are critical to any theory of culture.

Culture Is Learned

Although all human beings are born with the ability to learn culture, nobody is born as a fully formed cultural being. The process of learning a culture begins at birth, and that is partly why our beliefs and conduct seem so natural: we have been doing and thinking in certain ways since we were young. For example, the Ongee [ahn-gay], an indigenous group who live in the Andaman Islands in the Indian Ocean, learn from a very early age that ancestors cause periodic earthquakes and tidal waves, a fact that is as given to them as it would be strange to you, who were not raised with such

TABLE 2.1   PROMINENT ANTHROPOLOGICAL THEORIES OF CULTURE

Theory	Period	Major Figures	Definition
Social evolutionism	1870s–1910s	E. B. Tylor (1871), Herbert Spencer (1874–1896), L. H. Morgan (1877)	All societies pass through stages, from primitive state to complex civilization. Cultural differences are the result of different evolutionary stages.
Historical particularism	1910s–1930s	Franz Boas (1940), Alfred Kroeber (1923), Edward Sapir (2004)	Individual societies develop particular cultural traits and undergo unique processes of change. Culture traits diffuse from one culture to another.
Functionalism	1920s–1960s	Bronislaw Malinowski (1922)	Cultural practices, beliefs, and institutions fulfill psychological and social needs.
Structural-functionalism	1920s–1960s	A. R. Radcliffe-Brown (1952)	Culture is systematic, its pieces working together in a balanced fashion to keep the whole society functioning smoothly.
Neo-evolutionism	1940s–1970s	Leslie White (1949), Julian Steward (1955)	Cultures evolve from simple to complex by harnessing nature's energy through technology and the influence of particular culture-specific processes.
Cultural materialism	1960s–1970s	Marvin Harris (1979)	The material world, especially economic and ecological conditions, shape people's customs and beliefs.
Cognitive anthropology	1950s–1970s	Ward Goodenough (1965), Roy D'Andrade (1995)	Culture operates through mental models and logical systems.
Structuralism	1960s–1970s	Claude Lévi-Strauss (1961; 1949)	People make sense of their worlds through binary oppositions like hot–cold, culture–nature, male–female, and raw–cooked. These binaries are expressed in social institutions and cultural practices like kinship, myth, and language.
Interpretive anthropology	1970s–present	Clifford Geertz (1973), Victor Turner (1967), Mary Douglas (1966), Roy Wagner (1975)	Culture is a shared system of meaning. People make sense of their worlds through the use of symbols and symbolic activities like myth and ritual.
Post-structuralism	1980s–present	Renato Rosaldo (1989), James Clifford, George Marcus, Michael M. J. Fischer (Clifford and Marcus 1986; Marcus and Fischer 1986)	Not a single school of thought, but a set of theoretical positions that rejects the idea that there are underlying structures that explain culture. Embraces the idea that cultural processes are dynamic, and that the observer of cultural processes can never see culture completely objectively.

Figure 2.1   Do You Get It?
You were enculturated to read from left to right. But when speakers of Hebrew language are taught to read, such as those who might read this cartoon from a Hebrew language newspaper, they begin on the right and move left.

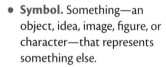

• **Enculturation.** The process of learning the social rules and cultural logic of a society.

beliefs. Anthropologists call this process of learning the cultural rules and logic of a society **enculturation**.

Enculturation happens both *explicitly* and *implicitly*. Your student experience illustrates how enculturation processes have shaped you. Throughout your schooling, your teachers have explicitly taught you many things you need to know to be a productive member of society: to write, to analyze a text, to do mathematics, and so on (Figure 2.1). But you have also learned many other things that are more implicit, that is, not clearly expressed. These lessons include obedience to authority and respect for social hierarchy, learned from sitting in class facing forward in rows so the teacher can control your attention and movement. Bells and announcements over the loudspeakers also regulate your activities and the flow of your day. These patterns are so ingrained that you take them for granted. Enculturation continues throughout your life.

Culture Uses Symbols

• **Symbol.** Something—an object, idea, image, figure, or character—that represents something else.

Clifford Geertz (1926–2006) was one of the best known American anthropologists of recent times. He proposed that culture is a system of **symbols**—a symbol being something that conventionally stands for something else—through which people make sense out of the world. Symbols may be verbal or nonverbal. Symbols are things that people in a given culture associate with something else, often something intangible, such as motherhood, family, God, or country. To illustrate this point, Geertz posed an interesting question: How do we know the difference between a wink and a twitch (1973:6-7)?

As movements of the eye, winks and twitches are identical. But the difference between them is enormous, as anyone who has experienced the embarrassment of taking one for the other can attest. A twitch is an involuntary blink of the eye, and generally speaking has no symbolic significance. A wink, however, communicates a particular message to a particular someone, and it takes a lot of implicit knowledge, first, to decide if it is a wink or a twitch, and second, to understand what it communicates.

In an instant, we must consider a number of questions: Is there intent? What is the intent—conspiracy, flirtation, parody, ridicule, or something else? Would it be socially appropriate for this person to wink at me, and under what conditions? Underlying our considerations, which may barely rise to the surface of consciousness, is a shared system of meaning in which we (and the winker) participate that helps us communicate with and understand each other. Interestingly, what sounds like a complex computational process when broken down into these many decision points actually comes quite naturally to the human mind. This is because of the human capacity for learning with symbols and signs that otherwise have little meaning outside a given culture.

• **Interpretive theory of culture.** A theory that culture is embodied and transmitted through symbols.

Geertz's concept of culture, often called the **interpretive theory of culture**, is the idea that culture is embodied and transmitted through symbols. This fundamental concept helped anthropologists clarify the symbolic basis of culture, something virtually all anthropologists take for granted today. Because culture is based on symbols, culture is implicit in how people think and act, so they rarely, if ever, recognize

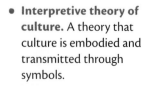

culture for what it is; it is simply natural to them. In fact, people express culture in *everything* they do—playing games, speaking a language, building houses, growing food, making love, raising children, and so on (Figure 2.2). The meanings of these things—and the symbols that underlie those meanings—differ from group to group, and, as a result, people do things and organize themselves differently around the world. These differing meanings are what make the Balinese Balinese, Zapotecs Zapotecs, and Americans Americans.

Cultures Are Dynamic, Always Adapting and Changing

In a globalized world with high levels of migration across cultural borders, communication flowing in all directions, and social and ethnic mixing, it is often impossible to say with any certainty where one culture or social group ends and another begins. As a result, many anthropologists today talk less about culture as a totally coherent and static *system* of meaning and more about the *processes* through which social meanings are constructed and shared.

Culture is a *dynamic* process. Social groups are not uniform or homogeneous, because not everybody interprets the events of everyday life in the same way, nor do they blindly act out scripts already laid out for them to perform. Cultural processes are emergent, fluid, and marked by creativity, uncertainty, differing individual meaning, and social conflict. Relations of power and inequality routinely permeate these cultural processes.

Culture Is Integrated with Daily Experience

As cultural beings, how we relate to the world seems natural to us, transparent, obvious, inevitable, and necessary. Our sense of passing time, for example, might contrast sharply with that of people in other cultures. In Western cultures, we think of time as an entity that moves from past to present to future. This concept—an element of culture—has a critical influence on our daily lives, because it helps us organize and regulate our activities every day. It also motivates us to make plans, since this concept of time leads us to believe that time must be used or it will be lost.

Understanding that culture comprises a dynamic and interrelated set of social, economic, and belief structures is a key to understanding how the whole of culture operates. The integration of culture across these domains leads to expectations that are specific to a given social group. For example, white middle-class American parents think it is "natural" for their babies to sleep in single beds, often in their own rooms (Small 1998:116–18). They believe that sleeping with their babies creates emotional dependence. Such dependence seems damaging to the child in a society which prizes personal independence and self-reliance. Other societies find these ideas strange and exotic. The Gusii of Kenya, for example, think it is "natural" to sleep with their babies, not to mention holding them constantly during waking hours, precisely because they *want* them to grow up to be dependent on others. For them, proper human behavior means constantly relying on other people.

Culture helps shape the basic things all humans must do for biological survival, like eating, sleeping, drinking, defecating, having sex, and so on. There is no better illustration of this fact than food preferences. As omnivores, humans can eat an enormous range of foods. But many Americans' stomachs churn at the thought of eating delicacies like rotten shark flesh (Iceland), buffalo penis stew (Thailand), or dogs (East Asia) (Figure 2.3).

Figure 2.2   It's Like Getting a Joke.   When a popular comedian like Jerry Seinfeld tells a funny joke, most of us barely think about what makes it so funny. Like other examples of culture Geertz discussed, we just "get it."

Figure 2.3   Yummy . . . or Not.   A meal of insect larvae might make some Americans vomit or wretch, which shows how powerful cultural beliefs are: they actually provoke a biological response to something that is perfectly digestible, if not healthy and delicious.

- **Cross-cultural perspective.** Analyzing a human social phenomenon by comparing that phenomenon in different cultures.

- **Cultural construction.** The meanings, concepts, and practices that people build out of their shared and collective experiences.

No other animal so thoroughly dwells in artificial, or human-made, worlds of its own creation. Anthropologists stress that a **cross-cultural perspective** (analyzing a human social phenomenon by comparing that phenomenon in different cultures) is necessary to appreciate just how "artificial" our beliefs and actions are.

Culture Shapes Everybody's Life

White middle-class North Americans tend to believe that they have no accent. But just as people from Dallas, Boston, or Oklahoma City may each feel they have no accent, they will likely feel their culture is not very distinctive either. These are understandable reactions to the transparency and naturalness of culture.

But the other side of the coin is the tendency to view minorities, immigrants, and others who differ from white middle-class norms as "people with culture," as compared with people who have what they understand as a fairly general American culture. In the United States, these ideas are tied to social and institutional power: the more "culture," in this sense of the term, one appears to have, the less power one wields; the more power one has, the less one appears to have culture (Rosaldo 1989). This power of mainstream culture over ethnic cultures is about the relationships of power and inequality mentioned earlier. By being in the minority and therefore "different," a group's culture becomes more visible to everyone. It is in this sense that groups with the most conspicuous cultures tend to be the least powerful.

Culture Is Shared

The notion that culture is shared refers to the idea that people, through their participation in social groups, make sense of their worlds and order their lives. Culture is not a product of individual psychology or biology, nor is it reducible to either individual psychology or biology. As a result, anthropologists generally accept that purely psychological and biological explanations of human experience are inadequate.

An individual's comprehension of anything is always based on what his or her group defines collectively as proper and improper. Anthropologists commonly refer to such definitions as **cultural constructions**, which refers to the fact that people collectively "build" meanings through common experience and negotiation. In the debate over college mascots, for example, both sides collectively "constructed" the significance of these images and symbols for both Indians and colleges through their debates, protests, and discussions. A "construction" derives from past collective experiences in a community, as well as lots of people talking about, thinking about, and acting in response to a common set of goals and problems.

Cultural Understanding Involves Overcoming Ethnocentrism

One of the key features of culture is that it makes us feel that the ways we do things are correct, that is, that we do things—or think things out—in the "right" way and everybody else thinks and does things incorrectly. As we mentioned in the previous chapter, feeling that everyone else does things the wrong way and that our way of doing things is right is called *ethnocentrism*. For anthropologists, who like all other humans have a culture, ethnocentrism presents a major problem. Overcoming ethnocentrism is the first step to understanding other cultures. Living with a community provides access to understanding what other people do, say, think, and believe, but if we are constantly judging their society and how it does things by our own goals, morals, and understandings, we cannot ever understand them in their own terms.

From the beginning of cultural anthropology in America, anthropologists have argued that the only way to understand other cultures is in terms of that other culture's own goals, ideas, assumptions, values, and beliefs. The concept of *relativism*, by which we interpret and make sense of another culture in terms of the other culture's perspective, using their own goals, values, and beliefs rather than our own to make sense of what people say and do, is a central means of overcoming ethnocentrism, and it is a major feature of the anthropological perspective on culture.

But understanding another culture in its own terms does not mean that anthropologists necessarily accept and defend all the things people do. Even though the job of an anthropologist is not to judge other cultures but learn to understand how and why other peoples do things as they do, anthropologists still carry basic values as individuals and as members of a particular society. A relativistic perspective is simply a useful tool that can help anthropologists overcome ethnocentrism and begin to see matters from the point of view of another culture.

A number of anthropologists, in fact, advocate "critical relativism," or taking a stance on a practice or belief only after trying to understand it in its cultural and historical context. Critical relativism also holds that no group of people is homogeneous, so it is impossible to judge an entire culture based on the actions or beliefs of a few (Merry 2003). For example, many North Americans practice male circumcision, which other societies consider abhorrent, including people in the German city of Cologne, who banned circumcision in 2012 as a human rights abuse. There is even a small but growing social movement in the United States that condemns the practice along similar lines. But when people from other societies or members of this movement criticize this practice, they are not condemning our entire culture.

Another motive for advocating critical relativism is that, in an extreme form, cultural relativism can be a difficult position to uphold. It can lead to **cultural determinism**, the idea that all human actions are the product of culture, which denies the influence of other factors like physical environment and human biology on human behavior. Some critics also argue that extreme relativism can justify atrocities like genocide, human rights abuses, and other horrific things humans do to one another. For some background on the origins of relativism in anthropology, see "Classic Contributions: Franz Boas and the Relativity of Culture."

• **Cultural determinism.** The idea that all human actions are the product of culture, which denies the influence of other factors like physical environment and human biology on human behavior.

Defining Culture in This Book

Although all anthropologists agree that these seven elements of culture are critical to any definition, in their research, different anthropologists emphasize or interpret these elements differently, which contributes to the diversity of culture theories expressed in Table 2.1. So while we too accept the importance of these key elements to any definition, reflecting our backgrounds as interpretive anthropologists working in regions of rapid social change due to globalization, as authors of this book we define culture in the following way: *Culture consists of the collective processes that make the artificial seem natural.*

This is a constructivist view of culture, by which we mean that culture is not a static set of rules or a totally coherent system of symbolic beliefs that people "have" or "carry" like a toolbox that gets passed down from generation to generation, which have been common views of culture among anthropologists. Culture, in fact, is more dynamic, emergent, and changing than these ideas allow, as cultures intermingle due to cross-border interconnections such as migration, global media, economic globalization, and other such dynamics of our contemporary world. So we emphasize

CLASSIC CONTRIBUTIONS

Franz Boas and the Relativity of Culture

GERMAN-BORN FRANZ BOAS (1858–1942) was a pioneer anthropologist and the major figure responsible for establishing anthropology in America. Although he had a doctorate in physics, he became interested in studying non-Western cultures while conducting research on Baffin Island (Newfoundland) on the color of ice and sea water. He befriended many Inuit (so-called Eskimos) and learned that they thought about the world differently; for example, they did not distinguish between the colors green and blue. From these conversations he learned a valuable lesson that would be at the heart of his work for the rest of his life: to learn about another people's perspective, one has to try to overcome one's own cultural framework. This perspective has come to be known as cultural relativism.

The data of ethnology prove that not only our knowledge, but also our emotions are the result of the form of our social life and the history of the people to whom we belong. If we desire to understand the development of human culture we must try to free ourselves of these shackles. This is possible only to those who are willing to adapt themselves to the strange ways of thinking and feeling of primitive people. If we attempt to interpret the actions of our remote ancestors by our rational and emotional attitudes we cannot reach truthful results, for their feeling and thinking were different from ours. We must lay aside many points of view that seem to us self-evident, because in early times they were not self-evident. It is impossible to determine a priori those parts of our mental life that are common to mankind as a whole and those due to the culture in which we live. A knowledge of the data of ethnology enables us to attain this insight. Therefore it enables us also to view our own civilization objectively. [Boas 1940:636; translated from the original German published in 1889 as Die Ziele der Ethnologie]

Franz Boas.   Posing for a museum display about the Hidatsa at the American Museum of Natural History.

Questions for Reflection

1. Do you think it is really possible to, as Boas said, "free ourselves of these shackles" (our own self-evident points of view)? Why and how? If you do not think it is possible, why not?

2. Do you think we can even know what our self-evident points of view are? How?

culture as the processes through which people in social groups collectively construct or accept certain ways of thinking and acting such that they feel "natural," that is, obvious, appropriate, or even necessary. This definition emphasizes that those feelings of naturalness people experience about their beliefs and actions are in fact artificial, that is, humanly constructed and variable across social groups, and they can change somewhat quickly. It also assumes that culture is emergent and even unstable, responding to innovation, creativity, and struggles over meaning. The power of this definition is that by presenting culture as a dynamic and emergent process based on social relationships, it leads anthropologists to study the ways cultures are created and re-created constantly in people's lives. Throughout this chapter and in subsequent chapters we illustrate how this approach to understanding culture works.

But this definition does raise an immediate question: If culture is a dynamic process, why doesn't it always feel that way to people? We deal with this question in the next section.

THINKING CRITICALLY ABOUT CULTURE

How can an understanding of the complexities of culture help us make sense of the day-to-day world in which we live? Give an example from your life to illustrate your answer.

If Culture Is Emergent and Dynamic, Why Does It Feel So Stable?

Imagine how chaotic life would be if you could not expect the same rules and processes for interacting with others from one week to the next. People need cultural stability. If we always had to stop and think about changes in the rules of social interaction, we could not function in our society. The very power of culture is that its processes feel totally natural and simultaneously predictable. Yet the previous section defined culture in a way that emphasizes its processes as dynamic and emergent. So how does something feel stable if it is so dynamic?

The concept of enculturation—the idea that people have been doing or believing things for much of their lives—only partly explains why culture feels so stable. There are a number of other features of culture—symbols, values, norms, and traditions—that help explain the sense of stability that people feel about it.

Symbols

One way of approaching the issue of cultural stability and change is by examining symbols (Sahlins 1999). A symbol, as we noted, is something that conventionally stands for something else. The relationship between the symbol and what it refers to is arbitrary, based on no particular rhyme or reason (Figure 2.3). Symbols can be more than just images or concepts, however; people also use their bodies as symbols. In Japan, for example, bowing is a form of greeting, but depending on how low one bows, it may also symbolize respect, apology, gratitude, sincerity, remorse, superiority, or humility.

Figure 2.4   Love, Affection . . . and Toilets.   Symbols are arbitrary. In the United States and several other countries, the heart conventionally symbolizes love and affection. But in rural Sweden and other parts of Scandinavia people also associate the heart with outhouses, or rustic toilets (Lonely Planet 2014).

- **Values.** Symbolic expressions of intrinsically desirable principles or qualities.

A society will store its conventional meanings in symbols because their meanings tend to be stable. But symbols and their meanings can and do change, sometimes dramatically. For example, during the Spanish conquest of the Peruvian Andes in the sixteenth century, the Spaniards carried banners of their patron saint, Santiago Matamoros, to ensure victory over the Indians. The Indians quickly absorbed Santiago into their native religion. They identified Santiago as their own god of thunder and lightning, Illapa, who they believed was a shape shifter and changed forms. To the Indians, Santiago symbolized the power of their own mountain gods and encouraged resistance against the Spaniards (Silverblatt 1988).

Values

Studying values also helps us understand how change and stability are so closely related. **Values** are symbolic expressions of intrinsically desirable principles or qualities. They refer to that which is moral and true for a particular group of people. For example, "Mom and apple pie" symbolize American core values (values that express the most basic qualities central to a culture), such as patriotism or loyalty to country. In the United States, "Mom" expresses the purity of selfless sacrifice for the greater good. "Apple pie," a common food since colonial times, expresses Americans' shared heritage. Of course, not everybody eats apple pie and not every mother is loyal to her family, much less sacrifices herself for the greater good. The point is not that these ideals reflect what actually happens in the real world. Rather, they orient thinking about one's obligations as a citizen, like putting aside differences with other Americans and being willing to sacrifice oneself for love of family and country.

Values are conservative in that they conserve prevailing ideas about social relations and morality. Yet this does not mean that a community's values do not change. Nor does it mean that within a society or community people will not have opposing values. It is not uncommon for people to hold conflicting values simultaneously.

Norms

- **Norms.** Typical patterns of actual behavior as well as the rules about how things should be done.

While values provide a general orientation for social relations, norms are more closely related to actual behavior. **Norms** are typical patterns of behavior, often viewed by participants as the rules of how things should be done. In our society, for example, it would be unimaginable to haggle over the price of toothpaste at the grocery store because everyone expects you to pay the listed price. But in many other societies, especially in the Arab world and in Indonesia, the norm is just the opposite: no matter how small the item, it is considered rude to *not* haggle. In such places, taking the first asking price disrespects the seller. For more expensive items, such as a digital camera, buyers and sellers may expect to haggle over the price for an hour. The norm is for the starting price to be three to five times the item's actual worth, and buyers may break off negotiations and leave the shop two or three times so the buyer can run after them, bringing them back into the shop with a lower price.

- **Social sanction.** A reaction or measure intended to enforce norms and punish their violation.

- **Customs.** Long-established norms that have a codified and lawlike aspect.

Norms are stable because people learn them from an early age and because of the social pressure to conform. Norms also tend to be invisible (we're usually not conscious of them) until they are broken, as visitors to a different society or even city often find when they do things the "wrong" way. The scowls or expressions of disapproval you might receive provide a **social sanction**, a reaction or measure intended to enforce norms and punish their violation. Long-established norms may eventually become **customs**, which have a codified and law-like aspect.

Traditions

Tradition usually refers to the most enduring and ritualized aspects of a culture. People often feel their traditions are very old, which justifies actions that make no logical sense in contemporary times. With such justifications individuals and groups go to great lengths to protect their traditions. The controversy between Indians and NCAA schools over mascots with which we opened this chapter illustrates how powerful such traditions can be.

But anthropologists are careful not to assume that traditions are as old as people may say, because appearances can be deceiving (Hobsbawn and Ranger 1983). For example, Scottish people often celebrate their identity with bagpipes and kilts made from tartans, plaid textiles made of stripes of different widths and colors that identify the wearers' clans. But these traditions, while indeed venerable, are not actually ancient. As a matter of fact, these objects, and the sense of a distinctive tradition they symbolize, emerged only during the eighteenth and nineteenth centuries (Trevor-Roper 1983). An English iron industrialist designed the kilt as we know it for his workers in the late 1700s. As the kilt caught on in the Scottish highlands, textile manufacturers began producing distinctive plaids to expand sales and found willing buyers among clan chiefs. The chiefs wanted to distinguish themselves and their ancestry as unique, so they adopted particular designs. When England's King George IV made a state visit to Scotland in 1822, the organizers heavily promoted the use of kilts and tartans to enhance the pageantry of the visit. This occasion legitimized highlands culture and established the look as a national institution. The power of tartans comes not from their antiquity, but from their association with the clans that have long been central to Scottish highlander social life. Figure 2.5 shows another example drawn from Japanese culture of a similarly recent and flexible tradition.

Such examples demonstrate that what we take as timeless and authentic examples of tradition may be quite recent innovations. But knowing that a particular tradition may be a recent invention does not mean people are any less protective of it (just ask defenders of Indian mascots on college campuses; most mascots came about only during the early twentieth century).

• **Tradition.** Practices and customs that have become most ritualized and enduring.

Figure 2.5   Another "Tradition" That Might Surprise You.   Like the use of tartans in Scotland, Sumo wrestling in Japan feels ancient, although key features of it—such as the practice of awarding one person champion—are less than one hundred years old.

Historically, anthropologists have emphasized that culture is "shared" among a group of people, implying a kind of uniformity and stability in culture. Clearly, people need a relatively stable and common base of information and knowledge in order to live together. But these different aspects of culture—symbols, values, norms, and traditions—are features that seem stable and common even though they may not be shared by everybody in a society. There is another reason culture feels stable. It is that culture is expressed through social institutions, a theme we turn to next.

THINKING CRITICALLY ABOUT CULTURE

Most students think it is easy to identify the symbols, values, norms, and traditions that support other people's practices. But they find it more difficult to think about their own daily practices in the same terms. Use any of your own daily practices to illustrate how these four features of culture reinforce your own behavior.

How Is Culture Expressed Through Social Institutions?

- **Social institutions.** Organized sets of social relationships that link individuals to each other in a structured way in a particular society.

The **social institutions** of any society are the organized sets of social relationships that link individuals to each other in a structured way in a particular society. These institutions include patterns of kinship and marriage (domestic arrangements, the organization of sex and reproduction, raising children, etc.), economic activities (farming, herding, manufacturing, and trade), religious institutions (rituals, religious organizations, etc.), and political forms for controlling power. Each culture has its norms, values, and traditions for how each of these activities should be organized, and in each case they can vary greatly from one society to another because each society has a different culture.

Let us consider how mid-twentieth-century anthropologists approached culture's relationship to social institutions. Then we will consider how changes in these institutions can shape cultural patterns, which ultimately transform the social institutions themselves.

Culture and Social Institutions

- **Functionalism.** A perspective that assumes that cultural practices and beliefs serve social purposes in any society.

From the 1920s to the 1960s, the dominant answer to this question about how culture was expressed in social institutions was that culture is like the glue that holds people together in ordered social relationships. Associated with British anthropologists Bronislaw Malinowski and A. R. Radcliffe-Brown, this theory, known as **functionalism**, holds that cultural practices and beliefs serve purposes for society, such as explaining how the world works, organizing people into roles so they can get things done, and so on. Functionalists emphasize that social institutions function together in an integrated and balanced fashion to keep the whole society functioning smoothly and to minimize social change.

As an illustration of functional analysis, think back to the case of the Ongee, the people who believe their ancestors make earthquakes and tidal waves. A functionalist would focus on how Ongee beliefs about their ancestors explain how the natural world works, and that these beliefs in turn help shape and are shaped by their migratory hunting-and-gathering existence. Working together with other structures of Ongee society, such as political organization, economics, kinship, and so on, these beliefs contribute to the maintenance of an ordered society.

For functionalists, cultures were closed, autonomous systems. But even at its height of popularity, critics insisted that functionalism's vision of culture was *too* stable. In fact, not all societies function smoothly, and functionalism's static view of culture could not explain history and social change. One of Britain's most prominent anthropologists, E. E. Evans-Pritchard, famously broke with functionalists in 1961 when he said that anthropology should not model itself on the natural sciences but on humanistic disciplines, especially history with its processual focus.

In spite of its shortcomings, functionalism has left important legacies, especially that of the **holistic perspective**, a perspective that aims to identify and understand the whole—that is, the systematic connections between individual cultural beliefs, practices, and social institutions—rather than the individual parts. This does not mean contemporary anthropologists still see a society as wholly integrated and balanced. Rather, the holistic perspective is a methodological tool that helps show the interrelationships among different domains of a society, domains that include environmental context, history, social and political organization, economics, values, and spiritual life. Thus, the life of a community becomes expressed through the social relationships among its members, organized as they are through their social institutions. To understand how changes in cultural values can lead to changes in social institutions, consider the relationship between diet, industrialization, and sexual deviance.

- **Holistic perspective.** A perspective that aims to identify and understand the whole—that is, the systematic connections between individual cultural beliefs and practices—rather than the individual parts.

American Culture Expressed Through Breakfast Cereals and Sexuality

Let us begin by posing a simple question: Why do so many Americans prefer cereal for breakfast? Most of us today prefer cereal because it is part of a "healthy and nutritious diet" (the standard industry line) or because of its convenience. In any event, eating cereal for breakfast has become a social norm for a majority of Americans. It builds on positive cultural values attributed to health and on the symbolism of "healthy food = a healthy body." But corn flakes began in the nineteenth century as a cure for sexual deviance, masturbation being the most worrisome.

Nineteenth-century religious leaders considered masturbation an abomination, and the emerging scientific disciplines of psychiatry and surgery claimed that masturbation caused shyness, hairy palms, jaundice, insanity, cancer, and murderous behaviors (Figure 2.6). From 1861 to 1932, the U.S. Patent Office issued some two dozen patents on antimasturbation devices to prevent boys from masturbating, among them a safety pin to close the foreskin of the penis, various kinds of male chastity belts, and an electric bell attached to the penis that would notify parents if

Figure 2.6   The Effects of Masturbation, Circa 1853. This image comes from a book called *The Silent Friend* about the "horrors of masturbation." At the time, common wisdom held that masturbation would lead to insanity.

their son got an erection during the night. As recently as 1918, a U.S. government brochure advised new parents to prevent their babies from masturbating by tying their hands and legs to the sides of their cribs. Circumcision became the most commonly performed surgery in the United States based on the view that it prevented masturbation.

John Harvey Kellogg (1852–1943), the inventor of corn flakes, was a physician from Battle Creek, Michigan. He was a nutritional enthusiast and a follower of the health food movement of vegetarian and dietary reformer Sylvester Graham (1797–1851), who had developed graham flour used in graham crackers. Kellogg became director of a Seventh-day Adventist sanitarium in Battle Creek, where he built on Graham's ideas, inventing corn flakes and various granolas as food for his patients (Figure 2.7). Both men were concerned with health and sexuality—they especially abhorred masturbation—which they attributed to animalistic passions that were enhanced by a rich, meaty, or spicy diet. Both believed that bland but healthy foods were the way to soothe these volatile and unhealthy sexual urges (Money 1985).

Of course, their solution to the perceived problems of sexual passion was based on the symbols of passion being fiery that could be quenched (symbolically) only with bland cereals. None of these efforts ever prevented masturbation, of course, and no one defends them for that purpose anymore. But these assumptions were enough to create corn flakes and graham crackers. The meanings we give to eating cereal and masturbation have changed as our lifestyles and diets have changed. In fact, an increasing number of medical professionals embrace masturbation as good for mental health.

During the nineteenth century, the American breakfast, like the rest of the diet, was a hearty meal of meat, eggs, fish, biscuits, gravy, jams, and butter. Although farmers worked off the calories in their fields, as America became more urban such rich meals became a sign of prosperity, just as the ideal body type was full-bodied for both men and women. But as American culture began to value healthy eating early in the twentieth century, industrial cereal makers, like C. W. Post and Kellogg's brother William, took advantage of this connection between cereals and good health to market their creations as nutritious foods. By the 1920s the American diet had shifted dramatically along with the ideal body type becoming much thinner. The result was an increased demand from consumers for convenient and tasty breakfast cereals, spawning a giant breakfast cereal industry associated with good taste and health rather than with preventing sexual deviance.

In answering our initial question, we see interrelationships between separate domains like beliefs (about sexual morality, good health), social institutions and power

Figure 2.7   Happiness Is Wellness in the Bowels. John Harvey Kellogg's Battle Creek Sanatarium, opened in 1876, served corn flakes, granolas, and yogurts to promote good bowel health. There was also an enema machine that could pump fifteen gallons of water through a person's bowel in seconds. It was a popular and fashionable vacation destination.

(expert knowledge, medical practices), and daily life (changes in labor organization and economic life, dietary preferences). This is the holistic perspective.

Second, it shows the integration of specific domains. For example, beliefs about sexual morality are intertwined with institutions of social authority, such as sanitariums and medical disciplines like psychiatry and surgery, and those institutions in turn regulate people's sexual relationships. Similarly, changes in people's economic relationships and work habits help shape and are shaped by their ideas about what is good to eat. At any historical moment, these domains feel stable because they are reflected in the other domains, even though some may be highly transitory and dynamic. The values, norms, and traditions in one domain are buttressed and supported by values, norms, and traditions in many other domains.

And herein lies the power of a cultural analysis: it shows how doing something that feels totally "natural" (pouring yourself a bowl of cereal in the morning) is really the product of intertwined "artificial" processes and meanings. In "Thinking Like an Anthropologist: Understanding Holism" we present a scenario to illustrate how simple innovations can lead to changes in social institutions.

Can Anybody Own Culture?

As we have defined culture, the question of owning culture may appear to make little sense. How can somebody own the collective processes that make the artificial seem natural? For the most part, owning culture is about power relations between people who control resources and (typically) minority communities who have been kept outside the mainstream. At one level, nobody can own culture, but many will claim the exclusive right to the symbols that give it power and meaning.

The debate over sports teams' Indian mascots is only one example of a conflict over who has the right to use, control, even "own," symbols, objects, and cultural processes. This conflict is related to the phenomenon of **cultural appropriation**, the unilateral decision of one social group to take control over the symbols, practices, or objects of another. Cultural appropriation is as old as humanity itself. The fact that people adopt ideas, practices, and technologies from other societies demonstrates the fluidity of social boundaries and partly explains why societies and cultures are changing all the time.

• **Cultural appropriation.** The unilateral decision of one social group to take control over the symbols, practices, or objects of another.

Yet cultural appropriation also often involves relationships of domination and subordination between social groups. For American Indians, for example, the pressure to assimilate into dominant white Euro-American society has coincided with the dominant society's appropriation of Indian cultural symbols. That appropriation goes beyond the use of Indian images as sports mascots and includes, among others, kids "playing Indian," New Age religion's imitation of Indian spirituality and rituals, Hollywood's endless fascination with making movies about Indians, even the use of the Zia Pueblo sun symbol on the New Mexico state flag (Strong 1996; Brown 2003). While some Indians do not mind, others find these uses of Indian symbolism degrading and simplistic because they ignore the realities of Indian communities and traditions or because nobody asked permission to use the culturally meaningful objects and symbols.

Some of these conflicts have taken shape as dramatic protests, as in the 2002 case of Australian Aboriginal activists who removed the coat of arms at the Old Parliament House in Canberra. They declared that images of the kangaroo and emu (a large flightless Australian bird resembling an ostrich) on the national seal are the cultural

Thinking Like an Anthropologist

Understanding Holism

ANTHROPOLOGISTS BEGIN THEIR research by asking questions. In this box, we want you to learn how to ask questions as an anthropological researcher. Part 1 describes a situation and follows up with questions we would ask. Part 2 asks you to do the same thing with a different situation.

PART 1: INTRODUCING CASH CROPS TO HIGHLAND NEW GUINEANS

When anthropologist Ben Finney (1973) studied coffee as a cash crop in the Eastern Highlands of Papua New Guinea, he observed that some younger men planted large fields in coffee and some had become coffee buyers. In the years since Finney's field research, many of these men became very successful coffee planters and buyers. Several acquired whole fleets of Isuzu and Toyota trucks, which they used to bring coffee beans to local warehouses and to coastal cities (Westermark 1998).

On the face of it, this program was dramatically successful in introducing a valuable cash crop to a region that only known subsistence horticulture. But a holistic approach illustrates that coffee also brought important social consequences for Highland communities.

In the 1950s an Australian colonial ban on tribal warfare opened up large tracts of no-man's-land between formerly hostile groups. Colonial officers brought coffee seedlings for villagers to plant in this formerly useless land. Some highlanders planted coffee, others rejected the whole idea, saying "what good is coffee, you can't eat it and pigs can't eat it either," pigs being an especially important form of wealth in Highlanders' political and economic lives. Most of the village leaders and prominent elders continued planting sweet potatoes and tending pigs as they always had. The pigs ate surplus sweet potatoes and were used in feasts and ceremonial exchanges with friends and rivals in other villages. Men with extensive exchange networks became village leaders called "big men." Big men achieved prominence and influence over others from their own hard work, assisted by the hard work in the gardens of their wives and female relatives. Traditional subsistence farmers made fun of their coffee-planting neighbors.

But after seven years, the coffee trees began to bear fruit, and the officers showed the coffee planters how to pick,

process, and sell the beans. The young coffee planters now had larger sums of cash than people had ever seen. Coffee profits increased as more and more trees matured. Unexpectedly, younger men found themselves with money that they would have had to work for months or years on a coastal plantation to earn.

These young coffee growers used this money to achieve social status because they, unlike the old men, had access to all sorts of imported goods in stores. In some cases, the prestige of these new big men was even greater than that of the older big men. Suddenly, everyone wanted to become a coffee planter, but after seven or eight years nearly all the open land was already planted in coffee.

Elimination of tribal warfare and the introduction of coffee did not eliminate the big man political system or the cultural logic upon which it is based. But a holistic perspective shows that it did have important ramifications throughout the society.

What questions does this situation raise for anthropological researchers?

1. How did Highland's society change as a result of coffee?
2. What were the unexpected effects of introducing coffee on this small-scale egalitarian society?
3. Which effects were positive? For whom were they positive? Who experienced negative consequences from the introduction of coffee?

PART 2: INTRODUCING SMARTPHONES TO AMERICAN COLLEGE STUDENTS

Consider the relatively recent rise in the use of smartphones by high school and college students. As little as ten or fifteen years ago, students were forced to use a land line if they wanted to talk to their friends, which usually meant that they were calling from home. Nowadays, most students have their own smartphones, not just for making phone calls but for taking pictures, surfing the Internet, texting, and so on. Students use their smartphones in a variety of ways not possible on their parents' land lines. They have brought lifestyle changes for young people that might be considered unexpected effects when cell phones were initially introduced.

Using a holistic approach, think about some of the changes that smartphone use and texting have introduced into the lives of high school and college students. What questions would you ask about this situation as an anthropological researcher? (Sample questions can be found at the end of this chapter.)

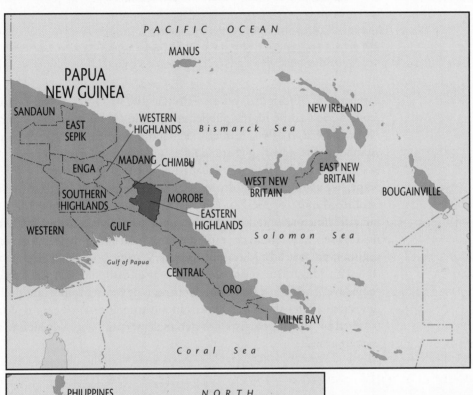

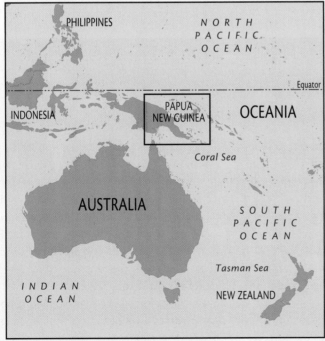

Eastern Highlands of Papua New Guinea.

THINKING CRITICALLY ABOUT CULTURE

Anthropologists feel that holism is one of the key aspects of culture because it links together lots of things that people in other disciplines do not routinely think about. Use an example of an object in daily life to show how it is holistically linked to other aspects of American life. (Consider, for example, an item you use in class—such as a book, a pencil and paper, or an iPad—to show how this object is linked to or breaks from our past but is connected to many other things in our lives.)

property of Aboriginal people (Brown 2003). Other conflicts have happened in courts, such as the highly publicized lawsuit Zia Pueblo brought against the state of New Mexico in 1994, formally demanding reparations for the use of the Zia sun symbol in the state flag (Figure 2.8).

Anthropologists have not escaped indigenous scrutiny and criticism for claiming expertise about native cultures. Anthropologist Kay Warren (1998), for example, studied the rise of the Pan-Maya ethnic movement in Guatemala. When she gave an academic presentation on Maya political activism, Maya intellectuals and political leaders in attendance responded by challenging the right of foreign anthropologists even to study Maya culture. As Warren points out, indigenous movements like Pan-Mayanism reject the idea that anthropological knowledge is neutral or objective. They insist that doing anthropology raises important political and ethical questions: Who should benefit from anthropological research? Why do the people studied by anthropologists not get an opportunity to help define and evaluate research projects?

Figure 2.8   The Cause of Indigenous Rights.
Indigenous groups forced the United Nations to establish the Permanent Forum on Indigenous Issues in 2000. The Forum's goal is to address the human, cultural, and territorial rights of indigenous peoples around the world.

Anthropologist as Problem Solver

Michael Ames and Collaborative Museum Exhibits

FOR SEVERAL DECADES indigenous activists in the United States and Canada have criticized museums for mishandling sacred indigenous artifacts and displaying objects without the permission of tribal leaders. Until the 1990s most museums paid little attention to these concerns. They rarely sought indigenous input into museum exhibits, and when they did, it was usually long after planning for an exhibit was complete.

In the United States, the passage of the Native Americans Graves Protection and Repatriation Act (NAGPRA) in 1990 changed the playing field substantially. The law provides a framework for the return of human remains, burial goods, and religious objects to tribes that can demonstrate a direct connection (Brown 2003). At first, museum professionals worried that their collections would be cleaned out by Indian claims. But for the most part museums and Indian tribes have made concerted efforts to find effective solutions to these problems. Anthropologists have played key roles as mediators and advocates—for both museums and Indians—in many of these situations.

One pioneer in creating a partnership between native communities and museums in Canada was Michael M. Ames (1933–2006), who was director of the Museum of Anthropology (MOA) at the University of British Columbia from 1974 until 1997. Ames made several changes in the relationships between museums and their publics, including museum visitors and native peoples. While he was director of the MOA, he put all of the museum's ethnographic collections on display in visible storage so that the ordinary visitor could see everything in the collection. This was a striking shift for a museum, but nothing compared with his efforts in the 1990s to establish a new relationship between the MOA and the local First Nations—as Indian communities are referred to in Canada. He pioneered collaborative exhibitions in the museum.

Two proposed exhibitions dealt with archaeological material excavated on the lands of First Nations communities. Early in the planning process, Ames contacted tribal leaders from the communities, who agreed to participate and wanted to participate fully in managing the exhibitions and interpreting the objects displayed. The tribal leaders insisted on meaningful consultation at every stage of the process, including selection of objects, the final design of the exhibition, interpretation of each object, installation, promotion, and exhibit maintenance.

Michael Ames and Margaret Mead.

Tribal leaders became so involved in developing these exhibits that some museum staff feared that MOA was giving up its scholarly role altogether. After extensive negotiations with tribal leaders facilitated by Ames, First Nations communities acknowledged that museum professionals were experts in research, interpretation, and exhibition design. But they asked that this expertise be used toward the Indians' educational goals (1999:46). For example, even though the objects displayed were prehistoric and archaeological, they had contemporary relevance for the native groups involved. Ames (1999:48) suggests that these archaeological pieces "have a powerful resonance for the living descendants and thus in a very real sense are contemporary as well as prehistoric" objects, especially since these prehistoric objects and sites are part of their historical record and thus part of their assertion of continuing sovereignty over their territories. These objects have current meaning in much the same way that documents and historic sites from the American Revolution have ongoing meaning for Americans.

Ames's efforts to have real participation by native groups in the museum's exhibitions have changed the museum's relationships with native communities throughout British Columbia. These communities feel that every object in the museum from their area is part of their own cultural patrimony. Museums may hold them, but they do so in trust for the native communities, who made, used, and continue to value these objects. Ames's work helped build bridges where previously there had been little more than suspicion toward anthropologists and museum professionals.

Questions for Reflection

1. From the perspective of museum curators, what might be lost if they make indigenous peoples partners in an exhibition?

2. What are the possible benefits to the museum of accepting indigenous input?

3. Even though museums may purchase cultural artifacts from members of indigenous communities, who really owns these objects?

Responding to such questions, a number of anthropologists like Warren have modified how they do cultural research, including inviting the subjects of their research to be collaborators in all stages of the research, from the definition of the study all the way through to publication. In "Anthropologist as Problem Solver: Michael Ames and Collaborative Museum Exhibits" we explore how one anthropologist collaborated with indigenous people in the creation of museum exhibitions.

THINKING CRITICALLY ABOUT CULTURE

Discuss whether people from one culture could "own" a dance—like the samba from Brazil—that originated with people from another ethnic group. Could anyone own a style of pop music?

Conclusion

At the heart of all anthropological discussions of culture is the idea that culture helps people understand and respond to a constantly changing world. As we have defined it, culture consists of the collective processes that make the artificial seem natural. Based on symbols and expressed through values, norms, and traditions, culture offers a relatively stable and common base of information and knowledge so that people can live together in groups. A holistic perspective on culture illustrates how different domains of a society interrelate. But culture is also dynamic, responding to innovation, creativity, and struggles over meaning.

In spite of the many difficulties involved in studying culture, it is more important than ever to understand culture, what it is, and how cultural processes work. The big and urgent matters of our time have cultural causes and consequences. These matters range from the problems posed by development and change for indigenous groups and heated conflicts about social identity over mascots and traditions on college campuses, to others like terrorism, environmental degradation and sustainability, ethnic diversity and racial conflict, religious intolerance, globalization, and health care. As you read this book, you will learn how anthropologists use cultural perspectives to understand, explain, and even contribute to resolving problems related to these matters.

KEY TERMS

Cross-cultural perspective
  p. 36

Cultural appropriation
  p. 45

Cultural construction
  p. 36

Cultural determinism
  p. 37

Customs   p. 40

Enculturation   p. 34

Functionalism   p. 42

Holistic perspective   p. 43

Interpretive theory
  of culture   p. 34

Norms   p. 40

Social institutions   p. 42

Social sanction   p. 40

Symbol   p. 34

Tradition   p. 41

Values   p. 40

Reviewing the Chapter

Chapter Section	What We Know	To Be Resolved
What is culture?	Culture is a central component of what it means to be human. Culture involves the processes through which people comprehend, shape, and act in the world around them.	Although most definitions of culture emphasize common themes, anthropologists have never agreed on a single definition of culture.
If culture is emergent and dynamic, why does it feel so stable?	Cultural processes are emergent, fluid, and marked by creativity, uncertainty, differing individual meaning, and social conflict. Yet culture is also remarkably stable.	Anthropologists continue to debate which is more important—dynamism or stability—in explaining how culture works in people's lives.
How is culture expressed through social institutions?	A holistic perspective enables anthropologists to understand how different social institutions and domains of a society are interrelated.	Anthropologists continue to debate how and why social institutions in any society change.
Can anybody own culture?	The phenomenon of cultural appropriation illustrates the tensions between cultural change and stability, and raises important ethical and political questions about anthropological knowledge itself.	Anthropologists continue to debate over which research and collaborative strategies are most effective to respond to the ethical and political issues raised by the creation of anthropological knowledge about culture.

Readings

For an overview of different theories of culture in anthropology and how and why they differ across schools of thought within the discipline, see Adam Kuper's *Culture: The Anthropologists' Account* (Cambridge, MA: Harvard University Press, 2000). In the book Kuper expresses deep skepticism about the centrality of the culture concept to anthropology and illustrates why anthropologists continue to debate what culture means.

● ●

For an intellectual history of the development of the culture concept in anthropology and its place in the discipline during the early twentieth century, the essays in George Stocking's book *Race, Culture, and Evolution: Essays in the History of Anthropology* (Chicago: University of Chicago Press, 1968) are classics and remain relevant today.

● ●

The book *Who Owns Culture?* by anthropologist Michael Brown (Cambridge, MA: Harvard University Press, 2003) is a highly readable account of the vexing legal, ethical, and methodological issues involved in who owns native cultural symbols and heritage.

● ●

SUGGESTED ANSWERS TO "THINKING LIKE AN ANTHROPOLOGIST"

Use these examples as a guide to answering questions for other "Thinking Like an Anthropologist" boxes in the book.

1. How has cultural life on campus changed because of smartphones?
2. Are there unexpected effects of introducing smartphones into college life?
3. How has the proliferation of smartphones changed college students' patterns of communication with their parents and friends?
4. Are people more connected socially than they were before?
5. Are there ways that people are less connected socially?
6. Does smartphone use have any impact on the ways university classrooms operate?

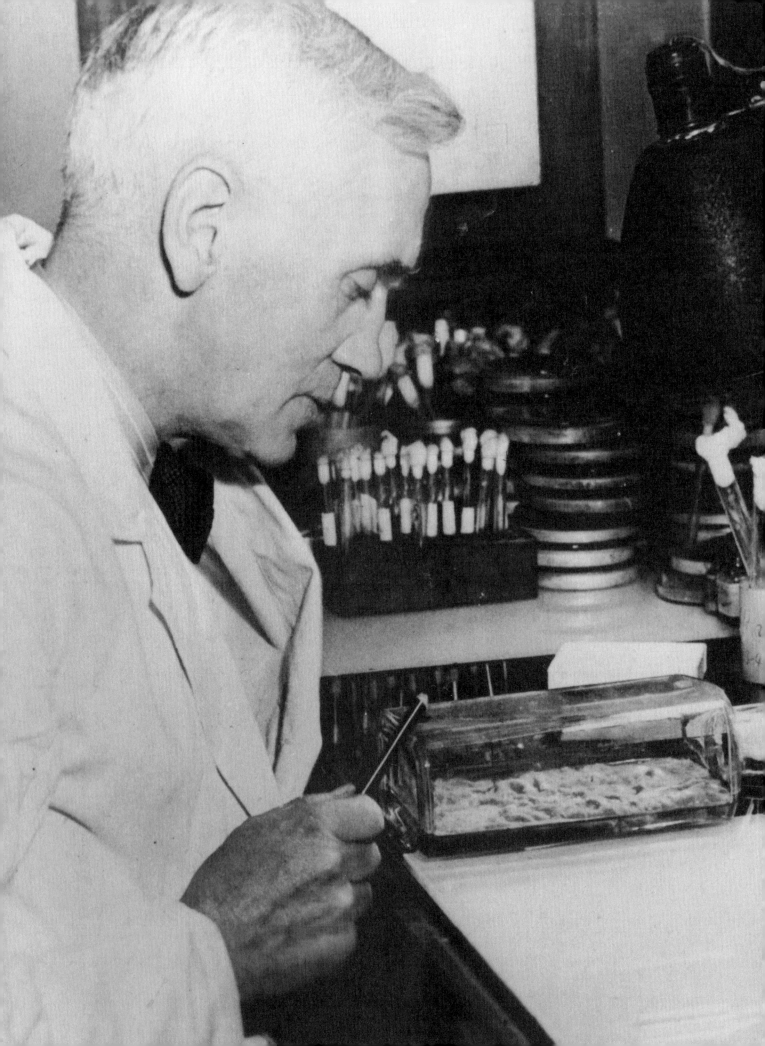

Evolution

Life Is Not Static

When the Scottish microbiologist Alexander Fleming accidentally discovered the bacteria-killer penicillin in his laboratory in 1928, he did not expect that it would revolutionize medicine. But, within a decade, penicillin was used widely to cure microbial infections that previously killed many people, and scientists began producing other antibiotics with similar miraculous properties. Since then, antibiotics have saved countless lives from infectious diseases like tuberculosis, pneumonia, typhoid fever, syphilis, and others.

Antibiotics kill bacteria by inhibiting their ability to synthesize proteins, produce cell walls, or replicate DNA. But over time, antibiotics can also decline in effectiveness, something Fleming found out early in his experiments with penicillin. In speeches he gave, Fleming cautioned that bacteria can rapidly develop the ability to resist the effect of antibiotics, especially when antibiotics are overused or applied for short periods or in quantities that are too small to work effectively.

If he were alive today, Fleming might wonder if anybody had paid attention to his warnings. As early as the 1940s, certain types of staphylococcal bacteria that cause infections in wounds were already resistant to penicillin. Today, there are also several dozen other varieties of bacteria that are now resistant to the antibiotics that were once effective against them. According to the Centers for Disease Control and Prevention, the U.S. government's primary public health agency, every year two million Americans are infected with antibiotic-resistant bacteria and at least 23,000 die as a direct result of these infections (CDC 2013). What happened?

🌱 **Scottish microbiologist Alexander Fleming.** Fleming understood both the power and limitations of antibiotics. He warned that bacteria could rapidly develop resistance to penicillin, thereby reducing its effectiveness in treating infectious disease.

What happened is that the bacteria have undergone evolution, which refers to the adaptive changes in populations of organisms across generations. Perhaps a random genetic mutation occurred in a single bacterium, or maybe it picked up new genetic material from its environment or another bacterium. Any of these could give it and its offspring a selective advantage, an ability to resist the effects of antibiotics that its ancestors did not have, allowing them to survive and reproduce. Mutations are generally rare, but because bacteria populations are so large with fast generation times (typically days, hours, or even minutes), these things can happen very quickly.

Human behavior also contributes to this problem, especially misuse of antibiotics. One of the most controversial is industrial farming's use of antibiotics among healthy chickens, cows, and pigs to promote growth and prevent disease. In addition, physicians sometimes prescribe them unnecessarily, and patients do not always take them properly. Hospitals are especially conducive environments for bacterial evolution given the high concentration of antibiotic use, and these environments have recently seen the emergence of fearsome "superbugs" with high levels of resistance to antibiotics. Even antibacterial soaps and hand lotions in restrooms and public places contribute to antibiotic resistance.

Antibiotic resistance is a good example of how humans can influence the evolutionary trajectories of other species. But we are not islands unto ourselves, and our own evolution is wrapped up with other species, bacteria being an excellent case in point. Infectious diseases have had important influences on the genetic structure of human populations, conferring selective advantage on humans able to resist those diseases. But evolution has also endowed us with useful bacteria and other microorganisms we require for our bodily processes, from digestion and growth to self-defense. Antibiotics work against that evolutionary history, disrupting those complex ecosystems in our bodies by also killing the bacteria on which our lives depend.

All of these facts suggest that evolution is an important and ongoing process in our lives and those of other species. At the heart of anthropology's interest in evolution is a key question: *How can understanding evolutionary theory inform our understanding of how humans and other species change and exhibit variation?* Embedded in this broader question are the following problems, around which this chapter is organized:

How and why did evolutionary thinking come about?

Life changes. But what does it mean to say it evolves?

What are the genetic and non-genetic mechanisms of evolution?

How and why do new species evolve and others go extinct?

How do evolutionary processes affect organisms?

Evolution explains how members of a species change and why variations exist from one species to another. It also provides anthropology the ability to understand how and why our own species emerged and changed over time. Nevertheless, as we will also see, evolutionary theory is also changing as new evidence and approaches have emerged over the past decade or two that complicate our understanding of evolutionary processes.

How and Why Did Evolutionary Thinking Come About?

All societies give some form of classification to their worlds, explaining how things came to be and why there are similarities and differences between groups of people, animals, plants, and landscapes. Underlying these concerns is a key question: How can we explain the origins and diversity of life? Natural and social scientists, among them anthropologists, have sought to explore this question with evolutionary theory.

Most people associate evolution with the English naturalist Charles Darwin, a point we highlighted in Chapter 1. But the theory did not occur to him out of thin air. He was building on a long history of intellectual thinking about the origins and diversity of life. We share the general outlines of that intellectual history here.

- **Essentialism.** The philosophical position that dictates that each organism has a true, ideal form, and that all living representatives of that organism are slight deviations from the ideal type.

The Intellectual Foundations of Evolutionary Thinking

Until fairly recently, the dominant explanation in Western culture about the origins and diversity of life on earth combined classical Greek and Roman philosophy and Judeo-Christian-Islamic theology. Aristotle's (ca. 384–322 BCE) *scala naturae*, or the Great Chain of Being, held that all forms of life exist in a ranked, hierarchical order (Figure 3.1). At the top are gods and demigods, followed by humans, animals and plants, and minerals. Another key concept was **essentialism**, which holds that organisms each have an ideal form, and that actually living versions of any organism are minor deviations from the ideal type. The result was an enduring explanation for the diversity of life on earth: everything is ranked in a specific order, and things do not change too much from their essential form.

Judeo-Christian-Islamic theology added an origin story to this intellectual foundation. As described in the biblical story of Genesis, all the world's creatures were created in an order that ends with a man, Adam, situated in a position of dominion over the other earthly creatures, and everything that exists was created exactly as it is now. In 1650, the archbishop of Ireland, James Ussher, calculated that the creation occurred in 4004 BCE, meaning the earth was about 6,000 years old. For centuries,

Figure 3.1 The Great Chain of Being. This 1579 drawing by Didacus Valades from a book called *Rhetorica Christiana* represents the ancient view of the hierarchy of all living things.

challenging this origin story and Ussher's date was not easy because of the belief that under God's power it had all been done flawlessly.

A number of intellectual changes during the sixteen and seventeenth centuries began to challenge these older notions and lay the foundations from which evolutionary thinking would emerge. Certain key institutions and figures, among them the Italian inventor Galileo Galilei (1564–1642), English philosopher Francis Bacon (1561–1626), and English physicist and mathematician Isaac Newton (1642–1727), began to emphasize the importance of gaining knowledge through the careful observation of nature, sensory evidence, measurement, hypothesis building, mathematical proof, and experimentation. Natural philosophers (who today we might call scientists) began to examine the geological history of the earth and to study and classify plants and animals on the basis of their similarities and differences, realizing that changes in life forms had occurred on the planet.

In this intellectual ferment, a number of individuals contributed specific ideas that would contribute to evolutionary theory, including the following:

- Carl von Linnaeus (1707–1778), Swedish naturalist, systematized scientific findings about the diversity of life forms by developing **taxonomy**, the system of naming and classifying organisms that we (more or less) still use today. He grouped together organisms with similar anatomy, suggesting that physical similarity indicates relationship. His taxonomy placed all organisms on the same level, chipping away at the Great Chain of Being.
- George-Louis Leclerc, Comte du Buffon (1707–1788), French philosopher and natural historian, argued that the relationship between organisms and their environment was a dynamic one. He argued that active forces of nature—not biblical creation—had created ever-proliferating forms of life.
- Erasmus Darwin (1731–1802), the grandfather of Charles Darwin, conducted systematic observations of domestic and wild animals, fossils, and their anatomies. In 1796, he argued that life had arisen from an original filament (God) and that groups of organisms could undergo gradual changes and become different from the first group, thus producing the diversity of forms we see on the planet.
- Jean Baptiste Pierre Antoine de Monet, Chevalier de Lamarck (1744–1829), articulated the first theory of biological evolution. Lamarck believed that when an organism confronts a challenging environmental condition, it could intentionally direct fluids or forces to change its body, developing, for example, new organs. He also believed that these physical changes were passed to its offspring, or if the new organs fell into disuse, would be modified into another form or gradually disappear, all within the lifetime of a single organism. His ideas about the mechanisms for change (the organism's will to change), inheritance patterns (inheritance of acquired characteristics), and time frame (within a lifetime) were all rejected. But the idea that creatures make modifications in form to meet environmental challenges was adopted by later scholars.
- Geologists James Hutton (1726–1797) and Charles Lyell (1797–1875) studied geological processes (erosion, the formation of mountains, and so on) and observed that an enormous amount of change has occurred on this planet. In his 1830 book *Principles of Geology*, Lyell referred to these processes as "evolution," meaning a gradual unfolding, marking the first use of the term in scientific literature. Both scientists also realized that, given how slowly geological processes occur, the earth must be older than 6,000 years. They introduced the concept of "deep time" to explain that slow pace.

● **Taxonomy.** A system of naming and classifying organisms.

Darwin and Wallace Propose a Theory

By the mid-1800s, the table was set for a new and refined scientific theory to account for the diversity and origins of life on earth. Two naturalists, Charles Darwin and Alfred Russel Wallace (1823–1913), drew on elements of this intellectual history to make this new theory. Darwin, whose story we introduced in Chapter 1, combined his observations of natural history made during his travels on the HMS *Beagle* with his knowledge of domestic-pigeon breeding (Figure 3.2).

Based on his observations of different plant and animal forms in different environments, Darwin saw these varieties as the result of interactions between organisms and their environment. He proposed that if some individuals had traits that helped them acquire more food and survive better in an environment, they would leave more offspring. If these traits were passed on to offspring, then the off-

Figure 3.2   The Naturalists and the Theory of Selection. Charles Darwin (*left*) and Alfred Russel Wallace (*right*). Each independently developed the idea of natural selection, based on observations of a variety of animal species and similar personal and intellectual trajectories.

spring who inherited the traits would benefit from them. He argued that variations do not arise from a desire to change, as Lamarck argued, but are found in the preexisting traits of individuals within a population.

By 1844, Darwin had thought through in some detail this new theory, which he called "*descent with modification via natural selection.*" He did not use the term "evolution" because he felt it could imply progress, improvement, and the possibility of an ultimate and perfect creation, all of which he rejected. Darwin held off on publishing his theory, knowing it might provoke outrage in conservative 1840s England. He was, after all, arguing that biological change occurred and biblical creation stories were allegorical, not literal—still a controversial idea among religious conservatives today.

Fifteen years later, he published his theory. Sometime during the previous decade, he began receiving letters from Wallace, a young English naturalist and museum collector traveling around island Southeast Asia. Wallace came up with ideas similar to Darwin's, based on similar experiences, and had read many of the same books and naturalist publications as Darwin. He had come to see in Darwin's writings hints of the same ideas he was developing. Wallace described these ideas in letters to Darwin, which convinced Darwin to publish his views in full or be scooped on the idea that he had spent years developing. In 1858, Darwin and Wallace both presented papers about their ideas of descent with modification via natural selection to the Linnaean Society of London and then had the papers published side by side in its journal. The next year, Darwin published what was to become one of the most famous books of all time, *On the Origin of Species* (1859), a book that uses the term evolution only once, in the last line. About a decade later, he published *The Descent of Man, and Selection in Relation to Sex* (1871), an account of how humans descended from non-human primates.

The Modern Synthesis

Although Darwin's fear that his ideas would be misinterpreted did indeed occur, they were nevertheless adopted in scientific fields during the late nineteenth century, including anthropology, because they offered a coherent theoretical framework with explanatory power, one that was open to empirical testing. Darwin developed his

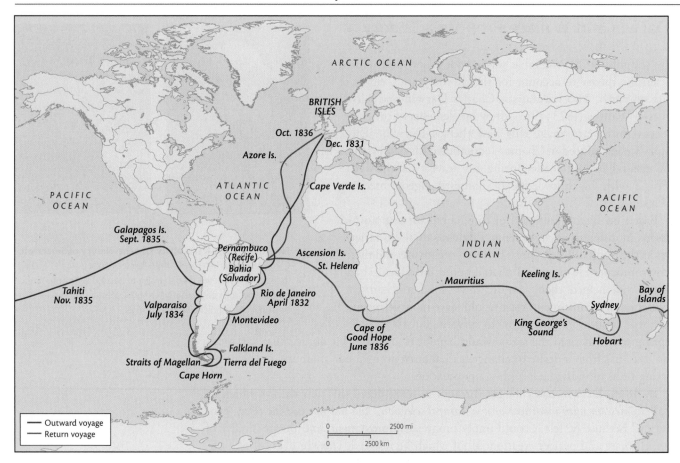

Figure 3.3   Voyage of the Beagle. In 1831, at the age of twenty-two, Darwin became the captain's companion and naturalist aboard the HMS *Beagle* during a five-year surveying voyage around South America and the Pacific. During the voyage Darwin was exposed to something that few other scientists had seen: natural diversity across a wide range of habitats, locations, and environments. (Fuentes 2007:32).

- **Modern synthesis.** The view of evolution that accepts the existence of four genetically based processes of evolution: mutation, natural selection, gene flow, and genetic drift.

- **Population.** A cluster of individuals of the same species who share a common geographical area and find their mates more often in their own cluster than in others.

theory without any knowledge of genetics, but by the 1930s and 1940s, new scientific fields like molecular biology and population genetics had shown there was a close relationship between genetics and evolution. A growing understanding of patterns of inheritance, coupled with statistical modeling of change and populations, allowed researchers to gain insights unavailable to Darwin and other early evolutionary thinkers. The expanded description of evolution put forward by these scientists has been called the **modern synthesis**.

A key feature of the modern synthesis is that evolution can only be measured across generations and within a **population**, a cluster of individuals of the same species who share a common geographical area and find their mates in their own cluster. In other words, individuals do not evolve within their own lifetimes, and changes in genetic variation require many generations.

The modern synthesis also recognizes four processes of evolution in populations—mutation, natural selection, gene flow, and genetic drift, each of which we discuss in more detail later—whereas Darwin and Wallace primarily understood only natural selection. These four processes form the basis for a single unified theory of evolution accepted during the second half of the twentieth century.

Evolutionary Thinking Is Still Changing

Scientific understandings of the origins and diversity of life have been anything but static, and evolutionary thinking is still changing. During the past decade, a number of scientists, among them anthropologists, have begun to argue that the primary legacy of the modern synthesis—that evolution occurs only through genetic processes—does not capture the full gamut of evolutionary processes that have been observed (Laland et al. 2014). Calling their approach the **extended evolutionary synthesis**, these scientists emphasize that a number of non-genetic processes also drive evolution, including the following:

- Developmental bias: physical development can influence the generation of variation.
- Plasticity: the environment directly shapes organisms' physical traits.
- Niche construction: organisms directly modify their environments.
- Extra-genetic inheritance: organisms transmit more than genes across generations.

These are critical innovations in evolutionary thinking with direct relevance to understanding human origins and diversity, and we explore them in more detail below and especially in Chapter 9. Pulling back from these details, however, the dynamic character of evolutionary thinking raises an important issue: What does it mean to say life is evolving?

- **Extended evolutionary synthesis.** The view of evolution that accepts the existence of not just genetically based, but also non–genetically based, processes of evolution: developmental bias, plasticity, niche construction, and extra-genetic inheritance.

THINKING CRITICALLY ABOUT EVOLUTION

How do continued changes to evolutionary thinking undermine—or strengthen—its legitimacy as a way of explaining the origins and diversity of life?

Life Changes. But What Does It Mean To Say It Evolves?

Living things change over time because of how they interact with environments and other life forms. Think back to the ways bacteria have developed antibiotic resistance in response to human behavior. Or think about the exotic shapes and behaviors of deep sea fish and how these characteristics allow them to cope with the intense pressures and low light conditions of the deep ocean. In both cases, the specific interactions the ancestral populations had with their surroundings generated changes in physical form and behavior that we can observe in present populations. Understanding those changes can help us understand ourselves and other life forms. But why call these things evolution and not simply change?

We can start differentiating evolution from simple change by clarifying that evolution is both a body of factual evidence and a theory. It is a body of factual evidence—observable and verifiable truths—because we can examine fossils (the preserved remains of past life), analyze the biochemistry of organisms, or study geological patterns, and each of these demonstrates empirically that change over time has happened. It is also a theory, that is, a set of well-supported, testable hypotheses that explain *how* such changes occur. In this sense, evolution provides an explanation and a model for how change occurs. The theory of evolution is supported today by repeated testing over the past century and a half across many different domains of life, from humans to microbes.

Darwin's Principles

Understanding several key principles underlying the Darwinian notion of "descent with modifications via natural selection" will take us further. One of the key issues Darwin and Wallace recognized is that change over time is intimately tied to *variation* in the present. That is, if you observe, as Darwin did during his journey to the Galápagos Islands, that finches have variably sized and shaped beaks, evolution provides a testable, if not also reasonable, explanation for that variation. The variations between physical traits that interest us from an evolutionary point of view are at the population level, as opposed to the individual level, and come about because of particular environmental challenges. So the reason for the variability in the beak size and shape of finches is closely related to the type and size of food sources available in each finch population's geographic area (Figure 3.4).

Because variations in physical traits are closely related to a life form's survival, what also interests us from an evolutionary perspective are *adaptive* changes. **Adaptation** refers to the development of a trait that plays a functional role in the ability of a life form to survive and reproduce. For Darwin, that mechanism of adaptation was natural selection, which is not a force or a guided process. It is a *process of selection* among traits that provide fitness in a particular environment.

Evolution is thus *non-directional*, that is, not progressive, linear, or necessarily leading toward improvement. Environmental changes can make a physical trait work against the population's survival and not all changes are adaptive. Some changes might enable individuals or a population to survive, while others might lead to death and extinction. What counts is the extent to which any changes enable a population to survive under very specific environmental conditions.

Another key principle is that those traits that enable successful adaptations are *inherited*, that is, passed on across generations. Although Darwin and Wallace did not understand exactly how inheritance worked, scientists had long recognized that parents often passed physical traits on to their children. By 1866, the Austrian monk

● **Adaptation.** The development of a trait that plays a functional role in the ability of a life form to survive and reproduce.

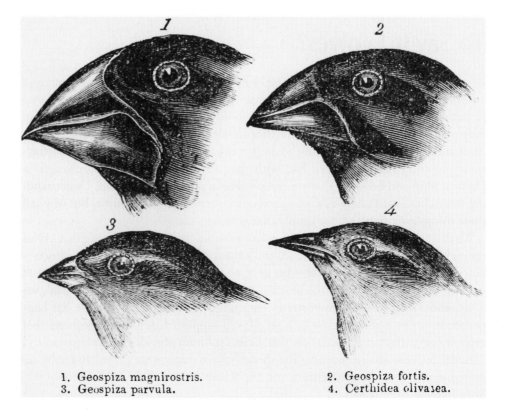

🌱 **Figure 3.4   Darwin's Finches.** The most important differences between the finches Darwin described in his book *On the Origin of Species* was in their beak sizes and shapes, which are adapted to specific food sources found in the environment.

1. Geospiza magnirostris.
2. Geospiza fortis.
3. Geospiza parvula.
4. Certhidea olivasea.

Gregor Mendel, an amateur scientist who doubled as his monastery's gardener, provided the first refined understanding of inheritance. He had identified seven traits in common edible peas, including a purple or white flower, tall or short stem, yellow or green pod, and so on. Based on close observations, he connected those traits to specific parents and learned that the characteristics of offspring could be controlled by selective breeding. From the theory of Mendelian inheritance we derive a general understanding of the inheritance of physical traits, such as the understanding that each parent passes separate genetic material to their offspring and that dominant traits will mask recessive traits.

A final point is that evolution directs our attention to *relational* change. Changes always happen in relationship with other factors, primarily environmental conditions and what other life forms are up to, but also the specific biological and genetic factors unique to a population's common ancestry. Understanding those relationships of common ancestry is thus critical to understanding the evolution of any life form.

What It Means to have Common Ancestry

To establish common ancestry, it is necessary to have some way of naming populations. This is where Linnaeus, to whom we referred in the previous section, returns to the story. Linnaeus developed the taxonomic system we use to organize and name organisms, called "binomial nomenclature," or a two-name naming system. It groups together those organisms with similar form into a *genus* (plural, *genera*) and those that share even more specific features into a *species*. In the Linnaen system, genera and species are the basic levels of classification, but the taxonomy also groups life forms into even higher and more general categories as we show in Figure 3.5. Using the methods established by Linneaus, scientists are able to produce a taxonomy of all living forms on earth.

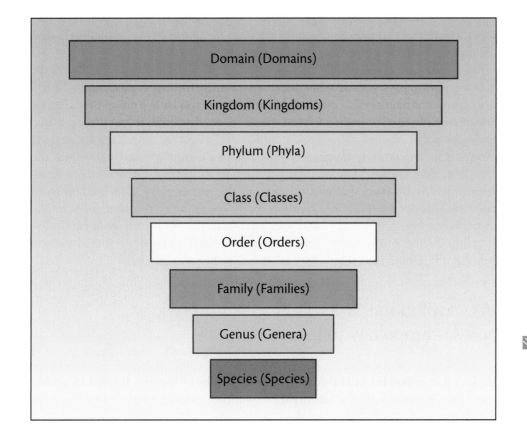

Figure 3.5 Classifying Life. The Linnaen taxonomy organizes life into hierarchical groups, from the most specific, in ascending order, to the most general.

Figure 3.6 A Basic Phylogeny. Like a family tree, you read from the root of the tree to branches and tips, which are called lineages. Each branching point is where a single ancestral lineage gives rise to two or more descendent lineages.

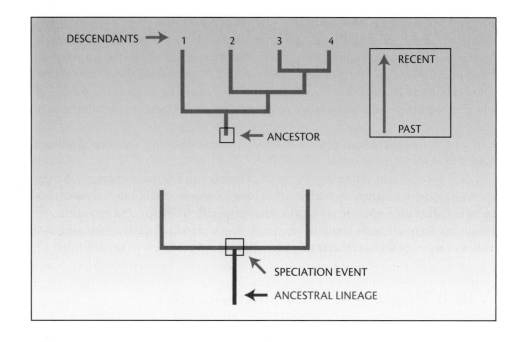

● **Phylogeny.** A graphic representation that traces the evolutionary relationships and identifies points when an evolutionary event or change occurred, such as the creation of a new species.

Linnaen taxonomies can imply suggestive ancestral connections, but morphological similarities alone do not provide useful information about evolutionary processes because they do not capture the dimension of time or the relationship between descendants and their ancestors. To describe those relationships, scientists create a **phylogeny**, a chart that looks somewhat like a family tree and traces the evolutionary history of a species or group, focusing specifically on points when an evolutionary event or change happens, such as the creation of a new species (Figure 3.6). Like a family tree, you read from the root of the tree to branches and tips (called lineages). At each branching point a single ancestral lineage—the common ancestry—gives rise to two or more descendant lineages. Those lineages each have their own unique histories. Because of this fact, no organism is higher or "more evolved" than others, and life forms evolve traits unique to their lineages.

Phylogenies are constructed using morphological, molecular, and fossil data. In creating phylogenies, scientists look for three features. The first is ancestral *characteristics*, traits or structures that are shared by all or most species in a group because they are inherited from a common ancestral species. A good example is hair among mammals. Second is *derived characteristics*, which are unique to a species. These traits evolved after two or more species who have shared a common ancestor diverged; the chin in modern humans is an example (see Chapter 8). Third is *shared derived characteristics*, which are traits that evolved after all the species being compared shared a common ancestor, but prior to some more recent speciation events, seen, for example, in the larger brains of humans and apes relative to the brains of monkeys. Understanding distinctions between traits that are ancestral, derived, or shared derived helps us understand the evolutionary relationships between species.

Why Evolution Is Important to Anthropology . . . and Anthropology to Evolution

Evolution is important to anthropology for a number of reasons. It helps us understand our origins as a species, identify the evolutionary changes that make our species distinctive, and specify traits we share with other creatures with whom we have

CLASSIC CONTRIBUTIONS

Clyde Kluckhohn and the Role of Evolution in Anthropology

CLYDE KLUCKHOHN (1905–1960) was an important theorist of culture. At Harvard University, where he spent his career, he was a key figure in the interdisciplinary Department of Social Relations, among whose faculty and graduates have come some of the most influential social scientists of the twentieth century. In 1959, toward the end of his life, he reflected on the relationship between evolutionary theory and anthropology in the concluding chapter of the volume entitled *Evolution and Anthropology: A Centennial Appraisal*, which brought together prominent anthropologists to assess the Darwinian legacy in anthropology. In his essay, Kluckhohn asserts that neither biological nor cultural aspects of humanity can be understood as a series of separate creations but only as a continuum of small changes, often cumulative, that bear some relationship to selective pressures. In the excerpt here, Kluckhohn outlines some of his main insights, which arguably hold as much relevance for the discipline of anthropology today as they did in 1959.

Clyde Kluckhohn.

If the future role of evolutionary thought in anthropological studies is to be an optimal one, I think the following conditions must be fulfilled:

1. More attention to the evolution of behavior and psyche;

2. Still greater fusion of the biological with cultural-social-psychological dimensions [of being human];

3. Bold and imaginative focus upon the constant interactions between the environment (both physical and cultural) and the constitution and experience of individuals;

4. The creation of models that are as embracive [inclusive] as possible. [Kluckhohn 1959:154]

Questions for Reflection

1. Kluckhohn suggests that culture influences human evolution. Can you think of a scenario in which cultural processes (like the use of e-mail or cell phones, or medical technologies, for example) might accelerate the rate of evolutionary change?

2. How do you think evolutionary processes could explain human "behavior and psyche?"

common ancestry. It also helps us make sense of biological and cultural variations between human populations. In "Classic Contributions: Clyde Kluckhohn and the Role of Evolution in Anthropology," we explore how one influential anthropologist understood its importance.

But the relationship between anthropology and evolution is not a one-way street. Anthropology brings some very important things to evolution, and anthropologists are at the forefront of contemporary evolutionary theory. Most significant is that anthropology challenges the biological reductionism of much evolutionary theory, offering the holistic (embrace) perspective that Kluckhohn called for. As Jonathan Marks (2012:148) observes, "While it may be attractively pseudoscientific to imagine human evolution as simply biological history driven by simple biological processes, the most fundamental aspects of human evolution belie that assumption. They are not biological features with biological histories, but biocultural features with biocultural histories." What he means is that culture also plays a critical role in human evolutionary history. Through culture, humans actively construct the worlds we live in, rearranging nature to suit our needs and using our cultures to imagine new ways to interact with the natural world. As a result, the selective processes emphasized in Darwin's approach are not the sole—or necessarily even most important—means through which human populations evolve. In Part II of this book, we explore this point in more detail. But we still have more to discuss about evolution itself, including the actual mechanisms through which evolution occurs.

THINKING CRITICALLY ABOUT EVOLUTION

A centerpiece of evolutionary theory since Darwin is that it is non-directional change, that is, it is change that could lead in a number of possible directions. Yet a misconception in popular usage is that the word "evolution" implies progress and improvement in one direction. What do you think might explain the gap in understanding? What can anthropologists do to communicate the more nuanced view that emphasizes its non-directionality?

What Are the Genetic and Non-Genetic Mechanisms of Evolution?

In this section we examine in closer detail how evolution actually works. DNA is a key part of the story. We also review the modern synthesis, which built on Darwin's theory as well as discoveries in molecular biology to expand our understanding of the genetic mechanisms through which evolution occurs. We then examine the non-genetic mechanisms presented by the extended evolutionary synthesis, an area where anthropologists are actively contributing new data and insights.

Basic Sources for Biological Change: Genes, DNA, and Cells

Gene. A segment of DNA that contains the code for a protein.

Genes are the building blocks of our bodies, the basic units of information for living things. They provide the primary means by which individuals pass on biological information to their children. Genes are found in the nucleus of every cell, the main unit of construction in our bodies. Variation in genes, which is at the heart of biological variation in organisms, acts as the basic source for biological change. Traits vary from one individual to another, and these differences result partly—but not entirely—from genetic variation. Without genetic variation in a population, evolution and biological change from generation to generation are very unlikely.

Genes are segments of the filaments of **deoxyribonucleic acid** (DNA), which consists of molecules that reside in each of our cells in the form of spiral-shaped strands (Figure 3.7). DNA is inherited from our parents, and with it the genes that make up the DNA. A significant part of what DNA does is related to its physical and chemical structure. The structure of the DNA molecule is a double helix, or spiral, which allows the molecule to be easily opened into a ladder-like shape and closed. Chemically, DNA is composed of three major units: nucleotide bases, sugars, and phosphates. Usually, DNA is condensed into chromosomes, which are supercoiled masses of DNA in the nucleus of cells (Figure 3.8).

The Functions of DNA

DNA has two main functions, replication and protein synthesis. **Replication** is the ability of DNA to copy itself. DNA's double helix structure enables it to unwind, which happens with the assistance of enzymes that respond to chemical cues. Once the ladder is opened, the chemical makeup and shape of the bases prove to be a strong allure for their complementary bases. The process of pairing up bases is repeated along the entire length of both sides of the opened ladder as shown in Figure 3.9.

DNA copies are necessary for two of the primary functions of cells: mitosis and meiosis. **Mitosis** is the creation of two new cells out of one cell, by a process of division. This is required for our bodies to grow and heal. We also constantly lose cells due to death or injury, and mitosis ensures their replacement. **Meiosis** is like mitosis but occurs in only one set of specialized cells that produce the gametes (sperm and eggs).

Protein synthesis is the other major function of DNA. The organic structures of our bodies are made up of proteins, which are strings of amino acids. By itself a string of amino acids is called a polypeptide. To become a protein, the polypeptide changes shape and folds itself in various ways, acquiring a specific chemical signature. The DNA is the "code," or set of assembly instructions, for the right sequence of amino acids to create a particular polypeptide which will serve as the basis for a protein (this "code" is, in essence, a gene).

Parents pass on to their offspring DNA segments that provide the information for constructing proteins. A unit of heredity is the segments of DNA that contain messages for a protein. These segments occur in the same places in the DNA (and thus on the chromosomes) in all humans. A gene, then, can be further defined as a segment of DNA that contains the sequence, or message, for a protein. All humans have the same genes, but for most genes, a number of different nucleotide sequences make up the protein message, each producing slight variants on the same final product, which are the observable physical traits. Variations in the sequences of the same gene are called **alleles**. For example, over twenty genes with hundreds of alleles are responsible for the variation in eye color across the human species. These alleles, or genetic variations, provide the fuel for evolutionary change.

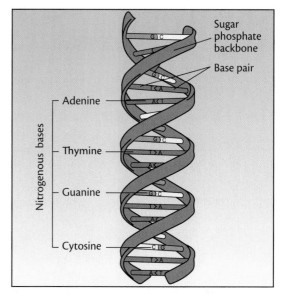

Figure 3.7 The DNA Molecule. This figure shows the molecule with its sugar-phosphate backbone. A series of sugar and phosphate groups make up the sides of the "ladder," and two nucleotide bases make up each rung. There are four nucleotide bases—adenine (A), cytosine (C), guanine (G), and thymine (T)—and each has a specific affinity, or chemical attraction, to one of the other bases. The rungs of the ladder of DNA are always composed of an A-T or a C-G pair.

- **Deoxyribonucleic acid (DNA).** Spiral-shaped molecule strands that contains the biological information for the cell.

- **Replication.** The process by which DNA makes copies of itself.

- **Mitosis.** The process of cell division and replication.

- **Meiosis.** The process of gamete production.

- **Protein synthesis.** How DNA assists in the creation of the molecules that make up organisms (proteins).

- **Alleles.** The variants in the DNA sequences for a given gene.

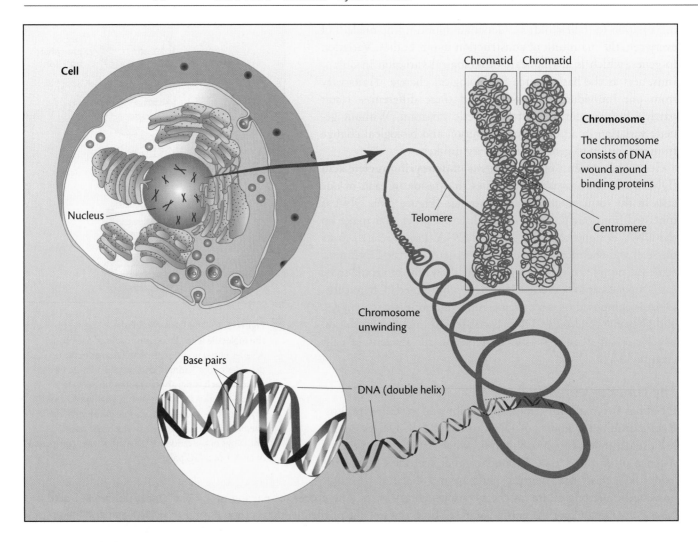

Figure 3.8   The Human Chromosome.   Human DNA is grouped onto 46 chromosomes, which come in the form of 23 pairs. Each of us has two copies of the first 22 chromosomal pairs, which we get from our mother and father. The 23rd chromosomal pair defines the sex (two X chromosomes being a female, and an X and a Y being a male).

Comparing the DNA sequences of individuals, groups, or species can help us understand molecular patterns. This approach provides a method independent of morphological comparison for testing hypotheses about the taxonomic status and evolutionary histories of different species—in other words, whether creatures are connected through common ancestry. We explore these ideas further in "Thinking Like an Anthropologist: Making Sense of Genetic Relationships."

Genetic Mechanisms of Evolution

The modern synthesis accepts that there are four major processes that contribute to biological change in groups of organisms over time. These processes are involved in the creation, movement, and shaping of genetic material, as well as the shape and function of living things. At the core of these processes is genetic variation. New genetic variation arises through mutation and three other evolutionary processes—natural selection, gene flow, and genetic drift—move genetic variation around; they do not create new genes or new traits.

Mutation

Variation initially arises with **mutation,** which is a change in a DNA sequence. The machinery of our cells normally repairs these changes, which usually have neutral or

● **Mutation.** Change at the level of the DNA (deoxyribonucleic acid).

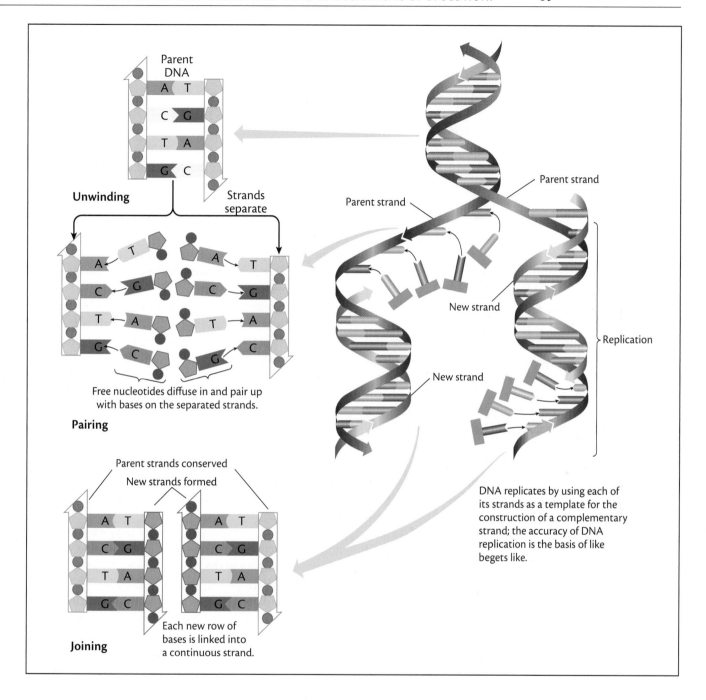

Parent
DNA

Unwinding

Strands
separate

Free nucleotides diffuse in and pair up
with bases on the separated strands.

Pairing

Parent strands conserved

New strands formed

Joining

Each new row of
bases is linked into
a continuous strand.

Parent strand

Parent strand

New strand

New strand

Replication

DNA replicates by using each of
its strands as a template for the
construction of a complementary
strand; the accuracy of DNA
replication is the basis of like
begets like.

no effects anyway. Also, an organism with negative mutations may not survive. Sometimes, however, changes are not repaired, creating variation. If there were no mutations among organisms in a population, each generation could only have the exact same genetic structure as its parent generation.

One example of a mutation-related variation is sickle cell anemia in certain human populations that trace their ancestry to West Africa. DNA is involved in producing a protein important for helping red blood cells carry oxygen around the body. The blood cells typically have a circular form, but one mutation in a section of DNA that changes the resulting protein causes red blood cells to bend and curve into a sickle-like form. The sickle-shaped cells cannot carry oxygen effectively, which affects proper bodily function. Mutations do not always have negative effects, however; sickle cells also provide a resistance to malaria, a potentially deadly tropical disease.

 Figure 3.9 Replication of the DNA Molecule. As the strands unwind, the base pairs attach to their complements. The rows of new bases are then linked into a continuous strand.

Thinking Like an Anthropologist

Making Sense of Genetic Relationships

ANTHROPOLOGISTS BEGIN THEIR research by asking questions. In this box, we want you to learn how to ask questions as an anthropological researcher. Part 1 describes a situation and follows up with questions we would ask. Part 2 asks you to do the same thing with a different situation.

PART 1: WHAT DOES IT MEAN TO BE 98% CHIMPANZEE?

One frequently cited comparison between humans and chimpanzees is that the two species share 98% identical DNA. This statement is generally taken to mean that chimpanzees share 98% of our genetic sequences, and by extension 98% of our genes. But this interpretation is not quite true. Humans and chimpanzees belong to the same family (Hominidae), and we are both a kind of ape, but we differ at many levels. The current trend of comparing sequences of DNA between species, or even between groups of humans, and expecting it to have functional significance, has the potential for serious misuse of already common misconceptions about DNA. University of North Carolina-Charlotte anthropologist Jonathan Marks has tackled this issue and its potentially dangerous genetic implications. In his books *What It Means to Be 98% Chimpanzee* (2002) and *Human Biodiversity: Genes, Race, and History* (1995), Marks reveals misconceptions and a few problematic generalizations that threaten an accurate understanding of genes, behavior, and evolution.

Marks approached this problem on three fronts. First, he has long questioned the notion that humans and chimpanzees are more closely related than humans and gorillas (or chimpanzees and gorillas). While many studies of proteins and DNA show humans and chimpanzees as having a slightly closer phylogenetic relationship, a few studies do show gorillas and chimpanzees or even humans and gorillas as being closer in molecular terms.

Second, Marks applies a theoretical perspective to the problem, demonstrating how we tend to forget some very basic aspects of DNA. For example, there are only four nucleotide bases in all DNA, so that *any* two randomly selected, very large DNA sequences will differ, on average, by no more than 25%. Of course, more closely related organisms share more sequences in common, as they have been separate species for less time and thus the forces of evolution have had fewer chances to shuffle existing sequences or allow mutations to occur. Because humans and chimpanzees have only about seven to nine million years of separate evolution, we are quite similar at the level of the DNA sequence.

Third, Marks points out that 98% similarity is a statement about the chemical structures of the DNA, not necessarily the actual function of the genes. Overall, only about 5% of the human DNA is actively coding for proteins.

Marks's work forces researchers to be very careful about making assertions about genetic differences or similarities between groups of people. All humans share 100% of the same DNA, but there are a huge number of variations in the frequencies and even the presence of certain alleles across the different human populations. What questions does this situation raise for anthropological researchers?

1. Are the same 5% of active human genes also active in chimpanzees?
2. If we accept the simplistic idea that all human–chimpanzee differences arise from 2% of our DNA, what are we to make of the differences in allele frequencies between human populations?
3. What do these similarities mean about changes in behavior and morphology relative to changes at the level of the DNA?
4. What do we gain and lose when we primarily construct our understanding of human and primate behavior through the analysis of DNA?

How Closely Are We Related?

PART 2: WHAT DOES IT MEAN TO BE 37% DAFFODIL?

Some biologists have compared the DNA sequences of humans with those of a variety of other species of animals and plants. We share large amounts of DNA with most other mammals, although the length of human DNA is considerably longer than mammals with much simpler morphology. It may surprise many that we also share DNA with plants. One estimate places the similarity of human and daffodil DNA at 37%. What questions would you ask about this situation as an evolutionary researcher?

Natural Selection

Getting enough food, avoiding predators, and finding a mate for reproduction are difficult, and some individuals do better than others at these things. Biologists sometimes speak of the "survival of the fittest," but what they really mean is competition for **reproductive success**—an organism's number of surviving off-spring. The greater the number of offspring that reach maturity and have offspring themselves, the better their reproductive success. If some individuals are better able to produce offspring than others, because of factors related to specific heritable traits, then over time the more successful (or "fit") genetic variants will become more common in the population. This mechanism of change is called **natural selection**.

According to natural selection, over many generations the interactions between organisms and their environment result in gradual genetic shifts within a population. We can understand these shifts as changes in **phenotype,** the observable and measurable physical traits of an organism. Phenotype, not DNA, interacts directly with the environment. The organism, or more specifically its physical traits, must successfully pass through the environmental filter by reproducing successfully so it can leave more copies of its **genotype** (the genetic component).

- **Reproductive success.** How many surviving offspring an organism has.

- **Natural selection.** The process through which certain heritable traits become more or less common in a population related to the reproductive success of organisms interacting with their environments.

- **Phenotype.** The observable and measurable traits of an organism.

- **Genotype.** An organism's genetic component.

Figure 3.10   Natural Selection of Peppered Moths. The peppered moth illustrates natural selection. Dark-colored moths were more visible to birds on light-colored bark and more often eaten until soot from factories during the Industrial Revolution made tree bark darker.

A classic example of natural selection is the peppered moth in England, which historically had two varieties, light and dark (Figure 3.10). The light moths were more numerous because they could hide on light-colored buildings and trees. The darker moths were more visible and thus more often eaten by birds. But during the Industrial Revolution (mid-1800s), factory pollution changed the environment by covering buildings, trees, and rocks with a dark-colored soot. The tables were turned: birds could now see the light-colored moths much more easily, and the dark moths now had the better fit. In both cases, selection was occurring.

Gene Flow

Gene flow is the movement of genetic material (DNA) within and between populations. Choosing a sexual partner affects the pattern and process of moving genetic variation around in two ways, through migratory movement and whom individuals choose as their mates. The migration of individuals from one population to another can alter genetic variation in all populations involved (Figure 3.11). Populations that are geographically distant from one another tend to experience less gene flow, while nearby groups usually have more. Gene flow can also occur through non-random mating. When individuals choose their mate, they can either stick with their group (inbreeding) or choose a mate with specific traits that are attractive to them (called assortative mating). A good example of gene flow based on non-random mating comes from anthropologist Michael Park's (2003) work with communities of Hutterites, a Protestant sect in Canada. The Hutterites, who resemble the Amish in the United States, live in small farming communities and follow lifestyles that date back centuries. Because of their cultural and religious beliefs, they seldom marry outside their group. Park examined over a thousand fingerprints as indicators of genetic variation from two Hutterite colonies formed when a larger founding colony split in 1958. Surprisingly, he found that these two colonies were more genetically similar to one another than either was to the founding colony. The reason is that the two new colonies were geographically close to one another, and individuals from each colony often found marriage partners in the other group. Gene flow had occurred between the two offshoot colonies, which reduced variation between them.

Genetic Drift

Genetic drift is a change in genetic variation from one generation to another caused by random factors, such as accidents, who gets to mate, or other events that change the makeup of a population. Small populations offer opportunities to see it in action, because random events are more likely to have a genetic impact. A well-known example is found among the people who live on Tristan de Cunha island, a small island in the Atlantic Ocean near South Africa, settled by fewer than fifty British subjects in

• **Gene flow.** The movement of genetic material within and between populations.

• **Genetic drift.** A change in genetic variation across generations due to random factors.

Figure 3.11   Simple Gene Flow Between Two Populations.   In this graphic, P1 through P6 represent geographically localized populations of the same species. All are linked through gene flow (or interbreeding between populations), although every population doesn't interbreed with every other population.

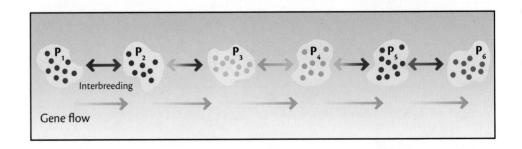

1816 (Roberts 1968). For almost a century, the islanders had little contact with the rest of the world. In 1961, a storm threatened to wipe out the island's 294 residents, and they were evacuated to the United Kingdom, where everyone was examined by medical personnel. These exams found an unusually high frequency of the specific genetic variant (allele) for a serious eye disease called retinitis pigmentosa, which leads to blindness. Though it is rare in the British and South African populations from which the islanders came, a few members of the original founding population carried the genetic variation responsible for the disease, but not the disease itself. Inbreeding on the island, as well as little gene flow, resulted in the high frequency of the alleles for the disease. This situation is known as the **founder effect**, which is the loss of genetic variation when a new population is founded by a small number of individuals (Figure 3.12).

Non-Genetic Mechanisms of Evolution

The key idea behind the extended evolutionary synthesis is that organisms are not simply robots programmed by their genes, but also constructed during the developmental process of life itself. They also do not necessarily "fit" into natural environments but can shape those environments or coevolve along with them. Not all scientists agree with these claims, but there is increasing evidence coming from fields like our own, anthropology, and others such as developmental biology, genomics, epigenetics, and ecology that recognizing these mechanisms is changing the fabric of evolutionary theory (Laland et al. 2014).

Developmental Bias

Developmental bias refers to the idea that not all variations come about randomly, because the developmental processes that organisms undergo during their lives tend to generate certain forms more readily than others (Arthur 2004). For example, there is a group of centipedes with over 1,000 species and all of them have odd-numbered leg-bearing segments, which is closely related to how those segments develop. Developmental processes can also explain how organisms adapt to their environments and become multiple species. A compelling illustration is that African

- **Founder effect.** A form of genetic drift that is the result of a dramatic reduction in population numbers so that descendent populations are descended from a small number of "founders."

- **Developmental bias.** The idea that not all variations are random, but a function of the developmental processes organisms undergo during their lives that tend to generate certain forms more readily than others.

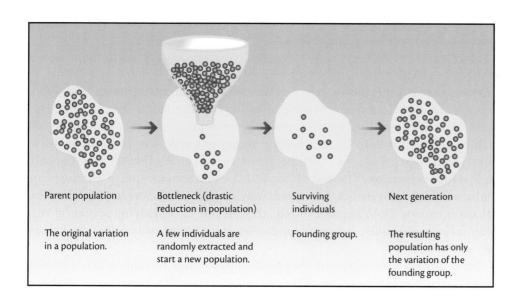

Parent population | Bottleneck (drastic reduction in population) | Surviving individuals | Next generation

The original variation in a population. | A few individuals are randomly extracted and start a new population. | Founding group. | The resulting population has only the variation of the founding group.

Figure 3.12   A Form of Genetic Drift: The Bottleneck Effect.   This form of genetic drift occurs when a large population undergoes a dramatic reduction in numbers so that only a small sample of the previous variation in the population remains. Following the bottleneck, the population increases, but the resulting large population only has the limited variation from the founding population that made it through the bottleneck.

cichlids (a type of fish commonly sold in pet stores) in Lake Malawi and Lake Tanganyika have different evolutionary histories yet have developed parallel forms, including similar body shapes, facial features, and jaws (Brakefield 2006). Although this process probably works in conjunction with natural selection, it demonstrates that selection is not a completely wide-open process but follows certain physical properties (Laland et. al. 2014).

Plasticity

- **Plasticity.** A particular form of developmental bias in which an organism responds to its environment by changing during its lifetime.

Plasticity is a particular form of developmental bias in which an organism responds to its environment by changing during its lifetime, such as how tree leaves will change their shape under certain water and soil conditions. This could be a first step in adaptation, and natural selection here can also play a role if the new traits enhance the survivability of the organism. But instead of changes in the genes driving this adaptive process, the modification may happen first and then through mutation or selection the genes follow to cement the change generations later (West-Eberhard 2003).

If something about this idea seems familiar, perhaps you are thinking it is a new version of Lamarckism described earlier. It is not, however. Something more subtle is at work, which involves the interaction of development with selection. An interesting illustration of that interaction is an experiment involving dragon fish, an unusual fish with lungs and the ability to breathe air, that were raised out of water. Through plasticity the fish developed the ability to move around on dry land using their fins. The fish have the hidden capacity to build stronger limbs, but in water they don't need them so that capacity remains invisible, or "cryptic" as scientists would say. When their environment changes, the relevant trait becomes visible, which exposes that genetic variation to selection (Myers 2014).

Niche Construction

- **Niche construction.** when organisms play an active role in their evolution by reshaping the environment to suit their own needs.

In **niche construction** organisms play an active role in their evolution by reshaping the environment to suit their own needs, which can bias selective processes. Organisms are still influenced by environmental dynamics, but their ability to control certain environmental factors plays a role in their success. For example, termites build mounds in systematic and repeatable ways, reflecting previous selective processes, but the mounds they actually build in turn shape future selective processes. As a species, humans are master niche constructors as we modify our environments through agriculture, technology, and other means in ways that have shaped our own evolution, a theme we elaborate on in later chapters.

Extra-Genetic Inheritance

- **Extra-genetic inheritance.** The socially transmitted and epigenetic factors that can aid in the adaptive success of organisms.

Extra-genetic inheritance refers to the observation that parents and social groups create environments for their offspring that can aid in their adaptive success. Socially transmitted behavior across generations is one of those inheritances. Chimpanzees, for example, teach their young to crack nuts and fashion sticks into rudimentary tools. The migratory patterns of certain fish are also transmitted across generations (Laland et. al. 2014). Another example of extra-genetic inheritance is epigenetics, in which environmental factors create chemical changes in how DNA expresses itself (though not its underlying sequence) that can influence fertility, longevity, and disease resistance in individuals (Laland et. al. 2014).

Now that we have explained the specific mechanisms through which evolution works, we can now turn to one of the big issues in evolution, which is how and why new species emerge and others go extinct.

••

THINKING CRITCALLY ABOUT EVOLUTION

The idea of niche construction emphasizes that human evolution today is affected by new conditions that select for different traits than those our prehistoric ancestors were selected for. Can you think of a human activity today that might not have existed during prehistoric times that is affecting our current evolutionary trajectory?

••

How and Why Do New Species Evolve and Others Go Extinct?

There is perhaps no better illustration of the role of evolutionary change over time than the disappearance of the dinosaurs. Approximately 70 to 80 million years ago, changing climates across the planet and the emergence of new creatures that could compete more effectively for the same environments produced a decline in the size and diversity of dinosaur populations. Then about 65 million years ago, a sudden global catastrophe (probably a major asteroid colliding with the earth) ended the dinosaurs, almost. A few lineages related to the dinosaurs not only made it past that extinction event; they have gone on to flourish. These living dinosaur descendants are birds. What happened is a basic pattern of life on this planet, extinction and speciation.

While the vast majority of species that have ever lived are extinct, most of their lineages still have living representatives. Rather than seeing extinction as the end (à la dinosaurs) and **speciation**, the process by which new species emerge, as the beginning (à la birds), our current understanding of evolution sees them both as part of the ongoing dynamism of life on this planet. All life is related at some level but also constantly changing in some form or another.

Within a population, genetic variation can become so considerable that one part of the population becomes quite different from others. That group might become so different that it is a separate species. Speciation is what we would expect from Darwin's notion of descent with modification: new forms of life are not created anew but arise from previously existing forms.

Clear enough, but there is more ambiguity here than commonly recognized. Most of us would readily agree that dogs, humans, and whales are different species, but just what a species is, is not easily definable. The concept of species derived from biology is perhaps the best known, defining a species as a reproductively isolated group of interbreeding populations so that, under natural conditions, individuals only mate with other members of the group.

This all seems straightforward enough when we think about distantly related creatures like dogs and whales. But more closely related animals, like a dog and a wolf, confound things a bit. A domestic dog (*Canis familiaris*) and a wolf (*Canis lupus*) can mate together, and sometimes they do. Yet we separate them as different species. All organisms share many common genetic elements (DNA), as well as the

• **Speciation.** the process by which new species arise.

biological similarities shared across orders (such as mammals). Thus, life forms sharing recent common ancestry may be similar enough to have compatible mating physiology. What is going on here is that what we think of as separate species are not yet totally distinct, because they are still undergoing speciation. It may seem ambiguous to us, but any ambiguity is an artifact of our taxonomic classification system. It can take hundreds or thousands of generations for evolution to take place. Thus, we can differentiate between dogs and whales, whose common ancestor was probably around 40 or so million years ago, but dogs and wolves probably diverged only 15,000 years ago, making those distinctions much more difficult to make. This point raises a new question, which is how do the processes of evolution affect organisms?

THINKING CRITICALLY ABOUT EVOLUTION

Do you think this evolutionary perspective on extinction and speciation has any sociopolitical implications. For example, regarding a course of action for preserving certain endangered species?

How Do Evolutionary Processes Affect Organisms?

Beginning in the 1950s, a team of Russian geneticists, among them Dimitry Belyaev and his assistant Lyudmila Trut, took on this problem by studying the ways wild animals are turned into human pets, using canines as their medium. They hypothesized that domestication involved patterns of evolutionary change at both the phenotypic and genotypic levels. They also wondered how you could get such wide variation in the same animal, as you recognize when you picture the difference between a Chihuahua and a Great Dane. Their work on domestication has demonstrated that evolutionary processes interact and overlap in complex ways (Fuentes 2009).

Domesticated and wild animals often differ in their behaviors and certain morphological traits. One of these differences is tameness among domesticated animals, that is, a lack of fear of humans and subordination to their commands. Domesticated animals also have morphological traits, such as dwarfism, gigantism, mixed coat color, curly hair, shortened tails, and floppy ears, not seen in their wild cousins.

Interested in understanding how these characteristics could come about, the scientists bred foxes—45,000 of them, over forty years and thirty-five generations—selecting for one trait, tameness (Trut 1999) (Figure 3.13). They selected out the tamest individuals of each generation, about 10–15% of the pups, and allowed them to breed. Today they have very tame foxes that behave remarkably like domestic dogs, whining, cuddling, and so on. The scientists also observed changes in morphology and physiology, including variations in size, skull shape, leg length, and the color of their coats. These foxes also have curled tails, floppy ears, lower levels of stress hormones, and slower rates of development compared with wild foxes.

Figure 3.13   Domesticating Foxes. Russian geneticists Dimitry Belyaev and Lyudmila Trut sped up evolution by breeding foxes and studying the molecular, behavioral, and morphological impacts of these processes on the canines.

This experiment is an intensive example of artificial (human) selection speeding up evolution, and it can help us understand the processes through which canines became domesticated and exhibit such wide variations in morphology. They also demonstrate how evolutionary processes interact to affect organisms, including the following.

Mutation   At some point in canine evolutionary history, a mutation occurred that caused an initial variation in alleles. These variant alleles had the capability to affect behavior and development, and the earliest foxes who exhibited more tameness toward humans likely had those variants.

Gene Flow   As the first domesticated canines spent more time with humans, over time they would have bred less with wild canines. Less contact between the populations would mean less gene flow, and eventually the populations would be cut off from each other. Restricted gene flow means that other factors, such as selection and drift, can more easily affect domesticates.

Genetic Drift   The population of domesticates, now cut off from gene flow with wild canines, have a set of common alleles. The gene pool is now more restricted and domesticates have only those common allele variants.

Selection   Extensive selection for tameness was involved in domestication. It probably occurred when ancestral canines hung around groups of humans. Over time, a mutually beneficial relationship took shape, the tamed dogs guarding against predators and in turn receiving more food and shelter from humans. Humans also began

Anthropologist as Problem Solver

Andrea Wiley on the Evolution and Politics of Human Milk Digestion

BEFORE 6,000 OR so years ago, humans could not digest milk beyond early childhood, an ability many of us take for granted today. In evolutionary terms, the ability to drink milk into adulthood is novel and it happened astonishingly fast. Yet it is not the norm for our species. Biological anthropologist Andrea Wiley, who teaches at Indiana University, set out to study the biological and cultural dimensions of this evolutionary story. Her findings not only demonstrate how evolutionary processes have affected certain human populations but also raise important questions about the social, cultural, and political dimensions of milk and dairy policy.

All mammalian babies produce an enzyme called lactase that allows them to digest lactose, a simple sugar found in their mothers' milk. For the majority of the world's humans, lactase production ceases before adulthood, and drinking fresh milk or eating dairy products can create symptoms of lactose intolerance such as bloating, diarrhea, and cramps. Although it is possible to process milk using bacteria or acid to break down lactose and make its nutrients available (think cheese and yogurt) without producing lactose intolerance, some populations developed the ability to digest lactose. East African herding groups were probably first, and then groups of herders in Northern Europe, South Asia, the Middle East, and the Arabian Peninsula. It appears to be a story of convergent evolution, of disparate groups developing a genetic trait independently of each other. These populations have high frequencies of a genetic mutation that enables lifelong lactase activity, referred to as "lactase persistence." The mutation would make the nourishment that milk provides available to them, presumably making them healthier and better able to produce more offspring, who also have the mutation. Natural selection would have caused the mutation to spread rapidly through these populations (Wiley 2011).

By employing a holistic anthropological perspective, Wiley observes there are also non-genetic factors at work here that derive from how diets interact with our biology. Among these are issues like what foods do people have access to? What ideas do they have about what foods are "good"? And how is the production, distribution, and consumption of a food like milk shaped and transformed by cultural processes? Wiley concludes that these cultural factors are as critical as the biological and evolutionary ones for understanding lactase persistence. She observes that the cultural process of domesticating animals some 9,000 years ago set the stage for lactase persistence, making fresh milk constantly available to those genetically able to take advantage of it. Other cultural factors, such as the central role of milk production in the domestic economy and a belief system that views the consumption of fresh milk and dairy products as a positive trait, also support lactase persistence.

▼ **The Ability to Digest Milk Is Unusual in the Human Species.**

Wiley's work raises important concerns about food policy in the United States, where the dairy industry influences federal and state nutritional standards. Official communications ("Got Milk?") emphasize that all U.S. citizens should consume milk and milk products throughout our lives (Wiley 2004). It is true that the Northern European ancestry of many North Americans means lactase persistence is widespread, yet a substantial minority (upward of 25%) do not have it. Wiley's view is that instead of promoting milk as a singular good and a privileged source of protein, fat, calcium, and other nutrients, government policy should recognize the biological variation in milk digestive physiology and build nutritional standards from that information. For reasons of economic self-interest, the dairy industry keeps these facts of biological variation hidden. As a result, the public is misinformed about the realities of lactase impersistence, and the many other dietary sources for these nutrients do not receive the same privileged political and economic attention in our policies as milk.

Questions for Reflection

1. Can you use elements of the extended evolutionary synthesis to understand the evolution of milk digestion among certain populations? For example, what roles do you think developmental bias or plasticity might have played in this story?

2. What effects does the domestication of animals have on human evolutionary processes?

selecting some dogs and restricting others from breeding. The genetic variations of these selected canines became the most common in the new domestic dog population.

The behaviors selected for have some genetic component, such as barking or not barking. But because genes do not necessarily shape behavior or morphology, behavioral and morphological variation are typical. These dynamics are apparent in extreme cases, such as the differences between Great Danes and Chihuahuas, which results from selecting for size.

Developmental Factors   As the extended evolutionary synthesis indicates, patterns of development and their flexibility are key aspects of evolution. As the fox experiments show, selecting for certain traits correlates with certain developmental patterns, such as or decreased levels of hearing response or stress hormones. The integration of genetic, behavioral, and developmental systems can create unanticipated effects.

In the "Anthropologist as Problem Solver: Andrea Wiley on the Biology and Politics of Human Milk Digestion," we ask how similar evolutionary processes can affect human populations in similarly complicated ways.

THINKING CRITICALLY ABOUT EVOLUTION

Belyaev and Trut studied how evolutionary processes affect organisms by studying domestication and the particular trait of tameness in canines. Can you imagine another experiment you could design with a different animal, plant, or life form that could also demonstrate how evolutionary processes affect organisms?

Conclusion

Even as we marvel at the complexity of humans and the things we can do, many scientists believe that bacteria are the most successful form of life on earth. Their remarkable biological and genetic simplicity, along with their large population sizes and the exotic ability some have to change their genetic makeup by ingesting genetic material from other bacteria, lend them great flexibility and resilience to respond quickly to changes in their environment. With such characteristics, it should not be surprising that human efforts to kill them through antibiotics are experiencing failures, and in turn, generating new threats for us. Yet bacteria are essential to our bodies, so much so that the number of bacterial cells in the human body is more than double the number of human cells! The widespread notion that humans are "more evolved" than bacteria crudely oversimplifies the complex stories of evolutionary history that bind us, as well as the ongoing evolutionary processes that are taking place in both life forms.

As we explored in this chapter, evolutionary thinking developed over time to address a basic concern, how to explain the origins and diversity of life on our planet.

Until Darwin and Wallace proposed their theory of descent with modification, the adaptive, inherited, and non-directional qualities of these processes had been under-appreciated, misunderstood, or ignored. Theirs was a powerful theory that was open to empirical testing and verification. And yet over time, the limits of the sole Darwinian emphasis on selection have also become apparent, as other mechanisms, both genetic and non-genetic, have been discovered and recognized. Today scientists in diverse fields—from biology and ecology to medicine and anthropology—rely on both the observable facts of evolution, as well as the theoretical power of evolution to explain how life changes, pushing the boundaries of our knowledge.

KEY TERMS

Reviewing the Chapter

Chapter Section	What We Know	To Be Resolved
How and why did evolutionary thinking come about?	Evolutionary thinking developed to understand the origins and diversity of life and is still changing. "Descent with modification via natural selection" provided the first coherent scientific theory of evolution. Through the modern synthesis, advances in genetics have been incorporated into evolutionary theory, and the extended evolutionary synthesis recognizes non-genetic dimensions of evolution.	Although an increasing number of anthropologists and other natural scientists accept the extended evolutionary synthesis, not all scientists do and debate continues over its details.
Life changes. But what does it mean to say it evolves?	Evolution differs from simple change because it is change that is adaptive, non-directional, inherited, and relational. Through the construction of phylogenies, we can understand how evolutionary change is rooted in relationships of common ancestry.	The particular meanings of evolution continue to develop as new facts are discovered and theoretical explanations and models are refined.
What are the genetic and non-genetic mechanisms of evolution?	The basic building blocks of evolution are genes and DNA. Genetic variation arises through mutation. Natural selection, gene flow, and genetic drift move that variation around. Non-genetic mechanisms include developmental bias, plasticity, niche construction, and extra-genetic inheritance.	Some scientists believe that recognizing the non-genetic mechanisms of evolution undermines the coherence of evolutionary theory under the modern synthesis.
How and why do new species evolve and others go extinct?	A basic pattern of life is extinction and speciation, dimensions of an ongoing dynamism in which life emerges from previously existing forms. Speciation is a process that may take many hundreds or thousands of generations before species are effectively distinct.	Scientists continue to explore how, when, and why species are formed, as well as the causes and evolutionary consequences of extinction events.
How do evolutionary processes affect organisms?	As experiments with canine domestication demonstrate, multiple evolutionary processes interact and affect organisms in behavioral, morphological, and molecular terms.	While the genetic and molecular dimensions of evolution are well established, the developmental dimensions of evolutionary change are still being understood.

Readings

Charles Darwin's *On the Origin of Species* is still available in in many reprint editions (a 150th anniversary edition was published in New York by Signet in 2003). Ernst Mayr's classic *What Evolution Is* (New York: Basic Books, 2002) offers an excellent accompaniment to Darwin's original.

• • • • • • • • • • • • • • • • • • •

Stephen Jay Gould wrote extensively on the history of evolutionary thinking and the biology of evolutionary processes, including a column for *Natural History* magazine, compiled into highly readable books of essays. A good place to start is his third volume of collected essays, *Hens Teeth and Horse's Toes: Further Reflections on Natural History* (New York: W. W. Norton, 1983), which has his classic essay "Evolution as Fact and Theory."

• • • • • • • • • • • • • • • • • • •

The journal *Nature* hosted a debate over whether "Evolutionary Theory Needs a Rethink" (http://www.nature.com/news/does-evolutionary-theory-need-a-rethink-1.16080), presenting arguments for and against the extended evolutionary synthesis.

• • • • • • • • • • • • • • • • • • •

The "Anthropologist as Problem Solver" box draws from Andrea Wiley's 2011 book *Re-imagining Milk: Cultural and Biological Perspectives* (New York: Routledge).

• • • • • • • • • • • • • • • • • • •

Anthropological Methods

CHAPTER 4

Researching Human Beings and Their Pasts

On a bluff overlooking Brush Creek in Adams County, Ohio, sits Serpent Mound, a 400-meter-long mound of earth and stone shaped like a snake. It is the most grandiose and distinctive of the 10,000 mounds or so constructed by Indians thousands of years ago or more in North America. But it was not a burial mound as nearly all the other mounds were. As a result, Serpent Mound has long captivated the attention of anthropologists seeking to unlock its mysteries. Who built it, and why? How was it used in the ritual and daily lives of people through its history? Which cultural group did it belong to?

The first anthropologist to take on these questions was Frederic Ward Putnam, famed professor and curator of the Peabody Museum of Archaeology and Ethnology at Harvard University. Putnam arranged to preserve the mound by purchasing the land on which it sat, becoming one of the first efforts to protect a prehistoric site in the United States. In 1887–1889 he and his team undertook to figure out who the people were who built it and what its relationship was to other mounds nearby and elsewhere in Ohio. Interviews with Indians from the area in the early nineteenth century revealed that Indians knew of the mounds but knew nothing about who built them. Putnam and his team excavated a cross-section of the serpent's body and two smaller mounds nearby (Putnam 1890). The great serpent contained nothing but soil and rocks. The two smaller mounds were burial mounds and contained skeletons and grave goods that differed stylistically from one another. Putnam concluded that these objects

Aerial View of Serpent Mound in Adams County, Ohio. One of a handful of mounds that take the shape of an animal. This site was the first prehistoric site in the U. S. to be protected from destruction as a park open to the public.

indicated that they came from different cultures. Objects in one mound revealed a connection to the Adena culture that flourished during the Early Woodland period (around 500 BCE to 200 CE) and the other appeared to belong to the much later Fort Ancient culture of the Late Prehistoric period (1000 to 1650 CE), long after the Adena culture had disappeared. This finding raised an intriguing question: Did the Adena people erect Serpent Mound or was it erected centuries later by people with very different cultural preoccupations?

Anthropologists are still struggling with this question, but over the years they have been able to use new and refined methods to bring more certainty to their research. For example, in 1991 archaeologist Bradley Lepper from the Ohio Historical Society (now the Ohio History Connection) and his team excavated small pieces of charcoal from Serpent Mound, using a technique called flotation in which the excavated soil is immersed in water and small bits of lighter charcoal and other organic material float to the surface where they can be collected. Analysis of the samples using **carbon-14 dating** techniques suggested a Late Prehistoric period date of from 1000 to 1140 CE (Fletcher et al. 1996), associating these samples with the Late Prehistoric Fort Ancient culture and challenging the earlier attribution of the mound to the Adena culture.

More recently, a team of researchers based at Indiana University extracted soil cores from various locations along Serpent Mound and in layers at the base of the mound. They found some organic material that they were able to date, again using carbon-14 techniques, and came up with a range of earlier dates: 639 BCE (two samples) and 360 BCE (four samples). From these data, Herrmann et al. (2014) concluded that the mound was built initially during the Early Woodland period and that it was refurbished during the Late Prehistoric period. But Lepper and his team have concerns about this interpretation, mostly because snake designs are essentially absent in objects found in the burial mounds from the Adena period but quite common among objects associated with the late Fort Ancient burial mounds.

Most recently, Lepper and his colleagues have begun using a new dating technique called optical stimulated luminescence on organic materials drawn from the mound in hopes of settling this question. Although Serpent Mound still remains something of an enigma, thanks to the development of such new research techniques, we know a lot more about Serpent Mound than Putnam ever could have in the 1880s.

As this example shows, the research methods archaeologists use to study the past have changed over time, thanks to technological innovation and new techniques used in field excavations and the laboratory. Archaeology is not the only subfield of anthropology to have developed and refined its methods over the past century. The three other subfields—physical, cultural, and linguistic anthropologies—have also seen the proliferation and refinement of their research methods. Compared to other social sciences, anthropology draws on the widest and most diverse range of methods to study humans. The questions

• **Carbon-14 dating.** A dating method that establishes the date or period of an organic artifact or feature from the relative proportions of radioactive carbon to non-radioactive isotopes.

we ask are only limited by the kinds of data available to researchers and the ingenuity of those who have developed more sophisticated methodologies.

At the heart of anthropology's approach to research methods is this question: *How can we study and learn about the human species in all of its diversity today, in the recent past, and in the very distant past?* Embedded within this larger question are a number of more focused problems around which this chapter is organized.

How do anthropologists study the origins and evolution of early humans?

What methods do archaeologists use to decipher the more recent past?

How do cultural anthropologists research the lifeways of contemporary peoples?

What methods are important to the study of human language within anthropology?

In this chapter we survey the primary quantitative and qualitative methods anthropologists in the four subfields use to interpret the bodies, sites, artifacts, environments, landscapes, social lives, and beliefs of people past and present. Because of subfield and research specializations, no single anthropologist will use all the methods that we discuss, but all will use one or more. Let us begin with how anthropologists study ancient primates and humans.

How Do Anthropologists Study the Origins and Evolution of Early Humans?

To understand ancient life forms we study them scientifically. Our primary line of evidence in this endeavor comes from fossils, the remains of past life. **Paleoanthropologists**—those physical anthropologists and archaeologists who study the fossilized remains of ancient primates and humans to understand their origins and evolution—have developed a number of research strategies to uncover and analyze fossils.

What Fossils Can (and Cannot) Tell Us

Technically, of course, fossils cannot "tell" us anything. They are mute. But drawing on a number of methods and disciplines, among them archaeological techniques and various specializations of geology, anatomy, and other scientific fields, paleoanthropologists can use fossils to develop clues and hypotheses about the lives of the ancient humans. It is not, however, very easy to find useful fossils.

Under special environmental conditions, hard tissues like bone and teeth can slowly turn to stone in a process called **fossilization** (Figure 4.1). When the body of an animal

- **Paleoanthropologists.** Physical anthropologists and archaeologists who study the fossilized remains of ancient primates and humans to understand their biological and behavioral evolution.

- **Fossilization.** The process by which hard tissues like bone and teeth slowly turn to stone as molecule by molecule the hard tissues turn to rock, keeping the shape of the original bone.

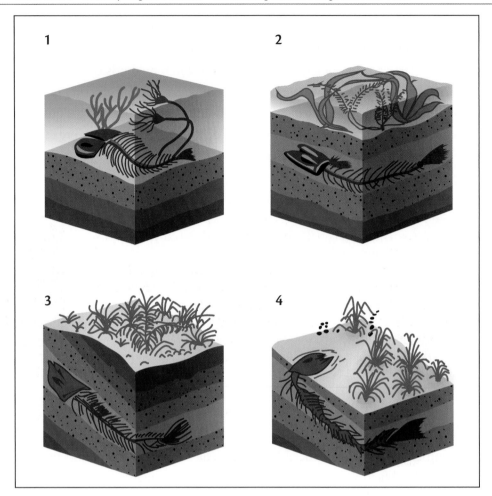

Figure 4.1   The Fossilization Process.   Once an animal dies (1), its body is buried in low-oxygen sediment such as mud (2), then geological processes create a dry environment (3), and because of erosion the fossilized remains are exposed to the surface (4).

- **Trace fossils.** Soft tissues such as organs, skin, and feathers that do not fossilize, but sometimes leave impressions, or traces on the sedimentary rock that forms around them.

becomes buried in mud or another oxygen-free sediment that prevents decay, over tens of thousands of years minerals in the animal's bone can be replaced by rock crystals.

Soft tissues such as organs, skin, and feathers do not fossilize but may leave impressions, or traces, providing clues to their physical characteristics or activities. These types of specimens are called **trace fossils**. Another form of trace fossil consists of footprints left in mud that turned to rock, such as footprints of ancient primates and humans (Figure 4.2).

Given the odds, discovering an ancient primate or human fossil is highly improbable. The conditions that produce fossilization are unusual, so only a very small percentage of anything that has ever lived will become a fossil. Most dead animals will be eaten or decay. Another improbable event is that it will be eventually exposed by erosion or some other geologic event. Most improbable of all, perhaps, is that the fossil will be found by a paleoanthropologist who can collect critical contextual data about it to apply to understanding the human past.

Because of the rarity of fossils, our understanding of the evolutionary lineage of humans is necessarily and always incomplete. It means that we are forced to base our understanding on the best fossil evidence to date, a situation that can change as more fossils are found (see Chapter 8). As we explore in "Classic Contributions: Richard Leakey and Roger Lewin on the 'Jigsaw Puzzle' of Studying Human Origins," the fossil-related challenges paleoanthropologists and archaeologists face are daunting indeed.

And yet the fossilized fragments of over 6,000 individual ancient primates and humans—not always complete skeletons per se, but in the form of individual teeth, collarbones, femurs, skulls, and so forth—have been found, suggesting perhaps that luck comes to those who are prepared. One way field researchers ensure they are

CLASSIC CONTRIBUTIONS

Richard Leakey and Roger Lewin on the "Jigsaw Puzzle" of Studying Human Origins

THE MOST FAMOUS family in paleoanthropology is the Kenya-born family of Louis Leakey (1903–1972), his wife, Mary Leakey (1913–1996), and their son, Richard Leakey (b. 1944). Richard and his wife, Maeve Epps Leakey (b. 1942), together with their daughter, Louise (b. 1972), continue the family's paleoanthropological research tradition in East Africa. Louis and Mary had started hunting fossils at Olduvai Gorge in the Rift Valley of Tanzania in 1951 and have made numerous famous discoveries (see Chapter 8). Their son, Richard, who is currently head of the Turkana Basin Institute and professor in the anthropology department at SUNY Stony Brook in New York, interspersed his career in paleoanthropology with work as a conservationist and politician in Kenya.

The Leakey Family has played an influential role in paleoanthropology.

In 1977, Richard and science writer Roger Lewin summarized the state of knowledge on human origins in a book called *Origins: What New Discoveries Reveal About the Emergence of our Species and Its Possible Future*. One section of the book explains how difficult it is to find, identify, and analyze the fossils of early human ancestors.

What was it actually like to be almost human, to be making tools of wood and stone, to live in organized social groups and to share the world with creatures who were also more human than ape, but who lived quite different lives? If we are honest we have to face the fact that we shall never truly know. We can guess, and the broad research approach encompassing study of the ancient and the modern is beginning to give those guesses some substance. But even if our guesses were absolutely right, there is no one to say, yes you have the correct answer! Inescapably, it is a matter of trusting our methods, and this makes the whole problem more challenging—and more exciting.

Our task is not unlike attempting to assemble a three dimensional jigsaw puzzle in which most of the pieces are missing, and those few bits that are to hand are broken! The jigsaw is multidimensional because, against a background of the physical evolution of our

ancestors, we are also trying to construct some semblance of their social and behavioral patterns.

The core of the problem then, is the fossil record, the fragments of bones which survived the combined destructive activities of the environment to become preserved for later discovery by one of the many teams of fossil hunters now scouring promising sites in Africa. Just as finding a key piece of the jigsaw can help you slot into place many others that have been something of a puzzle, so the lucky discovery at the East Turkana site of a remarkable fossil at the end of 1972 proved to be an important event in the emergence of a new picture of human evolution. In many ways the fossil skull . . . merely confirmed certain earlier ideas of the path of evolution, ideas that seemed reasonable in terms of a biologically sound scenario of human prehistory, but ones that lacked the important evidence of a reasonably complete specimen. [Leakey and Lewin 1977:84–5]

Questions for Reflection

1. Do you think the jigsaw puzzle is an apt metaphor for the challenges of paleoanthropology and archaeology? Why or why not?

2. What are some of the possible difficulties that come from having too few pieces of the puzzle?

🌱 **Figure 4.2   The Laetoli Footprints.**   These are among the most famous trace fossils in paleoanthropology. They are footprints left in ash, which were made by at least two individuals of different sizes, and show evidence for bipedalism in early hominins, probably *A. afarensis*.

- **Test pit.** A preliminary excavation, usually of a single 1-meter-by-1-meter square (or half-meter square) to see if artifactual material exists at the site and to assess the character of the stratigraphy.

- **Breccia.** A rock composed of broken fragments or minerals cemented together by a fine-grained matrix.

🌱 **Figure 4.3   Using an Accelerator Mass Spectrometer to Identify composition of a archaeological or paleontological sample.**   Recent technological advances and new digital-imaging techniques have allowed researchers more nuanced insights to all of these matters and have been used to extract additional evidence from the existing fossil record.

prepared is by reviewing geological, aerial, and satellite imagery surveys so they can concentrate their efforts in areas with good fossil-bearing sediments or that have yielded fossils before. For example, in Ethiopia, certain distinctive layers of volcanic ash known as tephra have been identified as good fossil-bearing sediments (Wood 2010). It is also useful to talk to miners and quarry workers, who also encounter (and often inadvertently destroy) fossils.

When a potential site of interest is identified, researchers conduct a survey of the area, collecting material evidence on the surface that might give clues that ancient humans lived there, such as animal bone fossils, or stones that appear modified by human activity. Researchers dig **test pits**, 1-meter-by-1-meter squares (or even squares that are 50 cm on each side), that can reveal information about the depth, contents, and stratigraphy (soil layers) of the site, recording the locational details of any artifacts or biological materials they find. Researchers will also typically create multidimensional virtual maps where they can plot their finds and layer the map with other information, including landscape features, types of sediments, and so on. As we discuss later, prehistoric archaeologists also utilize these techniques in their own field studies.

The type of excavation employed depends on the type of rocky sediment in which the fossils are encased. A range of tools—from jackhammers, crowbars, and sledgehammers to various kinds of sensitive air-powered drills—are used to release the fossils. Where fossil beds exist researchers might cut blocks of **breccia**, a rock composed of broken fragments or minerals cemented together by a fine-grained matrix, which are taken to the laboratory to be dissolved in baths of weak acid, or worked at with hammers and chisels, to release fossilized remains. These techniques are highly destructive, and excavations can often destroy the very evidence being recorded, leaving nothing but written testimony to back up key assertions.

In the laboratory, researchers glean useful information using various kinds of powerful microscopes, x-rays, and three-dimensional scanners to study the fossils up close. Knowing the physical characteristics of skulls, teeth, and bones—especially the indentations, channels, and cavities they exhibit—allows scholars to infer an individual's growth, age, injury, disease, cause of death, environmental conditions, and even possible intelligence or behavior (Figure 4.3).

Dating Fossils and Archaeological Sites

How do paleoanthropologists—and archaeologists, who draw on similar techniques—actually establish the age of fossils or another artifact? Both draw on multiple dating methods, but a primary consideration for both involves the object's provenience, or precise location and context in which a specimen is found. We are not talking about a location like a shelf in a museum storage facility or a rock shop, which have probably lost key contextual data. This contextual data includes what type of rock it is found in, the layers or strata of rock above and below the fossil or artifact, and other fossil and non-fossil items surrounding it. If the exact location of a fossil or artifact find is not known, it is difficult, perhaps impossible, to determine its age.

There are two general methods for determining how old a fossil or an artifact is: **relative dating** and **chronometric (or absolute) dating** (Table 4.1). Relative dating techniques provide us with rough estimation of a fossil's or artifact's age relative to other fossils, rocks, or features. Chronometric dating techniques, which have been improving with technological advancements, give us a more specific age for a fossil or piece of organic material, based either on analyzing a piece of the fossil, or of the rocks surrounding the fossil or artifact. Many objects contain radioactive components that slowly decay into another element at a constant rate over time, such as bone, which has carbon, and volcanic rocks, which have potassium or argon. Measuring the rate of decay in an element can yield a numerical value, which is the age of the object.

- **Relative dating.** Any dating techniques provide us with rough assessments of the age of a fossil, artifact, or archaeological feature relative to other fossils, rocks, artifacts or features.

- **Chronometric (or absolute) dating.** Any dating method that determines an age of a fossil, rock, artifact, or archaeological feature on some specified time scale.

- **Stratigraphy.** The study of layers of soil or rock and how they were deposited.

	Name of Method	Description	Practical Use
TABLE 4.1 BASIC DATING TECHNIQUES FOR FOSSILS, FOSSIL SITES, ARCHAEOLOGICAL SITES, AND ANCIENT MONUMENTS			
Relative Dating	**Stratigraphy**	Examines the layers of sedimentary or volcanic rock to establish correlation with geological events and processes.	Nearly all projects begin with a stratigraphic analysis. One of the earliest stratigraphic analyses was Flinders Petrie's (1891) excavation of an ancient village site known as a *tell* or mound in the desert.
	Seriation	Documents changes over time in styles of pottery, flint knapping, carving, etc.	Useful for dating archaeological sites, but rarely for fossil sites. It is especially useful for "horizontal" stratigraphy, such as when different sites were occupied at a variety of different, but slightly overlapping, times. Flinders Petrie (1899) first described this methodology for dating ancient graves in a cemetery in the Nile Delta. It has also proved useful for dating Pueblo pottery in the New Mexico region in what has been called the Pecos Classification proposed at the Pecos Conference in 1927 by Alfred Kidder (1927, 1931).
	Faunal correlation	Correlates a new fossil with another of a known age (Oakley 1964:33–40).	Based on the presence of certain animal bones known to be living in a region at a certain time. For example, the presence of a wooly mammoth bone places it at a certain period before these creatures went extinct, but it cannot tell us exactly when the artifact was used.
	Fluorine absorption	Measures the relative amount of fluorine in a bone that is absorbed from groundwater.	Can only be expressed as younger or older than something of known age (Taylor 1975).

(Continued)

	Name of Method	Description	Practical Use
	TABLE 4.1 (CONTINUED)		
Chronometric Dating	Carbon-14 (14C) dating	Measures half-life of decaying carbon-14 in artifacts of biological origin (5,730 years).	Useful for dating artifacts up to 60,000 years old. Only organic material can be subjected to carbon-14 dating because living organisms (both plants and animals) take in carbon atoms during eating (animals) or breathing (plants). Once an organism dies, it stops replenishing its 14C and the percentage of these atoms decay at a known rate (Renfrew and Bahn 2004: 141–49).
	Potassium-argon (40K/40Ar) dating	Measures decay of an isotope of potassium into argon.	Useful for dating minerals, clays, and sediments over 100,000 years old. Often used for dating fossils and very early stone tool, by dating a higher layer of igneous rock that was laid down as volcanic ash (Curtis 1975).
	Fission-Track	Measures damage trails, or fission tracks, left by fission fragments in uranium-bearing minerals.	Can distinguish young from older and very old rocks (especially useful for very old fossils); see Wagner and Van den Haute (1992).
	Thermoluminescence (TL)	Measures time elapsed since crystalline material was heated.	Useful for dating archaeological items like clay fired as pottery or exposed to fire in a hearth (Aitken 1985; Renfrew and Bahn 2004:154–56), or older items exposed to heat-like volcanic activity.
	Optical stimulated luminescence (OSL)	Measures the number of electrons trapped in the crystalline structure of minerals like quartz and feldspar after being buried in the earth for long periods. Crystals absorb energy from trace amounts of radioactive material in the soil and rock. When exposed to light the electrons are released and can be measured to estimate the date they were buried (Ahr, Nordt, and Forman 2013).	Useful for dating geological sediments and sometimes fired pottery and bricks.
	Tree-ring dating (or dendrochronology)	Counts tree rings, each of which represents a year.	Useful in very dry regions where trees are preserved, such as the American Southwest over the past 12,000 years. In some cases it has been used for much earlier samples (Douglas 1919; Bannister and Robinson 1975).
	Electron spin resonance	Measures the build-up of electrons trapped inside crystals after they were formed.	Commonly applied to tooth enamel several thousand to several million years old (Grün 2008).
	Textual evidence	Deciphering and analyzing writing systems such as hieroglyphs.	Egyptian hieroglyphics, Mesopotamian cuneiform, and Mayan glyphs, as well as some early writing systems in China often appear on ancient monuments, clay tablets, stelae, papyrus, and other surfaces discussing the heroic deeds of leaders. Where translations are possible, written evidence often provides more or less precise dates for events, buildings, and documents of financial transactions.

Studying Ancient DNA

In addition to the formal dating methods outlined in Table 4.1, genetic data can sometimes document in a rough way how old a sample is by estimating the rate of mutation in DNA molecules. This method assumes that mutations have occurred at stable rates over long periods of time. Genetics also makes it possible to link living populations with ancient ones, as long as we can recover DNA samples from fossils. These genetic samples from fossils are even more uncommon than the fossils themselves because over time they degrade significantly, but modern advances in genomic science have enabled the recovery of DNA samples from partly fossilized bones.

In practice today, paleoanthropologists and archaeologists are increasingly using several methodologies simultaneously for discerning how any new set of fossils or human skeletal remains relates to modern human groups. In "Doing Fieldwork: Studying the Genetic Continuity of Paleoamericans and Modern Native Americans at Hoyo Negro," we examine how one research team used multiple methods to make conclusions about the peopling of the New World.

● ●

THINKING CRITICALLY ABOUT ANTHROPOLOGICAL METHODS

Given the limitations and fragmentary nature of the fossil record, paleo-anthropologists can never provide a picture of the ancient primate and human past with complete certainty or precision. In addition to the methods described here, how do you think they build confidence in the validity of their insights?

● ●

What Methods Do Archaeologists Use to Decipher the More Recent Past?

Archaeologists try to reconstruct what life was like during the past 8,000 years or so. When a culture changes, the society does not completely disappear. People change how they do things—sometimes gradually, other times quite suddenly, such as when a natural disaster like an earthquake, flood, or drought makes the old way of living impossible. Archaeologists study those changes by analyzing the stone, bone, wooden, and ceramic remains people left behind. They also reconstruct the character of the prehistoric landscapes and environments in which human groups lived and worked. But how do archaeologists know where to work?

Knowing Where to Excavate

When we find great monuments, tombs, or the ruins of temples and palaces, archaeologists know where to conduct their research. But knowing where to excavate does not usually begin with the presence of artifacts or large structures. It begins with the questions an archaeologist wants to answer. Once clear questions are in mind, researchers seek sites that will help answer them. We then develop a plan for

- **Seriation.** A relative dating method that analyzes changing styles of pottery or other artifacts over time to situate any particular assemblage of artifacts into a time series of styles and designs.

- **Potassium-argon dating.** A dating method that measures the decay of an isotope of potassium into argon, used to date minerals, clays, and sediments over 100,000 years old in igneous rock that was laid down as volcanic ash.

- **Thermoluminescence dating.** A dating method for estimating dates of pottery that has been fired.

- **Optical stimulated luminescence (OSL).** A dating method that measures electrons trapped within the crystalline structure found in quartz and feldspar after being buried in the earth. Crystals in these grains absorb energy from trace amounts of radioactive material in the soil and rock. When exposed to light, the electrons are released and can be measured to estimate the date they were buried.

- **Sites.** Any location that shows evidence of human activity, including those with monuments and buildings.

- **Tree-ring dating (or dendrochronology).** A dating technique that counts years by establishing a standard pattern of thick and thin tree rings and matching the ring pattern in a wooden artifact to a point on this sequence.

Doing Fieldwork

Studying the Genetic Continuity of Paleoamericans and Modern Native Americans at Hoyo Negro

THE AMERICAS WAS the last major part of the planet occupied by humans. We know that by about 15,000 years ago modern humans had crossed to the Americas from northern Asia. They reached as far south as the bottom of South America surprisingly quickly. But anthropologists have yet to solve the actual timing of these settlement processes, how many waves of settlement there were, and whether it was by one group or many groups of people.

One piece of this puzzle has been the existence of morphological differences between the earliest Paleoamericans and modern Native Americans, specifically differences in cranial and dental traits (Steele and Powell 1999). Researchers have debated whether these differences are the result of separate migration events from Asia, separate migrations from groups already settled in North America, or evolutionary changes that occurred in the Americas after settlement (Chatters et al. 2014).

These debates represent the intellectual backdrop against which a group of cave divers were exploring a deep underwater cave system in Mexico's Yucatán Peninsula in 2007 and discovered an intact human skull with a very good set of teeth (Balter 2014a). The skull was sitting upside down on the cave floor, with other mammal bones, including those of saber-toothed tigers, gomphotheres, which are ancestors of elephants, and ground sloths. Led by paleoanthropologist James Chatters, a multinational and interdisciplinary team of paleoanthropologists, archaeologists, geneticists, and geologists was formed to study the site—now called Hoyo Negro (Black Hole)—and the fossils to determine who this individual was. In 2014, they published their findings in the journal *Science*, arguing that it was a Paleoamerican teenaged girl who lived between 12,000 and 13,000 years ago, and that modern Native Americans share ancestry with her. Their conclusions give weight to the third interpretation about the peopling of the Americas, that there were evolutionary changes, perhaps genetic drift, in American populations after settlement (Chatters et al. 2014).

What methods did they use to make this case? Two key methods in particular have to do with how they dated the bones and then analyzed the DNA they were able to recover from them. The bones were not easily accessible, so research divers made measurements in place and took pictures every 20 degrees around the skull to develop a three-dimensional image. Leaving the skeleton in place, they recovered several teeth, a rib, and a sample of carbonate mineral called calcite on the bones. Dating the calcite involved a technique called uranium-thorium dating, which is useful for dating, carbonate minerals such as coral up to 500,000 years old. Unlike other absolute-dating methods that measure the decay of a radioactive substance, this technique measures the degree of equilibrium between thorium and uranium. The researchers also performed a similar dating on calcite collected from gomphothere bones and found that both those and the girl's dated to 12,000–13,000 years ago, suggesting both were trapped in this hole during the late Pleistocene.

To identify genetic connections with modern humans, the researchers analyzed mitochondrial DNA (mtDNA). Mitochondrial DNA is not located in the nucleus of cells, but in the organelle of specific cells that create energy. It is easier to access than nuclear DNA because there are more copies of it, and it does not code or recombine. Inherited only through the mother, mtDNA mutations accumulate sequentially and create a **haplotype**, or group of distinctive inherited genes. Lineages that share haplotypes are called **haplogroups**. In the Hoyo Negro project, the researchers extracted DNA from the skeleton's upper-right third molar and utilized several specific techniques developed to sequence poorly preserved mtDNA. When the researchers analyzed the recovered sequences and compared them with living Native American haplogroups, they found a high frequency of overlap, especially with indigenous people

▼ **Hoyo Negro**

from Chile and Argentina. On this basis, they confirmed that these modern Native Americans share ancestry with this Paleoamerican.

Studies of ancient genetics are often limited because ancient DNA may be deteriorated and contaminated by soil microbes, fungus, and even the anthropologists and lab technicians who handled the bone (Hawks 2013). MtDNA studies are also limited by the fact that they can show only the mother's lineage. Studies of nuclear DNA and Y-chromosomes DNA (inherited from males) can show other ancestral connections that do not appear in mtDNA. But in cases such as this one where fossil findings are very limited or degraded, they can provide suggestive evidence of genetic continuity where morphological similarities no longer exist.

Questions for Reflection

1. How do you think paleoanthropologists guard against contaminating ancient DNA samples?

2. This project involved individuals from numerous disciplines. What do you think are some of the practical challenges involved in coordinating such a research project?

---

surveying, sampling, and testing within an area or region. Field research techniques include the following:

-   ***Preliminary Surface Surveys and Test Pits.*** Fieldwork typically begins by walking an area, collecting whatever scattered artifacts can be found on the surface (often referred to as "ground reconnaissance"). These artifacts are called **surface collections**. Also recorded is the presence of streams and other water sources, potential quarry sites, flat places where camps could have been situated, and points that offered protection from the elements or potential enemies. These features can suggest how people might have used a site and the natural resources surrounding it. Surface collections only tell us about what has happened on the uppermost few inches of the soil, surfaces that are still being acted upon by the environment—rain, wind, floods, sedimentation, rodents, farmer's plows, and the like. Surface collections may also reveal artifacts from several different periods, and archaeologists have to determine from the terrain or human activity how these objects ended up together. Professional archaeologists always keep careful records about the location of surface artifacts. Researchers usually follow up by digging several test pits that will offer a sense of how part of a site was used, how many different periods of occupation are represented, and whether it was continuously or sporadically occupied. After several test pits, the archaeologists may determine that the site seems suitable for addressing the research questions.

-   ***Regional Surveys.*** In 1946 American archaeologist Gordon Willey (1953) pioneered the study of regional settlement patterns based on research in the Virú valley of Peru. Instead of examining individual sites, Willey looked at the entire valley as a single interconnected set of villages. His research showed that particular communities exploited different ecological niches, and through trade and political relationships all the villages had access to the valley's diverse resources, including different crops that only grew at certain elevations or minerals that were only found in certain places. Willey's strategy involved surface surveys around many dozens of sites across the valley, requiring dozens of assistants to assist with the surveys. Regional surveys are now standard

-   **Haplotype.** A group of distinctive inherited genes.

-   **Haplogroups.** Lineages that share certain haplotypes.

-   **Surface collection.** A collection of pottery and stone artifacts made from the surface of the soil around a possible site.

practice for most archaeologists in the Americas. Typically these regional surveys were preliminary to a major excavation at one or two sites. But more recently, the strategy has developed from being a preliminary step in fieldwork into a field of inquiry all its own. As the costs of excavation have risen, regional surveys make it easier and less expensive to make surface collections over a broad region and are less destructive to potential sites than intensive excavating.

- *Aerial Surveys.* Another regional survey technique makes use of photographic surveys made from the air. Aerial photographs can be either vertical, from directly overhead, or oblique, shot from an angle. Each has its own advantages, providing either a ground plan from overhead or revealing texture in the terrain from angle shots (Reeves 1936) (Figure 4.4). Aerial photographs shot in sequence allow the archaeologist to view them stereographically (using pairs of photos with slightly different angles) to reveal the three-dimensional texture of landscapes. Recently, because of the easy accessibility of satellite imagery, aerial surveys have become a standard archaeological tool.

- **Geographical information systems (GIS).** A computerized methodology that brings together data from several sources and integrates them with a geographic reference map.

- *Geographical Information Systems (GIS).* GIS is employed for mapping archaeological sites and regions. GIS brings together many different databases of geographic information. Researchers map and digitize variables, such as vegetation, rocks, or geologic formations, onto different databases, several of which are linked to a baseline map. Digital maps with a separate overlay for each variable can be viewed individually or together to analyze any combination of variables on the landscape. Producing digitized maps is very labor intensive, but once physical features and other information have been digitized, GIS can identify patterns quickly and easily. For example, it may be useful to know which locations are within a certain distance of a stream, above a certain elevation, and near some possible source of flint. Then, during ground reconnaissance, the researcher can investigate whether such locations are viable archaeological sites.

- *Remote-Sensing Techniques.* During the past decade, technological improvements have enabled the use of remote-sensing techniques. Among the most productive are magnetic surveys, which allow researchers to walk systematically back and forth across a landscape with a magnetometer, the reading of which can now be linked to locational data. These data can reveal the original arrangement and structure of a site. This technique has been utilized in rural southern Ohio, where so many mound complexes and earthworks were leveled in the nineteenth century so that nothing remains visible on the surface to indicate human occupation. At a site called Junction Works site near Chillicothe, farmers had flattened the site for agricultural use during the previous century so that nothing of the original earthworks remained. In 2005 archaeologist Jarrod Burks conducted a magnetic survey of the entire site to reveal the underlying structure of the mounds and earthworks on the site. The magnetometer reads soils under the former earthworks that were more packed down differently from areas without any additional earthworks. When these magnetic images are plotted on a mapping of the site, they reveal the shapes of the original structure (Burks 2014; Lepper 2015). One of the main advantages of remote sensing techniques is that they don't disrupt a site (see Figure 4.5).

Figure 4.4   Aerial Survey of a Site.

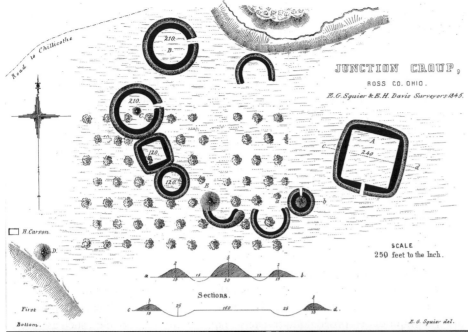

Figure 4.5 Remote Sensing at the Junction Works Site reveals the distribution of mounds and earthworks observed in the 1840s by E. G. Squier and E H. Davis (1846). Jarrod Burks recorded readings from a magnetometer on wheels that he pushed back and forth across a field where the early earthworks once stood (from Lepper 2015).

Analyzing Artifacts

One of the main challenges for archaeologists is making sense of what an artifact is, how it was made, how it was used, and its importance in the social lives of a group of people. Because archaeologists can never see firsthand how an object was made or used, we can only propose, or infer, plausible answers to these questions based on whatever bits and pieces of evidence are available in **habitation sites** (places where we presume people lived). Archaeological interpretation involves filling in details about what is not there, which usually means first figuring out if an object was really made or used by humans.

- **Habitation sites.** Places where people lived at some time in the past.

Use-Wear Analysis

Archaeologists examine closely the surfaces of artifacts—especially cutting tools—to identify patterns of wear. Since edges and cutting surfaces wear differently depending

- **Use-wear.** Patterns of wear and tear on an artifact that is presumed to be due to use.

- **Residue analysis.** Microscopic analysis of the residues of plant and animal foods, especially starches, on pottery or tools.

on the types of jobs they do, their **use-wear** pattern (pattern of wear) offers evidence about how the tool was used. Most use-wear analysis involves stone or bone artifacts because they preserve well. Of course, people used other materials such as hardwood, bamboo, or thorny vines, but because of rot they rarely appear in excavations.

Lithic analysis entails microscopic examination of a stone tool's cutting surfaces, revealing flaking, chipping, and abrasions that cause a blade to wear down during use. Determining what material the tool was used to cut requires setting up an experiment in which newly made stone blades are used to cut a variety of materials: soft and hard wood, bone, hide, meat, antler, and plants. Afterward, the blades are examined for microscopic differences in use-wear among the different materials. The archaeologist then compares what is found on the new, experimental stone blades with the microscopic wear on actual stone artifacts.

Residue Analysis

Another kind of microscopic analysis—usually called **residue analysis**—looks at the residues of plants and other foods left behind on the surface and edges of an artifact. For many years archaeologists scrubbed clean their potsherds and stone artifacts to study them. That was a mistake, because the soil caked on them may have had residues that never decomposed completely.

Australian archaeologist Richard Fullagar (2005) has recently pioneered the microscopic analysis of plant residues found on tools and pottery. Residues usually consist of microscopic grains of starch, resins, cellulose, bone, and blood. Comparisons of archaeological samples with modern plant and animal tissues allow researchers to identify the primary foods found in prehistoric diets. The most promising area residue analysis has been used is in distinguishing different starches, because corn, rice, wheat, sweet potato, taro, manioc, and sago—all starchy foods—each have unique signatures. Fullagar's analysis has demonstrated that early New Guineans were eating taro 2,000–4,000 years ago, something that had been supposed but never proven.

Analyzing Pottery: There Is More Than One Way to Make a Pot

Pottery is among the most important materials archaeologists can use to study the past. Pots break easily and often, revealing brief archaeological moments. They regularly mark different periods because clay is so easily shaped, incised, and decorated that pottery styles tend to change as the community that makes them changes. Once broken and discarded, pottery is almost indestructible, persisting as potsherds indefinitely.

Pottery consists of clay mixed with an added material called temper, which gives the pot added strength and keeps the clay from cracking or breaking when being fired. The finer the temper, the stronger the pot. The most common materials used as temper are sand, crushed rock, crushed shell, crushed potsherds, straw, and grass. Traditions of pot-making vary a great deal around the world, but in the same community these traditions also change over time, and the temper used in a pot may offer some clue that new styles of pottery making have arisen (Figure 4.6).

Reconstructing Prehistoric Environments

Whether people lived in a forest or a grassland, temperatures were warm or cool, the climate was wet or dry, there were rivers or lakes nearby, and plant and animal resources were available make a big difference in the possible lifeways a society may adopt. Besides, environments change, and we cannot assume that a past environment was similar to what we observe today. We can illustrate the complex relationships between global and regional environments archaeologically by considering three areas: changing sea levels, changing landscapes, and plant remains.

(a)

(b)

Figure 4.6 The Two Techniques for Making Pottery Without a Wheel: Coiling Technique and the Hammer and Anvil Technique. (a) Potter Teko of Serra village in Papua New Guinea demonstrates pot-making. She rolls a coil of clay that she will attach to the round base in front of her. When she is finished, the sides of the pot will rise another five or six inches as she repeatedly adds rolls of clay to build up the walls of the pot. She will smooth the rolls into a solid wall with her fingers. (b) Potter in Bilbil village near Madang in Papua New Guinea fashions a fine pot using the hammer and anvil technique. Here she holds a stone from the river in her left hand inside the pot (this serves as the anvil). In her right hand is a wooden paddle, which she uses to shape the wall of the pot (the paddle serves to hammer the clay into place).

Changes in Sea Level

One of the most important aspects of any prehistoric environment has to do with alternating periods of **glaciation** (ice ages) and warming that have occurred over the past million years. A large part of human history occurred during the **Pleistocene** epoch, informally known as the "Great Ice Age" (ca. 1.6 million years ago to 10,000 years ago). During the Pleistocene, global temperatures were generally much cooler than at present. But it was also punctuated with warm periods between the times when glacial ice reached it maximum extent, known as **interglacials**, causing sea levels to go up or down over time. For example, during the last glacial maximum, about 20,000 years ago, the mean sea level was about 400 feet lower than it is today.

Such significant changes in sea level had large impacts on human activity, and they may explain why it is so difficult to identify archaeological sites from the

- **Glaciation.** A condition when the land surface is covered with sheets of glacial ice.

- **Pleistocene.** A geologic period in which much of the land in the northern hemisphere was covered by glaciers. These ice sheets retreated about 12,000 years ago.

- **Interglacials.** Warm periods between ice ages, usually referring to warm periods during the Pleistocene.

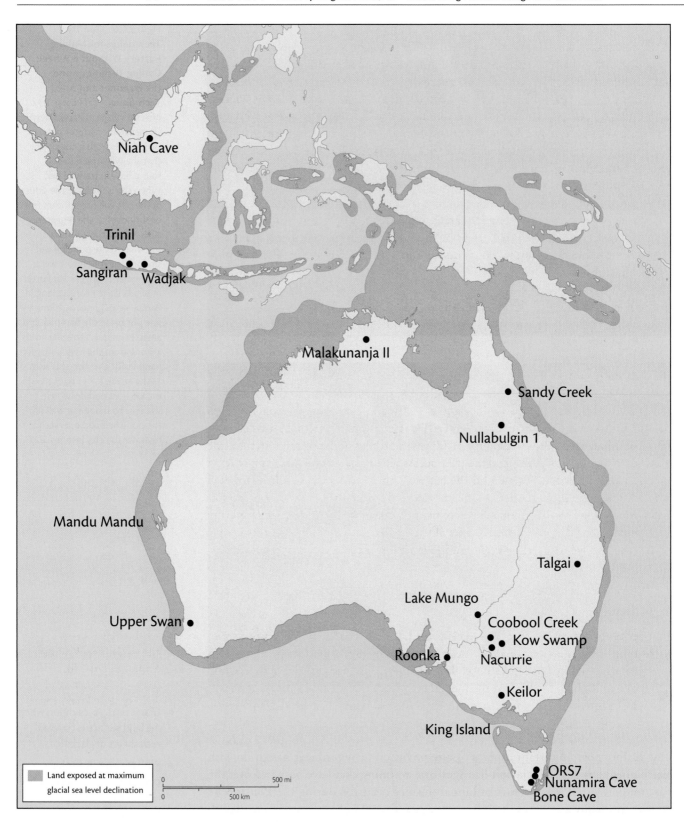

Niah Cave

Trinil

Sangiran   Wadjak

Malakunanja II

Sandy Creek

Nullabulgin 1

Mandu Mandu

Talgai

Lake Mungo

Coobool Creek

Upper Swan

Kow Swamp

Roonka   Nacurrie

Keilor

King Island

ORS7
Nunamira Cave
Bone Cave

Land exposed at maximum
glacial sea level declination

0   500 mi

0   500 km

🌱 **Figure 4.7   Ice Age Sea Level and Contemporary Sea Levels in Southeast Asia.** Late Pleistocene sea level circa 14,000 BP and modern coastlines in the islands and mainland of Southeast Asia, New Guinea, and Australia.

last glacial maximum (roughly 12,000–20,000 BP, or Before the Present). Coastal populations were likely larger than populations in interior regions because of the rich sources of fish, shellfish, and other resources found along coasts. But it is nearly impossible to find evidence today because most coastal sites from 14,000 BP and earlier are now covered by 300–400 feet of saltwater (Figure 4.7).

Studying the Landscape

Archaeologists often collaborate with geologists and **geomorphologists,** who study the origin and change of landforms, to reconstruct prehistoric landscapes. They know that most landscapes are constantly undergoing processes of subsidence (sinking); uplift (the movement and colliding of geotectonic plates to create hills and mountains); erosion (when sediments from mountains and hillsides become deposited in valleys, lakebeds, and the ocean floor); and floods. In addition, rivers often change course, leaving behind rich **alluvial soil** (rich, fine-grained soils deposited by rivers and streams). Because alluvial soils are so fertile, people have often chosen such areas for their settlements. When these streams empty into shallow bays and lagoons, they often produce abundant and varied plant and animal resources.

Because of environmental change, archaeologists need to be conscious of where streambeds were situated in relation to habitation sites during their occupation. The key is to sample enough of the sediments around a site to determine which are original or which have been eroded from other sites. Such patterns of deposition and erosion are critical in understanding the history of an archaeological site and how human action may have influenced these sediments.

A variety of other more specialized paleoenvironmental techniques have been developed to address particular environmental dynamics. These include ice cores in the arctic or high mountain regions, lake or sea varves (layers of silt or sand deposited by wave action), and volcanic strata in areas where volcanic activity has transformed the environment. An example of volcanic strata comes from obsidian samples found all along the north coast of New Guinea and the Bismarck Archipelago. Archaeologists have identified two obsidian quarries in the Bismarck Archipelago that provided most of the obsidian used in this region for 3,500 years. Studies of the volcanic strata at the quarries indicate when these quarries were accessible to humans before being covered with ash after an eruption sealed off the quarry with many meters of ash. Since each quarry produced obsidian with a different density, the density of obsidian flakes or fragments found in other parts of the country can be dated roughly by determining which quarry the flake came from. Thus, if the sample has one density, it is from one quarry site and we will know the period in which it was first used, if another density, we know it was obtained later from another quarry, in this particular case many centuries later.

Paleoethnobotany

Paleoethnobotany is the study of ancient plant remains to reconstruct a picture of prehistoric environments. It also focuses on human–plant interactions in archaeological settings to gain perspectives on prehistoric diets, crop production, land use, and seasonal occupation (Hastorf 1988). It can involve the study of coprolites (human and animal excrement), plant impressions in clay, and plant residues in cooking vessels. Another key method, developed by Norwegian geologist Lennart von Post (1946), involves the study of ancient pollen grains. Pollen grains normally decay like wood or leaves in many environments, but they preserve fairly well in acidic peat bogs and lake sediments. They have varied and distinctive shapes that allow researchers to identify the species to which a well-preserved grain belongs. Once samples of pollen from bogs or lake sediments are retrieved and their species identified, it is possible to calculate the relative proportion of grains from the identified species. Grasslands have an abundance of grasses represented, while forests have few grass pollens but large proportions of tree pollens. Rain forests typically have a wider variety of species than temperate forests. Because pollen is generally airborne and can travel several miles, a lakebed or bog some miles from an excavation can tell us what kind of vegetation was present in an area (Figure 4.8). The most difficult challenge in pollen analysis is to make sure

- **Geomorphologists.** Geologists who study the formation and structure of the earth's surface.

- **Alluvial soil.** Rich, fine-grained soils deposited by rivers and streams.

- **Paleoethnobotany.** The study of ancient plant remains in order to reconstruct a picture of prehistoric environments and human–plant interactions.

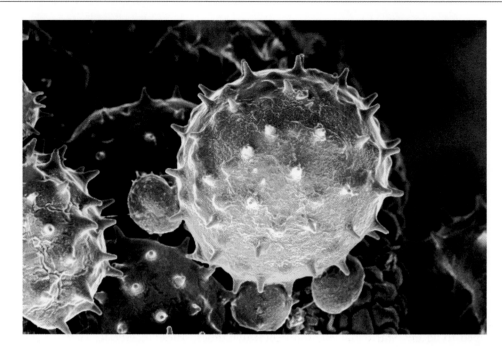

Figure 4.8   Pollen Under a Microscope.   High magnification shows that pollen grains are as varied as the diverse plant species they come from.

that the samples are from the same layer of sediment and have not been contaminated by the excavator or by some natural process.

In sum, environments in all parts of the globe have changed a great deal over the past 20,000 years, processes that have both affected and been affected by human action. To understand any changing lifeways demands understanding the changing environment and then inferring how people have adapted to these changing conditions. Most of the time we have much less evidence than we would like, but archaeology is about making sense of and drawing inferences from what disparate bits of evidence may be available.

THINKING CRITICALLY ABOUT ANTHROPOLOGICAL METHODS

Recent methodological innovations have made archaeological interpretations far more rigorous than a half century ago. But even though we can know where and how people lived in a certain environment, what aspects of prehistoric life can we still not know?

- **Intersubjectivity.** The realization that knowledge about other people emerges out of relationships and perceptions individuals have with each other.

- **Interview.** Any systematic conversation with an informant to collect field research data, ranging from a highly structured set of questions to the most open-ended ones.

How Do Cultural Anthropologists Research the Lifeways of Contemporary Peoples?

Although cultural anthropology shares some methods with other social sciences, such as economics, psychology, and political science, it is the most qualitative and has distinctive and effective methodological tools of its own. Cultural anthropology is holistic, traditionally studying multiple aspects of social life simultaneously. Research also involves long-term immersion and participation in a community. Along with an open mind, these methods yield insights we would never achieve had we started with preconceived ideas about a culture.

Fieldwork: Participant Observation and Interviewing

Long-term immersion in a community is called **fieldwork**. It is *the* defining methodology of the discipline. During fieldwork, anthropologists become involved in people's daily lives, observe and ask questions about what they are doing, and record those observations. Short visits or surveys are limited because people may say one thing but then do something completely different. Sticking around helps us put what people say in context. Fieldwork also helps us achieve one of our discipline's central goals, which Clifford Geertz (1973:28) once described as deciphering "the informal logic of everyday life," or the implicit assumptions people make and the tacit rules they live by. By participating directly in community activities, we can observe what is important to the community, what they discuss among themselves, and how these matters intertwine with social institutions. This approach can yield rich insights about people's behaviors, actions, and ideas that people themselves might not notice or understand, as we explore in "Thinking Like an Anthropologist: Fieldwork in an American Mall."

A key element of fieldwork is **participant observation**, a systematic research strategy that is, in some respects, a matter of just hanging out and going with the flow of everyday life. But what distinguishes anthropological "hanging out" is that anthropologists record much of what transpires while we are doing it. We are also in a different social position than we are normally accustomed to, and we must work hard to build collaborative relationships in a community (Figure 4.9). Establishing those relationships requires a lot of discipline, as well as acceptance of local customs and practices, however peculiar, unfamiliar, or uncomfortable to the fieldworker.

Participant observation makes the anthropologist a professional stranger and has been compared to living on the edge of a razor (Delaney 1988); it is neither pure observation nor pure participation. As observers, anthropologists cannot remove themselves from the action (Figure 4.10). Yet giving into participation too easily prevents one from noticing subtleties of behavior and learning to intuit their significance.

As anthropologist Johannes Fabian (1971) has suggested, fieldwork isn't simply about collecting "objective" data. Fieldwork data is created by the relationships between an anthropologist and his or her **informants**, the people from whom he or she gathers information. The anthropologist observes things, often multiple times, and inquires about them, gradually pulling together an enriched sense of what has been observed. Both the anthropologist and his or her informants have been actively creating this synthesis that becomes field data. For Fabian such observations and understanding are neither objective nor subjective, but the product of **intersubjectivity**, which means that knowledge about other people emerges out of relationships individuals have with each other.

Participant observation gives us many insights about how social life in another society is organized, but it is up to us as anthropologists to find systematic evidence for our perceptions. So another key goal of fieldwork is to flesh out our insights and gain new perspectives from **interviews**, or systematic conversations with informants, to collect data, which range from highly structured situations to casual conversations (Figure 4.11). Table 4.2 outlines the various interviewing strategies.

- **Fieldwork.** Long-term immersion in a community, normally involving firsthand research in a specific study community or research setting where people's behavior can be observed and the researcher can have conversations or interviews with members of the community.

- **Participant observation.** The standard research method used by sociocultural anthropologists that requires the researcher to live in the community he or she is studying to observe and participate in day-to-day activities.

- **Informant.** Any person an anthropologist gets data from in the study community, especially people interviewed or who provide information about what he or she has observed or heard.

Figure 4.9 Anthropologist Margaret Mead. Here she is wearing clothing typical of young Samoan women during her fieldwork in 1925–1926. This was not what she ordinarily wore, but something that she did to help build rapport.

Thinking Like an Anthropologist

Fieldwork in an American Mall

ANTHROPOLOGISTS BEGIN THEIR research by asking questions. In this box, we want you to learn how to ask questions as an anthropological researcher. Part 1 describes a situation and follows up with questions we would ask. Part 2 asks you to do the same thing with a different situation.

PART 1: OBSERVING THE USE OF SPACE IN THE AMERICAN SHOPPING MALL

We've all been to a shopping mall, but have you ever stopped to consider how people actually use malls? Anthropologist Paco Underhill (2005) has spent his career studying the American shopping mall and advising retail businesses on how to use space to sell products to the American consumer. From his observations it is clear that visiting a mall is a socially patterned experience, although visitors may not realize how their actions are being shaped by others.

Underhill begins his research on a mall, perhaps surprisingly, in the parking lot. There, he observes the possible entrances to the mall and the fact that, from the outside, the shopper can see little of what is inside. Landscaping is minimal, as is any other attraction that might keep the would-be shopper outside, and so they stream into the building. The goal of the mall, Underhill infers, is to get people inside to begin spending money.

Once people enter, Underhill observes, they need time to slow down and adjust to the space of the mall, so shops are rarely placed at the entrance; instead, these spaces are rented to doctors, accounting firms, and other businesses whose customers require appointments. After leaving this "decompression area," visitors come to the excitement of the mall proper: shop after shop with brightly colored merchandise pouring out into the hallways to attract attention.

Unlike the halls of a hospital or office building, those at the mall are extra wide. Underhill seeks to understand what goes on in these spaces that requires room for two broad lanes of foot traffic, often separated by stalls, carts, and tables filled with merchandise. While most people pop in and out of the many shops, others stop to look at the shop windows and the merchandise that lies on tables or hangs

along the way. Still others—particularly during cold or stormy weather—power-walk alone or in pairs, getting their exercise.

Underhill pays close attention to the people in these hallways and what they do, taking careful notes of his observations. He pays close attention to the ages and sexes of people there, if they walk by themselves or with others, who those others might be (children? middle aged?), and if these patterns change by day of the week and time of day. Entering the food court, Underhill observes the types of restaurants, the ways people interact with those restaurants, the kinds of shops near them, and how long people linger before returning to shopping. Underhill then turns his attention to the restrooms, observing where they are located, which is often hidden away in distant corners and corridors, intended not to affect the shopping experience negatively.

As Underhill wanders in and out of the large anchor stores, he makes other observations. Merchandise is piled up in the entryways, some on sale, some seasonal. He observes what grabs people's attention, getting them to slow down and pause. He observes how and where stores place different kinds of products, which influences how people move through the store, and what they are likely to see (and possibly purchase even though they did not come to buy that particular thing).

Underhill's research shows that by looking at the architecture and observing the flow of shoppers through it we can sense what kinds of behavior the store managers had hoped to encourage, what they might have hoped to discourage, and how people actually make use of these semi-public spaces.

The experience of walking through the mall with Paco Underhill raises important questions for anthropological researchers.

1. What might an anthropologist learn about the use of space from watching and observing what people do as opposed to interviewing them?
2. How can an anthropologist check the inferences he or she might make about the goals of store managers?

PART 2: OBSERVING THE USE OF SPACE IN THE COLLEGE LIBRARY

Consider your college library. Most libraries have a variety of tables, desks, and study carrels. The stacks may be open, or students may need to show their ID cards to get inside.

Audiovisual materials may be accessible to everyone in the student body, or professors may put some videos or DVDs on reserve. Modeling your work on Paco Underhill's, what kinds of questions would you pose to orient your observations of a college library?

Figure 4.10   Cultural Anthropologist Robert L. Welsch Being a Participant Observer.   Wearing appropriate clothing, whether traditional or contemporary, helps build rapport with the community by allowing the anthropologist to demonstrate that he or she respects traditional customs and culture. One of the authors wears traditional Mandarese clothing, including a silk sarong, batik shirt, and cap, to attend a wedding reception near Majene on the island of Sulawesi in Indonesia.

Figure 4.11   Interviews in the Field.   Interviews take place in all kinds of settings, from the most formal and sterile, such as an office, to settings like this one, in which coauthor Luis A. Vivanco (*left*, holding plants) interviews an environmental activist in rural Costa Rica about an agricultural demonstration project.

TABLE 4.2	CHARACTERISTICS AND NATURE OF DIFFERENT KINDS OF INTERVIEWS		
Kinds of Interviews	Nature of Interview	Clear Focus for Interview	Kind of Fieldnotes
Interview schedule	Questions are read from a printed script exactly as written to all subjects of the interview. Often used for survey data collection. Researcher decides what is important to ask.	Yes	Interview schedule form.
Formal interview/ Structured interview	Interviewer has a clear goal for the interview and writes down or tape-records the informant's answers. Often used for survey data collection. Researcher decides what is important to ask.	Yes	Transcript of answers or of questions and answers.
Informal interview/ Open-ended interview	Interviewer has a focus for the interview but may not have a clear goal of what information he or she wants. Interview may begin with certain questions, but new questions emerge as the interview proceeds. A notebook may be present, but most of the time is spent in conversation rather than writing notes.	Sometimes	Preliminary notes that outline the discussion. Later writes up a full description of context and content of discussion.
Conversation/ Casual conversation	Most people would not recognize this as an interview, notebooks are not present, and it would appear that the anthropologist and informants are simply having an ordinary conversation. Afterward the anthropologist takes a few jot notes so he or she can remember the topics discussed or goes somewhere private to write up more detailed raw notes that can be fleshed out later.	No	Headnotes and jot notes. Later writes up a full description of context and content of discussion. Notes often include topics to follow up on in future interviews or conversations.
Hanging out	At the heart of anthropology is participant observation, involving hanging out with members of the community in sex- and age-appropriate ways. It may involve helping with fishing, cooking, planting, or weeding in rural or traditional societies. Or it might be at a coffee shop, diner, or bar, or in a work environment such as an office or cafeteria. Anthropologists may occasionally make jot notes, but most of the time they record details in their notes later, when people are not around.	No	Headnotes and jot notes. Later writes up a full description of context and content of discussion. Notes often include topics to follow up on in future interviews or conversations.

Knowing What to Ask

How do cultural anthropologists know what questions to ask? From the 1870s until the 1950s, many British and American anthropologists relied on a volume published by the British Association for the Advancement of Science (1874) entitled *Notes and Queries in Anthropology* as a guide for what questions field researchers should use. It was initially created to help colonial-era travelers, missionaries, and administrators gather data to send back to Europe for "armchair anthropologists," people who never went to the field but relied on others for their ethnographic data (Urry 1972).

With the professionalization of anthropology in the early 1900s, however, such guides became less relevant since anthropologists themselves were collecting their own data. Today, anthropologists no longer have a prescribed set of good questions to ask. Usually we go with certain questions we want answered—drawn from theories and background literature, from an advisor or other colleague, or from simple curiosity. These questions change during fieldwork as we experience and confront new cultural realities. A solid education prepares us to ask insightful questions. As the expression goes, "99% of a good answer is a good question."

Taking Fieldnotes

Much of an anthropologist's time in the field is spent scribbling **fieldnotes**, information that the anthropologist writes down or transcribes (Lederman 1990). Some of this happens in the ebb and flow of everyday life, as we jot down notes in unobtrusive notebooks while conversing with others, or when a festival, ritual, or some other activity is taking place. With time and plenty of explanation about what we plan to do with the information, people become accustomed to it. Anthropologists have an ethical commitment to share our reasons for doing research, and explaining our goals often helps build rapport with informants.

In fact, many anthropologists only bring out a notebook when they are conducting structured interviews and surveys. We write down many details after the fact, or after we have had a chance to reflect more deeply on something. A lot of us also keep diaries where we express personal frustrations and keep what anthropologist Simon Ottenberg referred to as **headnotes**, which are the mental notes we make while in the field (Sanjek 1990:93–95), all of which can prove to be useful later. Writing down these details is essential because, as one anthropologist observed, if it's not written down, it didn't happen (Sanjek 1990). Think about it. You are in the field for at least a year. Once you get back home, settle in, organize and analyze all your fieldnotes, think about what you want to write, think about it again, and then write it, *several years* may have passed.

These techniques—becoming involved in people's lives, getting them to talk, and taking notes about it—enable anthropologists to pursue a major goal of fieldwork, which is to see the world from the point of view of the people who are the subjects of research.

Seeing the World from "The Native's Point of View" and Avoiding Cultural "Tunnel Vision"

The decision to live for a long period of time—a year or more—in an unfamiliar community in order to observe and record cultural differences emerged after 1914 and led to profoundly new kinds of understandings of native peoples. It had become clear that living in the community did not guarantee cultural relativism—that is, understanding a native culture on its own terms—or even eliminate ethnocentrism. But it increased the likelihood that the anthropologist could get some sense of the world in terms that local people understood.

Of course, nobody ever gets into another person's mind or has the same thoughts. Even in our own community, we rarely understand fully how classmates, neighbors, or colleagues think about some topic. Even when we think we do, a similar but new situation often produces an unexpected or contradictory reaction, usually triggered by different conditions or contexts.

As outsiders, we might initially think that our informants can be similarly contradictory. But after some time and effort to see things in terms of local context, the

- **Fieldnotes.** Any information that the anthropologist writes down or transcribes during fieldwork.

- **Headnotes.** The mental notes an anthropologist makes while in the field, which may or may not end up in formal fieldnotes or journals.

Figure 4.12   "The Native's Point of View." The ethnographer's tent on the beach of Nu'agasi, Trobriand Islands.

Figure 4.13   Conducting Participant Observation. Bronislaw Malinowski sits on a canoe chewing betel nuts with the white trader Billy Hancock and one of his Trobriand Islander informants, 1918.

things people say and do begin to make sense and we generally feel we are beginning to see the world from an emic (or insider's) perspective. Anthropologist Bronislaw Malinowski referred to this perspective as "the native's point of view" and asserted that it lay at the heart of the ethnographic method (Figures 4.12 and 4.13).

When we first interact with people from another culture, their reactions to nearly everything seem foreign and strange, and our own cultural "tunnel vision"— unquestioned tacit meanings and perspectives drawn from our own culture that prevent us from seeing and thinking in terms of another culture's tacit meanings and perspectives. But as we get to know them and see more of their culture, their reactions seem less puzzling and unexpected, even reasonable. We do not usually start thinking the way they do, and we may even continue to feel that their way of doing things is peculiar or even wrong, but we will gradually come to accept their reactions as making sense in terms of the local culture.

Of course, people in other societies have their own tunnel vision. They feel that their way of doing things, their moral, ethical, and legal codes, and their ways of thinking about the world are correct, while everyone else's are flawed. When anthropologists attempt to see the world "from the native's point of view" we are not claiming that the other culture's way of thinking is necessarily better than our own. Rather, we are attempting to unravel the cultural logic within which unthinkable actions in our own society become commonplace in another culture.

Other Methods That Cultural Anthropologists Use

Although participant observation and unstructured, open-ended interviews are the core research methods for cultural anthropologists, some projects require other strategies to understand particular social complexities as well as aspects of the native's point of view. Some of the most important of these other methods or strategies are summarized in Table 4.3.

Anthropologists have always drawn on any sources of data that may help them address and answer the questions they are pursing. More recently, anthropology as a discipline has benefited from being practiced by people who come from

TABLE 4.3 OTHER METHODS THAT ANTHROPOLOGISTS USE		
Name of Method	Description	Comments and Special Uses
Comparative method	Any anthropological research that involves systematic comparison of several societies. Often used to discern broad patterns in human societies.	Although a traditional method, today it is often associated with HRAF (Human Relations Areas Files), an online project based at Yale University. One of the earliest anthropological studies by Lewis Henry Morgan (1871) was a comparative study of kinship systems.
Genealogical method	A systematic methodology for recording kinship relations and how kin terms are used in different societies.	Originally developed by W. H. R. Rivers (1910) during the 1898 Cambridge Expedition to the Torres Strait. Today it is a standard strategy for many researchers.
Life histories	Reconstructing an informant's life, including such topics as residence, occupation, marriage, family, and difficulties, usually collected to reveal patterns that cannot be observed today.	Since anthropologists can never interview people who lived several generations ago, one way for accessing past lifeways has been collecting detailed life histories. Franz Boas's early students employed this method to reconstruct social patterns on Indian reservations long after traditional patterns had ceased (see, e.g., Radin 1920).
Ethnohistories	The study of historical change where a community had no written histories or historical documents, usually relying heavily on oral history for data. Ethnohistory may also refer to a view of history from the native's point of view, which often differs from an outsider's view of the same history.	Ethnohistories often provide insights into how an indigenous community views its relationships to other groups. Lurie (1961) provides an early statement on the benefits of ethnohistory. Native American scholars have used ethnohistory as a way of unraveling the pasts of tribes now on reservations (e.g., Sakiestewa Gilbert 2010), and the National Park Service often hires ethnohistorians to help interpret the national parks for visitors (see, e.g., Boxberger 2003).
Rapid appraisals	Short-term, focused ethnographic research typically lasting no more than a few weeks about narrow research questions or problems.	One of the best statements about specific techniques and goals involved in this fairly recent innovation is by James Beebe (1995).
Action research	Research in which the goal of a researcher's involvement in a community is to help make social change.	Sol Tax championed action anthropology, sending his students to the Fox Reservation during the 1940s and 1950s to bring positive social change (Tax 1975; Stapp 2012).
Participatory action research	Research questions, data collection, and data analysis are defined through collaboration between the researcher and the subjects of research. A major goal is for the research subjects to develop the capacity to investigate and take action on their primary political, economic, or social problems.	It is based on the idea that poor people, who usually have no voice in setting the policy that affects them, should do much of their own investigation, analysis, and planning (Chambers 1997). It not only aims to place the research and subjects on a more even plane but also encourages researchers to share their methods so people can act on them.
Research at a distance	Any method used to understand another society we cannot visit, because of war, devastation, or natural disaster	The most famous early example of this methodology was Ruth Benedict's *Chrysanthemum and the Sword* (1946) about the culture of the Japanese, conducted in the U.S. during World War II.
Analyzing secondary materials	Using any data that come from secondary sources such as a census, regional survey, historical report, and other research that is not compiled by the field researcher.	Many anthropologists have deposited their fieldnotes at one archive or another, so later anthropologists can make use of them. The most important repository is the National Anthropology Archives at the Smithsonian Institution (National Anthropology Archives 2015).
Focus groups	An interview strategy that brings several people together to talk about a focused topic, sometimes responding to the interviewer and sometimes responding to one another.	Focus groups add one key dimension that a simple, open-ended interview rarely provides, namely, the social context of an individual's views. Participants routinely adjust their comments in response to the views of others in the group, which mimics more natural social groups, even though the participants may have just met (see, e.g., Agar and MacDonald 1995).

different countries and from different cultures than several decades ago. Not surprisingly, these anthropologists have offered different approaches about how to frame the questions we ask and hope to answer. Anthropologists from developing countries have seen many uses for anthropological research that American or European researchers had not studied in quite the same ways, for example, pushing the limits of action anthropology and other kinds of engaged anthropological methods.

THINKING CRITICALLY ABOUT ANTHROPOLOGICAL METHODS

Using these methods, what special insights do you think anthropology offers that the other social sciences, such as psychology with its clinical psychology interview, sociology with its analysis of survey data, or economics with its quantitative data sets about the flow of goods and services, do not?

What Methods Are Important to the Study of Language Within Anthropology?

Linguistic anthropologists, like cultural anthropologists, work directly with their informants or research subjects. Much of their research therefore also involves long-term fieldwork and building rapport in another culture. But the specific field strategy that a linguistic anthropologist adopts will depend on the kind of question he or she is asking about the use of language in another culture.

In the early decades of the twentieth century, anthropologists saw language as central to understanding culture. Franz Boas (1911) and his team of researchers who were studying the tribes of the Pacific Northwest Coast (U.S. and Canada) in the late 1890s published many texts transcribed in their original Indian languages along with English translations. They insisted that the categories and concepts encoded in Native American myths and stories were distinctive to local cultural backgrounds. They pioneered a tradition—expanded by Boas's student Edward Sapir—that has come to be called **anthropological linguistics**, the branch of anthropology that studies human beings through their languages. In referring to this period, Harry Hoijer (1961:110) suggested that anthropological linguistics "is devoted in the main . . . to the languages of people who have no writing" (see also Teeter 1964; Voegelin 1965). Such anthropological linguists conducted systematic analyses of grammar, for example, the way verbs were constructed and inflected, how words are formed, and the range of meaning for particular words. These methods generally follow the methods of descriptive linguistics and are discussed in more detail in Chapter 5.

In the 1960s and 1970s linguistic anthropologist Dell Hymes (1962; 1972; 1973) pioneered a new anthropological approach to language that distinguished

- **Anthropological linguistics.** The branch of anthropology that studies human beings through their languages.

the ways people *actually* speak from the ideal ways people in any culture are *supposed* to speak. This approach has been called the **ethnography of speaking** (see Bauman and Sherzer 1974). This approach uses participant observation focusing on listening to what people say, the register they say it in, the words they use, and what they are hoping to communicate—both intentionally and unintentionally.

Linguistic anthropologist Dennis Tedlock (1972, 1988, 1993) has also focused on the ethnography of speaking, but he emphasized recording precisely what an informant or research subject utters, including the pauses, the mistakes, and the specific word choices. He viewed all speech acts as performances, an approach that has come to be known as **ethnopoetics**, referring to a method of recording oral poetry, stories, ritual language, and so on, as verses and stanzas rather than as prose paragraphs in order to capture the format and other performative elements that might be lost in written texts. In his studies of Zuni stories and ritual texts, Tedlock (1999) pioneered ways of analyzing every pause, silence, change in volume or tone, intentional sound effects, gestures, and props. For native speakers of the language, these variables would be perceived intuitively (Figure 4.14).

Over the last several decades many linguistic anthropologists have sought to understand how people use language to mark and communicate social position. These researchers are interested in how language is gendered, how language helps establish patterns of dominance and subordination, or how one person in a community can use a language cue to influence others. One applied example concerns how political advisors for national political parties sometimes use linguistic anthropology research and focus groups of potential voters to determine which words and phrases are most likely to generate appeal for voters. Several years ago the pollster and linguistic researcher Frank Luntz (2007) introduced a new way the Republicans could talk about the estate tax, a tax on the wealth (the estate) of a person who dies, before it is distributed among the heirs. Republicans wanted to eliminate the estate tax, which affected the wealthiest 2% of Americans. To muster

- **Ethnography of speaking.** An anthropological approach to language that distinguished the ways that people actually speak from the ideal ways that people in any culture are supposed to speak.

- **Ethnopoetics.** A method of recording oral poetry, stories, ritual language, and nearly any narrative speech act, as verses and stanzas rather than as prose paragraphs in order to capture the format and other performative elements that might be lost in written texts.

Figure 4.14 Linguistic Anthropologist Anna Luisa Daigneault. She is taking notes and conducting interviews with two Ayoreo elders in northern Paraguay.

the support of the 98% of voters who would not benefit from this change in tax law, Luntz suggested calling this tax the "death tax," a term that suggests that the government is taxing the act of dying—something everybody will experience. Opposition to the "death tax" soared in 2001 and the U.S. Congress even passed a bill that reduced the estate tax to zero by 2010, before a new bill reinstated the tax. Luntz typically uses focus groups as a methodology for learning about how ordinary people understand and perceive words, phrases, and concepts. As the title of Luntz's book suggests (*It's Not What You Say, It's What People Hear*), it is not what a politician says that matters, but what people think they hear him or her saying.

THINKING CRITICALLY ABOUT ANTHROPOLOGICAL METHODS

Although most linguistic anthropologists use linguistic transcription, many also incorporate various aspects of cultural analysis in their work. How might an understanding of the cultural background of greeting ritual or the expectations listeners have of song, poetry, stories, or even feature films shape the meaning these verbal performances might have for ordinary listeners?

Conclusion

The evidence on which all anthropologists base their interpretations of fossils, artifacts, and cultural practices comes from a wide range of standard methods. Each of the subfields has its own methods, but while the issues that biological anthropologists, archaeologists, cultural anthropologists, and linguistic anthropologists pursue are different, each invokes the kind of holism that is central to anthropology as a discipline.

As the example we began this chapter with suggests—how old is Serpent Mound?—even the most basic archaeological knowledge (e.g., how old is a site?) can often be complicated and ambiguous. Students sometimes ask us why archaeologists need *so many* different kinds of dating methods. Serpent Mound shows us how even "scientific" methods like carbon-14 dating aren't perfect, but depend on the quality of the sample, where the sample was taken from and the stratigraphy in that part of the mound, and even what the history of that tiny sample of organic material might have been. The issues in interpreting early fossils are quite similar, even if they involve several other variables.

These anthropologists who study the past collect artifacts and fossils as a way of interpreting sequences of artifacts and changing past lifeways, and not because the artifacts themselves are valuable in their own right, but because they provide evidence of the bigger picture of an ancient way of life. The most important factor for the researcher is the context in which the artifact or feature was found, which gives meaning to the site and any other artifacts found on it.

Cultural anthropologists and linguistic anthropologists confront a somewhat different set of problems because they often have too much data, rather than too little. But each interview or effort to gather data from living people presents the possibility of introducing a distortion of what our informants and research subjects feel and do because of our presence. Over time our informants get used to our presence, but even this fact does not make our presence irrelevant. Rather, it leads us to look for other confirmations in people's behavior, their activities, their preoccupations, and the like, much as archaeologists do to confirm their dates.

In the same way, an interview in a community one is studying is not valuable on its own, but as data for constructing a description of the society that would make sense to the residents. And while most people around the world do not consciously perceive many aspects of how they speak, a systematic study of actual speech says volumes about the society in which we live. It is this theme that we turn to next.

KEY TERMS

Reviewing the Chapter

Chapter Section	What We Know	To Be Resolved
What can fossils tells us?	Methods of dating fossils have improved in recent years, as have methods of morphological analysis. Genetic analysis of ancient DNA is also improving. Working together, these methods are illuminating the early history of human ancestors.	Despite improvements in how paleoanthropologists search for fossils, it is not clear how the process of fossilization creates sampling problems for paleo-anthorpologists. Key samples needed to fill in the story of human origins may never have been turned into fossils.
What methods do archaeologists use to decipher the past?	Archaeologists have developed many standard strategies for determining how prehistoric people lived, how their artifacts were made and used, and how to reconstruct the environment of prehistoric sites. But we are always dependent on sites that have survived and that have been discovered. Newly discovered and excavated sites can often change the conclusions we reach.	Studies of ancient environments and habitation sites are improving all the time, but subsidence and rising sea levels since the Pleistocene have made it difficult for archaeologists to reconstruct certain environments. We may never know about the nature of these early settlements and landscapes now under water.
What is so distinctive about cultural anthropology fieldwork?	Participant observation and immersion in another culture provide rich and nuanced insights about the social lives and cultural practices in a community. Immersion offers the researcher a chance to see what people do, not just what they say.	Although nearly all anthropologists accept participant observation as a reliable research tool, scholars in other disciplines, particularly economics, political science, and psychology, do not accept participant observation as reliable because it seems to them subjective.
What methods do linguistic anthropologists use?	In addition to descriptive analyses of grammar, how words are formed, and vocabulary, contemporary linguistic anthropologists study how people speak, using what has come to be called the ethnography of speaking or ethnopoetics. These methods offer nuanced insights into how people shape meaning by how they speak, not just by what they say.	The ethnography of speaking and ethnopoetics suffer the same criticisms that cultural anthropologists face in having systematic methods but unsystematic sampling strategies. This problem arises largely because linguistic anthropologists can rarely sample large numbers of individuals in an ethnography of speaking project.

Readings

H. Russell Bernard's *Research Methods in Anthropology: Qualitative and Quantitative Approaches*, 5th ed. (Lanham, MD: Altamira Press, 2011) provides a comprehensive overview of quantitative and qualitative methods across the four subfields. *A Companion to Biological Anthropology*, edited by Clark Spencer Larsen (Malden, MA: Wiley-Blackwell, 2010) offers historical and contemporary overview of theories and methods in biological anthropology.

•••••••••••••••••••••

There are many useful introductions to ethnographic methods, but Michael Agar's *The Professional Stranger: An Informal Introduction to Ethnography*, 2nd ed. (San Diego, CA: Academic Press, 1996) is a classic resource for the beginning student. There are also numerous histories of ethnographic methods, among them George W. Stocking, Jr.'s edited volume *Observers Observed: Essays on Ethnographic Fieldwork* (Madison: University of Wisconsin Press, 1983).

•••••••••••••••••••••

For a rich resource for exploring the intellectual and theoretical issues involved in the practice of writing and analyzing fieldnotes, see Roger Sanjek's *Fieldnotes: The Makings of Anthropology* (Ithaca, NY: Cornell University Press, 1990). A more practical guide to writing and analyzing fieldnotes is *Writing Ethnographic Fieldnotes,* by Robert Emerson, Rachel Fretz, and Linda Shaw (Chicago: University of Chicago Press, 1995).

● ● ● ● ● ● ● ● ● ● ● ● ● ● ● ● ● ● ● ●

For a focused approach to archaeological methods, see Jane Balme and Alistair Patterson, eds., *Archaeology in Practice: A Student Guide to Archaeological Analyses* (Malden, MA: Blackwell, 2006). A now-classic article aimed at explaining the method of seriation dating is provided in James Deetz and Edwin S. Dethlefsen's (1967) "Death's Head, Cherub, Urn and Willow," *Natural History* 76 (3): 29–37, which analyzes a series of gravestone carvings in New England to show how the method works in practice.

● ● ● ● ● ● ● ● ● ● ● ● ● ● ● ● ● ● ● ●

For general approaches to linguistic anthropology, see Susan D. Blum's *Making Sense of Language: Readings in Culture and Communication,* 2nd ed. (New York: Oxford University Press, 2012). For a more explicit example of how to record texts, see Dennis Tedlock, *Finding the Center: Art of the Zuni Storyteller,* 2nd ed. (Lincoln: University of Nebraska Press, 1999).

● ● ● ● ● ● ● ● ● ● ● ● ● ● ● ● ● ● ● ●

Linguistic Anthropology

Relating Language and Culture

In her well-known book *You Just Don't Understand: Women and Men in Conversation*, linguist Deborah Tannen (1990) describes the tensions that arise between young couples because of the different ways they use language. Consider the case of Josh, a college student who has been dating his girlfriend, Linda, for more than a year. One day, he received a text from his close high school friend, who was coming through town. Josh invited him to spend the weekend and to see the Red Sox play the Yankees. That evening, when Josh was over at Linda's he told her he was going to have a houseguest and wouldn't be able to see the film he had told her they would see on the day of the Sox–Yankees game. Linda became upset. Linda would never make such plans without talking about it with Josh first. In fact, she liked being able to say to her friends "I'll have to check with Josh" because it showed how close they were. Josh's failure to check with her suggested to Linda a lack of intimacy in their relationship.

Josh was equally upset by Linda's reaction, although for different reasons. When Linda asked him why he did not consult her first, he replied, "I can't say to my friend, 'I have to ask my girlfriend for permission!'" For Josh, checking with Linda would make him feel subordinate to her or, worse, like a child. He felt Linda was trying to limit his freedom as an adult and as a man.

Josh and Linda speak the same language, yet they were clearly talking past one another. In their case, the same words "I'll have to check with Josh (or Linda)" meant very different things to each person. What

---

🌱 **Talking Past Each Other?**   Men and women in the United States are socialized to communicate in different ways, which can produce tensions when one party doesn't recognize or appreciate differences in the other's approach to using language.

CHAPTER

5

IN THIS CHAPTER

Where Does Language Come From?
• Evolutionary Perspectives on Language
• Historical Linguistics: Studying Language Origins and Change

How Does Language Actually Work?
• Descriptive Linguistics
• Phonology: Sounds of Language
• Morphology: Grammatical Categories
• Sociolinguistics

Do People Speaking Different Languages Experience Reality Differently?
• The Sapir-Whorf Hypothesis
• Hopi Notions of Time
• Ethnoscience and Color Terms
• Is the Sapir-Whorf Hypothesis Correct?

How Can Languages Be So Dynamic and Stable at the Same Time?
• Linguistic Change, Stability, and National Policy
• Language Stability Parallels Cultural Stability

How Does Language Relate to Social Power and Inequality?
• Language Ideology
• Gendered Language Styles
• Language and Social Status
• Language and the Legacy of Colonialism

115

explains the miscommunication? While the expression "women are from Venus and men are from Mars" overstates the situation, in American culture, men and women do live in somewhat different worlds. We have different expectations of one another, expectations that help shape how we use language. If Linda were more direct, people would consider her harsh, aggressive, and unladylike. Josh's directness, however, would typically be a sign of his strength, independence, and maturity, the supposed ideal for a man in American culture. Taking this a step further, we can see how American patterns of gender inequality are built into how we use language. In some settings—the workplace, say—Linda's concern for preserving good social relationships could appear as a sign of weakness, dependence, and uncertainty, limiting her ability to climb the corporate ladder.

This perspective on language leads us to ask a question at the heart of anthropology's interest in language: *How do the ways people talk reflect and create their cultural similarities, differences, and social positions?* Embedded within this larger question are the following problems, around which this chapter is organized:

Where does language come from?

How does language actually work?

Do people speaking different languages experience reality differently?

How can languages be so dynamic and stable at the same time?

How does language relate to social power and inequality?

Language is one of the most rule-bound and structured aspects of human culture. Yet, ironically, language is also one of the least conscious aspects of culture. Moreover, while language is structured, it is also one of the most dynamic aspects of human life, because it can change so rapidly. Different languages have words for different sets of concepts, just as different words can be used for similar concepts. Furthermore, within a society social hierarchies and gender differences are both marked and reinforced by linguistic expressions. Before we get into these kinds of subtleties, it is important to find out where language comes from.

Where Does Language Come From?

- **Language.** A system of communication consisting of sounds, words, and grammar.

A **language** is a system of communication consisting of sounds, words, and grammar. This simple definition emphasizes three features: (1) language consists of sounds organized into words according to some sort of grammar, (2) language is used to communicate, and (3) language is systematic. But where does it come from? We can begin to answer this question in two ways: one is evolutionary, having to do with our biological heritage; and the other is historical, related to how languages have developed over time.

Evolutionary Perspectives on Language

The simple fact that we are able to make sounds and put them into meaningful sequences suggests two different biological abilities that both link us to and separate us from non-human animals. First is the ability to make linguistic sounds using the mouth and larynx. Second is the ability to reproduce these sounds in an infinite variety of ways to produce an equally diverse range of thoughts. To what extent do we share these capabilities with other animals?

There are clearly examples in which an animal appears to talk. Animal behaviorist Irene Pepperberg worked for several decades to train her famous African Grey Parrot Alex (1976–2007) to make similar simple sentences using symbolic concepts of shape, color, and number. Alex's ability to use language was quite rudimentary compared to human speech. He was one of the few non-primates to have an obituary published in the *New York Times* (Carey 2007). But do animals really talk?

Call Systems and Gestures

Most animals cannot talk because they do not have a larynx, which enables humans to make the meaningful sounds we call language. Yet most animals use sounds, gestures, and movements of the body intended to communicate. Anthropological linguists refer to these sounds and movements as **call systems,** which are patterned forms of communication that express meaning. But why is this communication not language? There are four major reasons:

● **Call systems.** Patterned sounds or utterances that express meaning.

1. *Animal call systems are limited in what and how much they can communicate.* Calls are restricted largely to emotions or bits of information about what is currently present in the environment, while language has few limitations in the content of what kind of information it can transmit.
2. *Call systems are stimuli dependent, which means that an animal can only communicate in response to a real-world stimulus.* Animal calls are responses to visible triggers in the external world and nothing more. In contrast, humans can talk about things that are not visible, including things and events in the past or future.
3. Among animals each call is distinct, and these calls are never combined to produce a call with a different meaning, while the sounds in any language can be combined in limitless ways to produce new meaningful utterances.
4. *Animal call systems tend to be nearly the same within a species with only minor differences between call systems used in widely separated regions.* In contrast, different members of our species speak between 5,000 and 6,000 different languages, each with its own complex patterns.

Humans are evolutionarily distinct from other animals in that we developed not just the biological capacity to speak through a larynx but the brain capacity to combine sounds to create infinite symbolic meanings. Both abilities form the basis of human language.

Teaching Apes to Use Sign Language

Nevertheless, it is clear that some apes have the ability to communicate, beyond the limits of a call system, as researchers who have attempted to teach American Sign Language (ASL) to apes have demonstrated. A well-known example is a chimp named Washo, who grew up in captivity but heard no spoken language from her human caregivers, R. Allen Gardner and Beatrice Gardner. The Gardners instead used ASL whenever they were with her, and Washo learned just over 100 signs that had English equivalents. Even more striking, she was able to combine as many as five signs to form

Figure 5.1   Koko with Penny Patterson.

complete, if simple, sentences (Gardner, Gardner, and Van Cant-fort 1989). Similarly, Penny Patterson (2003) worked with a female gorilla named Koko, who has learned to use some 2,000 signs and can also combine them in short sentences (Figure 5.1).

Chimpanzees and gorillas clearly have the cognitive ability to associate signs with concepts and then to combine them in original ways, comparable in some respects to the linguistic ability of a toddler. Such capabilities are not surprising among our nearest relatives in the animal kingdom, since the human capacity for language had to begin somewhere, and we would expect other advanced primates to have some limited abilities.

Several anthropologists have nevertheless challenged whether apes like Washo and Koko actually demonstrate any innate linguistic ability (Wallman 1992). These critics argue that the two apes are extremely clever and have learned to respond to the very subtle cues of their trainers, in much the way circus animals learn remarkable tricks and know when to perform them. But as linguistic anthropologist Jane Hill (1978) has noted, most of these critics have never worked with primates. Such studies of ape sign language suggest that our capacity for language may have begun to emerge with our ancestral apes. Most likely, from this rudimentary ability to associate meaning with signs and gestures, full-blown language evolved as human cognitive abilities became more complex.

Historical Linguistics: Studying Language Origins and Change

While primatologists take the evolutionary approach to the origins of language, historical linguistics focuses on how and where the languages people speak today emerged. This approach uses historical analysis of long-term language change. The approach began in the eighteenth century as **philology**, which is the comparative study of ancient texts and documents. Philologists like the German Jakob Grimm (1822), best known for his collections of fairy tales, observed that there were regular, patterned differences from one European language to another. To explain these patterns, he hypothesized that English, German, Latin, Greek, Slavic, and Sanskrit all came from a common ancestor. As speakers of languages became isolated from one another—perhaps because of migration and geographic isolation—the consonants in the original language shifted one way in Sanskrit, another way in Greek and Slavic languages, in a different direction in Germanic and English, and yet another way in Latin and the Romance languages, all of which came to be known as Grimm's Law (Figure 5.2). The supposed common ancestor language, which became extinct after these divergences took place, is called a **proto-language**.

Genetic Models of Language Change

Contemporary historical linguists call Grimm's approach "genetic," since it explores how modern languages derived from an ancestral language. To identify languages that have a common ancestry, historical linguists identify **cognate words**, which are words in two or more languages that may sound somewhat different today but would have changed systematically from the same word (Table 5.1). As speakers became isolated from one another for geographic, political, or cultural reasons, consonants, vowels, and pronunciation diverged until they were speaking two or more new, mutually unintelligible languages. For example, German, Dutch, and English are descended from the same proto-Germanic language, but speakers of these three languages cannot usually understand each other unless they have studied the other language.

- **Philology.** Comparative study of ancient texts and documents.

- **Proto-language.** A hypothetical common ancestral language of two or more living languages.

- **Cognate words.** Words in two languages that show the same systematic sound shifts as other words in the two languages, usually interpreted by linguists as evidence for a common linguistic ancestry.

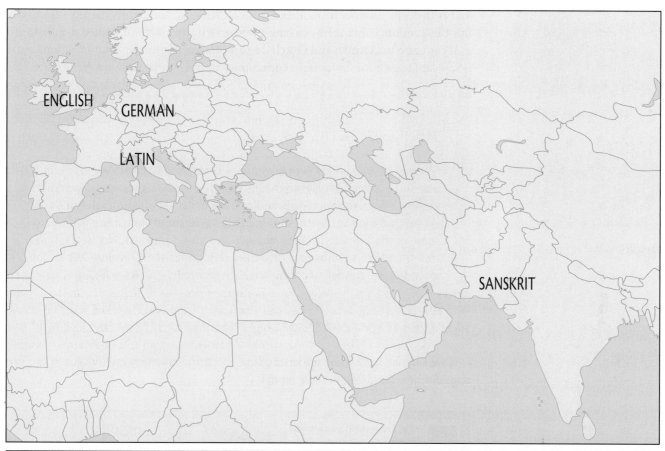

INDO-EUROPEAN INITIAL CONSONANT	ENGLISH	GERMAN	LATIN	SANSKRIT
*p	foot	Fuß	pes	pet
*p	father	Vater	pater	pita
*d	two	zwei	duo	dva
*d	tooth	zahn	dens	dan
*k	hundred	hundert	centum	satam
*k	heart	Herz	cor	sua
*k	hound	Hund	canis	sua

Figure 5.2   Grimm's Law.   Early Indo-European forms using *k* in Greek, Latin, and Irish shifted to *h* in the Germanic languages of English, German, Danish, and Norwegian. Many other examples include "head" and "heart."

TABLE 5.1 EXAMPLES OF COGNATE WORDS IN INDO-EUROPEAN LANGUAGES								
English	Dutch	German	Norwegian	Italian	Spanish	French	Greek	Sanskrit
three	drei	drei	tre	tre	tres	trois	tri	treis
mother	moeder	mutter	mor	madre	madre	mère	meter	matar
brother	broeder	bruder	bror	fra	hermano	Frère	phrater	bhrator

Non-Genetic Models of Linguistic Change: Languages in Contact

Languages also change by being in contact with another language, which is a "non-genetic" model of change. Such change generally takes place where people routinely speak more than one language. In the speech of multilingual persons, the use of one of the languages is subtly influenced by the other language's sounds, syntax, grammar, and vocabulary. Evidence of this process can be seen in the use of the flapped and trilled *r* in Europe. In southern parts of Western Europe, the trilled *r* is typical, but this pronunciation seems to have given way in the north of France to a flapped *r* as is common in German and Dutch. In this process, distinctive pronunciations move across language boundaries from community to community like a wave (Figure 5.3).

THINKING CRITICALLY ABOUT LANGUAGE

Many of us are familiar with how our pets respond to things we say in regular and predictable ways so that it often seems like they understand what we are saying. Although dogs and cats cannot make the normal sounds in English, we might sometimes think they understand simple English. Using some of the primate-language studies as a guide, how would you respond to a friend who claims that his or her dog understands English? What do examples like this tell us about language generally?

Now that we have some understanding about the emergence of language, we can consider how language actually works.

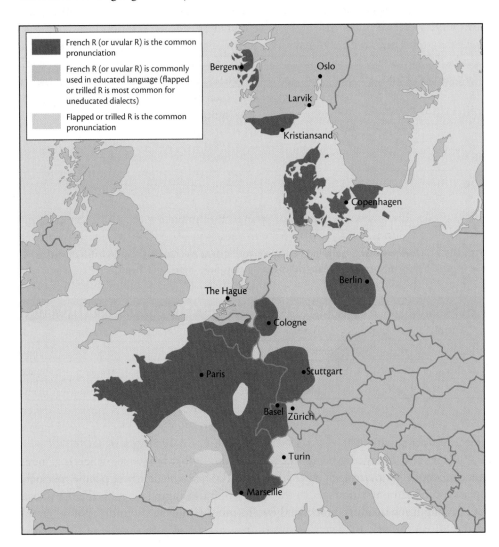

Figure 5.3   The Wave Theory of Language Change.   Uvular, trilled, and flapped *r* in European languages. Note that pronunciation patterns sweep across language boundaries from French to German and even to Scandinavian languages.

French R (or uvular R) is the common pronunciation

French R (or uvular R) is commonly used in educated language (flapped or trilled R is most common for uneducated dialects)

Flapped or trilled R is the common pronunciation

Bergen

Oslo

Larvik

Kristiansand

Copenhagen

Berlin

The Hague

Cologne

Paris

Stuttgart

Basel   Zürich

Turin

Marseille

How Does Language Actually Work?

Over the past century, linguists and linguistic anthropologists have studied the majority of the world's languages and have found that each is highly structured. Moreover, most people, even those who speak unwritten languages, are largely unaware of the structure of their language until someone makes a mistake. Even then, they do not always know what is wrong; they just know the sentence sounded wrong.

To explain such reactions, the French linguist Ferdinand de Saussure (1916, 1986) suggested a distinction between the structure, or formal rules, of a language (*langue*) and how people actually speak it (*parole*). Distinguishing *langue* (language) and *parole* (speech) allows linguists to separate the rules and expected usage of language from what people actually say. The distinction is useful because it helps us realize that the rules we use to produce the sounds, word formation, and grammar as native speakers of a language can differ from how we actually speak, which is as much a social and cultural phenomenon as it is a function of language's structure. Here we explore how language is formally structured, which is the field of descriptive linguistics, and then sociolinguistics, the field that studies the social contexts of language use.

Descriptive Linguistics

The study of *langue,* or the formal structure of language, is called **descriptive linguistics**, which refers to the systematic analysis and description of a language's sound system and grammar. Linguists distinguish three types of structure in language: (1) **phonology,** the structure of speech sounds; (2) **morphology,** how words are formed into meaningful units; and (3) **syntax,** how words are strung together to form sentences and more complex utterances, such as paragraphs. (High school grammar classes mostly focus on morphology and syntax). All languages have predictable phonological, morphological, and syntactic structures.

- **Descriptive linguistics.** The systematic analysis and description of a language's sound system and grammar.

- **Phonology.** The systematic pattern of sounds in a language, also known as the language's sound system.

- **Morphology.** The structure of words and word formation in a language.

- **Syntax.** Pattern of word order used to form sentences and longer utterances in a language.

Phonology: Sounds of Language

The sounds of language are organized by marking systematic contrasts between pairs or groups of sounds. The majority of both these sounds and the contrasts appear in many of the world's languages, and yet each language has its own unique pattern of sounds. When linguists listen to natural language, such as when people talk unselfconsciously in ordinary conversations, they identify minimal pairs, which are pairs of words that differ only in a single sound contrast.

Sound Contrasts: Pan, Ban, and Man

Consider, for example, the initial sounds in the English words "pan," "ban," and "man." Three sounds, [p], [b], and [m], distinguish these three words, while the other sounds in these words are the same. The consonants *p*, *b*, and *m* are formed at the front of the mouth at the lips. The differences among three consonants parallel differences among the initial sounds in the words "tab," "dab," and "nab," or the final sounds in the words "pig," "pick," and "ping."

These nine contrasts distinguish three series of what linguists call **stops,** sounds that are made by an occlusion, or stopping, of the airstream though the oral cavity or mouth. But in addition, [b], [d], and [g] differ from [p], [t], and [k] in that the first group are voiced, formed by the vibration of the vocal cords (glottis), at the Adam's apple. The triplet of nasal consonants, [m], [n], and [ng], are also voiced

- **Stops.** Sounds that are formed by closing off and reopening the oral cavity so that it stops the flow of air through the mouth, such as the consonants *p, b, t, d, k,* and *g.*

consonants that stop the airflow through the mouth but allow the air to pass through the nasal cavity.

Mind you, these are examples from English. Other languages have different sounds. One of the most distinct from our language's point of view is the click (!) sound of Southern African peoples like the !Kung (Bushmen). Most speakers of English, !Kung, or for that matter any language, are not fully aware of how they form the different sounds they use when speaking, yet linguists recognize that sound systems are surprisingly systematic.

Dialects and Accents

Another interesting way to think about phonology is to consider dialects, which are regional or social varieties of a single language. Differences in vocabulary, grammar, and pronunciation, as well as regional accents such as those found in Brooklyn or Alabama in American English, are examples of a fairly minor dialect variation. Sometimes the variation occurs between generations or among people of different social classes. Part of the difference between these forms of speech is intonation, the pattern of rising and falling pitch, but usually careful analysis of the sounds shows that they also have systematic differences in their respective sound systems.

Up to the 1970s linguists assumed that American language was becoming increasingly homogeneous. It seemed that, owing to schools or to national broadcasts on television and radio where the accent is standardized, regional dialects would disappear. In fact, variation in sound systems seems to be greater now than ever before. The sociolinguist William Labov (1990; Labov, Ash, and Boberg 2006) observed in the 1980s that language change in the sound system of American English was concentrated in the cities. He also noted that sound change was most pronounced between generations in the same communities. Such findings suggest a much stronger role for peer groups in the transmission of linguistic forms than linguists had previously noticed.

Morphology: Grammatical Categories

The elements of grammar—tense, word order, which genders are marked, and so on—are also structured. Just like cultural patterns, grammatical patterns learned during childhood feel extremely natural to native speakers in any language, even though the same forms and structures would seem quite unnatural to speakers of most other languages. A couple of examples illustrate how varied even the most basic grammatical categories can be.

Tenses

Americans tend to assume that there are only three natural tenses: past, present, and future. But not all languages use this same set of tenses, and some languages do not even require that tense be unambiguously marked in any particular sentence.

For example, the Ningerum language of Papua New Guinea uses five tenses: present, future, today-past, yesterday-past, and a-long-time-ago-past. Events that happened earlier in the day receive a different tense marking from those that happened yesterday or the day before. Similarly, events that happened several weeks, months, or years ago take a different tense marking altogether.

In contrast, Indonesian has no regular tense marking in its verbs but uses adverbs or other time references to emphasize when something has happened or will happen.

Pronouns

American English has fewer pronouns than many other languages. We distinguish between singular and plural, and among three persons (first person, second person, and third person). English also has two cases used when the pronoun is either the subject or the object. If we consider only person and number, we should have six basic pronouns, plus two extra pronouns for gender marking in the third person singular (he, she, and it).

This set of pronouns does not even begin to exhaust the possible pronoun distinctions that could be used. In French, for example, the second person singular pronoun,"you," takes two forms, *tu* and *vous* (an informal and a formal form). The Awin language of Papua New Guinea has singular, dual, and plural forms of its pronouns, meaning "you" (one person), "you two," and "you" (more than two).

Such basic examples as pronouns and tenses illustrate some of the wide range of possibilities that are possible in natural languages. Each configuration suggests certain distinctions that represent meaning encoded in the language's grammar. But such patterns do not alone create meaning.

Sociolinguistics

Sociolinguistics is the study of how sociocultural context and norms shape language use and the effects of language use on society. Sociolinguists accept whatever form of language a community uses—which de Saussure referred to as *parole*—as the form of language they should study.

When one examines the actual speech (*parole*) used in any community, one often finds that different people may use the same grammar and sound system (*langue*), but the actual sentences they make (*parole*) often carry different assumptions and connotations. This is because meaning emerges from conversation and social interaction, not just the formal underlying rules of language. We can see how sociocultural context shapes meaning by looking at signs, symbols, and metaphors.

- **Sociolinguistics.** The study of how sociocultural context and norms shape language use and the effects of language use on society.

Signs

Signs are words or objects that stand for something else, usually as a kind of shorthand. They are the most basic way to convey meaning. A simple example is the ordinary traffic sign that tells motorists to stop or not to park along a certain stretch of roadway (Figures 5.4 and 5.5).

Symbols

Symbols, which we introduced in Chapter 2, are basically elaborations on signs. When a sign becomes a symbol, it usually takes on a much wider range of meanings than it may have had as a sign. For example, most colleges and universities in America have mascots and colors associated with their football teams. A mascot, such as a wildcat or panther, is a sign of the team, but mascots also readily become a symbol for the whole school, so that the wildcat represents all the distinctive features of the institution and its people. But note that symbols work because signs themselves are productive, capable of being combined in innovative and meaningful ways.

Anthropologist Sherry Ortner (1971) distinguished three kinds of key symbols, or culturally powerful symbols. These are summarizing symbols, elaborating symbols, and key scenarios. Summarizing symbols sum up a variety of meanings and experiences and link them to a single sign. An example would be the American flag, which many Americans see as summarizing everything good about America, especially such

Figure 5.4 One of the Most Common Signs in American Life. Even without words on it, we all know the meaning of this sign.

Figure 5.5   The Productive Use of Signs Around the World.   This sign in front of a business in Papua New Guinea bans the sale of betel nut. When chewing betel nut, a common practice in that island nation, one needs to spit out bright red spittle frequently.

things as "democracy, free enterprise, hard work, competition, progress, and freedom" (Figure 5.6).

Elaborating symbols work in exactly the opposite way from summarizing symbols, by helping us sort out complex feelings and relationships. For example, the cow is an elaborating symbol among the Nuer and Dinka peoples of southern Sudan. By talking about cows, the Nuer and Dinka can talk about social relations within the community (Figure 5.7).

The key scenario differs from the other two kinds of symbols because it implies how people should act. A common American key scenario is the Horatio Alger myth. In Horatio Alger's many novels, this scenario often involves a young boy from a poor family, who works hard to become rich and powerful. It does not matter that most of us will not become these things, but the scenario does have meaning for how we feel about and evaluate hard work and persistence.

Metaphors

Metaphors are implicit comparisons of words or things that emphasize the similarities between them, allowing people to make sense of complex social relations around them. For example, in our culture we metaphorize ideas as food, as in "this textbook gives you *food* for thought, and some things to *chew* over, although you probably can't *stomach* everything we tell you here." Another example is how we metaphorize love as a disease, as in "he got over her, but she's got it bad for him, and it broke her heart" (Sheridan 2006:54).

Through signs, symbols, and metaphors, language thus reinforces cultural values that are already present in the community. Simultaneously cultural norms and values reinforce the symbols that give language its power to convey meaning. Such relationships between language and culture raise a very interesting and old question: Do speakers of different languages see the world differently, just as people from different cultures might? We turn to this issue in the next section.

Figure 5.6   Making Use of a Summarizing Symbol. The Marine Corps War Memorial in Arlington, Virginia, pictured here is based on the famous photograph "Raising the Flag on Iwo Jima" by Joe Rosenthal. The image of Marines raising the flag has become a symbol of the American struggle for freedom.

THINKING CRITICALLY ABOUT LANGUAGE

How might paying attention to the metaphors and symbols we use in our daily language allow us to frame important issues in more or less appealing ways? An example from national public life is the use of the term "downsizing" rather than "firing" staff. Consider an undesirable change at your college or university and think of different ways the administration might have made the change seem more appealing by talking about it differently.

Figure 5.7   An Elaborating Symbol to Make Sense of Social Relations.   Dinka cattle have various kinds of markings and colors, and the Dinka use them to make sense of social differences in their community.

Do People Speaking Different Languages Experience Reality Differently?

Most Americans generally assume that the world is what it is, and our experience of it is shaped by whatever is actually happening around us. But as we saw in Chapter 2, our culture predisposes us to presume some features of the world, while other people's culture leads them to assume something different. For many decades anthropologists and linguists have been debating a similar point in relation to language: Does the language we speak shape the way that we perceive the physical world? According to the Sapir-Whorf hypothesis, which we examine next, it does.

The Sapir-Whorf Hypothesis

In the 1920s, the linguistic anthropologist Edward Sapir (1929) urged cultural anthropologists to pay close attention to language during field research. Recognizing that most non-European languages organized tense, number, adjectives, color terms, and vocabulary in different ways from English, French, or German, he argued that a language inclines its speakers to think about the world in certain ways because of its specific grammatical categories. We explore this hypothesis further in "Classic Contributions: Edward Sapir on How Language Shapes Culture." It is anthropology's first expression of **linguistic relativity**, which is the idea that people speaking different languages perceive or interpret the world differently because of differences in their languages.

- **Linguistic relativity.** The idea that people speaking different languages perceive or interpret the world differently because of differences in their languages.

Sapir's student Benjamin Lee Whorf (Carroll 1956) expanded on Sapir's work. Whorf had studied the language of the Hopi Indians and found that his knowledge of the grammars of European languages was little help in understanding Hopi grammar. He concluded that people who speak different languages actually do—are not just "inclined to," as his teacher Sapir would have said—perceive and experience the world differently. By the 1950s, linguistic anthropologists saw the ideas of Sapir and Whorf as related and began referring to them as the "Sapir-Whorf hypothesis." Let us illustrate the hypothesis with one of Whorf's best examples, the lack of tenses in Hopi.

Hopi Notions of Time

Whorf studied Hopi language and concluded that it lacked tenses like those we have in English. Hopi uses a distinction not expressed grammatically in European languages, which he called "assertion categories." These include (1) statements that report some fact (e.g., "he is running" or "he ran"); (2) declaration of an expectation, whether current or past (e.g., "he is going to eat" or "he was going to run away"); and (3) statements of some general truth (e.g., "rain comes from the clouds" or "he drinks only iced tea"). These three assertion categories do not overlap and are mutually exclusive. When translating these Hopi concepts into English, most people will use our tenses (past, present, and future), partly because we have to express tense in English to make a sentence, and partly because this is the only convenient way to express these different types of assertions in English.

Whorf argued that the structure of the Hopi language suggested different ideas to Hopi than their translations would to Englishspeakers. He also linked these grammatical categories to Hopi "preparing" activities that surrounded certain rituals and ceremonies, arguing that "[t]o the Hopi, for whom time is not a motion but a 'getting later' of everything that has ever been done, unvarying repetition is not wasted but

CLASSIC CONTRIBUTIONS

Edward Sapir on How Language Shapes Culture

THE LINGUISTIC ANTHROPOLOGIST Edward Sapir (1884–1939) was the only professionally trained linguist among the students of Franz Boas, a founder of American anthropology. Sapir believed that language "provided the ethnographer with a terminological key to native concepts, and it suggested to its speakers the configurations of readily expressible ideas" (Darnell and Irvine 1997). In this excerpt we see Sapir's strongest statement about how language shapes the cultural expectations of the individual speaker:

Edward Sapir.

It is an illusion to think that we can understand the significant outlines of a culture through sheer observation and without the guide of the linguistic symbolism which makes these outlines significant and intelligible to society. . . .

Language is a guide to "social reality." Though language is not ordinarily thought of as of essential interest to the students of social science, it powerfully conditions all our thinking about social problems and processes. Human beings do not live in the objective world alone, nor alone in the world of social activity as ordinarily understood, but are very much at the mercy of the particular language which has become the medium of expression for their society. It is quite an illusion to imagine that one adjusts to reality essentially without the use of language and that language is merely an incidental means of solving specific problems of communication or reflection. The fact of the matter is that the "real world" is to a large extent unconsciously built up on the language habits of the group. No two languages are ever sufficiently similar to be considered as representing the same social reality. The worlds in which different societies live are distinct worlds, not merely the same world with different labels attached. . . . We see and hear and otherwise experience very largely as we do because the language habits of our community predispose certain choices of interpretation. . . . From this standpoint we may think of language as the symbolic guide to culture. [Sapir 1929:209–210]

Questions for Reflection

1. Can you think of an example, either from your native language or another language you know, in which language predisposes you to think in certain ways?

2. How does thinking of language as a "symbolic guide to culture" impact how you think about culture?

accumulated" (Carroll 1956). Americans, in contrast, might see repetitive actions before a celebration as a sapping of effort or as inefficiency (Figure 5.8).

Several linguists have challenged his interpretation of Hopi grammar. Malotki (1983), for example, argues that Hopi does, in fact, have tenses that resemble English tenses. Malotki's claims have not gone unchallenged, but if true, such a finding would call Whorf's example into question, although not necessarily his theory of the relationship between language and culture. Moreover, in the time between Whorf's and

Figure 5.8   A Hopi Ceremony of Regeneration. Tendencies in language are reflected in and reinforced by social action, such as this ritual which emphasizes regeneration and the recycling nature of the world. Non-Hopi people are now prohibited from seeing most Hopi rituals and religious dances today; this historic image of one of these celebrations of renewal is from a century ago, when outsiders were permitted to see them.

Malotki's research, Hopi have become more knowledgeable and conversant in English, suggesting that if Hopi now has tenses, these may be evidence of language change since the 1930s.

Ethnoscience and Color Terms

In the 1960s anthropologists began to explore how different peoples classified the world around them, focusing on how people conceptually group species of plants and animals or other domains, such as planets or colors. The study of how people classify things in the world became known as **ethnoscience** (see also Chapter 15). These studies began with a very different set of assumptions about the relationship between language and culture from those accepted by Sapir and Whorf. These scholars assumed that the natural world was a given, and that all human beings perceived it in the same way. Differences in classification were simply different ways of mapping categories onto empirical reality.

For example, anthropologists Brent Berlin and Paul Kay (1969) analyzed the color terms of more than 100 languages and found that basic color terms are consistent across languages. For example, if a language has only two basic color terms, they are terms for dark (black) and light (white). But if a language has three terms, they were black, white, and red. The third term is never green, blue, purple, or orange. An example of a language with three basic color terms is Lamnso, spoken in the Central African country of Cameroon (see Figure 5.9). If a fourth color is present, then the terms are black, white, red, and blue/green. Some anthropologists suspect that these patterns are universal and may have to do with the way our optic nerve responds to light of different wavelengths (Figure 5.9).

This universal pattern does not disprove the Sapir-Whorf hypothesis or linguistic relativity more generally. But when informants with limited numbers of basic color terms were given paint chips displaying a wide range of colors, they could distinguish the different colors from other chips, but they classified them into groups that corresponded to their basic color categories. People speaking different languages did not

• **Ethnoscience.** The study of how people classify things in the world, usually by considering some range or set of meanings.

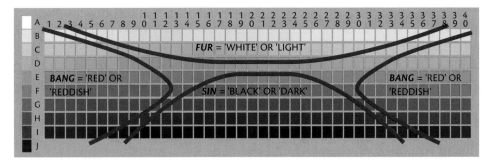

Figure 5.9 The Munsell Color Chart.   The Cameroon language of Lamnso has three basic color terms that center on the colors called *sin, fur,* and *bang,* which we would gloss as 'black' (or 'dark'), 'white' (or 'light'), and 'red' (or 'reddish'), respectively. But as we can see from the plot of these three color terms on a standard Munsell color chart, our American sense of black, white, and red is not at all typical of the range of colors included in each of these Lamnso terms.

appear to see colors any differently; they just classified them differently. For example, as Franz Boas discovered early in his career, Inuit would not make a distinction between blue and green as he and other Europeans did because they did not separate the colors into distinct categories. But the Sapir-Whorf hypothesis would not necessarily have predicted that people see color differently anyway.

Is the Sapir-Whorf Hypothesis Correct?

By the late 1960s ethnoscience had largely dismissed the Sapir-Whorf hypothesis as having no significance for understanding human cognition. The most powerful argument against the idea that our language shapes our thought is that we have no way of knowing for sure what cognitive processes are involved when we distinguish different sets of pronouns or have no English-style tenses. All we have is the language, which is where we started in the first place, plus the researcher's intuition (Pinker 1994).

Today most anthropologists accept what has come to be called the weak or non-deterministic version of the linguistic relativity argument, which suggests (much as Sapir wrote) that the language habits of a community lead people to think about the world in certain ways and not others. Such a reading of the Sapir-Whorf hypothesis supports the idea that some ways of thinking are guided and encouraged by the language we use while others are not.

There are implications here for language change. Over the long term such suggested ways of thinking would lead to a preference in each language for some kinds of linguistic change over others. If we take a rather static view of language, this issue might lead us to believe that languages are very stable, slow to change; and yet throughout this chapter we have suggested that language is dynamic. Let us now consider how language can constantly be changing, yet seem so stable.

THINKING CRITICALLY ABOUT LANGUAGE

How might the coarse slang used in daily conversations by college students be interpreted differently by parents or grandparents?

How Can Languages Be So Dynamic and Stable at the Same Time?

A striking paradox in linguistics is that, like culture, language constantly changes, yet most people experience their own language as stable and unchanging. We tend to notice the changes only when we hear other people in our communities using different words, pronunciations, or grammatical forms from our own. Usually national policies come into play to enforce or support the use and stabilization of certain linguistic forms over others, leading to language change within a strong framework of stability.

Linguistic Change, Stability, and National Policy

The increase of commerce, communication, and migration around the world over the past few centuries has produced new environments for language change. Colonial powers such as Great Britain, France, and Spain learned about new plants, peoples, and ways of living in their far-flung colonies. In the Americas, these powers also introduced slave labor from Africa, resulting in the blending of diverse African cultures, which were also blending with Native American cultures. These societies developed dynamic new languages, such as creole and pidgin languages, and implemented national language policies, in some cases to stabilize rapid linguistic change.

Creole and Pidgin Languages

In the Americas, local colonized societies developed hybrid languages that linguists call **creole languages,** languages of mixed origin that developed from a complex blending of two parent languages. A prominent example is the language commonly spoken in Haiti that combines several African languages with Spanish, Taíno (the language of Caribbean native peoples), English, and French.

In Asia and the Pacific, these hybrid forms have generally been called **pidgin languages**, which refers to a mixed language with a simplified grammar that people rarely use as a mother tongue (which is the case of Haitian creole) but to conduct business and trade. In the independent Melanesian countries of Vanuatu, the Solomon Islands, and Papua New Guinea, for example, local forms of Pidgin that combine various local languages and English have become national languages along with the colonial languages of English or French. In all three countries, ability to speak Pidgin has positive social status.

National Language Policies

Different countries have tried to control language change through the creation of national language policies. Short of making one particular regional dialect the national language, however, countries have found it nearly impossible to dictate what language or what form of the national language the public will speak. Three examples—taken from the Netherlands, France, and Quebec (Canada)—demonstrate different approaches to controlling processes of language change.

In the Netherlands during the twentieth century, Dutch linguists recognized that pronunciation and vocabulary had changed so much that spelling no longer reflected how people pronounced words. Dutch linguists recommended that spelling be changed to keep up with changing language use, and twice in the twentieth century the ruling monarchs, Queen Wilhelmina and Queen Juliana, issued royal decrees changing the official spelling of Dutch words to parallel actual use. The Dutch approach is quite tolerant of changing language.

- **Creole language.** A language of mixed origin that has developed from a complex blending of two parent languages that exists as a mother tongue for some part of the population.

- **Pidgin language.** A mixed language with a simplified grammar, typically borrowing its vocabulary from one language but its grammar from another.

In contrast, the French spent much of the twentieth century trying to preserve traditional French words that were being replaced by English loans, such as "le hamburger." The French parliament has passed several laws restricting English words from formal French documents, and prominent leaders have spoken out against the use of foreign words in proper French. But such laws have had little effect on the everyday speech of French people—especially the young, who readily borrow from English when discussing music, the arts, film, and anything trendy (Figure 5.10).

French Canadians in the province of Quebec have been considerably more successful in preserving Quebecois (the form of French spoken in Quebec) against the pressure of English-speaking Canadians, who have historically considered English to be the superior language. Although government officials throughout Canada must be bilingual in English and French, the province of Quebec conducts government business in French. To stem the tide of Anglicization (the creeping influence of English), the provincial parliament passed laws that require signs in public places to be in French. If English is also used, the English words cannot be longer than their French translations (Figure 5.11). In this case, language use coupled with nationalist control of the provincial parliament has encouraged the use of French throughout the population of Quebec.

Figure 5.10   Mock Language and Exoticization. The American firm that produces LeSportsac uses mock French words to exoticize its products.

Language Stability Parallels Cultural Stability

As the situations of language use in France and Quebec demonstrate, the potential loss of a native language can be a critical issue for a group of people. In such cases, people view the use of a particular language not just as a means of communication but as integral to their cultural identities and worldviews as well. As a result, the preservation of language and culture are often seen to go hand in hand.

The connection between cultural stability and the ongoing use of language is an especially critical one for many indigenous peoples around the world, who are striving to protect their languages and distinctive ways of life in face of rapid social change. In many cases, the cultural disruptions created by rapid social changes such as colonization and globalization have undermined the use of native languages. As a result, many indigenous groups around the world are facing what scholars call "language death," referring to the dying out of many minority languages. Some linguists argue that nearly half of the world's 5,000 or 6,000 languages are in jeopardy of dying out within a century (Hale 1992).

In many cases government actions have systematically set the stage for native language death by discouraging younger members of the community from using their indigenous language in favor of the national language. For example, in the United States the Bureau of Indian Affairs sent many American Indians to schools where until the 1970s they were prohibited from using their native languages and were taught that their languages were inferior and stupid. The effect has been that many Indians stopped using their native tongues and most indigenous North American languages are spoken by only small numbers of old people.

Many scholars believe that these dramatic losses will have considerable impact on the world's linguistic diversity, even as new languages are created all the time. And because of the close relationship between language and culture, the world's cultural diversity will suffer as well. As our discussion of the Sapir-Whorf hypothesis suggests, language is the primary medium through which people

Figure 5.11   Defending Quebecois from Anglicization. In Quebec, on many store signs English words must by law be smaller than French ones.

experience the richness of their culture, and loss of language suggests a genuine loss of a culture's fullness.

As we have seen in this section, issues of language stability and change are closely tied to questions of domination, control, and resistance, a theme we explore in more detail in our final section.

THINKING CRITICALLY ABOUT LANGUAGE

What is it about our language that makes it feel so personal and so much a part of us? How is it that our language actually changes so seamlessly as we hear and adopt new words and expressions?

How Does Language Relate to Social Power and Inequality?

Anthropological linguists established long ago that language use influences the cultural context and social relationships of its speakers. But in recent years, they have become especially attuned to issues of power and inequality in language use, specifically how language can become an instrument of control and domination. We explore these issues here by introducing the concept of language ideology.

Language Ideology

• **Language ideology.** Widespread assumptions that people make about the relative sophistication and status of particular dialects and languages.

The concept of **language ideology** refers to the ideologies people have about the superiority of one dialect or language and the inferiority of others. A language ideology links language use with identity, morality, and aesthetics. It shapes our image of who we are as individuals, as members of social groups, and as participants in social institutions (Woolard 1998). Like all ideologies, language ideologies are deeply felt beliefs that are considered truths. In turn, these truths are reflected in social relationships, as one group's unquestioned beliefs about the superiority of its language justifies the power of one group or class of people over others (Spitulnik 1998:154). In the accompanying "Thinking Like an Anthropologist," we explore how the use of mock Spanish by Anglo-Americans in the United States reflects and reinforces the impression of social inferiority of Latinos.

Gendered Language Styles

In our daily interactions, men and women often experience miscommunication as Josh and Linda did in the vignette at the beginning of this chapter. Typically, each speaker feels that she or he has expressed things correctly and that the other speaker is at fault. When a man feels that his way of speaking is better, and the woman's is wrong, a language ideology about gendered use of language has come into play.

Despite what your high school English teachers may have told you, there is no "proper" way to speak English or any other language. From the anthropological perspective of language ideology, there are only more and less privileged versions of language use. Language use either legitimates an individual or group as "normal," or even "upstanding," or defines that individual or group as socially inferior. Consider, for example, the findings of a classic study in sociolinguistics that explores how gendered expectations of how women speak English in our culture can reflect and reinforce the idea that women are inferior to men. In her research, Robin Lakoff described how "talking like a lady" involved the expectation that a woman's speech patterns should include such things as tag questions ("It's three o'clock, *isn't it?*"); intensifiers ("It's a *very* lovely hat!"); hedge ("I'm *pretty* sure"); or hesitation and the repetition of expressions, all of which can communicate uncertainty and were largely absent in expectations about men's speech (Lakoff 1975).

Lakoff argued that the social effects of speaking in this way can marginalize women's voices in contexts like a courtroom or a workplace, where speaking in a way that implies uncertainty—even if the speaker is not intentionally expressing uncertainty—can undermine a woman's testimony (as in a court of law) or trustworthiness (as in a workplace). Such situations, she suggested, are used to justify elevating men to positions of authority over women.

Lakoff recognized that some men may communicate in female-preferential ways, and not all women use the patterns just described, since language ideologies are not hard and fast for every speaker. Indeed, more recent research of e-mail communications between men and women (Thomson, Murachver, and Green 2001) suggests that men and women can be quite flexible in their use of gendered language styles, changing these depending on whom they are talking to. As a result, men may use female-preferential language when interacting with a woman, and vice versa, further suggesting that language ideologies do not always exercise total control over how people speak.

Language and Social Status

As we saw with gendered language, language ideologies are closely tied to the creation of social difference. They are also closely tied to the creation and maintenance of social status. Let us see how this works in a particular society by considering language and social status among the Javanese, for whom language use reflects and reinforces a highly stratified and unequal society.

The people of the Indonesian island of Java are among the most status conscious people on earth. In any social setting one person has a higher social position, while the other is lower. Politeness—and through it, social position—is expressed in Javanese in nearly every sentence. Nearly every word takes on a different form in each of three different registers (varieties or levels of speech used by people of a certain social status or social class): *Ngoko* (informal speech), *Madya* (intermediary register), and *Karya* (polite speech). Throughout Java, every sentence marks the speaker's social status in relation to his or her listener, both by choice of vocabulary and by the pronoun used to refer to the listener. Most verbs and many nouns have at least three different forms representing the lower, intermediate, and polite registers. Younger people use the more polite words with their elders, and peasants or other low-status people use the more polite forms to nobles. But elders and nobles usually respond with informal word forms. In Java, the vocabulary used in any conversation differs for speaker and hearer.

Thinking Like an Anthropologist

Exploring Relationships of Power and Status in Local American Dialects

ANTHROPOLOGISTS BEGIN THEIR research by asking questions. In this box, we want you to learn how to ask questions as an anthropological researcher. Part 1 describes a situation and follows up with questions we would ask. Part 2 asks you to do the same thing with a different situation.

PART 1: MOCK SPANISH IN THE AMERICAN SOUTHWEST

Anthropological linguist Jane Hill (1993, 1998), who lives and teaches in Arizona, noticed that white Anglo residents of southwestern states, who were monolingual speakers of English, incorporated a large number of Spanish words and phrases in their everyday speech. Hill notes that these borrowings are not just random uses of Spanish or Spanish-like words in English, but they are often used in jokes or in contexts intended to be humorous. Usually such utterances are grammatically incorrect both in English and in Spanish. Nor would these sentences be acceptable in Spanglish, dialects that employ elements of both Spanish and English. Hill describes these utterances as "Mock Spanish."

Speakers and hearers can only get jokes in Mock Spanish if they already assume that Mexicans or Mexican Americans have traits that are viewed as negative in mainstream Anglo culture. Although Hill found that working-class whites used and understood some Mock Spanish jokes, she feels that the most productive use of Mock Spanish was found among middle- and upper-income, college-educated whites. The domain of Mock Spanish is instead found in the university

seminar, in the board room, or the country club party. For Hill, Mock Spanish serves as a covert form of racism in which the jokes or utterances implicitly disparage Latinos, simultaneously identifying the speaker and hearers as members of different social classes. To many listeners these jokes may not seem overtly racist, and in any event, they can be dismissed as merely evidence that the speaker had lived around Spanish-speaking people, or that it was just a joke.

Examples of Mock Spanish include such phrases as "no problemo," "cojones" used as a euphemism for the vulgar English "balls," the use of "mucho" to mean "much," "numero uno" and its Mock Spanish variants like "numero ten-o," as well as more seeming benign words "amigo," and "Comprende?" Hill suggests that it is the seemingly innocuous nature of these Mock Spanish forms that creates a powerful racist distinction between the superior Anglo-speaker and the inferior Mexican American.

What questions does this raise for anthropological researchers?

1. How does language use serve to create or at least reinforce social distinctions?
2. What is it about Spanglish that makes its speakers seem neither mainstream American nor mainstream Mexican, Cuban, Salvadoran, and so on?
3. What is it about the use of Mock Spanish that allows white Anglos who are monolingual in English to feel superior to their Spanish-speaking neighbors?

Examples of Mock Spanish.   "Hasta la vista" is a common expression used in a mocking way (right). On the left is another type of Mock Spanish, in this case by Hispanicizing an English word (cheap) that doesn't exist in Spanish. In these examples Mock Spanish marks Hispanic Americans, their culture, and their language as inferior.

PART 2: LANGUAGE USE ON YOUR CAMPUS

On your campus, students and faculty most likely use colloquial forms of English, most likely words and phrases that you and your friends use that your parents and surrounding community members would likely not understand. What kinds of questions could you pose about how this colloquial dialect draws boundaries between different groups of people or enhances and builds on distinctions between social groups, social classes, ethnicities, and the like?

As the linguist Robbins Burling (1971) noted, poorer and low-status people may only know the lowest and crudest register of Javanese, while higher status people are conversant with a much wider range of registers. Using these registers, with their different choices of words, helps Javanese sort out a wide variety of social positions beneath theirs (see Table 5.2).

Note that Javanese registers differ from the distinctive vocabulary of occupational or youth dialects in the United States, which tend to be unfamiliar to speakers of mainstream English. In these American dialects, distinctive words indicate common membership in a group, occupation, or cultural movement. For example, in the hip-hop youth subculture, speakers use a shared vocabulary—words like "crib" (place of residence) and "fly" (cool)—to build solidarity within the group in opposition to mainstream American culture. By contrast, the Javanese words used by each speaker and hearer will be different and mark their relative social positions in society.

Language and the Legacy of Colonialism

In places like sub-Sarahan Africa, nineteenth-century European colonial powers introduced their own language as the official language, because they viewed indigenous languages as socially inferior to their European languages. When these countries acquired independence, many of these languages became one of several national languages. As a way of building a national identity, many newly independent nations have had to make decisions about which language or languages among its many vernaculars to select as its official language. In Zambia, for example, which gained independence from Great Britain in 1964, the government recognized seven of the most important of its seventy-three local languages, plus English, as national languages, since nearly everyone in Zambia knows one or another of these languages. In theory

TABLE 5.2	THE THREE BASIC REGISTERS OF JAVANESE THAT MARK SOCIAL STATUS						
	Are	you	going	to eat	rice	and	cassava	now?
3 (high)	menap	sampéjan	bade	neḍa	sekul	kalijan	kaspé	samenika
2 (middle)	napa	sampéjan	adjeng	neḍa	sekul	lan	kaspé	saniki
1 (low)	apa	Kowe	arep	mangan	sega	lan	kaspé	saiki

All three registers are Javanese, but the vocabulary changes depending on a person's social class. Elites use the highest register with higher ranking people. They use the second register with one another, and the lowest register with servants. Servants use the highest register with high-status people but the lowest register within their families. The point is that the vocabulary and pronunciation mark one's social status with respect to the person he or she is speaking to. Unlike English, there is no neutral register; a speaker must mark social position.
Source: Burling (1970:82–87).

Doing Fieldwork

Untangling Language Ideologies in Contemporary Egypt

IN RECENT YEARS the Middle East has taken on an important role in American business and diplomacy, but few American businessmen or diplomats have a firm grasp of Arabic, the most important language in this region. Each of the dozen or so Arab countries has its own vernacular, or locally distinct, form of Arabic that is the mother tongue of its citizens. These forms of Arabic vary widely from Morocco to the Persian Gulf, and most people from other Arab countries have difficulty understanding the vernaculars of other Arab countries.

Each of these Arab states has chosen Classical Arabic—the language of the Quran—as its official language. Most Arabs feel that Classical Arabic is more sophisticated and appropriate for official business than any of the local versions of Arabic. But nobody has spoken Classical Arabic as his or her mother tongue for a thousand years. What people learn to speak from childhood is a vernacular Arabic.

For the anthropologist concerned with language ideologies, this situation raises questions about how language use is linked to political power in a region that is so important in international affairs and the world's economy. To address some of these concerns and to offer policymakers and others insight into the relationship between language and patterns of dominance and politics in Arab countries, linguistic anthropologist Niloofar Haeri (1997, 2003) has studied the use of language in Cairo, Egypt, the largest and most cosmopolitan Arab city. During nineteen months of fieldwork she interviewed dozens of native speakers from a diverse set of social classes. These informants ranged from those with no schooling to physicians, diplomats, professionals, and bureaucrats.

She found that nearly all the educated Cairo elite had studied at private schools where the medium of instruction was a foreign language such as English, French, or Italian. Nearly all of these people had studied Classical Arabic only a few hours a week, and nearly all felt they had very weak skills in the official language. Most had good command of colloquial Egyptian Arabic, which gave them credibility in the national arena. But nearly all of these professionals had succeeded because of their command of a foreign language, which has much higher caché than the vernacular.

Haeri observed a very different pattern among the middle class, who took midlevel jobs as clerks and secretaries in government or business. These middle-class people had good command over Classical Arabic, which they had studied in national schools. Unlike the elites, the middle class used Classical Arabic as their road to success in work; often it was their ability to write the official language that landed them their jobs. Ironically, Haeri found that nearly all of the high-ranking bureaucrats and professionals succeeded because they relied heavily on their secretaries and aides for drafting any formal written documents, which were necessarily written in Classical Arabic.

Thus, contrary to the pattern in Europe and America, where command of the official language helps elites remain elite, in Egypt it is command of a foreign language that serves this role. One implication of Haeri's research is that if one wishes to succeed in an Arab country, knowledge of Classical Arabic may not be sufficient. In such cases, however, familiarity with the county's vernacular form of Arabic may be helpful, since this is the language of the financial and political elite.

Questions for Reflection

1. Why would Classical Arabic, a language nobody speaks, seem a better choice as an official language than one of the vernacular forms of Arabic?

2. What significance should we give to the fact that all Arab countries have chosen Classical Arabic as their official language? How does this choice of a common official language help create or reinforce a pan-Arab identity?

3. Why do Egyptian elites not bother to learn Classical Arabic? What does this say about the relative importance of the official language in Egypt as compared with other languages?

🌱 **Secretaries Working in an Office in Cairo.**

each is equal to the others, but in practice they are not, as listening to Zambian radio broadcasts reveals (Spitulnik 1998).

Although all eight Zambian languages were given airtime, English dominated the airwaves, both in the number of hours per week and in having a more sophisticated and cosmopolitan content. Certain of the more widely spoken indigenous local languages also got more airtime than minority languages. Over the past decades, broadcasters have presented to their ethnically diverse listening public what they feel are appropriate topics in each of the different languages, such as themes related to subsistence farming for certain language groups considered less sophisticated, and themes related to business and politics for others deemed linguistically superior. These broadcasting decisions have shaped how the public evaluates each indigenous language, presenting some as more sophisticated than others, but all as less sophisticated than English. In this case, broadcasts not only become models of language hierarchy in Zambia but also reinforce these views of different languages and the ethnicities associated with them.

The broader point about language ideologies that comes across in each of our examples is that language can be used to exclude or marginalize some people in workplaces and social programs. In "Doing Fieldwork: Untangling Language Ideologies in Contemporary Egypt," we consider the practical implications for anthropologists concerned about the implications this situation has for democracy and social justice.

THINKING CRITICALLY ABOUT LANGUAGE

Students often feel they will never be able to participate in the professional lives of their advisors because their advisors and other professors seem to speak a language that many students do not understand. Of course, they are speaking English, but they use many complex words that few students know. How does language in this situation become a tool of control and power over students?

Conclusion

The capacity for language is one of the central features that distinguishes humans from other animals. Whatever the particular language being spoken, human languages are universally structured and rule bound, as descriptive linguistics demonstrates, and they change in fairly uniform ways, as historical linguistics tells us. But to end there—with the idea that language is something that all humans have access to and use in the same ways—misses the crucial fact that sociocultural context and norms shape language use and that the use of language has important impacts on everyday social relationships. To separate language from culture leads to an impoverished understanding of *both* language and culture.

This point, of course, is one that Sapir and Whorf made many decades ago when they advanced the idea that particular languages guide ways of thinking and acting. We can see a more updated illustration of the relationship between culture and language—and perhaps a more recognizable one to all of us—in the vignette that opens this chapter, in the different ways that Josh and Linda communicate with each other. Their particular miscommunication is not the result of a universal human situation in which women and men cannot understand each other, but the product of a particular culture that expects girls and women to speak in some ways, and boys and men in others. On its own, this insight is interesting and reveals something about how our culture socializes us to communicate in certain ways.

But we should not forget the social consequences of language use, especially when certain ways of talking and expression imply the correctness or superiority of one group, gender, or social class, and the incorrectness or inferiority of another. The broader point here is that language has great power to shape not just our meanings and comprehension of the world but our experiences as social beings as well.

KEY TERMS

Call systems   p. 117

Cognate words   p. 118

Creole language   p. 130

Descriptive linguistics
     p. 121

Ethnoscience   p. 128

Language   p. 116

Language ideology   p. 132

Linguistic relativity   p. 126

Morphology   p. 121

Philology   p. 118

Phonology   p. 121

Pidgin language   p. 130

Proto-language   p. 118

Sociolinguistics   p. 123

Stops   p. 121

Syntax   p. 121

Reviewing the Chapter

Chapter Section	What We Know	To Be Resolved
Where does language come from?	Animals do not have language, but some primates have a rudimentary ability to use signs, which is a necessary but not sufficient condition for language to develop.	Although most linguistic anthropologists accept both genetic and non-genetic models, the relative importance of these models remains unclear, and we currently have no unified models that draw on both.
How does language actually work?	Language is systematic, but most descriptive linguistic models are static and do not express the dynamic nature of language.	By and large, linguistic anthropologists have not found that historical models of language change fully explain why particular sound systems or grammatical patterns have taken the forms they do.
Do people speaking different languages experience reality differently?	Meaning is conveyed through symbols, but particular meanings have their roots in the social processes of daily life.	Although the structures of language vary widely in different languages, anthropologists and linguists have never reached a consensus about whether the structure of language actually shapes the ways we perceive the world.
How can languages be so dynamic and stable at the same time?	Languages are always changing in small ways as sound systems gradually change and as new words are borrowed from other languages or created anew.	Although anthropologists recognize that languages change as cultures change, there is no current consensus about how these changes emerge.
How does language relate to social power and inequality?	A language ideology links language use with identity, morality, and aesthetics. It helps us imagine the very notion of who we are as individuals, as members of social groups and categories, and as participants in social institutions.	Despite efforts of governments to control their populations by shaping language policies, creole and pidgin forms of languages are far more important than was thought to be the case half a century ago. Yet anthropologists do not have a full understanding of the precise conditions under which a creole or pidgin language can assert its own importance.

Readings

William A. Foley's book *Anthropological Linguistics: An Introduction* (Malden, MA: Blackwell, 1997) provides a general introduction to linguistic anthropology. A more classical approach to the basics of language and its relation to culture was published by Edward Sapir in his 1921 book, *Language: An Introduction to the Study of Speech* (New York: Dover, 2004). Unlike most linguistics texts, because Sapir was an anthropologist as well as a talented linguist, this early work is much more sensitive to cultural factors than the books written by most linguists.

• • • • • • • • • • • • • • • • • • •

Linguistic anthropologist George Lakoff has published a number of books dealing with the symbols and metaphors that provide meaning in the words and phrases we hear. One of his classic studies is *Metaphors We Live By* (Chicago: University of Chicago Press, 1980). Several of his more recent publications pursue these ideas more fully.

• • • • • • • • • • • • • • • • • • •

A key survey of how governments create and promote nationalism through language policy can be found in Bambi B. Shieffelin, Katharyn A. Woolard, and Paul V. Kroskrity's book *Language Ideologies: Practice and Theory* (New York: Oxford University Press, 1998).

• • • • • • • • • • • • • • • • • • •

One of the best introductions to gendered speech can be found in Deborah Tannen's *Talking from 9 to 5: How Women's and Men's Conversational Styles Affect Who Gets Hired, Who Gets Credit, and What Gets Done at Work* (New York: W. Morrow, 1994).

• • • • • • • • • • • • • • • • • • •

Globalization and Culture

Understanding Global

Interconnections

In the early 1980s, Walpiri [Wal-*peer*-ee] Aborigines living as hunter-gatherers in the remote Central Desert of Australia began watching movies and television in their temporary camps near cattle stations. By 1985, one observer wrote, "the glow of the cathode ray tube had replaced the glow of the campfire in many remote Aboriginal settlements . . . Of all the introduced Western technologies, only rifles and four-wheel-drive Toyotas had achieved such acceptance" (Michaels 1994:91). During the past century of contact with Europeans, the Walpiri had maintained their distinctive culture and language. Many observers began to worry, however, that the introduction of mass media would finally destroy their traditions.

But that was not what happened. The Walpiri turned this alien technology toward more familiar ends, by incorporating the genre of film and filmmaking into their own traditions of storytelling and by imposing their own meanings on the videos they watch. In Walpiri settlements, viewing a video is a social event where people participate and collaborate in ways that are similar to how they view their traditional sand paintings or tell stories. If a movie—like *Rambo*, a DVD

 Representing the Walpiri Landscape   Walpiri people of northern Australia have taken to watching—and producing—their own television programs. Their cinematic productions reflect particular social dynamics and cultural perspectives. (Image courtesy of PAW Media/Warlpiri Media Association.)

141

that continues to circulate in rural Australia, fails to say who the main character's grandmother is, or who is taking care of his sister-in-law—meaningful kinship information for this hunting-gathering people—they debate the matter and fill in the missing content (Michaels 1994:92). Walpiri people view films in socially appropriate kin groups, on video players that are collectively owned and shared according to traditional patterns. These practices help reinforce rather than diminish their culture.

Walpiri people of northern Australia have taken to watching—and producing—their own television programs. Their cinematic productions reflect particular social dynamics and cultural perspectives.

Walpiri also began making films to tell their traditional stories. Their films are disappointing to or misunderstood by Western audiences because of the slow and subtle way they unfold, taking their meaning from the Walpiris' own cultural style and aesthetic criteria. The camera pans slowly across a landscape, and the long, still shots seem empty of meaning to Westerners. But Walpiri examine these films closely for the important stories they are supposed to reveal, with the camera tracking locations where ancestors, spirits, or historical characters are believed to have traveled (Michaels 1994:93). Walpiri also pay close attention to what happens behind the scenes, because to them the authenticity of a film depends on whether the family that "owns" the story gave its permission to retell it and supervised its production. In short, the Walpiri use this global technology to express their own local traditions and worldviews, borrowing from the outside world what they want to maintain or even revitalize on their own.

The Walpiri fascination with television and film is not unique. Around the world, people living in even the most remote places now have television sets connected to video players or satellite dishes, wear Western clothing, or migrate to and from distant lands. These international borrowings are happening everywhere, but does this mean that the world is losing its rich cultural diversity? Examples such as the Walpiri lead us to the question at the core of anthropologists' interest in globalization: *Are all the world's different cultures becoming the same because of globalization?* Embedded in this larger question are a number of problems, around which this chapter is organized:

Is the world really getting smaller?

Are there winners and losers in globalization?

Doesn't everyone want to be developed?

If the world is not becoming homogenized, what is it becoming?

What strategies can anthropologists use to study global interconnections?

We aim to deepen your understanding of culture as a dynamic process by showing its importance for understanding contemporary global processes. For anthropologists, the cross-border connections we refer to as globalization are not simply a matter of cultural homogenization. It is a process that illustrates how people create and change their cultures because of their connections with others. Not everybody participates equally in these diverse kinds of global connections, which means we also have to consider power relationships and social inequality.

Is the World Really Getting Smaller?

Asian hip-hop in London. American retirement fund investments in a South Korean steel conglomerate. Indian "Bollywood" movies in Nigeria. Mexican migrants cooking Thai food in a North Carolina restaurant. Each of these situations confirms our sense that the world is getting smaller and cultural mixing is on the rise. This sense extends to anthropologists, who recognize that the people whose lives we study are often profoundly affected by global interconnections, migratory flows, and cultural mixing. During the past several decades, understanding how those processes of global interconnection affect culture has become an important issue for all anthropologists. For a discipline that has long tried to understand the differences and similarities between human groups and cultures, the idea that the world is getting smaller might suggest that the differences, in particular, are melting away. But is the world really getting smaller? To answer this question, we first need to understand what globalization is. Unfortunately, defining globalization is, as one scholar has observed, like eating soup with a fork (Nederveen Pieterse 2004). Why?

Defining Globalization

Defining globalization is a challenge for two reasons. First, different academic disciplines define globalization differently because they study different things. Economists focus on investment and the activity of markets, political scientists on international policies and interactions of nation-states, and sociologists on non-governmental organizations (NGOs) and other international social institutions. But there is a second problem. Is globalization a general *process* or a trend of growing worldwide interconnectedness? Is it a *system* of investment and trade? Or is it the *explicit goal* of particular governments or international trade bodies that promote free trade? Or is it, as some say, "globaloney," something that does not actually exist at all (Veseth 2005)?

Anthropologists define **globalization** as the contemporary widening scale of cross-cultural interactions owing to the rapid movement of money, people, goods, images, and ideas within nations and across national boundaries (Kearney 1995; Inda and Rosaldo 2002). But we also recognize that social, economic, and political interconnection and mixing are nothing new for humanity. Archaeological and historic records show that humans have always moved around, establishing contacts with members of other groups, and that sharing or exchanging things, individuals, and ideas is deeply rooted in human evolutionary history.

Early American anthropologists also recognized these facts. Franz Boas and his students Alfred Kroeber and Ralph Linton developed a theory of culture that emphasized the interconnectedness of societies. The Boasians thought of themselves as **diffusionists**, emphasizing that cultural characteristics result from either internal historical dynamism

- **Globalization.** The widening scale of cross-cultural interactions caused by the rapid movement of money, people, goods, images, and ideas within nations and across national boundaries.

- **Diffusionists.** Early twentieth-century Boasian anthropologists who held that cultural characteristics result from either internal historical dynamism or a spread (diffusion) of cultural attributes from other societies.

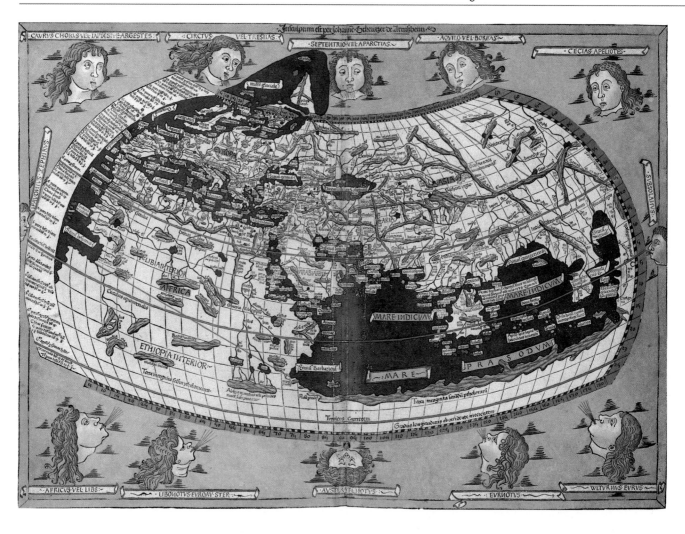

Figure 6.1   A Global Ecumene. The Greeks referred to an ecumene as the inhabited earth, as this map shows. Much later, anthropologist Alfred Kroeber (1876–1960) used the term to describe a region of persistent cultural interaction. The term became current again in the 1980s and 1990s as anthropologists adopted it to describe interactions across the whole globe.

or a spread (diffusion) of cultural attributes from one society to another (Figure 6.1). Later, beginning in the 1950s, Marxist anthropologists like Eric Wolf argued against the isolation of societies, suggesting that non-Western societies could not be understood without reference to their place within a global capitalist system, which reaches across international boundaries with abandon. And yet, until the 1980s, such themes of interconnectedness rarely interested most cultural anthropologists.

Mainstream anthropology was locally focused, based on research in face-to-face village settings. But as encounters among societies have seemed to increase, anthropologists have realized that paying attention only to local settings gives an incomplete understanding of people's lives. It also gives an incomplete understanding of the causes of cultural differences. As we will see, differences often emerge not in spite of, but *because of,* interconnections.

The World We Live In

How do anthropologists characterize the world in which we live today? Several factors stand out, including the scale of human interconnections and a growing awareness of these interconnections (Nederveen Pieterse 2004). But even if we acknowledge the intense interconnections, anthropologists know that these changes hardly mean that everybody is participating equally in the same globalizing processes. Further, the word "globalization," unfortunately, tends to make us think of the entire globe, exaggerating the scale and expanse of financial and social interconnections, which, while

Figure 6.2   Bollywood in Africa. "Bollywood" movies—musicals produced in India, which has the largest film industry in the world—have become popular in countries like South Africa (pictured here) and Nigeria because of recent increases in the global distribution of media.

great, are typically more limited and often more subtle than the word implies. Indeed, some anthropologists prefer the term **transnational** to describe the circulation of goods and people instead of the word "global" because *transnational* imagines relationships that extend beyond nations without assuming they cover the whole world (Basch, Schiller, and Blanc 1993). Nevertheless, it is useful to think of globalization as indicating persistent interactions across widening scales of social activity in areas such as communication, migration, and finances.

- **Transnational.** Relationships that extend beyond nation-state boundaries without assuming they cover the whole world.

Communication

At the heart of globalization are rapid increases in the scale and amount of communication. With cell phones, the Internet, and e-mail possible in most parts of the world, it is clear that the scale of contact has made a quantum leap forward over the past generation. Such rapid and much more frequent communication means that people in very remote places can be in contact with people almost anywhere on the globe (Figure 6.2). Never before has this capability been possible.

But access to these innovations is extremely limited for some, while readily accessible for the wealthier and better educated. In sub-Saharan Africa (excluding South Africa), for example, only one in 5,000 people has computer access. As a result, some observers—to highlight real inequalities of access—prefer to talk about the globalization of communication in terms of wealth and poverty.

Migration

Another key feature of the changing scale of globalization is the mobility of people. Whether **migrants** (who leave their homes to work for a time in other regions or countries), **immigrants** (who leave their countries with no expectation of ever returning), **refugees** (who migrate because of political oppression or war, usually with legal permission to stay), or **exiles** (who are expelled by the authorities of their home countries) (Shorris 1992), people are on the move. These movements of people bring larger numbers of people in contact with one another, offering many possibilities for intercultural contact (Figure 6.3).

- **Migrants.** People who leave their homes to work for a time in other regions or countries.

- **Immigrants.** People who enter a foreign country with no expectation of ever returning to their home country.

- **Refugees.** People who migrate because of political oppression or war, usually with legal permission to stay in a different country.

- **Exiles.** People who are expelled by the authorities of their home countries.

Finance

In the modern era, financial globalization involving the reduction or elimination of tariffs to promote trade across borders began in the 1870s. Although the two world wars disrupted those processes, the past sixty years have seen their reemergence. In

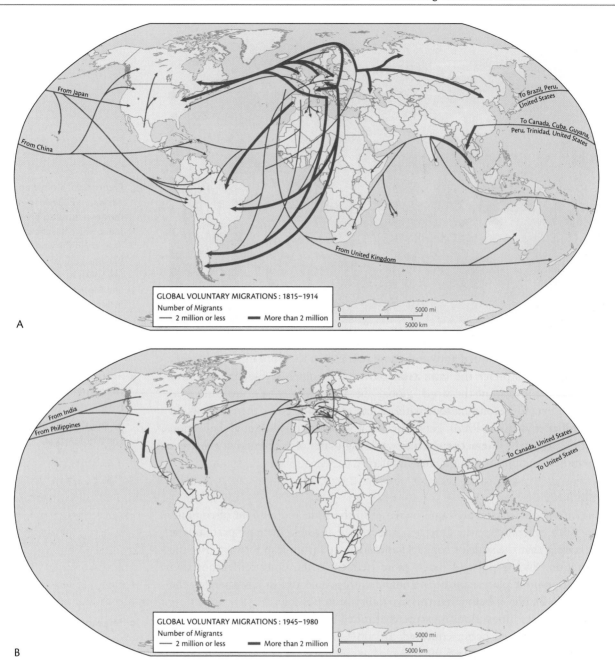

Figure 6.3   Global Voluntary Migrations. These two maps show dramatic differences in the directions of migratory flows. In Map A, during the European colonial era, Europeans were motivated to migrate out of Europe because of opportunities in the colonies. In Map B, after the Second World War, decolonization saw a reversal in the flow, as non-Europeans and non-U.S. Americans began moving into Europe and the United States in search of new opportunities for themselves.

recent decades, finance and the rapid movement of money across national boundaries have allowed corporations to move factories from one country to another. A generation ago, U.S. factories moved their operations to Mexico and China, but now many of these same factories have been shuttered and relocated to Honduras or Vietnam because of rising hourly labor costs in Mexico and China.

Under these conditions of globalized capital, many transnational corporations have accumulated vast amounts of capital assets. A number of these corporations now exceed entire governments in terms of their economic size and power. For example, if WalMart, the world's largest retailer, were its own economy, it would rank 24th in the world, just ahead of Norway (D. S. White 2010). Because powerful corporate interests often influence the policies of governments, some see in this situation a movement of power away from nation-states (Korten 1995). But this economic growth and trade are also highly uneven. "Thinking Like an Anthropologist: Understanding Global Integration Through Commodities" explores the complexities of contemporary economic globalization.

Thinking Like an Anthropologist

Understanding Global Integration Through Commodities

ANTHROPOLOGISTS BEGIN THEIR research by asking questions. In this box, we want you to learn how to ask questions as an anthropological researcher. Part 1 describes a situation and follows up with questions we would ask. Part 2 asks you to do the same thing with a different situation.

PART 1: THE T-SHIRT ON YOUR BACK

Concepts like the "global economy," "economic integration," even "globalization" are pretty abstract. Here, by considering the common T-shirt as a concrete example of economic globalization, we can show how your life is touched by seemingly remote and abstract economic, social, and political forces.

The things people want and need depend increasingly on the interactions of numerous institutions, individuals, states, and corporations, many of which are anonymous to consumers. To understand these diffuse interconnections, it is helpful to start with some concrete object that circulates through and between these actors. All objects, such as the humble T-shirt, have biographies, that is, particular life stories and trajectories. You can learn a lot about a social system—especially global integration—by following the trajectory of an object such as a T-shirt: who produced it, how it has changed hands, who has used it, and the uses to which it has been put (Kopytoff 1986).

Let us begin in the most obvious place, the tag on your shirt. Chances are pretty good it says "Made in . . ." followed by an exotic port of call: Bangladesh, Malawi, Malaysia, the Philippines, Mexico, or maybe China, which since 1993, has been the world's largest producer and exporter of clothing, about 30% of the world's share. Each year, Americans buy about one billion garments from China, four for every U.S. citizen (Rivoli 2005:70).

To tell the full story of your T-shirt, though, we have to get the whole picture, which includes understanding the commodity chain, or the linked elements—labor, capital, raw materials, and so forth—that contribute to the manufacture of a commodity. Quite likely, your T-shirt originated in a cotton field around Lubbock, Texas. The United States has dominated cotton production markets for 200 years, thanks largely to our ability to be highly productive while controlling labor costs. Before the Civil War, slavery kept these

Chinese Garment Factory. T-shirts are made in this garment factory.

costs down; now tractors and government subsidies do. Raw cotton is then shipped off, quite likely to China, to be made into thread and cloth, and then, if it does not stay in China to be manufactured into a T-shirt, off to somewhere else to be cut and sewn. The manufacturer then sells the T-shirts to a distributor, probably a U.S.-based business, and maybe after changing hands once again for silk-screening, it goes to the retailer, who sells it to you.

But let's keep going. After you wear it for a while, you might toss it in the trash, where it finds its way into a landfill. Or you might donate it to a used clothing charity bin like those in the parking lots of grocery stores. The charities themselves rarely handle your clothing, but in turn sell it to companies like Ragtex or the Savers Company that sort, bundle, and ship used clothing in 1,000-pound bales to sub-Saharan Africa (the largest market for used U.S. clothing), Eastern Europe, East Asia, or Latin America. A whole new series of wholesalers and small traders take over from there (Veseth 2005).

In these markets, people rarely think of these clothes as cast-offs or rags, as we do. For example, in Zambia, in southern Africa, where anthropologist Karen Tranberg Hansen (2000) has researched the local trade in used clothing, people call this clothing *salaula*, which means opportunity, choice, and new chances. At the same time, the arrival of so many inexpensive T-shirts and other clothing to places like Zambia undermines the local clothing industry, which cannot compete with the low cost of these used items.

What questions does this situation raise for anthropological researchers?

1. Is the supply chain that created your T-shirt really "global"?
2. Why are T-shirt production facilities no longer in the United States, and why are these facilities in the places they are?
3. Who are the different actors who participate in the processes of manufacturing and using your T-shirt, both before and after you own it?
4. What are the consequences for local people of this global trade in t-shirts?

PART 2: CHILEAN TABLE GRAPES

In industrialized economies like the United States and Europe, food is also quite likely to come from faraway. This is especially true of fruits and vegetables, which can be harvested in the Southern Hemisphere during the North American winter when domestic fruits and vegetables are not available in the United States. Chile is a major exporter of fruits to the United States and Europe, because its summer harvests coincide with the winter off-season in the Northern Hemisphere. If you wanted to understand global economic integration through table grapes such as those produced in Chile, what questions would you ask as an anthropological researcher?

Such analyses raise a key question: Who benefits from and who pays the costs of global interconnections? We turn to this important question in the next section.

THINKING CRITICALLY ABOUT GLOBALIZATION

Beyond communications, migration, and finance, what are some other culturally significant forces that make the world feel smaller?

Are There Winners and Losers in Global Integration?

In public debates, the most common way of framing globalization is in terms of winners and losers. Globalization's promoters focus on winners, arguing that greater economic integration brings unprecedented prosperity to millions. They cite evidence that the more open a country is to foreign trade, the more rapidly its economy grows (Norberg 2006). Critics focus on losers, invoking images of sweatshops and poverty. They offer evidence that the gap between rich countries and poor countries has actually widened, and we are witness to a "globalization of poverty" (Chossudovsky 1997). In the face of such arguments, it is useful to remember that both sides are often discussing fairly narrow economic policy questions such as free trade, labor conditions, outsourcing of jobs, and so on. These are important issues, but they tend to ignore the cultural nuances of global interconnections, which include inequality, confrontation, domination, accommodation, and resistance.

World Systems Theory

For several decades, **world systems theory** has provided the social sciences with an important theoretical lens for understanding global inequality. Developed by economic historians André Gunder Frank and Immanuel Wallerstein, world systems theory rejects the idea that global interconnections are anything new, identifying the late fifteenth century as the beginning of a new capitalist world order that connected different parts of the world in new ways. During this historical period, according to world systems theory, European powers created a global capitalist market based on unequal exchange between a "core" (the home countries) and a "periphery" (the rest of the world). The core (the winners) develops its economy by exploiting the periphery (the losers), whose role is to provide labor and raw materials for the core's consumption. The result is the periphery's long-term poverty, underdevelopment, and dependency on the core. Anthropologists have made a particular contribution to world system studies by posing a question other social scientists had not: How has this world system affected the native peoples and cultural systems of the periphery?

In his influential book *Europe and the People Without History*, anthropologist Eric Wolf took on this question. Wolf argued that long-distance trade and cultural interaction were around long before the development of capitalism, but that the expansion of European colonialism and capitalism drew non-European people into a global market, in which, as producers of commodities, they were to serve the cause of capital accumulation as a subordinate working class (Wolf 1984:352–3). These processes disrupted, even destroyed, many societies (Bodley 1999).

But Wolf rejected the customary divisions we make between "West" and "non-West." He insisted that people in the periphery also have helped shape the world system because they have not responded passively to capitalist expansion. In fact, they have often resisted it. These are the common people usually ignored by the victorious elites when they wrote their histories. Wolf argued that we need to pay close attention to the peripheral people's active role in world history. As we explore in "Classic Contributions: Eric Wolf, Culture, and the World System," Wolf's argument not only challenged popular stereotypes of indigenous people as isolated and passive, but he also challenged anthropology's bias toward the local, that is, the traditional ethnographic focus on villages and other small groups.

Because world systems theory focused on the rise of capitalism as a global system, this perspective did not readily lend itself to ethnographic research of smaller communities and non-global economics. But the theory helped anthropologists better explain the historical emergence and contemporary persistence of uneven development patterns around the world and has been of critical interest to scholars of **postcolonialism**, the field that studies the cultural legacies of colonialism and imperialism. It has also helped anthropologists understand the linkages between local social relations (families, kin networks, communities) and other levels of political-economic activity, like the regional, national, and transnational.

Resistance at the Periphery

As Wolf observed, expansion of the capitalist world system did meet resistance from the peripheral peoples affected. Anthropologists have devoted considerable attention to this resistance, finding examples that range from open rebellion and mass mobilizations to more subtle forms of protest and opposition.

Many forms of resistance may not be obvious to us. For example, in one factory in Malaysia, spirit possession episodes have erupted, disrupting work and production

- **World systems theory.** The theory that capitalism has expanded on the basis of unequal exchange throughout the world, creating a global market and global division of labor, dividing the world between a dominant "core" and a dependent "periphery."

- **Postcolonialism.** The field that studies the cultural legacies of colonialism and imperialism.

CLASSIC CONTRIBUTIONS

Eric Wolf, Culture, and the World System

ERIC WOLF (1923–1999) studied issues of power, inequality, and politics in Latin America. He insisted that the discipline needed to discover history, "a history that could account for the ways in which the social system of the modern world came into being" (1984:ix). He was interested in the origins and workings of peasant and tribal societies, but always in relation to the powerful governmental and business interests that so often kept peasants poor. In this selection, Wolf presents why anthropologists should view most societies over the past 500 years as societies linked to other societies, often with tragic consequences for some of the people involved.

🌱 **Eric Wolf.**

While some anthropologists thus narrow their focus to the ever more intensive study of the single case, others hope to turn anthropology into a science by embarking on the statistical cross-cultural comparisons . . . drawn from large samples of ethnographically known cases. . . .

What, however, if we take cognizance of processes that transcend separable cases, moving through and beyond them and transforming them as they proceed? Such processes were, for example, the North American fur trade and the trade in native American and African slaves. What of the localized Algonkin-speaking patri-lineages, for example, which in the course of the fur trade moved into large nonkin villages and became known as the ethnographic Ojibwa? What of the Chipewayans, some of whose bands gave up hunting to become fur trappers, or "carriers," while others continued to hunt for game as "caribou eaters," with people continuously changing from caribou eating to carrying and back? . . . What moreover, of Africa, where the slave trade created an unlimited demand for slaves, and where quite unrelated populations met that demand by severing people from their kin groups through warfare, kidnapping, pawning, or judicial procedures, in order to have slaves to sell to the Europeans? In all such cases, to attempt to specify separate cultural wholes and distinct boundaries would create a false sample. These cases exemplify spatially and temporally shifting relationships, prompted in all instances by the effects of European expansion. If we consider, furthermore, that this expansion has for nearly 500 years affected case after case, then the search for a world sample of distinct cases is illusory. [Wolf 1984:17–18]

Questions for Reflection

1. What happened about 500 years ago that changed the relations between societies from what they had been?

2. Why does Wolf feel that most societies have been in touch with Europeans and others outside their society for the past 500 years?

3. How would you explain to your younger brother or sister why Wolf feels anthropologists should not view societies as bounded and unconnected to other societies?

goals (Ong 1988). According to the factory women of Malaysia, the facility violated two basic moral boundaries: close physical proximity of the sexes, and male managers' constant monitoring of female workers. Young female workers, who as Muslims are expected to be shy and deferential, believe these two factors force them to violate cultural taboos that define social and bodily boundaries between men and women. They also believe that the construction of modern factories displaces and angers local spirits, who then haunt the toilets. For the women, these three transgressions combine to provoke spirit possession, in which the women become violent and loud, disrupting work in the factory. Spirit possession episodes help the women regain a sense of control over both their bodies and social relations in the factory (Ong 1988:34). Such resistance interests anthropologists because it shows how people interpret and challenge global processes through local cultural idioms and beliefs.

Globalization *and* Localization

Perhaps greater global integration also creates opportunities for local cultures to express themselves more vividly. This is a phenomenon that some anthropologists call **localization**, and it's the flip side, or side effect, of globalization. Localization is the creation and assertion of highly particular, often place-based, identities and communities (Friedman 1994). This is evidenced by the recent rise of autonomy movements among Hawaiian separatists and the Zapatistas in Mexico, movements that seek self-determination; nationalist and ethnic movements like the Basques in Europe; and other movements engaged in reinforcing local control, such as community-supported agriculture and local currencies (Friedman 1994). Each of these movements seeks to recuperate and protect local identities and places in the face of greater economic and cultural integration within a nation or a transnational network.

Other evidence of localization lies in people's patterns of consumption, which is a common way people express their local identities and ways of being. In our own society, people choose certain clothing and shoe brands because they believe it says something about them as individuals: their social status, lifestyles, and outlook on the world, in particular. People in other countries do this too, but because of local culture and history, patterns of consumption can communicate very different things.

For example, among the Bakongo in the People's Republic of Congo, a former French colony in Central Africa, poor Bakongo youths in urban shanty towns of the capital city, Brazzaville, compete with each other to acquire famous French and Italian designer clothes (Figure 6.4). Calling themselves *sapeurs* (loosely translated as "dandies"), the most ambitious and resourceful go to Europe where they acquire fancy clothes by whatever means they can. By becoming hyper-consumers, *sapeurs* are not merely imitating prosperous Europeans. Europeans may believe that "clothes make the man," but Congolese believe that clothes reflect the degree of "life force" possessed by the wearer (Friedman 1994:106). The *sapeur*'s goal is not to live a European lifestyle; his goal is to accumulate prestige by linking himself to external forces of wealth, health, and political power. In highly ranked Congolese society, the poor Bakongo urbanite ranks lowest. By connecting to upscale European fashion trends, the *sapeur* represents an assault on the higher orders of Congolese society who normally dismiss him as a barbarian.

Whether they are Walpiri Aborigines watching videos, Malay factory women, or Congolese *sapeurs,* people continue to define their identities locally. What is different today from previous generations, perhaps, is that people increasingly express their local identities through their interaction with transnational processes, such as communications or consumerism, and with institutions, such as transnational businesses. In today's world, people participate in global processes *and* local communities

• **Localization.** The creation and assertion of highly particular, often place-based, identities and communities.

Figure 6.4   Bakongo *Sapeur*.
The *sapeur*'s engagement in both transnational fashion worlds and local processes of social stratification destabilizes any strong local-global dichotomy.

simultaneously. But they rarely participate in global processes on equal footing, because of their subordinate place in the world system or in their own countries. Nevertheless, many anthropologists feel that to identify them in stark terms as *either* winners *or* losers of global integration greatly simplifies the complexity of their simultaneous involvement in globalization and localization processes.

As these examples show, people can be accommodating to outside influences, even while maintaining culturally specific meanings and social relations, whether because of defiance or because they actively transform the alien into something more familiar (Piot 1999). In these circumstances, cultural differences exist not in spite of, but because of, interconnection. But it still seems difficult to deny that so many millions of people are striving to become developed and pursue lifestyles similar to middle-class Americans.

THINKING CRITICALLY ABOUT GLOBALIZATION

Who should define who is a winner or loser in the processes of global integration? What kinds of criteria (financial, social, political, etc.) do you think are most appropriate for defining such a thing?

Doesn't Everyone Want To Be Developed?

Long before the current globalization craze, discussions about global integration were often framed as the problem of bringing "civilization" (Western, that is) and later economic development to non-European societies. But the question we pose here—Doesn't everyone want to be developed?—has no easy answer. Ideas differ about what development is and how to achieve it, so first we must ask: What is development?

What Is Development?

In 1949, U.S. President Harry Truman gave his inaugural address in which he defined the role of the United States in the post–World War II world, when the West confronted the communist nations. He said, "We must embark on a new program for making the benefits of our scientific advances and industrial progress available for the improvement and growth of the underdeveloped areas" (Truman 1949). He defined two-thirds of the world as "underdeveloped" and one-third as "developed." Truman believed that if poor people around the world participated in the "American dream" of a middle-class lifestyle, they would not turn toward communism (Esteva 1992).

The Cold War is over, but development is still with us. It is a worldwide enterprise that was never solely American. Many European nations give aid to their former colonies. The stated goals of this aid range from expanding capitalist markets through trade and new construction to alleviating poverty, improving health, and conserving natural resources. Key actors include the United Nations, the government aid agencies of most industrialized countries, lending agencies like the World Bank, and non-governmental organizations (NGOs) like CARE International.

Contemporary international development still aims to bring people into the "modern" world and correct what it identifies as undesirable and undignified conditions like poverty and lack of modern conveniences. And, just as in the colonial era, "advanced" capitalist countries still provide the economic and social models for development.

But there is ambiguity in the concept of development. Is it a means to a particular end? Or is it the end itself? Who defines the shape and course of development? More important for our purposes, development has an ambiguous relationship with cultural diversity. Is its goal to foster the unfolding potential and purposeful improvement of people—from their own local cultural perspective? Or is it a program of forced change that is eliminating cultural diversity to create a world ordered on the universal principles of capitalist societies? Is it an effort to remake the world's diverse people to be just like us?

There are two distinct anthropological approaches to development: **development anthropology** and the **anthropology of development** (Gow 1993). While development anthropologists involve themselves in the theoretical and practical aspects of shaping and implementing development projects, anthropologists of development tend to study the cultural conditions for proper development or, alternatively, the negative impacts of development projects. Often the two overlap, but at times they are in direct conflict.

- **Development anthropology.** The application of anthropological knowledge and research methods to the practical aspects of shaping and implementing development projects.

- **Anthropology of development.** The field of study within anthropology concerned with understanding the cultural conditions for proper development, or, alternatively, the negative impacts of development projects.

Development Anthropology

Development anthropology is a branch of applied anthropology. It is a response to a simple fact: many development projects have failed because planners have not taken local culture into consideration. Planners often blame project failures on local peoples' supposed ignorance or stubbornness (Mamdani 1972). But it is often planners themselves who are ignorant of local issues or set in their ways. Projects are more likely to meet their goals when they are fine-tuned to local needs, capacities, perspectives, and interests.

A classic example recognized by many anthropologists is the work of Gerald Murray on deforestation in Haiti. In the 1970s and 1980s, the U.S. Agency for International Development (USAID) invested millions of dollars in Haitian reforestation projects that consistently failed (Murray 1987). Poor farmers resisted reforestation because it encroached on valuable croplands. Worse yet, aid money directed to farmers kept

Figure 6.5   Haitian Farmers Planting Saplings for Reforestation.

disappearing in the corrupt Haitian bureaucracy. Murray saw that planners misunderstood the attitudes and needs of local farmers, not to mention the most effective ways to get the resources to them. He suggested a different approach. Planners had conceived of this project as an environmental one. He convinced USAID instead to introduce it to farmers as planting a new cash crop and to avoid involving the Haitian bureaucracy. Farmers would plant trees along the borders of their lands, allowing crops to continue to grow (Figure 6.5). After several years, they could harvest mature trees to sell as lumber. It was a very successful project: within four years, 75,000 farmers had planted 20 million trees, and many discovered the additional benefits of having trees on their land.

Development anthropologists often think of themselves as advocates for the people living at the grassroots—the poor, small farmers, women, and other marginalized people—who could be most affected, negatively or positively, by development but who lack the political influence to design and implement projects (Chambers 1997). As a result of pressure from anthropologists and other social activists, governments and major development organizations like the World Bank began to commission social impact studies to understand the potential impacts of their projects and to try to alleviate the negative effects on local populations. Today, many anthropologists work in development agencies, both internationally (such as in USAID) and domestically (in community development organizations). One indication of how anthropologists' contributions to development have been successful is that the current director of the World Bank, Dr. Jim Yong Kim, is an anthropologist.

And yet there are limits to what anthropologists can do. Policymakers and development institutions may not pay attention to their advice. Or the anthropologist may not have enough time to fully study a situation before having to make recommendations (Gow 1993).

Anthropology of Development

A number of anthropologists have supported the work of development anthropology by analyzing the social conditions that might help projects succeed. Other anthropologists have examined the development enterprise itself and challenged its unpredictable and often harmful impacts on local cultures. These critics argue that no matter how well intentioned the developers, the outcome of most development projects is to give greater control over local people to outsiders or the worsening of existing inequalities as elites shape development projects to serve their own political and economic interests (Escobar 1995). They also charge that the notion of development itself is ethnocentric and paternalistic (Escobar 1991).

Anthropologist James Ferguson applied some of these perspectives in his study of the Thaba-Tseka Rural Development Project. This project was a World Bank and U.N. Food and Agriculture Organization (FAO) project that took place between 1975 and 1984 in the southern African country of Lesotho (J. Ferguson 1994). Its goal was to alleviate poverty and increase economic output in rural villages by building roads, providing fuel and construction materials, and improving water supply and sanitation. But the project failed to meet its goals.

Ferguson argued that plans like this one never turn out the way their planners expect because project planners begin with a distinctive way of reasoning and knowing that nearly always generates the same kinds of actions. In this particular case, the planners believed that Lesotho's problems fit a general model: its residents are poor because they are subsistence farmers living in remote and isolated mountains, but they could develop further if they had technical improvements, especially roads, water, and sanitation.

But, according to Ferguson, this perspective has little understanding of on-the-ground realities. He noted that people in rural Lesotho have been marketing crops and livestock since the 1840s, so they have already been involved in a modern capitalist economy for a long time. They are also not isolated, since they send many migrants to and from South Africa for wage labor. In fact, most of the income for rural families comes from family members who have migrated to South Africa.

Ferguson's point is that people in rural Lesotho are not poor because they live in a remote area and lack capitalism; they are poor because their labor is exploited in South Africa. By viewing poverty as a lack of technical improvements in the rural countryside, the project failed to address the socioeconomic inequalities and subordination that are the underlying causes of poverty in rural Lesotho. All of this misunderstanding led to one major unexpected consequence: the arrival of government development bureaucrats to put the development project's technologies in place undermined the power of traditional village chiefs. Ferguson concluded that development exists not to alleviate poverty, but to reinforce and expand bureaucratic state power at the expense of local communities.

Not all anthropologists, especially those working in development, are comfortable with such critiques. Some anthropologists counter that we cannot sit on development's sidelines; we have a moral obligation to apply our knowledge to protect the interests of the communities we study. Others insist that critics ignore the struggles within development institutions that indicate that there is not simply one discourse of development but a variety of perspectives among developers (Little and Painter 1995). Still others insist that development is less paternalistic and more accountable to local communities than it has ever been (Chambers 1997).

These debates remain unresolved, but now that we have some background, we can begin to answer the bigger question: Do people really want to be developed? The answer often depends on how much control over development processes people will have.

Change on Their Own Terms

In indigenous and poor communities around the world, it is not uncommon to hear variations on the following phrase, originally attributed to Lila Watson, an Australian Aboriginal woman: "If you have come here to help me, you are wasting your time. But if you have come here because your liberation is bound up with mine, then let us work together." According to this perspective, outside help is not automatically virtuous, and it can undermine self-determination. Some scholars view this basic desire—to negotiate change on one's own terms—as a fundamental challenge to development's real or perceived paternalism and negative effects on local culture (Rahnema and Bawtree 1997). As confirmation of that fact, they point to the explosion of grassroots social movements throughout the Third World that challenge capitalist development schemes and seek alternatives such as social justice and environmental sustainability (Escobar, Alvarez, and Dagnino 1998).

Understandably, in the face of forced change, people want to conserve the traditions and relationships that give their lives meaning. This point is one of the keys to understanding culture in the context of global change. Culture helps people make sense of and respond to constant changes in the world and is itself dynamic. But culture also has stable and conservative elements, and different societies have different levels of tolerance for change, both of which mean that cultural change is not a uniform process for every society. This situation of uneven change partly explains why we see the persistence of cultural diversity around the world in spite of predictions that it would disappear.

● ●

THINKING CRITICALLY ABOUT GLOBALIZATION

Are anthropologists ethically obligated to help communities develop if members of the community want it?

● ●

If the World Is Not Becoming Homogenized, What Is It Becoming?

Like the previous question about whether everyone wants development, this one has no simple answer. Anthropologists are divided on this question. The interaction of culture with political, economic, and social processes is complex, and in many ways the world's material culture and associated technologies are becoming homogeneous. Anthropologists who study these processes pursue one or another form of cultural convergence theory. Other anthropologists, however, see conflict and a clash of cultures. And still others see hunter-gatherers like the Walpiri using aspects of modern technology in their own ways and on their own terms. These scholars use an approach called hybridization theory. In this section we examine the strengths and relevance of each theory.

Cultural Convergence Theories

In the 1960s the famous media scholar Marshall McLuhan suggested that the world was becoming a "global village" in which cultural diversity was in decline. Many social scientists agree. The British philosopher and social anthropologist Ernest Gellner, for example, believed the spread of industrial society created a common worldwide culture, based on similar conditions of work within the same industry. Making T-shirts in a factory is going to be similar whether situated in Honduras, Tanzania, or Vietnam. Gellner wrote that "the same technology canalizes people into the same type of activity and the same kinds of hierarchy, and that the same kind of leisure styles were also engendered by existing techniques and by the needs of productive life" (1983:116–17). Gellner's view was that local distinctions and traditions will gradually fade as Western ideas replace those in non-Western communities.

Another version of convergence theory envisions a worldwide convergence of consumer preferences and corporate practices, invoking the image of "McDonaldization." Advocates of this version assert that the principles of the fast food restaurant—efficiency (quick service at a low cost), calculability (quantity over quality), predictability, tight control over production, and using technology over human labor—characterize American society and, increasingly, the rest of the world (Ritzer 1996).

Still another variation on this theme imagines "Coca-Colonization," alternatively called Westernization or Americanization (see Foster 2008). This model proposes that the powerful and culturally influential nations of the West (especially the United States) impose their products and beliefs on the less powerful nations of the world, creating what is known as **cultural imperialism**, or the promotion of one culture over others, through formal policy or less formal means, like the spread of technology and material culture.

The appeal of these theories is that they address the underlying causes of why the world feels smaller, as well as how rich societies systematically exploit poor societies by drawing them into a common political-economic system. They also appear to explain the appearance of a common **world culture**, based on norms and knowledge shared across national boundaries (Lechner and Boli 2005; Figure 6.6).

But many anthropologists disagree with the basic assumptions convergence theorists make about culture, and in fact most proponents of convergence are not anthropologists. As we discussed earlier in this chapter, the fact that people might consume the same goods, wear the same clothes, or eat the same foods does not necessarily mean that they begin to think and behave in the same ways. A major limitation of convergence theories is that they underestimate variability and plasticity as key features of human culture and evolutionary history (J. Nash 1981).

Figure 6.6   World Culture and the Olympic Games.   The Olympic Games is a quintessential global event. Currently 203 countries participate in the Olympic Games, even more than are members of the United Nations. Drawing on certain core values—competitiveness, internationalism, amateurism, and so on—they foster an awareness of living in a single world culture.

- **Cultural imperialism.** The promotion of one culture over others, through formal policy or less formal means, like the spread of technology and material culture.

- **World culture.** Norms and values that extend across national boundaries.

Clash of Civilizations

One alternative to convergence theories is the "clash of civilizations" theory. Advanced by political scientist Samuel Huntington, it offers a direct challenge to convergence theorists by explaining why cultural differences have not disappeared. It argues that consciousness of culture is becoming greater around the world and that states and people band together because of cultural similarities, not because of ideological similarities, as in the past (Huntington 1996). As a result, the world is divided into civilizations in perpetual cultural tension with each other. For example, Huntington pits Western civilization against Islamic and Confucian (Chinese) civilizations, arguing that their divergent values and worldviews generate geopolitical conflicts.

American neoconservatives used this theory during the early 2000s to justify the "war on terror" as a clash between what they saw as an enlightened and democratic West versus a closed and autocratic Islam. Although a handful of anthropologists accept Huntington's premises (Wax and Moos 2004), most have dismissed this theory and its mosaic vision of the world as crude, ethnocentric, and inaccurate. Not only does it assume that cultural difference automatically generates conflict—which is not supported by historical facts—but it also denies overwhelming evidence of cultural mixing and fluidity.

Hybridization

An alternative theory that many anthropologists prefer is **hybridization**, which refers to open-ended and ongoing cultural intermingling and fusion. The word is actually drawn from nineteenth-century racial thinking, which idealized "racial" purity and abhorred racial mixing as hybridism (Nederveen Pieterse 2004). The difference is that

- **Hybridization.** Persistent cultural mixing that has no predetermined direction or end-point.

Figure 6.7   Kabuki Meets Shakespeare.   As an illustration of hybridization, consider how in recent years a quintessential Japanese theater form, Kabuki, has been used to stage the plays of William Shakespeare, such as this performance of *Twelfth Night*.

anthropologists have reimagined the word so it is no longer perceived as a negative process but is descriptive of a key feature of human existence. While the convergence and clash of civilization theories imagine a world based on or moving toward cultural purities, hybridization emphasizes a world based on promiscuous mixing, border crossing, and persistent cultural diversity (García Canclini 1995; Piot 1999) (Figure 6.7).

Hybridization has several aliases, including syncretism and creolization. Anthropologists have usually applied the word *syncretism* to the fusion of religious systems; *creolization* is used to mean the intermingling of languages. Still another metaphor is the notion of "friction," which anthropologist Anna Tsing (2005) employs: just as rubbing two sticks together creates light and heat, the coming together of diverse and conflicting social interactions creates movement, action, and effects. Tsing's broader assertion is that globalizing processes produce important effects around the world but that these effects are rarely predictable given the particularities of how people situated in their local cultures relate to those effects. Debates continue over the relative usefulness of each of these terms. But anthropologists recognize that each revolves around a common theme: the synthesis of distinct elements to create new and unexpected possibilities.

Hybridization theory does have critics. Some argue that cultural mixing is merely a superficial phenomenon, the real underlying condition being convergence. Others charge that all the talk about boundary-crossing and mixture ignores the fact that boundaries—national, social, ethnic, and so on—have not disappeared (Friedman 1999). At the heart of this criticism is the charge that hybridization theory ignores real political and economic power and inequalities. Others assert that these three approaches do not have to be mutually exclusive, but that convergence is happening in some places, cultural conflict in others, and hybridization everywhere, all at the same time.

Although these debates can be contentious, for a discipline historically accustomed to studying culture from a local vantage point (the stereotype of the anthropologist in a village), there is widespread consensus that taking on big questions like these opens up exciting new possibilities for research.

THINKING CRITICALLY ABOUT GLOBALIZATION

Can you identify any practical difficulties or ethical dilemmas involved in multi-sited research that might be different from traditional ethnographic research in a single community setting?

What Strategies Can Anthropologists Use To Study Global Interconnections?

Today nearly every anthropologist accepts that it is impossible to make sense of local cultural realities without some understanding of the broader political, economic, and social conditions that also shape people's lives (Kearney 1995). The problem is that anthropologists have typically conducted their studies in a single field site (a village, community, tribe, or district), while the transnational or transregional connections may be very faraway. So how can anthropologists simultaneously study a local phenomenon in a community and the national or international factors and forces shaping that community?

Defining an Object of Study

Some anthropologists, such as Eric Wolf, have defined their object of study as the world system itself. They focus on the role of culture in that system. Others who take a global system more or less for granted have focused on specific components within that system, especially objects, money, and ideas that "flow" and "circulate" around it (Appadurai 1996), or the "cosmopolitan" people (journalists, city people, world travelers) who move within and through it (Hannerz 1992). Some go a step further, observing that in a transient world, the migrant offers the most productive object of study (Kearney 1995; García Canclini 1995).

But some reject the notion of a unified global system altogether and propose investigation of what Tsing (2000:348) describes as "interactions involving collaboration, misunderstanding, opposition, and dialogue" between transnational and local actors. A key component of this approach is learning how people find meaning in their places within broader political, economic, and cultural systems. For example, in September 2012, riots erupted throughout many Muslim countries after a crude video produced in the United States was posted on YouTube that portrayed the Muslim Prophet Muhammad in a highly negative light. These riots ended in many injuries and even deaths. While American officials scrambled to communicate their agreement that the video was reprehensible, such arguments had little effect on Muslim publics who invoked a longer history of frustration with what they perceive to be a pattern of Western disrespect of Islam throughout the twentieth century.

Each of these approaches raises questions about the adequacy of anthropology's most distinctive methodological tool, ethnographic research. Understood as intensive participation and observation in the everyday life of a single place over a long period of time, ethnographic research has yielded incredibly rich insights into how people live and make sense of their lives. Yet ethnographers also assume that to learn about a community one should stay in one place. But what if the community or the issues one wants to study extend beyond that place?

Multi-Sited Ethnography

One technique is to use **multi-sited ethnography**, which is a strategy of following connections, associations, and putative relationships from place to place (Marcus

- **Multi-sited ethnography.** An ethnographic research strategy of following connections, associations, and putative relationships from place to place.

Doing Fieldwork

Studying Chernobyl's Aftermath with Adriana Petryna

IN APRIL 1986, the worst nuclear disaster of the twentieth century occurred in the Soviet Union, when Unit Four of the Chernobyl nuclear reactor exploded. Its radioactive cloud spread over Belarus, Ukraine, Russia, and Western Europe, exposing millions of people to dangerous levels of radiation. Three years later the Soviet Union and its socialist economy collapsed, leaving the newly independent country of Ukraine, where the ruined reactor lies, to deal with the reactor's technical maintenance, extensive radioactive contamination, and a major health crisis. Some 3.5 million Ukrainians (one of every twenty people) are suffering from the effects of radiation poisoning.

University of Pennsylvania anthropologist Adriana Petryna was one of the first to examine the political, scientific, and social aftermath of the disaster systematically (Petryna 2002). She was particularly interested in how technical, scientific, and political actors understood and responded to the disaster as well as its impacts on the everyday lives of the people.

How did Petryna go about studying a topic as complex as the way science, politics, and people intersected in their everyday lives in the aftermath of a nuclear disaster? The radiation did not simply involve Ukrainians; Petryna writes, "It became apparent that in order to do a fair analysis of the lived experience of Chernobyl, I had to do multi-sited work" (2002:17). First, between 1992 and 1997, she lived and worked for several brief and long periods of time in Kiev, the capital of Ukraine. There, she conducted participant observation among resettled families, radiation-exposed workers, and mothers of exposed children. Next, she interviewed government officials and civil servants in charge of dealing with Chernobyl's aftermath, as well non-governmental disability rights organizations. During some of this time she also did participant-observation research in the state-supported Radiation Research Center, where she studied the everyday activities and interactions of medical personnel and patients.

In between her stints in Kiev, the research also took her to other countries. She went to Russia to study the scientific knowledge and technical experience nuclear and radiation experts gained from the disaster. She conducted interviews and participant observation in the United States at the International Atomic Energy Agency in New York and in

🌱 **Chernobyl Nuclear Power Plant Accident, Ukraine.**

government laboratories such as the Lawrence Berkeley Laboratory in California, where she learned techniques for measuring the biological impact of radiation at the cellular and genetic levels, which helped her better understand the scientific dimensions of these matters.

Multi-sited research like Petryna's requires following certain common themes and processes across widely dispersed research settings. Its goal is not to study the world system in its totality but to identify the connections that link these dispersed settings. The settings can be geographically dispersed, both within and across nation-states. But they can also be socially dispersed, as in the social distance that exists between a state-run research clinic and a neighborhood where resettled families live.

Her transient method provided rich perspectives on the complex changes in people's lives that came following the breakdown of state socialism following the collapse of the Soviet Union and the sudden rise of global capitalism and new laws. On the one hand, citizens gained new democratic opportunities, including the right to information and the ability to pressure their government to provide benefits for their suffering. On the other hand, to deal with the suffering, the Ukrainian state's welfare system had to expand instead of contract, defying any predictions that the end of state socialism would automatically lead to a capitalist, free-market economy.

These complex changes have expressed themselves through what Petryna calls "biological citizenship." In the normal sense of citizenship, citizens bear certain natural and legal rights as their birthright. But in Ukraine, themes like biological damage, scientific knowledge, and suffering have become the grounds upon which many people claim citizenship.

Questions for Reflection

1. What would Petryna have gained if she had stayed in one place to do her research? What would she have lost?

2. What do you think are some of the practical problems facing an anthropologist who wants to conduct multi-sited research?

3. Do you think that multi-sited research raises any particular ethical issues?

1995). Its goal is not a holistic representation of the world system as a totality. Rather, it seeks to track cultural themes as they express themselves in distinct places and settings that are typically connected in some concrete way. Its goal is to describe relationships and connections between these different places. In this sense, multi-sited ethnography offers a comparative method. Comparisons emerge from juxtaposing phenomena that were once thought "worlds apart" (Marcus 1995:102). "Doing Fieldwork: Studying Chernobyl's Aftermath with Adriana Petryna" considers how one anthropologist has taken advantage of the opportunities multi-sited ethnography presents for studying culture in transnational contexts.

Multi-sited fieldwork has been productive for studying transnational phenomena like environmentalism and other social movements, the media, certain religious societies whose membership extends across the borders of many countries, and the spread of science and technology. As the object of anthropological research has expanded to include topics like these, more and more anthropologists are doing multi-sited research. Multi-sited research is not appropriate for every research topic, but it is now becoming a common anthropological research strategy.

THINKING CRITICALLY ABOUT GLOBALIZATION

Can you identify any examples of cultural hybridization in your community? How does the example you came up with connect to transnational dynamics and processes?

Conclusion

No anthropologist can claim to have easy answers to the dilemmas, dislocations, and problems raised by globalization. But anthropological research can provide critical perspectives on how and why people relate to large-scale social, economic, and political changes in the ways they do.

As we have established in this chapter, culture helps people make sense of and respond to constant changes in the world, which is itself dynamic. But cultural change is not a uniform process. There are many reasons for this. Different societies have differing levels of tolerance toward change, and some are more protective of their cultural traditions than others. In addition, as the story about Walpiri watching television demonstrates, people can be open to outside influences even while maintaining culturally specific meanings and social relations. They do this by actively transforming the alien into something more familiar. Even more important, perhaps, is that not all people participate in global processes on equal terms. Their position within broader political-economic processes helps shape their consciousness and experience of global cultural integration.

For these reasons alone, it is possible to see why cultural diversity continues to exist in the world. But there is another key reason. It is because cultures are created in connection with other cultures, not in isolation, as many anthropologists had previously thought. This is not to say that there are not certain elements that make the world feel smaller, including empirical changes in communications, migration, and finances. But does this mean we live in a global village as Marshall McLuhan once claimed? Only if we think of a village as a place in which diversity, and not uniformity, is the defining feature of that village.

KEY TERMS

Anthropology of
   development   p. 153

Cultural imperialism
   p. 157

Development anthropology
   p. 153

Diffusionists   p. 143

Exiles   p. 145

Globalization   p. 143

Hybridization   p. 157

Immigrants   p. 145

Localization   p. 151

Migrants   p. 145

Multi-sited ethnography
   p. 159

Postcolonialism   p. 149

Refugees   p. 145

Transnational   p. 145

World culture   p. 157

World systems theory
   p. 149

Reviewing the Chapter

Chapter Section	What We Know	To Be Resolved
Is the world really getting smaller?	It is impossible to make sense of local cultural realities without some understanding of the broader political, economic, and social conditions that also shape people's lives.	Anthropologists do not have easy answers for the cultural, economic, and political dilemmas raised by globalization.
Are there winners and losers in global integration?	Not everybody participates equally in the diverse kinds of interconnections that make up globalization, and taking globalization seriously means taking power relationships and social inequality seriously.	While some anthropologists emphasize the destructive and dominating effects of global capitalism's spread for many non-Western societies, others have argued that the expressions of resistance and creative localization are meaningful and important responses.
Doesn't everyone want to be developed?	Development raises complex and politically charged issues about socioeconomic and cultural change for anthropologists and the indigenous and poor communities that are the target of development initiatives.	Anthropologists are deeply divided over the positive and negative impacts of development, and they continue to debate the merits and drawbacks of anthropological involvement in development and other projects that promote globalization.
If the world is not becoming homogenized, what is it becoming?	Globalization is a complicated matter that illustrates how people create and change their cultures not in isolation but through connections with others.	Although many anthropologists accept that globalization is a process primarily of hybridization, others argue that it is a process of cultural convergence.
What strategies can anthropologists use to study global interconnections?	Multi-sited ethnography is one approach for tracking cultural themes as they express themselves in distinct places and settings, and it seeks to identify concrete connections between those places and settings.	Anthropologists continue to debate whether or not multi-sited research is as effective for understanding culture as traditional community-based ethnographic methods.

Readings

Although anthropologists have been interested in cultural transmission from one society to another for more than a century, very few of these studies are studies of globalization as anthropologists now understand the concept. *The Anthropology of Globalization: A Reader,* edited by Jonathan Xavier Inda and Renato Rosaldo (Malden, MA: Blackwell, 2007) offers a rich overview of the history, topics, and debates in the anthropological study of globalization, including essays on themes such as migration, the creation of transnational identities, and the movement of goods and capitalist economic structures across political, economic, and cultural boundaries.

• •

Although he is not an anthropologist, Pico Iyer's book *The Global Soul: Jet Lag, Shopping Malls, and the Search for Home* (New York: Vintage, 2001) captures rich description of many of the cultural dilemmas and situations that draw anthropological attention about global processes. Anthropologist Michael Jackson's book *At Home in the World* (Durham, NC: Duke University Press, 1995) is a rich ethnographic and philosophical counterpart to Iyer's book, juxtaposing the author's global travels and sense of uprootedness with how Australian Walpiri construct a concept of home as hunter-gatherers who move across large geographic distances.

• •

Many anthropologists have written noteworthy ethnographic monographs exploring the intersections of culture and globalization. Among the more thought-provoking are Anna Tsing's book *Friction: An Ethnography of Global Interconnection* (Princeton, NJ: Princeton University Press, 2005), which examines the many global institutions and interactions that shape the problems facing Indonesian rain forests and indigenous peoples; Charles Piot's *Remotely Global: Village Modernity in West Africa* (Chicago: University of Chicago Press, 1999), which explores how village life among the Kabre of Togo is shaped by a complex mixture of local traditions and colonial and postcolonial histories; and Adriana Petryna's *Life Exposed: Biological Citizens After Chernobyl* (Princeton, NJ: Princeton University Press, 2002), which is described in the "Doing Fieldwork" box.

● ●

Part II

Becoming Human

One of anthropology's principal tasks is figuring out when, how, and under what conditions our earliest ancestors evolved and became "human," and how our humanity differentiates us from other species. Thanks to new field discoveries, technological progress in studying ancient fossils, and theoretical advances, our knowledge of human origins has grown by leaps and bounds in recent years. They all point to a critical finding: that the material and symbolic cultures our ancestors created over time had—and continue to have—an influence over our evolution as a species. A new biocultural paradigm is reshaping not only our understanding of humanity's evolutionary past, but also how we approach contemporary human behavior, biological variations among human populations, and people's ideas and experiences of bodily health and illness.

The first chapter in this section examines why and how anthropologists study nonhuman primates, a central goal being to identify what in human behavior is general to primates, what is restricted to a few kinds of primates and humans, and what is uniquely human. We then present a chapter describing the latest paleoanthropological findings and theories about the human family tree and the lives of the first humans. A chapter exploring the importance of the biocultural paradigm follows, explaining how intertwined biological and cultural factors shape human behavior and our ongoing evolution as a species. The next chapter takes stock of contemporary human biodiversity, offering a biocultural perspective on how and why human populations vary in physiology, immunity, and body type. In that chapter, we also examine the biological fallacies and embodied consequences of race and racism. The final chapter examines complicated linkages between culture, biology, and human health and illness from the perspective of one of our discipline's most dynamic branches, medical anthropology.

Living Primates

Comparing Monkeys, Apes, and Humans

During 2014, an epidemic of Ebola virus disease in West Africa dominated news headlines around the world. Ebola produces fearsome effects in humans, including the hemorrhaging of blood and other bodily fluids, with an average mortality rate of 50%. The 2014 outbreak was the largest in history. Within a year, some 25,000 cases were confirmed and over 10,000 deaths recorded, mostly in the countries of Guinea, Sierra Leone, and Liberia. Extreme poverty, years of armed conflict, broken public healthcare systems, and burial practices involving the handling of infected bodies all conspired in these countries to produce a situation that U.S. President Barack Obama described as "spiraling out of control" as he and other international leaders scrambled to organize a humanitarian intervention.

Beyond the headlines, another Ebola epidemic was also spiraling out of control, among chimpanzees and gorillas in Western and Central equatorial Africa. The Ebola virus is thought to be harbored in fruit bats and passed to gorillas and chimpanzees when they make contact with bat secretions, such as saliva on half-eaten fruits. Humans and great apes are susceptible to many infectious diseases in common—from the common cold to polio—and can pass them to each other. One likely avenue of Ebola transmission to humans is through contact with infected apes that have been hunted for bushmeat.

Infectious Dangers   Because of our close evolutionary histories, great apes, like the ones pictured here, are susceptible to many infectious diseases that also affect humans. Understanding disease-transmission patterns between human and ape communities is an increasingly critical concern to public health officials and conservationists.

Ebola has been devastating for apes, producing higher rates of mortality than among humans. Although accurate data collection is difficult because of their remoteness and mobility, it appears that since the 1990s Ebola outbreaks have reduced the world's gorilla and chimpanzee populations by as much as one-third. In some dramatic cases, such as Minkébé Park in northern Gabon, over 90% of the gorilla population has died. Compounding the viral threat are histories of deforestation, civil war, and hunting for bushmeat in ape territories. Long reproductive cycles mean it is difficult for ape populations to rebound from these pressures, leading Peter Walsh, a primatologist who works in the Division of Biological Anthropology at the University of Cambridge, to warn, "without aggressive investments in law enforcement, protected area management and Ebola prevention, the next decade will see our closest relatives pushed to the brink of extinction" (Walsh et al. 2003:611).

Walsh and his colleagues have been testing a vaccine for chimpanzees and gorillas. They conducted trials on captive chimpanzees using an experimental virus-like particle vaccine developed for use in humans. To date, the trials have not involved injecting the vaccinated chimps with the live virus, which is a critical step in the development of vaccines. The reason is that medical research involving great apes in Europe is highly restricted because of their cognitive and behavioral similarities to humans (Inglis 2015). An ethical debate continues about whether exceptions should be made in this case.

These immunological connections and similarities between humans and great apes are but one example of the close relationships between our species, which exist because of the extensive evolutionary history we share as primates. These connections and similarities interest biological anthropologists, who study human biological adaptations, variability, and evolution in the context of human culture and behavior. Biological anthropology encompasses the study of primates with a goal of identifying what in human behavior is general to primates, what is restricted to a few kinds of primates and humans, and what is uniquely human.

Central to biological anthropology's interest in living primates is the question: *What can studying other living primates tell us about what it means to be human?* Embedded in this larger question are the following problems, around which this chapter is organized.

What does it mean to be a primate, and why does it matter to anthropology?

What are the basic patterns of primate behavioral diversity, and under what conditions did they develop?

How do behavior patterns among monkeys and apes compare with humans?

What can studying monkey and apes really illustrate about human distinctiveness?

Primates are of importance to anthropology because they provide us with a comparative baseline for understanding ourselves as humans. And yet, due to our distinctive evolutionary trajectories, there is a wide array of possibilities involved in being a primate, and no single primate provides a totally adequate model for human evolution or behavior.

What Does It Mean To Be a Primate, and Why Does It Matter to Anthropology?

Throughout history and across cultures, the similarities between monkeys, apes, and humans have been recognized, celebrated, condemned, and puzzled over. It was Carl Linnaeus (see Chapter 3) who formalized those similarities for science, by classifying humans along with other apes and monkeys. In his taxonomy, he placed humans within the genus *Homo*, as well as chimpanzees and orangutans, the only other large apes known to European scientists at the time. He placed *Homo* in a family he called Primates, including in that family two other genera he called Simians and Lemurs. Later scientists would discover new species and refine the taxonomy, but the fact that Linnaeus slotted humans into his system was—and continues to be—important, and for some, controversial. Darwin faced that controversy when critics charged that his theory of natural selection communicated that humans evolved from monkeys (Figure 7.1). Humans are not monkeys, nor did we evolve from them. But monkeys and humans are both primates, and we explore what that means here.

What It Means To Be a Primate

The word *primate*, derived from the Latin word for "of the first rank," implies that these creatures are a higher order than other life forms. Linnaeus used it because as a Christian he took for granted the Great Chain of Being that placed humans and similar beings closer to divine powers. As you know from Chapter 3 on evolution, no creature is "more advanced" than any other from an evolutionary perspective. All organisms are evolving along trajectories relative to their environments and ancestries.

Primates are social mammals with grasping hands, bony and enclosed eye sockets, and relatively large brains. They share a common ancestry that split from other mammals some 65 million years ago, and live in mostly tropical and subtropical areas of the Americas, Africa, and Asia (Figure 7.2). The number of living non-human primate species is not certain: new discoveries are still being made (58 since 2010), many species are endangered and on the verge of extinction, and taxonomists still disagree over relations between primates. For some researchers, a good working number ranges between 250 to 300 species, while the International Union for the Conservation of Nature recognizes 612 species and subspecies (Rowe 2015). What does it actually mean to be a primate?

Perhaps two of the most important things are manual dexterity and visual acuity. Being a primate means being adept and skillful with the hands, and in many cases, feet. Having five individually moveable fingers involving an opposable thumb, as well as large toes, allows for fine movements—peeling, grooming, manipulating things— that having paws or fixed claws does not provide. Primates are generalists, which

Figure 7.1   Questioning Darwin.   After he published his book *The Descent of Man* in 1871, which explains human origins in terms of natural selection, the satirical magazine *The Hornet* published this caricature called "A Venerable Orang-outang." Darwin's evolutionary theory, and especially his book, insisted that humans and apes had common ancestors, which provoked widespread social outrage.

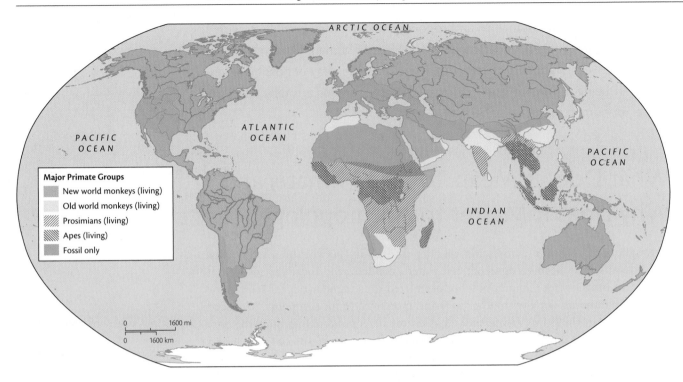

ARCTIC OCEAN

PACIFIC OCEAN

ATLANTIC OCEAN

PACIFIC OCEAN

INDIAN OCEAN

Major Primate Groups
- New world monkeys (living)
- Old world monkeys (living)
- Prosimians (living)
- Apes (living)
- Fossil only

0   1600 mi
0   1600 km

🌱 **Figure 7.2   Geographic Distribution of the Living Primates.**   Except for a few species of Old World monkeys and humans, primates live in tropical regions.

means they are able to live in a wide variety of environments and make use of many different resources, which manual dexterity supports.

Primates also have excellent vision, not relying as much on smell as other animals. Their eyes face forward and are close together, and though each eye captures its own information, together they create stereoscopic vision, or three-dimensional vision with depth perception. Stereoscopic vision has many advantages, especially helping primates to know with precision where objects such as food or predators are in relation to themselves, and for moving around in their environments effectively. Unlike other animals, the eyes are protected by either being fully enclosed by bone (picture a human skull) or with a postorbital bar, which is a ring of bone that surrounds the eyeball and protects it from being jostled by chewing.

There are several other shared characteristics. General intelligence, related to a larger brain size than similarly sized creatures. Locomotive flexibility and a collar bone at the shoulders, both of which provide greater mobility—running, climbing, jumping, walking, and so on—than creatures that have to walk on all four legs. And longer gestation times and childhoods, the second of which in numerous primate species involves training to live in complex social groups.

These characteristics are still quite general, and primates vary among themselves, sometimes greatly. To get at that variation and the multiple possibilities involved in being a primate, it is helpful to break down the distinctions between the different groups of primates and to describe their characteristics in more detail.

- **Strepsirrhini.** The infraorder of primates including lemurs, galagos, and lorises.

- **Haplorrhini.** The infrorder of primates including monkeys, apes, and humans.

The Distinctions Between Strepsirrhini and Haplorrhini

Taxonomists identify two suborders in the order Primates, which are the **Strepsirrhini** [strepp-**sur**-en-eye], consisting of prosimians, and the **Haplorrhini** [hap-**plor**-en-eye], which includes all species of tarsiers, monkeys, apes, and humans. Here we identify briefly the distinctions between these suborders, as well as the general characteristics of the primates that fall within them.

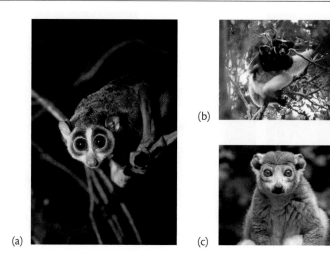

The Strepsirrhini

There are two groups of Strepsirrhini, or prosimians, the lemurs and a group that includes the lorises and galagos. Strepsirrhines have smaller body sizes than other primates, a smaller brain-to-body-size ratio (but a larger one than most other mammals), and a keener sense of smell (olfaction) than other primates. A large portion of their brain is devoted to smell and they have a rhinarium, or wet nose, enhancing their ability for receiving chemical particles associated with scents. Most Strepsirrhines are **arboreal** (tree-dwelling), and many are **nocturnal**, active at night, with large eyes and excellent night vision (Figure 7.3).

Lemurs live exclusively on the island of Madagascar, off the southeastern coast of Africa, where they arrived approximately 54 million years ago. Like most Strepsirrhines, they have a grooming claw (a special nail on their feet) and a tooth comb (lower incisors) used for cleaning their own and others' fur. Because there were no other primates on Madagascar until the arrival of humans, lemurs spread out, adapting to different food sources and habitat types. Today forest destruction has caused the extinction of many lemur species and threats to others.

Galagos are a group of small, nocturnal species found across forests in central Africa. They have specialized arms and legs that provide great leaping ability. They mostly eat fruit and insects, spending their time in vocal and olfactory communication. The range and diversity of their vocalizations are so important that differentiating species might be based on vocal structure and not physical features because they look so alike (Bearder et. al. 1995).

Lorises consist of the Asian lorises and the African pottos. They are mostly nocturnal and fully arboreal, eating insects and other small animals. The lorises do not leap in the trees but move slowly through them, using all four limbs to grasp branches.

The Haplorrhini

There are two infraorders (groupings below the level of the order) of Haplorrhini, these being the Tarsiiformes and the Simiiformes. The Tarsiiformes include the tarsiers (family Tarsiidae). The Simiiformes include three superfamilies: Ceboidea, or monkeys of the Americas; Cercopithecoidea, or Asian and African monkeys; and Hominoidea, or apes and humans. In this book, we use two specialized terms to refer to the Simiiformes: **anthropoid** is a term referring to all monkeys, apes, and humans, and **hominoid** refers only to apes and humans. The term **hominine** applies to *Homo sapiens*, our own species.

Figure 7.3   Strepsirrhines. Shown are slender loris (a); indri with young (b); adult male crowned lemur (c); ringtailed lemurs (d).

- **Arboreal.** Living in the trees.

- **Nocturnal.** Active during the nighttime.

- **Anthropoid.** A Primate superfamily that includes monkeys, apes, and humans.

- **Hominoid.** The Primate superfamily Hominoidea that includes all the apes and the humans.

- **Hominine.** The division (called a tribe) in the superfamily Hominoidea that includes humans and our recent ancestors.

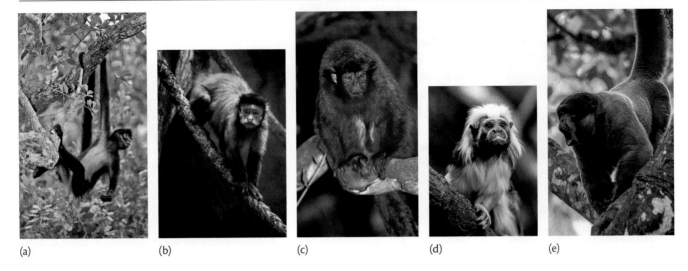

(a)　　　　　(b)　　　　　(c)　　　　　(d)　　　　　(e)

🌱 **Figure 7.4   New World Monkeys, or Ceboidea.**
Shown here: spider monkey (a); capuchin monkey (b); titi monkey (c); cotton-top tamarin (d); and wooly monkey (e).

• **Prehensile.** The ability to grasp things, usually referring to hands or tails.

• **Terrestrial.** Living on the ground.

The Haplorrhines have larger bodies and larger brain-to-body-size ratios than Strepsirrhines. They lack a wet nose, and have more brain devoted to vision than olfaction. They show greater diversity in lifeways (tree-living, ground-living, and a mix of both), so their skeletons are more varied.

Tarsiers and Monkeys

The tarsiers of Southeast Asia are small-bodied and nocturnal. Their elongated tarsal bones (ankles) endow them with extreme leaping abilities and gives them their name. They spend their lives in small groups, typically two adults with their young. With their large eyes (whose combined weight is larger than their brain!), the tarsiers move about in dense tropical forests at night.

The Ceboidea, or New World Monkeys, are widely dispersed from Southern Mexico to Southern Argentina. Though there is a lot of diversity between them, the majority are arboreal and relatively smaller than anthropoids found in Africa and Asia. They differ from other anthropoids in other ways, including having certain dental and other anatomical characteristics (three premolars, for example) (Figure 7.4). An important skeletal adaptation for life in the trees is the **prehensile** tail, which grasps and clings to branches and foliage. A fleshy pad at the tip of the tails even has its own "fingerprint."

The Cercopithecoidea, or Old World monkeys, are found in Asia and Africa (Figure 7.5). There are two subfamilies, the cercopithecinae and the colobinae. Baboons and macaques are cercopithecinae, and are each active in the daytime in both **terrestrial** (ground-living) and arboreal contexts. The cercopithecinae also have small pockets inside their cheeks for food storage, and so they are sometimes called "cheek pouch" monkeys. The other group, the colobines, do not have cheek pouches and are typically more arboreal. Known as "leaf monkeys," they carry special bacteria in large stomachs with multiple internal folds that help them digest plant matter that other primates can't digest.

Apes and Humans

African apes (gorillas and chimpanzees), Asian apes (orangutans and gibbons), and humans are all members of Hominodiea. Hominoids have large bodies and brains, except for gibbons. The apes and humans don't have tails and carry various adaptations in the upper body permitting full rotation of the arm and greater hand movement, which allow them to hang and swing among branches. The initial adaptation for

(a)   (b)   (c)

swinging from limb to limb (so-called brachiation) laid the groundwork for changes that eventually led to bipedal walking, which is unique to the human lineage.

Now that we have described taxonomic distinctions between the primate suborders and their characteristics, we can bring evolution back into the picture. In Figure 7.6 we present a primate phylogeny, which uses a combination of morphological, fossil, and genetic evidence to show what scientists traditionally accept as the evolutionary relationships between primates.

Figure 7.5   Old World Monkeys, or Cercopithecoidea. Shown here: black and white colobus (a); olive baboons (b); and hanuman langurs (c).

Primatology as Anthropology

Why do all these details about primate suborders and creatures like lemurs and tarsiers matter to anthropology? Anthropologists who study primates often have to address this question, explaining why their studies of primates do not belong in other fields that also study primates, including biology, zoology, ecology, and psychology.

Primate studies within anthropology began in the 1950s, thanks to the efforts of physical anthropologist Sherwood Washburn, who asserted, "Since man is a primate who developed from among the Old World simian stock, his social behavior must have also evolved from that of this mammalian group. Thus the investigation of man's behavior is dependent on what we know of the behavior of monkeys and apes" (1961, quoted in Sussman 2014:41). Since the 1960s when it became a field science—rather than simply a lab science studying bones and fossils—biological anthropologists have been key players in the creation of primatology as an interdisciplinary field, identifying and describing new species, standardizing methods, and performing long-term studies (Sussman 2011).

Several features distinguish anthropologically specific approaches to primates. One is that anthropologists have often approached the study of living primates as a window into the evolution of social behaviors among humans, much as Washburn suggested. Prior to World War II, physical anthropology was closely associated with efforts to measure and categorize different human races, which anthropologists had come to disavow as racist (see Chapter 10). For Washburn and his students, those older approaches were disconnected from the exciting findings of the modern synthesis in evolutionary thought (Chapter 3), and studying the behaviors of living primates could support the creation of hypotheses about human evolution (Haraway 1989).

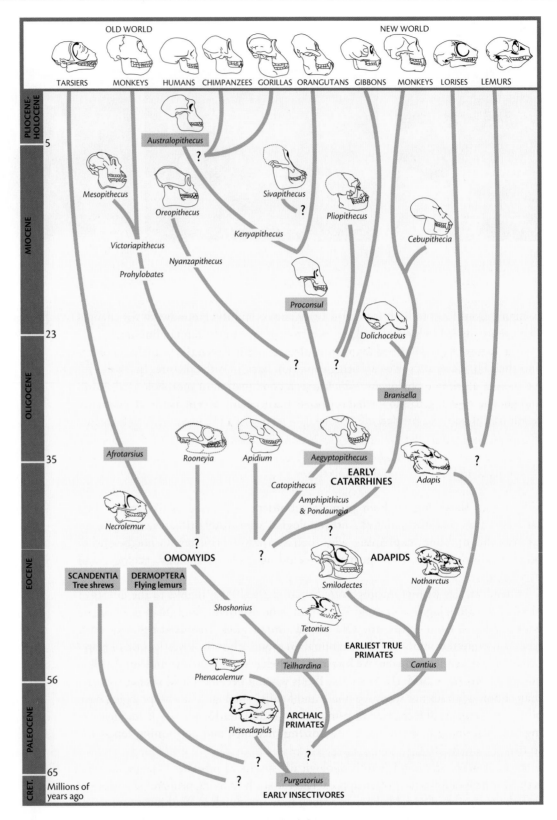

Figure 7.6   Evolutionary Relationships in the Primate Order.   There is still debate over specific evolutionary relationships among primate taxa across some time periods, but this phylogeny gives a traditional overview.

Doing Fieldwork

Anthropological Primatology Among Owl Monkeys with Eduardo Fernandez-Duque

YALE UNIVERSITY–BASED BIOLOGICAL anthropologist Eduardo Fernandez-Duque was born in Argentina and returns there often to do fieldwork among owl monkeys. As an anthropologist, he is interested in understanding how, when, and why male–female relationships, pair-bonding, and paternal care may have evolved. He studies these topics among living primates because it has been suggested that pair-bonding could be a fundamental adaptation of early humans. It is also difficult to study these things directly among contemporary humans, given the incredible cultural diversity of marriage and kinship patterns. The question is do other primate species create male–female bonds similar to humans, and if they do, what factors shape how and why they these bonds may have evolved? What light might these case studies shed on the evolutionary basis of male–female relationships among all primates?

In his fieldwork with owl monkeys, Fernandez-Duque employs a number of methods, including hands-off observational studies in which he and his field assistants observe and record monkey behaviors and interactions for long periods during the day and night (Fernandez-Duque 2014). He also uses capture-and-release techniques. For example, in his research on owl monkeys living on a private ranch in northeastern Argentina, he and his field assistants have used a blowgun with tranquilizer darts to capture monkeys living in the tree canopy, who fall into a net after being tranquilized. The research team then take hair samples for genetic analysis, rub Q-tips on the pectoral and perianal glands for analysis of olfactory communication, and take small skin biopsies from the inner thighs for establishing live cell lines (Fernandez-Duque 2014). They also conduct a complete physical exam of each monkey, including taking body measurements, getting its weight, and checking its fur for parasites. As they finish, they fit radio collars to track remotely the monkey's movements using telemetry equipment. Some of these collars have motion sensors to collect more detailed information about how their movements relate to light conditions. The overall approach here is a quantitative one whose goal is to identify and analyze different data sets to see what patterns emerge.

It is notoriously difficult to identify the sex of owl monkeys because males and females look and act very similar. It was often only when they conducted a physical exam of a captured individual or when they received lab results that Fernandez-Duque and his team knew for certain what the sex of a particular individual was. Over a period of intensive capturing, marking, and sampling, Fernandez-Duque and his team were finally able to identify enough individuals and track their move-

Eduardo Fernandez-Duque

ments so that, as he says, "the soap opera of their lives began to unfold" (2014:87). They discovered that monkey "families" included not just biological parents and offspring but also regularly included step-parents. They also discovered that after individuals left the group they were born into, they fought with other individuals of the same sex over reproductive opportunities, sometimes to the death. It was a surprising finding because it was not known until then that most owl monkeys spend part of their lives as solitary individuals.

Owl monkeys have a slow life trajectory, including four years of childhood and adolescence living with their birth groups, reaching reproductive maturity after six years of age. Collecting data about pair-bonding over these life trajectories requires a long-term commitment to these animals, as well as to the community of people who live with and near these monkeys. A key dimension of Fernandez-Duque's commitment is his establishment of a conservation foundation to protect the monkey's habitat, educate about owl monkeys, and involve local community members directly with the monkeys through participation in fieldwork. This attentiveness, sense of obligation, and commitment to work intensively with human communities at least partially distinguish Fernandez-Duque as an anthropologist. The other part comes from the fact that he derives his research questions about pair-bonding, and his comparative approach to primates, from his home discipline of anthropology.

Questions for Reflection

1. What ethical questions are involved in monkey capture-and-release studies like those Fernandez-Duque has conducted in Argentina?

2. How do you think a case study of owl monkeys might or might not be applicable to understanding pair-bonding in other primates, such as humans?

In "Doing Fieldwork: Anthropological Primatology Among Owl Monkeys with Eduardo Fernandez-Duque," we examine how one contemporary anthropologist conducts research among primates to explore questions of relevance to human evolution.

Anthropologists also bring holistic, comparative, and cross-cultural perspectives to the study of primates. Instead of viewing primates as programmed by their biology and evolution, anthropologists are attuned to the flexibility and plasticity of primate behaviors, which are rooted in cognitive and social complexity (Strier 2003; Ellwanger 2011). Anthropologists often document the social coordination and individual choices involved in primate group membership, which are variable not just across different primate species but also within a single species.

Finally, anthropological studies of primates recognize that humans and primates share historically deep and complicated relationships with each other. Our species compete with each other for food and space, and have shaped each other's ecologies, health, and evolutionary histories (Fuentes 2014b). One clear example is the case of Ebola described earlier, where the destinies of human and ape communities are intertwined through the transmission of infectious disease, hunting, and habitat reduction.

- **Ethnoprimatology.** The study of the interface between human and ape communities.

An emerging approach to primate studies called **ethnoprimatology**, which comes out of anthropology, focuses on the interface between human and ape communities, envisioning human and non-human primates as members of a dynamic ecosystem (Riley, Wolfe, and Fuentes 2011). Ethnoprimatology recognizes that many cultures around the world have strong and variable connections to primates—expressed in religious beliefs, local attitudes, and informal, everyday interactions—that are not merely competitive but also based on building intricate relationships. In numerous societies, primates have sacred status and live in religious temples, live as pets in homes, participate in tourism economies by interacting with tourists, and are hunted by humans. Not all people place primates in "nature" as Western culture and sciences do, but see primate communities as extensions of the social worlds in which they participate as humans (Haraway 1989; Fuentes 2012).

From an ethnoprimatological perspective, studying the coexistence of primate species with humans is thus as much about studying primate behaviors as it is understanding how humans think about them and under what conditions the different species come into contact with each other. In methodological terms, ethnoprimatologists are as likely to document quantitative details of primate behavior through field observations and genetic analyses, as they are to document qualitative perspectives through interviews and participant observation with people (Haraway 1989; Fuentes 2012).

Now that we have considered what primates are and why anthropologists are concerned with them, we can now turn our attention to how they actually behave. In the next section we consider the diversity of basic primate behavior patterns.

● ●

THINKING CRITICALLY ABOUT LIVING PRIMATES

Can you think of some concrete ways anthropologists might approach the study of primates holistically? Cross-culturally? Comparatively?

● ●

What Are the Basic Patterns of Primate Behavioral Diversity and Under What Conditions Did They Develop?

In creating a comparative baseline for understanding humans, anthropologists look for three kinds of behavioral patterns in primates: primate-wide trends, hominoid-wide trends, and unique human characteristics. Explaining the patterns of primate behavioral diversity and the conditions under which behavioral diversity emerges can help us begin to move toward what might be unique to apes and ultimately to humans.

Common Behavior Patterns Among Primates

Primates share a number of common behavioral patterns, all of which are connected to the requirements of living in groups and negotiating social relationships. There is likely some genetic basis to these shared patterns (Figure 7.7), which include the following.

Mother–Infant Bond

Primates have a long period of infant dependency. The infant relies totally on others for its nutrition, movement, regulation of body temperature, and its protection from predators. Mothers and other relatives have a clear evolutionary interest in ensuring the offspring will reach maturity. In primates, this interest creates intensive caregiving behaviors called the mother–infant bond (although this doesn't mean males can't also be caregivers). Through this relationship, the infant is in frequent physical and vocal contact, and is exposed to the mother's behavior and relationships. In this way, infants learn crucial information about other group members, foods, and appropriate behaviors. Caregiving is a learned behavior, gained through individual experience and observations of how other group members handle infants.

Affiliation and Grooming

The ability to get along with others is critical for primates, given that they live in social groups. Individuals in frequent contact with each other usually have a tolerant, even friendly, relationship called **affiliation**. In contrast, an agonistic relationship exists where individuals are in conflict with each other. Primates create affiliations and avoid agonism through **grooming**, or moving their hands or licking the fur to remove dirt, insects, and so on. There is a hygienic dimension here, but they do it more than is necessary. When conflicts erupt, primates engage in grooming to reduce

- **Affiliation.** A relationship between individuals who are frequently in close association based on tolerance, even friendliness.

- **Grooming.** Touching another individual to remove dirt, insects, and debris, usually as a way for individuals to bond.

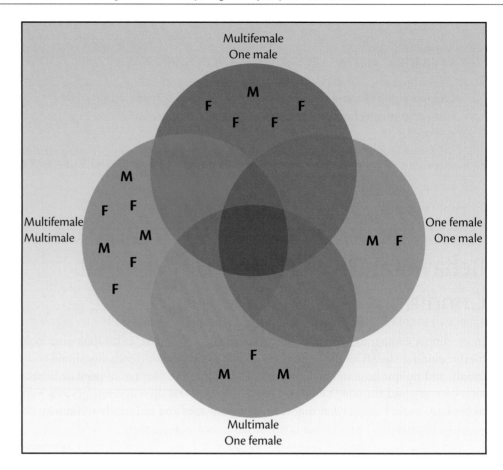

Figure 7.7   Basic Primate Grouping Patterns.   Many of the primate behaviors observed are closely related to the demands of living in groups.

🌱 **Figure 7.8   Grooming Macaques.**   Macaques, such as this adult, seen here grooming an immature macaque, engage in grooming behaviors to build and maintain social relations.

- **Dominance hierarchy.** The ranking of access to desired resources by different individuals relative to one another.

- **Sexual dimorphism.** A difference between the sexes of a species in body size or shape.

stress. Grooming relationships closely follow affiliations; in other words, grooming takes place among animals who want to associate, and agonism where they refuse to groom (Figure 7.8).

Dominance Hierarchies

Unequal access to resources is typical in primate groups. A **dominance hierarchy** is the ranking that individuals have relative to others for access to resources. Often the hierarchy is obvious, and an "alpha animal" has priority over other members of the group. In these situations, individuals have priority over others except those who outrank them. Dominance is a social role, not an inborn trait, that an individual occupies for a period in their life. In many primate societies, **sexual dimorphism**—where males are larger than females—means that males are often dominant over females (Figure 7.9). Nevertheless, there are circumstances in which, due to environmental circumstances, females are dominant, males and females are co-dominant, or individuals do not compete openly with one another and so dominance is not clear. Dominance hierarchies are also complicated by collective alliances.

Dispersal Patterns

The life cycle of a primate involves several main stages, including growth and development, reproductive maturity, and old age and death. At some point, usually as they begin to enter reproductive maturity, members of one sex leave the group, which is called **dispersal.** They might join other groups, while those of the opposite sex remain with the group in which they were born. Dispersal is a risky process: individuals must create relationships with non-kin, and moving between groups makes them susceptible to predation or unable to access food.

Cooperation and Conflict

It is rare for primates to spend much time alone, and they maintain social relationships through acts of cooperation. Dominance relationships tend to maintain social order, and serious fighting for resources is rare (Garber and Sussman 2007). Conflicts, of course, do occur, damaging alliances that must be repaired. Reconciliation is achieved by behaviors such as sharing, embracing, or other forms of postconflict physical contact (Arnold and Aureli 2007).

Figure 7.9 Sexual Dimorphism. Male and female macaques exhibit important differences in size.

The Emergence of Primate Behavioral Diversity

These basic common patterns evolved over millions of years and are shared by all primates. They do not mean any of us behave as a promsimian like a galago does, and there are, obviously, important differences in behavior among primates. But if primates have a set of common behavioral patterns, it leads us to ask: How and why do *differences* in behavior emerge out of those basic common patterns?

Primate behaviors involve complex interactions between morphology (physical characteristics of the body), learning and experience, environmental circumstances, and chance occurrences. **Behavioral ecology** is a branch of ecology that studies how ecological conditions challenge organisms, and how those organisms deal with environmental pressures through behavioral evolution. It offers useful tools for understanding how, why, and under what circumstances certain behaviors emerge. Behavioral ecologists typically look at two general kinds of pressures, socioecological pressures and energy costs and benefits.

Socioecological Pressures

Socioecological pressures on primates come in four primary forms:

1. *Nutrition*, or the necessity of sufficient food and water. The pressure to obtain key dietary items—fruits, leaves, insects, or other mammals—affects how and where a primate will find its food, as well as how it will capture and process it.
2. *Locomotion*, or the necessity to move around in an environment. Primates are arboreal, terrestrial, or both; yet there is still a lot of variability between and within species in terms of locomotion. For example, imagine two different species of arboreal primates. One might move around the lower, densely foliated branches, while the other uses the upper levels, moving around the smaller terminal branches. Pressures on their bodies and behaviors are quite different.
3. *Predation*, or the necessity to avoid predators. Avoiding predators is probably one of the reasons for group living. The higher the number of individuals in a group, the lesser the odds of being eaten. Predator detection also increases.
4. *Competition*, or the necessity to gain access to resources in a context in which members of the same species (intraspecific competition), or other species (interspecific competition), compete for the same resources. Imagine, for example, monkeys and birds wanting the same fruit source (van Schaik 1989).

- **Dispersal.** A pattern of one sex leaving the group they were born into about the time of reproductive maturity.

- **Behavioral ecology.** The study of behavior from ecological and evolutionary perspectives.

Sometimes these socioecological pressures act individually on an organism but, more often than not, particularities in that organism's environment intersect in unique ways to present individuals with a range of challenges. Differences in behavior emerge out of the ways organisms respond to those particularities.

Behavioral Costs and Benefits

Within behavioral ecology, understanding an organism's response to socioecological pressures also involves the concept of **costs and benefits**. It is a basic economic model (cash in and out) for measuring energy expenditure. It strives to determine whether a certain behavior gives back to the organism what it expended; if the organism loses energy because of the behavior, thus incurring a net loss of energy; or if it gains energy, thus benefiting from the behavior. Behavioral ecologists typically assume that it is in the interest of organisms to maximize their net energy gains and minimize their costs. In theory, this should support their reproductive success. Patterned behaviors that become common within a population are known as a **strategy**.

One of behavioral ecology's goals is to predict how animals should behave if the patterns of behavior benefit the primates (Hamilton 1964). An important aspect of behavioral ecology is **kin selection**, which consists of favoring one's close genetic relatives over more distant relatives or non-relatives. This idea was proposed to explain **altruism**, or seemingly "selfless" acts. In evolutionary terms it doesn't make sense to maximize the fitness of other individuals, because it reduces the energy available to an individual. But kin selection offers a simple way of predicting when an individual organism behaves in a way that looks altruistic. If an individual receiving a benefit from another individual is related, then their shared genotype benefits (depending on the degree of relatedness). It amounts to a simple equation. Close relatives, which include parents, offspring, siblings, and even first cousins, share much of their genotype, so aiding each other makes genetic sense. The most obvious examples of this pattern are when parents assist their offspring or when siblings collaborate and help one another.

The Limitations of Cost-Benefit Analyses

One of the limitations of cost-benefit analyses is their inability to deal with great complexity. One complication is the fact that organisms develop different kinds of traits that are subject to different kinds of pressures. For example, certain primates use both arboreal and terrestrial environments. Being in the trees tends to favor the evolution of curved fingers for grasping, while being on the ground favors straighter fingers (or at least toes) for more efficient walking. Cost-benefit analysis would have a hard time explaining this situation. And behavioral evolution is even more complicated.

It is extremely difficult to identify direct causal links between genes and behavior. Ecological conditions create a range of selection pressures for which certain behavioral responses might be appropriate, but some behaviors will be more successful than others. Those possible behaviors exist along a spectrum. Factors like natural selection (fitness costs/benefits) and morphology (body size and shape) establish the ends of the spectrum, that is, what might be practical behaviors. The spectrum itself merely establishes the *potential* for a trait or behavior. But the actual expression of the trait or behavior is its *performance*. Potential and performance are complexly intertwined. As a simple example, think about how people express physical aggression. Factors like an individual's body size, muscle density, and health might set the range of possible aggressive acts. But other factors, such as cultural ideologies about appropriate conditions for violence (see Chapter 16) shape its actual performance. In "Thinking Like an Anthropologist: The Flight or Fight Response," we consider another illustration of the complexity of the relationship between a behavior's potential and performance.

- **Costs and benefits.** An analytical approach that considers the caloric cost of obtaining food and the calories obtained.

- **Strategy.** A set of behaviors that has become prominent in a population as a result of natural selection.

- **Kin selection.** The behavioral favoring of your close genetic relatives.

- **Altruism.** Seemingly "selfless" acts that have a net loss of energy to the actor but a net gain in energy to the receiver.

Thinking Like an Anthropologist

The Flight or Fight Response

ANTHROPOLOGISTS BEGIN THEIR research by asking questions. In this box, we want you to learn how to ask questions as an anthropological researcher. Part 1 describes a situation and follows up with questions we would ask. Part 2 asks you to do the same thing with a different situation.

PART 1: FLIGHT OR FIGHT RESPONSE IN ZEBRAS

Imagine you are walking down the street at night, and you hear noises behind you. You glance around and see no one. You walk more quickly and hear footsteps. Your heart beats faster and you break into a run. The physical response to fear or danger is basically the same in all humans and, in fact, across all mammals. Why would this be?

Some behavior patterns that are widespread in a taxonomic group serve clear functions. These patterns are easily observed, described, and tested, and we assume that they developed at some point as adaptations to a particular combination of socioecological or cost-benefit pressures. The flight/fright/startle response in mammals is a good example, as the research of Robert Sapolsky (2004) of Stanford University illustrates. His work asks us to imagine what happens when a zebra standing on the savannah looks up from the grass it is eating to see a lion charging at it, mouth open and teeth glistening. The zebra immediately stops eating and starts moving. Its heart beats faster, the blood flows away from its stomach and intestines toward its legs, and it sprints away as fast as it can. If successful, it escapes the lion and then slowly calms down and returns to eating. If the situation is slightly different—for example, the lion is old and has a bad leg—the zebra may choose to stand and fight. Either way, the physiological response (e.g., changing heartbeat and blood flow) is the same; it is part of the zebra's phylogeny. The decision to flee or fight, however, is based on learning and is part of the zebra's life experience.

Sapolsky and other researchers have also noted that low-level flight/fright/startle responses that are chronic (occur over long periods of time or are repeated frequently) can have very negative effects on the body. This finding suggests that something that is beneficial in one context might not be in another.

What questions does this situation raise for anthropological researchers?

1. At what point and under what socioecological and genetic conditions in mammalian evolutionary history did the fight or flight response emerge?
2. What factors in mammalian lives might lead to long-lasting low-level fear/stress responses?
3. How do zebras learn to make decisions about whether to fight or flee?
4. What role might mental capacity play in producing and managing term chronic fear and other stresses?

🌿 **To Fight or Flee, That Is the Question.**

PART 2: FLIGHT OR FIGHT RESPONSE
IN PRIMATES

A similar pattern happens in primates, including humans. If a friend or foe sneaks up on you and scares you, your heart pumps faster, your stomach feels queasy, and you may yell or jump. A whole genre of movies (suspense/slasher movies) relies on this startle response. Because the fight/flight/startle physiological pattern and its generalized behavioral response are very old and found in most animals, it stands to reason that those individuals who did not respond to predators in this way did not do so well in their overall evolutionary success. But in primates, in contrast with zebras, social learning and even culture play a critical role in how primates evaluate and respond to pressures and threats. What questions would you ask about this situation as an anthropological researcher?

When it comes to primates, we need to appreciate the fundamental complexity of behavior. It is also important to remember a key tenet of evolutionary thinking: our focus should not be simply on individual behaviors or traits but on how a whole population of organisms deals with environmental challenges in patterns over a lifetime. The reproductive success of those organisms as a group will affect succeeding generations. Models of energy cost and benefit tend to oversimplify these population-level dynamics, as well as lifetime patterns.

With this background, we can move to biological anthropology's interest in developing a comparative baseline for understanding humans. In the next section we examine the behavior patterns of primate relatives nearer to us in evolutionary terms and offer some comparisons with humans.

THINKING CRITICALLY ABOUT LIVING PRIMATES

Factors other than natural selection affect behavioral evolution. Chance events, such as those involved in genetic drift, can influence an individual's life in ways not predictable from energy models, giving rise to new behaviors. Can you think of any other factors that might give rise to new behaviors among primates?

How Do Behavior Patterns Among Monkeys and Apes Compare with Humans?

As we said before, humans are not monkeys, and we did not evolve from them. The same is true of apes like chimpanzees, gorillas, or orangutans. Even while there are certain behavioral commonalities across all primates, monkey behavior patterns and morphology differ in key respects from hominoid (ape and human) patterns. The same is true about the behavior patterns of hominines (humans) and apes. While behavioral ecology attempts to offer theoretical explanations for *why* these patterns vary, we will use the comparative approach to show *how* these patterns vary among actual primates. Here we examine a kind of monkey called a macaque and a kind of ape called a chimpanzee and then reflect on how the behavior patterns of each compare with our own behavior as humans.

The Lives of Macaques

Macaque monkeys (members of the genus ***Macaca***) are among the most widely dispersed of all primates, being found in Asia, central Eurasia, and northern Africa. The spread of the genus about two million years ago was similar to that of our own genus, *Homo,* at the same time, although we are currently more widespread. But among the non-human primates, macaques have adapted to the widest and most diverse environmental conditions.

Macaque Social Life

The feeding pattern of macaques is a generalist one. They prefer fruit but will eat a wide variety of other foodstuffs, including leaves, insects, and occasionally even vertebrates. They spend most of their time in the trees, but most species also move along the ground.

Most macaques live in groups with adult males and adult females, commonly between twenty to fifty individuals, but sometimes as few as ten or as many as one hundred. These groups usually have more adult females than males, and the social life of these groups is focused around related females (Thierry 2007). Males leave their birth groups and join other groups, while females stay throughout their lives with their female relatives (sisters, cousins, aunts, mother, grandmother, and so on). These clusters of related females and young are called **matrifocal units** (Wheatley 1999) (Figure 7.10). Most males are relatively solitary, only occasionally interacting with females and other males, and living just beyond matrifocal units.

- *Macaca.* The genus of macaque monkeys.

- **Matrifocal unit.** A cluster of individuals generally made up of related females.

Figure 7.10   A Macaque Matrifocal Unit.   Much of the life of a female macaque is spent interacting with maternal kin.

Dominance Relationships

Dominance relations among macaques are closely aligned with sex. Between matrifocal units, more dominant units tend to push others from the best sources of food. Larger groups are typically dominant over smaller groups, although members of a subordinate cluster can usually dominate a lone female that has strayed from her unit. Macaques have a unique ranking system among primates, in which a mother's rank is passed to her youngest daughter. Because of this situation, younger females who are the daughter of a high-ranking female can take resources from older, lower ranked females.

Male macaques also have relationships involving dominance of one individual over another, but these change frequently within any particular group or cluster. Since males leave their birth groups, they have to form associations with other individuals to help them resolve and negotiate disputes. Higher ranked males can act aggressively toward some individuals in the group, while simultaneously building bonds with other males through grooming. Often males of lower rank will create coalitions to defend their position in the group or gain access to preferred food resources. Because males move between groups, their rank is always fragile compared with that of females. That movement exposes them to risk, which may explain why most groups of macaques have more adult females than males.

Sexual Behavior

Sexual behavior in macaques varies a great deal. Nevertheless, most females mate with more than one adult male, and they sometimes mate with all the males in a group. Many macaques are seasonal breeders, which means they are receptive only at certain times of the year. At these times, females often seek out and solicit sex from males. In some groups a high-ranking male can restrict access to females though a process described as "mate guarding," which involves sticking closely to the females whose sexual access they want to restrict. In slightly more than half the macaque groups where researchers have been able to determined genetic relationships among members, high-ranking males fathered the majority of infants born while they were dominant.

The Lives of Chimpanzees and Bonobos

Since Jane Goodall's groundbreaking research at Gombe in Tanzania (1971, 1986), which focused the world's attention on behavior patterns among chimpanzees and how similar they were to human patterns of behavior, researchers have asked comparative questions about primates and the evolution of human behavior. The primate they focus on most often is the chimpanzee (genus ***Pan***). Together with the gorilla, the chimpanzee is, evolutionarily speaking, our closest relative. Chimpanzees therefore share many primate-wide behavioral traits as well as shared-derived (hominoid and homininee) morphological and behavioral traits with humans.

- ***Pan.*** The genus of chimpanzees.

There are two species of chimpanzee: the common chimpanzee is *Pan troglodytes*, and the bonobo is known as *Pan paniscus*. Both species are found across Central Africa. Chimpanzees are large and weigh 35–50 kilograms (75–130 pounds), while their smaller cousins *P. paniscus* weigh 32–40 kilograms (70–90 pounds). All members of the genus are primarily fruit eaters, and as a result their lives and behaviors are oriented toward the seasons and the times when particular fruits are available (Figure 7.11).

Chimpanzee and Bonobo Social Lives

Both species live in communities consisting of many adult males and females. These range from 20 to about 150 individuals. But even though we may think of these communities as a group, they are only rarely all in the same place at the same time. Most individuals spend the majority of their time in subgroups characterized by a mix of

(a)

(b)

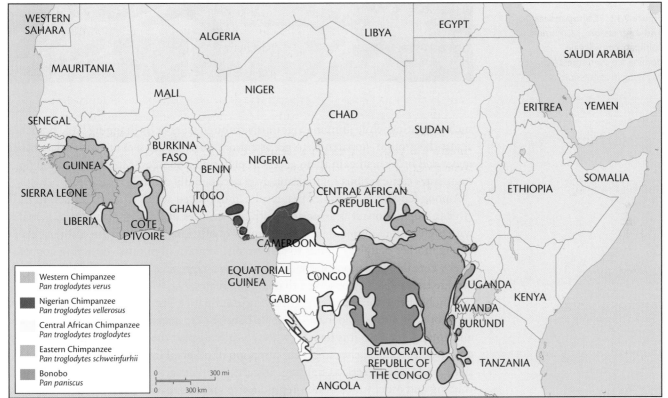

Western Chimpanzee
Pan troglodytes verus

Nigerian Chimpanzee
Pan troglodytes vellerosus

Central African Chimpanzee
Pan troglodytes troglodytes

Eastern Chimpanzee
Pan troglodytes schweinfurhii

Bonobo
Pan paniscus

(c)

ages and sexes. Groups tend to be larger when fruit is plentiful and disperse when fruit is scarce. Females from both species typically leave their birth group when they become adults and disperse to other groups (Stumpf 2011). Both species exhibit a number of behavioral patterns remarkable among non-human primates, including what we may think of as empathy and fairness (de Waal 2013).

Dominance Relationships

Males are more often dominant over females among common chimpanzees, but both males and females typically establish dominance relationships within their sex. These hierarchies affect access to preferred foods as well as sexual partners (Stumpf 2011). Males generally attain high rank from the alliances they form with other males (usually males of a similar age). They also employ a strategy of using spectacular displays,

Figure 7.11 The Two Chimpanzee Species.
Pan troglodytes, or common chimpanzees (a); and *Pan paniscus*, or bonobos (b); and their distribution (c).

Figure 7.12 Chimpanzees and Aggression.   Common chimpanzees will gain dominance over others by engaging in aggression.

such as hooting while jumping vigorously through trees or by dragging large branches across the ground, apparently to get attention. Such tactics seem to intimidate other males and help them gain them access to preferred resources. Male competition does sometimes cause serious injuries and even occasionally death (Figure 7.12).

Among females, high rank often results in improved access to food sources. In East African populations it is associated with higher rates of infant survivorship. Females with high rank tend to have a larger number of offspring, and mothers often use these strong mother-daughter bonds to achieve or maintain high rank, by acting cooperatively. Females can also achieve dominance via aggressive displays, but these behaviors are less frequently observed than among males.

Bonobo behavioral patterns involving dominance are somewhat different from those of common chimpanzees. Female bonobos are generally dominant over males, and among bonobos it is females who typically display their dominance by dragging objects like tree branches to get the attention of others. However, dominance interactions rarely lead to serious fighting. Instead, conflicts are resolved via genital-genital rubbing and other kinds of non-reproductive sexual behavior. Among male bonobos, dominance hierarchies do exist, but most commonly a male's rank is linked to the rank of his mother. Males can compete aggressively, but the overall rates of bonobo aggression are substantially lower than those of common chimpanzees.

Sexual Behavior

Females in both species show observable signs of fertility. During periods of sexual receptivity their anogenital region becomes filled with fluid, provoking interest from other members of the community. During these times, females can be observed soliciting copulation, often with several males. Primatologists observing common chimpanzee males in natural settings have reported high rates of aggression toward females, which may be a coercive strategy intended to get females to mate with them. This strategy is not, however, present among bonobos. Female choice in sexual partners plays an important role in both species, yet there is little evidence that bonobo males can effectively restrict female mating choices, since the females are usually dominant over males.

Most copulation occurs during the female's swelling periods, but most individuals in both species engage in sexual activity at other times, most notably bonobos. Bonobo males and females engage in frequent genital contact and stimulation as a common means of social interaction. This is especially the case when conflicts among females occur.

Group Aggression

Because it superficially resembles human patterns of fighting, chimpanzee and bonobo incidents of intergroup fighting have received a great deal of attention in the popular press (see, e.g., Wrangham and Peterson 1996). Among common chimpanzee populations, researchers have reported incidents of intercommunity conflict that end with some deaths. "Border patrols," or groups of males circulating around the community's geographic perimeters, have been seen in most populations. Occasionally, when these groups encounter individuals from another community, they attack as a mob, sometimes resulting in the death of the attacked individual(s) (Stumpf 2011). But the pattern of chimpanzee and bonobos patrolling their perimeters seems quite different from the broader patterns of aggression and violence found in many human communities, and violent incidents seem much less significant among both *Pan* species than in our own.

Social Traditions and Using Tools

In the 1950s and 1960s tool use was thought to be a hallmark of humanity (see, e.g., Oakley 1958), but we now know that many organisms use objects aside from their limbs or mouths to get food. Both chimpanzee species exhibit a wide variety of tool modification and use. They use stone hammers and anvils for cracking nuts, carefully selected sticks and blades of grass for extracting termites from mounds, pointed sticks (like spears) for stabbing and catching small mammals, and forked branches for skimming moss off the top of ponds. Although all chimpanzee and bonobo populations use tools, different groups have different ways of using similar tools, and some don't use certain tools at all. Both male and female chimpanzees use tools, but females appear to be the more prolific tool users. Tool use is a learned behavior that, in some cases, takes years to acquire (Figure 7.13).

So How Do They Compare with Us?

Being a human, you already have a pretty good sense of our general behavior patterns. As you read about the lives of these other primates, it is possible that you began to identify some of the ways our behaviors are similar to or different from theirs. But now let's get more systematic about the comparison.

First, consider macaques. Humans and macaques do share some general characteristics, such as the existence of mixed groups of males and females, social interactions around kin relations, and widespread dispersal based on remarkable adaptability. Our dominance hierarchies have certain similarities, including how we establish and maintain them. Both of our species are able to survive in diverse habitats, which is rooted in our foraging and behavioral flexibility.

But there are critical differences as well. These differences include our body morphologies, how we move around through locomotion, the size of our brains, and, most notably, the scale and complexity

Figure 7.13   Tool Use Among Chimpanzees. Chimpanzee tool use is learned, not inborn. Here common chimpanzees who are using specially prepared twigs to fish for termites from a termite mound.

of social organization. There are also significant differences between male and female life patterns, which most human societies don't have, except in extreme cases.

Chimpanzees and bonobos present a more interesting, if more complicated, comparison. Obviously we have more in common with them than we do with macaques. One commonality is living in a community. The ways we divide into subgroups and the types of relationships between individuals in communities have elements of similarity.

Other behavioral patterns bear resemblance to our own. Male-to-male bonding in the context of aggression is one similarity, as is the social use of sex. Another is the hunting of meat and other foods among certain group members.

Sexual aggression, mate guarding, and aggression between communities might superficially seem like rape, marriage laws, and war in humans. But debate continues over whether human and chimpanzee social patterns are **analogous** (similar in appearance but not because of shared ancestry), **homologous** (similar because of a shared ancestry), or not comparable because they are totally distinct behaviors.

An important issue, as we noted earlier, is that the two chimpanzee species exhibit behavioral diversity, both within their species and between them, which muddies comparisons with humans. Furthermore, for more than six million years, humans and chimpanzees have been on different evolutionary paths, and the chimpanzee species and subspecies are more evolutionarily similar to one another than they any are to humans. More important, perhaps, is that humans have dispersed more widely, adapting to many more environments on the basis of adaptations that are not genetically rooted, but culturally mediated.

So what does this all add up to? Can we really understand what it means to be human by turning to primates, and what do we learn about ourselves when we do? The last section takes up these issues.

- **Analogous.** Similar in appearance or function, not the same due to shared ancestry.

- **Homologous.** Similar due to shared ancestry.

• •

THINKING CRITICALLY ABOUT LIVING PRIMATES

Do you see advantages or limits in comparing monkeys, apes, and humans solely in terms of their behaviors? What are those advantages or limits?

• •

What Does Studying Monkeys and Apes Illustrate About Human Distinctiveness?

During the past few decades, claims about how humans and primates overlap in morphological, genetic, and especially behavioral terms have proliferated and become more refined. Putting these claims simply, primatologist Frans de Waal (2013:16) has observed, "Just like us, monkeys and apes strive for power, enjoy sex, want security and affection, kill over territory, and value trust and cooperation." Certain apes, like gorillas and chimpanzees, can recognize themselves in mirrors, use sign language to create new words (see Chapter 5 on language), and use sophisticated problem-solving skills to escape enclosures.

Where does this leave us in terms of understanding human distinctiveness? The different natural and social scientific disciplines that conduct primatological studies are likely to answer this question somewhat differently, resulting from distinct theoretical and methodological trajectories. Most anthropologists would argue that this is not simply a descriptive problem, that is, it is not just a matter of simply listing the behavioral characteristics of primates and humans and checking off those that appear similar and crossing off others that do not. Rather, it is necessary to take a holistic and comparative approach that brings biological *and* anthropological data and theories into synergistic communication with each other. As we explore in "Classic Contributions: Sherwood Washburn and the New (Integrative) Physical Anthropology," Washburn signaled the importance of an integrative approach decades ago.

Primate Social Organization and Human Behavior

What does the integration of biology and anthropology tell us about human distinctiveness vis-à-vis monkeys and apes? In general terms it links our distinctiveness to the characteristics of the social behaviors and organization we have developed. Most of human evolutionary history has involved humans living in small groups of mostly genetically related individuals, cooperating together in foraging, defense, and raising the young. Some two million years ago or so, these early humans began moving out of Africa and encountered new environmental challenges. To meet those challenges, those humans relied on tools and basic forms of social cooperation and alliances (a theme discussed in more detail in Chapter 8).

When anatomically modern *Homo sapiens* appears, social behavior changes quite radically. Human social groups grow and tend to become more sedentary (staying in the same place). They also seem to develop divisions of labor within the group and create new social roles. Sometime between 20,000 to 40,000 years ago, permanent settlements appear. The practice of agriculture enables population growth and environments begin to change and cultural differences between groups grows (see Chapters 12 and 13).

What this all says is that, when compared with other primates, humans have certain unique qualities. We live in groups of mixed adult males and females, organizing ourselves into subgroups and a division of labor. Although much depends on demographic factors and cultural specificities, both males and females tend to stay with their birth groups. Most of us (but not all) live in permanent settlements, eating both plant and animal food, much of which we now grow or raise. Our bonds, both moral and social, with kin are strong, but we can also develop deep relationships with non-kin. These bonds are sometimes about mating, but often not. Because of culture, there is great variation in our mating patterns, but in general we will mate with multiple individuals through our lives, and choice can play a big role in that decision. Although certain elements of all this resemble what we see in primates, no single primate exhibits them all. There is also no primate species that mediates these relationships and behaviors so thoroughly through culture.

We Have Culture. Do They Too?

During the past several decades, the idea that non-human primates have "culture" has become more popular. Certain macaques, and especially gorillas, orangutans, and chimpanzees do exhibit patterns of behavioral variation across groups, based on specific behaviors that are shared, learned, and maintained on a group-by-group basis. Among chimpanzees, for example, primatologists have observed several dozen behavior patterns—from tool use to grooming and courtship practices—that are customary or habitual in a particular community but not others. These observations suggest that these behavioral patterns are not reducible either to genetic or to ecological factors (Whiten et al. 1999; Caldwell and Whiten 2011). If these particular behaviors observed in one community but not others are not driven either by genetics or by the local ecology, then could they be a simple form of culture?

CLASSIC CONTRIBUTIONS

Sherwood Washburn and the New (Integrative) Physical Anthropology

IN 1951 SHERWOOD WASHBURN, then at the University of Chicago and later at the University of California at Berkeley, published a short but visionary article entitled "The New Physical Anthropology." In it he set forth a view that began integrating primatology and anthropology, clarifying the core role of evolutionary theory for anthropology generally at a time when the modern synthesis was generating excitement. Washburn's primary goal in this essay was to move physical anthropology away from the purely descriptive approaches and measurements of individual anatomical traits (such as skull features) that characterized the field from the mid-1800s though the mid-1900s. He realized that integrating evolutionary theory and the study of primates with the (then) new theory and practice of genetics would create an entirely new framework for physical anthropology. Washburn saw the value of integrating these different perspectives and envisioning humans (and other primates) as both the products of an evolutionary history and as currently evolving beings. In this excerpt from his conclusion, he emphasizes the fundamentally integrative motivations of the new physical anthropology.

Sherwood Washburn.

The purpose of this paper has been to call attention to the changes which are taking place in physical anthropology. Under the influence of modern genetic theory, the field is changing from the form it assumed in the latter part of the nineteenth century into a part of modern science. The change is essentially one of emphasis. If traditional physical anthropology was 80 per cent measurement and 20 per cent concerned with heredity, process, and anatomy, in the new physical anthropology the proportions may be approximately reversed. I have stressed the impact of genetics on anthropology, but the process need not be all one way. If the form of the human face can be thoroughly analyzed, this will open the way to the understanding of its development and the interpretation of abnormalities and malocclusion, and may lead to advances in genetics, anatomy, and medicine. Although evolution is fascinating in itself, the understanding of the functional anatomy which may be gained from it is of more than philosophical importance. The kind of systemic anatomy in which bones, muscles, ligaments, etc. are treated separately became obsolete with the publication of the "Origin of Species" in 1859. The anatomy of life, of integrated function, does not know the artificial boundaries which still govern the dissection of a corpse. The new physical anthropology has much to offer to anyone interested in the structure or evolution of man, but this is only the beginning. To build it, we must collaborate with social scientists, geneticists, anatomists, and paleontologists. We need new ideas, new methods, and new workers. There is nothing new we do today that will not be done better tomorrow. [Washburn 1951:303–304]

Questions for Reflection

1. What are the different intellectual threads that Washburn is saying need to be integrated?

2. Washburn refers to the "integrated function" involved in the "anatomy of life." What do you think he means, and how will the new physical anthropology study it?

The use of the term "culture" to describe these behavior patterns has been controversial, not unexpectedly among social and humanistic scholars, but also among scientists who study other non-primate animals. Part of the problem is an empirical one, which is whether there is enough reliable data, or data of the right kind, to declare that non-human primates have culture. What is the threshold to decide that enough behaviors are "cultural" to declare that the species as a whole exhibits culture?

Another problem has been the tendency to reduce culture to socially transmitted learning. Such learning is not unique to primates; Norway rats and Japanese quail (among others) also exhibit social learning (Grant 2007). Primatologists have countered that in those species social learning relates to only single behaviors, while in chimpanzees and bonobos, the social transmission of behaviors is more complex and extensive. Of course, given their brain sizes relative to these other animals, it should be not surprising that chimpanzee social learning is more extensive.

But from an anthropological perspective, reducing culture to the social transmission of behaviors and variation across groups involves a vast oversimplification of how much language and symbolic abstraction lie at the heart of what culture is and how it works, a theme we explored in Chapters 2 and 5. Symbolization, personification, metaphorization, abstraction, all of these things are mediated through culture and provide humans with a capacity not simply to interact with actual worlds but to imagine and then construct other worlds, or for that matter, hold two competing thoughts simultaneously. The fact that humans do these things with such diversity across cultures suggests that studying behavior alone is not sufficient to understand culture; we also need to understand and interpret how people think and how those thoughts inform and guide their actions. The tremendous variability and flexibility of ways of thinking and living across our species as documented by sociocultural anthropologists calls into question whether there is a universal human or human behavior against which we can compare any other primate (Haraway 1989).

None of this is meant to deny that non-human primates like chimpanzees exhibit remarkable behavioral flexibility and plasticity, or that they can use a version of human sign language in limited ways, both which are rooted in cognitive and social complexity relative to other primates and mammals. But anthropologists insist that culture and language enable humans to communicate content not accessible to other organisms and, combined with our use of symbolic representation, allows us to acquire, manipulate, and disseminate knowledge—and alter our environments—more extensively than any primate species.

The evolutionary changes that define us as human arose over time and continue to arise. So watching a chimpanzee or a macaque can tell us a great deal about what it takes to be a successful chimpanzee or macaque, but rather little about what it means to be a human. In the same way, watching humans can tell us rather little about being a macaque or chimpanzee. Quite simply, all three primates have distinct bodies and minds that are the result of separate evolutionary trajectories.

THINKING CRITICALLY ABOUT LIVING PRIMATES

If, as anthropologists argue, "culture" is ultimately not applicable to describing non-human primate behaviors, are there other terms you could think of that might work, such as "tradition?" What would be the advantages and disadvantages of the other term(s)?

Conclusion

Humans are primates. Understanding what we have in common with the other living primate species provides an important comparative baseline for understanding ourselves and what we have inherited biologically as a species. As we explored in this chapter, there are certain primate-wide physical trends—excellent vision, grasping hands, relatively large brains, for example—as well behavioral trends, including caregiver–infant bonds, grooming, dominance hierarchies, dispersal patterns, and conflict and cooperation. Using the information generated by studying non-human primates, anthropology is in a better position to reconstruct aspects of human evolution, to better understand what is general to primates, what is restricted to a few kinds of primates and humans, and what is uniquely human.

But anthropology's interest in primates does not stop there. We are also interested in the interface between primates and humans. In the interdisciplinary spirit of integration Washburn had once called for framing a "new physical anthropology," ethnoprimatologists, for example, draw on ethnographic and primatological research methods to better understand these interfaces. As the movement of Ebola viruses between and among West African human and ape populations demonstrates, understanding those interfaces has important practical and public health dimensions.

The findings of biological anthropology tell us that as compelling as it may be to look at primates and want to see reflections of ourselves, no other primate is a perfect model for human evolution because even our closest relatives, the chimpanzees, have experienced millions of years of separate evolution. Humans are similar to other primates in a number of ways, yet specific aspects of our evolutionary history have resulted in a distinct trajectory of biocultural adaptation. In the next chapter, we begin telling that story of human evolution in more detail.

KEY TERMS

Affiliation   p. 177

Altruism   p. 180

Analogous   p. 188

Anthropoid   p. 171

Arboreal   p. 171

Behavioral ecology   p. 179

Costs and benefits   p. 180

Dispersal   p. 179

Dominance hierarchy   p. 178

Ethnoprimatology   p. 176

Grooming   p. 177

Haplorrhini   p. 170

Hominine   p. 171

Hominoid   p. 171

Homologous   p. 188

Kin selection   p. 180

Macaca   p. 183

Matrifocal unit   p. 183

Nocturnal   p. 171

Pan   p. 184

Prehensile   p. 172

Sexual dimorphism   p. 178

Strategy   p. 180

Strepsirrhini   p. 170

Terrestrial   p. 172

Reviewing the Chapter

Chapter Section	What We Know	To Be Resolved
What does it mean to be a primate, and why does it matter to anthropology?	Primates are social animals with excellent stereoscopic vision, grasping hands, and relatively large brains. The two suborders of primates—the Strepsirrhini and Haplorrhini—differ from each other in relative body and brain-to-body sizes, and greater relative emphasis on smell or vision.	Anthropologists have long approached the study of living primates as a window into the evolution of our species, but new areas like ethnoprimatology, which studies the human–primate interface, have created promising new research directions that integrate primatological and sociocultural perspectives.
What are the basic patterns of primate behavioral diversity, and how did they develop?	All primates share certain common behavior patterns, including mother–infant bonding, affiliation and grooming, dominance hierarchies, dispersal, and cooperation and conflict. From those basic patterns, differences in behavior have probably emerged in response to certain socioecological pressures and the energetic costs and benefits of a behavior.	Cost-benefit analyses within behavioral ecology have been dominant for several decades, but they can oversimplify the complexity of behavior. More nuanced approaches are emerging that seek to understand the complicated relationship between the potential for a behavior and its actual performance.
How do behavior patterns among monkeys and apes compare with humans?	A comparison between macaques, chimpanzees, and humans can identify certain general commonalities between humans and macaques, and a more specific set of commonalities between humans and chimpanzees.	Primatologists and anthropologists continue to debate whether human and chimpanzee behaviors are analogous (similar in appearance or function, but independent of shared ancestry) or homologous (similar because of shared ancestry).
What does studying monkeys and apes illustrate about human uniqueness?	The uniqueness of humans vis-à-vis other primates has to do with the relative complexity, flexibility, and variability of our social behaviors and relationships, as well as the formation and expression of human thought and action through language and culture.	The debate over primate "culture" has not been resolved, and it seems likely to continue as more primatological experiments and field studies are conducted on the subject.

Readings

The book *Primates in Perspective*, 2nd ed. (New York: Oxford University Press, 2011) edited by a team of top primate researchers (Campbell et al.) provides a comprehensive overview of all areas of contemporary primatology.

• • • • • • • • • • • • • • • • • • • •

A useful and readable introduction to primatological methodology is Karen B. Strier's recent book *Primate Ethnographies* (Boston: Pearson, 2014) which has short essays by prominent anthropologists and primatologists reflecting on their research on monkeys and apes.

• • • • • • • • • • • • • • • • • • • •

Although now somewhat dated, Noel Rowe's book *The Pictorial Guide to the Living Primates* (East Hampton, NY: Pogonias Press, 1996) is very accessible, with many color photographs and basic information on the behavioral patterns of individual primate species. Recognizing that his book is out of date, Rowe has initiated a website called All the World's Primates (http://www.alltheworldsprimates.org/Home.aspx), which is a comprehensive—and updated—resource on primate information.

• • • • • • • • • • • • • • • • • • • •

Frans de Waal is one of the most recognizable names in primatology, and his book *The Ape and The Sushi Master: Cultural Reflections of a Primatologist* (New York: Basic Books, 2001) explores his perspectives on primate "culture."

• • • • • • • • • • • • • • • • • • • •

Ancestral Humans

Understanding the Human Family Tree

In 2008, a nine-year-old boy named Matthew Berger was chasing his dog in the Malapa Nature Reserve, north of Johannesburg, South Africa, and he found a fossilized bone. Malapa is a U.N.–designated World Heritage Site known as "The Cradle of Humankind" because of the many discoveries of ancient fossils that have been made in its dolomite limestone sediments since the 1930s. Matthew showed the fossil to his father, Lee Berger, an American paleoanthropologist who was working nearby on an excavation. The senior Berger realized it was a human-like clavicle, or collarbone, and further inspection uncovered a mandible, or jaw, with a canine tooth.

During subsequent excavations, Berger and fellow researchers from the Institute of Human Evolution at the University of the Witwatersrand in Johannesburg uncovered the rest of that skeleton, which proved to be a boy, and discovered several other mostly complete adult and infant skeletons. In 2010, they announced that these individuals were members of a new previously unknown species of early human ancestors, *Australopithecus sediba* (Berger et. al. 2010). Sediba means "fountain" or "wellspring" in the language of the Sesotho people who live in the area, and refers to the location where Berger and his colleagues found the bulk of the skeletal remains, at the bottom of a pit that was once a deep wellspring into

Excavating *Australopithecus sediba*. Since the initial find of a clavicle in 2008, several thousand fossilized specimens of this new species have been found. These finds represent exciting new possibilities for understanding human ancestors and have added a new branch to the family tree.

195

which these creatures probably fell, drowned, and were quickly covered with sediment.

But the findings would not stop there. In 2013, Berger organized a National Geographic Society–sponsored expedition at the Rising Star cave system near where these initial discoveries were made, which brought international researchers and amateur cave explorers to the site. Covering their work in real time using social media like Twitter, Facebook, and blog updates, they uncovered thousands of new fossils. Among them were numerous similarly intact individuals that exhibited important differences from *A. sediba*. In 2015 Berger and his team announced that these individuals were members of yet another previously unknown ancestral species, which they named *Homo naledi*, "naledi" referring to a chamber in the cave where they found the remains.

Many details remain ambiguous about these early human ancestors, including their geographic range and their relationship with each other. But they both exhibit a mix of physical traits with similarities to *Australopithecus* and *Homo*, two genera of known human ancestors. *A. sediba* lived some 1.7 to 1.9 million years ago, and like other members of its genus had ape-like qualities and were at least partly arboreal, but like members of the genus *Homo*, they also had the ability to walk upright and had human-like hands (Balter 2010). *H. naledi*, which has not yet been dated, had similar human-like hands but a distinct skull shape and was probably more of a full-time walker, similar to other early members of the genus *Homo*. Although the taxonomic order of each is not settled, the significance of these finds is that they both represent new branches in our family tree, affecting understanding of our past.

Because of the scarcity of fossils, much less such complete ones, identifying a new species of early human ancestors is rare for **paleoanthropologists**, those physical anthropologists and archaeologists who study the fossilized remains of ancient primates and humans to understand their biological and behavioral evolution. But these are exciting times for paleoanthropology. Thanks in part to discoveries like those in Malapa and improved field excavation techniques, our understanding of ancestral humans and our family tree has been growing by leaps and bounds in recent years (Zimmer 2015). Advancements in genomic science and technology, including the use of DNA evidence recovered from fossils in the lab, have also had a major influence on the field (Hawks 2013). Recently such technology was a key element in the discovery of a new group of 40,000-year-old humans called the Denisovans, as well as the announcement in 2013 that a transnational scientific initiative called the Neanderthal Genome Project had completed mapping the **genome** (the complete set of an organism's DNA) of the Neanderthals. One momentous discovery in all this is that modern humans share a small amount of genetic ancestry with Neanderthals and Denisovans, pointing to some level, perhaps, of interbreeding.

At the heart of anthropology's interest in our human ancestors is a key question: *When, where, and how did our human ancestors emerge, and under what*

• **Paleoanthropologists.** Physical anthropologists and archaeologists who study the fossilized remains of ancient hominids to shed light on their biological and behavioral evolution.

• **Genome.** The complete set of an organism's DNA.

conditions did modern humans evolve? Embedded within this larger question are a number of more focused problems around which this chapter is organized:

Who are our earliest possible ancestors?

What does walking on two legs and having big brains mean for us?

Who were the first humans and where did they live?

How do we know if the first humans were cultural beings, and what role did culture play in their evolution?

In this chapter we meet our immediate evolutionary family. The fossil record shows that the genus to which we belong, *Homo*, emerged some two million years ago and began to diversify between 1.8 million and 300,000 years ago, exhibiting a growing "humanness" in our ancestors. Although many details and connections between ancestral humans remain fuzzy, the story of ancestral humans shows the growing role of culture in shaping our evolution, making us what we are today. We begin with a look at what is known about our very earliest ancestors.

Who Are Our Earliest Possible Ancestors?

In order to answer this question, it is necessary to address two issues: our evolutionary relationship to the other apes, and how that relationship affects how we view and name certain fossils found from six to one million years ago (**mya**). In other words, we have to figure out where humans sit in the family tree of the apes. The current view is that we are hominins, a small branch that is part of the large African branch that includes the gorilla and the chimpanzee.

Our Earliest Ancestors Were Hominins

Current knowledge of both morphological (e.g., structural) and molecular (genetic) relationships among the living apes and humans indicates that chimpanzees, gorillas, and humans are actually more similar to one another—and thus more closely related—than any of them is to the orangutan (Begun 1999; Wood 2010). This knowledge affects how paleoanthropologists reconstruct the evolutionary trajectory of our early human ancestors.

All great apes and humans are placed together in the family **Hominidae**. Within the Hominidae, chimpanzees, gorillas, and humans belong in the subfamily **Homininae** (an African-derived branch of Hominidae), and orangutans are placed by themselves as the subfamily **Ponginae** (an Asian-derived branch of Hominidae). See this illustrated in Figure 8.1. The distinction between the hominines, or chimpanzees, gorillas, and humans, is placed at the taxonomic level below subfamily and just above genus. Humans and our direct human ancestors are then classed as representatives of the tribe **Hominini** and referred to as hominins. In this classification, all

- **mya.** Million years ago.

- **Hominidae.** A family of primates that includes the Hominids, namely humans and their ancestors.

- **Homininae.** The African subfamily of the Family Hominidae, which includes humans, chimpanzees, and gorillas.

- **Ponginae.** The Asian derived subfamily of Hominidae to which the Orangutan belongs.

- **Hominini.** The tribe to which humans and our direct human ancestors belong, who are referred to as hominins.

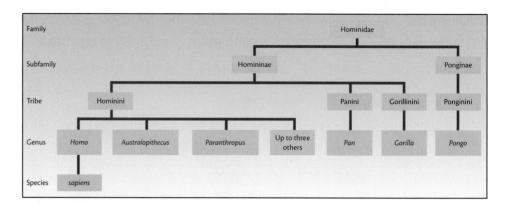

Figure 8.1   The Family Hominidae.   In this classification, great apes and humans are placed in the same family.

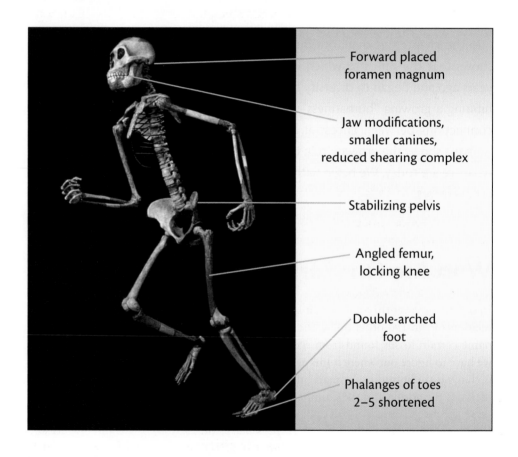

Forward placed foramen magnum

Jaw modifications, smaller canines, reduced shearing complex

Stabilizing pelvis

Angled femur, locking knee

Double-arched foot

Phalanges of toes 2–5 shortened

Figure 8.2   General Characteristics of Hominins. Hominins have various modifications in the skull, pelvis, legs, and feet that support bipedalism, as well as modifications to their jaws and teeth that differentiate them from their evolutionary relatives.

hominins are hominines, but the reverse is not true: only some hominines are hominins, these being modern humans and our direct lineage.

The hominins share in common several unique traits (Figure 8.2). These include:

- modifications in the lower body, the upper arms, and the backbone that make them capable of **bipedal locomotion** (walking on two legs)
- smaller canine teeth than other members of the Hominidae family
- a forward-placed **foramen magnum,** the hole in the base of the skull where the spinal cord enters, which supports bipedalism.
- a reduced **Canine/Premolar-3 shearing complex,** in which the lower first premolar tooth rubs against the upper canine as the mouth closes, which sharpens or flattens the tooth

Thus, you the reader and we the authors are hominins, and the fossils that show many or all these traits are considered hominin as well.

- **Bipedal locomotion.** The use of two legs rather than four for movement.

- **Foramen magnum.** The opening at the base of the skull (cranium) where the spinal column enters and connects to the brain.

The Fossil Record of Hominins in Africa

Fossil evidence of ancestral hominins comes from Africa. During the end of the Miocene epoch (22 to 5.3 mya), we find primitive hominin-like primates emerging in East Africa, with a few in the Mediterranean region near North Africa. This pattern suggests that the transition by one or more very old hominoid lineages toward a hominin form took place in these two areas (Benefit and McCrossin 1995). Three of the most important fossils are summarized in The Evolution of Humans 8.1 (see pp. 200–201). Debate persists whether these fossils are undoubtedly hominin. One of the reasons is that when paleoanthropologists study morphological differences in fossils, they often translate these differences into taxonomic designations. But it is not unusual among living ape species to exhibit peculiar anatomical quirks, which are simply normal variations within a species, and this sparks debate about whether morphological differences are as meaningful as they seem (Zimmer 2015). Indeed, this point is an important one to keep in mind as we examine all the examples of human ancestors, because it is not unique to these transitionary hominines but to later hominins as well.

The Three Hominin Genera

Numerous identifiable hominins emerged during the Pliocene epoch (5.3–2.5 mya) and the Pleistocene (2.5 mya to 11,500 years ago). The evolutionary relationships between these and earlier Miocene hominoids remain unclear. During the Pliocene, Africa collided with Europe, creating the Mediterranean Sea, and North America became linked to South America through the Isthmus of Panama. Though the Pleistocene didn't see such great continental movements, it did see significant periods of glaciation with cooling effects on global temperatures. The Plio-Pleistocene hominins are divided into three genera: *Australopithecus*, *Paranthropus*, and *Homo*. Numerous species of these genera overlapped in time, and in some cases geography, suggesting that there were multiple forms of coexisting hominins, and that the human family tree during this period was "bristling with new branches" (Zimmer 2015). Here we summarize the general characteristics of each genus and in The Evolution of Humans 8.2 (see pages 204–209) examine the individual species in more detail.

Genus Australopithecus

Of all the hominins, the genus *Australopithecus* ("Southern Ape," as many have been found in South Africa) has the longest presence in the fossil record, a span of over two million years. Originally discovered in the 1920s and found distributed widely throughout eastern and southern Africa, we have more information about these ancient hominins than we have about any other early hominin. Most researchers hypothesize that the human lineage emerged from the **australopithecines** (a word that refers to the genus *Australopithecus*).

Australopithecines were **gracile** (a paleoanthropological term referring to a slender build), between 1.2–1.4 m (3 ft. 11 in.–4 ft. 7 in.) tall, and exhibited a fairly high degree of sexual dimorphism, with males larger than females. Their relatively large brain sizes, while still only 35% of the brain size of modern humans, distinguish them from their primate ancestors. They also had a gripping hand. The discovery at several australopithecine fossil sites of stone flakes and mammalian bones with cut marks on them suggests that at least several members of this genus put their brain and hand power to processing food, perhaps as early as 3.3 million years ago (Balter 2014b).

Like their primate ancestors, their arm length suggests at least a partially arboreal existence, although they also had bipedal stature that allowed them to walk on two legs.

- **Canine/Premolar-3 shearing complex.** A condition in which the lower first premolar tooth is somewhat sharpened or flattened from rubbing against the upper canine as the mouth closes.

- **Australopithecines.** A word that refers to the genus *Australopithecus*.

- **Gracile.** A body of slender build.

The Evolution of Humans 8.1

The Late Miocene Transitionary Hominines, 7 to 4 MYA

Australopithecus (various)

MYA—> **7**   **6**   **5**   **4**   **3**

Sahelanthropus tchadensis

Orrorin tugenensis

Ardipithecus ramidus

Australopithecus afarensis ("Lucy")

KEY	= The Late Miocene Transitory Hominines, 7 to 4 MYA	= The Plio-Pleistocene Hominins, 4 to 1.8 MYA	= Homo erectus, Archaic humans, and Modern Homo sapiens 2.6 MYA–Present

	SPECIES	DISCOVERY	RANGE
1	***Sahelanthropus tchadensis*** Name means "Sahel man from Chad"	Discovered in Chad in 2001 by French-Chadian team led by Brunet (Brunet et al. 2002)	West-Central Africa
2	***Orrorin tugenensis*** "Orrorin" means "original man" in Tugen language of Kenya	Discovered in 2000 in Kenya by French team led by Senut and Pickford (Senut et al. 2001)	E. Africa
3	***Ardipithecus ramidus*** "Ramid" means "root" in Afar language of Ethiopia	Discovered in 1992 in Aramis site, Awash River, northern Ethiopia by Ethiopian team led by Y. Haile-Selassi (Haile-Selassie 2001)	E. Africa

1 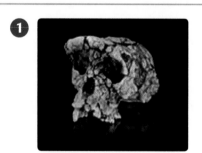   **2** 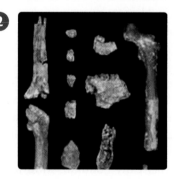   **3**

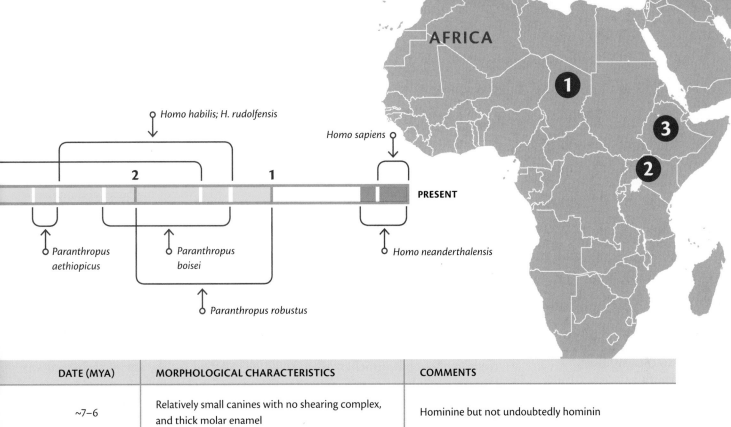

DATE (MYA)	MORPHOLOGICAL CHARACTERISTICS	COMMENTS
~7–6	Relatively small canines with no shearing complex, and thick molar enamel	Hominine but not undoubtedly hominin
~6	Thick molar enamel, small brain and prominent brow-ridges, small canine teeth, forward-placed foramen magnum	Hominine but not undoubtedly hominin
5.8–4.4	Thin molar enamel, relatively large canines, forward placed foramen magnum	Hominine but not undoubtedly hominin

We do not know how much time they lived on the ground or in trees, but fossilized bipedal footprints found in Tanzania—the famed Laetoli footprints (see Chapter 4)—have been attributed to one of the best known australopithecines, *Australopithecus afarensis.*

Genus Paranthropus

Between ~2.7 and 1 mya, we find a cluster of hominin fossils that differ in morphology from the australopithecines, primarily for their large chewing bones and muscle. There are three known species in this genus, *Paranthropus*, which means "beside" or "near" humans. Discovered originally in 1938 in South Africa and found in East Africa as well, paleoanthropologists have long debated whether these hominins were actually australopithecines or a different genus. The latest taxonomic orders split them because of important morphological differences.

Paranthropines had larger brains than the australopithecines. They had broad, "dish-shaped" faces, almost small foreheads, widely flared cheekbones, a pronounced **sagittal crest** (ridge in the center of the skull produced by chewing muscle attachment), and a forward jutting jaw. They exhibit **megadontia**, or larger postcanine teeth (molars and premolars) than would be expected for the size of their bodies. Given the grinding structure of their teeth and studies of their tooth enamel, it seems they may have relied more heavily on plant foods than australopithecines. Standing 1.3–1.4 m (4 ft. 3 in.–4 ft. 7 in.) tall, all three species were bipedal, and they probably lived in open woodland or savannah landscapes. They were almost certainly tool users.

Genus Homo

The genus *Homo* emerged out of one of the australopithecine lineages sometime between three and two million years ago. When Linnaeus originally designated the genus *Homo* in 1758, our own species *Homo sapiens* (wise ones) was the only species in the genus. As increasing numbers of hominin fossils have been found and studied during the past forty years, paleoanthropologists continue to add more species to the genus, as we saw in the introduction to this chapter. Most hominin fossils found in Africa and Asia dating to younger than about 1.8 mya are generally considered members of the genus. But disagreement persists about how many species they represent, even in some cases whether the earliest ones should be assigned to the genus *Homo* or the genus *Australopithecus* (Wood and Collard 1999).

To be placed definitively in the genus *Homo*, fossils must display certain characteristics, a primary one being large cranial capacity. Although the two species of *Homo* that appear early in the fossil record—*H. habilis* and *H. rudolfensis*—have brain cavities about half the size of a modern human, their brains are both relatively and absolutely larger than the brains of any of the *Paranthropus* species. Intriguingly, the part of the human brain associated with speech in modern humans appears to be present in one of the species, *H. habilis.* Early members of *Homo* were also competent bipeds, who probably lived in mixed savannah-woodlands landscapes. In addition, their fingers are slightly curved and strongly built, and their hands suggest the ability to use a precision grip, an important requirement for making tools. They made and used stone tools, called **Olduwan tools** (edged choppers named after their initial discovery in the Olduvai Gorge of Tanzania) (Figure 8.3).

Both species of early *Homo* display a mix of ancestral and derived (unique) characteristics, and these are expressed differently in each species. For example, *H. habilis* displays no sagittal crest, and has large incisors, smaller postcanine teeth, and a narrower tooth row than is seen in the australopithecines (Conroy 1997; McHenry and Coffing 2000). The face of *H. rudolfensis* is broad and flat, and the cranium has no

- **Sagittal crest.** A ridge running along the top of the cranium, usually representing increased bone area for the attachment of chewing muscles.

- **Megadontia.** The characteristic of having large molar teeth relative to body size.

- **Olduwan tools.** Rocks that were modified to produce sharp flakes and edged choppers.

Figure 8.3   Olduwan Tools. Named after Olduvai Gorge in Tanzania where this type of stone tool was discovered, Olduwan tools were made by striking the edge of a stone with a hammerstone, producing the kinds of hammering stones shown here, as well as sharp flakes useful for cutting food and other objects.

distinct brow ridge, but it does have a sagittal crest. The postcanine teeth exhibit megadontia and are absolutely larger than those of *H. habilis*, but because of the larger body size of *H. rudolfensis*, the premolars and molars are relatively smaller (McHenry and Coffing 2000).

Who Is Our Most Direct Ancestor?

To recap, our very earliest ancestors were bipedal hominins who lived in eastern and southern Africa by at least four million years ago and probably earlier. They did not yet have the big brain that characterizes modern humans, but what we do see aligns with what we would expect our early ancestors would look like. From this assortment of forms arise our direct ancestors.

But which one is most directly related to us? Is it the "missing link?"

The notion that there is a "missing link" out there awaiting discovery has long captured popular imagination, suggesting that once we identify that link a lot of uncertainties about our past will fall into place. Yet, while paleoanthropologists agree that we do have a common ancestor, deciding which one is a major challenge, if not impossible, because the fossil record is still so incomplete. Furthermore, evolutionary theory rejects the possibility of a "link" because that metaphor assumes a straight and linear series of relationships—a chain—which is not really how species evolve (Chapter 3). A missing link will thus never be found. What we have instead are many "missing links," and what paleoanthropologists are looking for are further linkages (evolutionary relationships) between the hominins we have identified.

We can be reasonably certain that by 2 mya our own lineage had arisen. Because the members of the genus *Australopithecus* mostly predate members of our own genus in eastern and southern Africa, and because of similarities in anatomy, our genus *Homo* probably emerged from *Australopithecus* lineage. Strong similarities in anatomy indicate that most, if not all, hominins from ~3 million years ago on are derived from the *A. afarensis* lineage. But dating issues with *A. africanus* as well as the existence and classification of *Kenyanthropus* and *A. deyiremeda* do pose some problems for seeing *A. afarensis* as our direct ancestor.

What about the genus *Paranthropus*? This group had slightly larger brains than earlier forms and seemed capable of making stone tools. But their massive chewing anatomy seems to be very specialized relative to more recent members of the genus *Homo*, making it unlikely that they are our ancestors. *Paranthropus* was perhaps a sister genus that coexisted with our own for almost 1.5 million years. They might have even competed for similar resources, and predators saw both genera, at least early on, as targets (Hart and Sussman 2005). If we could understand why *Homo* flourished as *Paranthropus* went extinct, we might gain a valuable insight into what it means to be human. A recent attempt to model this process emphasizes that *Homo* might have gained selective advantage over *Paranthropus* through increasingly complex patterns of cooperation and niche construction (Fuentes, Wyczalkowski, and MacKinnon 2010).

At the same time, we still do not know which of the early members of the genus *Homo* is our most direct ancestor. *Homo habilis* has the right head (smaller teeth and a large brain) but the wrong body (smaller body size, pelvic and limb anatomy, and the relatively flexible feet of the australopithecines). *Homo rudolfensis* has the wrong head (megadontia similar to *Paranthropus*, but relatively smaller teeth owing to its larger body size and an absolutely larger but relatively similar brain) but the right body, including pelvic anatomy more like that of later humans than that of the australopithecines.

The Evolution of Humans 8.2
The Plio-Pleistocene Hominins, 4 to 1.8 MYA

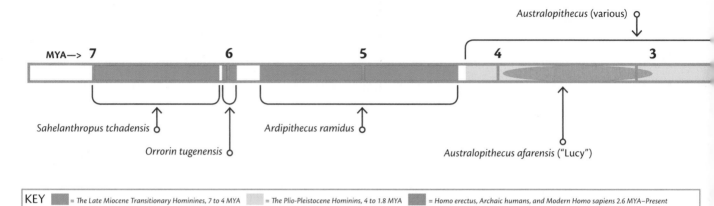

Australopithecus (various)

MYA—> 7   6   5   4   3

Sahelanthropus tchadensis

Orrorin tugenensis

Ardipithecus ramidus

Australopithecus afarensis ("Lucy")

| KEY | = The Late Miocene Transitionary Hominines, 7 to 4 MYA | = The Plio-Pleistocene Hominins, 4 to 1.8 MYA | = Homo erectus, Archaic humans, and Modern Homo sapiens 2.6 MYA–Present |

	SPECIES	DISCOVERY	RANGE
1	***Australopithecus anamensis*** "Anamensis" means "of the lake" in the Turkana language	Discovered in in 1995 near Lake Turkana in northern Kenya by team led by M. Leakey (Leakey et al. 1995, 1998; Ward, Leaky, and Walker 2001)	E. Africa
2	***Australopithecus afarensis*** "Afarensis" means "from Afar" (a region in Ethiopia)	Discovered in 1974 near Hadar, Ethiopia by American team led by T. Gray and D. Johanson. Some remains found as early as 1930 added to this species	E. Africa
3	***Australopithecus deyiremeda*** "Deyiremeda" means "close relative" in language of Afar people	Discovered in 2011 in Afar region of Ethiopia by an Ethiopian team led by Y. Haile-Selassie (Haile-Selassie et al. 2015)	E. Africa
4	***Australopithecus bahrelghazali*** "Bahrelghazali" refers to "Bar El Ghazal" (a region in Chad)	Discovered in 1995 in by M. Brunet	N. Central Africa

1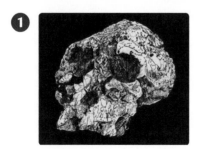

2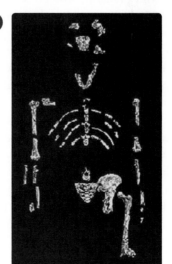

3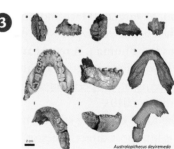

Australopithecus deyiremeda

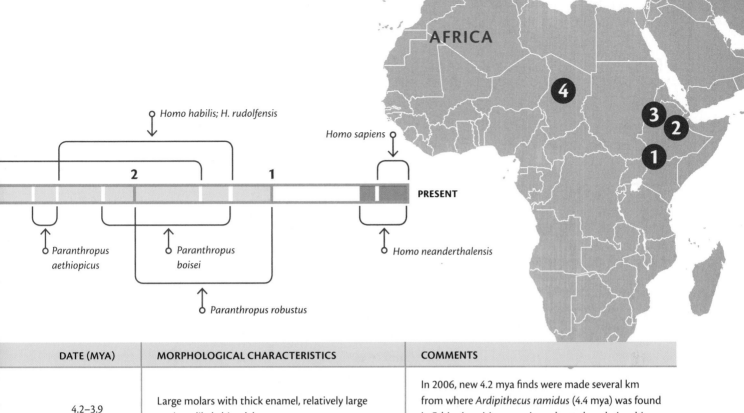

DATE (MYA)	MORPHOLOGICAL CHARACTERISTICS	COMMENTS
4.2–3.9	Large molars with thick enamel, relatively large canines, likely biped, long arms	In 2006, new 4.2 mya finds were made several km from where *Ardipithecus ramidus* (4.4 mya) was found in Ethiopia, raising questions about the relationships between them.
3.9–3.0	Large molars with thick enamel, relatively large canines, gracile, bipedal anatomy, long arms so probably partly arboreal	One of best known fossils (over 300 found in numerous sites). Team of D. Johanson discovered one in 1974 and nicknamed it "Lucy," after the Beatles song playing at the camp. Laetoli footprints in Tanzania attributed to *A. afarensis* (Conroy 1997; Stern 2000; Simpson 2002).
3.5–3.3	Similar in respects to *A. afarensis*, but its teeth are smaller, the cheekbones are more forward-facing, the lower jaw is larger, and some teeth have thicker outer enamel.	Possibly a descendent of *A. afarensis*, but fossil evidence is fragmentary and some have argued that it is not a new species at all but an illustration of diversity within *A. afarensis*.
3.3	No clear characteristic	Only a mandible fragment has been found. Some argue it may not be another species but member of *A. afarensis*.

The Evolution of Humans 8.2 *continued*

The Plio-Pleistocene Hominins, 4 to 1.8 MYA

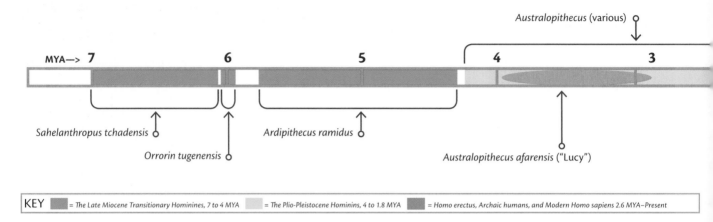

Australopithecus (various)

MYA—> **7**   **6**   **5**   **4**   **3**

Sahelanthropus tchadensis

Orrorin tugenensis

Ardipithecus ramidus

Australopithecus afarensis ("Lucy")

| KEY | ░ = *The Late Miocene Transitionary Hominines, 7 to 4 MYA* | ░ = *The Plio-Pleistocene Hominins, 4 to 1.8 MYA* | ░ = *Homo erectus, Archaic humans, and Modern Homo sapiens 2.6 MYA–Present* |

	SPECIES	DISCOVERY	RANGE
5	***Australopithecus (or Kenyanthropus) platyops*** "Platyops" means "flat faced" in Greek	Discovered in 1999 near Lake Turkana in Kenya by Justus Erus of M. Leakey's team (Leakey et al. 2001)	E. Africa
6	***Australopithecus africanus*** "Africanus" means "African" in Latin	Discovered in 1924 in Taung, near Kimberley, South Africa, by Australian anthropologist Raymond Dart	S. Africa
7	***Paranthropus aethiopicus*** "Aethiopicus" means "Ethiopian" in Greek	Species name proposed in 1960s by French team based on find in Ethiopia, but too little evidence until skull was discovered in 1985 in West Turkana in Kenya by Alan Walker	E. Africa
8	***Australopithecus garhi*** "Garhi" means "surprise" in Afar language	Discovered in 1995 in the Middle Awash of Ethiopia's Afar Depression by Ethiopian Berhane Asfaw and American Tim White (Asfaw et al. 1999)	E. Africa
9	***Paranthropus boisei*** "Boisei" honors Charles Boise who funded Louis Leakey's fossil	Discovered in 1959 in Olduvai Gorge in Tanzania by Kenyan team led by M. Leakey. Previous discoveries made in 1955 were assigned to this species.	E. Africa

5    **6** 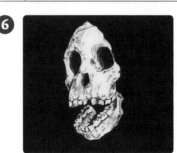   **7**

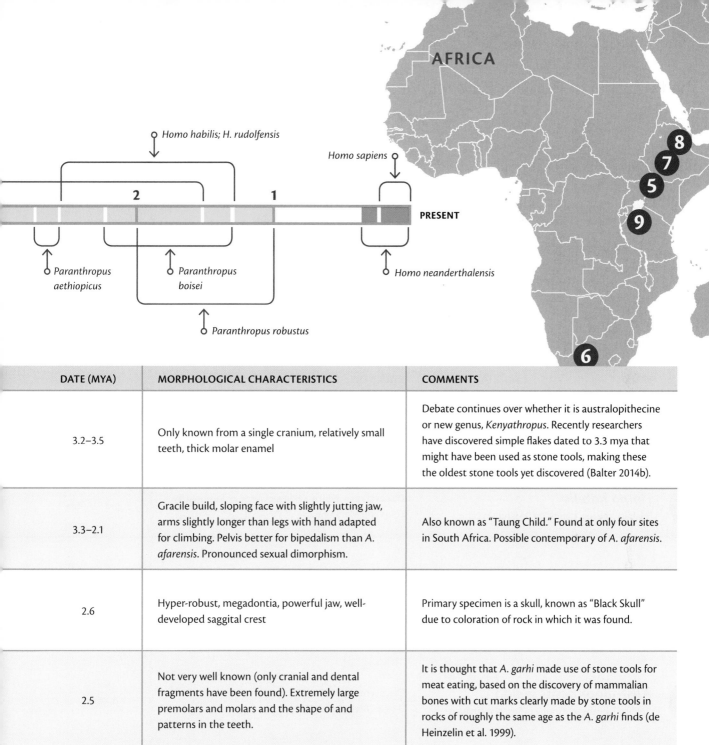

AFRICA

Homo habilis; H. rudolfensis

Homo sapiens

2   1   PRESENT

Paranthropus
aethiopicus

Paranthropus
boisei

Homo neanderthalensis

Paranthropus robustus

DATE (MYA)	MORPHOLOGICAL CHARACTERISTICS	COMMENTS
3.2–3.5	Only known from a single cranium, relatively small teeth, thick molar enamel	Debate continues over whether it is australopithecine or new genus, *Kenyathropus*. Recently researchers have discovered simple flakes dated to 3.3 mya that might have been used as stone tools, making these the oldest stone tools yet discovered (Balter 2014b).
3.3–2.1	Gracile build, sloping face with slightly jutting jaw, arms slightly longer than legs with hand adapted for climbing. Pelvis better for bipedalism than *A. afarensis*. Pronounced sexual dimorphism.	Also known as "Taung Child." Found at only four sites in South Africa. Possible contemporary of *A. afarensis*.
2.6	Hyper-robust, megadontia, powerful jaw, well-developed saggital crest	Primary specimen is a skull, known as "Black Skull" due to coloration of rock in which it was found.
2.5	Not very well known (only cranial and dental fragments have been found). Extremely large premolars and molars and the shape of and patterns in the teeth.	It is thought that *A. garhi* made use of stone tools for meat eating, based on the discovery of mammalian bones with cut marks clearly made by stone tools in rocks of roughly the same age as the *A. garhi* finds (de Heinzelin et al. 1999).
2.3–1.2	Robust, canines that appear like incisors. Sometimes known as "Nutcracker Man" due to flattest cheek teeth and thickest tooth enamel among hominins. Pronounced sexual dimorphism.	One of the best known early hominins. Probably made some very rudimentary stone tools, which were found in the same area.

The Evolution of Humans 8.2 *continued*
The Plio-Pleistocene Hominins, 4 to 1.8 MYA

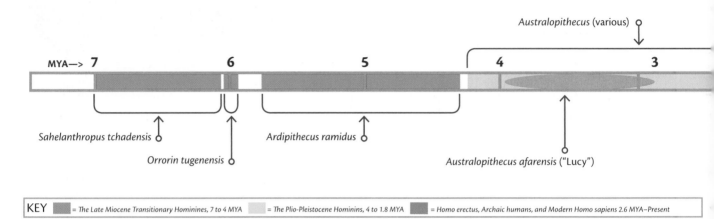

Australopithecus (various)

MYA—> 7 6 5 4 3

Sahelanthropus tchadensis

Orrorin tugenensis

Ardipithecus ramidus

Australopithecus afarensis ("Lucy")

KEY | = The Late Miocene Transitionary Hominines, 7 to 4 MYA | = The Plio-Pleistocene Hominins, 4 to 1.8 MYA | = Homo erectus, Archaic humans, and Modern Homo sapiens 2.6 MYA–Present

	SPECIES	DISCOVERY	RANGE
10	***Paranthropus robustus*** "Robustus" means "strongly built" in Latin	Discovered in 1938 in Kromdraai in South Africa by Scottish doctor Robert Broom	S. Africa
11	***Homo habilis*** "Habilis" means "handy" or "skillful" in Latin	Discovered in 1960 in Olduvai Gorge in Tanzania by Louis and Mary Leakey	E. and S. Africa
12	***Homo rudolfensis*** "Rudolf" refers to Lake Rudolf	Discovered in 1986 near Lake Rudolf (now known as Lake Turkana) in northern Kenya by Louis Leakey	E. Africa
13	***Australopithecus sediba*** "Sediba" means wellspring in Sesotho language	Discovered in 2008 in Malapa, South Africa, by Lee Berger (Berger et al. 2010).	S. Africa
14	***Homo naledi***	Discovered in 2013 in Rising Star cave system by amateur cavers working with Lee Berger	S. Africa

10

11

12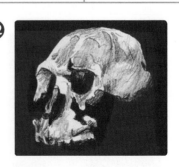

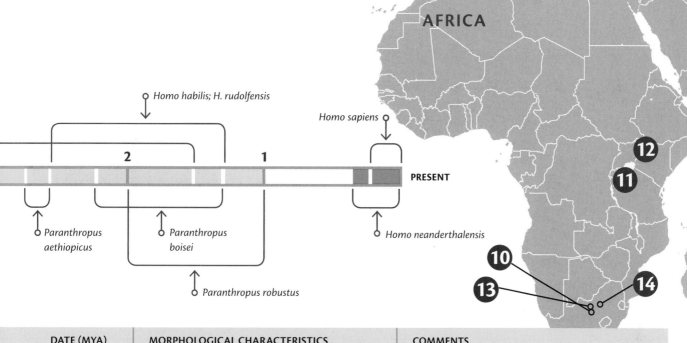

AFRICA

PRESENT

Homo habilis; H. rudolfensis

Homo sapiens

2

1

Paranthropus aethiopicus

Paranthropus boisei

Homo neanderthalensis

Paranthropus robustus

DATE (MYA)	MORPHOLOGICAL CHARACTERISTICS	COMMENTS
2–1	Robust, fairly large brain, large chewing muscles, large molars. Arms were longer than the legs, but feet and hands displayed remarkable similarities to those of later hominins.	Given its precision gripping hands, it may have been a tool user. Some bone tools have been found at *P. robustus* sites.
2.4–1.4	Large incisors, larger brain than australopithecines and paranthropines, moderately prognathic face, gripping hand for tool use	Was long considered to be first hominin to use tools, though recent evidence suggests hominin tool use was earlier.
2.4–1.6	Larger than *H. habilis* in body size, brain case, and molars, as well as a longer face	The majority of *H. rudolfensis* material comes from about twelve fossils, with very little postcranial material, and researchers are still debating whether the postcranial material that does exist belongs to this species or to *Paranthropus* (Wood and Collard 1999; McHenry and Coffing 2000).
1.9–1.7	Larger cranial capacity than other australopithecines, similar to *Homo* in tooth and jaw size, grasping hand suggests possible tool use, longer arms suggest partly arboreal existence, bipedal capacity	Example of mosaic evolution, having characteristics of both *Australopithecus* and *Homo*.
No date yet	Human-like hands and feet. A small brain case more similar to *Australopithecus*.	At least fifteen individuals were found. Most experts contend more analysis is needed at this point to determine their classification.

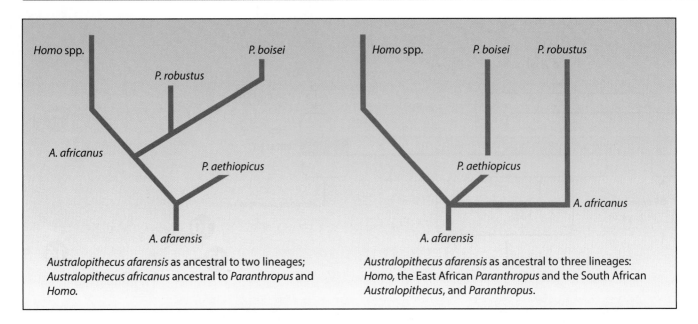

Figure 8.4   Possible Hominin Phylogenies.   Traditional phylogenies propose linear relationships between early hominin and modern *Homo sapiens*, but not enough information is available to support such details about our ancestry.

A Possible Phylogeny, with Caveats

Given the present fossil evidence, we have no completely right answers about the specific relationships among early hominins, though we do have proposals for several possible phylogenies, some supported by more evidence than others. But we still do not know how many early species existed prior to 3 mya or how these several early species are related to later ones. Figure 8.4 illustrates two possible phylogenies.

As the fossil record grows, some of these phylogenetic ambiguities may clear up. In the meantime, we can focus on what two defining features of our lineage—bipedalism and big brains—mean for hominin evolution.

THINKING CRITICALLY ABOUT ANCESTRAL HUMANS

The current picture of our family tree suggests that multiple hominins of the different genera—*Australopithecus*, *Paranthropus*, and *Homo*—had periods of overlap in their existence, but only one genus exists today. In evolutionary terms, what are the different possible things that could have happened to the others?

What Did Walking on Two Legs and Having Big Brains Mean for the Early Hominins?

Bipedalism is a major component of being human. It is one of the determining traits of the hominins and is directly linked with our emergence and our separation from the apes. Increased brain size is also significant as it has enabled us to acquire a degree of social complexity and tool use not seen in other apes. In this section, we explore why and how these changes occurred and their consequential effects on the evolution and behavior of early hominins.

The Benefits of Upright Movement

Most of the australopithecines and *Homo habilis* have longer arms than would be expected for a biped. This feature would have allowed these forms to move through the trees as well as bipedally on the ground. But there is a difference between a bipedal-*allowing* anatomy that still enables the use of four limbs for movement and climbing and a bipedal-*enforcing* anatomy, as modern humans have. The big question is why this shift took place, in other words, how and why did full-time bipedalism evolve? The latest thinking is that bipedalism is a consequence of multiple, independent selections that have some relation to the following points paleoanthropologists have considered (modified from Fuentes 2006):

- *It aids carrying objects.* Because it frees the arms, objects like food, tools, and infants can be carried, although these benefits would only be realized after bipedalism evolved. So it can't be the reason it arose.
- *It benefits hunting.* It is efficient for long-distance locomotion and enables weapon carrying. Unfortunately, the archaeological evidence for hunting comes later than the development of bipedalism.
- *It favors upright reaching.* Changes in the upper and lower body enabling bipedalism enhanced the ability to reach for hanging fruit and plants. But erect posture benefits both arboreal or terrestrial forms, so again, it doesn't explain why it arose.
- *It aids vigilance and visual surveillance.* The ability to stand on two legs gives a better view of potential predators, especially in savannas where early hominins lived. Because it aids predator avoidance, natural selection might be at work.
- *It aids long-distance walking and running.* Although early hominins didn't move bipedally as effectively or efficiently as we do, it would nevertheless have made the search for food or mates over large areas easier. In "Anthropologist as Problem Solver: Were We Born to Run?" we explore the relationship between walking, running, and evolution further.
- *It aids heat regulation.* It minimizes the amount of skin exposed to the sun and it could increase heat loss, especially in the challenging sunlight conditions of open savannas. However, the earliest hominins appear to have lived in forested or mixed forest-savanna settings, so it doesn't explain why it arose.

By itself no single explanation is entirely satisfactory, probably because, as we explained in Chapter 3, evolutionary processes have overlapping dimensions and complex effects on any species. Whatever the case, what we do know is that as the end of the Pliocene and the beginning of the Pleistocene epoch approached, hominins became progressively better at walking on two legs.

The Effects of Big Brains on Early Hominin Behavior

The growth of cranial capacity in hominins over several million years gave it greater brain power. But big brains require a lot of energy (upward of 20% of the entire energy intake in modern humans), so the metabolic costs (in calories) for keeping the body operating also increased. If this began with *H. habilis* and *H. rudolfensis*, we would expect to see dietary changes toward more energy-dense foods. All the species

Anthropologist as Problem Solver

Were We "Born to Run?"

If you haven't caught on to the "barefoot running" craze in recent years, it could be that you are not one of the estimated 65 million Americans who jog at least once a year. If you are a serious runner, perhaps you have even tried it out. This fad took off after the publication of the popular 2011 book *Born to Run*, by journalist and endurance runner Christopher McDougall. In the book he describes what seem like superhuman feats of long-distance endurance running involving hundreds of miles by Mexican Tarahumara Indians. Incredibly, the Tarahumara run barefoot or with simple leather sandals, report few injuries, and run throughout their lives into old age (McDougall 2011). These facts do not seem to square with the constant reports of chronic pain and injuries in the knees, hamstrings, heels, and feet of American runners, who run many fewer miles.

The book draws on the research of paleoanthropologist Daniel Lieberman at Harvard and his colleague biologist Dennis Bramble from the University of Utah to argue that thanks to our evolutionary history, humans are natural endurance runners. Their research suggests that adaptations for endurance running are derived capabilities of our genus that originated about two million years ago (Bramble and Lieberman 2004). Among these evolutionary adaptations are skeletal and muscular changes that differ from the requirements of walking, especially those that allow for greater spring, reduce the impact of running on the joints, and provide stability. These adaptations include the arch of the foot and our big knee joints; the development of spring-like tendons in the legs and heel (such as the Achilles heel) that generate force economically; sweat glands that help our overheated bodies cool down; and large muscles in the gluteus maximus and upper shoulders that help stabilize us. Working together, these things allow *Homo* (and us as its sole modern representative) an unusual ability to run for longer distances and more sustained time periods than any other animal.

Walking is still more efficient than running, but there are multiple theories as to why these adaptations may have evolved (Bramble and Lieberman 2004). One of these is that as scavengers early *Homo* may have gained selective advantage in the search for resources by being able to cover large distances quickly and economically. Another suggests that before the development of hunting technologies like bows and arrows, *Homo* practiced persistence hunting, which means forcing a quadrapedal animal to run until it either dies from heat exhaustion or slows to the point where humans could easily kill it. Few four-legged animals have the ability to sweat and will overheat if they do not slow down

to pant. Humans, on the other hand, do sweat and we carry water, and we could literally run an animal to death by forcing it to keep running. Some contemporary hunter-gatherer groups have been observed conducting persistence hunts.

The fact that the genus *Homo* did not evolve to do these things with modern running shoes on its feet amplifies one argument for barefoot running. Lieberman and Bramble's biomechanical research on the running bodies of contemporary individuals shows that modern running shoes with thick heel pads encourage heel strike first instead of engaging our complex and springy foot arch, which does a better job than the heel does in absorbing and distributing impact. One possible implication (drawn out explicitly in McDougall's book) is that the high rates of knee and other injuries seen among habitual American runners may be at least partly due to the interference of running shoes in engaging that evolved system.

Naturally, this claim has not gone over well with athletic shoe companies. A number of medical doctors have also spoken out against it, who have been treating injured runners who decided to try barefoot running and hurt themselves, a not very surprising situation since most of us who have worn shoes our whole lives have not developed the techniques and musculature for barefoot running, which involves rotating foot strikes on the front and middle edge of the foot, not the heel. Lieberman—himself a barefoot runner—and his collaborators at Harvard have taken an official position that more research is necessary on these issues, announcing, "Please note that we present no data on how people should run, whether shoes cause some injuries, or whether barefoot running causes other kinds of injuries. We believe there is a strong need for controlled, prospective studies on these issues" (Harvard University Skeletal Biology Lab 2015). Whatever the outcomes of these debates, it is clear that paleoanthropological research is relevant to the discussion about contemporary human athletic abilities and injuries.

Questions for Reflection

1. Other than the selective advantages discussed here, can you think of other evolutionary processes that could have played a role in the evolution of endurance running capacity in the genus *Homo*?

2. What do you think are the limits of using paleoanthropological evidence to address contemporary human problems?

of *Homo*, including us, are omnivores, but it is likely that expanding the amount of meat consumed in the diet could have helped meet the added energy expenditures of having larger brains. The consumption of meat is supported by findings in fossil sites where processed remains of antelopes and antelope-like mammals exist alongside tools probably made by these early hominins.

Still, paleoanthropologists believe that meat was a small portion of the diet for our early omnivorous ancestors, including *Homo*. Because of their abundance and the relative ease of gathering them, roots, tubers, nuts, and fatty fruits—all sources of high-quality nutrition—were probably staple elements of their diets. We are still not certain what their foraging patterns looked like, but they probably revisited food-rich sites, scavenged meat and did some hunting, and used their growing brain power to develop tools to support their ability to gain access to and process nutritious foods.

Increasing brain capacity probably also supported cooperative social behaviors and group action, because it bolstered greater capacity for communication among individuals. For example, we know from the fossil sites of *A. afarensis* found at the AL-333 site at Hadar, Ethiopia, and those of *A. sediba* and *H. naledi* in South Africa, that these groups consisted of several adults, children, and infants. These hominins probably moved as groups and interacted with each other through grooming and various kinds of communicative acts, such as gestures and vocal utterances. Because predators such as giant leopards and hyenas roamed the savannas and foraged in the trees, they probably also figured out ways to deal with predators, perhaps by running away or organizing cooperative defense. Either way, avoiding predation was an essential behavior in the life of these australopithecines and continued with *Homo* (Hart and Sussman 2005).

Paleoanthropologists hypothesize that among the early hominins bipedalism and increasing brain power, with associated changes in diet, tool use, and social relations, contributed to evolutionary changes that led to the later forms of *Homo* (De Heinzelen et. al. 1999; Tattersall 2012). If true, this hypothesis points to something quite powerful and new, the interaction of biology and culture through biocultural evolution to meet selective challenges. In the next sections, we examine these later forms of *Homo*—among whom we can identify the first humans—where that interaction is quite important.

THINKING CRITICALLY ABOUT ANCESTRAL HUMANS

Scholars are still working through the actual sequence of evolutionary changes in hominins that led to the development of bipedalism, large brains, social complexity, and tool-making abilities. Knowing what you now know about early hominins and how evolutionary processes work, can you theorize a possible sequence of evolutionary changes?

Who Were the First Humans, and Where Did They Live?

Throughout the Pleistocene epoch, we see increasing qualities of "humanness" in our lineage, ranging from upright, large-brained physical qualities to, eventually, the modern body type we have today, sophisticated language, complex social formations, and aesthetic imaginations. Our lineage also begins to spread out of Africa and populate other corners of the earth. In this section we review who these first humans were, with greater species detail in The Evolution of Humans 8.3 (see pp. 220–225).

Introducing *Homo erectus*

Originally, it was thought that humans came out of Asia, not Africa, as is now known. In 1891, a Dutch military surgeon named Eugène Dubois excavated ancient hominoid skeletal remains near a river bank on the Indonesian island of Java. Estimated to be 700,000 to 1 million years old, the presence of thigh bones much like our own indicate that this figure walked upright. Dubois dubbed it an evolutionary "missing link" between humans and apes. It was quite an international sensation, especially since Darwin's new theory of evolution was still fresh in people's minds. Dubois gave it the name *Pithecanthropus erectus* (upright ape-human), though it was known popularly as "Java Man." During the next half-century, the "missing link" theory was discredited and similar finds elsewhere precipitated a taxonomic reordering. In 1950, the species were placed in the genus *Homo*, directly within our own evolutionary lineage, and became known as *Homo erectus*.

Thanks to 150 years of excavations that have yielded hundreds of useful fossils, paleoanthropologists have learned a lot about *H. erectus*. They appeared about 1.8 mya, lived in numerous locations around the globe, and became extinct (perhaps) as

CLASSIC CONTRIBUTIONS

Davidson Black and the Brain Capacity of *H. erectus*

IN 1926 THE Canadian anatomist Davidson Black, then working in China, heard that two fossil human teeth had been unearthed by mine workers at a site called Zhoukoudian near the Chinese city of Peking (now called Beijing). Black wanted to investigate further, but the Peking Union Medical College where he worked denied him. With some cajoling and a grant from the U.S.-based Rockefeller Foundation, he organized a large excavation at Zhoukoudian in 1927. By 1929 the group working for Black had unearthed a number of human fossils which Black named *Sinanthropus pekinensis*, which became known popularly as "Peking Man." We now know these were the first *H. erectus* fossils found in East Asia, and the taxonomic name was later changed to *H. erectus*. Black continued uncovering *Sinanthropus/H. erectus* fossils at the Zhoukoudian site, but in 1934 he died of heart failure at the age of fifty. Before his death Black created plaster casts of a number of skulls to analyze them. In this excerpt of a 1933 paper, he discusses one of the adolescent endocranial casts (from inside the skull) which allowed him to assess the brain capacity of this individual. As he indicates here, their "cerebral superiority" probably allowed for "articulate speech."

Davidson Black.

The extraordinarily marked development of the opercular portion of the inferior frontal region of the left side in Sinanthropus is a matter of particular interest in view of the known location in this region of the modern brain of the motor speech centre. Thus in view of this peculiar development of Broca's convolution, it is considered probable that the mechanism of articulate speech was elaborated in Sinanthropus...

In conclusion, it may be said that the endocranial cast of Sinanthropus presents both in its general form and in the details of its morphology an interesting blend of archaic, generalized and progressive characters quite *in keeping with what is already known about the external skull morphology of this form. From the evidence furnished by a detailed study of this cast but little room for doubt remains that this early hominid was provided with the essential nervous mechanism for the production of articulate speech. Finally, concerning the probable significance of the cerebellar and cerebral asymmetries noted above it is of interest to add that in their recent memoir Teilhard and Pei have shown that not a few of the Choukoutien artifacts "seem to have been handled with the right hand."* [Black 1933:276]

Questions for Reflection

1. Are there differences between what we can learn from casts and actual fossils?

2. Paleoanthropologists are skeptical that *H. erectus* had anything more than a simple proto-language because it is not cranial features and capacity alone that enable "articulate speech." What other bodily characteristics do you think would need to be in place for language to develop?

recently as 30,000 years ago. They had human-like body proportions and height, lived their lives on the ground as obligatory bipeds, appear to have cared for their young and the weak, made and used stone tools, and controlled fire. As we explore in "Classic Contributions: Davidson Black and the Brain Capacity of *H. erectus*," they may have even had some kind of simple proto-language.

- **Sagittal keel.** A raised area in the mid-cranium.

All of these qualities make *H. erectus* appear human. Of course, you would immediately notice obvious differences if one were to walk down the street. Their bones were thicker and the skeleton more robust. Their heads were different too: the shape of the cranium was long and low, with a massive brow ridge. Some of the fossils also have a **sagittal keel**, a raised area in the mid-cranium, and most have a pronounced ridge at the base of the skull. Their jaws were robust compared to those of modern humans, and they had no chin.

H. erectus fossils have been found throughout Africa, Europe, India, Indonesia, and China. It was long assumed that *H. erectus* evolved out of *H. habilis*, but recent finds in Kenya increasing *H. habilis's* temporal range suggest that the two may have coexisted. As *H. erectus* spread geographically, cranial differences emerged, and paleoanthropologists distinguish between African and Asian forms. Some scholars argue that Asian forms, for example, have larger teeth, sagittal keels, and neurocrania (part of the skull that protects the brain and face) than African forms. These scholars have used the name *Homo ergaster* for African forms to formalize that distinction.

Not all scholars accept the distinction, though, and the exact taxonomic ordering of *H. erectus* has never been totally resolved. There are three main hypotheses in the debate that continues today as we write this (modified from Fuentes 2006). See Table 8.1.

Although the current evidence appears to support the first position, the sparse nature of the fossil record and the fact that new findings and evidence can challenge existing interpretations continue to fuel the debate.

The Emergence of Archaic Humans

- **Postorbital constriction.** An indention of the sides of the cranium behind the eyes.

Around 500,000–300,000 years ago, changes in both morphology and material culture suggest that one or more new variety of *Homo* had emerged—supporters of Hypothesis #1 and #2 (Table 8.1) see this as the emergence of a new species, while proponents of Hypothesis #3 suggest it was simply another variation of the same species. The classic *H. erectus* traits of robustness decreased and cranial capacity increased (Figure 8.5). Over the next several hundred thousand years, the brow ridges of these humans became smaller and more separated, and the **postorbital constriction** (indention of sides of the cranium behind the eyes) reduced in size. The face became less prognathic, or forward-projecting. These humans were also known for making tools that were more refined and specialized than previous tools. We refer to individuals with these traits as archaic humans.

Figure 8.5   Two Archaic Human Crania. When compared, it is possible to see the differences in robustness. The Bodo cranium (above) dates to approximately 600,000 years ago; the Kabwe cranium (below) dates to approximately 300,000–30,000 years ago.

TABLE 8.1	THREE HYPOTHESES ON THE TAXONOMIC ORDER OF *H. ERECTUS*
Hypothesis #1	*H. erectus* was a single species that dispersed out of Africa between 1.8 mya and 300,000 years ago. Variations between Asian and African varieties are a result of genetic drift within the species. All are ancestral to modern humans.
Hypothesis #2	Genus *Homo* had three or four species between 1.8 mya and 300,000 years ago that moved out of Africa in waves. African *H. ergaster* and *H. erectus* are ancestral to modern humans, and Asian forms are not.
Hypothesis #3	All members of *Homo* after 1.8 mya are *H. sapiens*, exhibiting variations over time. Current humans are a subspecies known as *H. sapiens sapiens*.

Anthropologists classify archaic humans in one of two ways. The first is to lump them all into one category of archaic *Homo sapiens*, a broad category that assumes that we evolved directly out of this group. Another is to separate them into two different species, *Homo heidelbergensis* and *Homo neanderthalensis*, both of which were originally discovered in Germany during the 1800s. Regardless of their taxonomic status, archaic humans are almost—but still not quite—us (Conroy 1997).

The oldest archaic human specimens are found in Africa, and of these, the very oldest is the Bodo cranium, discovered in 1976 in Ethiopia. Their geographic spread includes the Middle East, Mediterranean, East Asia, Siberia, and Eastern and Western Europe. The Spanish site of Atapuerca has abundant archaic human finds, representing thirty-two individuals who lived between 200,000 and 300,000 years ago. Some paleoanthropologists argue that these fossils represent a distinct species (*Homo antecessor*) and that they were the ancestors of the Neanderthals (archaic humans found across Western Eurasia), modern humans, or perhaps both (Arsuaga et al. 1997; Bermudez de Castro et al. 1997). And a curious find on the Eastern Indonesian island of Flores has generated some surprises about the diversity of archaic humans. In 2004, a short, *erectus*-like hominin was discovered that dates to 95,000 and 12,000 years ago. These unusual hominins, which their discoverers named *Homo floresiensis* (Brown et al. 2004) and popularly referred to as "hobbits," are approximately three feet tall with a very small cranium.

Who Were the Neanderthals and Denisovans?

Few issues in human evolution have sparked as much attention and debate as the fossils of *Homo neanderthalensis* that occur in many parts of Europe and the Middle East dating from about 300,000 to 30,000 years ago. The surprising discovery between 2008 and 2010 of a coeval archaic human dating to 41,000 years in Denisova cave in the Altai Mountains of Siberia has added new evidence and interest in the ongoing debate.

The Neanderthals were stockier than modern humans, but in our same range of height and weight. The Denisovans may have been similarly robust, but the sparseness of skeletal evidence (a finger bone and two teeth) has prevented any morphological description and most of what we know about them comes from analyzing their mitochondrial DNA (see Chapter 4). The Neanderthals' large noses and husky features were probably adaptations to the harsh cold of the Pleistocene era when glaciers were extensive throughout the northern latitudes where many Neanderthal remains are found.

There is strong fossil evidence that Neanderthals, Denisovans, and modern humans overlapped during a period of 10,000 years or more, especially in the Middle East as well as the cave in Denisova, Siberia, which shows remains of all three groups though not necessarily at the same time. Some sites in Europe and the Middle East have even yielded evidence of Neanderthals using modern human-like tool kits and modern humans using Neanderthal-like tool kits.

The story of the relationships among these varieties of *Homo* has grown more complicated and intriguing as ancient human genomics has exploded during the past fifteen years thanks to technological innovations in sequencing, informatics, and improved recovery of mitochondrial DNA from fossilized bones less than 100,000 years old (Hawks 2013). Most startling of all is that there is even sufficient DNA from the few Denisovan bones uncovered in Siberia to reconstruct their genome. Ancient human genomics is still a new science and old DNA is often terribly degraded,

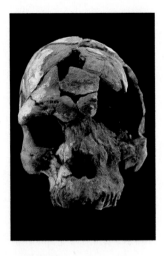

Figure 8.6   Anatomically Modern Human Cranium. This cranium is one of the oldest found that is considered to be anatomically modern. Dating from 160,000 years ago, it was found with other fossils in the Herto and Bouri region of eastern Africa.

- **Recent African origin model (RAO).** Modern humans arose as a new species in Africa about 150,000 year ago, during the late Pleistocene.

- **Multiregional evolution model (MRE).** Modern humans are only the most recent version of a single species, *Homo sapiens,* that had been in Africa, Asia, and Europe for nearly 2 million years.

- **Multiple dispersals model (MD).** Incorporates complexities in genetic datasets to argue that humans left Africa in multiple waves.

but the latest findings point to some level of interbreeding and gene flow between Neanderthals, Denisovans, and modern humans, suggesting perhaps that the Neanderthals and Denisovans never completely disappeared because they shared genetic material with modern humans (Sankararaman et. al. 2012). Puzzling through the genetic relationships between these groups is currently one of the most dynamic areas of paleoanthropology.

Anatomically Modern Humans Hit the Scene

Sometime between 200,000 and 25,000 years ago, the archaic features in the fossil record begin to change, and we see the emergence of features identified with modern humans (Figure 8.6). We see further changes in morphology (a high, rounded cranium; relatively slender skeletal structure; and the appearance of a chin) and dramatic changes in the types and complexity of tools and other aspects of material culture and behavior. Language as we know it probably appeared with anatomically modern humans (Berwick et. al. 2013). Paleoanthropologists continue to debate whether these changes represent the emergence of a new species or if archaic humans were essentially *Homo sapiens.* As recently as 35,000–12,000 years ago, there may have been at least two, if not more, species or subspecies of humans on the planet. However, today all anthropologists agree that only one human species remains, and all humans today belong to the same species of *Homo.*

Where did these humans—us?—actually originate? Anthropologists have long debated this question, developing three explanatory models. The **Recent African origin model** proposes that modern humans arose as a new species in Africa between 200,000 and 180,000 year ago, during the late Pleistocene (Cann et. al. 1987). The **Multiregional evolution model** proposes that modern humans are only the most recent version of a single species, *Homo sapiens,* that had been in Africa, Asia, and Europe for nearly two million years (Thorne and Wolpoff 1992). Both have lines of evidence to support them. But a third model, **Multiple dispersals model** (MD) (Templeton 2002), which argues that modern humans left Africa in multiple waves, edges out the others given the current fossil and DNA evidence. In this model the initial movement out of Africa occurs approximately 1.8 mya. *Homo* spread around western, central, and southern Eurasia, with back-and-forth gene flow across Africa and Eurasia, and possibly with some isolation of peripheral populations. Other dispersals include (adapted from Fuentes 2007):

- 800,000 to 400,000 years ago, influencing Eurasian populations through interbreeding, and affecting genetic patterns in the genus *Homo.*
- 150,000 to 80,000 years ago, also affecting genetic patterns throughout the genus *Homo.*
- 60,000 years ago, influencing the genetic patterns of central Eurasian and African populations. This event is also followed by back-and-forth gene flow as well as isolation by distance.
- 50,000 years ago, populations move into northern Eurasia, Australia, the Pacific Islands, and eventually the Americas (15,000 years ago) via migration.

This model predicts that African populations would have had forceful and recurrent effects on the genetic characteristics of humans over the past 1.7 million years. It also predicts that gene flow would be an important recurrent dynamic, with groups living closer to each other most affected by that flow.

It is admittedly difficult to pinpoint an exact dividing line between humans that are "anatomically modern" and archaic humans. From an evolutionary point of view, changes in complex organisms like humans may take hundreds or thousands of *generations* to occur, and closely aligned species can reproduce and pass genetic material between one another, as appears to have happened between modern humans, Neanderthals, and Denisovans. Working with ancient genomes has already begun to help clarify the genetic relatedness and biological variability of these human populations, and it promises to do more as DNA sequencing technologies advance. But genetics and morphology alone will never give us a holistic picture of the first humans, because we also know that culture played a critical role in their evolution. In the next section, we explore how we know that.

THINKING CRITICALLY ABOUT ANCESTRAL HUMANS

What are the pros and cons of approaching the first humans as a single species that goes way back to *H. habilis*, as some paleoanthropologists have suggested, or to differentiate them into distinct species as many other paleoanthropologists do? What kind of evidence could help support each position?

How Do We Know If the First Humans Were Cultural Beings, and What Role Did Culture Play in Their Evolution?

The answer to this question is *not* that culture suddenly appeared and transformed everything, like turning on a light switch transforms a dark room. Such a view is based on an erroneous conception of human evolution, that it is at its roots simply a story of biological transformation, with the spark of culture being a very recent add-on to that biological foundation. In fact, the cultural capacity of hominids emerged over a long period of time and interacted with biology to meet selective demands, in a process we call **biocultural evolution** (see Chapter 9).

When **paleolithic** humans (the long epoch of human prehistory from about 2.5 mya to 10,000 years ago) tackled the challenges of the environment with something more than their hands and teeth, real changes occurred in the way the pressures of natural selection affected them. The material and symbolic cultures that humans have invented over time have and continue to influence our evolution. These processes are, to an important extent, a reflection of how much human biocultural evolution is a story of niche construction, that is, about how humans have changed and constructed the world around them for a long time (Fuentes et. al. 2010). So what was the cultural capacity of the first humans?

- **Biocultural evolution.** The interaction of cultural capacity and biology to meet selective demands.

- **Paleolithic.** Literally "old stone," refers to a long epoch in human prehistory from about 2.5 mya to 10,000 years ago, and roughly corresponds with the Pleistocene geological epoch.

The Evolution of Humans 8.3

Homo erectus, Archaic Humans, and Modern Homo sapiens, 1.6 MYA to the present.

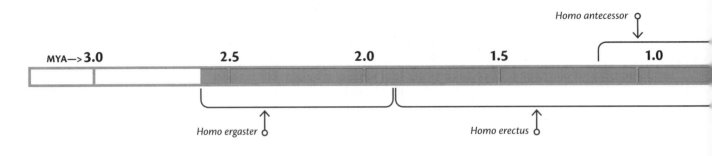

Homo antecessor

MYA—> 3.0   2.5   2.0   1.5   1.0

Homo ergaster

Homo erectus

KEY ▨ = *The Late Miocene Transitionary Hominines, 7 to 4 MYA*   ▨ = *The Plio-Pleistocene Hominins, 4 to 1.8 MYA*   ▨ = *Homo erectus, Archaic humans, and Modern Homo sapiens 2.6 MYA–Present*

SPECIES	DISCOVERY	RANGE
1 *Homo ergaster* "Ergaster" means "working" in Latin	New species proposed in 1975 based on analysis of already-discovered *H. erectus* jawbone	Africa
2 *Homo erectus* "Erectus" means "upright" in Latin	Discovered in 1891 in Java, Indonesia, by Dutch doctor Eugène Dubois	Northern, Eastern, and Southern Africa, Western Eurasia, and East Asia (China, Indonesia)

1 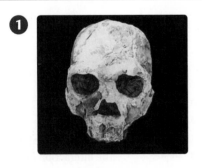 **2**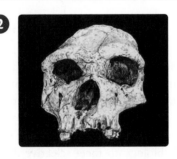

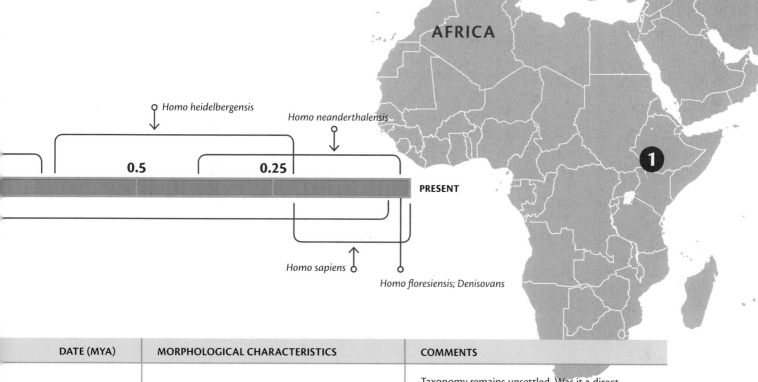

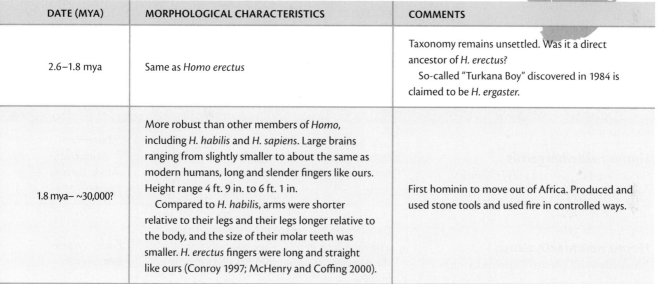

DATE (MYA)	MORPHOLOGICAL CHARACTERISTICS	COMMENTS
2.6–1.8 mya	Same as *Homo erectus*	Taxonomy remains unsettled. Was it a direct ancestor of *H. erectus*? So-called "Turkana Boy" discovered in 1984 is claimed to be *H. ergaster*.
1.8 mya– ~30,000?	More robust than other members of *Homo*, including *H. habilis* and *H. sapiens*. Large brains ranging from slightly smaller to about the same as modern humans, long and slender fingers like ours. Height range 4 ft. 9 in. to 6 ft. 1 in. Compared to *H. habilis*, arms were shorter relative to their legs and their legs longer relative to the body, and the size of their molar teeth was smaller. *H. erectus* fingers were long and straight like ours (Conroy 1997; McHenry and Coffing 2000).	First hominin to move out of Africa. Produced and used stone tools and used fire in controlled ways.

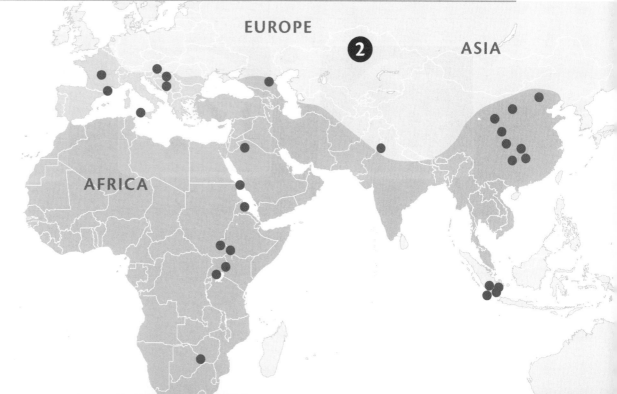

The Evolution of Humans 8.3 *continued*
The Late Miocene Transitionary Hominines, 7 to 4 MYA

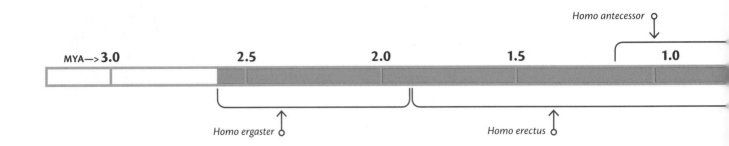

SPECIES	DISCOVERY	RANGE
3 **Homo antecessor** "Antecessor" means "explorer or pioneer" in Latin	Discovered in 1995 in Atapuerca, Spain, by Eudald Carbonell, Juan Luis Arsuaga, and J. M. Bermúdez de Castro	Europe (Spain)
ARCHAIC HUMANS		
4 **Homo heidelbergensis** "Heidelbergensis" refers to a city in Germany	Discovered in 1908 near Heidelberg, Germany, by a worker, and named by scientist Otto Schoentensack.	Eastern and Southern Africa, Europe, possibly Asia
5 **Homo neanderthalensis** "Neaderthalensis" refers to a region in Germany	Discovered in 1829, although nobody knew it was a hominin fossil. In 1856, a new discovery caught the attention of German scientists who named it in 1864.	Europe, Middle East, Siberia

3
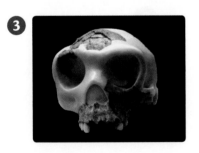

4

5

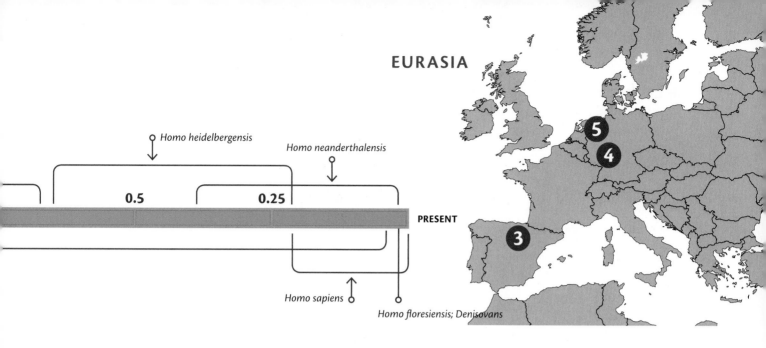

EURASIA

Homo heidelbergensis

Homo neanderthalensis

0.5

0.25

PRESENT

Homo sapiens

Homo floresiensis; Denisovans

DATE (MYA)	MORPHOLOGICAL CHARACTERISTICS	COMMENTS
1.2 mya–~800,000	Same as *Homo erectus*	Taxonomy remains unsettled. Was it a direct descendent of *H. erectus*?
700,000–200,000	Brains a bit smaller than modern humans. Robust; thick cranial walls; separated brow ridges; average height of 5 ft. 9 in. (males) and 5 ft. 2 in. (females).	Appears to be the first hominin to live in colder climates and has robust adaptations probably related to the cold. Used fire, made spears and other tools, hunted large game.
300,000–30,000	Brains slightly larger on average than modern humans. Stocky body; very large incisors, and large gap behind third molar (retromolar gap); average height 5 ft 5 in. (males) and 5 ft 1 in. (females).	Lived in cold climates, used tools similar to anatomically modern humans, almost certainly used language and other symbolic communication. Today most people who live outside of sub-Saharan Africa have ~1%–4% Neanderthal genetic ancestry.

The Evolution of Humans 8.3 *continued*

The Late Miocene Transitionary Hominines, 7 to 4 MYA

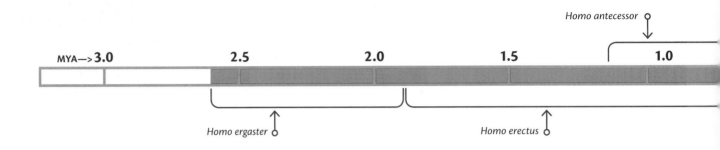

Homo antecessor

MYA—> **3.0**   **2.5**   **2.0**   **1.5**   **1.0**

Homo ergaster

Homo erectus

SPECIES	DISCOVERY	RANGE
6 **Denisovans**	Discovered in 2008 in the Altai Mountains of Siberia by a Russian team led by Michael Shunkov	Siberia

	SPECIES	DISCOVERY	RANGE
7	**Homo floresiensis** "Floriensis" refers to the island of Flores in Latin	Discovered in 2003 on the Island of Flores in Indonesia by joint Australian-Indonesian team led by Mike Morwood	Flores island, Indonesia
	ANATOMICALLY MODERN HUMANS		
8	**Homo sapiens**		Global

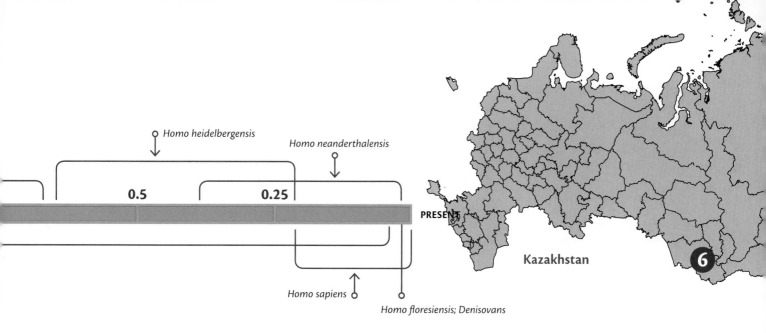

DATE (MYA)	MORPHOLOGICAL CHARACTERISTICS	COMMENTS
40,000 +/-	Physical evidence still too limited to know	Do not know if it was a distinct species. What we know at this point is based on analysis of mitochondrial DNA. Up to 6% of the genome of Melanesians, Australian Aborigines, and some East Asians derives from Denisovans.
95,000–12,000	Short bodies, very small heads, absence of a chin, different teeth form than modern humans	Some controversy has swirled over whether or not it is a distinct species; some claim it could have been modern humans with some kind of anatomical pathology.
~200,000–present	Large brain; high, rounded cranium; chin; no retromolar gap	Only living species of hominin

The Emerging Cultural Capacity of *H. erectus*

Beginning with *H. erectus*, we see a greater capacity for culture. We know that culture played a greater role in their lives than earlier hominins because:

Figure 8.7   The Acheulian Toolkit.   Acheulian tools appeared 1.6-1.4 mya. The technique of bifacial flaking creates a sharp edge, as can be seen with this hand-axe, a versatile tool for cutting, chopping, and various other tasks..

- **Acheulian tools.** A more complex and diverse stone-tool kit than earlier Olduwan tools. The main characteristic was bifacial flaking, a process that produced strong, sharp edges.

- ***Their diets changed.*** The increased brain and body size of *H. erectus* over previous *Homo* involved higher metabolic rates, requiring more and higher quality food (Aiello and Wells 2002). *H. erectus* responded to these new pressures by ratcheting up its reliance on tools and other cultural behavior to increase the quality of its diet. This dietary pattern was omnivorous, although Aiello and Wells (2002) hypothesize that *H. erectus* relied more heavily on meat and other high-energy foods. Support for this hypothesis comes from sites in East Africa where fossils of animals and stone tool assemblages appear around the time that early *H. erectus* fossils show up in the fossil record (O'Connell et al. 2002). It appears that as brains grew in size, the guts (digestive organs) became smaller in *H. erectus* than in the earlier *Homo* species. Smaller guts require higher energy foods, most likely meat, which would have required more efficient food gathering or hunting.

- ***Their tools changed.*** When members of the genus *Homo* first spread from Africa into Eurasia and beyond, they used Olduwan tools. With these sharp flakes and stout-edged choppers, they were able to process both animal and plant matter to reduce the pressures on the teeth and jaw. About 1.6–1.4 mya, a new type of stone tool began to show up in the fossil record, first in East Africa and then throughout the rest of Africa, in western and central Eurasia, and in at least one location in East Asia. Known as **Acheulean tools** (named after St. Acheul in France where they were first discovered in 1847), these tools had better edges and were more varied in style. A classic example is a hand-axe with bifacial flaking, which is produced by flaking chips off of each side of the base stone to produce strong, sharp edges (Figure 8.7). They were likely used to process meat and hides, and probably for modifying wood and bones. Acheulian tools show up in many (but not all) *H. erectus* sites as far apart as southern Africa, the British Isles, and India. But they remain extremely rare at *H. erectus* sites in East and Southeast Asia. It is possible in these places that *H. erectus* used biodegradable material such as wood, bamboo, or bone as tools, but evidence is very thin since these things don't last like stone tools do.

- ***They used fire.*** *H. erectus* and archaic humans created and maintained small fires. Evidence for controlled use of fire exists in France, Spain, China, and Hungary, dating to 500,000 to 300,000 years ago. We also have possible evidence—although it is still controversial—of fire use from before 1 mya in East Africa and later in South Africa. Since indications of fire use (fire pits and ashes) and fire-blackened animal bones do show up with more regularity in the archeological record by about 400,000 years ago, however, it is possible that, at least in some places, *H. erectus* was using fire before then. Fire enables the consumption of a wider variety of foods and a higher energy return on foods eaten. It also marks the beginning of cooking, a process that involves a transformation of raw food that anthropologists have long considered a unique hallmark of cultural capacity (Wrangham 2009).

- ***Cooperative behaviors increased.*** *H. erectus* relied heavily on hunting and gathering high-quality plant material, both of which require coordination and cooperation among group members. With an increase in caloric requirements, the energetic costs of reproduction, and especially breast feeding (lactation), shoot up. One group of researchers estimated that the amount of energy invested in lactation was 45% greater in *H. erectus* than in earlier hominins (Aiello and Wells 2002). This situation probably enhanced cooperative behaviors, as group members shared caregiving responsibilities and collaborated in foraging activities. Although we have no evidence of what their speech was like, these activities also require a level of symbolic communication beyond the limits of a simple call system typical of nonhuman animals (see Chapter 5, "Linguistics").

By themselves, none of these changes would have been sufficient to enable *H. erectus* to successfully adapt to a wide variety of landscapes across Africa and Eurasia, but together they generated an important adaptive capacity. That capacity played an even greater role in the adaptability and biology of archaic humans.

Culture Among Archaic Humans

Evidence for archaic human material culture and behavior comes from Neanderthal sites from between 300,000 and about 50,000 years ago. We see the emergence of more complex tools than the prior Acheulian style. We also see evidence of organized group hunts, such as at Atapuerca, Spain, where archaic humans forced large game animals over cliffs (Dennell 1997). The regular use of controlled fire was widespread, and we see evidence of shelters of wood and possibly hide.

By 200,000 years ago, a new tool-making technique emerged. This new method, called the **Levallois technique**, involves flaking off pieces around the outline of a desired flake, producing higher quality blades capable of many more uses (Figure 8.8). In many Neanderthal sites, we see an even more effective method for creating tools, based on a disk-core technique, called the **Mousterian industry** (Figure 8.9). This technique requires little effort to quickly create stone flakes from a single core. These flakes have many uses and expanded opportunities for tool use. At least sixty types of Mousterian tools have been identified, hinting at regional cultural variation. Although Neanderthals never developed the technology of blade tools (a stone flake that is at least twice as long as it is wide) and therefore did not have needles for sewing, they did use clothing made of hides and probably plant materials, meaning that they were relying less on purely biological adaptations to deal with the environment and turning more and more to cultural ones.

All of these changes gave archaic humans improved access to nutrition and new pressures on the body to process the richer foods. Cooking with fire took pressure off the need for big teeth and massive chewing muscles, and we see the gradual reduction of size in both of these in the morphology of modern humans. The use of fire and refined tools also helped archaic humans deal with climatic challenges that exposed them to new selective pressures.

Social Cooperation and Symbolic Expression

Everything that we do as humans is based on social interdependence and intensive cooperation. Most cooperation depends on communication well in excess of anything our chimpanzee cousins are capable of, even if we see the rudimentary

- **Levallois technique.** Stone tool-making technique that involves complex preparation of the stone and provides a higher quality toolkit than previous types with more uses.

- **Mousterian industry.** A disk-core technique of stone tool making that allowed the tool makers to produce many good flakes with little effort and then turn those flakes into a wide variety of fine tools. Associated with the Neanderthals.

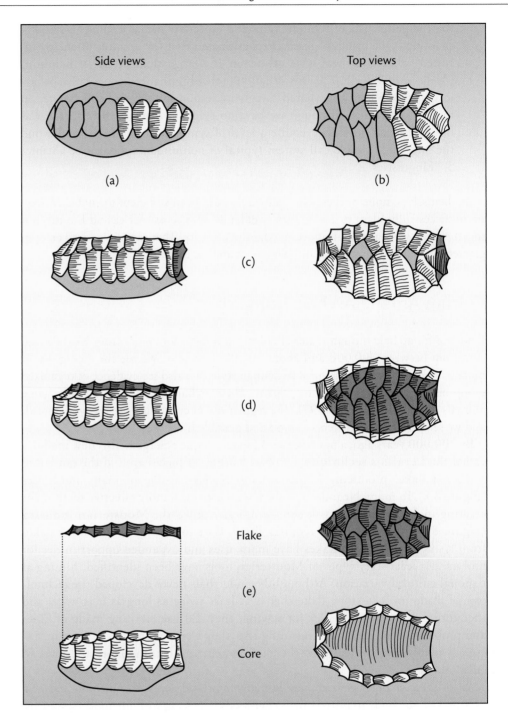

Figure 8.8   The Levallois Technique.   This image shows the technique step-by-step. It starts by producing a margin along the edge of the core (a); shaping the surface of the core (b); preparing the striking platform (the surface to be struck) (c, d); removing the flake (e). The photo on the next page is a replica of a Levallois core and tool.

beginnings of intergenerational learning and the simplest evidence of culture among some primates.. Having the capacity for culture was essential because cultural meanings allow for group memory, establishing patterned ways of doing things, and metaphysical thought (Fuentes 2014). We cannot say with any certainty when these characteristics appeared. Because it is impossible to really know the non-material processes of culture from material objects alone, many crucial details about the culture of archaic and early anatomically modern humans remain unknown. But we do know that archaic humans such as Neanderthals, who lived and worked together in communities, already exhibited social interdependence and even appear to have had

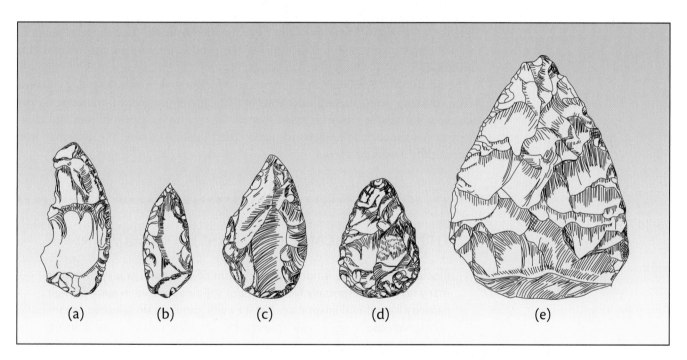

(a)   (b)   (c)   (d)   (e)

rich symbolic lives rooted in some level of (still unknown) linguistic ability. One indication is the existence of nonfunctional items of personal or group jewelry, such as the 130,000-year-old modified white-tailed eagle claws found in present-day Croatia (Radovčić et al. 2015). Neanderthals possibly cared for the sick and injured, as evidenced by the high number of healed injuries and relatively aged individuals, although this interpretation of these data are disputed. The Neanderthals also treated their dead with an apparent reverence that suggests symbolic thinking and production of collective memory. More than thirty-five Neanderthal grave sites have been identified, many of them with "grave goods," especially stone

Figure 8.8 (Continued)

Figure 8.9   Mousterian Tools. Mousterian tools, which date from 600,000 to 40,000 years ago were a refinement of the Levallois technique. Pictured here are scrapers (a, c); points (b,d), and a hand-axe (e).

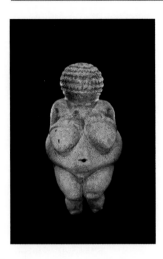

Figure 8.10   Upper Paleolithic Carved Objects. Some of these objects have a practical function and others appear to have primarily symbolic value, such as the famous "Venus" figurine pictured here.

cutting tools near the bodies and even the presence of flowers in the grave. Yet there is still far too little evidence for any viable hypotheses about their actual belief systems.

The First Humans and Artistic Expression

At least 50,000 years ago, anatomically modern humans were creating images on cave shelter walls and rocky outcrops that some scholars interpret as art. Over the next 20,000 years, art and other symbolic forms became much more common. Some of the most famous are in the caves in Altamira in Spain (18,000–14,000 years ago), and in Lascaux in southern France (17,300 years ago). A recent find of 40,000-year-old cave art in Sulawesi, Indonesia, expands the geography of the first artists beyond Europe (Vergano 2014). The type of imagery in early visual art includes both abstract and realistic representations of bison, deer, boars, horses, birds, cats, bears, rhinoceroses, and humans. These images include etchings and elaborate paintings on cave walls, carvings on the handles of tools, and carved figurines. It is difficult to know why these things were created and if they had some intentional purpose. But they indicate that by 50,000–30,000 years ago, all humans were fully capable of symbolic thought and almost certainly language (Figure 8.10).

Yet we have to be careful about using present-day views and experiences to interpret that artistic expression. The "Thinking Like an Anthropologist: Challenging Stereotypes of 'Cave Men' and Other Prehistoric Humans" box suggests some of the dilemmas involved in understanding the production and significance of this ancient art.

The cultural and symbolic capacities we take for granted as humans today emerged over a very long time. Although elements of that capacity precede *H. erectus*, it is clear that the cultural adaptations it made shaped the evolutionary possibilities and characteristics of the archaic humans who succeeded them, including Neanderthals and anatomically modern humans.

THINKING CRITICALLY ABOUT ANCESTRAL HUMANS

Biocultural evolution is not a "better" form of evolution, as it is clear that many hominins (especially Neanderthals) still disappeared in spite of their capacity for cultural adaptation. Yet it clearly gives certain selective advantages over the evolutionary trajectories of other non-primate animals. What do you think those selective advantages are?

Conclusion

Understanding of our human ancestors and the hominin family tree has been growing by leaps and bounds in recent decades. We have more ancient primate fossils than ever, and due to technological advancements in the lab, we also have new tools that allow researchers to access the subtle information they contain about human origins. And yet, due to the rarity of primate and hominin fossils, there is still so much to

Thinking Like an Anthropologist

Challenging Stereotypes of "Cave Men" and Other Prehistoric Humans

ANTHROPOLOGISTS BEGIN THEIR research by asking questions. In this box, we want you to learn how to ask questions as an anthropological researcher. Part 1 describes a situation and follows up with questions we would ask. Part 2 asks you to do the same thing with a different situation.

PART 1: RECONSTRUCTING PALEOLITHIC ART

When most of us think of archaic humans, we conjure up images like those in Hollywood movies, newspaper cartoons, and popular television commercials of "cave men" with unruly hair and big clubs, dressed in ragged skins, and a communicational ability that amounts to grunting. From an anthropological perspective these stereotypes are counterproductive, not simply because they reduce the complexity of those past lives but because they also reinforce

an unquestioned sense of superiority we as "moderns" have over them. The same point is applicable to cave art, where the image of the "cave *man*" painting a bison on the cave wall or maybe sculpting a figurine is a common one.

Cave art and figurines are important to understanding our biocultural evolution, but relatively few anthropologists have systematically considered how we have depicted the making of such art. Feminist archaeologist Margaret Conkey (1999) indicates two ways to think about ancestral human art: (1) the form and content of the art itself, and (2) the reconstructions (usually drawings or paintings by modern artists and researchers) of our ancestors making the art. Dr. Conkey asks whether these reconstructions are based on archaeological data or on current cultural ideas about who makes art and why.

Surveying a broad range of reconstructions, Conkey found that they tend to reflect our deeply embedded perspectives on race, class, and gender. For example, regardless of the

▼ **A Typical Artistic Interpretation of the Stereotypical Cave Person.**

Thinking Like an Anthropologist (continued)

absence of gender information in the fossil record about art, most reconstructions portray archaic human artists as males; the females, if present at all, are assisting or standing by carrying infants or preparing food. However, a few more recent reconstructions reverse this biased conception of gender roles, replacing the males, often left out of the picture entirely, with females who are depicted as shamans or priestesses. Conkey points out that neither of these extremes has any basis in the data about cave artists. She notes that we do not know whether only adults made art, whether art-making was a communal process, or whether it was confined to only select individuals in a group. One thing is certain, however, which is that for tens of thousands of years, imagery such as that in the cave art and symbolic works in general have been central to human lives, our communication, and our view of reality. One reason, Conkey believes, is that making these images long ago became a critical part of sustaining human communities and social memory.

The bottom line? In thinking about the place of artistic and imaginative expression in our biocultural evolution or approaching how and why our ancestors used art, we must not let our current preconceptions about art and artists color our representations of the past. The fossil and archaeological data have to drive our reconstructions; otherwise, we see only what we want to see.

What questions does this situation raise for anthropological researchers?

1. What are the hallmarks of human "artistic" ability?
2. Is there a functional role that art plays in human social behavior?
3. If we abandon our stereotypes, is there evidence that we might look for that would confirm whether men or women (or both) created cave art?
4. Does it matter if men, women, or both created cave art?
5. What are the more important aspects of human abilities that cave art demonstrates for our species?

PART 2: DETERMINING THE GENDER OF PREHISTORIC POTTERS

Between 7,000 and 10,000 years ago, pottery starts appearing in the prehistoric record. This simple technology uses clay mixed with straw, sand, or crushed shell as a fixative (archaeologists call it temper) to hold the clay together and strengthen it. After forming it into the shape of a pot or bowl, it is fired, usually with wood and dry leaves around the pots. Most potters in tribal societies today are women, but as specialization increases, we see more men becoming potters. This pattern suggested to early proponents of cultural evolution to see women as the first potters, followed by men as pottery became more complex. What questions would you ask about this situation as an anthropological researcher?

learn about the lives of those ancient creatures and their relationships to us. Set against that backdrop, it makes sense why the recent discoveries of *A. sediba* and *H. naledi* specimens in South Africa have generated so much excitement in and beyond paleoanthropology: they have the potential to fill in critical gaps and reshape our understanding of the details of our human origins.

While we cannot yet say for certain that any specific fossil older than two million years represents our direct ancestral species, we do know that the human lineage arose in Africa and emerged to confront the ecological challenges of the planet in a totally new way. These hominins had certain distinctive qualities that set them apart from their own ancestral apes, especially physical changes in the lower and upper body to support bipedal locomotion, modifications to teeth and other facial structures, and increasingly larger cranial capacity. These adaptations supported and in turn influenced increasingly important cultural capacity in the first humans, including *H. erectus*, archaic humans, and our own species of anatomically modern humans.

While fossils, genetics, and morphology are critical elements of biological anthropology, alone they will never give us the holistic picture of humans that anthropologists strive to develop, because we also know that culture played a critical role in the evolution of the first humans. The story of biocultural evolution goes way back in time and, as we saw here, clearly shaped the social and biological lives of the first humans in complex ways. In the next chapter, we will dive even deeper into the dynamics of biocultural evolution, including showing how they also shape our present.

KEY TERMS

Reviewing the Chapter

Chapter Section	What We Know	To Be Resolved
Who are our earliest possible ancestors?	They are hominins, who began emerging in Africa 5 mya. The three relevant genera—*Australopithecus*, *Paranthropus*, and *Homo*—exhibit varying degrees of bipedal locomotion, smaller teeth than apes, and various other physical particularities. In some cases, they exhibit tool making and use.	Paleoanthropologists continue to debate evolutionary relationships between the different genera and their species, as well as the interpretation of individual fossil discoveries. We will never find a single "missing link" but continue to look for further linkages between the hominins already identified.
What does walking on two legs and having big brains mean for the early hominins?	The development of bipedalism conferred a number of benefits on hominins and was followed sometime after by the development of greater brain capacity. Although big brains carry certain energetic costs, they also enable more complex social organization and more sophistication in the manufacture and use of tools.	Paleoanthropologists continue to explore basic questions about the complex interrelationships between diet, environment, and the development of bipedalism and large brains in early hominins.
Who were the first humans, and where did they live?	The first humans include *H. erectus* (1.8 mya–~30,000 years ago), the archaic humans (500,000–27,000 years ago), and anatomically modern humans (200,000 years–present), who all share certain common physical traits that differentiate them from earlier hominins. The origins of the first humans were in Africa, but they dispersed throughout Eurasia and eventually other locations around the globe.	There is long-standing disagreement over how many species the fossils of early *Homo* represent and how they are related to modern humans. The increasing use of genetic data from recovered ancient DNA promises to clarify these issues, but ancient human genomics is still a new science and old DNA is often terribly degraded.
How do we know if the first humans were cultural beings, and what role did culture play in their evolution?	Biocultural evolution is a very old phenomenon among hominins, and especially important for *H. erectus*, archaic, and anatomically modern humans. Material culture, social interdependence, and symbolic thinking enabled archaic and modern humans to survive and thrive in a wide range of environments. These cultural dynamics drove certain morphological changes seen among anatomically modern humans.	Paleoanthropologists are still working through the fossil evidence to identify the complex ways culture interacted with biology, as well as the particularities of cultural capacity among the first humans. Largely because it is impossible to really know the non-material processes of culture through material objects alone, many crucial details remain unknown. New insights may come from discoveries of new physical evidence or by reinterpreting existing evidence, but some argue that challenging our own cultural stereotypes about the first humans is also necessary.

Readings

The book *Human Evolution: A Very Short Introduction* by evolutionary scholar Bernard Wood (2006, New York: Oxford University Press) traces the history of paleoanthropology from the eighteenth century to recent fossil finds. A similar but more extensive treatment is Ian Tattersall's *Masters of the Planet* (New York: Palgrave Macmillan, 2012, which examines the role of bipedalism and social cooperation in the evolution of *Homo*.

•••••••••••••••••••••••

The 2011 PBS television program NOVA has an excellent three-part series called "Becoming Human" that covers some of the latest finds and thinking about human evolution (http://www.pbs.org/wgbh/nova /evolution/becoming-human.html).

•••••••••••••••••••••••

The book *Man the Hunted: Primates, Predators, and Human Evolution* (New York: Basic Books, 2005) by biological anthropologists Donna Hart and Robert Sussman explores compelling evidence that humans evolved not as we tend to think—as hunters dominating over other creatures—but as the hunted, that is, the vulnerable prey of other animals that drove certain kinds of adaptations that allowed our species to survive.

•••••••••••••••••••••••

British paleoanthropologist Richard Wrangham's 2009 book *Catching Fire: How Cooking Made Us Human* (New York: Basic Books, 2009,) provides a compelling analysis of the profound evolutionary effects of controlled use of fire and cooking among the first humans.

•••••••••••••••••••••••

The discovery of genetic connections between modern humans, Neanderthals, and Denisovans has been widely covered in the media. Science journalists have covered the story extensively, and non-technical writings appear in the blogs of science journals like *Nature*, *Science*, science-interest magazines like *National Geographic* and *Discovery*, and even non-science outlets like *Atlantic Monthly* and the *New York Times*. Articles from any of these outlets are easily accessible online using key word searches.

•••••••••••••••••••••••

Human Biocultural Evolution

Emergence of the Biocultural Animal

CHAPTER 9

Sleeping is one of the most important aspects of human life. We spend about a third of our lives doing it, and our daily well-being is shaped by how much of it we get. Over time, regular sleep deprivation can lead to more serious maladies like memory loss, depression, chronic illness, and even death. Because our bodies need it, it is common to think of sleeping in terms of its biological functions. This view is supported by research that shows the critical role of sleeping in human cognitive development, hormonal regulation, long-term memory and learning, energy conservation, and physical restoration.

But sleep also has complex cultural and behavioral dimensions. How, when, where, and with whom people sleep are patterned by collective social expectations, moralities, and available paraphernalia such as bedding, head rests, and so on (Mauss 1973; Glaskin and Chenhall 2013). Because they are learned, sleep practices are a key site of enculturation in every society. Although North Americans tend to think of sleep as something to do in private, many people around the world view it as a social activity and sleep in groups. The cross-cultural diversity surrounding how people think about and engage in sleep argues against viewing it as a solely biological phenomenon.

For all of these reasons, sleep is, from a holistic anthropological perspective, a complex **biocultural** phenomenon that intertwines

 Sleeping as a Biocultural Phenomenon The human behavior of sleeping is variable and plastic across our species. Because sleeping involves the complex intertwining of biological, evolutionary, and cultural processes, it is useful to approach it as a biocultural phenomenon.

● **Biocultural.** A phenomenon that intertwines dynamics of human biology with processes of culture.

human biology with the processes of culture (Worthman 2012). Among hominins, sleep evolved under particular environmental and social conditions. Because it creates vulnerability to predators, social animals like primates adapted by sleeping in groups, and developing a pattern of restful deep sleep interspersed with light sleep for maintaining vigilance. The evolution of hominin sleep patterns was especially affected by bipedalism (Worthman 2007). Bipedalism generated two conflicting evolutionary trends, one of structural refinements that saw the pelvis and birth canal get smaller to support bipedalism, and the other of increasing brain size to accommodate greater learning and social complexity. The adaptive compromise was the birth of neurologically immature infants for whom the majority of brain growth occurs outside the womb (McKenna 1993). This created the need for increased and sustained parental contact with infants, what biological anthropologist James McKenna refers to as a "dynamic, co-evolving interdependent system" between infant needs and parental response, which includes parents and infants sleeping together in close contact.

McKenna and his research team at the University of Notre Dame's Mother-Baby Behavioral Sleep Laboratory team have studied the intricacies of that interdependent system up close. They have learned that the touch, vision, smells, vocalizations, movement cues, breathing sounds, exchange of CO_2 gas, and breast milk involved in parent-infant co-sleeping provide critical physiological and neurological conditions for infant development. These things can even reduce the risk of sudden infant death syndrome (SIDS) (McKenna et al. 2007). These studies support the notion that co-sleeping, along with breastfeeding, evolved as critical elements of human infant development, and both are involved in our reproductive success as hominins.

The majority of human societies continue this close-contact sleeping with infants. One exception is postindustrial Western countries such as the United States and Canada, where cultural attitudes, supported by a century of pediatric medical and public health beliefs, emphasize that babies should sleep alone. These attitudes are partly based on fears that an adult will roll over and suffocate the baby and partly on the belief that co-sleeping will create too much emotional dependency in the individual as it grows up. Some hospitals even disallow newly born infants to be in bed with the mother at all.

From an evolutionary perspective, these beliefs and the behaviors that stem from them put mothers and babies at odds with their bodies. They are based on often flawed or insubstantial evidence and can even be detrimental to infant development, making them urgent issues for public discussion. For anthropologists, they also raise some important issues about the relationship between evolution, culture, and behavior. These issues include whether behavior evolves; how to explain the incompatibilities between lifestyles and cultures today and the conditions under which humans evolved; and what evolutionary impacts our behaviors today might have in the future.

At the heart of these issues is the question around which this chapter is organized: *How should we make sense of the biological and cultural factors that together shape our evolutionary trajectories?* Embedded in this broader question are the following problems this chapter explores:

How do biocultural patterns affect evolution?

How does behavior evolve?

Are modern humans evolving?

Where are culture and evolution leading us?

Because of our capacity for culture, the evolutionary processes humans experience differ from those of other species. In order to understand how human behavior evolves, we need to bring biology and culture into the same frame—a biocultural frame—and consider their intertwined role in shaping evolution. We begin by examining how the latest developments in evolutionary theory have contributed to the construction of the biocultural perspective.

How Do Biocultural Patterns Affect Evolution?

As we introduced in Chapter 3, contemporary evolutionary theory has been developing new understandings of the complex relationships between organisms and biological patterns that are not fully encompassed by the four genetic evolutionary mechanisms of mutation, natural selection, genetic drift, and gene flow. Within the framework of the extended evolutionary synthesis, scientists have begun to recognize how extra-genetic inheritances, developmental biases, and niche construction also contribute to evolutionary processes. These ideas provide the foundations for recognizing the biocultural patterns that affect human evolution. The approach we present here is known as a **constructivist approach**, emphasizing that a core dynamic of human biology and culture lies in processes of construction—the construction of meanings, of social relationships, of ecological niches, of developing bodies, and so on, all of which interact in complexly intertwined ways (see also Fuentes 2009a, 2009b).

- **Constructivist approach.** Emphasizes that a core dynamic of human biology and culture is processes of construction: the construction of meanings, social relationships, ecological niches, and developing bodies.

Inheritance Involves Multiple Systems

Not long ago, biologists Eva Jablonka and Marion Lamb (2005) pointed out that explanations of human evolution have traditionally focused on only one system of inheritance—the genetic system—which relies on explanations at the level of genes. Observing that this approach is too narrow to appreciate evolutionary complexity, Jablonka and Lamb argued that evolution actually involves four systems of inheritance (Figure 9.1). In addition to the genetic system, human evolution also works in the epigenetic, behavioral, and symbolic inheritance systems.

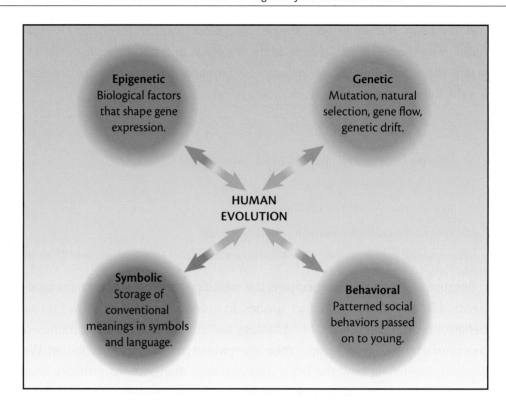

Figure 9.1   The Four Types of Inheritance.

- **Epigenetic system of inheritance.** The biological aspects of bodies that work in combination with the genes and their protein products, such as the machinery of the cells, the chemical interactions between cells, and reactions between types of tissue and organs in the body.

The Epigenetic System of Inheritance

The **epigenetic system of inheritance** involves biological factors outside the genes that affect gene expression. This system consists of the biological aspects of our bodies that work in combination with the genes and their protein products, such as the machinery of the cells, the chemical interactions between cells, and reactions between tissue and organs in the body. The epigenetic system works by attaching chemical tags (known as epigenetic marks) to DNA, which turns genes on or off. One common process is called methylation, where an epigenetic mark called a methyl group blocks the attachment of proteins that normally turn on the gene. The epigenetic system helps the information in the genes actually get expressed, and therefore it impacts genes as well as the whole body by altering an individual's physical traits.

Offspring may inherit those altered traits due to the past experiences of their parents. This process has been observed in various experiments, including in rats, where rat pups receiving high or low levels of nurturing developed epigenetic differences. The highly nurtured rats give the same high level of nurturing to their own offspring, and the low-nurtured rats give the same low level of nurturing to their offspring. Those epigenetic differences and the behaviors associated with them were carried on through succeeding generations.

In humans, epigenetic inheritance is more difficult to observe because of our long life spans, genetic diversity, and the fact that we don't live in highly controlled laboratories like rats. Nevertheless, epigenetic inheritance may be taking place, for example, in historical variations in access to food that can result in health effects on offspring. One study in Sweden analyzed 200 years of food harvests, observing that the ups and downs of harvests had impacts on diabetes and heart disease rates in succeeding generations, possibly caused because certain epigenetic marks caused by variations in diet were passed to offspring (Bygren et al. 2014). The study of the influence of the epigenetic inheritance system is still a young field, and much remains to be understood about how these processes shape human health.

The Behavioral System of Inheritance

The **behavioral system of inheritance** refers to the patterned behaviors that parents and adults pass on to young members of their group via learning and imitation. For example, most birds need to learn from their parents which foods to eat and which to avoid, since there are no genes telling them what to eat. In humans, we call these learned and patterned behaviors norms, customs, and traditions (see Chapter 2). The cross-cultural variability of human norms, customs, and traditions demonstrates the behavioral flexibility and plasticity of humans. That variability has long shaped the adaptive possibilities of our species.

Throughout our lives as members of a society, we learn a wide variety of behaviors—how to get food, when and how to talk to strangers, how to act when visiting a government office, and so on—from authority figures and peers, simply by observing and being corrected in everyday life. We also construct elaborate and formalized social institutions to mediate, manage, and control the behaviors of group members. Among humans, these activities occupy a huge amount of our energy, thought, worries, and creativity, and none of this activity is located in any specific genetic sequences.

The Symbolic System of Inheritance

Taking their cues from cultural anthropologists, Jablonka and Lamb (2005) acknowledged that in humans there is also a **symbolic system of inheritance**. This idea refers to the fact that humans store and communicate their knowledge and conventional understandings through extensive use of symbols and language. Symbols are the origins and basis of human behavior, and as such this system of inheritance is intimately tied to the behavioral system of inheritance. Symbols are rooted in our linguistic abilities. With some exceptions caused by extreme disability, all humans are capable of learning a language—enabled by a certain genetic makeup that only other humans share—but the actual language we do learn from our parents and peers then helps shape the way we perceive and interact with the world around us (see Chapter 5). As we explained in Chapter 2, the specific symbols and the meanings people attribute to them are arbitrary and socially constructed and are not coded in the genes.

Evolutionary Processes Are Developmentally Open-Ended

Another foundation of the biocultural perspective is the shift in thinking about evolution that came with the introduction of **developmental systems theory** (DST), which is a version of the concept of developmental bias we introduced in Chapter 3 (Oyama, Griffiths, and Russell 2001). DST focuses on the development of biological and behavioral systems over time rather than on genes as the core of evolutionary processes. Indeed, DST rejects the idea that there is a gene "for" anything, and that evolutionary processes are fundamentally open-ended and complex because they involve the ongoing assembly of new biological structures interacting with non-biological structures.

In this sense, development comes from the growth and interaction of several distinct systems (Fuentes 2014a). These systems include genes and cells, muscles and bone, and the brain and nervous system, all developing over the lifetimes of individuals. From this point of view, evolution is not a matter of the environment shaping fundamentally passive organisms or populations, as suggested by natural selection theory. Rather, it consists of many other developmental systems simultaneously changing over time. In humans, evolution is thus characterized by a complex set of interactions among the various biological systems that occurs throughout an individual's lifetime, all of which interact with factors like human demography, social interactions, cultural variations,

---

- **Behavioral system of inheritance.** The types of patterned behaviors that parents and adults pass on to young members of their group by way of learning and imitation.

- **Symbolic system of inheritance.** The linguistic system through which humans store and communicate their knowledge and conventional understandings using symbols.

- **Developmental systems theory (DST).** An approach that combines multiple dimensions and interactants toward understanding the development of organisms and systems and their evolutionary impact.

language, and environmental change. As such, these processes make it much more difficult to describe our evolution, but they recognize the actual complexity involved in how human biocultural systems work.

Niche Construction and Ecological Inheritance

As we explored in the previous chapter on the first humans, a critical aspect of our biocultural existence involves changing and constructing the world around us. A niche is the relationship between an organism and its ecology, which affects how that organism makes a living within a particular environment. F. John Odling-Smee, Kevin Laland, and Marcus Feldman (2003) describe the construction of niches as the process through which living creatures remake and reorganize their own niches though their metabolism, their activities, and their behavior. The scale of niche construction and niche destruction can occur at the narrow local level, such as shaping an environmental region such as a valley or body of water, or on a global scale, as we are currently experiencing with global warming. Each of these processes can change the kinds of natural selection pressures placed on the organisms involved.

Many different types of organisms engage in niche construction. Consider, for example, earthworms and their relationship with the soil. If you introduce earthworms to a patch of soil where there have never been earthworms (which is actually what happened when the first Europeans arrived in the Americas, since there were no native earthworms), that first generation begins to consume and defecate in the soil, changing its chemical properties. This changes the soil so that the next generations of earthworms are born into a soil that is more conducive to their ways of living, and they keep maintaining that ecology by their actions. As a by-product, what is good for worms is also great for plants; thus, gardeners put worms into their gardens to do a bit of niche construction themselves.

Much of what we take as "natural" in a landscape is actually an artifact of human niche construction and its effects (see Chapter 15). It can be relatively easy to see how the species composition of plants and animals in a landscape is directly shaped by humans (think of agriculture, for example), while in other cases it may be less obvious because it is the result of previous historical human involvement in a landscape. Reflecting the view that human influence over ecosystems is the defining dynamic of our world today, a number of scholars have begun referring to our current geological epoch as the **Anthropocene**.

When humans reorganize ecosystems they create the conditions for a coevolutionary process in which humans, plants, animals, and microorganisms can mutually shape each other's evolutionary prospects. The humans born into that set of relationships inherit particular challenges and opportunities for making a living. Similarly, if we change ecologies (say, by building cities), children born into those environments inherit the kinds of ecological challenges and opportunities that come with those ecological arrangements. Put in terms that Jablonka and Lamb might use, niche construction creates a kind of "ecological system of inheritance" (Figure 9.2).

The Importance of Constructivist Evolutionary Approaches for Biocultural Anthropology

The approaches laid out here go well beyond privileging genetic mechanisms as the main or sole force in evolution. But they do fit well with the ways in which some researchers have long seen selection interacting with environments over the course of

- **Anthropocene.** Refers to the geological epoch defined by substantial human influence over ecosystems.

Figure 9.2 Niche Construction and the Loss of Wetlands. The conversion of wetlands illustrates the effects of environmental alteration with evolutionary dimensions. Environmental change creates new selection pressures on organisms, and those species that cannot adapt to the new conditions may go extinct, especially if there is no other environment in which they can live.

evolutionary time without reducing those processes to natural selection. The biologist Sewall Wright's ideas about selection laid the groundwork for this perspective in the 1930s with his notion of the "adaptive landscape," which we discuss in "Classic Contributions: Sewell Wright, Evolution, and Adaptive Landscapes."

In a field as diverse as biological anthropology—which brings together specialties ranging from primatology and paleoanthropology to human population genetics—it would be unreasonable to assume that all the details discussed earlier are accepted in equal measure. Much less should we expect the constructivist approach to be shared by all, given the range of philosophical approaches among scholars. Nevertheless, in terms of meeting the challenge of constructing a holistic biocultural perspective—one that takes culture *and* biology equally seriously—these positions provide critical theoretical fuel for a productively complicated understanding of human evolution. Further, the constructivist approach here acknowledges that biocultural dynamics are open-ended and involve interactions between diverse forces and agents. In the next section, we explore how to apply these insights to the evolution of human behavior.

THINKING ABOUT HUMAN BIOCULTURAL EVOLUTION

Throughout this book, not just in this section, we take a broadly constructivist view of human culture, biology, language, and prehistory. What are some of the strengths and weaknesses of the constructivist perspective? How is it possible to reconcile a constructivist definition of culture, such as that found in Chapter 2—"culture consists of the collective processes that make the artificial seem natural" (p. 37)—with the constructivist approach toward evolution presented here?

CLASSIC CONTRIBUTIONS

Sewall Wright, Evolution, and the Adaptive Landscape

SEWALL WRIGHT (1889–1988) was a geneticist and theoretical biologist who played a central role in developing the modern synthesis (see Chapter 3) and creating the field of population genetics. Although he was not an anthropologist, some of his ideas anticipated evolutionary complexities with which anthropologists today are grappling. One of these is his idea of the "adaptive landscape," which fits well with ideas about niche construction and especially ecological inheritance (Skipper 2004). The concept of adaptive landscape employs the metaphor of "peaks" and "valleys" to represent the various beneficial and not so beneficial genetic combinations in a population. The peaks represent the gene combinations that create high fitness in a given environment, and valleys represent low fitness in the same environment. It uses a three-dimensional imaging technique to simplify our understanding of the ways genes interact with each other and the environment, and can be instructive in viewing evolutionary dynamics as a kind of "rugged landscape" that varies over time and across space. Wright's theoretical insistence on what he calls "balance" in evaluating the influences over these processes is also important. In this excerpt from a 1932 essay, Wright discusses some general conclusions he reached from using this kind of peaks and valleys model.

Sewall Wright at Harvard University.

Summing up: I have attempted to form a judgment as to the conditions for evolution based on the statistical consequences of Mendelian heredity. The most general conclusion is that evolution depends on a certain balance among its factors. There must be gene mutation, but an excessive rate gives an array of freaks, not evolution; there must be selection, but too severe a process destroys the field of variability, and thus the basis for further advance; prevalence of local inbreeding with a species has extremely important evolutionary consequences, but too close inbreeding leads merely to extinction. A certain amount of crossbreeding is favorable but not too much. In this dependence on balance the species is like a living organism. At all levels of organization life depends on the maintenance of a certain balance among its factors.

More specifically under biparental reproduction, a very low rate of mutation balanced by moderate selection is enough to maintain a practically infinite field of gene combinations within the species. The field actually occupied is relatively small though sufficiently extensive that no two individuals have the same genetic constitution. The course of evolution through the general field is not controlled by direction of mutation and not directly by selection, except as conditions change, but by a trial and error mechanism consisting of a largely nonadaptive differentiation of local races (due to inbreeding balanced by occasional crossbreeding) and a determination of long time trend by intergroup selection. [Wright 1932:365–66]

Questions for Reflection

1. Why is having a simple visual tool to explain evolution both a positive and a negative thing?

2. What does Sewall mean when he uses the notion of "balance" in considering evolutionary processes?

How Does Behavior Evolve?

It is not uncommon these days to encounter sensational media reports claiming that scientists have discovered the evolutionary or genetic origins of certain human behaviors, such as warfare, courtship, love-making, and so forth during the ancient past. They might explain that men cannot be loyal to their wives because they are driven by a deep impulse to have more offspring or that women are domestic and nurturing because of evolutionary pressure to care for the young by the campfire. With their sound-bite qualities and the fact that they often quote scientific authorities, such stories play well in the media. But what are the scientific bases of claims about the evolution of human behavior? In this section, we explore some of the prominent approaches, discuss why they often oversimplify matters, and articulate a biocultural framework for understanding the evolution of human behavior.

Prominent Approaches

Researchers have been proposing scientific theories to understand the evolution of human behavior since Darwin's era. In recent decades these discussions have been dominated by sociobiology, developed in the 1970s, which focuses on social behavior from a neo-Darwinian point of view. Other approaches include human behavioral ecology, evolutionary psychology, and dual-inheritance theory. We discuss each in turn.

Sociobiology

Sociobiology uses principles drawn from the biological sciences to explain human social behavior and social institutions. One strand, known as human ethology, argues that evolution has programmed animals, among them humans, to behave in specific ways in response to certain environmental triggers. In explaining human warfare, for example, a human ethologist might emphasize that it is an expression of a basic imperative that all animals share, which is to expand or protect one's territory to ensure a secure resource base. Another strand of sociobiology emphasizes that pressures of natural selection and the maximization of reproductive success explain the evolution of human behavior. This approach was initially framed by E. O. Wilson in his 1975 book *Sociobiology*. As an ant biologist, Wilson was attuned to the complex social dynamics of ants, and he suggested that the same principles used to explain the evolution of social behaviors among insects and animals should also apply to humans. In developing his case, he asserts three basic points: (1) understanding behavior can be done in more or less the same way as understanding a simple genetic system, (2) natural selection is the main force behind the evolution of behavior, and (3) genes promoting a variety of human social behaviors have been favored over time (Fuentes 2009b).

The approach that Wilson developed brings together the main hypotheses of human evolution and the fossil datasets available in the 1970s. He argued that when humans became big game hunters, the process of mental evolution was accelerated, and human social groups developed a sexual division of labor. That division of labor was rooted in special bonds between males and females (eventually formalized as marriage), and while males went out and hunted big game, females stayed at base camps and were responsible for caregiving and basic foraging (Figure 9.3). Over the past thirty years, some researchers in the biological and social sciences have incorporated elements of Wilson's assumptions in their work to explain matters ranging from why some people are violent to generosity among relatives.

- **Sociobiology.** An approach that uses principles drawn from the biological sciences to explain human social behavior and social institutions.

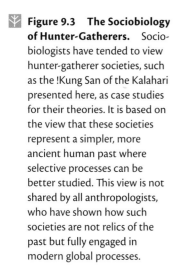

Figure 9.3 The Sociobiology of Hunter-Gatherers. Sociobiologists have tended to view hunter-gatherer societies, such as the !Kung San of the Kalahari presented here, as case studies for their theories. It is based on the view that these societies represent a simpler, more ancient human past where selective processes can be better studied. This view is not shared by all anthropologists, who have shown how such societies are not relics of the past but fully engaged in modern global processes.

- **Human behavioral ecology (HBE).** A perspective that focuses on how ecological and social factors affect behavior through natural selection.

- **Evolutionary psychology (EP).** A perspective focused on understanding the evolution of psychological mechanisms resulting in human behavior.

- **Psychological modules.** Adaptive clusters of cognitive function or information-processing mechanisms situated in human minds.

Human Behavioral Ecology (HBE)

Human behavioral ecology, or HBE, focuses on how ecological and social factors affect behavior. HBE applies sociobiology's neo-Darwinian approach toward natural selection to behavior, focusing on how ecological pressures affect an individual's fitness as well as energy expenditure and gain. In this approach each behavior or set of related behaviors (e.g., hunting, food sharing, caring for young, etc.) has evolutionary costs and benefits.

HBE assumes that organisms strive for optimal—that is, the best possible—adaptive responses to environmental problems. Those behaviors with lower success (fewer offspring produced, or more energy lost) will eventually disappear from the population, leaving only the most successful behaviors. HBE researchers recognize that most behavior in the real world does not reflect optimal responses, so HBE models can create a baseline to identify any particular constraints that interfere with optimal responses. Because behavior is a collection of adaptive responses, HBE sees flexibility in individual behavior as itself adaptive—a result of individuals striving to optimize lifetime reproductive success in diverse ecological circumstances. For example, it is unlikely that at any time in our evolution any group of humans has been able to optimize their hunting strategy to get the largest possible bounty of food for the energy expended during a hunt. But HBE assumes that groups try to achieve these ends.

Evolutionary Psychology (EP)

The basic goal of **evolutionary psychology**, or EP, is to understand the evolution of the psychological mechanisms guiding human behavior throughout history. EP fuses basic ideas from sociobiology with the concepts of universal **psychological modules**, which are areas of the mind specifically targeted toward certain functions. EP's main idea is that the human mind evolves in the face of resolving the challenges of natural selection (Barkow et al. 1992). It is based on three premises: (1) all humans possess the same basic set of evolved psychological mechanisms; (2) these psychological mechanisms are adaptations resulting from natural selection; and (3) the human mind is adapted, not to modern circumstances, but to the lifeways of our hunter-gatherer ancestors, because 99% of our evolutionary history was spent in this fashion. So EP considers the minds of present-day humans to be adapted to problems like food acquisition, territory selection and shelter, and protection from threats.

Dual-Inheritance Theory (DIT)

Focusing on culture as the mechanism through which behavior evolves, **dual-inheritance theory (DIT)** is more rooted in anthropology than either HBE or EP. DIT makes five basic assumptions: "(1) Culture is information that people acquire from others by teaching, imitation, and other forms of social learning. . . . (2) Culture change should be modeled as a Darwinian evolutionary process. . . . (3) Culture is part of human biology. . . . (4) Culture distinguishes human evolution from the evolution of other organisms; and (5) Genes and culture co-evolve" (Boyd and Richerson 2005:3–4).

Dual-inheritance theorists see culture as a set of information just as geneticists see the genetic code as a set of information. In this perspective, culture is an evolving pool of ideas, beliefs, values, and knowledge transmitted between individuals, similar to a gene pool. DIT holds that culture variants and genetic variants (genes) interact, under pressures of natural selection, to shape the evolution of human behavior. As such, DIT emphasizes that processes of natural selection can result in genetic variants and culture variants, both in varying frequencies.

Why These Approaches Oversimplify Matters

Although they differ in their details, each of these approaches shares a common characteristic, which lies in their understandings of culture—if they even recognize culture as a relevant category at all. They ignore or dismiss the complexity of how much culture's symbolic processes shape and guide human behavior, viewing human behaviors as expressions of an underlying universal genetic imperative, the outcome of a selective process, or a phenomenon that maximizes reproductive fitness. Even dual-inheritance theory, which does recognize the existence of culture, views cultural processes as mimics of universal biological processes. None of these approaches recognizes that human evolution could involve the construction of meanings, niches, bodies, and so on in open-ended ways.

Also all of these approaches are on some level deterministic, which is to say, they reduce the causes of human behavior to one determining factor, such as a search for reproductive fitness or an attempt to optimize an energetic expenditure for maximum benefit to the organism. More specifically, they are all variations on **biological determinism**, which is the idea that human behaviors and beliefs are primarily, if not solely, the result of biological characteristics and processes. Determinism reduces complexity and is the opposite of the alternative approach we have been advocating in this chapter, an approach that seeks to explain complexity without oversimplifying it. Our approach is one that emphasizes qualities of **emergence**, which refers to important processes and events that arise from interactions of wholes that are not explainable by the action of their parts. In "Thinking Like an Anthropologist: Emergence, Reductionism, and Human Behavior," we examine the differences between these two approaches.

A Contemporary Biocultural Approach to the Evolution of Human Behavior

Having considered the prominent approaches and their limitations, and combined with what we have covered in this and the preceding chapters, we can now frame our

- **Dual-inheritance theory (DIT).** The perspective that culture is evolutionarily important, that culture evolves in a Darwinian fashion, and that understanding gene-culture co-evolution is the key to understanding human behavior.

- **Biological determinism.** The idea that human behaviors and beliefs are primarily, if not solely, the result of biological characteristics and processes.

- **Emergence.** Refers to important processes and events that arise from interactions of wholes that are not explainable by the action of their parts.

Thinking Like an Anthropologist

Emergence, Reductionism, and Human Behavior

ANTHROPOLOGISTS BEGIN THEIR research by asking questions. In this box, we want you to learn how to ask questions as an anthropological researcher. Part 1 describes a situation and follows up with questions we would ask. Part 2 asks you to do the same thing with a different situation.

PART 1: EMERGENCE AND REDUCTIONISM IN EVOLUTION

Reductionism is the process of dividing wholes into constituent parts and looking at the parts to explain the whole. Biology, and much of evolutionary theory, includes a long history of thinking about life using reductionism. But the philosopher and theologian Loyal Rue (2007) describes reductionism as a problem because it does not adequately explain how or why complexity emerges; it merely views complexity in nature as a bunch of piled-up simplicities. Traditional or neo-Darwinian evolutionary approaches are reductionistic because they focus on genes and natural selection as the most basic explanation for why organisms do what they do.

Anthropologists, however, try to avoid reductionism and instead practice holism—an approach in which the whole and the parts are equally the focus of study. Another key concept here is emergence—the idea that important processes and events arise from interactions of wholes that are not explainable by the action of their parts. For example, human societies are not really discrete measurable entities. They emerge from the communal interactions of the individuals in them and their shared cultural assumptions and practices.

The theoretical ecologist Robert Ulanowicz (2007) tells us that although emergence in nature might be rare, it can play an important role in how we understand the world. He outlines three aspects of systems that can lead to emergence—that is, to things being more than the sum of their parts. His first element is that every now and then, wild and out of the ordinary things happen, such as major shifts in local ecologies or mutation that lead to novel genetic structures. The second element is "self-influence," or how "a process in nature, via its interaction with other natural processes, can influence itself." This idea resembles the concept of niche construction, since organisms alter their surroundings which in turn alter the kinds of ecological pressures on themselves. Finally, Ulanowicz suggests that history plays a role in the structure and patterns seen in organisms. By this he means that the culmination of past changes in organisms

and systems influences the way they interact and the processes that emerge from those interactions.

To restate Ulanowicz's three points in the simplest terms: stuff happens, many processes affect themselves and the world around them, and the history of life affects the way life works today. So some parts of what humans or dogs or frogs do are not reducible to their genetics, to natural selection, or to any specific parts of their bodies or worlds. Rather, some patterns simply emerge from the interactions of whole bodies to ecosystems and to societies.

This concept of emergence helps us see how we can weave together biology with human cultures, feelings, language, and behavior, while recognizing that there may be more than one way to explain all of them.

What questions does the concept of emergence raise for anthropological researchers?

1. How might using the concept of emergence help us understand relationships between biology and culture?
2. What would be a concrete example of emergence in human evolutionary history?
3. What kinds of factors and patterns would we seek to identify in approaching human behavior from an emergent perspective?
4. What role do historical contingencies play in shaping emergent phenomena?
5. What methods would be appropriate to study emergent processes?

PART 2: AVOIDING REDUCTIONISM IN UNDERSTANDING OUR BEHAVIOR

The problem of altruistic behavior among humans has been one that sociobiologists have struggled over because it seems to have no tangible (i.e., genetic, selective, or energetic) benefits for the individual who behaves that way unless it is performed for genetic kin (see Chapter 7). This view of altruism is reductionistic because it assumes humans engage in transactions with each other primarily to maximize the biological fitness of themselves or their close genetic relations. An emergent view of altruism would emphasize that there is greater complexity in altruistic behaviors that goes well beyond purely biological dynamics. If you wanted to understand the problem of altruism using an emergence perspective, what questions would you ask as an anthropological researcher?

approach to human behavioral evolution using the following seven assumptions (adapted and modified from Fuentes 2004, 2009):

1. *The evolution of human behavior is not a matter of single, independent behaviors evolving, but of a system evolving.* Instead of just asking why specific behaviors exist and come into being, all behaviors must be seen within a broader context. Human behavior and culture are not individual actions but rather a constellation of systematic actions, experiences, and innovations.

2. *Niche construction is a core factor in the evolution of human behavior.* Any explanation of human behavior must recognize how much we rearrange the environments in which we live. We can respond to challenges in flexible and innovative ways with behavioral, niche constructing, and non-genetic effects all at once. For example, the controlled use of fire may have come as a response to pressures of cold weather, predation risks, the need to make the nutrition in food more accessible, and to provide some level of warmth and safety for sleeping in groups. These processes mean selective pressures on humans are more complicated than for other animals.

3. *Social and ecological inheritances are central elements of human behavior and its change.* For at least the past 20,000 years—and much longer in areas of Africa and Asia—humans have been born into places where humans already lived. Everything about our lives is affected by the previous generations. Thus, we inherit huge amounts of information as well as previous transformations in local ecology.

4. *Our sophisticated capacity for communication and information transfer is central to understanding human behavior.* Humans have unparalleled linguistic ability, with all of its symbolic and meaning-making possibilities. We cannot ignore this critical factor in our approach to human evolution.

5. *Human behavioral evolution involves a lot of feedback.* Rather than humans adapting directly to a local environmental challenges over time, they may alter small parts of the environment, prompting new types of interactions with the environment. For example, a technological change in weaponry might change hunting success, but it simultaneously changes the population of the animals hunted. Changes in animal populations in turn alter the presence of predators, which might allow humans to expand their range, possibly encountering new kinds of ecologies and pressures including the extinction of other species. This interactive feedback occurs within lifetimes, not just across generations.

6. *A diverse set of biological and sociocultural processes shuffles genetic variation in evolutionary change.* Contemporary research suggests that gene flow and genetic drift, in addition to the cultural, social, and symbolic practices that alter human demography, residence, movement, and interaction patterns have roles in genetic, phenotypic, and behavioral changes. Thus, natural selection is not the only relevant evolutionary process.

7. *Human behavior is plastic, flexible, and emergent.* The majority of human behavioral changes are unlikely to be optimal. Even if they do allow adaptation, they are rarely the best strategy possible. Further, any particular behavioral adaptation is unlikely to have come in response to a single selective pressure. Instead, the majority of successful human responses likely reflect a pattern of behavioral plasticity, flexibility, and emergence.

In the next two sections, we aim to put this biocultural framework to work by exploring some ways that we can see evolutionary processes at work in human populations today. We turn first to an intriguing issue, which is whether and how humans are evolving right now.

Are Modern Humans Evolving?

There is a common notion that circulates around evolution, which is that "it happened in the past." Underlying this view is the belief that evolutionary processes are driving toward a goal, a plateau where the species is in tune with its environment, and that most species we encounter have reached it. This is simply not the case. Evolution continues, unabated, until a species becomes extinct. It has no particular direction and there is no intrinsic value of one adaptation over another except survivability. As humans, we are continuing to evolve. But because we can extend the ability to survive and flourish beyond the mere genetic, human evolutionary patterns are complex, and there is often a fuzzy line between biological and cultural influences. In this section we consider aspects of our ongoing evolution as a species.

The Impact of Disease on Evolution

We've all had a cold. Colds are widespread in our species, and we have no effective means to eradicate them. Rhinoviruses, the group of viruses that cause colds, do not seem to pose a great existential challenge for us. But every now and again, viral outbreaks can be deadly. For example, in 2002 a variant of the common cold caused deadly outbreaks of a disease called SARS (Severe Acute Respiratory Syndrome) (Perris et al. 2003). The SARS virus is common among birds and mammals, and it is believed that it was passed to humans through close contact, butchering, or undercooked meats, probably in southern China. Human cultural behavior combined here with an evolving virus to threaten members of our species, creating a new evolutionary pressure on humans (Figure 9.4).

Human history is marked by the constant circulation of population-shaping diseases. Millions of Europeans died from bubonic plague during the Middle Ages. Millions of American Indians died from smallpox carried to the Americas by European explorers and settlers. Until recent decades, in fact, smallpox continued to be a major killer around the world. Many other infectious diseases—the flu and cholera, for example—continue to hit many human populations hard. Every time a major disease outbreak occurs in which members of a population die, a set of genetic complexes disappears from that population. An individual death might be due to chance, or it may be because of a lack of immune-system resistance. Evolution is taking place here: when the

Figure 9.4   The SARS Epidemic.   SARS represents a new disease that arose because of evolutionary change combined with cultural change.

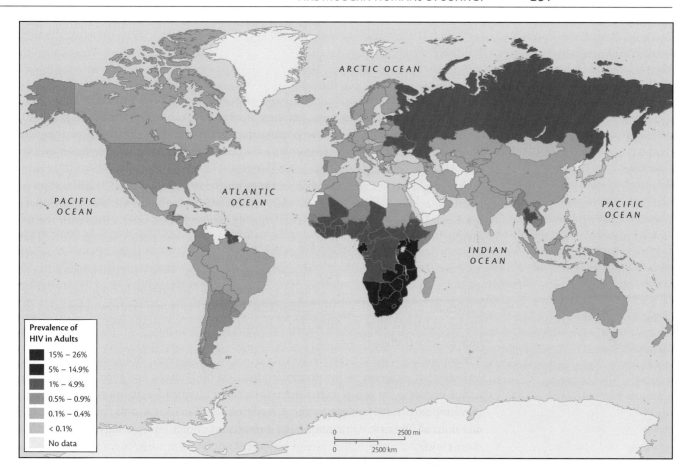

Prevalence of
HIV in Adults

■ 15% – 26%

■ 5% – 14.9%

■ 1% – 4.9%

▨ 0.5% – 0.9%

▨ 0.1% – 0.4%

▨ < 0.1%

□ No data

0   2500 mi

0   2500 km

epidemic subsides, the surviving population is genetically different from before because there has been a change in allele frequencies.

It is important to note, however, that biocultural practices strongly shape the experience and effects of disease. We explore this issue in more depth in Chapter 11, but consider, for example, the human immunodeficiency virus, or HIV, which causes AIDS. Although there is no cure, medicines now exist that make it possible for afflicted individuals in many Western countries to stay alive. The selective impacts of HIV are decreased if those individuals reproduce. But the effects of any disease, as well as access to those biocultural medical practices, are uneven. So in many less economically developed nations, AIDS remains a fatal disease, not the manageable chronic condition it is in North America and Europe. In sub-Saharan Africa, for example, AIDS is a disease of young adults—important years in the reproductive life of any individual—and is having important impacts on the evolutionary trajectory of that continent's populations, although it's not yet clear what those effects are (Figure 9.5).

What is important here is that the evolutionary pressures of diseases affect different populations differently, but not necessarily because there are any underlying genetic conditions in the populations. Rather, it is due to the differential access people have to healthcare because of broader socioeconomic and political relationships and processes.

Figure 9.5 The Global Distribution of HIV Infection. This map shows the percentage of the adult population estimated living with HIV infection in each region as of 2012.

Culture, Morphology, and Evolution

Morphology refers to the shape and form of the human body. Cultural practices, such as diet, body modifications, and patterns of daily activity, have the capacity to alter human morphology. Whether these changes translate into long-term evolutionary change, however, depends on the ways in which such changes affect human lives across generations.

Diet

Although all humans need certain basic nutrients and calories to survive, grow, and reproduce, different populations get those nutrients in varying quantities (Figure 9.6). Thanks to culture and important socioeconomic patterns like globalization, there are huge variations across populations in how people obtain and prepare food, and in what they eat (see Chapter 15).

One might expect that variable access to nutrition can help explain differences in bodily shape and form between and within human populations. An individual's height and weight range are inherited, but dietary practices, interacting with the individual's physiology and morphology, strongly shape the body's actual form. That body shape and form can be quite plastic. A well-known example of that plasticity comes from the documentary *Supersize Me* (Spurlock 2004), which follows a man who eats all his meals at McDonald's for a month. His extremely high fat/high carbohydrate diet had him gain 25 pounds (13% of his initial body weight), and his cholesterol levels shot up 40%. He suffered numerous physiological effects, and his morphology changed.

Most dietary changes are less extreme, but the relative caloric, dietary fat, and carbohydrate contents of any given diet do affect body shape and physiology. During recent decades, we can see this pattern in the widespread expansion of obesity. In "Anthropologist as Problem Solver: Clarifying the Biocultural and Evolutionary Dimensions of Obesity," we examine the interactions of diet, morphology, and evolution more closely.

Body Modification

In addition to shaping our bodies through diet, humans have, for a very long time, adorned themselves with things that change their appearance. The issue here is if, and how, these biocultural changes might affect human evolution.

Figure 9.6   Cultural Differences in Food Preparation and Diet.   A San woman from southern Africa prepares bird eggs that have been foraged (left); and college students share a pizza meal (right). There are big differences between these two groups terms of how they obtain and share food, and their actual diets also differ quite dramatically. In Chapter 15 we examine these issues in more detail.

Anthropologist as Problem Solver

Clarifying the Biocultural and Evolutionary Dimensions of Obesity

🌿 **Obese Morphology.**

The past sixty years have seen a dramatic global rise in obesity, which is the creation of excess body fat to the point of impairing bodily health and function, and of people being overweight, or having abnormal fat accumulation. There are now more overweight and obese people in the world than undernourished people, and several dozen countries have obesity rates exceeding 10% of their populations. Because these conditions can cause chronic diseases—diabetes and heart disease among them—health officials and researchers consider them to be among the most serious public health crises facing our world today. Because of our detailed knowledge of human relationships with food, morphology, and socioeconomic patterns, holistic anthropology has important contributions to make to address this crisis.

The ability to become obese is a universal human trait. But it was essentially non-existent until about 10,000 years ago (Brown 1991). Although historically obesity is associated with the wealthy, the situation is reversed in industrialized nations like the United States, where rates of obesity among the poor have far surpassed those of the wealthy. This fact has led to two explanations that have captured the public imagination and shaped national dialogue about the matter. One is that cheap, processed fast foods cause obesity and that some people simply cannot resist the temptations of food that is bad for them. In these terms, obesity is a problem of simply not having the individual willpower to control oneself in the face of tempting and inexpensive foods.

The other explanation is some version of the "thrifty gene hypothesis," which holds that certain groups of people evolved to metabolize energy efficiently, which helps them when food is scarce. But in times of abundance, these same people are predisposed to gain weight quickly because their bodies are ill-equipped to handle the extra calories (Neel 1962). Both of these explanations assume that eating "bad" foods that diverge from the normal human diet causes obesity (Leonard 2002). As appealing as these explanations may sound, however, they wrongly assume that humans have a "normal" diet, which is not the case. As omnivores, our dietary physiology evolved to be open-ended, leaving our needs to be met within the natural environments and socioeconomic and cultural contexts in which we live.

Deep in our evolutionary past, hominins evolved traits that promote the accumulation and storage of energy as adipose tissue, or fat. These traits likely developed for lean times when food was less available, but they are also linked to the demands of our developing brains, and, among females, to fertility. As a result, there are genetic dimensions to obesity (Choquet and Meyre 2011), but there is no single gene (thrifty gene) that causes individuals to gain a lot of weight, and obesity is definitely not genetically determined anyway.

From a biocultural perspective, obesity is a complex metabolic syndrome, or combination of medical conditions, that has some genetic dimensions but also non-genetic ones. Factors like maternal health and diet during pregnancy as well as local environmental conditions can influence an individual's predisposition. For example, smoking, insufficient nutrition during pregnancy, socioeconomic class, high temperatures in the natural environment, and certain environmental toxins all appear to be linked to a higher likelihood of developing obesity later in life. Cultural factors also shape access to food and how much is consumed at a meal. Furthermore, obesity is not inevitable. Although individuals may be predisposed to gain weight more easily than others, it can only develop if a person eats a lot of food while expending little energy (Ulijaszek and Lofink 2006). We now understand that it is a mix of biological and cultural factors that contributes to weight gain.

What contributions do biocultural insights have on public efforts to tackle obesity? One major point is that obesity cannot be successfully addressed as a public health issue by reducing it to a matter of an individual's willpower, "thrifty genes," and/or genetic predispositions, all of which have often led to failed diets or inappropriate medical solutions. Obesity is a complex emergent phenomenon that

(continued)

Anthropologist as Problem Solver (continued)

involves developmental processes in the body, socioeconomic networks and inequalities, and behaviors shaped by culture. Thus, as biocultural anthropologist Daniel Lende suggests (2008), it is necessary to address the broader systemic dynamics that prioritize cheap low-quality food, inactive lifestyles, and what he calls the "cultural biology system" that shapes eating patterns, body image, and expectations about exercise. Anthropologist Alexandra Brewis (2011) adds that the connection between obesity and socioeconomic disadvantage means that obesity needs to be framed as a social justice issue. In her view a fair society will do a much better job of distributing amenities—such as parks, walkable neighborhoods, and healthy food sources—in low-income areas, which would lower obesity rates. In practical terms, these anthropologists support a call to intervene in public discussions and policy debates promoting more holistic biocultural perspectives than currently exist.

Questions for Reflection

1. The idea that an individual can change his or her motivations through willpower is one version of a broader "self-help" culture that exists in North America. Why do you think this view is so persistent?

2. What role do you think evolutionary arguments should play in our public and policy debates over matters like obesity?

Different populations have distinct genetically based differences in physiological and morphological patterns. For example, in many human populations men have a physiological pattern that gives them facial hair, while in others (such as in Southeast Asia), men have minimal facial hair. Gene flow within and across populations probably played a role in creating these genetically inherited differences. But then, men alter these patterns through cultural behavior. We call it shaving.

People usually modify their bodily appearance because of cultural beliefs about attractiveness. Around the world, these practices are quite variable: people scar their skin, get tattoos, modify their genitals, have breast enhancements or reductions, change their teeth or get a new jawline, work out at the gym to build muscles, and any number of other things (Fuentes 2007). Do these things have evolutionary significance? Maybe, because they can enhance an individual's reproductive fitness. But unless the practice actually affects fitness—for example, sterility because of these practices is one scenario in which it does—it may not have any long-term evolutionary impact (Figure 9.7).

Daily Activity Patterns

Peoples' daily activity patterns—of work, movement, and so on—can have evolutionary consequences, since they can directly affect reproductive physiology. Mass rural-urban migration, modern transportation using motorized vehicles, and other factors have changed how people use their bodies. Sitting for long periods in an office or auto, especially when combined with longer periods of social stress and poor dietary patterns, can greatly impact individual physiology. The consequences range from chronic high blood pressure and heart disease to reduced fertility (Figure 9.8).

Human Migration Patterns

Gene flow is our most easily observable evolutionary process today. High rates of transnational migration, which bring diverse populations into contact, produce important changes in alleles. Cultural changes contribute to migration and the movement of alleles, including improvements in travel technology; social changes promoting mobility; wars, terrorism, civil unrest, and environmental problems that drive

Figure 9.7 Body Modifications and Evolution. In practically every human society, people modify their bodies through practices like tattooing, piercing, scarification, and other practices. Under what conditions might these practices have evolutionary impacts?

out-migration; even government actions, such as creating resettlement programs welcoming refugees. In northern European countries such as Germany, for example, where an aging population is stoking fears of a declining workforce, the invitation of foreigners through guest worker programs and refugee resettlement programs can have long-term evolutionary effects on the population.

The overall effects of such migrations for modern humans include (1) reduced differences in allele frequencies between populations; and (2) increased overall genetic variation within populations as specific, new alleles are added (Fuentes 2007). But the long-term impacts of cultural practices of diet, body modification, and daily activity level are less predictable. Perhaps these things affect the course of human evolution. But it is more likely that they only influence the expression of human variation, displaying our capacity as a species for behavioral and morphological diversity, without really affecting the species as a whole. So, where is this all headed? In the last section, we address that issue.

Figure 9.8 Shifting Physical Activity Patterns. In traditional and agricultural societies (left), people tend to be much more physically active than in contemporary urban settings (right), where people tend to live sedentary lives. When the shifting activity patterns begin to affect reproductive physiologies we can begin to see evolutionary consequences.

● ●

THINKING CRITICALLY ABOUT HUMAN BIOCULTURAL EVOLUTION

Social scientists tend to think of migration patterns primarily in socioeconomic terms, as involving "push-pull" factors like lack of opportunity back home (push) and greater opportunities in a new place (pull). If you had to articulate a biocultural perspective on migration patterns, what key points would you raise?

● ●

Where Are Biocultural Evolutionary Patterns Taking Us?

If you are a fan of science fiction films, you are no doubt familiar with what that genre thinks about our future: we will develop giant brains, using our telepathic capability to communicate with each other, or, as the movie *Wall-E* visualizes, begin losing our ability to walk as we lie about in lounge chairs while robots do everything for us. From the perspective of biocultural anthropology, these things are—for better or worse—unlikely to happen. During the last 300,000 years, brain size has stopped growing and only slight changes in the basic form of the body have occurred, suggesting that for the time being we have approached a relatively static basic body shape. And as we discussed at the beginning of this chapter, due to the trade-offs involved with bipedalism—including structural refinements to the pelvis that narrowed the birth canal—our heads are unlikely to grow any larger.

During the past 50,000–40,000 years, most evolutionary changes have occurred through gene flow, adaptive immune responses to new diseases, and cultural changes in behavior. However, evolutionary change is a constant of nature, and looking ahead, three biocultural issues could affect our evolutionary future as a species: population growth, genetic manipulation, and adaptive behaviors.

Global Population and Human Density

The global human population has grown dramatically in recent decades. Only 10,000 years ago, between 5 and 20 million humans inhabited the planet. By about 1804 our planet's population reached 1 billion, and by 1970 it was approximately 3.6 billion. Today the population numbers over 7 billion, doubling in only 40 years. This situation is unprecedented for our species, and we are just beginning to grapple with its evolutionary implications.

Our species faces important challenges because of this growth. One of these, of course, is the ability to feed ourselves. Up to this point, technological progress in food production has met the challenge, although there is considerable unevenness in access to food across populations due to social inequalities and socioeconomic dynamics like globalization (see Chapter 15). Thanks to developments in medical technology, infant mortality rates are generally falling as life expectancy rates continue to increase. These patterns are averages, and as is the case with food, who you are in global socioeconomic processes shapes any social group's actual experience. The situations of both food and healthcare point to a crucial fact: it is unequal distributions of technology, wealth, and access—not genetic causes—that will shape how human populations meet these new challenges.

An increasingly large population, coupled with greater reliance on technology, means that members of our species rely more and more on specialized socioeconomic systems such as industrial agriculture and manufacturing to get us the goods and food we need to live. Even as we marvel at the sophistication of the tools we now create to meet whatever challenges we face as a species, it is increasingly obvious that these processes are having significantly negative effects on air, water, and soils. In evolutionary terms, it is difficult to tell where industrialization will take us since it's only a couple of centuries old.

Another effect of our population growth is an increase in our population densities (the number of people per unit of space). For much of human evolutionary history, people were widely spread out and densities were low, but during the last several hundred years we have seen intensive urbanization and the rise of large cities that bring millions of humans in close daily contact. Although it is still too early to tell what the long-term evolutionary impacts of high population densities might be, we do see changing patterns of non-infectious diseases in these areas. There are also demographic dimensions here, one aspect being that the age structure of many human societies is changing, which carries important socioeconomic implications (Figure 9.9).

Against this backdrop of great uncertainties, we do know that as a population grows, genetic diversity tends to increase. Although recent research using new genetic sequencing techniques suggests that humans have lower rates of genetic mutation than the fossil record seems to suggest (Scally and Durbin 2012), as more individuals are born, the rate of novel genetic combinations increases. This has adaptive potential for the species in the long term, but only as long as individuals reach reproductive age and have children to pass on that genetic material.

Genetic Manipulation

Beyond all the evolutionary forces we have discussed in this chapter, humans have added yet another force of evolution: direct genetic alteration. Scientists can alter allele frequencies and even create new alleles for transgenic (across species) insertion into an organisms. Transgenic and genetically modified foods, cloning, and genetic therapies are increasingly important dimensions of our evolutionary future as a species, as well as the plants and animals we interact with.

Much of this work has focused on non-human animals—making crops more productive for agriculture, for example—but experimental research is increasingly focused on humans. In gene therapy, sequences of DNA are altered by inserting a specific sequence into a non-coding region of DNA to replace a non-functional gene. Gene therapies have shown only mixed success, however. Why? Because although we may know more about the human genome than ever and can isolate particular genes to manipulate them, having that genomic knowledge is a bit like having a list of parts for a Boeing 747 without necessarily knowing how they go together or what the principles of aeronautics are (Lock 2005). In other words, as we have shown throughout these chapters, genes never operate in isolation but are always expressed in relation to developmental, environmental, and sociocultural contexts. Pulling back and putting this all in an evolutionary perspective, hundreds of generations will probably have to pass before we can tell if genetic manipulations have long-term effects on our species.

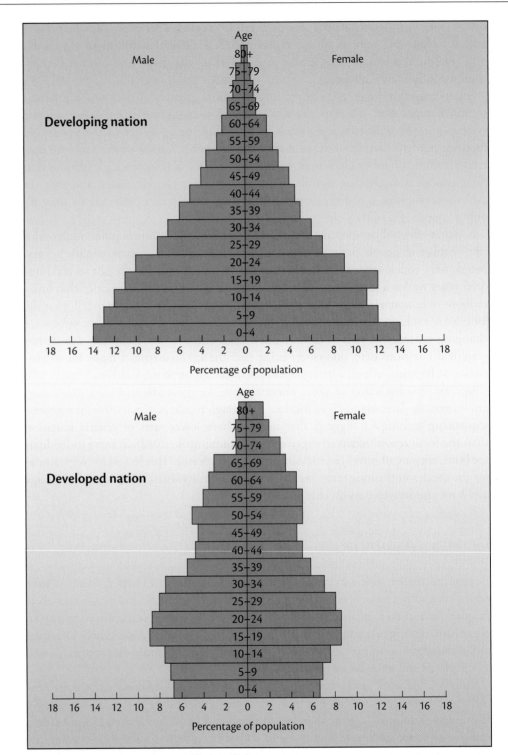

Figure 9.9   Population Distributions and Age.
The top graphic shows the age distribution of a typical developing nation, where there are large numbers of young people. The bottom shows the pattern of an industrialized country, where the number of children is smaller, and more people live to old age. These demographic patterns have distinct effects on an economy, political system, and migration patterns.

- **Geneticization.** The use of genetics to explain health and social problems over other possible causes.

Nevertheless, one effect of the hype around genetic manipulation is the creeping **geneticization** of health, intelligence, personality, and the like, which involves the use of genetics to explain health and social problems rather than other possible causes (Lippman 2001). One recent illustration is a situation in which the Burlington Northern Santa Fe railroad ran genetic tests on thirty-six employees who suffered from carpal tunnel syndrome, a painful wrist condition brought on by repetitive motion. Although the company claimed no wrongdoing, critics accused it of seeking to deny injured individuals compensation benefits on the basis that they were genetically predisposed to the condition. While there may be certain genetic dimensions to a condition like carpal tunnel syndrome, they alone do not define the problem. Geneticizing diverts attention from the social causes of the condition, which in this case had to do with the type of repetitive labor these workers were performing. Because of possible abuses, ethical, legal, and social justice concerns about who controls genetic information are expanding and likely to grow more important in coming decades.

Adaptive Behavioral Patterns

When a behavior emerges that gives individuals within a population some kind of reproductive advantage, it is considered adaptive. One of the big debates about adaptive processes in humans is how much of current behavioral patterns emerged during our evolutionary past and how much expresses our broad behavioral potential that is made possible by specific current environments (Fuentes 2007). As we discussed earlier, some researchers (such as evolutionary psychologists) argue that many human behavioral patterns—things like sexual attraction, jealousy, male aggression and competition, marriage, and so forth—were adaptive responses of Pleistocene humans. Others (such as the authors of this book) argue that rather than reflecting specific past adaptations, most modern human behavior emerges through the life experiences of individuals and the political, economic, and historical contexts in which they live. Through culture, our species has the capacity to express a wide range of social behaviors. Some of these behaviors might have adaptive significance, others will be non-adaptive, and yet most behaviors will simply be irrelevant to reproductive success.

This point means that predicting our behavioral futures is tricky, at best. One of anthropology's hallmark findings is that human behavior is not "hardwired," that is, genetically determined and inflexible. If it is true, however, that much of our behavioral patterns emerged as adaptations to past environments, then we should not expect these behavioral patterns to change much over the next millennia, regardless of whatever changes technology might create for our species. But if it is the case that our behavioral patterns are not rooted in past adaptations, then we would expect to observe continuing diversity and variation in how people behave. We take this position.

What all of this tells us is that human biocultural dynamics have become so complex that it is simply too difficult to separate biology from culture in understanding why people behave the ways they do. This does not mean that inquiry into behavioral evolution is a fool's errand—by any stretch—but it does mean that whatever progress we make will happen through greater commitments to anthropology's holistic and integrative potential.

THINKING CRITICALLY ABOUT HUMAN BIOCULTURAL EVOLUTION

During the last three centuries of industrialization, all the biocultural forces and processes we discuss here have been present since all humans were hunter-gatherers, with one exception: genetic manipulation that comes from biogenetic engineering. How is this dynamic, new factor likely to change the human evolutionary trajectory in different ways from all the other evolutionary processes?

Conclusion

Patterns of evolutionary change are complex. We can see these complex patterns in something as apparently straightforward as sleeping, the theme with which we opened this chapter. Hominin sleep evolved by favoring group sleeping, and our shift to bipedalism produced neurologically immature infants, leading to close parent-infant sleeping arrangements. Our own culture's message that babies should sleep alone is not universal among contemporary humans and pits our behavior against our deep evolutionary history. As this example shows, the intersections of biology, evolution, and culture mean that mundane behaviors, like sleeping, are not as straightforward as they seem.

A holistic biocultural approach to human evolution has benefited from developments in contemporary evolutionary theory that move us away from reductionistic accounts of human behavior. These new theories focus on multiple inheritances, social learning, changing relationships with the environment, and the power of human culture when asking questions about human evolution and behavior. They help us approach biocultural dynamics as open-ended, emergent, and characterized by interactions between diverse forces and agents.

Humans are still evolving and will continue to do so. We know that disease, diet, activity patterns, medical practices, and global migration impact our morphologies and physiologies in diverse ways. Whether they have evolutionary implications is in many cases still unclear because the complex intersections between culture, behavior, and biology make predictions about human evolutionary trajectories difficult. But these processes do generate important variations among contemporary human populations. In our next chapter, we explore how holistic anthropology approaches that human variation.

KEY TERMS

Anthropocene   p. 242

Behavioral system of
   inheritance   p. 241

Biocultural   p. 237

Biological determinism
   p. 247

Constructivist approach
   p. 239

Developmental systems
   theory (DST)   p. 241

Dual-inheritance theory
   (DIT)   p. 247

Emergence   p. 247

Epigenetic system of
   inheritance   p. 240

Evolutionary psychology
   (EP)   p. 246

Geneticization   p. 258

Human behavioral ecology
   (HBE)   p. 246

Psychological modules
   p. 246

Sociobiology   p. 245

Symbolic system of
   inheritance   p. 241

Reviewing the Chapter

Chapter Section	What We Know	To Be Resolved
How do biocultural patterns affect evolution?	The intertwining of biology and culture in human evolution has produced biocultural dynamics that are open-ended and emergent. Key elements of these processes include multiple inheritances, developmental openness, and niche construction.	Although the constructivist approach presented here strives to take biology and culture equally seriously, not all biological anthropologists share that philosophical orientation to human evolution, and debates continue about the relative influences of biology or culture on human evolution.
How does behavior evolve?	A contemporary biocultural approach to the evolution of human behavior emphasizes the non-reductionistic and emergent qualities of behavior. It also emphasizes that behaviors are shaped by multiple inheritances (genetic, behavioral, symbolic, ecological), niche construction, feedback, and human plasticity and flexibility.	Reductionist paradigms such as sociobiology continue to exercise influence among some biological anthropologists, and appreciation for qualities of emergence are not universal in the field.
Are modern humans evolving?	Modern humans are continuing to evolve, and they do it in biocultural contexts. Although humans can change their morphology quite readily, it is not always clear what the evolutionary implications of those actions might be. Nevertheless, migration and disease transmission have clear evolutionary impacts on contemporary humans.	Although no anthropologist would take seriously the idea that humans stopped evolving, those influenced by evolutionary psychology assume that most of our behavioral traits developed in the evolutionary past.
Where are culture and evolution taking us?	Human morphology has seemed to stabilize during the past 300,000 years, so it is unlikely that we will see big evolutionary changes in our bodily form anytime soon. A focus on population growth, genetic manipulation, and dynamics of behavioral adaptation can yield insights into possible evolutionary futures.	Given the complexity and emergent qualities of biocultural processes, any predictions about our species' evolutionary trajectories are riddled with uncertainties.

Readings

In his book *Tales of the Ex-Apes: How We Think About Human Evolution* (Berkeley: University of California Press, 2015), Jonathan Marks offers an approach to human evolution similar to the one we take in this book. He critiques biological reductionist approaches and explains how and why we are a biocultural species.

• • • • • • • • • • • • • • • • • • • •

The book *Race, Monogamy, and Other Lies They Told You: Busting Myths About Human Nature* (Berkeley: University of California Press, 2015) by this book's coauthor Agustín Fuentes challenges widely circulating myths about human nature, such as the idea that humans are naturally violent, that women and men are fundamentally different because of

biological differences, and that races are rooted in biology. It is an excellent tool kit to help readers bust simplistic scientific myths about humans.

• • • • • • • • • • • • • • • • • • • •

As Alexandra Brewis reports in *Obesity: Cultural and Biocultural Perspectives* (New Brunswick, NJ: Rutgers University Press, 2011), the study of the causes and consequences of obesity is a relatively new area of research for anthropologists. This book provides an overview of the issues as they relate to biocultural anthropology.

• • • • • • • • • • • • • • • • • • • •

Melvin Konnor's book *The Evolution of Childhood: Relationships, Emotion, Mind* (Cambridge, MA: Harvard University Press, 2011) explores how

an evolutionary perspective can shed light on why and how humans developed a long period of dependency and cognitive development during infancy and childhood.

• • • • • • • • • • • • • • • • • • • •

Douglas Fry's book *The Human Potential for Peace: An Anthropological Challenge to Assumptions About War and Violence* (New York: Oxford University Press, 2006) challenges biological determinists who claim violence and war are innate human characteristics resulting from our evolution as a species. It shows that the capacity for aggression and the ability to prevent and limit violence are rooted in human cultural processes.

• • • • • • • • • • • • • • • • • • • •

Contemporary Human Biodiversity

Understanding Our Differences and Similarities

In 2005, the U.S. Food and Drug Administration (FDA) approved a new drug called BiDil for the treatment of congestive heart failure among African Americans. Congestive heart failure is a chronic condition in which the heart muscle is too weak to circulate blood normally, producing symptoms like shortness of breath, tiredness, and swelling in the legs. BiDil is the first drug ever intended and approved for a particular racial group. It works well, too: one rigorous set of studies demonstrated its positive benefits for African American patients. For some scientists, medical researchers, and policymakers, the fact that African Americans respond well to this treatment confirms that racial groups have specific biological and genetic characteristics that can be treated with specific drugs.

But these claims do not hold up to critical scrutiny, and nothing about this situation proves that African Americans have biologically or genetically significant differences from other racial groups. How can this be? The answer lies in the political, economic, and social reasons this drug was developed and approved (Inda 2014). In recent years, the medical profession and the FDA have been under pressure from Congress and the public to reduce disparities in medical treatment among minority groups. Racialized minorities—African Americans, Latinos, Native Americans, and so on—are afflicted at higher rates than whites by illnesses like heart disease, diabetes, cancer, and asthma, yet they are more likely to receive serious obstacles to treatment, poor treatment, or no treatment at all.

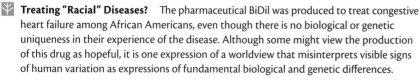

Treating "Racial" Diseases? The pharmaceutical BiDil was produced to treat congestive heart failure among African Americans, even though there is no biological or genetic uniqueness in their experience of the disease. Although some might view the production of this drug as hopeful, it is one expression of a worldview that misinterprets visible signs of human variation as expressions of fundamental biological and genetic differences.

263

Responding to this pressure and seeing an economic opportunity, the drug manufacturer targeted its efforts in developing BiDil exclusively for African Americans. After demonstrating the success of the drug, the company was able to gain a favorable patent from the FDA, which gave it special commercial protection and enabled it to raise capital for the expensive trials among investors who saw the opportunities of marketing to a particular group of people (Brody and Hunt 2006). The approval has also brought a measure of hope to a community that has been denied access to many of the benefits of modern medicine (India 2014).

But here's the issue: the drug was only tested on African Americans. The drug's manufacturer and various experts have admitted that BiDil will likely work just as well on non–African Americans, but they have not tested it on these population groups (Brody and Hunt 2006). At no point have any unique biological or genetic features of African Americans been identified that explain why BiDil works on them in particular. The reason is that congestive heart failure does not work differently among blacks than among other social groups.

Most solutions to racial inequalities in health have focused on social and environmental problems—better access to healthcare, better living conditions, better diet, and so on—but in the wake of successful efforts to map the human genome, genetic thinking has come to exercise increasing influence over how such inequalities are imagined (Inda 2014). While the development of pharmaceuticals for racial minorities may be new, attempts such as this one to biologize race as part of the natural order of things are not. Since the eighteenth century, there have been numerous efforts within Western science and medicine to frame human variation in racial terms. Many of these efforts have had serious social consequences, lending scientific credibility to the perpetuation of an unequal social order and even racial discrimination. But they have also been proven to be consistently fallible in empirical and factual terms. One reason is that biological traits and genetic features never vary in neat and easily defined ways, much less in ways that correspond to the set of racial categories that Americans are used to recognizing.

The situation leads us to ask the question at the heart of this chapter: *How should we understand biological and genetic diversity among contemporary human populations?* Embedded in this broader question are the following problems, around which this chapter is organized.

In what ways do contemporary humans vary biologically?

Why do human bodies look so different across the planet?

Are differences of race also differences of biology?

What biocultural consequences do discrimination and stress have on human bodies?

In this chapter we explore what biological anthropologists know about contemporary **human biodiversity**, a term that refers to the similarities and differences within and across human groups that have biological dimensions. Among other things, that knowledge challenges simplistic notions about the biological or genetic origins of racial differences. But it also demonstrates that cultural processes like racism and social stress can have important impacts on human biology. We begin by exploring the general patterns of human biological variation.

- **Human biodiversity.** The similarities and differences within and across human groups that have biological dimensions.

In What Ways Do Contemporary Humans Vary Biologically?

All humans share mostly identical genetic material—100% of the same genes and 99.9% of their variations—and have common physiological processes. Any differences are typically related to ancestral mutations or developmental processes that play out within an individual's lifetime. The primary interest of anthropologists is not so much individuals as it is understanding species-wide patterns, which means focusing on how that biological diversity works at the population level. If you remember from Chapter 3, a population is a cluster of individuals of the same species who shares a common geographical area and who typically find their mates in that same cluster. In this section we examine four key dimensions of population-level human biodiversity: patterns of genetic variation, the role of gene flow in genetic variation, physiological differences, and immune responses to disease.

Genetic Variation Within and Between Human Populations

For most mammals, the typical pattern of genetic variation is one in which variation exists between different populations, and most individual populations are more genetically uniform. This stands to reason: individuals mating within their population spread particular alleles around their group. Over time and depending on its size, a population can develop a specific genetic profile that differs from other populations, as long it remains separate from those other populations. In humans, this situation is—uniquely—reversed. Almost all our species' genetic variations are found *within* populations, not between them. In other words, you might be Scandinavian on both sides going back as many generations as anybody can remember, but you would have the same basic genetic makeup as someone who is Senagalese, Japanese, and Melanesian.

The first serious proposal that genetic variation exists between, not within, human populations came from evolutionary biologist Richard Lewontin in 1972 and was based on a statistical analysis of the appearance across human populations of certain known genes (Lewontin 1972). More extensive empirical evidence to support this proposal, however, took another quarter-century to compile. A key contribution came from the **Human Genome Project**, an international scientific research project between 1990 and 2003 whose goal was to identify all the genetic material in humans. When the first draft of its findings were published in 1998, it established clearly that humans demonstrate relatively little genetic variation, or allele differences, between populations. Since then, whether by looking at nuclear or mitochondrial DNA,

- **Human Genome Project.** An international scientific research project between 1990 and 2003 whose goal was to identify all the genetic material in humans.

amino acid sequence variation in proteins, or non-coding regions of DNA, many research teams have repeatedly confirmed this finding (Long et al. 2009; Kittles and Weiss 2003; Relethford 2002; 2009; Templeton 1998). What this research shows is that between 83 and 97% of genetic variation is found *within* human populations, and between 3 and 17 percent is found *between* populations.

These numbers are quite surprising for a mammal like ours that is large bodied and well dispersed. As a simple comparison, there are greater genetic differences between white-tailed deer populations in North Carolina and Florida than between human populations from Central America, Central Asia, and Central Africa. Another way to view this is if you compare any two humans from anywhere in the world, you will find, on average, one-quarter the amount of genetic variation between them than you would if you compared any two chimpanzees, which are found in only a limited distribution in Africa (Kittles and Weiss 2003; Fuentes 2007).

Genetic Variation Is Tied to Gene Flow

One of the major reasons we find this pattern of genetic variation among humans is because of gene flow due to migration. A brief example drawn from Central America will show the important role of gene flow in producing variation within a population.

The Culí are a small population of less than 100 people who live in the Costa Rican province of Limón, a humid tropical landscape perched on the edge of the Caribbean Sea (Castri et. al. 2007). They are originally descended from indentured servants brought to the Caribbean from the Indian subcontinent to work on plantations (Figure 10.1). Historically, Limón province had a small Amerindian population. But beginning in the nineteenth century with the construction of a railroad line and the establishment of a banana industry, it attracted new settlers, among them the East Indian ancestors of the Culí, Afro-Caribbeans, Europeans, and Chinese. Though

Figure 10.1 Labor Migration and Gene Flow in the Caribbean. The movement of indentured servants from the Indian subcontinent to the Caribbean during the nineteenth century as labor contributed new allelic variations to the ongoing mixture of populations in the region.

they phenotypically resist inclusion in any racial category, the Culí are a barely recognized and marginalized social community in Costa Rica.

Most anthropological fieldwork conducted among descendants of East Indians living in the Caribbean has focused on their distinctive cultural, religious, and musical practices, not their biological anthropology. Seeking to expand knowledge about the population-level dynamics of that community, in 2003 a research group headed by the University of South Florida and the Universidad de Costa Rica began collecting genetic, genealogical, and ethnographic data on the remaining Culí population (Castri et. al. 2007). The goal of the study was to understand the historic, cultural, and genetic stories of the largely overlooked population. It turns out that the Culí population has a lot of genetic variation within it.

The researchers conducted in-depth interviews, developing a history and genealogy of the community from the perspective of its members. They also collected hair follicles and buccal (inner cheek) swab samples from forty-four Culí individuals to assess the relative degree of admixture within the population. The samples were sent to a laboratory for DNA analysis. Comparing these samples with samples from other contemporary populations yielded evidence that the Culí gene pool includes allele patterns that characterize Native American, African, and Eurasian populations. In short, the Culí genotype shows a much more complex pattern than anyone would have imagined.

The researchers wrote of their results, "What is remarkable about the Culí families is that they can all be linked into one single pedigree. Our analysis of the community genealogies indicated that all living individuals descend in one way or another from a few initial founding couples, that migration continued through several generations, and that gene flow with non-Culí has been very common" (Castri 2007:176). Complemented by ethnographic, historical, and genealogical data, this study revealed not just an interesting history of a specific population but also how and why migration and gene flow are tied to the production of genetic variation within a population.

Physiological Diversity and Blood Types

Genetic variation is not the only kind of biological variability among humans. There are also physiological variations—in blood factors, enzymes, organ functions, and so on—which powerfully shape how our bodies work. If there were any good reason to divide humans into biologically defined groups—such as efforts to divide people into biological races discussed in the introduction—any one of the many thousands of physiological traits could provide a more valid basis for meaningful classification than a morphological feature such as the color of one's skin (Cohen 1998). In fact, we do classify people into biologically defined groups—blood type is one example—it's just that we don't assign that trait with any racial significance.

The study of blood types offers a way to investigate human physiological diversity and can also help us understand certain human evolutionary dynamics. During the American Civil War (1861–1865) doctors began using the technique of blood transfusions to help save the lives of patients who lost a lot of blood. It became apparent that something in blood made some people's blood incompatible with the blood of some others. By 1900, these processes of blood rejection were better understood, and they could be explained by the high level of diversity in the human immune system.

Red blood cells are coated by proteins that serve a variety of functions in the human body, including delivering oxygen to tissues and producing antibodies as an immune response. We call these protein sets **blood types**. Differences between these protein sets affect our ability to exchange blood from one person to the next, since when confronted with a different blood type, those proteins produce a self-defense reaction. The ABO system, along with the Rhesus blood type (expressed as Rh+ or Rh-), are the best

- **Blood types.** Sets of proteins that coat the red blood cells, which serve a variety of functions in the human body, including delivering oxygen to tissues and producing antibodies as an immune response.

known. The blood type you probably identify with—for example, O- or A+—comes from this system. Scientists now know of more than fifteen blood-type systems whose alleles exist across populations and affect the transfer of blood between individuals.

The variability in blood types is likely due to mutation, natural selection, and gene flow. O is the most common blood type, probably as the original allele. That original allele mutated at some point, into A and B, which are more recent variants. This relationship is suggested by the chemical structure of A and B, which are the same as the O molecule with the addition of a terminal sugar. Significantly, the different ABO phenotypes can support disease resistance, meaning that in some environments, specific blood types may increase or decrease one's chance of surviving a pathogen attack, such as malaria. Gene flow between populations over the past 50,000 years or so, have left their marks on the distribution of the ABO alleles across human populations (Figure 10.2).

Disease Environments and Human Immunity

As we discussed in the previous chapter, diseases can directly shape our evolutionary trajectory. The other side of that equation is the complex adaptive response of the human immune system to disease pressures that aid survival. As a globally dispersed species, we live in a great variety of environments on the planet, and encounter many pathogens, or infectious diseases. Our species' immune system has responded with both flexibility and the ability to resist. We can see evidence of adaptive responses on two levels, the first a generalized one across our species endowing flexibility to deal with pathogens, and the second providing certain populations with resistance to specific diseases.

Flexibility: The HLA System

- **Human leukocyte antigen system (HLA).** A series of proteins on the surface of white blood cells that recognize foreign particles or infectious agents.

A vital component of human immunity is the **human leukocyte antigen system (HLA)**, a series of proteins on the surface of white blood cells that recognize foreign particles or infectious agents. These proteins differentiate between "self" (the body) and "other" (outside proteins, such as pathogens), communicating to the immune system that foreign substances are in the body. The HLA system involves many genes, each having just a few to more than 100 alleles, producing many possible genetic combinations. Even members of same family may not share the exact same HLA genotype and subsequent phenotype. As a result, within any human population great variation exists in immune system response.

At the species level, this variation gives humans flexibility to handle different disease environments. Natural selection probably favored this adaptation, since the more variations we have in our immune systems the better our chances of fighting off any new pathogens we might encounter. The other side of the coin here is that this same variation makes organ transplants very difficult. Because of different HLA phenotypes between individuals, tissue from one human to another are often rejected.

Resistance: Sickle Cells and Malaria

Sickle cell disease is a blood disorder occurring in individuals with two copies of a recessive allele for a protein in hemoglobin, which carries oxygen in red blood cells. This protein can cause some red blood cells to become sickle-shaped, which affects their ability to transport oxygen. The resulting illness can be lethal.

Many human populations have this mutation, but because of its negative impact on fitness it tends to be selected out of the population over time. However, we see fairly high frequencies of one or more forms of the sickle-cell-inducing allele in some populations in western Africa, the Arabian Peninsula, southern India, and parts of Melanesia. The allele's persistence is related to the presence of malaria in an environment, a mosquito-borne disease caused by a family of parasitic microorganisms. In areas

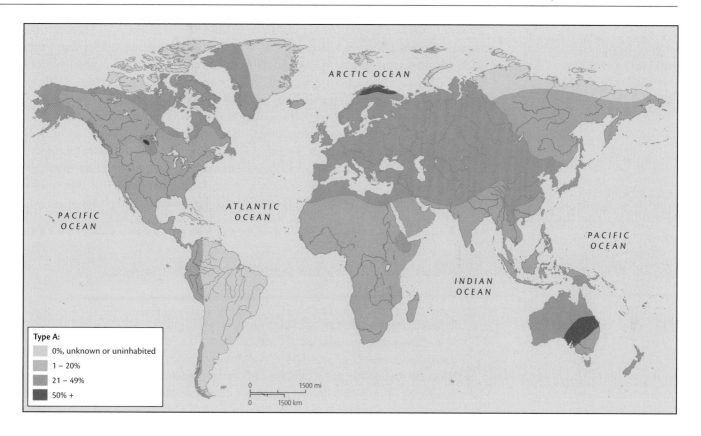

Type A:

- ░ 0%, unknown or uninhabited
- ░ 1 – 20%
- ░ 21 – 49%
- ░ 50% +

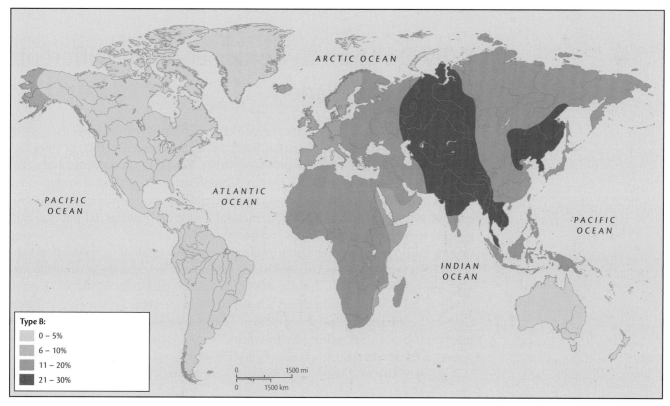

Type B:

- ░ 0 – 5%
- ░ 6 – 10%
- ░ 11 – 20%
- ░ 21 – 30%

where malaria is endemic, individuals with sickle cell disease usually do not get malaria, because sickled red blood cells interfere with the reproduction of the parasites.

One theory about this capacity to resist malaria is that human activity—especially the alteration of habitat for settlement and agriculture—increased breeding opportunities

Figure 10.2   Distribution of A and B Blood Types. These maps show the distribution of blood types A and B. There is no obvious pattern to this distribution.

for mosquitoes, which in turn increased the likelihood that humans will contract the malarial parasite. Natural selection favored the persistence of the alleles that cause sickle cell disease because it allowed individuals to resist malaria. Due to migrations from both India and western Africa, the frequency of the recessive sickle cell alleles present in North American populations has been increasing as a result of gene flow.

Up to this point, we have been discussing human biodiversity mostly in terms of substances and processes—proteins, genes, cells, immune responses, and so forth—that we can't see, except perhaps with the aid of powerful microscopes or laboratory tests. But what about the most obvious expressions of human biodiversity that literally stare us in the face? In the next section we examine what biological anthropologists know about how and why humans look so different across the planet.

THINKING CRITICALLY ABOUT CONTEMPORARY HUMAN BIODIVERSITY

Sickle cell disease offers an example in which biocultural dynamics (in this case landscape transformation) shape the evolutionary trajectories of both humans and the pathogens. Can you think of ways in which biocultural dynamics might affect one or another of the other issues we explored in this section, including genetic variation within human populations and physiological diversity?

Why Do Human Bodies Look So Different Across The Planet?

People across the planet vary, sometimes quite dramatically, in their looks. In areas of the United States where immigration levels are high—especially in large cities like New York, Los Angeles, Miami and so on—that variability is on display every day. While some might view that display as a celebration of multicultural diversity, others see it as troubling or threatening. In our society, and indeed in many others, powerful cultural judgments and prejudices are heaped onto bodily characteristics like skin pigmentation, hair, facial features, and body type.

From the perspective of biological anthropology, these kinds of morphological variations are often overemphasized and widely misunderstood, and are, generally speaking, less significant for everyday bodily function than the kinds of genetic, physiological, and immunity issues discussed in the previous section. Nevertheless they are important dimensions of human biodiversity. Because our bodies interact most directly with the natural environment, morphological traits can reflect evolutionary adaptations. In this section, we explain what two key morphological traits—skin pigmentation and body shape and size—can tell us about human biodiversity.

Is Skin Really Colored?

- **Melanin.** A complex polymer that is the main pigment in human skin, occurring in two colors, black and brown.

One of the most widely misunderstood aspects of skin is the feature that most of us take for granted, its "color." Skin does not have color, per se. What it does have, just under its outer layers, are cells called melanocytes that produce **melanin**, a complex

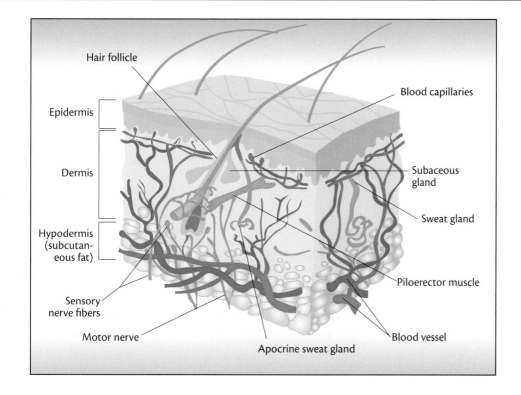

Hair follicle

Epidermis

Dermis

Hypodermis
(subcutan-
eous fat)

Sensory
nerve fibers

Motor nerve

Apocrine sweat gland

Blood capillaries

Subaceous
gland

Sweat gland

Piloerector muscle

Blood vessel

Figure 10.3   The Layers of Human Skin.   Melanocytes lie between two layers of skin, the (inner) dermis and the (outer) epidermis.

polymer whose color is either black or brown. Melanin works as a pigment providing a protective tint from the rays of the sun for what lies underneath. The density and distribution of melanin, along with the thickness of the skin, blood vessels, and another orange-ish pigment called carotene, create variations in reflection and absorption of light in the skin, contributing to the perception that skin has "color" (Figure 10.3).

Melanin is a natural sunscreen that evolved through natural selection. Thanks to satellite data of the earth's climate and radiation of the earth's surface, we know that the highest levels of ultraviolet (UV) radiation from the sun are concentrated in the same equatorial latitudes where hominins evolved (Jablonski 2006; Jablonski and Chaplin 2000; Relethford 1997). UV radiation destroys DNA and undermines other bodily functions, but it also catalyzes the production of vitamin D, which supports strong bones and healthy skin. Melanin blocks the worst of the UV rays while letting in enough for vitamin D production. Through natural selection, early hominins almost certainly had high levels of melanin to regulate their UV exposure, and thus they had dark skin complexions. This adaptation was all the more important after humans lost their fur, which probably happened a million years ago.

The dispersal of hominins out of Africa and into northern latitudes brought new variation to skin pigmentation. Because UV concentration levels are much lower at those higher latitudes, over time northern populations (among them probably Neanderthals) lost their melanin pigmentation and skin complexions lightened.

Of course, as anyone with light skin pigmentation who has gotten a tan can attest, short-term variations in skin pigmentation are possible. All humans have the capacity (albeit limited) to tan, which is a response to UV stress. When we tan, we temporarily increase melanin output, although that output (the actual tan we get) is affected by our age, health, and certain diseases (Jablonski 2004). While natural selection and one's ancestry sets the range of possible skin "color," what people actually look like in any given population is modified and distributed by gene flow and cultural patterns such as the use of clothing, sunblock, and artificial or natural tanning (Jablonski 2004; 2006).

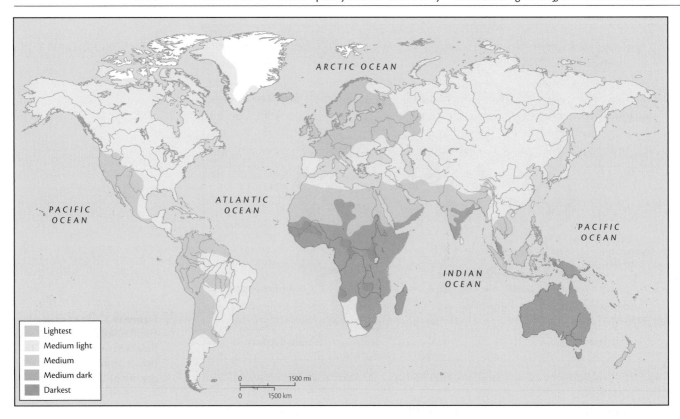

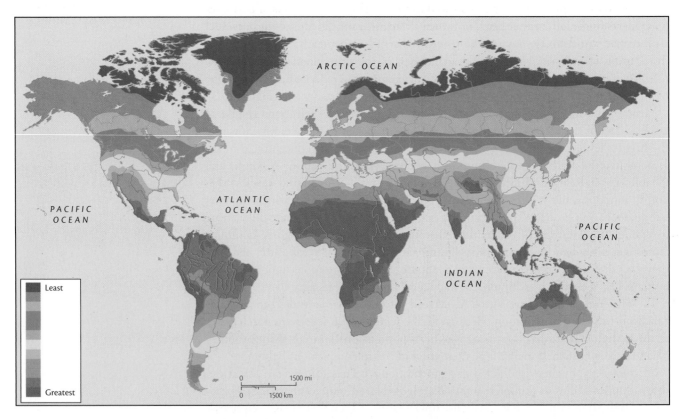

Figure 10.4   The Global Distribution of Skin Pigmentation.   The top map a shows general patterns in the global distribution of human skin pigmentation, based on five arbitrary categories. The bottom map shows the global distribution of UV light intensity. It is possible to see certain general patterns here, in terms of correlations between UV light intensity and skin pigmentation. What are they?

The variation we see today globally in skin pigmentation can be traced to the latitude where one's ancestors spent the most time (Figure 10.4). Generally speaking, darker skinned populations either live in or can trace their ancestry to lower latitudes, including sub-Saharan Africa, South Asia, Southeast Asia, and Polynesia. Lighter skinned populations are found in higher latitudes, including the Americas, Northeast Asia, and Northern Eurasia/Europe. Of course, there are exceptions to these patterns, such as in the United States, where large, recent migrations from various regions around the planet have created many shades. As we know, human movement mixes up genetic material producing new variations. The best we can say is only that skin pigmentation is not an accurate way to describe any population and that it only correlates in very general terms with latitude.

Variations in Body Shape, Stature, and Size

Humans vary greatly in body shape, stature, and size. Some groups of people are quite tall and slender, including Nilotic peoples of Sudan such as the Shilluk and Dinka who are among the tallest people in the world. Or they can be short and somewhat stocky, such as the Baka people of Central Africa and other so-called pygmies. The differences between them, not to mention the range of other bodily types seen globally, raise questions about the adaptive significance and biological dimensions of that variability for our species (Figure 10.5).

These variations can be quantified with **anthropometry**, which measures body parameters to assess physical variation, as well as the relative contributions of particular body parts to overall body shape. These measurements take the form of indices, such as the **cormic index,** the ratio of sitting height to standing height, and the **intermembral index,** the ratio of arm length to leg length. Measurements of body fat (adipose tissue) are also common. The body mass index (BMI), a measurement of weight over height (squared), also identifies patterned variations in human size and shape.

- **Anthropometry.** The measurement of body parameters that assess physical variation and the relative contributions of particular body parts to overall body shape.

- **Cormic index.** Standing height divided by sitting height.

- **Intermembral index.** The ratio of arm length to leg length.

Figure 10.5 Types of Human Body Builds. There are big differences in body shape, size, and stature when comparing the body builds of a Shilluk of Sudan (left) and Baka of Central African country of Gabon (right).

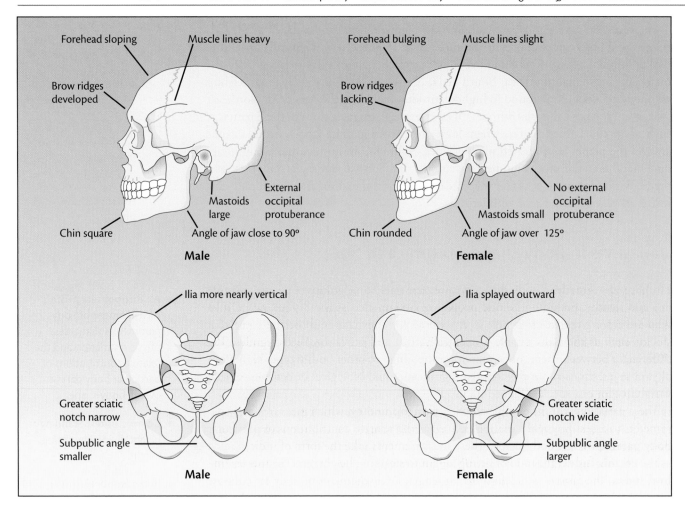

Figure 10.6 Identifying Sexual Differences in the Body. These images show distinct differences between male and female crania and pelvises. Knowing these differences helps biological anthropologists identify whether skeletal remains belong to a woman or man.

Modern humans vary quite a bit in size and shape. That variation is as much as 50% in average body mass (measured as weight within each sex), meaning that the smallest humans are half as heavy as the largest. At the pelvis, human width varies by about 25% across our species (Ruff 2002), and average heights range from about 150 to 185 cm (just under 5 feet to about 6 feet). There is about 10% variation in height among humans, although there are also extreme ends of the height spectrum. The difference between males and females in size (sexual dimorphism), is about 15%, so men's bodies, on average, are typically larger than female bodies (Figure 10.6).

While these variations seem important, they pale in comparison to the variability among early hominins and members of the genus *Homo* who had even greater sexual dimorphism and differences in size and mass. Those differences in sexual dimorphism reached levels we see today about 500,000 years ago. The late archaic humans (Neanderthals) had greater body mass than us, but then it started to decrease about 50,000 years ago (Ruff 2002). The reason is that humans' ability to reduce environmental stresses on the human body through culture—better access to food, protective shelter, clothing, and so on—improved. In recent decades, improvements in healthcare and the proliferation of high-calorie processed foods has reversed these trends and generated some pronounced increases in height and body mass (including historically high levels obesity and overweight) in numerous populations (Figure 10.7).

Body size and shape have played a role in how certain populations have adapted physiologically to living in extremely cold or hot climates. People who live in the extreme North (such as Alaska) and South (such as southern Chile) tend to be stocky and have a high metabolic rate, fat insulation around vital organs, and blood-flow patterns that produce and conserve heat. Alternatively, a body shape with a large

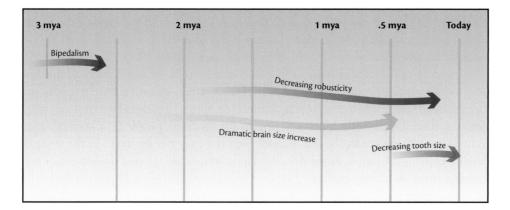

Figure 10.7 The Genus *Homo* and its Shifting Body Shape. During the past two million years, Homo has experienced decreasing robustness, changes in the size and shape of the cranium (related to increases in brain size), and decreasing tooth size. Robustness has declined even more during the past 10,000 years. Can you explain why this more recent decrease in robustness happened?

surface area such as that exhibited by the tall and slender Shilluk of Sudan enables efficient cooling in a hot climate.

It has to be said, though, that when it comes to these kinds of patterns, it is difficult to get much beyond suggestive generalities. One reason has to do with migration, and the fact that a population may have entered a climatological region too recently for evolutionary adaptations to have occurred. Bodies can also change within individual lifetimes: if you move to the Arctic, for example, over time your body would develop certain metabolic adaptations that help keep you warm based on our physiological flexibility and plasticity. Even more important is that people adapt to climate through cultural processes, including diet, activity patterns, and the use of clothing and shelter, which affect the ability to adapt to extreme climates no matter what the body shape, stature, or size.

Indeed, one of challenges of describing and explaining variations in how people look is just how much those variations can pass through and be shaped by cultural filters. And yet the idea that it is possible to organize humans into definable biological groups based on their looks is a persistent and enduring belief and is closely aligned with ideas about human races. In the next two sections, we examine the history of this idea and explore whether it has any biological significance.

THINKING CRITICALLY ABOUT CONTEMPORARY HUMAN BIODIVERSITY

One of the central arguments about how and why human looks vary across the planet has to do with the adaptive relevance of a physical trait. But do all traits have to serve a direct adaptive purpose? Can you think of any physical features on our bodies that may not have a direct adaptive purpose?

Are Differences of Race Also Differences of Biology?

Most Americans have a worldview that assumes that **race**, which organizes people into hierarchical groups based on physical traits thought to reflect differences rooted in biological differences, is a natural and inevitable aspect of human society. Although

- **Race.** A system that organizes people into hierarchical groups based on specific physical traits that are thought to reflect fundamental and innate differences that are rooted in genetic and biological differences.

Figure 10.8 "Equal Burdens." This 1874 image from the cover of *Harper's* magazine represents caricatures of a black man from the South and an Irishman from the North. Although the Irishman here is identified as "white," Irish immigrants to the United States were not really fully accepted as "white"—and shared the equal burden of racial discrimination with blacks—until the end of the nineteenth century. The rapid transformation of Irish into "white" people points to how dynamic and unstable racial identities can be.

- **Scientific concept of race.** A population or group of populations within a species that has measurable, defining biological characteristics and low statistical measures of similarity.

- **Subspecies.** A population that meets the criteria defined within the scientific concept of race.

- **Culturally-constructed concept of race.** A set of cultural or ethnic factors combined with easily perceived morphological traits (e.g., skin reflectance, body shape, cranial structure) in an artificial "biologized" category.

they may feel real, powerful, and unchangeable, there is nothing fixed or inevitable about racial categories. The markers upon which racial distinctions are made are especially arbitrary, and they can and often do change (Figure 10.8).

In order to make critical sense of race and its relevance (or irrelevance, as the case may be) for understanding human biodiversity, we first examine how the idea has been framed scientifically and how it connects to human biological variability, showing that there are no valid biological origins for grouping people into human races. But, as we will explore in the last section, even if it may not be "real" in the sense of having biological origins, racial discrimination and other stresses do have very real consequences on human bodies.

The Biological Meanings (and Meaninglessness) of "Human Races"

Biological anthropologists work with two concepts of race. The **scientific concept of race** is one of these, referring to a population, or group of populations, within a species that has measurable, defining biological characteristics (Edgar and Hunley 2009; Kittles and Weiss 2003; Templeton 1998). In biology this is known as a **subspecies**, or a unit within a species on an evolutionary path that diverges from that of other populations within the species.

The other concept is a **culturally constructed concept of race,** in which cultural ideologies and dynamics are linked with morphological traits (things like skin pigmentation, body shape, or cranial structure) to create an artificial, "biologized" category (Marks 1995). The culturally constructed conceptions of race we take for granted today originated during the period of European colonial expansion from the fifteenth to the nineteenth centuries, with the expansion of global maritime travel and new kinds of sustained contact between geographically distant people. Europeans explained and justified their dominance and control through colonialism by developing racial classifications that evaluated non-Europeans as less human or less civilized (see Chapter 16). Beginning in the eighteenth century, these differences were **naturalized**—made part of the natural order of things—through the production of scientific theories, schemes, and typologies about human differences. Indeed, the early years of physical anthropology (roughly 1850–1950) focused on attempts to discover the biological basis for classifying humans into races, typically through various kinds of anthropometric measurements. Although some anthropologists turned these ideas on their heads, using those same techniques to demonstrate that one could *not* classify humans into races based on morphological traits (Marks 1995), the basic notion of race in humans was adopted in mainstream scientific studies about human differences.

The Problem of Categorizing Humans Racially

Scientists came up with four general approaches to categorize human races. The first approach is trait based, which isolates certain physical features, such as head size and shape, bodily structure, facial features, lip shape, eye folds, or skin pigmentation, to divide people into races according to what seems physically most typical of the group (Johnston 2004). This approach is closely associated with German taxonomist and anthropologist Johann Friedrich Blumenbach (1752–1840), who identified five racial groups: Mongoloid, Caucasoid, Negroid, Malayan, and American Indian (Figure 10.9). American folk classifications do something similar with skin color, for example, making distinctions between white, black, red, and yellow skin to denote certain racial groups. Of course, nobody's skin is really any of these colors; they are just convenient symbolic markers of much more complex patterns of difference.

FIG. 339. — Apollo Belvidera.[553]

FIG. 340.[556]

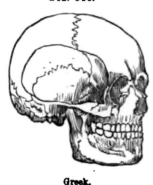

Greek.

FIG. 341. — Negro.[554]

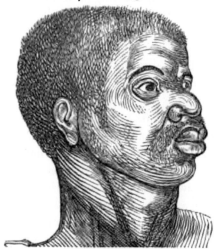

FIG. 342.[357]

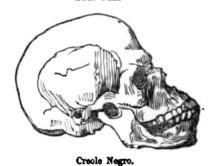

Creole Negro.

FIG. 343. — Young Chimpanzee.[555]

FIG. 344.[558]

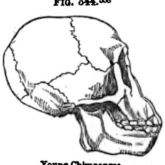

Young Chimpanzee.

Figure 10.9 Eighteenth-Century Racial Science. This image, from a book called *Types of Mankind* published in 1854, claims a close relationship between chimpanzees and Africans.

- **Naturalized.** Made part of the natural order of things through the production of scientific theories, schemes, and typologies.

A second approach to categorizing races is based on geographic origins. The Swedish taxonomist Linnaeus developed such a scheme, dividing humans into four races: African, Asian, American, and European. North American racial models also reflect some elements of this approach, with our division into African Americans, Asians, Native Americans, Hawaiians/Pacific Islanders, and so forth. In recent years the U.S. Bureau of the Census has used the racial category "Asian and Pacific Islander." The obvious weakness of this model is that political designations, such as Hawaiian and Pacific Islander, and vast continents with tremendous ethnic diversity like Asia, are made into racial groups.

Some anthropologists have refined this geographic approach into a third way of categorizing race called the adaptational approach to racial classification, which refers to the notion that people adapt to the environments in which they live and pass on those adaptations through inheritance (Coon, Garn, and Birdsell 1950). One illustration of this approach can be found in melanin's role in creating fitness and adaptability in regions of the globe with high UV concentrations. Nevertheless, as we saw, this point suggests only a very general correlation between biology and latitude and does not translate neatly to the four or five commonly defined races.

A fourth approach builds on advances in population dynamics since the 1950s and defines races as reproductively isolated breeding populations. This approach moved beyond trait-based and geography-based approaches by focusing on who mates with whom, which allows for the influence of cultural factors, such as religious affiliation or economic status, on the formation of racial groups (Garn 1961). With this approach, the number of races exploded from four to dozens, mainly because there are so many separate breeding populations in the human species. Taken to the extreme, it would also mean that every population qualifies as a race, which muddies the waters between the two concepts (Long 2003).

Each of these four approaches has their own specific limitations. But there is a common problem shared by all of them, and for that matter, any attempt to categorize humans into natural races: these typologies rarely describe an actual individual, and they do not characterize whole groups of people. What looks like patently obvious "racial" differences come from a special way of sampling people. This sampling process isolates one or more arbitrarily chosen visible traits and marks that trait as representative of a whole group of people. More troubling, is that one trait can come to be representative of other characteristics, such as intelligence, aptitude, and personal character. Moreover, the categories themselves are just not that stable and they shift over time, a theme we explore in "Thinking Like an Anthropologist: Counting and Classifying Race in the American Census."

Race and Variability in Human Populations

Biological traits and genetic features never vary in neat and easily defined ways, much less in ways that correspond to the "racial" categories Americans are used to recognizing. Because of historical movement, intermingling, and gene flow, human genetic and biological variations occur in a continuous fashion. Anthropologists call such variations **clinal** variations, which means that change is gradual across groups and that traits shade and blend into each other (Marks 1995). Take any physical trait that people use to identify racial groups—facial features, skin pigmentation, body shape, and the like—and there are never clearly definable lines between any of those features in an actual population.

Genetic and biological traits also tend to vary independently of each other. For example, there is no connection between skin pigmentation and any other supposed "racial" trait, such as certain facial features, cranial size, or body shapes. There is also absolutely no physiological parallel or relationship between these traits and the biological and social phenomena we call character and intelligence.

- **Clinal.** A type of variation in which change is gradual across groups and that traits shade and blend into each other.

Thinking Like an Anthropologist

Counting and Classifying Race in the American Census

ANTHROPOLOGISTS BEGIN THEIR research by asking questions. In this box, we want you to learn how to ask questions as an anthropological researcher. Part 1 describes a situation and follows up with questions we would ask. Part 2 asks you to do the same thing with a different situation

PART ONE: RACE AND THE 1850 CENSUS

Censuses interest anthropologists because they reveal the role of governments in classifying and categorizing groups of people. In addition, over time census categories change, reflecting broader shifts in social categories. The U.S. census has noted the "color" of American residents from the very first census in 1790, but these categories have changed over the next two centuries.

The U.S. Constitution requires a census every ten years to determine how many members each state should have in the House of Representatives. The Constitution mentions three kinds of people relevant to the population counted in the allocation of seats in Congress: free persons (each counted as one person), slaves (each counted as two-thirds of a person), and Indians (who were not taxed and not counted until 1860).

The first American census (1790) recorded the head of each household and the number of individuals in each household in basic categories: Whites (by age group and gender), Other Free Persons, and Slaves. From 1800 to 1840 the census expanded the age groupings but used the same basic categories in each household (U. S. Census Office 1853).

In 1850, for the first time the census recorded the name of every person in the United States and its territories. It also recorded the age, gender, color, occupation, and place of birth of every individual. Color is the most interesting classification because the census form mentions three possible categories: White, Black, or Mulatto. The figure shows a form that was filled out in New Orleans' 4th Ward.

Few Americans use the word "mulatto" anymore. It refers to mixed-race people, typically those who are part white and part black. Although the 1850 census doesn't show them, in some parts of the South people informally used even finer grained terms, such as "Quadroon," referring to a person who is one-fourth black and three-fourths white, and "Octoroon," a person who is one-eighth black.

All of these terms are obsolete and now considered offensive. But their use in that era suggests some important points. One is that Americans acknowledged the existence of people who are racially mixed and sought to classify them. Their use also reflects the same ideology that produced

1850 U.S. Census Numeration Sheet from New Orleans, Louisiana. In southern states like Louisiana, census takers were more sensitive to subtle differences in ethnicity than in most northern states. While northern states distinguished only between black and white as categories, the southern states routinely recognized an intermediary category of mulatto. In this copy of the 1850 enumeration of New Orleans Ward 4, Precinct 3, whites are left blank, blacks are marked "B," and mulattos are indicated with "M." Note that although social status marked by these arbitrary racial categories was clear to everyone, these status differences did not keep whites, blacks, and mulattos from living in the same neighborhoods and even in the same households.

the "one-drop rule," in which individuals were defined as "black" if they were believed to have just "one drop" of African blood, meaning a single African ancestor, thus mixed-race people are categorized as non-white.

After taking the census, the government produced an official summary of what it learned about the population to share with the public (something it still does). Interestingly, the summary never uses the terms "Black" or "Mulatto." Instead, it distinguishes people in terms of "White," "Free Colored," and "Slave," despite the fact that the terms "Colored" or "Free Colored" never appear on the enumeration forms, as we see in the image (U. S. Census Office 1853).

What questions does this situation raise for anthropological researchers?

1. What does the fact that the census forms used one set of categories but the public summary made use of a different classification tell us about American racial categories in the 1850s?
2. Why is it that it wasn't until the 1850s that the government wanted to record "Mulatto" and "Black?"

3. Although the terms "Mulatto" and "Black" might seem more precise than "Colored," do these competing terminologies suggest an (aborted) effort to change public understandings of race?

PART TWO: THE 2000 AND 2010 CENSUSES
Following categorizations first established in the 2000 census, the 2010 census asked, "What is this person's race? Mark one or more Races to indicate what this person considers himself/herself to be." Its list of races includes "White," "Black, African Am., or Negro," and "American Indian or Alaska Native," and uses a wide variety of other "races," including Asian Indian, Chinese, Filipino, Japanese, Korean, Vietnamese, Other Asian, Native Hawaiian, Guamanian or Chamorro, Samoan, Other Pacific Islander, or Some Other Race. In contemporary censuses race is no longer an "either/or" category, and Americans can now check off any number of boxes to reflect the complicated interethnic blending now recognized by Americans. If you wanted to understand the dynamism of racial categories in the contemporary American census, what questions would you ask as an anthropological researcher?

Anthropological skepticism about the utility of race for understanding human variation runs deep in the discipline's history. In "Classic Contributions: Ashley Montagu and 'Man's Most Dangerous Myth,'" we examine the perspective of one of anthropology's most prominent critics of the race concept.

Is It Possible to Tell Someone's Race from a Skull?

So where does this all leave the scientific concept of race? To test the hypothesis that modern humans can be categorized according to the scientific concept of race, we just need to identify the biological characteristics that define a subspecies within *Homo sapiens* and then assess how those characteristics map onto human variations. If you watch television programs featuring forensic scientists and detectives, they appear to do these things all the time, such as when they announce that the skull they have discovered is that of a black male or white woman. What is the actual evidence for making these claims?

Genetic Evidence
The genetic differentiation needed to classify a population or group as a subspecies in animals like birds, squirrels, or non-human primates, simply doesn't exist in humans. The variation levels are well below the statistical limits biologists use. Moreover, no single genetic marker can be used to sort people into races; that is, scientists have not found any specific Asian, black, or white genes or alleles. Nearly all alleles are found in some members of nearly every population. Genetically speaking, humans show up as one biological race, so "races" do not exist (Templeton 2013).

CLASSIC CONTRIBUTIONS

Ashley Montagu and "Man's Most Dangerous Myth"

FIRST PUBLISHED IN 1942 and now in its sixth edition, Ashley Montagu's book *Man's Most Dangerous Myth: The Fallacy of Race* stands as a cornerstone in the history and practice of anthropology. Montagu (1905–1999) was an English biological anthropologist who saw the abuses and misuses of race and racism as central concerns not only for anthropology but also for humankind. Although he wasn't the first anthropologist to take a critical perspective on race—Franz Boas and his students were doing it several decades earlier—Montagu's assertions were the most direct, public, and strident. In a sense, Montagu was arguing against his own discipline, since prior to World War II, physical anthropology was closely associated with efforts to measure and categorize different human races. But he felt an obligation as a scientist, an anthropologist, and a humanist to investigate the claims that races existed, whether the people who were so categorized actually varied in biological abilities, and whether any data existed to support those assertions. He explored the vast biological and anthropological data, theories, and perspectives available to him and concluded that race not only has no biological basis but it also is as a powerful myth. In the opening paragraphs of his book, reprinted here, he gets right to the point.

Ashley Montagu

The idea of race represents one of the most dangerous myths of our time and one of the most tragic. Myths are most effective and dangerous when they remain unrecognized for what they are. Many of us are happy in the complacent belief that myths are what uncivilized people believe in, but of which we ourselves are completely free. We may realize that a myth is a faulty explanation leading to social delusion and error, but we do not necessarily realize that we ourselves share in the mythmaking faculty with all people of all times and places, or that each of us has his own store of myths derived from the traditional stock of the society in which we live, and are always in ready supply. In earlier days we believed in magic, possession, and exorcism; in good and evil supernatural powers; and until recently we believed in witchcraft. Today many of us believe in race. Race is the witchcraft, the demonology of our time, the means by which we exorcise imagined demoniacal powers among us. It is the contemporary myth, humankind's most dangerous myth, America's Original Sin.

In our own time we have lived to see the myth of race openly adopted by governments as an expedient fiction. Myths perform the double function of both serving as models of and models for cultural attitudes and behavior. Thus myths reflect the beliefs and give sanction to the actions of society, while at the same time providing the forms upon which belief and conduct are molded. Built, as they are, into the structure of social relationships, racial myths often have a force which exceeds even that of reality itself, for such myths, in addition to the social encouragement they receive, draw upon both false biology and even worse theology for their sustenance. [Montagu 1997:41–42]

Questions for Reflection

1. Montagu understands "myth" both in it popular sense—as falsehood—as well as the anthropological sense, as a powerful narrative shaping understanding of how the world works. In what senses does he believe the myth of race shapes understanding of how the world works? What evidence about race do you think supports his view?

2. If as long ago as 1942 we knew that the idea of race was based on (in Montagu's terms) "false biology," why does this misconception persist?

Figure 10.10   The Problem With Identifying "Race" in a Skull. The relationships among genes, environment, development, and phenotype are very complex, rendering any effort to locate race in a skull highly problematic.

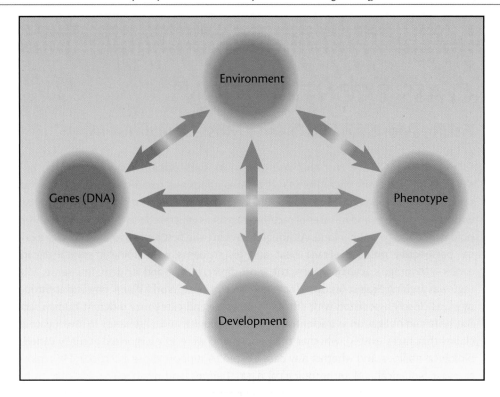

- **Forensic analysis.** The identification and description of dead people.

Morphological Evidence

Forensic analysis, the identification and description of dead people, often uses cranial measurements to sort people into populations. Forensic experts can frequently classify a skull's race (Asian, black, or white) about 80% of the time. Does this mean these categories are biologically based?

Not really. Health, nutrition, and evolutionary factors like gene flow create cranial variation between individuals. In humans, levels of cranial variations are similar to the levels of variation in our DNA (Figure 10.10). That is, about 80% of any variations in cranial shape would be found *within* a human population, and about 20% *between* populations (Relethford 2002).

So how do forensic scientists classify skulls into culturally constructed racial categories? The answer lies in how the crania are classified, and how many categories there are for classification. Scientists will place them in the categories that are available; the fewer the categories, the more simple it is to sort. For example, in one project forensic scientists took crania from white American males in two periods, 1979 and 1840, and easily sorted them into two groups. It was as simple as sorting the crania of modern American white and black males into separate groups (Jantz and Meadows Jantz 2000). Of course, white American males in 1979 did not belong to a different race from white American males living in 1840, but the limited number of categories scientists worked with predetermined how they would classify the skulls, and the differences seemed clear enough. But how do we explain the differences in skull measurements between the white males? The reason is that they had differences in their health and nutrition across time, as well as gene flow, especially if any of these individuals had some ancestors from other parts of the planet.

Things get even more uncertain when you look at skull measurements indicating "black" in the United States and compare them with crania from African continent, with all its human diversity. They just don't match up. More importantly, the cranial measurements used to identify "racial" groups are not specific or unique to any of the culturally constructed racial categories. Because the cranial measurements for each group are based on averages and ranges, any specific cranium will usually diverge from the "correct" range. As a result, forensic experts can't always place crania in the "correct" category—this happens as much as one in five times. The differences here are of degree, not kind (Fuentes 2015).

All of this evidence indicates that race is a powerful cultural *and* scientific construction, in the sense that any certainties about it have to be actively built—constructed upon—a set of assumptions that anthropology shows are flawed when applied to humans. Unfortunately, a lot of people—scientists among them—still believe that erroneous racial classifications are real, largely because they do not understand how processes of natural selection, population genetics, and human variation work (Harrison 1998; Gould 1996; Marks 1995; Peregrine et al. 2003; Fuentes 2014c). Nevertheless, it is important to recognize that even if the origins of racial groups are not genetically or biologically determined, race can *become* biology, by shaping peoples' biological outcomes. We explore how in the final section.

● ●

THINKING CRITICALLY ABOUT CONTEMPORARY HUMAN BIODIVERSITY

The idea that racial differences are genetically and biologically determined is widely accepted by the U.S. public, and the contrary and more complicated view just presented has failed to gain widespread traction even as it offers a more empirically valid understanding of the relationship between race and biology. How do you think anthropologists can communicate these ideas and findings to the broader public?

● ●

What Biocultural Consequences Do Discrimination and Stress Have on Human Bodies?

One of the criticisms of the idea that race is a myth or is culturally constructed is that it might give the impression that race is not "real" (Hartigan 2006). Race is very real because racial groupings are accompanied and supported by marginalization, exploitation, and stigma for some, and privilege for others. **Racism**, the repressive practices, structures, beliefs, and representations that uphold racial categories and social inequality, is a potent force in making race an objective reality. It works through the prejudice that people express against people who are different from them, and **discrimination**, which is negative or unfair treatment of a person because of his or her group membership or identity.

From a biocultural perspective, these processes powerfully shape a community's exposure to factors that create certain kinds of embodied health outcomes, including sickness, long-term chronic disease, stress, and suffering. Studying the ways people experience social stresses and discrimination through their bodies has become an increasingly important area of biological anthropology research because it shows how cultural processes can contribute to the production of biological variation in human populations. In this section, we examine two expressions of these concerns, eugenics and the embodied consequences of being a racialized minority.

- **Racism.** The repressive practices, structures, beliefs, and representations that uphold racial categories and social inequality.

- **Discrimination.** Negative or unfair treatment of a person because of his or her group membership or identity.

Eugenics: A Weak Theory of Genetic Inheritance

- **Eugenics.** The study of genetics with the notion of improving human biology and biological potential; often associated with simplistic, erroneous assumptions about the relationship of behavior or cultural traits with simple genetic systems.

One illustration of Ashley Montagu's concerns about the dangers of race comes from the field of **eugenics,** an early and misguided attempt at making biological anthropology an applied science whose goal was to improve human biology through selective mating. In the early 1900s, some geneticists sought to improve humanity by making it more disease resistant and smarter. They understood social, cultural, and racial differences among peoples to be the result of genetic differences. Through the promotion of selective mating and sterilization programs, their intention was to protect and promote "good genes" and eliminate "bad genes" from the population.

Although at the time, these ideas were viewed as progressive and were supported by prominent social reformers, philanthropists, and government agencies, the track record of eugenics included numerous human rights abuses. It was also based on a totally incorrect way of thinking about genetics. Eugenicists believed that inheritance was a simple function of dominant and recessive genes. That is, you simply get one thing from dad and one from mom, and the one that is dominant becomes your phenotype. Using this idea—that we now know is bad science—eugenicists offered an explanation for stereotypical racial traits. For example, they argued that certain groups of social undesirables had low intelligence ("feebleminded" is the word they used) based on the belief that they inherited certain dominant traits in high frequencies.

After World War II, eugenics lost its social legitimacy when it became clear that the Nazis in Germany had used their own eugenicist ideology to identify and standardize their ideas about the superiority of Nordic and Aryan racial types. This ideology fueled the Holocaust, which took the lives of millions of Jews, Slavs, Romani (Gypsies), and homosexuals and forced the surgical sterilization of people who suffered from what Nazi doctors defined as "hereditary" illnesses—among others, epilepsy, schizophrenia, body malformations, blindness, and deafness (Lifton 1986). These actions had important individual and population-level consequences that historians, biologists, and anthropologists are still documenting and striving to understand.

Germany was not the only country where eugenics was sanctioned as official state-supported ideology. Several states in the United States developed eugenics programs, including Vermont between 1925 and 1936. In Vermont it began with a statewide survey of "bad heredity" and identification of "degenerate families"—primarily Abenaki Indians, French Canadians, and handicapped people—and culminated with the 1931 passage of "A Law for Human Betterment by Voluntary Sterilization" (Gallagher 1999). Under this law, dozens of forced, not "voluntary," sterilizations occurred. To avoid sterilization, many Abenaki abandoned any obvious signs of their Native American past, which is a key factor that currently prevents them from being recognized as a tribe by the federal government. As the example of eugenics shows, when aligned with powerful social institutions, racist ideologies can have profound biocultural consequences on ordinary people's lives.

The Embodied Consequences of Being a Racialized Minority

Another context in which we can examine these biocultural consequences is by understanding racial inequalities in health. The existence of these inequalities is, to some extent, what the makers of BiDil, discussed in the introduction to this chapter, were responding to, and it has become an important area of biological and cultural research among anthropologists as well. The anthropological approach, however, makes opposite assumptions about the relationship between racial groups and biology than the drug makers. Instead of projecting preexisting biological differences between groups that can be treated with drugs, anthropological research lends support to a more a complex view that human health results from biocultural factors and is subject to phenotypic plasticity and epigenetic effects (Gravlee 2009).

Epidemiological studies in the United States indicate well-defined differences between racial groups in terms of morbidity and mortality, which refer to incidence of disease and life expectancy. One illustration of this fact is that African Americans and other minority groups like Latinos and Native Americans have higher rates of many diseases, such as hypertension, diabetes, cancer, stroke, renal failure, and cardiovascular disease, among others (Gravlee 2009). There is also a gap in black–white life expectancy that has been recognized for many decades. Although the gap has closed, from 17.8 years in 1903 to just under five years today, it continues to be a problem (Gravlee 2009).

Race is not the *cause* of these health inequalities. Rather, these health inequalities are the *result* of race, or more specifically, of racism and the complex environmental influences racism creates on human biology (Gravlee 2009). One expression of racism is residential segregation by racial group, which has been shown to produce inequalities in health because it constrains opportunities such as access to education, certain occupations, and quality healthcare. It can also create social environments that influence the spread and distribution of disease, poor diets, illegal drug use, gang violence, and gunshot wounds. All of these problems are linked to poverty and social marginalization, not the biology of the populations affected. Discrimination has also been shown to have bodily consequences on individuals, producing a range of effects from high blood pressure to lower birth weights. Although they are still not understood very well, these conditions can also have epigenetic dimensions, in other words, producing lingering effects throughout childhood and well into adulthood of the next generation.

This work shifts attention toward the ways experiences of racism are embodied. **Embodiment** is a concept that refers to how people biologically incorporate "the material and social worlds in which they live," from the act of conception until death (Krieger 2005). This work also recognizes how embodied inequalities reinforce racialized understandings of human biology (Gravlee 2009). Recognizing how biological variations are produced through social processes has been a productive avenue for biocultural research beyond the study of racial inequalities. One key area has been the study of the embodied consequences of rapid cultural and economic change. In "Doing Fieldwork: Rapid Social Change and the Embodiment of Psychosocial Stress in Samoa," we examine how one biological anthropologist has studied the effects of social change among Samoan youths.

The broader point is that if we want to understand human biological variation, it is necessary to take into account the role that social relationships and cultural attitudes—such as those that produce discrimination and psychosocial stress—play in shaping biological processes and health outcomes. Biocultural research along these lines is still relatively young. But its importance is that it challenges reductionistic biological and genetic perspectives that reproduce the same myths of separate human races that anthropologists long ago disproved, while recognizing that race does have certain kinds of objective realities.

● **Embodiment.** A concept that refers to how people literally incorporate, biologically, the material and social worlds in which they live, from conception to death.

Doing Fieldwork

Rapid Social Change and the Embodiment of Psychosocial Stress in Samoa

ANTHROPOLOGISTS HAVE LONG studied the social and health effects of rapid cultural and political-economic change. In addition to producing changes in diet, nutrition, and general health, rapid social change can produce stress, which has well-documented consequences like high blood pressure, reduced immune function, and depressive symptoms (Daltabuit and Leatherman 1998; Dressler 2005). Under some circumstances, these embodied stresses are related to what anthropologists and sociologists call "lifestyle incongruity," which is the situation that exists when an "individual aspires to a certain lifestyle that is inconsistent with his or her occupational or educational status and cultural traditions, resulting in psychosocial stress" (Dressler 1995).

Biological anthropologist Thomas McDade (2001; McDade et. al. 2000) set out to study whether young people in the Polynesian island country of Samoa were experiencing a version of lifestyle incongruity, and what effects it might be having on their bodies. Their traditional society has been undergoing a period of unprecedented cultural change due to, among other things, an influx of Western consumer goods, the migration of young people to New Zealand and the United States, longer periods of schooling for kids, and a shift from subsistence farming to wage labor. These changes have undermined traditional sources of power and status in a society where children are socialized to be highly status conscious and are linked to a steady increase in the number of suicides among young people, especially males (McDade 2001).

McDade designed a study in which he would compare the experience of psychosocial stress among young people in three geographic regions of Western Samoa. His team recruited 240 individuals between the ages of ten and twenty. In addition to taking participants' anthropometric measurements (weight, height, etc.), the team collected basic demographic data and conducted qualitative interviews of participants about their household's level of material wealth and their social relationships. Using a sterile, disposable lancet they then pricked each participant's finger to collect two to five drops of blood for later analysis of immune function, much as people with diabetes do several times a day. This relatively non-invasive blood collection was designed to minimize pain and inconvenience, while making it possible to collect a large number of samples.

In order to conduct this work, McDade's research proposal had to pass ethics reviews both at his home institution of Emory University and through the Western Samoa Health Research Council. As we discussed in Chapter 1, such ethical reviews have become standard during the past several decades to prevent abuses of research subjects participating in anthropological, social science, and medical research. Their primary goal is to protect the rights of human subjects, an especially critical issue among socially vulnerable and marginalized groups. Informed consent is required in this kind of research because individuals are asked to provide biological samples for laboratory analysis, and they need to understand why the research is being done as well as the possible impacts of it on their lives. The researchers also have to demonstrate to both the individuals providing the samples and the institutional review boards that they have protocols in place to protect the data, ensure its anonymity, and (in projects like this one) prevent its commercialization.

The dried blood samples were sent for laboratory analysis where they were tested for antibodies against the Epstein-Barr Virus (EBV). This is a ubiquitous herpes virus to which over 98% of Samoan youths have been exposed, but very few suffer from the disease because they have adequate immune suppression of it. Knowing from other

Thomas McDade

researchers that increases in EBV antibodies correlate with negative life events and stresses, McDade used statistical methods to identify connections between increases in antibodies and the data they had collected about social and material conditions of each individual. Various confounding factors were monitored and controlled, including undernutrition and current infections, but certain statistically relevant correlations in the data did emerge. The most important of these is that individuals living in households with material goods beyond their social status had elevated levels of antibodies, a sign that they had experienced stress (McDade 2001).

According to McDade, his research suggests that although young Samoans may not necessarily contribute directly to their household's material wealth, they do share in the anxieties associated with not having the economic means necessary to support the new kinds of material lifestyles associated with Western consumer goods and other social changes. Often times, to achieve those material lifestyles, households have to enter into certain kinds of undesirable debts and obligations, and the pressures and stresses related to these relationships extend to all members of the household. That they are embodied in certain kinds of ways among youths shows how people can incorporate, biologically, the social and political-economic worlds in which they live.

Questions for Reflection

1. What are some of the ways Samoan youths participating in the study might be made vulnerable by their participating in a study like this? Aside from securing informed consent from participants, how can biological anthropologists mitigate those vulnerabilities?

2. Do you think there are any public health initiatives targeted to the Samoan population that could come out of a research project like this one?

THINKING CRITICALLY ABOUT CONTEMPORARY HUMAN BIODIVERSITY

The approach presented here about embodiment suggests that the important thing about race is not that it is a myth, but that it is deeply entrenched in social relationships and culture. Is it possible to hold both views simultaneously? Why or why not?

Conclusion

A lot of Americans believe that thanks to the civil rights era of the 1960s and that a black man, Barack Obama, was twice elected the country's president race does not matter anymore. Many would also probably view the production of a heart drug like BiDil for African Americans as a positive sign of progress in redressing historical injustices or any lingering effects of racism. But even though overt racism—like segregated schooling and notorious Jim Crow laws in the South that prevented blacks from voting—may finally be deemed unconstitutional by the Supreme Court, race and racially based discrimination have hardly disappeared from American life. The unequal health outcomes between whites and blacks and other racialized minorities are but one expression of the ongoing problem.

There are many reasons racial inequalities persist, but one of the main ones is that they emerge out of a worldview that interprets visible signs of human variation as expressions of fundamental biological and genetic differences. With knowledge of human biodiversity, anthropologists have demonstrated over and over again how wrong this worldview is, showing that there is much less genetic variation between populations than within them; there is no single gene that codes for race; in scientific terms, humans are a single race; there are never clearly definable lines between physical traits in an actual population because variation is clinal; racial differences are culturally constructed upon arbitrary and shifting physical markers; the construction of racial typologies comes from a special way of sampling people and rarely describe an actual individual or group; morphological differences in humans are typically expressions of adaptability, not inferiority; and if there are any biologically more relevant ways to group humans, others such as blood type or immunity, are much more consequential in terms of bodily function. The latest biocultural research adds one more element to this body of knowledge: in spite of the fact that race has no biological or genetic origins, race can *become* biology through the embodiment of inequalities, dangerously reinforcing racialized understandings of human biology.

KEY TERMS

Reviewing the Chapter

Chapter Section	What We Know	To Be Resolved
In what ways do contemporary humans vary biologically?	There is greater genetic variation within populations than between them, which is largely a function of gene flow between populations. Humans exhibit important physiological diversity, especially in immune responses that enable flexibility and resistance to disease in variable ways.	Given how much humans move around geographically and due to the influence of cultural factors on reproduction, it can be challenging to identify and define stable human populations in a biological sense.
Why do human bodies look so different across the planet?	Because our bodies interact most directly with the natural environment, morphological traits such as skin pigmentation and body shape, size, and stature can reflect evolutionary adaptations to certain environmental pressures. They also influence biocultural outcomes for individuals and populations.	One of challenges of describing and explaining variations in how people look is contextualizing how much those variations can pass through and be shaped by cultural, not strictly biological or genetic, filters.
Are differences of race also differences of biology?	There are no valid biological justifications for dividing people into racial groups. Race is a powerful cultural *and* scientific construction, in the sense that any certainties about it have to be actively built—constructed—on a set of assumptions that anthropology shows are flawed when applied to humans.	Some scientific and medical authorities continue to produce biologized accounts of racial difference, suggesting that anthropologists still have important and unfinished work to do in challenging efforts to naturalize race.
What biocultural consequences do discrimination and stress have on human bodies?	Social relationships and cultural attitudes shape biological processes and health outcomes through embodiment. For this reason, race can become biology through the embodiment of racial discrimination, stress, and other factors.	The biocultural dynamics and consequences of embodiment represent a relatively new area of anthropological research, and the specifics of those processes are still being worked out. Anthropologists are also grappling with how dynamics of embodiment can actually reinforce racialized understandings of human biological variation.

Readings

In 2009 the *American Journal of Physical Anthropology* published a special issue entitled "Race Reconciled: How Biological Anthropologists View Human Variation" (139, no. 1). The ten articles provide comprehensive and relatively up-to-date perspectives on current anthropological thinking about human variation.

• • • • • • • • • • • • • • • • • • • •

Human Biodiversity: Genes, Race, and History (New York: Aldine de Gruyter, 1995) by Jonathan Marks offers a witty perspective on the history of thinking about human variation and race.

• • • • • • • • • • • • • • • • • • • •

Nina Jablonski's book *Skin: A Natural History* (Berkeley: University of California Press) is a fascinating and masterful exploration of the 300-million-year evolution of skin, with a specific focus on its place in human biology and cultural expression.

• • • • • • • • • • • • • • • • • • • •

The American Anthropological Association project "Race: Are We So Different?" is a national initiative to educate about anthropological perspectives on race. Its online portal examines the history of the race concept, race and its relationship

with human variation, and the lived experience of race: http://www .understandingrace.org/.

• • • • • • • • • • • • • • • • • • • •

The story of Vermont's eugenic movement is told in Nancy Gallagher's book *Breeding Better Vermonters: The Eugenics Project in the Green Mountain State* (Hanover, NH: University Press of New England, 1999). It examines the ties of eugenics with progressive social reform and the shifting scope, limits, and meanings of eugenics in America.

• • • • • • • • • • • • • • • • • • • •

The Body

Biocultural Perspectives on Health and Illness

In April 2009, breaking news headlines flashed across Americans' TV screens and newspapers, announcing that a deadly new strain of influenza, identified as swine flu, had killed more than 100 people in Mexico City. Influenza virus spreads rapidly through direct contact between individuals, especially hand to hand. But the response to this outbreak demonstrates that disease, even when the biological agent is clear, is about more than viruses and human biology. People in Mexico, the United States, China, and Egypt responded differently to the same outbreak.

In Mexico the epidemic produced a rapid and vigorous response. The government closed schools and universities. The busy streets of Mexico City were practically empty as Mexicans hunkered down in their homes. People wore surgical masks if they went out into the streets.

Soon a few cases were confirmed in several American cities among people who had recently visited Mexico. Intense TV and radio coverage prompted the White House and the Centers for Disease Control (CDC) to issue daily reports. But they seemed to heighten rather than calm public anxiety. Several prominent anti-immigration politicians called for sealing the border with Mexico. Even after six months there had been many fewer deaths in the United States than the more than 20,000 deaths each winter from ordinary seasonal flu.

Swine Flu and Cultural Differences In Mexico City, many people responded to the threat of swine flu by wearing surgical masks in public spaces, such as the subway pictured here. In other countries, where ideas about contagion and illness differ, people responded differently.

In China, the government reacted to the apparent—but false—association between the disease and pigs suggested by the name "swine flu." The Chinese government called for bans on imports of American and Mexican pork. Although this outbreak had nothing to do with pigs, banning American imports of pork made sense as a way of protecting China when they already blamed Americans for the worldwide recession at the time.

An unexpected response came from Egypt. Egyptian politicians directed killing their country's pigs to prevent the epidemic from infecting its population. Egypt is a largely Muslim country where, because of Muslims' restriction on its consumption, few people eat pork. Only the Coptic Christians, a small minority group, tend pigs and eat pork. Most of the pigs belong to poor Copts, who live around the enormous city dump that serves Cairo, where the pigs consume garbage and waste. Killing the country's pigs would affect only a stigmatized group. Whether responsible or not, such groups are often blamed for problems in many cultures.

And then, as suddenly as it had started, swine flu dropped off our TV screens and newspapers as if it had never happened. The initial worldwide response now seems exaggerated, because the epidemic never developed into the deadly worldwide pandemic so many had feared. In each country, officials and ordinary people reacted according to their society's cultural expectations of diseases and their regional experiences of other epidemics. Like all illness episodes, this outbreak was about how people in different cultures respond to disease in distinctive ways they consider reasonable.

These incidents and reactions lead us to ask a general question about medical and biocultural anthropology that is central to this chapter: *How does culture influence our experience of health and illness?* We can help answer this question by considering a number of more focused questions, around which this chapter is organized.

How should we make sense of biological and cultural factors that jointly shape our bodily experiences?

What do we mean by health and illness?

How and why do doctors and other health practitioners gain social authority?

How does healing happen?

What can anthropology contribute to addressing global health problems?

The swine flu epidemic shows how anthropology has a great deal to say about bodily experiences of health and illness. As we examined in the previous chapter, biological anthropologists have begun to develop useful tools for understanding how bodies are shaped through processes of embodiment. This chapter explores these issues more from the perspectives of cultural anthropologists, where the links between culture and disease hold long-standing interest. Some of that knowledge has been put to work in addressing real-world health crises. Let us first consider how biology and culture jointly shape how we experience of our bodies.

How Should We Make Sense of the Biological and Cultural Factors That Jointly Shape Our Bodily Experiences?

Since at least the 1920s cultural anthropologists have struggled with questions about the relative importance of our human biology as compared with the profound effects that culture has on individuals. In the nineteenth century, anthropologists like Edward B. Tylor (1871) and Lewis Henry Morgan (1877) thought that biology could explain why indigenous peoples in Africa, Australia, or the Americas had such modest toolkits to work with when compared with Europeans and white Americans. Their answer: the bodies and minds of "primitive" people were not as developed as those of Europeans. For a number of decades after 1920 it looked as if culture could shape who and what people were (e.g., Mead 1928). But in recent years, especially since the emergence of genetic research as a prominent branch of biology, it has appeared to many Americans as if it is "all in our genes" or our biological "hardwiring." Now biology, genes, and hormones are used to explain sexual orientation, criminality, IQ, wealth, education, and who becomes CEO of a Fortune 500 company.

Anthropologists are skeptical of grandiose claims about biological destiny. As the previous chapters in this section explain, a full appreciation of the human condition requires that we avoid thinking of ourselves as *either* cultural *or* biological (natural) beings, but through a new and emerging paradigm that emphasizes humans as biocultural beings in which biological, psychological, and cultural processes interact in complex ways. How does this affect cultural anthropology?

Uniting Mind and Matter: A Biocultural Perspective

One place cultural anthropologists have sought to mend the divide between biology and culture is in the human **mind**, the emergent qualities of consciousness and intellect that manifest themselves through thought, emotion, perception, will, and imagination. There is increasing biocultural evidence indicating that even our most basic cognition does not happen separately from our bodies. The human nervous system is a complex neurological network that reads and regulates chemical and biological conditions throughout the entire body, not just our thinking brains. Human biology sets certain broad outer limits that all humans share, but the actual character of cognitive processes differs from one individual to the next and across cultures because of the influence of external factors.

These external factors include social context and culture, with which the nervous system interacts through individual cognition. For example, culture shapes some basic aspects of perception. People growing up in societies with little two-dimensional

- **Mind.** Emergent qualities of consciousness and intellect that manifest themselves through thought, emotion, perception, will, and imagination.

art must learn how to understand photographs after first seeing them (Shore 1996). Cultural differences in perception suggest that mental development varies with cultural practices.

And as we explained in the precious chapter, research has also demonstrated that the mental stresses that people experience because of rapid social and political-economic change have physiological consequences, including raising blood pressure, affecting immunity to disease, and creating symptoms of fatigue or feelings of inadequacy (Dressler 2005). These mental stresses may accompany other biological impacts, including changes in diet, nutrition, and general health (Daltabuit and Leatherman 1998). The mind manifests itself through the whole person, throughout an individual's lifetime (Toren 1996).

Culture and Mental Illness

Studies of people with psychological problems across the globe have brought into question whether the psychological dynamics observed in Western countries are universal, that is, based purely in human biology. Numerous conditions, among them schizophrenia, anxiety, depression, attention deficit disorders, and narcissistic personality disorders vary greatly in their incidence in different cultures, suggesting that culture has a profound effect on the ways humans think about their psychology and display mental disorders. Such cross-cultural differences require us to approach mental illness in a culturally relative way.

Psychological abnormality is always defined culturally because what is considered abnormal is based on socially accepted norms. Not all societies define the same conditions as psychologically abnormal, nor do they necessarily share the same mental illnesses. A well-known example of a so-called **culture-bound syndrome** (a mental illness unique to a culture) is *koro*, the condition unique to Chinese and Southeast Asian cultures in which an individual believes his external genitalia—or, in a female, nipples—are shrinking and even disappearing.

Societies can even change what they consider a disorder, homosexuality being one such example. Although today few people view it as an illness, until 1974 American psychiatrists classified homosexuality as a mental disorder, and the U.S. Immigration and Naturalization Service used the classification of homosexuality as "abnormal" as a reason for excluding immigrants until 1990.

The ability to define any condition or behavior as a psychiatric disturbance reflects great social power and can have serious consequences for the course of an individual's life and for his or her experience of self. As we see in "Anthropologist as Problem Solver: Kim Hopper, Homelessness, and the Mentally Ill in New York City," anthropologists have paid close attention to the relationship between psychiatry and social power.

Because different societies define mental illnesses differently based on different cultural understandings of individual psychology, treatments differ accordingly. For example, on the Indonesian island of Bali, persons are not conceived of as isolated or indivisible, as we conceive of them in the West. Spirits and deceased ancestors commonly reside in individuals. Madness (*buduh*) can be caused by inherited factors, congenital influences, an ancestral or divine curse, or the blessings of gods (Connor 1982). The task of the village-level healer, called the *balian*, is to identify the specific causes of madness, which are usually related to some kind of social disruption or family conflict. The *balian* then resolves the conflict or disharmony in the family or neighborhood (Connor 1982) (Figure 11.1). Western psychiatry's approach, which often involves isolating the individual through institutionalization or providing pharmaceuticals, would clearly be inappropriate, if not socially disruptive, in these circumstances.

- **Culture-bound syndrome.** A mental illness unique to a culture.

Anthropologist as Problem Solver

Kim Hopper, Homelessness, and the Mentally Ill in New York City

HOMELESSNESS DID NOT become a recognized social problem in the United States until the late 1970s. Before then, of course, there were people who had nowhere to live, but homelessness was commonly understood as an extension of their poverty, the result of alcoholism, or lifestyle choices (Beriss 2005). Few researchers tried to understand how and why some people were homeless or what Americans thought about people without homes. One exception was anthropologist Kim Hopper of the City University of New York.

Since the 1970s, Hopper has lived among, studied, and worked as an advocate for homeless people in New York City. He has spent most of his professional life outside academia, working in non-profit agencies, advocacy organizations, and government (Hopper 2002). He helped draft legislation and legal briefs, submitted affidavits, served as a court-appointed monitor, testified as an expert witness, and served as a board member of the National Coalition for the Homeless.

According to Hopper, anthropology's strength in this arena is its ability to focus attention on the cultural concepts that shape our thinking about homelessness, the social and policy conditions that prevent adequate solutions, and the social control that service institutions exert on homeless people.

One area where these concerns come together is in the connection between homelessness and mental health. In the 1970s, the closing of mental hospitals, asylums, and psychiatric clinics led to an explosion of homelessness in large cities, leading many people to believe that most homeless people are mentally ill. Social service institutions were built on the assumption that people become homeless because of psychiatric problems. Their model suggests that the best way to approach homeless people is to treat them as mental patients.

Hopper has been highly critical of this model. Not only is there little evidence to prove its assumptions, there is no way of knowing if a perceived disorder is a *cause* or a *consequence* of homelessness. In other words, are the homeless people's patterns of behavior "symptoms" of mental illness or caused by, if not adaptations to, the homeless way of life (Hopper 1988:158)? According to Hopper, homelessness typically has its roots in larger developments, like housing crises, increases in unemployment, changes in household composition, and the reduction of government assistance programs. Defining all homeless people as deviant mental patients is an exercise in social control and leads to coercive policies of hospitalization. These actions preempt questions

Kim Hopper.

both about the quality of immediate assistance offered such people and about the long-term subsistence alternatives to the hospital (Hopper 1988).

From Hopper's point of view, the issue is not whether the problem of homelessness will be solved, because it will not. One reason, Hopper argues, is that industrialized societies produce "surplus people," which means that there are more people than positions in technology-driven industrial economies, so there will always be people on the margins of the economy and out of work. One key issue is to recognize that the opposite of homelessness is not a homeless shelter. Rather, it is a home, which is currently lacking in treatments of homeless people.

Hopper insists that ethnographic research offers useful on-the-ground insights into these matters, because policymakers, judges, and social service bureaucrats are unlikely to find these things out for themselves. But, he argues, fieldwork is not enough: anthropologists also need to familiarize themselves with clinical knowledge and the government's legal, regulatory, and procedural constraints to be able to evaluate proposed interventions.

Questions for Reflection

1. How and why do you think homeless people might develop traits of mental illness?

2. Why would social institutions want to define people as mentally ill if they are not?

3. What might you say to officials in your hometown to explain American cultural attitudes toward homelessness?

Figure 11.1   Balinese *Balians*.
Balians are ritual specialists and healers who use a mix of traditional herbs, prayers, and other rituals.

Nevertheless, as documented in Ethan Watters's book *Crazy Like Us: The Globalization of the American Psyche* (2011), Western psychological terms, notions, and illnesses are globalizing rapidly in recent years. For example, mental illnesses such as depression, anorexia, and post-traumatic stress disorder seem to now exist in places that have never had them before, such as Hong Kong, Sri Lanka, and Tanzania. Watters suggests that much of this is taking place because of global flows of Western media and psychiatric practices, and the expansion of pharmaceutical companies into new markets throughout the globe. Watters argues that such practices, which are usually based on an assumption of "hyper-individualism," destabilize indigenous notions and ways of treating mental illness in social context.

We can take this issue even further with a biocultural approach that combines cultural and biological insights. Rebecca Seligman has conducted research on Candomblé, a spirit-possession religion in Brazil (Figure 11.2). Seligman's question was, Why do certain people become spirit mediums and others do not? Biomedicine explains mediumship as a psychological disturbance with a biological basis but fails to explain how and why such a disturbance might express itself specifically through mediumship. The cultural approach argues that oppressed and marginalized individuals gravitate toward mediumship, but it fails to explain why not all dispossessed people become mediums (Seligman 2005).

Seligman found that there is no single pathway to mediumship, but the interaction of biological, psychological, and cultural factors plays a crucial role. Among these are a physiological ability to achieve dissociation (trance states); conditions of poverty and oppression that cause emotional distress, which is often experienced through bodily pain; and a cultural outlet and social role that reward people who exhibit the qualities of mediumship. Seligman concludes that without this holistic perspective on a medium's experience, we cannot appreciate the complexity of how people become mediums.

Now that we have explained how even the most basic matters of human cognition and psychology are not simply the function of our biological hardwiring, we can productively understand more broadly how *all* matters of disease, health, and illness are powerfully shaped by culture.

Figure 11.2   Candomblé Mediumship.   In Brazil, where some two million people practice Candomblé religion, temples where rituals are carried out are managed by women priests, known as "mothers-of-saint," often with support from men priests ("fathers-of-saint").

● ●

THINKING CRITICALLY ABOUT THE BODY

What are the implications of cross-cultural differences in psychology for the academic and clinical disciplines of psychology in which most psychologists treat patients who are Americans? What might these psychologists consider when dealing with recent immigrants from Africa or Asia?

● ●

What Do We Mean by Health and Illness?

Health and illness seem to be straightforward concepts. Dictionaries often define the word *health* as the "soundness of body and mind" or as "freedom from disease" and *illness* as being "unhealthy," or having a "disease," "malady," or "sickness." The problem is that ideas like "soundness of body" and "malady" do not suggest any objective measure of when we have health and when it has left us. For example, soreness after a hard workout at the gym or mild seasonal allergies and sinus conditions rarely impair one's daily life. These can be annoying, but are they signs of poor health?

The borderland between health and illness is more ambiguous than we might have originally assumed. This ambiguity results from two interlaced dynamics: the "subjectivity of illness," which is how people perceive and experience their condition on a personal level, and the "**sick role**," the culturally defined agreement between patients and family members to acknowledge that a patient is legitimately sick.

These issues are at the heart of medical anthropology, which is the branch of anthropology that tries to understand how social, cultural, biological, and linguistic factors shape the health of human beings (Society for Medical Anthropology 2016). Doctors tend to focus on treating sickness and disease, while public health officials have traditionally focused on preventing outbreaks of disease. Medical anthropologists look at the diverse aspects of illness, its prevention, and its treatment. At its core, medical anthropology begins with the fact that, as much as we might like health and illness to be objective categories, health and illness are subjective states.

● **Sick role.** The culturally defined agreement between patients and family members to acknowledge that a patient is legitimately sick.

The Individual Subjectivity of Illness

Illness is a subjective experience, but it is also shaped by cultural and social expectations. This insight is credited to sociologist Earl L. Koos, who in the 1940s conducted a classic study of attitudes toward health and illness in a mainstream American community he called Regionville. Koos interviewed thousands of ordinary Americans about being sick. For example, he asked one working-class woman about being sick, to which she replied:

> I wish I really knew what you mean about being sick. Sometimes I've felt so bad I could curl up and die, but had to go on because the kids had to be taken care of, and besides, we didn't have the money to spend for the doctor—how could I be sick? . . . How do you know when you're sick, anyway? Some people can go to bed most any time with anything, but most of us can't be sick—even when we need to be. (Koos 1954:30)

This statement demonstrates both the subjectivity of illness and how health and illness are inherently linked to social behavior and expectations, especially when our symptoms impair us so much that we cannot perform the normal social and economic duties expected of us—jobs, school, and, in this case, caring for her family.

To understand when a particular symptom is considered significant enough to provoke someone to seek medical care, we have to understand people's ordinary expectations. In the United States, these expectations are linked to issues like social class, gender, age, the kind of work people perform, and their routine lifestyles. The poor and working class routinely work more physically, eat less healthy food, and pay less attention to their health concerns than do wealthier people. It is not that lower class people do not care about health, of course. They simply have less time for doctors' visits, work in jobs they could lose if they miss a day, and eat the least expensive foods, which as we will discuss in Chapter 15, are the processed foods made available by the industrial food system. And they often have less adequate health insurance or no health insurance at all.

A number of cross-cultural anthropological studies confirm that cultural background also shapes the subjectivity of illness. For example, anthropologist Katherine Dettwyler (2013) conducted research in Mali, a West African nation at the southern edge of the Sahara. There she observed high infection rates of schistosomiasis, a liver and bladder problem caused by a parasitic worm that lives in water. This worm enters the human body through the feet and legs, causing sores on the skin and releasing blood into the urine. Dettwyler found this condition so common in Mali that by puberty nearly all rural men have blood in their urine. Instead of viewing red urine as a shocking symptom, as Americans would, Malian men understood it as a normal condition typical of the transition to adulthood. For these adolescents it meant they were becoming men, not that they were diseased (Figure 11.3).

Americans might interpret Malian understandings as ignorance, and perhaps there is some lack of biomedical knowledge among youth in Mali. But the important point is that people rarely worry about conditions that are common. Just as manual laborers rarely worry about lower back pain, Malian youth never worry about dark urine but see it as normal and even desirable.

The "Sick Role": The Social Expectations of Illness

In all societies around the world, when a person is ill there are expectations of how that person, as well as friends and family, should behave. For Americans this typically means the sick person should skip school or work, stay in bed and rest, be given chicken soup, and so on. But these patterns vary cross-culturally. One of this book's authors, Robert Welsch, experienced this kind of cultural difference while conducting field research in Papua New Guinea among the Ningerum people.

One day Welsch noticed that his body ached all over and his forehead burned with a high fever. It was malaria. At first he retired to his bed to rest, but the fever turned into chills, followed by sweats and an even worse body ache. He took antimalarial pills and aspirin, but the headache became so bad it was unbearable to lay his head on a pillow. Like most Americans he wanted to be by himself and endure this agony alone.

But Ningerum villagers did not sit idly by. As Welsch's condition worsened, more and more of his friends in the village came by the house to sit and chat and smoke. He later realized that most people in the village attributed his sudden symptoms to sorcery: someone

Figure 11.3   Undernourished Adolescent in Mali.
This condition is caused by a heavy disease load as much as poor nutrition in the diet.

in the area had used magic to hurt him, and people expected him to die. If it were sorcery, there was nothing anyone in the village could really do for him, but nobody wanted to be accused of having caused his death. The only sure way to avoid suspicion of being a sorcerer was to demonstrate concern. Fortunately for everybody, by the eighth day, the fever broke, and the headache and body aches subsided. The villagers who had been keeping vigil for several days went back to their normal activities.

Welsch and the villagers clearly had very different ideas of how they expect patients and caregivers to behave. Anthropologists and sociologists refer to these unwritten rules as the sick role, or the responsibilities and expected behaviors of sick people by their caregivers (Parsons 1951). To be considered legitimately sick—rather than as malingering, or faking sickness—one must accept specific responsibilities and a new social role, which exempts one from his or her ordinary daily roles and responsibilities such as school or work. Two key aspects of the sick role are to want to get well and to cooperate with medical experts.

A great example of this phenomenon comes from our own childhoods. During cold and flu season in the winter, many schoolchildren feel under the weather and want to stay home. When a parent agrees to it, many kids may decide later in the day that it would be fun to go out and play in the snow. But "Dr. Mom" steps in with her authoritative zeal to explain that if you are sick enough to stay home, you are too sick to go outside to play. Playing outside does not demonstrate that you want to get well—which is a key aspect of American ideas of the sick role—and slipping out of the house in defiance of Dr. Mom's explicit orders to stay in bed is not compliance with her medical expertise.

Welsch found that Ningerum people had a different sick role model, believing that if patients still enjoy a minimum of physical strength, they should themselves deal with the illness. For the Ningerum patient to get help with his or her care and treatment, the patient is obliged to display to family and friends precisely how sick and disabled he or she is. Patients convey this information through their actions or visible physical signs of illness rather than through their words. Startling symptoms such as fainting, bleeding, vomiting, shrieking, and sudden weight loss call family members to action. Patients can also display the severity of their condition by using props like a walking stick to limp cautiously across the village plaza, shedding clothing, refusing to eat, or smearing their chests and legs with mud and dirt. All these actions communicate to family and friends that the patient is sick and (silently) demand that family members show their sincere concern for the patient. Not to do so would suggest that one was not sensitive to a relative's needs—an indifference that, to the Ningerum, whose culture prescribes very close kinship ties, would suggest not being fully human.

While culture shapes a community's expectations of the sick role, our medical schools and hospitals have created a culture of medicine that often leads to tensions between the views of professionals and those of laypeople. These tensions often have to do with the social authority given to doctors that makes the relationship asymmetric, a topic we consider next.

THINKING CRITICALLY ABOUT THE BODY

The "sick role" concept works well for acute diseases like measles, bad colds, and chicken pox. But how might the sick role from an acute infection compare with a chronic condition like diabetes, chronic shortness of breath, or severe arthritis?

How and Why Do Doctors and Other Health Practitioners Gain Social Authority?

Figure 11.4   Improvements in Public Health.   Although use of antiseptics made surgery much safer in the late nineteenth and early twentieth centuries, improvement in life expectancy came from better sanitation and hygiene across the United States, including (a) street cleaning and the development of improved sewers, such as those implemented in the 1890s in New York that kept the public away from waste of all kinds (note that the street cleaners wore white uniforms in an effort to instill the sense of cleanliness in the public); (b) using antiseptics in the operating room, as this photo from 1900 shows; (c) the use of soaps to promote personal hygiene, as this Lifebouy soap ad from 1900 promises.

Medical doctors in the United States have one of the most prestigious, respected, and well-paid occupations. The prestige and social authority doctors enjoy, however, is relatively new. Throughout most of the eighteenth and nineteenth centuries, American doctors had low social status. Medicine was not sophisticated, and doctors often doubled as barbers. During the Civil War, surgeons were little more than butchers who amputated with large, dirty saws, using no antibiotics, few pain killers, and no antiseptics (Starr 1982).

Many people assume that doctors gained prestige and authority because new medical discoveries and technologies improved their ability to heal people. Antibiotics like penicillin, for example, have made a huge difference in treating disease. But the major advances in health we take for granted today were mostly improvements in *preventing* diseases rather than curing them. Clean water, sanitation, and other public hygiene programs saved more lives than doctors' treatments have (Figure 11.4). So how do we explain the social authority of doctors? Medical anthropologists have studied the social authority of healers in many societies. They identify several processes at work, the most important being the social processes that privilege the healers' perspectives over their patients and the designation of otherwise normal conditions as health problems.

The sociologist Eliot Freidson (1970) was among the first to identify the professionalization of the field of medicine as responsible for giving the doctor's perspective privilege over the understandings of ordinary people. It is not that doctors necessarily knew more about what the patient experiences during an illness, but doctors had been trained

(a)

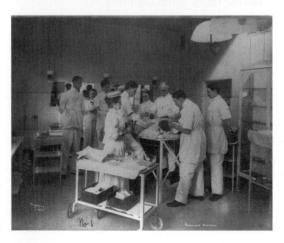

(b)

(c)

how to treat a wide variety of diseases. Subsequently, the medical sociologist Paul Starr (1982) argued that during the twentieth century medical doctors in the United States had used their professional status to increase their incomes, the level of respect they received from the public, and the exclusive right to determine the course of treatment for particular patients. Forming professional associations like the American Medical Association allowed them to control how many new doctors were being trained. But while American physicians had achieved professional privileges, great respect, and high salaries, few of these perks are enjoyed by doctors in most other countries.

The Disease–Illness Distinction: Professional and Popular Views of Sickness

Around the world, patients often view their illnesses differently from the doctors or healers who treat them. In the Western world, patients often feel that their doctors do not understand the intensity of their pain and other symptoms. What frequently emerges is a clash of professional and popular (or layperson's) understandings that we call the disease–illness distinction, in which doctors focus on **disease**, the purely physiological condition, and patients focus on **illness**, their actual experience of the disease (Eisenberg 1977); see Figure 11.5.

In our culture the doctor, not the patient, has the greater authority in identifying and defining health and illness. Sociologist Eliot Freidson (1970:205) explained this authority as the result of a social process: "In the sense that medicine has the authority to label one person's complaint an illness and another's complaint not, medicine may be said to be engaged in the creation of illness as a social state which a human being may assume."

American social structure also upholds the doctor's view as the officially sanctioned one. Because of the doctor's professional training, hospitals, governments, insurance providers, and, in extreme cases, even the courts recognize the diagnosis of the physician as legitimate. At the same time, the patient who has to live with the symptoms generally lacks any ability to authorize a prescription or treatment, or even offer an official diagnosis.

Understanding the distinction between doctor and patient perspectives is a key approach in contemporary medical anthropology. In the 1950s and 1960s anthropologists typically accepted Western medicine as superior and authoritative in much the same ways that Freidson suggests. Anthropologists generally assumed that health problems in developing countries were due to ignorance of medical knowledge and technology. A breakthrough came when Arthur Kleinman, a medical anthropologist who conducted research in Taiwan, argued that the key to understanding such differences in perspective is that healers and patients often have different **explanatory models of illness**, which are explanations of what is happening to the patient's body. Kleinman asserted that the goal of medical anthropology research was not to decide who was right in their explanation, but to accept that different people would come to the illness with different concerns and different kinds of knowledge. In "Classic Contributions: Arthur Kleinman and the New Medical Anthropological Methodology," we show an example of this approach.

Kleinman's approach also helped medical anthropologists realize the limitations of scientific knowledge, and they began to

- **Disease.** The purely physiological condition of being sick, usually determined by a physician.

- **Illness.** The psychological and social experience a patient has of a disease.

- **Explanatory model of illness.** An explanation of what is happening to a patient's body, by the patient, by his family, or by a healthcare practitioner, each of which may have a different model of what is happening.

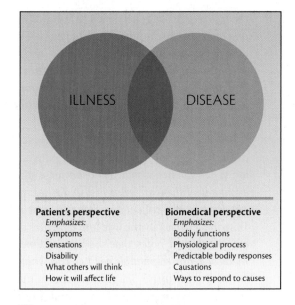

Patient's perspective	Biomedical perspective
Emphasizes:	*Emphasizes:*
Symptoms	Bodily functions
Sensations	Physiological process
Disability	Predictable bodily responses
What others will think	Causations
How it will affect life	Ways to respond to causes

Figure 11.5   The Disease-Illness Distinction.
Patients are concerned with the illness: symptoms, how they feel, and how their activities are affected by these symptoms. Doctors tend to focus on underlying causes of symptoms that they speak of as disease.

CLASSIC CONTRIBUTIONS

Arthur Kleinman and the New Medical Anthropological Methodology

IN THE MID-1970s physician, psychiatrist, and medical anthropologist Arthur Kleinman (b. 1941) published an essay on the history of medical anthropology. In it he added a short appendix where he introduced a new methodology around the concept of explanatory models, highlighting several cases he had come across in his work at the Massachusetts General Hospital in Boston. One case, excerpted here, offers an especially compelling illustration of his point.

For medical anthropologists, identifying the patients' explanatory model (EM) offered a new way of looking at how culture influenced a community's response to symptoms and illness. Rather than seeing an entire community responding uniformly to a set of symptoms, anthropologists now recognized that different individuals in varying relationships to the patient or with different positions in the society held quite varied views, or EMs. Kleinman's approach allowed medical anthropologists to shift the focus of their studies from the society to individuals within the society. And this methodology allowed anthropologists to make sense of how patients in non-Western settings use Western medicine. This new approach allows us to see healthcare decisions as a tension among different explanatory models.

Arthur Kleinman.

Mrs. F. is a 60-year-old white Protestant grandmother who is recovering from pulmonary edema secondary to atherosclerotic cardiovascular disease and chronic congestive heart failure on one of the medical wards at the Massachusetts General Hospital. Her behavior in the recovery phase of her illness is described as strange and annoying by the house staff and nurses. While her cardiac status has greatly improved and she has become virtually asymptomatic, she induces vomiting and urinates frequently in her bed. She becomes angry when told to stop these behaviors. As a result of this, psychiatric consultation is requested.

Review of the lengthy medical record reveals nothing as to the personal significance of the patient's behavior. When queried about this behavior, and asked to explain why she is engaging in it and what meaning it has for her, the patient's response is most revealing. Describing herself as the wife and daughter of plumbers, the patient notes that she was informed by the medical team responsible for her care that she has "water in the lungs." She further reports that to her mind the physiology of the human body has the chest hooked up to two pipes, the mouth and the urethra. The patient explains that she has been trying to be

helpful by helping to remove as much water from her chest as possible through self-induced and frequent urination. She analogized the latter to the work of the "water pills" she is taking, which she has been told are getting rid of the water on her chest. She concludes, "I can't understand why people are angry at me." After appropriate explanations, along with diagrams, she acknowledges that the "plumbing" of the body is remarkable and quite different from what she had believed. Her unusual behavior ended at that time.

This amusing but true case study is but a very striking example of the important role played by alternative explanatory models in health care. I use it because it derives from the still poorly understood and inadequately studied popular culture health-care domain, rather than from the far better appreciated and researched folk medical domain (i.e., that section of the health-care system composed of non-orthodox profession and paraprofessional healers—religious healers, quacks, practitioners of chiropractic and osteopathy, and other specialists). Yet it is the former, family- and community-centered beliefs and practices, which has the greatest impact on all forms of health-care-related behavior. [Kleinman 1975:652–3]

Questions for Reflection

1. How might Kleinman's explanatory models methodology help anthropologists understand healthcare choices in non-Western communities?

2. How does Kleinman's explanatory models methodology build on the disease–illness distinction?

challenge whether the doctors always had such special insights. Perhaps the patient understood some aspects of his or her body that the physician did not and, perhaps, could not understand. We have already discussed the subjectivity of pain and other symptoms. But in addition, medical knowledge is constantly changing, so how could doctors always have all the answers for how to treat their patients?

For example, consider what the medical profession has advised about breastfeeding for infants. Breastfeeding was universal until the 1950s, when baby formula was developed, and most American pediatricians promoted formula as a technologically superior way to raise a healthy baby. By the 1970s new scientific analyses of the contents of breast milk indicated that it contained antibodies that helped the child ward off infections. Rather than viewing breast milk as unsophisticated, the medical world began to see it as nature's way of protecting the child. About the same time in many developing countries, international aid workers were promoting baby formula as a way of producing strong, healthy babies. But by the 1990s, it had become clear that many babies suffered from malnutrition because their poor mothers could not afford enough formula or high rates of fatal diarrhea because clean drinking water for making formula was scarce (Figure 11.6).

With the spread of AIDS in the developing world, we now know that mothers infected with HIV can give the infection to their infants through breast milk. So, as a result, aid workers are once again, at least in communities where incidences of HIV infection are high, recommending baby formula. Who knows where the science of breast milk will settle in another generation? But as with nearly every other aspect of medicine, few scientific facts have remained, or will remain, static.

Since medical knowledge is constantly changing, it is no wonder that new diseases and drugs to treat them are constantly emerging. One way these changes emerge is when the professional medical system casts its net of authority even farther to cover conditions that were not previously understood as medical problems.

The Medicalization of the Non-Medical

Over the past fifty years the healthcare industry has expanded dramatically, taking over more and more of our individual personal

Figure 11.6 Changing Views on Breastfeeding. Dr. Benjamin Spock published a series of books beginning in the late 1940s (top) that promoted giving baby formula to infants rather than breast milk. Since the 1970s breastfeeding has had a resurgence in the United States after it became known that a mother's breast milk gave antibodies and partial immunity to infections to her baby (bottom).

Figure 11.7 The Temperance Movement. Alcohol use was condemned by members of the early twentieth-century movement as a moral failing.

• **Medicalization.** The process of viewing or treating as a medical concern conditions that were not previously understood as medical problems.

concerns. It has done so by redefining social, psychological, or moral problems as medical concerns. This process of viewing or treating as a medical concern conditions that were not previously understood as medical problems is called **medicalization**.

Alcoholism is a good example of this phenomenon. Excessive use of alcohol has been a problem throughout the history of the United States, producing opposition to it in the form of the temperance movement in the nineteenth and early twentieth centuries and prohibition in the 1920s. For a long time, alcoholism was seen as a moral failing that caused (usually) men to abandon their jobs and families (Figure 11.7). By the 1980s, psychiatrists, HMOs, and health insurance companies began to view alcoholism as a disease defined as "recurrent substance use resulting in failure to fulfill major role obligations at work, school, home" (American Psychological Association 1994). Defining alcohol abuse as a disease, rather than as a crime, socially inappropriate behavior, sinful behavior, or moral failing, reclassifies it as a medical concern.

Three major reasons have been suggested for medicalizing the non-medical. The first is financial: pharmaceutical companies, hospitals, and insurance companies stand to make larger profits when they can define a new disease for which they can provide treatment, care, and coverage. A second explanation is that medicalization enhances the social authority of physicians. A third explanation concerns Americans' current preference for viewing social problems in scientific rather than moral or social terms. In "Thinking Like an Anthropologist: The Emergence of New Disease Categories," we explore how patients and social institutions together created a new disease out of the so-called Gulf War syndrome.

Up to now we have largely considered how people and their professional healers make sense of and diagnose illness. But a key aspect of the illness experience has to do with how the treatments we get for our illnesses actually help us heal. As with the distinction between health and illness, healing is much more complicated than we might at first assume.

Thinking Like an Anthropologist

The Emergence of New Disease Categories

ANTHROPOLOGISTS BEGIN THEIR research by asking questions. In this box, we want you to learn how to ask questions as an anthropological researcher. Part 1 describes a situation and follows up with questions we would ask. Part 2 asks you to do the same thing with a different situation.

PART 1: MAKING SENSE OF THE SYMPTOMS OF GULF WAR SYNDROME

In 1990 Iraqi president Saddam Hussein sent his army to invade the independent country of Kuwait. In response, President George H. W. Bush sent some 700,000 American soldiers to the Persian Gulf. During the war the Iraqi army set fire to hundreds of oil wells that spewed dark smoke into the atmosphere. Adding to the perception of environmental devastation, many troops worried that American bombing of Iraqi troop positions had released toxic chemicals into the already putrid atmosphere. As it turned out, American bombing did not do this, but anxieties over what the air was doing to soldiers' health ran high.

After returning home, more than 10,000 veterans became ill with medically unexplained symptoms, such as chronic fatigue, loss of muscle control, headaches, dizziness, loss of balance, problems with memory, pain in muscles and joints, shortness of breath, and skin problems of various kinds. Most veterans who reported these symptoms attributed their poor health to their service in the Persian Gulf. Most military doctors who examined them found that their conditions resembled what came to be known during the Vietnam War era as post-traumatic stress disorder (PTSD) (called "battle fatigue" during World War II, and "shell shock" during World War I). These war-related conditions are considered anxiety disorders with psychological or psychosomatic roots.

When doctors diagnosed Gulf War veterans' problems as PTSD, most patients objected, claiming that their medical conditions were real and not "in their heads." Veterans had a variety of explanations for their symptoms: long-term contact with nerve agents or chemicals from the burning oil wells or brief encounters with volatile chemical agents. Others interpreted their symptoms as caused by a vaccine for anthrax, which all military personnel were injected with before leaving for the Gulf. Although repeated medical examinations could not confirm the explanatory models these patients had developed for their symptoms, and PTSD seemed the most likely cause, veterans began to refer to all these cases as the Gulf War syndrome.

From a medical perspective, most of the symptoms veterans reported are subjective, consisting of diffuse pain, fatigue, malaise, and indigestion. Moreover, the range of symptoms seemed so varied that physicians systematically rejected any single diagnosis as adequate. In addition, researchers have found the same mortality rates among veterans and other men who never visited the Gulf, suggesting that while the symptoms may be real, they are not causing higher than normal death rates among veterans of the Persian Gulf conflict. Nevertheless, veterans formed advocacy groups to defend their definition of these diverse health issues as Gulf War syndrome.

As we have seen, doctors and patients often have very different ways of understanding and interpreting patients' health concerns. And doctors' more authoritative interpretations are difficult for patients to challenge. But in this case there were so many vets with self-diagnosed Gulf War syndrome that veterans groups were able to get congressional attention. The Department of Veterans Affairs formed a study group to investigate the matter, and a federally mandated Research Advisory Committee on Gulf War Veterans' Illnesses (2008) concluded that these illnesses have real biological causes and serious consequences for affected veterans.

▼ **Gulf War Syndrome, a New Disease Category.**   Though its origins are in debate, some have associated the prevalence of Gulf War syndrome with burning oil wells in Iraq and Kuwait.

(continued)

Thinking Like an Anthropologist (continued)

The U.S. government now officially recognizes Gulf War syndrome as a disease, even though it has no single cause and no common symptoms. And while the official report of the Advisory Committee acknowledged it as a group of real illnesses with genuine effects on veterans, their classification is not a medical classification in the usual sense. But, of course, from the beginning, Gulf War syndrome was no simple health problem.

What questions does this situation raise for anthropological researchers?

1. Why should an environmental explanation—exposure to harmful chemical agents—be more appealing to veterans than PTSD?
2. Why would physicians and researchers initially have rejected Gulf War syndrome as a genuine disorder?
3. What role did political pressure by veterans' advocacy groups play here?

PART 2: MAKING SENSE OF RESTLESS LEG SYNDROME, ERECTILE DYSFUNCTION, AND OTHER PROBLEMATIC DISEASE CLASSIFICATIONS

Consider any one of the new health conditions that have emerged over the past thirty or forty years, such as restless legs syndrome, erectile dysfunction, premenstrual syndrome, acid reflux disease, or any of a number of other conditions for which pharmaceutical companies have now developed pills, tablets, or capsules as treatments. The American public considers many of these conditions as standard medical diagnoses, even though physicians have not always recognized them. What questions would you ask about the rise of new health conditions as an anthropological researcher?

THINKING CRITICALLY ABOUT THE BODY

Fifty years ago alcoholism was considered a moral failing, a behavioral problem found when people have no strong moral code to live by and do bad things to their families and others. Compare this earlier understanding of alcoholism with the most common view that alcoholism is a disease. How do you think this shift happened?

How Does Healing Happen?

When Robert Welsch was studying healing practices among the Ningerum, one of his informants came down with malaria. Welsch offered him some antimalarial tablets, but his informant could not swallow them because they tasted bad. After several days of lying in bed, the man's nephew performed a traditional ritual, smearing clay on his uncle's painful chest, reciting magic words, and apparently removing a packet consisting of some small object wrapped in a banana leaf from the sick man's chest. Within two hours, the man was up and about with his walking stick heading for the spring where he showered, a visible sign to everyone in the village, including the anthropologist, that he was feeling better (see Welsch 1983).

To the Western mind, such examples of traditional healing strain credibility. But anthropologists around the world have observed similar responses to a wide variety of non-medical treatments. We do know that the human body is remarkably resilient. If we cut ourselves superficially while chopping vegetables, the wound will bleed, scab over, and gradually new skin will cover the cut. We do not fully understand how healing works, but we know that healing is more complex than most Americans recognize. Healing is a biocultural process: it is not just about pills and surgeries, but about the meaning that the sick person and the healers give to treatments in a specific cultural context. Medical anthropologists generally accept that treatments help our bodies heal in four distinct therapeutic processes: (1) clinical processes, (2) symbolic processes, (3) through social support, and (4) through persuasion (Csordas and Kleinman 1996).

Clinical Therapeutic Processes

Most professionals working with Western medicine assume that effective treatment comes from **clinical therapeutic processes**, which involve a doctor observing a patient's symptoms and prescribing a specific treatment, such as a pill. The medicines have some active ingredient that is assumed to address either the cause or the symptom of a disorder. Thus, an antibiotic is thought to kill a type of bacterium, while a vaccination inserts a small amount of the virus or bacterium—usually already dead—into the blood, which triggers the body's immune system to react by creating antibodies so the body can fight off the infection in the future.

Sometimes doctors understand how these physiological processes work; at other times they may not understand the healing process but assume that it works by some plausible but unproven process. Whatever the case, there is still more to understand because these clinical processes do not account for healing such as when the Ningerum perform a ritual to drive away spirits.

Symbolic Therapeutic Processes

In most tribal societies that medical anthropologists studied in the twentieth century, there were some treatments that used herbs, teas, and potions. The explanatory models used in these societies sometimes drew on clinical models, but often the herbs and potions were important not so much for their chemical properties but for their symbolic ones. Although the chemical composition of the herb or leaf might help the patient heal, people were largely unaware of these properties and used them in rituals for other reasons.

In such cases, healing rituals act as a **symbolic therapeutic process** by virtue of their role in structuring the meanings of the symbols used. The symbolism of healing rituals comes from a number of sources, invoking our olfactory senses and our senses of taste and touch. It can also involve chanting, drumming, singing, and other sounds that set particular moods. Typically, the rituals provide a symbolic temporal progression, as in the form of a mythological story, that the affliction is supposed to follow for the patient to recover and heal (Figure 11.8).

For example, the French anthropologist Claude Lévi-Strauss (1961) documented a healing ritual among the Kuna [**koo**-nah] Indians of Panama that shows how over a period of many hours the shaman sings, produces smells, and touches a woman in the midst of a difficult birth. The ritual chanting recounts a mythological story in which

- **Clinical therapeutic process.** The healing process in which medicines have some active ingredient that is assumed to address either the cause or the symptom of a disorder.

- **Symbolic therapeutic process.** A healing process that restructures the meanings of the symbols surrounding the illness, particularly during a ritual.

Figure 11.8 The Power of Non-medical Healing. A Ningerum healer in Papua New Guinea removes a magical packet from a man's leg with magical words, rubbing magical leaves, and sucking to relieve pain in his leg.

a child overcomes diverse obstacles to reach its goal. These things relax the mother and her baby so the child can emerge from the womb, just as the hero of the story reaches his final goal. This kind of ritual is very common around the world because so many societies have found it efficacious.

Social Support

- **Social support therapeutic process.** A healing process that involves a patient's social networks, especially close family members and friends, who typically surround the patient during an illness.

The **social support therapeutic process** involves a patient's social networks, who typically surround the patient, much like Welsch's experience among the Ningerum. Although relatives and friends may perform some (usually) minor treatments on the patient, the major thrust of this therapeutic process comes from the presence of family members who provide comfort and aid to the sick person. Feeling aided and supported by his or her relatives may affect the patient's bodily functions. For example, diabetics often have better control of their blood sugars when they are with supportive family members but poorer control when feeling isolated.

Persuasion: The Placebo Effect

- **Placebo effect.** A healing process that works on persuading a patient he or she has been given a powerful medicine, even though the "medicine" has no active medical ingredient.

Persuasion is another powerful therapeutic process. Consider the **placebo effect**, in which a patient is given a non-medicine as if it were a medicine. The classic example of a placebo is a sugar pill given instead of some prescription drug with an active pharmaceutical ingredient. What makes it a placebo is that the sugar pill has a beneficial effect, even though it has no pharmacological or clinically active component. Usually, patients are told that they will receive a powerful medication or procedure, even though they will actually receive the placebo. This strategy, however, worries many people, including doctors, because it amounts to lying to a patient; dispensing placebos challenges professional ethical codes of behavior and even some federal laws in the United States.

Up to now it has been hard to explain the placebo's effect clinically, since the placebo seems to work through persuading the patient that the drug is effective. Something must be happening within the patient's body, but it seems to lie outside the bounds of ordinary medicine.

A dramatic illustration of the power of the placebo effect comes from a French study conducted in the 1990s. Researchers divided a group of hospitalized cancer patients with mild to moderate cancer pain into four groups to test the effectiveness of naproxen, a new painkiller now known by the brand name Aleve. None of the patients experienced so much pain that they required opiates, and the study put none of the patients in significant distress. At first these patients were randomly assigned to one of two groups as they came out of cancer surgery. One group was told they would be in a random trial of a powerful new pain reliever and would receive either the test drug or an inert placebo. Members of the second group were told nothing. This second group was unaware they were in a test and would assume that they were receiving standard hospital care. Half of the patients in each group were randomly given either an inert placebo or naproxen, thus creating four groups in all. Nurses, who were unaware of the details of the study, asked patients to evaluate their pain reduction hourly using a pain scale from 1 to 100 that represents the pain experienced (Bergmann et al. 1994; Kaptchuk 2001).

All the patients given naproxen showed a reduction in pain, confirming that naproxen works physiologically. But patients who were given the placebo, and were told they were in the study, had greater pain relief than those patients who were given naproxen but were told nothing about their pain treatment regimen. Figure 11.9

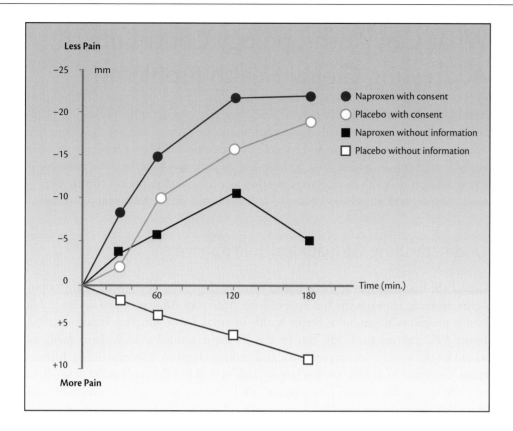

Figure 11.9 **Evidence of the Placebo Effect on Pain after Surgery.** Everyone in the study who received naproxen experienced pain reduction, but people told about the study who received only the placebo experienced more relief from pain than patients who received naproxen but were not told about the study. (After Bergmann et al. 1994)

illustrates this study's findings. Even more remarkable: this study suggests something that most researchers were not anticipating and had not appreciated. Figure 11.9 shows the large gap in the experience of pain relief between the two groups who were given naproxen. Theoretically, if we assume that naproxen works physiologically, both groups should have experienced similar levels of pain relief. But they did not; the placebo effect enhanced the pain relief in the test group who received naproxen and were told they were in the trial. In other words, those patients in the test group knew they were in the study and expected to get good results from their painkiller. What this tells us is that the placebo effect probably enhances all clinical interventions whether they are pharmaceuticals, surgeries, or other procedures. When patients *believe* that a pharmaceutical or medical procedure is effective, they regularly see improvements.

The insight that culture and social processes influence the healing process is a powerful insight of medical anthropology. So how do anthropologists put such insights to work? We consider this question in our last section.

THINKING CRITICALLY ABOUT THE BODY

The naproxen study demonstrates the power of the placebo effect. Discuss what this study might mean for a doctor prescribing a "powerful" antibiotic or some brand new treatment for a condition in a patient he or she sees in his or her clinic.

What Can Anthropology Contribute to Addressing Global Health Problems?

Anthropologists have long recognized that they can contribute to alleviating global health problems by understanding different healthcare systems around the world, how diseases are transmitted within and between communities, and how people use therapies available to them. In recent years anthropologists have also become more proactive in trying to improve health conditions where they work. We explore both of these themes—understanding and actively addressing global problems—in the following subsections.

Understanding Global Health Problems

One of the first attempts at this problem came in the 1950s when medical anthropologists, working through the Institute of Inter-American Affairs, helped design public health programs to promote better health in rural Latin America (Erasmus 1952; Foster 1952; Simmons 1955). But by the 1970s, it seemed that Western medicine would fix the world's health problems, and anthropology's role in explaining different cultural systems of healthcare was largely irrelevant. After the eradication of smallpox in 1979, the World Health Organization (WHO) believed that eradication of polio and other infectious diseases was simply a matter of time, and WHO's planners called their program—unrealistically—"Health for All by the Year 2000." But as AIDS and other public health crises erupted worldwide, and even polio proved more intractable than researchers had expected, medical anthropologists increasingly saw the need to double their involvement in understanding what were rapidly becoming global health problems with important biocultural dimensions. We explore two issues here: the issue of medical pluralism and patterns of disease transmission.

Understanding Medical Pluralism: Comparing Different Healthcare Systems

Medical anthropologists have long recognized that there are many sophisticated non-Western systems of medicine—in places like India, China, and the Arab world—that had been effective for centuries before the medical systems of the United States and Western Europe had developed antiseptics, antibiotics, and vaccines. As India, China, and the Arab world began to establish modern industrial societies, their healthcare facilities were integrating Western medicine with traditional practices. Medicine was not replacing these ancient traditions, but supplementing them. Nearly all other societies draw on more than one medical tradition simultaneously, a concept called **medical pluralism**, which refers to the coexistence and interpenetration of distinct medical traditions with different cultural roots.

An example of medical pluralism comes from anthropologist Carolyn Nordstrom (1988), who studied Ayurveda, a traditional medical system developed in India and Sri Lanka. Ayurvedic practitioners diagnose health problems using the classical Ayurvedic practice of reading the pulse, and they mix herbs in specified ways. But practitioners also draw upon traditional Sinhalese (referring to the people of Sri Lanka) medical ideas and practices in what Nordstrom refers to as a mediation of Ayureveda and local Sinhala medicine. She learned that they often mix traditional Sinhalese herbal preparations along with those they have learned at an Ayurvedic college, and that many Ayurvedic healers frequently use stethoscopes and thermometers and dispense standard Western medicines along with their herbal preparations.

- **Medical pluralism.** The coexistence and interpenetration of distinct medical traditions with different cultural roots in the same cultural community.

She also observed that some Sinhalese Buddhist monks incorporated Ayurvedic and Buddhist principles in their therapeutic work, sometimes adding Sinhalese preparations as well (Figure 11.10).

The broader point here is that in an increasingly globalized world, medical anthropologists are learning that all medical systems are now plural systems. Successfully addressing global health problems must take this fact into account.

Understanding Patterns of Disease Transmission

Medical anthropologists have also played a key role in making sense of how infectious diseases spread within a population, which is as much an anthropological or sociological task as it is a medical one. For example, anthropologists have played a key role in helping researchers understand the transmission of HIV, which causes

Figure 11.10   Medical Pluralism. Modern Ayurveda often adopts elements from biomedicine.

AIDS. In the United States and Europe, public health officials have promoted the use of condoms to interrupt the spread of HIV. But promoting condoms has not proved so effective in Africa, Haiti, and certain Southeast Asian countries, each of which had distinct cultures of sexuality and patterns of transmission. By studying these patterns of transmission, anthropologists helped medical researchers understand how culture was shaping HIV transmission.

In Africa, for example, HIV was first noticed along major highway routes where long-haul truckers became infected through heterosexual contacts with infected prostitutes, taking the infection to women in the next truck stop town (Nyamwaya 1993). Truckers, prostitutes, and truck stops produced ideal conditions for transmission of HIV through these wide-ranging and international social networks. Anthropologist and geographer Ezekiel Kalipeni (2004) suggests that epidemiologists and medical researchers had completely missed seeing these patterns. He argues that medical researchers explained the observed distribution of cases in terms of traditional patterns of African sexuality, which the medical community assumed was radically different from those of Western Europe. Traditional culture was demonized; the appearance of modern lifestyles, population growth, social inequality, and mounting poverty that was sending African villagers to urban centers and new forms of employment all went ignored. Anthropologists provided detailed observations of people's ideas about the disease, their explanatory models, and specific information about the sexual practices and behaviors of women and men, helping illuminate the patterns of HIV transmission (McGrath et al. 1992; Nyamwaya 1993).

Anthropological Contributions to Tackling the International HIV/AIDS Crisis

As their understanding of global health problems has become more sophisticated, anthropologists have become more assertive in putting their ideas to work. One way they do this is by working with communities to design aspects of the public health system to meet the needs, understandings, and cultural expectations of people in the community. To continue with the example of the HIV/AIDS crisis, we examine the work of Paul Farmer.

Using anthropology's holistic perspective to understand communities and their social problems, anthropologist and physician Paul Farmer (1992) began research for his dissertation in Haiti. As an undergraduate, Farmer majored in anthropology at Duke University. In 1983, before beginning medical school at Harvard, he spent some time in Cange, a community in the mountainous central plateau of Haiti. In this extremely poor area, he could see firsthand that the social, economic, political, and health

Figure 11.11   Partners in Health at Work in Haiti.   The organization co-founded by anthropologists Jim Yong Kim and Paul Farmer (pictured here with a shovel during a ceremony to build a health center) has had important positive impacts on Haitian public health. It now works in other countries where it brings a holistic perspective to improve public health.

problems were interconnected. Farmer saw these connections before HIV/AIDS had been identified and before large numbers of AIDS cases had been diagnosed in Haiti. When the AIDS epidemic broke out, the connections between the health of Haitians and socioeconomic and political conditions became even more obvious (Figure 11.11).

Working with another M.D.-Ph.D. student, Jim Yong Kim, Farmer helped found an organization in the highland district of Cange in 1987. (Kim went on to head the World Bank.) They called this organization Partners in Health (2010) and developed a small health center. The international health community was initially focused on treating AIDS patients and on other public health concerns to slow the spread of AIDS. But Farmer and Kim had larger goals that they saw as related to health in the Haitian community. They began encouraging local people to plant trees in the once lush forested region that had been devastated from poverty and rapid population growth, which led to deforestation as poor Haitians turned to their last resource (trees) to make into charcoal. Farmer and Kim put together an integrated program that attacked the causes of poverty and environmental degradation as a way of improving health. After twenty years of execution of this program, Farmer and Kim saw the district returned to something like its lush original environment, along with solid improvements in local health (Kidder 2003).

THINKING CRITICALLY ABOUT THE BODY

Medical anthropologists have traditionally been involved in public health efforts to vaccinate children, to provide clean drinking water, and more recently to assist with combating HIV/AIDS. Public health efforts appear to offer a natural role for anthropologists, but clinical settings that include physicians and their patients in modern urban settings less so. Why?

Conclusion

This chapter's focus on bodily experience reflects what most of us feel, implicitly, is the most natural part of our beings. But how we understand our bodies and minds and how we make sense of impairments to them are inevitably shaped by the culture.

As we saw with the Spring 2009 outbreak of H1N1 influenza (swine flu), discussed in the chapter opener, people living in different cultures, with varying views and cultural expectations, react differently to essentially the same set of facts. In an effort to protect their citizens, each country's leaders approach problems of health and epidemics somewhat differently because in each case it is not the virus or the epidemiology, but the local cultural assumptions that shape these leaders' actions. When individuals become ill in different cultures, they and their families also respond in locally appropriate ways, interpreting the signs, symptoms, and implications in locally meaningful ways.

Recent research even suggests that our bodies respond according to our expectations about the effectiveness of a treatment. Western physicians have nonchalantly dismissed such responses as merely the "placebo effect," but for millennia societies have looked after their sick with herbs and local rituals that seem to bring relief to the sick.

The research that medical anthropologists are conducting today comprises some of the most important applied projects in the discipline. These research projects have demonstrated that global health concerns and modern epidemics are much more than medical problems. Like everything else in life, health and illness are linked to the kinds of society we live in, our biology, the historic traditions that have motivated and shaped our communities, and the meaning and significance we give to these biological and social facts. These biocultural linkages taken together are what make us human.

KEY TERMS

Clinical therapeutic process p. 307

Culture-bound syndrome p. 294

Disease p. 301

Explanatory model of illness p. 301

Illness p. 301

Medical pluralism p. 310

Medicalization p. 304

Mind p. 293

Placebo effect p. 308

Sick role p. 297

Social support therapeutic process p. 308

Symbolic therapeutic process p. 307

Reviewing the Chapter

Chapter Section	What We Know	To Be Resolved
How should we make sense of the biological and cultural factors that jointly shape our bodily experiences?	Biocultural perspectives and evidence are breathing new life into classic anthropological interests in cognition, psychologies, and our bodily experiences.	Anthropologists continue to debate the relative and variable relationships between culture and biology involved in people's psychology, emotions, and mental states.
What do we mean by health and illness?	A person's culture shapes his or her interpretation of symptoms and understanding of the illness condition.	How people in any particular society will interpret the symptoms of illness can be determined only by detailed evidence from illness episodes in a particular society.
How and why do doctors and other health practitioners gain social authority?	By dealing with human concerns as medical or biomedical problems, our society implicitly gives power to health practitioners who can prescribe drugs and other therapies.	It is not entirely clear why some peoples around the world are so ready and willing to give authority to healers, while people in other societies are unwilling.
How does healing happen?	Not all healing can be explained by the clinical processes familiar to physicians and medical students. Healing has important social and cultural dimensions.	While the power of the placebo effect is demonstrated, we still don't understand why it can work on our bodies.
What can anthropology contribute to addressing global health problems?	Clinical solutions to global health problems cannot work effectively without understanding the local culture of the people whose health-related behavior we want to improve, and that due to medical pluralism most societies combine distinct healing systems.	Up to now there is no single solution to a health problem that will work in all societies; it is not clear if there are general strategies applicable to most societies.

Readings

For an excellent and readable overview of recent developments in the anthropology of cognition and the opportunities of closing the gap between cultural anthropology and the brain sciences, see Bradd Shore's book *Culture in Mind: Cognition, Culture, and the Problem of Meaning* (New York: Oxford University Press, 1996).

• • • • • • • • • • • • • • • • • • • •

As the biocultural synthesis has gained steam in anthropology, several books have emerged that treat it in detail. These include Alan H. Goodman and Thomas L. Leatherman's edited volume *Building a New Biocultural Synthesis: Political-Economic Perspectives on Human Biology* (Ann Arbor: University of Michigan Press, 1998) and Susan McKinnon and Sydel

Silverman's edited book, *Complexities: Beyond Nature and Nurture* (Chicago: University of Chicago Press, 2005).

• • • • • • • • • • • • • • • • • • • •

Katherine Dettwyler's *Dancing Skeletons: Life and Death in West Africa*, 2nd. ed. (Long Grove, IL: Waveland Press, 2013) gives students a sense of what it is like to be a medical anthropologist in a developing country. Anne Fadiman's *The Spirit Catches You and You Fall Down: A Hmong Child, Her American Doctors, and the Collision of Two Cultures* (New York: Farrar, Strauss and Giroux, 1997) offers a glimpse into the tensions between American biomedical culture and an Asian immigrant medical culture.

• • • • • • • • • • • • • • • • • • • •

Arthur Kleinman's classic *Patients and Healers in the Context of Culture: An Exploration of the Borderland Between Anthropology, Medicine, and Psychology* (Berkeley: University of California Press, 1980) provided the first modern formulation of medical anthropology as a systematic branch of anthropology. Mary-Jo Delvecchio Good, Paul E. Brodwin, Byron J. Good, and Arthur Kleinman's volume *Pain as Human Experience: An Anthropological Perspective* (Berkeley: University of California Press, 1992) explores applications of Kleinman's work to chronic pain.

• • • • • • • • • • • • • • • • • • • •

Part III

Human Social Relations

Human social relations are characterized by interdependence, intensive cooperation, and sharing, all of us as individuals relying on others to meet our basic needs. Our capacity for social cooperation has undoubtedly been one of the critical reasons for the evolutionary success of the human species. Until 7,000 or so years ago, most prehistoric human groups met the challenge of living in society in more or less the same ways, living in small face-to-face groups, using simple technologies and collective effort to gather and hunt what they needed to survive. When people began to grow their own food and create more complex social formations like cities and states characterized by social inequality, however, social relations underwent dramatic change. Yet these processes were not uniform, and since then, matters of feeding, organizing, and controlling people have varied greatly across our species, always carrying distinctive consequences for the actual lives that individuals will lead.

This part opens with a chapter that examines what anthropological archaeology has found out about why and how prehistoric humans shifted from living in small family groups based on lives of gathering and hunting to producing their own food. In the next chapter we turn to the story of how, why, and when larger scale social groupings in which social complexity—understood as inequalities of power and social hierarchy—began to emerge. From those largely archaeological chapters, we shift toward what the branch of cultural anthropology called economic anthropology knows about the diverse ways people make, share, and buy things to create value and get what they want and need. A chapter on the closely related matter of sustainability—encompassing food production and human-nature relations—follows, which explores the diverse ways people interact with their environments. We end this part with a chapter that examines what political anthropology knows about the diverse forms that power, politics, and social control take in the world today.

Early Agriculture and the Neolithic Revolution

12

Modifying the Environment to Satisfy Human Demands

In 1930 two Australian prospectors set off in search of gold in the Central Highlands of Papua New Guinea. No Westerner had been there before, and the widespread assumption was that these highlands were uninhabited. But the prospectors were surprised to find many thriving villages surrounded by extensive gardens. It turns out that this region had over a million inhabitants, with the population densities in some areas reaching as high as 700 people per square mile, equivalent to an American suburb.

The most surprising aspect of this story was that the gardens were mostly growing sweet potatoes (*Ipomoea batatas*), a tuber which originated in South America, not Melanesia. Sweet potatoes were *the* staple food not just for all these people but also for huge herds of domesticated pigs. **Domestication** refers to converting wild plants and animals to human uses by taming animals and raising them for meat or milk, or making plants able to be grown for food or other uses. How could such large populations in the center of New Guinea be cultivating huge areas with a crop that did not originate there? When and how did the changes enabled by sweet potato cultivation happen?

This evidence sparked a new debate about the history of human settlement and agriculture in Papua New Guinea. Cultural anthropologist James B. Watson (1965) suggested that dense highland populations resulted from a major shift from hunting and gathering to food

Horticulture in New Guinea. Kuk World Heritage Site in Papua New Guinea, site of the earliest known drainage ditching for draining swampy land on the island of New Guinea. **Inset:** Ditching used to drain fields in historic times among the Dani in the highlands in West New Guinea now a part of Indonesia.

317

- **Domestication.** Refers to converting wild plants and animals to human uses by taming animals or turning them into herds that can be raised for meat or milk or making plants able to be grown for food or other uses.

production and pig domestication. He hypothesized that food production started as a response to this new crop, the sweet potato, which everyone assumed Europeans had brought from South America to the island 400 years ago. Archaeologists dismissed Watson's idea, following the discovery of 10,000-year-old drainage ditches and digging sticks (Brookfield and White 1968; Golson et al. 1967). It turns out that Highlanders had been gardening for millennia, probably even growing sweet potatoes that arrived there much earlier from trade networks connecting them to Polynesia and the Americas. It seems likely that the first cultivated plants were varieties of wild tubers that had existed in New Guinea for many thousands of years, now largely abandoned except in hard times. The imported taro and sweet potato replaced them because they were more efficient to grow.

The unexpected dominance of sweet potatoes in the Central Highlands of Papua New Guinea added a new dimension to an old debate among anthropologists about how, when, and why ancient humans, who lived by hunting and gathering, shifted to food production. In the 1920s the Australian archaeologist V. Gordon Childe, who had studied this shift in the Middle East, described it as the **Neolithic Revolution**. The Neolithic refers to the so-called new stone age when humans had begun growing crops and raising animals for food using stone-tool technology. According to Childe, this transformation was revolutionary because it allowed for population expansion and change in almost all aspects of society. But Childe and his successors focused on the domestication of grains, which can be stored for long periods, and so it came as a surprise that tubers could also sustain such large populations. The main problem with tubers is that, unlike grains, they tend to rot after a couple of weeks. In fact, New Guinea highlanders *did* store the tubers, but they did so in the form of animal protein, by feeding them to their large herds of pigs.

- **Neolithic Revolution.** The "new" stone age when humans had begun growing crops and raising animals for food, using a stone-tool technology.

Watson may have been wrong to conclude that horticulture was so recent, but he was surely correct about the profound effect cultivation had on how people lived. These changes range from population growth and the ability to settle in one place to the development of sophisticated social hierarchies, agricultural systems, political systems, and the arts. These issues lead us to ask: *How did raising plants and animals change the ways people lived in their environments?* Embedded within this larger question are a number of smaller questions around which this chapter is organized.

How heavily did prehistoric people depend on hunting?

Why did people start domesticating plants and animals?

How did early humans raise their own food?

What impact did raising plants and animals have on other aspects of life?

For more than a century, archaeologists have viewed the transition from hunting and gathering to agriculture as one of the most intriguing puzzles, raising questions about how early humans learned to plant crops or how to tame wild animals to become a domestic herd. We now know that there was no single Neolithic Revolution, affecting all humanity in the same ways or at the same time. Instead, multiple transformations have played out differently in distinct times and places around the globe. The story of how and why these transitions happened must begin with how early humans got their food, and this brings us to the matter of hunting.

How Heavily Did Prehistoric People Depend on Hunting?

As we explained in Chapter 8, anatomically modern humans have been around for approximately 200,000 years. During about 95% of that time people ate only what they could hunt, gather, or scavenge from the natural environment. Without claws or sharp fangs like other animals, the only way early humans could hunt large game was by using tools made from sharpened wood, bone, antler, and stone. We know that small animals like possums, rodents, snakes, and lizards can be obtained by the hands alone or with the simplest of tools. People also used tools such as digging sticks and stone scrapers to hunt, gather, and prepare wild foods. But most of the time the only archaeological evidence that early humans hunted comes from their stone tools and bones with signs of cutting they left behind. From cave art in the later Paleolithic period we have some evidence of how some groups hunted, and studies of the skeletons of ancient hunters and gatherers have offered insights into both the foods people ate and how they acquired these foods, particularly from **osteology,** the study of bones, and from paleopathological studies that tell us about a variety of diet-related health problems (e.g., Cohen and Crane-Kramer 2007; Eshed et al. 2010). But the information is scant, so archaeologists have turned to living hunter-gatherers for ideas and insights about early practices.

Taking Stock of Living Hunter-Gatherers

When anthropology emerged in the nineteenth century, most of the world's people had been growing their own food for at least a few thousand years. It was only in the remote deserts, rain forests, and polar regions that small bands of people practiced **foraging,** or obtaining food by searching for it, as opposed to growing or raising the plants and animals people eat. For the most part, agriculture and animal husbandry had not penetrated these regions because the environment and climate were not suited to these activities. Explorers, travelers, and eventually anthropologists often described these environments as harsh, depicting their inhabitants' technologies as simple and their ways of life as crude and brutish. These were the deeply held cultural stereotypes rooted in urban European and American worldviews, and they rarely reflect the perspectives of the desert-dwelling Australian Aboriginals and the people of the Kalahari Desert, or any of the Inuit groups living in the Arctic. Most Westerners—including early anthropologists—assumed these people, who still hunted in the Arctic or the deserts, represented examples of the most primitive human societies. They must

- **Foraging.** Obtaining food by searching for it, as opposed to growing or raising the plants and animals people eat.

therefore resemble the human ancestors of contemporary peoples living in Europe, the Middle East, India, and China who once had similar hunting practices but had evolved into more complex and sophisticated forms (Figure 12.1).

But just how difficult was it for early hunter-gatherers to get their food? And just how similar were contemporary hunter-gatherers to their prehistoric ancestors? These topics and many others were at the heart of an international gathering of anthropologists and archaeologists titled "Man the Hunter."

"Man the Hunter"

In April 1966 anthropologists Richard Lee and Irven DeVore (1968:vii) hosted a conference at the University of Chicago with the title "Man the Hunter" to address the state of anthropological knowledge about hunting and gathering ways of life. To current readers, the conference's title may sound sexist, but it was unintentionally so, because at the time the conventional term for all humans was "man." Yet the dominant anthropological model of these societies in the decades leading up to the conference held that hunter-gatherers live in **patrilocal bands** (small groups where men controlled resources and hunting territories). The assumptions included three key features: (1) hunting was an activity principally undertaken by men, (2) hunting was more important than gathering, and (3) men's subsistence activities were more significant than women's.

In spite of its title, what emerged from the conference was a resounding rejection of the old male-dominated model. A key revelation in toppling this old view was the consensus among participants that hunting was not *the* defining feature of these societies, as the old model held, but in fact were based on women's subsistence activities (Table 12.1). For example, Richard Lee's (1968) research in the Kalahari Desert among contemporary !Kung San hunter-gatherers had shown that women

• **Patrilocal bands.** Small groups where men controlled resources and hunting territories.

Figure 12.1   Hunter-Gatherers.   Some of the Best Known Contemporary Hunter-Gatherers Around the World.

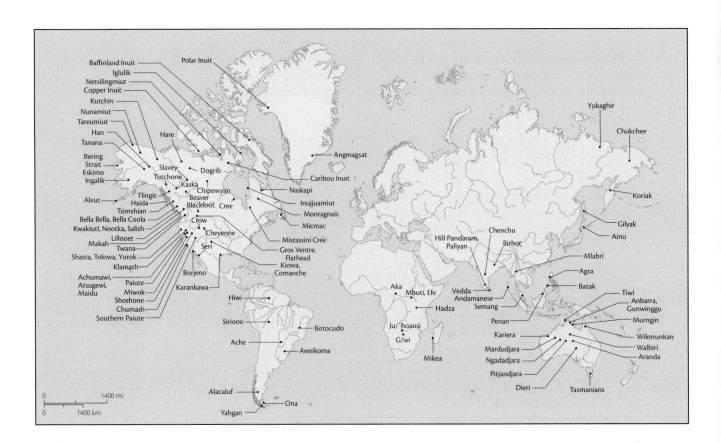

Region	Ethnic Group	Effective Temperature	Percentage of Diet Provided by Men	Population Density (per km²)
TABLE 12.1 THE RELATIVE IMPORTANCE OF MEN'S AND WOMEN'S CONTRIBUTIONS TO THE BASIC DIET IN CONTEMPORARY HUNTER-GATHER COMMUNITIES				
EXTREMELY COLD CLIMATES				
Siberia	Yukaghir	8.9	90%	0.5
Alaska	Nunamiut	9.8	85%	2.0
Canada	Copper Inuit	9.1	90%	1.2
Greenland	Angmagsalik	9.0	100%	8.0
S. America	Ona (Selk'nam)	9.0	75%	
S. America	Yahgan	9.9	50%	4.6
COLD CLIMATES				
Siberia	Gilyak	10.4	70%	19.2
Alaska	Chugach Eskimo	10.5	80%	18.0
Alaska	Kaska	10.5	80%	
Alaska	Eyak	10.5	80%	
Alaska	Ingalik	10.8	80%	2.5
Alaska	Aleut	11.6	90%	65.0
NW Coast	Tlingit	10.0	90%	10–40
NW Coast	Bella Coola	10.5	80%	10
NW Coast	Tsimshian	11.1	70%	32–83
NW Coast	Quileute	11.3	70%	64.5
Hunter-Gatherers Canada	Chilcotin	11.2	60%	13
Canada	Chipewyan	10.3	100%	0.4
Canada	Pikangikum (Ojibwa)	11.0	90%	3.2
Canada	Sekani	11.1	95%	1.0
Canada	Beaver	11.3	68%	0.5
Canada	Saulteaux	11.7	70%	0.6
Canada	Montagnais	11.6	70%	
COOL CLIMATES				
Japan	Ainu	12.0	50%	
NW Coast	Klallam	12.3	75%	
NW Coast	Squamish	12.6	90%	
NW Coast	Nootka	12.6	65%	66–77
NW Coast	Cowichan	12.6	60%	34
Plateau	Flathead	12.1	60%	
Plateau	Gros Ventre	12.4	80%	
Plateau	Coeur d'Alene	12.7	70%	1.5
Plateau	Kutenai	12.7	70%	2.0
Plateau	Sanpoil	12.7	58%	
California	Washo	12.3	75%	28
California	Tubatulabel	12.9	58%	30
Canada	Micmac	12.7	85%	2.3
S. America	Tehuelche	12.8	85%	
TEMPERATE CLIMATES				
California	Achumawi	13.3	60%	17.5
California	Yurok	13.3	58%	180

(Continued)

TABLE 12.1   (Continued)

Region	Ethnic Group	Effective Temperature	Percentage of Diet Provided by Men	Population Density (per km²)
California	Chimariko	13.5	80%	34.1
California	Maidu	13.5	58%	103
California	Wintu	14.6	78%	281
California	Diegueno	14.6	50%	18.1
California	S. Yokuts	14.7	73%	90
California	E. Pomo	14.7	63%	196–633
California	Wappo	14.7	63%	163
Plateau	Umatilla	13.3	70%	4.5
Plateau	Tenino	13.3	50%	
Great Basin	Tosawihi	13.0	50%	15
Great Basin	Kaibab (S. Paiute)	14.0	48%	3–4
Plains	Crow	13.0	80%	2.6
Plains	Arapaho	13.3	70%	3
Plains	Comanche	14.4	63%	5
S. America	Botocuido	14.4	78%	
WARM CLIMATES				
Great Basin	Panamint	15.0	40%	2.1
Great Basin	Shivwits (S. Paiute)	15.1	48%	1.3
Australia	Aranda	15.9	30%	3.0
Australia	Dieri	15.9	30%	1.9
SW U.S.	N.E. Yavapai	16.0	55%	1.4–4.0
S. America	Aweikoma	16.5	70%	
Africa	Hadsa	17.7	20%	15
HOT CLIMATES				
Africa	Ju/hoansi (Dobe)	18.8	40%	10–16
Africa	G/wi	19.3	30%	8.0
Australia	Walpiri	18.4	30%	1.0
Australia	Wikmunkan	19.6	35%	18.7
VERY HOT AND HUMID CLIMATES				
Australia	Tiwi	22.6	38%	
Australia	Murngin	23.5	53%	5
Malaysia	Semang	23.7	80%	5–19
Africa	Mbuti	23.7	41%	17
SE Asia	Andamanese	24.4	30%	86

Source: After Kelly (1995:265).

• **Generalized foraging model.** A model asserted that hunter-gatherer societies have five basic characteristics

often provided more than 60% of the calories people eat. Similar findings were reported from many other living hunter-gatherer societies, where women may only rarely hunt for large game but provided the bulk of plant foods, fish, crustaceans, shellfish, and small game. Recognizing these facts, participants offered what has come to be known as the **generalized foraging model** (Kelly 2013:10). This model asserts that hunter-gatherer societies have five basic characteristics, shown in Table 12.2.

TABLE 12.2	THE GENERALIZED FORAGING MODEL: THE FIVE BASIC FEATURES OF HUNTER-GATHERERS
Egalitarianism	Mobility constrains the amount of property that can be owned and thus serves to maintain material equality.
Low population density	Population is kept below carrying capacity through intentional, conscious controls such as sexual abstention, abortion, and infanticide.
Lack of territoriality	Long-term adaptation to resource variability requires that hunter-gatherers be able to move from one region to another, so defending territories would be maladaptive.
A minimum of food storage	Since the group is nomadic and food plentiful relative to population density, food storage is unnecessary; hence the potential for food storage to create social hierarchy is thwarted.
Flux in band composition	Maintaining social ties requires frequent movement and visiting among groups, which discourages violence since disputes can always be solved through groups breaking up rather than fighting.

Source: After Kelly (2013:10).

The conference also challenged the notion that hunter-gatherer lives were harsh; instead, they were examples of the "original affluent society" (Sahlins 1968, 1972). Previously, anthropologists had assumed that a hunting-gathering lifestyle was so difficult and precarious that people had to work long hours and had no time to develop elaborate cultural artifacts. But in his presentation for the conference, Marshall Sahlins rejected this image, pointing out that hunter-gatherers worked only a few hours a week. Playing on the title of economist John Kenneth Galbraith's (1958) book on U.S. capitalism, *The Affluent Society*, Sahlins showed how ethnographic data supported the view that hunter-gatherers had more than enough food resources available to them. Further, he asserted, most people in a foraging band spent many hours each day in leisure activities, socializing, or sleeping. Their nomadic lifestyle meant that they neither needed nor desired material goods, which they would have to carry from camp to camp. Sahlins also insisted hunter-gatherers did not view their natural environments as scarce and harsh (as we might) but as abundant and always providing for their needs, even in times of objective scarcity such as drought (Bird-David 1992). The importance of Sahlins's analysis was to insist that a different cultural logic underlies how and why foraging societies think about and relate to their natural environments. It also undermined the assumption that switching to farming and herding was necessarily an improvement in human welfare.

Recent Developments

While participants in the 1966 conference dismissed the "hunter" model in favor of a generalized forager model, more recent research has shown that there is considerable variation among hunter-gatherer groups. For example, it has become clear that women often contribute a great deal to a band's subsistence needs in some places but provide much less in many others (see, e.g., Peterson 2002).

For instance, in colder climates, such as among the Inuit and other Arctic groups, foraging adds little to basic subsistence since diets are based mainly on large animals, and women contribute little to food procurement. But even in these societies, women spend as much time working as men do—much of their time being devoted to food and clothing preparation—so we should not imagine that Inuit women contribute little to the community's livelihood. Not surprisingly, when archaeologists considered the role of men and women in early agricultural societies, they similarly assumed that men performed the lion's share of the work, while more recent analyses suggest that in most horticultural and agricultural societies, women's effort is typically greater than that of men.

The new view of hunter-gatherers raised an interesting question: If they could procure sufficient food with just a few hours of labor each day (as the "original affluent society" concept emphasizes), why did they not spend an extra hour each day to amass a surplus—more goods than people need—as people living in settled communities regularly do?

Anthropologists have suggested two answers to this question. The first was proposed by Lorna Marshall, a pioneer researcher among the !Kung San (also known as Ju/hoansi) of the Kalahri in southwestern Africa. Marshall noted that the !Kung women she observed were not lazy, but they only gathered as much as they needed for their own families because if they had more, they would be expected to share it with the entire band (Lee and DeVore 1968:94). Knowing that her labor would not help her family, most of these women intentionally avoided collecting too much. The key feature of this explanation is that among the !Kung, as in many other hunter-gatherer communities, people place great emphasis on sharing, which is viewed as a moral obligation (Marshall and Miesmer 2007).

The second was suggested by anthropologist Bruce Winterhalder (1993; see also Winterhalder and Smith 1981), whose research showed that even if only a few members of the band decided to harvest more than they needed on a regular basis, their actions could threaten the survival of the entire community as they depleted local resources that everyone relied upon—especially in years of environmental stress, such as drought. Winterhalder, along with Eric Smith, developed a model they called the **optimal foraging strategy,** which suggests that people capture just enough calories from the environment as they (and their families) need to survive comfortably. Any additional calories would, over time, stress the resources of the area and threaten the survival of the community.

In fact, not all societies using hunting and gathering as their subsistence strategy avoided accumulating surpluses. The best known examples of these are the Indian communities of the Pacific Northwest that had attracted so much attention because of the work of Franz Boas. These groups include the Tlingit, Haida, Tsimshian, Kwakiutl, Nootka, and Coast Salish. When Europeans first visited them, all of these peoples relied primarily on fishing, especially on the annual migration of salmon returning to inland spawning grounds. Men were responsible for most of the salmon catch, but women played the largest role in cutting, cleaning, drying, and preserving it. These Indian groups—unlike nearly all other contemporary hunter-gatherers—developed elaborate art traditions, large ceremonial houses, enormous totem poles that bore images representing their ancestors and clan affiliations, and ceremonial exchange relations involving gifts of large quantities of material objects.

Uniquely among hunter-gatherers, they also amassed large surpluses above their subsistence needs. Fish and other valuable objects were given away or sometimes destroyed in competitive exchanges called **potlatches,** opulent ceremonial feasts intended to display wealth and social status by giving away or destroying valuable possessions like carved copper plates, button blankets, and baskets of food (Codere 1950; Drucker and Heizer 1967; Kan 1989). Unlike exchanges in other hunter-gather societies, the goal of these gift exchanges was not to provide food or material goods to other groups, but to assert political, economic, and social superiority by giving away more than the recipients could pay back at some later potlatch (Figure 12.2).

● **Potlatches.** Opulent ceremonial feasts intended to display wealth and social status by giving away or destroying valuable possessions like carved copper plates, button blankets, and baskets of food. These were characteristic of the communities on the Northwest coast of North America.

Figure 12.2 Nineteenth-Century Kwakiutl Potlatch. Note the rich material culture available to this sedentary hunting and gathering community, made possible by the harvest of migrating salmon that swim the same rivers each spring and summer. The surplus of salmon allowed competitive exchanges called potlatches between rivals.

The large number of ethnographic studies of contemporary hunter-gatherers provides many insights about life under these non-agricultural conditions. But do these societies represent the actual lifestyles of our prehistoric ancestors during Paleolithic times?

Back to the Past: Understanding Prehistoric Hunter-Gatherers

No anthropologist or archaeologist today expects contemporary hunter-gatherers to be identical to prehistoric communities. One key reason is that in almost every contemporary case, hunter-gatherers are linked to sedentary agricultural and industrial societies through trade and other social ties, which would obviously not have been the case before the development of agriculture. For example, the Punan, who live in the rain forests of Borneo, have been gathering forest products like rattan for the world market for perhaps a thousand years (Hoffman 1984); and Central African pygmies had been involved in trading ivory toward the coast long before Europeans reached their forests (Bahuchet 1988). Some anthropologists have even wondered whether any of the contemporary hunter-gatherer groups could actually have survived without contact with farmers and industrial societies.

Despite these concerns, some contemporary groups do have features that are important for archaeological understanding of prehistoric hunter-gatherers. First is the fact that hunting and gathering can occur in a variety of forms, with hunting and fishing making up as much as 100% of the diet or as little as 10%, while foraging makes up the rest.

The second is that our anthropological models of the typical hunter-gatherers have changed. Before the "Man the Hunter" conference, anthropologists and archaeologists saw these societies as male-dominated and focused almost solely on hunting. After the conference, anthropologists came to see them principally as egalitarian foragers, relying primarily on plant foods, where women's roles are equal in importance to those of men. Today, the image of hunter-gatherers is complex, emphasizing variability between groups (Kelly 2013). But for archaeologists to make sense of how heavily prehistoric peoples relied on hunting, they needed to abandon these earlier stereotypes and open themselves to possibilities not found in the ethnographic record, even when it proves difficult to find clear evidence in the archaeological record.

In the next section, we apply these lessons to one of the biggest questions of all: What led people to shift from a foraging lifestyle in the first place?

THINKING CRITICALLY ABOUT THE RISE OF AGRICULTURE

Why do you suppose that until the 1960s, anthropologists generally assumed that hunting was more important than gathering and foraging to pre-agricultural societies? How is this assumption linked to American and Western European ideas about appropriate gender roles? Do you think the growing number of women professional anthropologists had an impact on how archaeologists and cultural anthropologists understood prehistoric gender roles?

Why Did People Start Domesticating Plants and Animals?

Sometime during the past 10,000 years, ancient societies developed more or less independently in the Middle East, China, India, Mesoamerica, and South America (Figure 12.3). One feature all of these societies had in common was that at some point the people who created them abandoned their hunting and gathering lifestyles in favor of regular food production that involved some sort of horticulture, farming, or herding. What led them to do so?

It is not because hunter-gatherers suddenly "discovered" how to plant seeds, nor is it because they abruptly learned that by feeding certain wild animals they could control their behavior. Although it is not easy to demonstrate archaeologically, most hunter-gatherers were likely aware of several methods they could use to improve the foods they gathered by burning, weeding, and modest tending.

One key fact is that simple agriculture emerged in the Fertile Crescent of the Middle East about 10,000 to 12,000 years ago, with similar forms emerging in the Indus valley at roughly the same period. Chinese development of simple rice agriculture emerged in the same period, almost certainly independent of the other two. In the New World, cultivation of **maize**, the species that evolved into modern corn, emerged somewhat later, and the Peruvian potato was being cultivated by at least 8,000 years ago. And the various tubers of the New Guinea highlands, as noted, were being raised in small fields drained by ditches 10,000 years ago. No matter what the **cultigen.** Any plant that is intentionally grown for human use. humans across the globe were beginning to cultivate useful plants almost simultaneously, suggesting that the knowledge of plants long preceded systematic cultivation. What seems lacking until roughly 10,000 years ago was some reason to grow one's own food.

Archaeologists have long struggled to understand the reasons hunter-gatherers shifted to agriculture. Theories range from the influence of certain geographic features to the growth of populations, which we examine in turn.

• **Maize.** The indigenous species of corn that was first domesticated in Mexico—the term is often used for any variety of corn, since all current varieties are thought to have been derived from this early version of so-called Indian corn.

Cultigen. Any plant that is intentionally grown for human use.

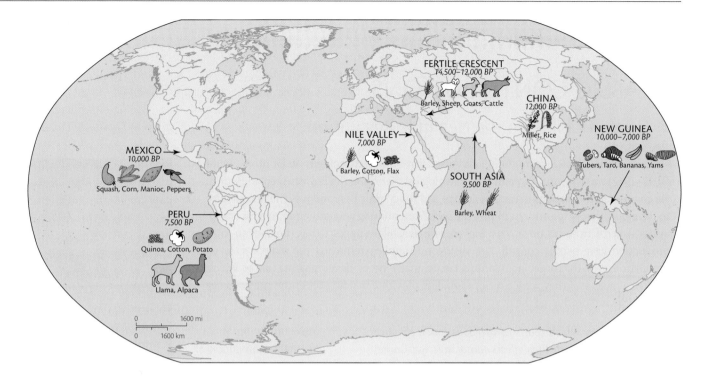

Figure 12.3 Early Domestication. Major areas of early plant and animal domestication, and the approximate date when widespread domestication began.

Defining the Neolithic Revolution

Archaeologist V. Gordon Childe (1936) was the first to recognize that the shift from hunting and gathering to food production had significant consequences for the development of more sophisticated technologies, larger populations, and more complex forms of social organization—including the formation of cities, state governments, and social hierarchies. In "Classic Contributions: V. Gordon Child on the Neolithic Revolution," we explore his thoughts on the matter.

For Childe, food production was not a single *event* but a *process* that set in motion a variety of changes, each of which encouraged other socioeconomic, political, and technological changes. Childe favored the notion that food production arose around oases in the Mesopotamian lowlands. But while Childe was correct that food production was associated with other social changes, he did not understand what actually led hunters and gathers to begin producing their own food, and some scholars questioned whether his oasis hypothesis was correct.

The Hilly Flanks Hypothesis

In the late 1940s, the American archaeologist Robert J. Braidwood (1952) was the first to tackle this why-did-they-do-it question in a systematic way. The first evidence archaeologists had of early humans actively and intentionally planting seeds for their own food comes from excavations in the Middle East in what has come to be known as the Fertile Crescent, a curved swath of land that includes Mesopotamia; the Mediterranean coast of Syria, Lebanon, and Israel; and the Nile valley (Figure 12.4). Here we find the beginnings of sedentary lifestyles and archaeological evidence that early humans—through planting crops and domesticating animals—were transforming the foods they ate.

Braidwood noted that few of the plants first cultivated in the Fertile Crescent were indigenous to the lowland plains where archaeologists had been excavating early

CLASSIC CONTRIBUTIONS

V. Gordon Childe on the Neolithic Revolution

FROM THE 1920S until the 1950s Australian-born archaeologist V. Gordon Childe (1892–1957) was the most prominent archaeological theorist in the English-speaking world. He conducted excavations in eastern Europe and the Middle East and was the first scholar to develop a theory for understanding the shift from hunting and gathering to agriculture. In this excerpt from his book *Man Makes Himself,* Childe suggests that the shift to food production gave people control over their food supplies, removing the main barrier to population growth. Larger populations led to many other developments, all of which emerge almost as if they were a set of cascading tiles, one building off of the previous development and producing the next.

V. Gordon Childe.

The steps by which man's control was made effective have been gradual, their effects cumulative. But [some] stand out as revolutions. The first revolution that transformed human economy gave man control over his own food supply. Man began to plant, cultivate, and improve by selection edible grasses, roots, and trees . . . [and] certain species of animals in return for the fodder he was able to offer, the protection he could afford, and the forethought he could exercise. . . .

As a revolution the introduction of a food-producing economy [was also] reflected in the population curve. . . . The community of food-gatherers had been restricted in size by the food supplies available—the actual number of game animals, fish, edible roots, and berries growing in its territory. . . .

Two other aspects of the simple food-producing economy deserve attention. Firstly, [it] provides an opportunity and motive for the accumulation of a surplus. Secondly, the economy is entirely self-sufficing . . . not dependent on the necessities of life on imports obtained by barter or exchange from another group. . . .

The co-operative activities involved in "Neolithic" life found outward expression in social and political institutions . . . and [these were] reinforced by magico-religious sanctions, by a more or less coherent system of beliefs and superstitions. . . . Finally, cultivation may have required a closer observation of the seasons, a more accurate division of time, the year. Agricultural operations are essentially seasonal. [Child 1936:59–60]

Questions for Reflection

1. What kind of archaeological data do you think Childe drew on to come up with the idea that the Neolithic Revolution was a sequence of "small revolutions"?

2. To what extent were Childe's sequence of innovations likely derived inductively from his field data? To what extent were they deductive hypotheses?

towns and fields. He reasoned that the upland fringes (the so-called hilly flanks in the title of the hypothesis) of the Fertile Crescent were the natural habitat of these prehistorically cultivated species. There, on the hilly flanks, not only were the necessary cultigens present but environmental conditions were conducive to cultivation because of higher rainfall than the dry lowlands. Braidwood hypothesized that once

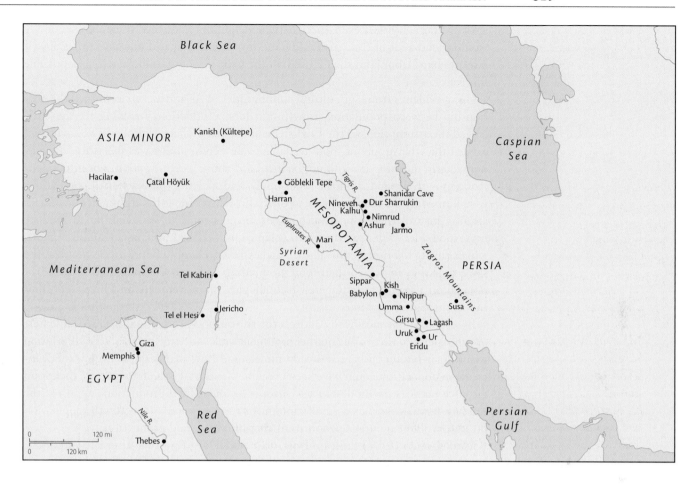

Certain plants had been domesticated in the uplands, their use as food spread to neighboring groups in the lowlands, where population growth, cities, and states eventually emerged.

To test this hypothesis, Braidwood undertook a series of excavations across the hilly country of Iraqi Kurdistan, southern Turkey, and western Iran. He found cave sites from hunter-gatherers who may have just begun to produce some of their own food, open sites that people had used as temporary encampments with tents, and one of the earliest villages at a site known as Jarmo. This last site produced traces of two species of wheat, one of barley, one of peas, and a certain variety of pistachios. Braidwood also argued that the domestication of sheep and goats took place here, evidenced by the large proportion of teeth found in the site from yearlings, a finding that suggested that residents were culling their herd and eating the less desirable individual animals (a process of selection, designed to improve the herd).

Braidwood's analysis suggested where people were starting to domesticate plants and animals in the Middle East, what they were domesticating, and why domestication began in these areas. But he did not explain why people started to produce their own food when they did rather than a few thousand years earlier or later. It was an agricultural economist who took this next step.

The Pressure of Population Growth

In the 1960s the agricultural economist Esther Boserup (1965) developed a model to explain why societies with simple economies had not taken up intensive

Figure 12.4 Fertile Crescent. The Fertile Crescent showing major archaeological sites providing evidence of early agriculture and later political centers.

agricultural activities, even though their neighbors had. She argued that nobody would spend a lot of time gardening and farming if they did not have to because it requires hard labor, and she focused on the issue of population growth as a possible motivator.

Using evidence from agricultural communities in Asia, Boserup examined the relationship between population growth and food production. In doing so, she challenged the assumptions of the English demographer Robert Malthus (1798), who had argued that the supply of food available to any community was inelastic—an economic term meaning it could not be increased above a certain point. For him, population growth depended on the food supply, and societies that had small populations were limited by the food available to them. Boserup turned this argument on its head, arguing instead that population growth forced people to work harder to produce more food. Her evidence came from Asian countries like India, Japan, and Indonesia, which during the nineteenth century had experienced rapid population growth at the same time they increased their food production. She argued that similar processes of population growth had triggered technological improvements and increased labor inputs throughout recorded history.

Boserup did not specifically address the rise of food production in the Middle East or other parts of the world. But her argument's relevance to the Neolithic Revolution was this: if hunter-gatherers already understood how plants grow, even a small increase in population could have been enough to encourage them to manage their food resources, at least in modest ways. Then, if incipient food production supported the existing population plus a small amount of further population growth, population pressure would encourage people to further intensify food production.

Mark Cohen (1977) built on Boserup's model, arguing that after the end of the last ice age around 12,000 years ago, environmental conditions stabilized and improved. At this point human populations were still widely scattered around the globe as they had been for hundreds of thousands of years, but these better environmental conditions probably allowed a small but gradual population increase. Domestication of animals in this model emerged only when populations of wild game declined.

A related model came from archaeologists Lewis Binford (1968) and Kent Flannery (1969), who suggested that in the Middle East and Mesoamerica postglacial populations increased in coastal areas that had favorable wild resources for fisher-foraging groups. Population growth, however, put pressure on some coastal residents to move away from these resource-rich coastal areas to less favorable environments. Some of these environments were situated along Braidwood's hilly flanks of the Fertile Crescent, where wild resources were less reliable. So cultivation was an obvious way to control uncertain food supplies. Thus, in Binford and Flannery's model, food production did not begin where resources were most plentiful or most scarce, but in environmental zones that were less predictable (see Bellwood 2005).

Some Other Explanations for the Beginnings of Food Production

Beyond population pressure, two other kinds of theories have been offered. The first is the fact that if food production began in diverse parts of the world almost simultaneously, then it likely had to do, at least partly, with the gradual warming of the planet after the last ice age. Sea level was rising, the climate was warming, and in many places the environment was becoming more habitable. Which or which combination of these changing conditions may have prompted food production is unclear, but this early phase of global warming was felt everywhere.

A second family of theories suggests that social processes were key to the beginning of food production (Bender 1978; Hayden 2003). Humans may have experienced some changes in cognitive ability that allowed them to perceive some longer term advantages that came with regular food production, although what that actual cognitive shift might have been remains elusive (see, e.g., Mithen 2007). Finally a neoevolutionary symbiosis model offered by David Rindos (1984) suggests that irrespective of why people in one region or another began cultivating plants, the people and the plants they began cultivating began to evolve together. In other words, once people started planting crops, the plants began domesticating the people. A similar process occurs with animal husbandry; as soon as one begins to domesticate wild animals, the animals and people begin to coevolve. Such has been most obviously the case with cattle, which have coevolved with certain human populations, so that people's bodies gradually adapted to the lactose in the milk, and cattle have evolved to suit the needs of their human owners (see Chapter 3).

A recent discovery that might lend some support to one or another of these social explanations was found at Gobekli Tepe, where the community began to construct some of the earliest monumental architecture associated with complex rituals (Dietrich et al. 2012). This fact would not be surprising except that it was happening before people had actively begun food production, all of which supports some of these theories built around social elements.

Now that we have covered some of the major theories about *why* humans made the shift from foraging to agriculture, we can address the *how* of the actual transition.

• •

THINKING CRITICALLY ABOUT THE RISE OF AGRICULTURE

What evidence can you think of for why archaeologists and cultural anthropologists assume that hunter-gatherers understood that plants sprouted from seeds or from leaves, roots, or tubers? How successful would early humans be if they were not already aware of the patterns of animal behavior and how plants grew?

• •

How Did Early Humans Raise Their Own Food?

Hunter-gatherers and their ancestors have an extraordinary knowledge of their natural environment. They are able to eat because they know where they will find foods and at what times certain foods ripen and become edible. They understand the fact that seeds grow into mature plants and that birds and game animals deposit seeds on the soil in feces, which then sprout and grow. This information was not the result of accidental discovery, but of careful observation made in their daily lives. Similarly, to be successful hunters of game, large or small, people needed to know the places animals ate or drank, and develop a fairly sophisticated understanding of animal behavior—ask any modern hunter, most of whom know considerably less than early humans before the Neolithic era. Given the details we discussed in Chapters 8 and 9 about human biocultural evolution and the emergence of human cognitive sophistication, it is highly likely that our human ancestors knew some or all of these things for hundreds of thousands of years, if not longer. Archaeologists have developed some plausible explanations of how people put this knowledge to work, which we review here.

Domesticating Plants

Almost immediately after humans started consciously planting wild grains from locally occurring grasses, the edible seeds became larger than their wild cousins. By tending and planting wild grass seeds, early humans were selecting the best seeds, which were also seeds from the most hardy and productive plants. These choices rapidly improved the planting stock in subsequent seasons. In fact, it is precisely these kinds of changes in indigenous grasses that allow archaeologists to trace the earliest evidence of domesticated grains and to be able to demonstrate that domestication had happened in the first place (Zohary and Hopf 2000).

In the Middle East, archaeologists have excavated sites where they found charred kernels of slender grains from wild varieties of wheat. The earliest sites date at least to 17,000 BCE. Their small size suggests that hunter-gatherers had harvested these grains from wild stands of native grasses. But by at least 7,800 BCE, charred seeds of a plumper variety from the same species appear in other sites, suggesting that humans were already selecting wheat with larger seeds. Several other wild species of wheat and barley later spread to Europe after being domesticated to become the principal cereals throughout the Middle East and Europe over the next 2,000 or 3,000 years (Figure 12.5).

EINKORN   **EMMER**

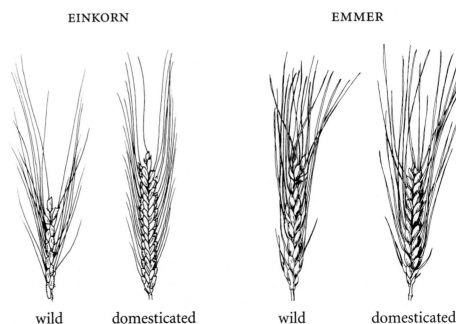

wild   domesticated   wild   domesticated

Figure 12.5   Wild and Domestic Grains of Wheat and Barley in Palestine.

Figure 12.6 Domesticated Corn Over Time. Examples of domesticated corn from the Tehuacán valley of Mexico showing how domestication gradually produced larger and larger cobs.

The process by which seeds became larger through selection can also be seen in the Americas with early varieties of maize. In the early 1960s, archaeologists Richard S. MacNeish (1967) discovered a series of caves in the Tehuacán [Tay-wah-**kahn**] valley of Mexico. When he excavated these sites, he found what looked like tiny corn cobs, the size of a cigarette filter, which proved to be ancestors of the modern corn species *Zea mays,* which has been the key staple food across Mesoamerica, the subtropical and tropical regions between what is now the United States and South America. He also found evidence of squash and bottle gourds, as well as beans, tomatoes, chili peppers, and avocados. Carbon-14 dates from these caves and rock shelters convincingly documented the domestication of these important cultigens at Tehuacán at least by 7,000 years ago (Piperno and Flannery 2001), making the site one of the earliest known evidence for cultivated maize in the Americas. Archaeologist Michael Blake (2015) has recently found an even earlier site in the Balsas River valley of western Mexico, where domesticated corn has been dated to 9,000 years ago from a wild grass he identifies as belonging to the grass species *Balsas teosinte* (Figure 12.6).

While we have less evidence about the earliest domestication of tubers in the New Guinea Highlands, Jack Golson, discussed in this chapter's opening story, identified evidence of trenching and swamp drainage by about 9,000 BCE. Poor preservation of tubers makes it difficult to know exactly which species were cultivated in the Neolithic period. Some have suggested taro or one of several other indigenous root crops occasionally planted today. But current horticultural practices offer little help in explaining which plants were domesticated so long ago. The most common species cultivated in the same region today, for example, is the sweet potato, which originates in South America. Its introduction to the Pacific Islands is likely much earlier than James Watson (1965) and Peter White (Brookfield and White 1968) had originally assumed; it was probably introduced by some early contacts between people of the Peruvian coast and eastern Polynesia perhaps a thousand years ago. Nevertheless, the New Guinea Highlands case demonstrates that the earliest cultigens in a region need not be grains but can be tubers or other root crops that propagate from cuttings.

Watson (1977) suggested another reason why cultivation might have spread so rapidly once people started growing their own food. His argument was developed to account for the rapid spread of sweet potato growing in New Guinea, where violence and tribal fighting was quite marked (see, e.g., Gardner and Heider 1969; Gardner 2004), but his model is broadly applicable even in regions without the high levels of violence found in New Guinea. Watson called it the "Jones effect," because once a neighboring group started increasing their food—in potatoes and pigs—by planting sweet potatoes, there was pressure on neighbors to "keep up with the Joneses" in order to solidify alliances, better maintain friendships, and the like. The problem with this model is there is little archaeological evidence that can either support or contradict it.

Of course, humans did not domesticate plants just for food; they have also domesticated plants for other uses, such as fiber-bearing plants for basket-making. We consider one such example in "Thinking Like an Anthropologist: Unpacking the Dynamics of Plant Domestication."

Domesticating Animals

Similar processes occurred with domesticated animals as they did with plants: selective breeding to favor certain qualities, such as to increase size or to favor certain other qualities and characteristics like docility, protectiveness, and appearance. But not every animal species (or plant, for that matter) can be domesticated effectively. The ancestors of modern sheep, goats, horses, and cattle were suitable for domestication because their dispositions were generally docile. As we explored with the example of foxes in Chapter 3 on evolution, canines can readily bond with a dominant individual in a pack, which can be transferred to their human owners as an animal becomes tame. Other species, for reasons not well understood, like zebras, lions, tigers, and bears, have not been domesticated, partly perhaps because of their mean or unpredictable disposition (Diamond 2002).

Domesticating animals is not necessarily an all-or-nothing proposition. We can see examples of semi-domestication in Papua New Guinea today among the Ningerum people who catch feral piglets soon after they are born and keep them tied near a house while they are young. Later the pigs are released but fed every afternoon, and while they may have foraged for food during the day, they always return for food in the afternoon, where they can easily be caught when they are big enough to be part of a local pig feast. Even domesticated pigs in this community still breed in the wild because all the male piglets are gelded (castrated), so the boars in the breeding stock are all feral. But as was likely true in prehistoric times, semi-domesticated animals do not improve as quickly from selection even though regular feeding may have a positive effect on their appearance and phenotype.

Raising animals is also an especially useful practice for people who have domesticated plants. Animal dung can be used as fertilizer to nurture the crops, and some animals, such as oxen, horses, and mules can help till the soil. One of the most common animals domesticated very early was the dog, which was originally used for hunting, but could also help with herding sheep and goats. As mentioned earlier and in Chapter 3, the evolutionary effects of selective dog breeding is quite

Thinking Like an Anthropologist

Unpacking the Dynamics of Plant Domestication

ANTHROPOLOGISTS BEGIN THEIR research by asking questions. In this box, we want you to learn how to ask questions as an anthropological researcher. Part 1 describes a situation and follows up with questions we would ask. Part 2 asks you to do the same thing with a different situation.

PART 1: THE COGNITIVE DYNAMICS OF A RECENT DOMESTICATE

Most of us assume that the domestication of plants happened in some distant prehistoric past, but nothing could be further from the truth. People today continue to select wild plant varieties with qualities they find appealing, collect their seeds and transplants, and breed them with a goal of cultivating them. One such example is a fiber plant called Devil's Claw, which is one of only a handful of native plants domesticated by American Indian farmers and gardeners (Nabhan and Rea 1987). Within the past century or two, O'odham [oh-**oh**-dum] people of the Sonoran desert region of southern Arizona and northern Mexico began selecting seeds and cultivating Devil's Claw. The domesticated plant produces a more robust fruit and longer, more pliant fiber strings, preferred for economically important basket-making, than wild varieties. One plausible hypothesis for Devil's Claw's domestication has to do with the decreasing availability of the wild varieties due to overgrazing by Anglo cattle ranchers and the increasing marketability of Indian baskets.

Although recent and current attempts to domesticate a plant variety do not necessarily offer straightforward analogs for prehistoric times when many major foods and plants we use today were domesticated, unpacking the dynamics of Devil's Claw's domestication can reveal clues as to the causes, modes, and effects of domestication more broadly. One issue of interest to anthropologists in this case is the cognitive aspects of domestication, in other words, how people involved in domestication perceive and classify plant characteristics, and how their perceptions and classifications change over time (Nabhan and Rea 1987).

Addressing these concerns requires knowledge of how O'odham perceive and group Devil's Claw with similar and related plants. One way O'odham classify plants is in terms of their mode of establishment, making a distinction between a seed a person intentionally sows or transplants and a plant that grows on its own. Devil's Claw sits ambiguously between these categories because its seeds can be planted, but it may

also drop seeds that grow by themselves. Wild plants, if transplanted, can be considered intentionally sown (although they typically don't survive). And although they may look different, when grown together cultivated and non-cultivated varieties can mix genes. The O'odham recognize that there is no clear discontinuity, and so their view does not easily map Devil's Claw onto the categories "wild" or "domesticated." Native speakers grapple with this ambiguity and use a variety of terms to describe the plant. For example, some people who know of the domesticate will still refer to Devil's Claw with the same term for known non-cultivated varieties. Others will use specific terms for each, marking domesticates from non-cultivated. And still others use adjectives that mark the plant as "more" or "less" cultivated or not-cultivated.

This situation should not be interpreted as confusion among the O'odham, many of whom have as sophisticated an understanding of how this plant grows and reproduces as any scientist. Rather, native speakers are still working out how to classify this plant because its domestication is so recent. The broader point here is that domestication processes involve changes in the ways people perceive, understand, and classify plants.

What questions does this situation raise for anthropological researchers?

1. Why would O'odham decide to cultivate Devil's Claw, and who would have been the most likely people to undertake its domestication?
2. How have O'odham terms for Devil's Claw changed over time? Do changing terms reflect different ways of perceiving the plant?
3. What implications might the cognitive dynamics discussed above have for understanding prehistoric domestication processes?

PART 2: DOMESTICATING YAMS IN SOUTHWEST ETHIOPIA

In a remote corner of southwest Ethiopia, the Sheko and Dizi people practice horticulture, apiculture (honey production), and limited plant gathering. Some farmers also transplant wild-growing, indigenous yams in their home gardens, indicating that an incipient process of domestication may be under way (Hildebrand 2003). What questions would you ask about this situation as an anthropological researcher?

marked, but there is ample evidence that cattle, horses, donkeys, llamas, and even ducks and chickens, have all evolved in the context of the human societies in which they were raised.

Recent Findings on Arboriculture

Archaeologists and anthropologists have recently begun to consider how humans may have begun manipulating their food sources in more subtle and less comprehensive ways than with wheat, barley, and maize long before these grains were domesticated. For example, archaeologist Kyle Latinis (2000) suggests that arboriculture, or planting and tending tree crops whose fruits are edible, likely occurred considerably earlier than domestication of other crops in Southeast Asia. Unlike cereals and tubers, trees last a long time and can easily be tended in minor ways, such as by planting a shoot, seed, or sucker, or by weeding, pruning, and clearing vegetation so the tree gets just a little more sun. These activities take little time or energy and yet have considerable impact on the productivity of the tree or the size of its fruit. Modest tending of sago palms, for example, can increase the amount of starch produced by the palm, doubling or even tripling the starch content as well as speeding up the maturation process.

While it is hard to find firm evidence of just when people started manipulating their tree-crop resources, in many tropical areas, it was likely very early. Even today, to the casual observer, rain forests inhabited by small human populations may look like vast tracts of primary forest, when in fact they more closely resemble low-intensity orchards or tree gardens. In "Anthropologist as Problem Solver: Michael Heckenberger on the Amazon as a Culturally Managed Landscape," we consider whether the Amazon was a pristine, primeval forest or a culturally managed landscape in prehistoric times.

To return to the question of how early humans learned to grow their own food, it is likely that the earliest efforts to manipulate plants came with simple tending of useful trees. Once people began to plant seeds, roots, or cuttings, the improvements in the seeds or tubers would have been obvious because by choosing the best planting stock they would have selected for the best varieties. Such manipulations of the natural environment are very modest at best, so modest that we may not be able to detect these manipulations in the archaeological record.

But other kinds of management or modification of the environment and its indigenous species can and often have a much more significant impact on the species and on the ways that people live in their environment. More important, producing food for one's community has often meant significant changes in human lifeways, the topic we turn to next.

● ●

THINKING CRITICALLY ABOUT THE RISE OF AGRICULTURE

There is a big difference between lightly tending tree crops in a rain forest and the intensive work of raising animals like horses, cattle, goats, pigs, chickens, and dogs. What was it about these domesticated animals that required a great deal of human effort once domesticated that was not present when they were wild animals?

● ●

Anthropologist as Problem Solver

Michael Heckenberger on the Amazon as a Culturally Managed Landscape

One of the enduring intellectual puzzles that archaeologists have confronted for the past century was: Just how densely populated was the New World when Columbus first reached the Americas? This question is important because for many years population estimates were drawn from early European accounts, mostly written after epidemics of European diseases had killed large sectors of the indigenous population. Clarifying this situation has major implications for how we view the history of humans in the vast and ecologically critical Amazon basin.

Archaeologists have long assumed that the rain forest in the region of the Amazon River, the largest rain forest in the world, was sparsely populated (Meggers 1971). Archaeologists have recognized that rain forest dwellers in the Amazon proper and the Bolivian Amazon had been manipulating their environment for a very long time (see, e.g., Roosevelt 1999; Erickson 2000). But until fairly recently, most believed that the shift from hunting and gathering to food production had come very late, largely because the environment was not a naturally fertile region. When farmers cut down the rain forest for gardens the heavy rainfall quickly leaches most of the nutrients out of the soil, leaving behind very little, if any, rich topsoil. As a result, anthropologists assumed that people had long been hunter-gatherers but had begun a very simple slash and burn farming, cutting down and burning off the forest to provide nutrients. For the most part, the region appears to be a vast pristine wilderness, a primeval forest that had supported human settlements for only the last thousand years.

University of Florida archaeologist Michael Heckenberger (2005; Heckenberger et al. 2003) addressed the question of how long people have been living in this region while working at the periphery of the Amazon in the upper reaches of the Xingu [shing-**goo**] River, one of the main southern tributaries. The Xingu is one of the least densely populated parts of the Amazon basin, and a large part of it is a Brazilian national indigenous park more than 10,000 sq. miles in area (about the size of Massachusetts). Drawing on more than a decade of field surveys and excavations in the region, Heckenberger asked whether the area inside Xingu Indigenous Park was a pristine natural rainforest or should best be understood as a carefully managed landscape for the last thousand years.

Heckenberger conducted extensive regional research in the Xingu from 1993 to 2002, residing at one time for eighteen months in Kuikuro village. In his excavations and regional surveys he found an unexpectedly complex pattern of regional settlement within the upper Xingu. His carbon-14 dates confirmed human settlement around 1000–1200 CE. If people had lived in the region previously, they had likely been hunter-gatherers. The archaeological sites he found were likely associated with some sort of food production. Heckenberger concludes that within a century or so the region was supporting larger populations than anybody had assumed. He found evidence of nineteen prehistoric settlements connected by paths or roads in his study area where simple slash and burn could not possibly have supported the entire population. His conclusion was that prehistoric Xingu were carefully managing their forests, partly by bringing in a kind of soil called *terra preta*, which is a rich topsoil found in certain other parts of the forest.

Recent research in the Upper Xingu, as well as excavations in many other parts of the Amazon, seems to suggest that the rain forest supported much larger populations prehistorically than archaeologists had expected because they were managing their forests—and their topsoil—to create vast park-like gardens that we might see as essentially virgin forests. But in Xingu, by intensifying their efforts on their fields and environment, prehistoric peoples had transformed a fairly barren environment into one that could support substantial populations.

Questions for Reflection

1. What evidence would have led early archaeologists and anthropologists to conclude that when Columbus reached the New World the Amazon was sparsely populated?

2. Why might food production in the Upper Xingu area have made it possible to support larger populations than the same region with a hunting-and-gathering lifestyle?

3. In what sense might the Amazon be a thought of as a culturally managed landscape? What implications might these findings have for contemporary conservation strategies in the Xingu?

What Impact Did Raising Plants and Animals Have on Other Aspects of Life?

Knowing that the Neolithic Revolution happened over time in a series of "small revolutions"—Childe's idea that is still with us today—it is likely that the first efforts to raise food changed people relatively little. Quite likely, hunter-gatherer groups, who ranged across large territories in search of food, planted and harvested plants during the annual movements within their territory in much the same way they did with naturally occurring plants.

Herding may have brought a greater change in people's way of life, because livestock always need new food from new fields in which to graze or forage. And as the number of livestock increased, the needs of the animals may have led some food producers to turn to **transhumance,** the practice of moving herds to different fields or pastures with the changing seasons.

Transhumance

In some respects, transhumance represents a fairly simple transformation of the nomadic lifestyle of hunter-gatherers. Instead of moving from one territory to another to hunt game, a family moves itself and its livestock from one set of pastures to another to take advantage of seasonal changes. For example, the Bakhtiari people of southwestern Iran adapted their transhumant lifeways to local environments. This movement included a strenuous journey from their highland summer quarters over steep mountain passes to their lowland winter quarters (Paramount Pictures 1999). More than 50,000 people and half a million animals crossed rivers and mountains during these semiannual treks. Like other societies that practice **pastoralism**—or the breeding, care, and use of domesticated herding animals such as cattle, camels, goats, horses, llamas, reindeer, and yaks—raising herds of livestock is a key component of such a group's subsistence economy and does not necessarily require people to settle in one place (see also Chapter 15). But pastoralism tends to lead to larger populations and much more complex patterns of social interaction that resemble what has typically happened whenever humans become sedentary (Figure 12.7).

Sedentism

Still, pastoralists are relatively few in number worldwide. Most people in the world are settled and dependent on agriculture, either directly or indirectly. Archaeologists understand that the most significant changes that accompany food production are largely the combined result of **sedentism**, or year-round settlement in a particular place, and population growth. But during the **Mesolithic,** which is the period from the end of the last ice age until the beginning of agriculture or horticulture, a number of hunter-gatherer-forager groups had established lakeside or seaside settlements that seem to have been year-round sites (Arnold 1996).

As we have seen, the technological shift from hunting and gathering to simple domestication of plants and animals was a fairly minor one. But once people started settling down to tend these crops, their populations grew, leading gradually to greater intensification of food production (Zvelebil and Rowley-Conwy 1984).

- **Transhumance.** The practice of moving herds to different fields or pastures with the changing seasons.

- **Pastoralism.** The practice of animal husbandry, which is the breeding, care, and use of domesticated herding animals such as cattle, camels, goats, horses, llamas, reindeer, and yaks.

- **Sedentism.** Year-round settlement in a particular place.

- **Mesolithic.** The period from the end of the last ice age until the beginning of agriculture, a number of hunter-gatherer-forager groups had established lakeside or seaside settlements that seem to have been year-round sites during this period.

Figure 12.7 Transhumance. Transhumance among the Bachtiari of Iran.

Larger communities required more labor inputs for food production, typically resulting in periodic shortages of food because of the growing population. These shortages in turn led to what we might call true agriculture, involving, for example, fertilizing with dung or mulches and the development of new technologies altogether, such as plows and the use of draft animals to pull them across a field (see also Chapter 15).

One of the most striking aspects of sedentism is that with population growth it tends to lead to permanent social inequality. But since the rise of social inequality is also one of the characteristics commonly associated with the rise of early cities and the emergence of state-like political formations, we will defer our discussion of these topics to Chapter 13, where we examine them more directly.

Dietary Consequences of Sedentism

The shift to sedentism also brought with it a change from relying on a large variety of plants and animals typical of hunting and gathering societies to relying on a small number of plant species. Indeed, the more intensive the horticulture or agriculture, the smaller the list of cultigens becomes.

For example, the few hunting-and-gathering groups in New Guinea exploit nearly every edible plant in their environment as well as nearly all the species of birds, marsupials, bats, rodents, and insects that inhabit the rain forests. In horticultural communities, in contrast, where people typically plant mixed gardens with fifteen to thirty species of plant cultigens, most people eat fewer than a dozen species of plants on a regular basis and have access to animal protein only sporadically in spite of the fact that they have access to many of the same wild foods available to hunter-gatherers. Bolstering this food culture are complex patterns of food taboos in which individuals from various social categories, ages, and genders are prohibited from eating particular foods, while others may enjoy them. This is true even though most people have regular access to wild animal proteins from marsupials and birds they have hunted or from small fish and crayfish in the many streams.

Sedentism and Epidemic Diseases

Sedentism and population growth also have had an impact on people's health with evolutionary consequences for our species (see Chapter 9), since larger numbers of people living together allowed certain bacteria, viruses, and parasites to move from one host to another more easily. The immediate impact of these microbes was to spread quickly as epidemics throughout the population. At first such epidemics would kill off a substantial part of the population, leaving those who survived with antibodies that naturally provided an acquired or partial immunity. When the epidemic returned some years later, only young children, born since the last epidemic, were unprotected by the acquired immunity—though many of these children would have obtained partial immunity from antibodies in their mothers' breast milk.

The Fertile Crescent, where agriculture and sedentism arose earliest, was also at the crossroads of Africa, Asia, and Europe. Here, peoples from all three continents interacted through trade and marriage more often after sedentary villages had formed, and there were more people around to interact. As a result, historian William McNeil (1976) has suggested, diseases repeatedly swept through the Fertile Crescent, and these microbial parasites left behind immunity-conferring antibodies in their surviving hosts. Such antibodies later protected the community from the most serious effects of plagues, while most populations that had not been exposed to these microbes typically suffered much more severe losses.

European colonization of the New World, where many American Indians had long before become sedentary, demonstrates the effect of sedentism on epidemic diseases. These settled New World communities had experienced their own plagues and had developed some immunity to indigenous microbes such as syphilis. But they had no immunity whatsoever to common European diseases like measles and smallpox. When Europeans arrived to explore these new lands, they found large settlements along much of the coast of New England, where they stopped only briefly in the decade or so after 1600. But these early fleeting contacts were enough to pass along European microbes to the indigenous people. Diseases spread rapidly through the population, killing large numbers, perhaps as much as 90% of the coastal population (Loewen 1995:77ff; see also Segal and Stineback 1977:54–55). The effect of foreign plagues did not stop at the Atlantic shore but spread to inland groups who had contact with coastal peoples through trade and travel (Figure 12.8).

THINKING CRITICALLY ABOUT THE RISE OF AGRICULTURE

What are some of the costs and benefits of sedentism? Why might sedentism set off a chain of both positive and negative consequences for humans living in year-round settlements that they did not experience when living a hunting-foraging life?

Conclusion

The Neolithic Revolution was not a single event occurring during a set span of years; it was many events in many parts of the world occurring at different times, each with its own unique features. In some regions, the shift to horticulture or agriculture

Figure 12.8 **Mandan Epidemic** One of the large Mandan villages visited by the artist and explorer George Catlin in the early 1830s. A smallpox epidemic killed most of the inhabitants in 1837.

occurred independently of similar transitions in other regions, as in the Fertile Crescent, the Highlands of New Guinea, and Mesoamerica. In other places and times, the motivation to cultivate one's food came from neighboring groups. For example, cultivation in the Indus valley of India was likely linked to what was happening in the Fertile Crescent, but the rise of rice growing in China along the Yellow River was probably independent. And cultivation of plants among the Aztecs of Central Mexico, the people of the Mississippi Valley, and those of the Southeast were probably influenced by patterns that had emerged after domestication of corn in Mexico had spread to the Maya of Central America and southern Mexico. Even if the particular crops were quite different and growing techniques were quite independent, it was the likely the idea of active food production that allowed neighbors to innovate.

Cultivation and animal husbandry typically led to sedentism and the production of food surpluses as well as new ways of storing grains and other crops. Since people were not always on the move, they did not need to limit the food they acquired, as they did when they collected everything they ate. Growing population pressures together with the ability to amass surpluses led to radical, new ways for groups to interact. In the Fertile Crescent, intensification led to the growth of villages and towns and finally cities.

A somewhat different, but nevertheless related, pattern emerged in the New Guinea Highlands. Raising tubers began with simple cultivation plots, but quickly led to draining swamps and other kinds of intensification. When the New World sweet potato reached the island, rapid growth allowed New Guineans to expand production, providing surpluses that could support both growing human populations and increasingly large local pig herds. Soon, people began using their surplus sweet potatoes and pigs as valuables they could exchange with neighboring groups.

Elsewhere, of course, where grains and other crops could be stored for months or years, surpluses led to other developments, most notably the rise of cities, the formation of states, and the introduction of social hierarchies with essentially permanent patterns of social inequality. In the next chapter we will explore these issues in some depth.

KEY TERMS

Cultigen   p. 326

Domestication   p. 317

Foraging   p. 319

Generalized foraging model
    p. 322

Maize   p. 326

Mesolithic   p. 338

Neolithic Revolution
    p. 318

Pastoralism   p. 338

Patrilocal bands   p. 320

Potlatches   p. 324

Sedentism   p. 338

Transhumance   p. 338

Reviewing the Chapter

Chapter Section	What We Know	To Be Resolved
How heavily did prehistoric people depend on hunting?	Early humans relied on a mix of hunting and foraging strategies, and women's contributions to the total diet from gathering were often as much or greater than men's contributions, even though men (and many early male anthropologists) may have given more emphasis to men's hunting.	It is still unclear how similar the living conditions and knowledge of contemporary hunter-gatherers resemble those of prehistoric humans before they began to produce their own food.
How did early humans raise their own food?	Hunter-gatherers knew a great deal about their environments and certainly knew that plants sprout from seeds. It was a simple matter to plant seeds. The hard part was weeding, tending, and managing the crop.	Although we know that domesticated plants and animals evolved together with humans, there is relatively little archaeological evidence about the earliest food production.
What impact did raising plants and animals have on other aspects of life?	The Neolithic Revolution did not occur at a single moment when humans started producing food. It consisted of many small revolutions in which different societies started producing their own food at different times and in a variety of ways.	Finding archaeological evidence for the beginnings of food production is difficult and still developing. Mostly we can see evidence of food production from the gradual improvement in seeds or other characteristics of the domesticates and the social consequences of sedentism.

Readings

For a summary of the most current thinking about the foraging activities of hunter gatherers, see Robert L. Kelly's *The Lifeways of Hunter Gatherers: The Foraging Spectrum* (Cambridge: Cambridge University Press, 2013) and Peter Bellwood's book *First Farmers: The Origins of Agricultural Societies* (Malden, MA: Blackwell, 2005).

•••••••••••••••••••••

Jane Peterson's *Sexual Revolutions: Gender and Labor at the Dawn of Agriculture* (Walnut Creek, CA: AltaMira Press, 2002) remains an important assessment of how the rise of early agriculture influenced gender relations in prehistoric societies. Another kind of change that came with the rise of agriculture was changes in people's health resulting from changing diets. This is the subject of Mark Nathan Cohen and Gillian M. M. Crane-Kramer's *Ancient Health: Skeletal Indicators of Agricultural and Economic Intensification.* (Gainesville: University of Florida Press, 2007).

•••••••••••••••••••••

The Rise and Decline of Cities and States

Understanding Social Complexity in Prehistory

Beginning about 1050 CE, prehistoric archaeologists have determined that a dramatic transformation took place in the Mississippi River bottom lands near what is now St. Louis. At a place called Cahokia, a number of loosely affiliated and egalitarian agricultural communities changed suddenly, possibly in the span of a single generation, ushering in a new hierarchical social and political order. At the top of this new order sat ruling chiefs and an elite social class who relied on other peoples' labor to provide food and to construct massive new earthen mounds, temples, plazas, and defensive stockades.

By 1250, Cahokia was a major urban center, with between 5,000 and 10,000 inhabitants organized into a complex social order of ranked groups. Its social, economic, and political influence spread along the Mississippi River valley from what is now Minnesota in the north to Louisiana in the south, making it the most important center of pre-European Indian social life in what is now the United States. But by 1400, a century and a half before the first European explorers arrived in the area, the stratified society that was Cahokia had disappeared.

 Cahokia Mounds. The mounds at Cahokia, just east of St. Louis, constituted the largest complex of mounds in the Ohio and Mississippi valleys. This mound complex is also the most recent, suggesting that they had learned things about mound construction from other groups. From their political center at Cahokia, the leaders had economic relationships with people across Indiana and Ohio for flint and pipe stone, up the Mississippi River to Lake Superior from which they received copper, along the Missouri River as far as Yellowstone from which they received agates, and down to the Gulf Coast from which they received sea shells, all exotic goods that expressed and enhanced the appearance of power of the Cahokia leadership.

The puzzle Cahokia represents for prehistoric archaeologists is to understand how and why such social complexity emerged there when it did, and why it didn't last, because there are no written records. One way to see how it emerged is in the rise of status markers in material culture and changes in architecture (Pauketat 1994). In certain burial sites, for example, many objects appear after 1050 marking the high status of the person. These items include shell beads, war clubs, sandstone tablets, pottery, and special projectile points, many of these things made with hard-to-get exotic materials drawn from distant lands—such as copper from Lake Superior, pipe stone from Ohio, agate from Yellowstone, and shells from the Gulf of Mexico—decorated with special colors and designs associated with political and sacred powers. As the center grew, Cahokians also tore down traditional housing—tightly clustered groups of small houses built around courtyards in which family groups lived—replacing them with large new plazas and earthen mounds, rectangular and circular buildings, and temples, all using new styles of wall construction. Over time, elites used the center of the city—a six-square-mile area where over 100 mounds were built—for residences and for religious and political purposes. Non-elites were pushed out to live in settlements nearby, outside the center of Cahokia.

It is much more difficult to figure out why this transformation took place. Why would people who governed themselves give up their independence to be ruled by others? Based on the physical evidence, it seems likely that the new class of leaders gained authority gradually over time. They created regional alliances and exploited conflicts between political and economic factions within their community, and supported a new division of labor in which small numbers of craftsmen manufactured tools and peasants served as laborers. The emerging elite in control of the society associated themselves with certain powerful religious and ideological symbols (Pauketat 1994).

In Cahokia, political struggle and instability were common, a condition that likely contributed to the city's eventual disappearance. Some archaeologists also point to an environmental collapse, caused by population growth, deforestation, and the erosion of agricultural soils (Dalan et al. 2003). Others suggest that warfare played a role, pointing to evidence of burials with weapons, burned buildings, sacrificial victims, and defensive stockades (Chappell 2002). Still others (Pauketat 1994; Pauketat and Emerson 1997) observe that Cahokian society didn't so much "collapse" as split into different groups that moved off in different directions to take advantage of resources and opportunities elsewhere.

At the heart of prehistoric archaeology's approach to understanding the rise and decline of complex societies like Cahokia is a key question: *How and why did cities and states emerge and sometimes disappear?* Embedded in this broader question are the following problems, around which this chapter is organized.

- When archaeologists talk about social complexity, what do they mean?
- How can we identify social complexity from archaeological sites and their artifacts?
- Why don't cities and states always survive?

An archaeological focus on the rise of cities and states reveals much about how, why, and when humans shifted from small-scale face-to-face societies to larger scale social groupings in which inequalities of power and social hierarchy are more common. Yet social complexity is not always associated with social inequality and hierarchy. We begin by presenting what archaeologists mean when they talk about social complexity.

When Archaeologists Talk About Social Complexity, What Do They Mean?

The earliest archaeologists were Europeans educated in the classic civilizations of Greece, Rome, Egypt, and Mesopotamia. Part of the fascination these ancient societies held for nineteenth-century Europeans was that they saw themselves as linked more or less directly to these older societies, which had provided the inspiration, if not the precise basis, for European legal codes, constitutions, and philosophies. As the Egyptians, Mesopotamians, Greeks, and Romans were expanding their empires throughout the ancient world, however, the people of northern Europe lived in small-scale tribal groups, with no obvious markers of what European scholars considered to embody civilization, such as writing, cities, great monuments, occupational specialization, or social ranking. These early scholars wanted to know: What caused these changes to occur in Europe? When and where did civilization emerge?

Early archaeologists sought answers to these questions by excavating these ancient societies because they believed their findings would better help them understand the principles of how societies, including their own, became civilized and complex, as well as why some societies—societies that still existed around the world during the nineteenth century—remained small and relatively simple.

In addition to excavating ancient sites, much of this early research focused on definitional issues, especially identifying the key traits and characteristics of civilizations. In Table 13.1 we present one influential analysis of the particular culture traits associated with the rise of complex societies produced by American anthropologist Alfred L. Kroeber, who saw the great civilizations emerging from the accumulation of particular items of material culture. We contrast Kroeber's material culture model with that of Australian archaeologist V. Gordon Childe's view that the origins of cities and city-states was less about material things than about organizational arrangements (Table 13.1).

TABLE 13.1   CHARACTERISTICS OF CIVILIZATIONS ACCORDING TO A. L. KROEBER AND V. GORDON CHILDE

Kroeber understood the emergence of states as a consequence of increasingly sophisticated material culture, while V. Gordon Childe saw urbanization as a consequence of new arrangements of how people interacted with one another, leading to social stratification (see Smith 2009).

A. L. Kroeber (1923)	V. Gordon Childe (1950)
Pottery & bow/arrows (Neolithic)	
Bone tools (Neolithic)	
Use of dogs (Neolithic)	
Hewn stone axes (Neolithic)	
Domesticated plants and animals (Neolithic)	
Use of metals (Bronze Age)	
Sun-burned brick	Larger population in settlements
Stone masonry	Full-time specialist craftsmen
Potter's wheel	Producers give surplus to leaders as tax to deities (via priests)
Astronomical records	Monumental public buildings
Development of iron	Priests, civil leaders, military leaders use surplus for own benefit
Writing	Writing
Elaboration of science (math, geometry, etc.)	
Conceptual and sophisticated styles of art	

• **Social complexity.**
A society that have many different parts organized into a single social system.

Most archaeologists recognized that there were different degrees to which specific cases fit with either Kroeber's or Childe's model. But it was also clear that the social, political, and economic lives of people living in societies characterized as civilizations were very different from those of people living in small-scale societies. Nowadays, archaeologists have moved away from using the word "civilization" because of its ethnocentric assumptions about the superiority of our society's arrangements over other social forms. The dialogue with cultural anthropologists who also study politics and economics has also refined archaeological perspectives on these issues (see Chapters 14 and 16). Most anthropologists and archaeologists refer to the differences between these societies as differences of **social complexity**, by which they mean "the multiplicity of different parts on a social system" (Kowalewski 1990). In other words, social complexity is when people divide themselves or are divided into many separate subgroups. These groups exercise power over others, control resources, and experience inequalities relative to other groups.

It is important to note that *all* societies experience some level of social complexity. No human society is "simple": even the most egalitarian face-to-face societies have ways of exercising power, controlling resources, and grouping people into smaller units for specific purposes, such as hunting parties, religious rituals, and so forth. In fact, some of the societies with the simplest technologies can have highly complex theologies and kinship systems. Anthropologists do not usually talk of complexity when referring to kinship terminologies or a complicated set of religious rituals, but only when the material arrangements of a society are differentiated into social or occupational classes or differences in wealth, power, and control, all of which are lacking in the egalitarian hunter-gatherer communities of Australia, the Kalahari, and the Arctic.

But not all societies are **complex societies**, that is, societies in which socioeconomic differentiation, large populations, and centralized political control are pervasive and defining features. In these societies there are many different social roles that people can play, especially specialized occupations, including people who produce food, craftspeople that make things, soldiers, leaders, and so on. Complex societies typically have political formations called **states**, which are societies with forms of centralized political and economic control over a particular territory and the inhabitants of that territory. **Cities**—relatively large and permanent settlements, usually with populations of at least several thousand inhabitants—are also characteristic of complex societies. The emergence of cities containing thousands of residents from much smaller villages and towns needed to be organized so residents were not constantly at odds with one another. Small cities did not require elaborate legal codes any more than tribes did; they already had customary ways of handling problems, disputes, and contention within the community. But as cities grew in size, one faction or another typically took control of key resources and asserted its will on the others. Thus, in most cases, like Cahokia in the New World and across Mesopotamia, these cities developed as **city-states,** autonomous political entities that consisted of a city and its surrounding countryside, with some form of centralized authority. And it was from these city-states that proper states and their larger cousins, kingdoms and empires, arose.

All of this is polite language to say that complex societies are characterized by dynamics of wealth, power, coercion, and status, in which social stratification—elites and non-elites—ensures that the labor of the non-elites benefits the lifestyles of the elites.

So, what led to the emergence of cities, city-states, states, and empires in the first place, and where did they emerge (Figure 13.1)? Early on, archaeologists recognized that for complex societies to form, more intensive food production was necessary.

- **Complex societies.** Societies in which socioeconomic differentiation, large populations, and centralized political control are pervasive and defining features of the society.

- **States.** Societies with forms of political and economic control over a particular territory and the inhabitants of that territory.

- **Cities.** Relatively large and permanent settlements, usually with populations of at least several thousand inhabitants.

- **City-state.** An autonomous political entity that consisted of a city and its surrounding countryside.

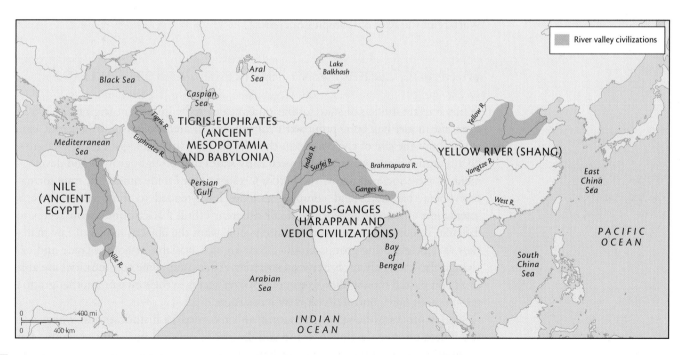

Figure 13.1   The Four Great River Valleys That Produced the Earliest State Societies.   They largely emerged as city-states; and in the Indus and Mesopotamia regions, these states remained city-states for much of their history, only occasionally developing larger empires. By 2000 BCE urban centers had arisen along the Tigris and Euphrates Rivers in Mesopotamia (modern Iraq and Turkey), along the Nile River (Egypt), along the Indus and Ganges Rivers in India and Pakistan, and along the Yellow River in northern China.

It means that the societies had made the Neolithic transition from foraging and hunting to food production, typically producing enough of a surplus that the farming groups could provide for the dietary needs of the more powerful elites. It is also clear that the elites in early cities and states began to construct a state ideology and religious ideas that explained and justified why the political elites deserved the special treatment they received and groups with less power deserved fewer resources. Several other features have been suggested that we will consider here: population growth, contact with other cultures, and specialization and the differentiation of social roles.

Population Growth and Social Complexity

All the complex societies that archaeologists examined had large populations ranging from thousands to even hundreds of thousands of people. Nearly all had central locations that we could talk about as cities, even though some were much larger than others, ranging from 30,000 to 50,000 people in some ancient Egyptian cities, to perhaps as many as 65,000 in Ur at its height, to about half a million people in Rome when Augustus Caesar established the Roman Empire (27 BCE). The Greek city-states were somewhat smaller.

Large populations require a corresponding sophistication and scale of food production. Importantly, societies with cities and the early hints of what would become centralized states lived side by side with small-scale and tribal societies that also produced their own food, often the same foods that were part of the diet of people in these early towns and cities. Food production to feed a growing population was thus a necessary, but not sufficient, characteristic that led some societies to become complex.

Another way to think about population growth's relationship to complexity is that as a population grows, social conflict over essential resources such as land and water can also increase. This social conflict that results can trigger the rise of complexity. We consider this argument in "Classic Contributions: Robert Carneiro on the Role of Warfare in the Rise of Complex Societies."

Trade and Contact with Peoples of Different Cultures

While warfare models of state formation continue to be important (e.g., Haas 1990), a second model has been proposed by a number of archaeologists. In a recent case study about the rise of civilization in the Middle East, archaeologist David Wengrow (2010) argues that it was trade between early states that brought growth and development in these societies across the Fertile Crescent. The "trade model" of state formation holds that states and complex societies have tended to form where there is interaction among groups of people of different ethnic backgrounds with access to different resources. Trade arises because people want the objects, foods, or raw materials that neighboring groups produce that are not available at home. Trade and exchange also create alliances between societies. After time, some communities are able to exploit partial monopolies, exert control over access to their own or another group's resources, or take control over a busy trade route.

Similar processes have been observed and recorded in historic times, where it is possible to observe the flow of trade and the rise of political power more vividly. For example, we know that some communities exploited control over different segments of the Silk Road trade to amass great wealth. The most extreme case of state formation centered on the silk trade was the Mongol empire of Gengis Kahn which used its monopoly to enhance its wealth and its army to conquer powerful states. In the

CLASSIC CONTRIBUTIONS

Robert Carneiro on the Role of Warfare in the Rise of Complex Societies

DURING THE LATE 1960s, many archaeologists began to develop models to explain social change, especially models that could explain why societies at certain times and places had shifted from tribal societies to become chiefdoms and states. One of the best examples of this trend in archaeology is the work of Robert Carneiro, who developed a model he called circumscription theory to explain what forces propelled societies to change and take on more social complexity. Carneiro (1974) turned to the problem of what happens when limited resources need to be exploited by a growing number of people. According to Carneiro's model, as populations grew they put pressure on the land, leading to competition and warfare. The victors in these confrontations could eventually place themselves in control of more resources, allowing them to rise in status over their less successful neighbors.

The same squeeze in available arable land that led to the development of more intensive farming in certain areas of the world gave rise to another important cultural phenomenon as well: competition between one tribe and another over land.

Warfare has entirely different consequences in an area of restricted arable land and dense population than it does where land resources are extensive and population is sparse. In a circumscribed, densely settled area a defeated group could not make a strategic withdrawal. There would be no place for it to go; all of the arable land would be occupied. It would have to remain where it was and suffer the consequences. And the consequences of defeat under these conditions would generally be, first, the payment of tribute, and, at a later stage, outright incorporation into the territory of the victor. Having to pay tribute in kind, the vanquished group would have to work their lands even

more intensively then before. While food production had not as a rule previously exceeded domestic consumption, a clear surplus would now have to be wrought from the soil to meet the demands of the dominant group.

The ever-increasing need for more arable land would continue to act as a stimulus to war; and warfare, through the process of conquest and amalgamation, would lead to an increase in the size of political units. At the same time it would also give rise to confederacies and alliances, as each tribe or chiefdom sought to strengthen its military position. The culmination of this process locally would be the political unification of an entire valley under the banner of its strongest chiefdom. The ultimate military and political result of the process over part or all of a continental area would be the formation of a large conquest state encompassing and controlling many valleys. [Carneiro 1974:86–87]

Questions for Reflection

1. Is it inevitable that some form of subjugation through tribute or enslavement would follow from conquest? What other ways might the victorious group respond?

2. What evidence might we look for in an archaeological site that might confirm or support Carneiro's model?

fourteenth century, the entrepôt of Malacca on the Malay Peninsula (just west of modern Singapore) was able control nearly all trade through the Strait of Malacca between India, China, and the Indonesian islands. When the Portuguese conquered Malacca in 1511, more than a hundred different languages were spoken in the city. In both of these historic examples, states emerged because by controlling trade they could establish control over surplus resources.

Most trade models of state formation focus on the key role that a specialized class of traders plays in managing markets and marketplaces, and providing military protection of markets and caravans, all of which they are able to do by collecting taxes and tribute. And, as populations in cities grew in Mesopotamia, there arose the need for record-keeping, which led to the development of cuneiform writing using a stylus in clay. The vast majority of early written documents in ancient Mesopotamia were records of debts owed for food and other resources (see, e.g., Graeber 2011). In this model, varying kinds of trade, differing geographies, different volumes of goods, and the like meant that the trajectory of each state's emergence was somewhat different. But in all cases having contact with diverse groups of people added to the social complexity by bringing new trading opportunities, technological innovations, and new social possibilities to the emerging state.

Specialization and Production Models

Another model archaeologists have used is called the "production model" of state formation. The driving force in this model is craft specialization, which led to new social roles for food producers and craftspeople who produced useful objects like stone tools and pottery. As food production and especially yields increased, the surpluses could feed the new specialist craft-producing class of non-producers. Surpluses gave rise to a military class of full-time warriors, and these warriors supported a full-time class of elite leaders.

True control of production came with construction of irrigation canals and systems that developed in many early states in the Middle East. Even the Nile valley, with its seasonal floods that enriched the soil with silt, provided the basis for a network of drainage ditches that acted as an irrigation system. Control over the system gave the governing elites tremendous control over the fertility of the land and thus over the people.

- **Hydraulic despotism.** Denotes empires built around the control of water resources by a despotic, or all-powerful, leaders.

The level of political and social control exerted by ancient elites lays the basis for what early archaeologists referred to as **hydraulic despotism**, which denotes empires built around the control of water resources by despotic, or all-powerful, leaders. In ancient Egypt we see in the ruins of temples, tombs, and pyramids ample evidence of what appears to have been a centralized leadership that controlled vast numbers of laborers. For years at a time these workers toiled building extensive palaces at centers like Thebes, Luxor, and Amarna (Figure 13.2). The basis of these dynasties' control lay in their ability to control water resources.

Another model of ancient despotism is visible in the centralized empire of Ur in Mesopotamia. For much of its history Ur was a large but typical city-state rather than the powerful kingdom we think of from historical writings. But one particular phase of state formation at the city of Ur represents the flourishing of just this kind of society. Known as Ur III, because it emerged after two earlier social formations on the same site, this empire was a central state with a broad reach. The seat of strong kings with large bureaucracies of accountants, tax collectors, and scribes, the elites at Ur III controlled the circulation of goods, services, and information (Yoffee 1995:299). The bureaucrats collected tribute and taxes from producers, arranged for the distribution and redistribution of grain and other products, sold rights to particular parcels of land, and wrote of the great accomplishments of their rulers (Kramer 1963). Thus, the

Figure 13.2   **Temples at Luxor along the Nile River.**   Such structures required a great deal of labor to erect the many columns, statues, and other architectural features, all of which demonstrate the pharoah's control over a large laborer class.

need for financial record-keeping on clay tablets or on papyrus prompted the development of writing systems, later providing a useful way of promoting the state histories and accomplishments of increasingly powerful leaders.

These images of ancient despotism are undoubtedly reasonable at various times and places, but they are biased because there were so many Mesopotamian scribes writing about everything imaginable in cuneiform script on clay tablets that survive well in the arid lands of the Middle East (Figure 13.3). Much of what we can infer about these states comes from what the rulers, their scribes, and stoneworkers left behind in the form of relief carvings, palace art, and monumental stonework engraved with cuneiform writing. Egyptian rulers and nobles left tombs carved with similar accounts, which we assume is partly the same kind of "spin" that our politicians and their supporters provide today to enhance their image and status, and control how later generations would view them.

The scholars who studied these cuneiform tablets were most interested in compiling lists of kings and their accomplishments as much as the scribes were intent on preserving these interpretations of the (for them) historical record. Only in recent years, and mostly in a few of the settlements for craftsmen, workers, and laborers do we have examples of graffiti on the wall of well-preserved houses and back chambers used to construct tombs and the like, that tell of the lives of ordinary people and their sometimes less-than-flattering views of their leaders.

Rethinking the Scale of Mesopotamian Kingdoms
Recent archaeological findings have motivated a reinterpretation of the so-called kingdoms and empires of bronze age Mesopotamia. Most of these formations were rather short-lived and really city-states rather than vast empires. The evidence suggests that most of the kingdoms were organized more like estates that served the needs of particular temples. For the period 3200–1600 BCE in

Figure 13.3   **Carved Relief from the Northwest Palace of Ashurnasirpal II at Nimrud, Assyria, Dating to ca. 883–859 BCE.**   Cuneiform characters are chiseled into the stone across the images of the king and other important people.

Mesopotamia, for example, populations abandoned residence in the countryside near their fields in favor of the protection afforded by rapidly growing cities, largely it would seem by elites who controlled the temples and who provided military protection from hostile neighbors. Agricultural labor was coordinated from these cities to work sets of fields near particular streams or irrigation canals, leaving other fields to lie fallow for planting in subsequent years. Such activities allowed protection for agricultural laborers and the hydrologic system that supported agriculture all in the name of the divinities celebrated in the temples. In return for all this religious and military protection, farmers made payments in the form of tribute or taxes and allegiance.

Two processes were at play in these city-states: **urbanization** in which towns grew as residential centers, and **ruralization** in which the countryside was configured as a contested no-man's land lying between city-states (Yoffee 1995:284). At this period monumental architecture associated with religious shrines, temples, and leaders flourished along with the emergence of record-keeping devices like cylinder seals and cuneiform tablets (Figure 13.4). We have much richer "historical" documentation of these early city-states than in ancient Egypt because the latter documented the minutia of their daily lives on papyrus that does not easily survive the elements even in dry climates.

The question that arises in these ancient Middle Eastern cities, city-states, and states is why would previously independent people, working fields and herding sheep, goats, or cattle, surrender their independence to a local leader in their own community or, even more surprisingly, to a leader in a city some distance away? One likely reason is that leaders with armies and police forces at their disposal would have the power to enforce their control over farmers. But developing a warrior class of loyal men probably started in simple ways when somewhat larger clans began coercing less powerful neighbors. As specialization in the crafts and trades emerged, these skilled workers needed protection and willingly followed the wishes of more powerful elites who could protect them.

- **Urbanization.** Process by which towns grew as residential centers as opposed to being trading centers.

- **Ruralization.** Process in which the countryside was configured as a contested no-man's land lying between competing city-states.

Figure 13.4   Ancient Mesopotamian Cylinder Seal and the Impression It Leaves on a Clay Tablet.   These seals were status symbols in themselves, and they often attempted to enhance the status of their owners.

Does Complexity Always Imply Social Inequality?

As we have suggested, the Mesopotamian city-states were likely much smaller in their reach than the great kingdoms and empires that anthropologists and archaeologists wrote about a century ago as ancient despotism. It does not mean that ancient Mesopotamian rulers were never despotic, but rather that the rise of early states seems more plausibly linked to social arrangements that allowed farmers and agricultural laborers to yield some control over their land and labor in exchange for protection from potentially hostile neighbors.

In the later Neolithic (7,000–5,000 BCE), settlements were growing in size and density, but many suggest little evidence of social inequality. The important site of Çatal Höyük in southern Turkey, for example, shows little evidence for hereditary inequality yet was a rather large settlement. This site appears quite egalitarian compared with most later Mesopotamian sites (Hodder 2006).

As more control over agricultural production was given to ruling elites and their bureaucrats, these systems might develop into despotic kingdoms. But such situations are more tenuous for ruling elites than one might suspect. For example, archaeological evidence at some of these Mesopotamian formations suggests that agricultural laborers could and perhaps often did shift their allegiances to a neighboring city-state and its leaders, when protection might be more secure or when provided other perks and benefits.

Importantly, social complexity does not always emerge from social inequality. Some societies may have social groups organized into broad regional relationships by building on individual relationships rather than relying on a central authority to organize societies. These units can coordinate their productive activities through individual arrangements, and they can even specialize in certain kinds of production. But because they view one another as social equals, these communities do not emerge as highly stratified societies. Consequently, they often lack monumental architecture, professional militaries, and writing.

One example of this kind of social complexity is found along the north coast of Papua New Guinea today. Nearly 200 politically independent communities over some 400 miles of coast are economically integrated through individual exchange relationships between pairs of friends. These friendships persist because they are inherited by children and sometimes other relatives. We have ethnographic, ethnohistorical, and archaeological evidence that these relationships have persisted for at least 300 years and probably much longer. In this region, each community specializes, producing fish, sago, pottery, shell ornaments, bows, arrows, nets, canoes, and a host of other products. Yet despite this specialization, everyone along the coast has essentially the same material culture and the same diet. Islanders living on islands such as Tumleo, Ali, and Seleo have no sago whatsoever, but they get sago and many vegetables from friends on the mainland where sago grows abundantly. Tumleo islanders produce pots—as they have for at least ten centuries—while the other islanders provide smoked fish and shell ornaments—as they likely have for a similar period. The pattern of specialization is quite complex, but an ideology of equality has prevailed, even when a few communities occasionally try to control a monopoly on certain products (Terrell and Welsch 1990; Welsch and Terrell 1998). The social system is too diffuse for any sort of monopoly to persist for any length of time.

Such an example challenges the idea that social complexity and specialization always take on some single universal form. But it also raises another question: How do archaeologists identify evidence of complexity in the first place?

• •

THINKING CRITICALLY ABOUT THE RISE OF SOCIAL COMPLEXITY

Many archaeologists have long seen the rise of cities with specialized occupations like warriors, leaders, farmers, and those who make special products as progress and advancement. But could we also see the rise of ancient cities, states, and empires as based on the rise of social inequality? How is complexity in political structure linked to inequality?

• •

How Can We Identify Social Complexity from Archaeological Sites and Their Artifacts?

Suppose a future archaeologist excavating the site of your childhood home uncovers several plastic toys, a computer chip, metal eating utensils, and assorted fragments of ceramic plates. Based on such a limited number of admittedly mundane objects, how could an archaeologist know anything about your life, much less the complexity that characterized your society? This challenge confronts *all* archaeologists interested in social complexity, not just those who might excavate centuries from now.

Archaeologists know that material objects are an expression of people's social relationships. The objects themselves also help shape social relationships, including those related to wealth, power, and status (Love 1999:129). In other words, how we use houses, jewelry, and other daily objects expresses our wealth, power, and status as individuals or as members of a group, and these objects in turn affect our daily lives in various ways. But by itself, in isolation, an object recovered in an excavation can't necessarily tell us much about dynamics of wealth, power, and status. As we show in this section, evidence of such things usually comes from close analysis of different kinds of objects, often as an **assemblage** or collection of objects found together, as well as evidence of their manufacture and distribution in a site or region, and contextual clues that can connect individual artifacts to similar or related artifacts—all of which can involve various forms of archaeological, ecological, geological, and forensic expertise. Only after pulling together these different pieces of evidence and analysis does a picture of social complexity begin to emerge.

• **Assemblage.** A group or collection of objects found together at an excavation or site.

Identifying Social Complexity in Western Mexico

The best way to convey how archaeologists develop a picture of social complexity from handling different kinds of artifacts is to present a case study: the Tarascan empire in what is now the western Mexican state of Michoacán. It is a fresh example—only during the last few decades have archaeologists intensively studied its rise, scale, and social complexity (Figure 13.5). Beginning in the Classic Period (400 CE–900 CE) and culminating in the Post-Classic period (1000–1400s), the Tarascans organized the second-largest state in Mexico, most likely to counter the military and political pressures exerted on them by Mexico's largest empire, the Aztecs.

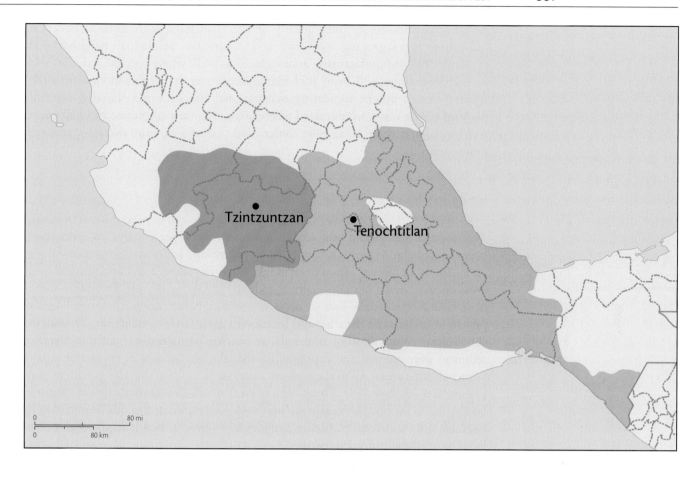

By 1522 when the Spaniards arrived, the Tarascan king ruled a vast territory that included some 1.3 million people divided into numerous social rankings, ethnic groups, and occupational specialties, as well as a state bureaucracy that controlled the extraction of raw materials, trade, and the distribution of many goods. Evidence of the state's emergence, as well as the social distinctions and power relations within it, comes from diverse sources, among them several we review here: population growth and settlement patterns; soils and land use patterns; monuments and buildings; mortuary patterns and skeletal remains; and ceramic, stone, and metal objects (Pollard 1993, 2003).

Figure 13.5   The Tarascan Empire (Green).   The Tarascan state was the second largest in the New World when Spanish colonists conquered the largest, the Aztec state (orange) in 1521.

Population Growth and Settlement Patterns

The political, economic, and social center of the Tarascan empire was in the Lake Pátzcuaro [**pahts**-quahr-oh] basin in a city called Tzintzuntzan [cheen-choon-**chahn**], whose ruins still stand today. Beginning in the period before 1000 CE, people lived on the lakeshore but eventually moved to higher ground, apparently to maximize access to agricultural land, hold a better defensive position against enemies, and gain closer access to obsidian mines for toolmaking. This move sets the stage over the next few centuries for political consolidation under single authority (Pollard 2003a:227). In the new site, an increase in the number of households and outlying settlements, as well as the construction of monuments, suggests population growth and the city's rise as the administrative and religious center.

Archaeologists also observe that over time the growing city became spatially segregated and divided into special function zones. For example, analyzing domestic trash deposits, which hold discarded foods and broken tools and pots, has revealed assemblages of finer quality objects associated with certain residences, indicating the segregation of elite and commoner residential neighborhoods (Pollard 1993). Manufacturing zones appear as well, where specific activities such as pottery-making and stone-tool manufacture were practiced in specific settlements but not others, indicating occupational specialization. Finally, carefully planned public zones were created where large monuments, plazas, and ball courts were built, and these areas were under direct control of administrative and religious authorities.

Soils and Land Use

The study of soils in and near settlements offers useful perspectives on connections between population growth, agricultural expansion, and soil degradation (Fisher et. al. 2003). In recent years, a drop in lake levels has allowed archaeologists to study areas once occupied but eventually abandoned as lake levels rose. In addition, they have taken cores of lake soils in order to conduct pollen analysis, especially maize pollen, to understand the scale and location of agricultural production. By studying the mineral composition of lake soils, archaeologists have discerned that layers of sediment were released and deposited on the lake bed because of erosion of soils in higher altitude areas. All of these pieces of evidence indicate that the growth of population centers, especially Tzintzuntzan, created soil degradation. In the centuries leading up to the Spanish conquest, land managers responded to this degradation by implementing soil conservation techniques like terraces, which required abundant labor most likely controlled by elites.

Monuments and Buildings

Because they transform a landscape and require substantial engineering and collective labor, monuments and buildings are important symbols of power, wealth, and connection to the divine order. In Tzintzuntzan, specialized stone platforms consisting of rectangles with circular extensions called a *yácatas* [**yah**-kah-tahz] were constructed (Figure 13.6). The discovery of ritual paraphernalia in rooms inside these structures indicates their function as religious temples. The region also had abundant wood resources, and as a result many of the city's buildings were constructed of wood. Archaeologists have found elaborately carved wooden lintels, portals, and posts, as well as painted posts and walls, mainly in temples and elite residences (Pollard 2003b:85). Analyzing monuments and the characteristics of their construction is an important means by which archaeologists can consider dynamics of complexity in ancient societies, as we explore in "Thinking Like an Anthropologist: Deciphering How Monuments Were Erected."

Mortuary Patterns and Skeletal Remains

Archaeologists have observed changes in the location and contents of Tarascan burial sites over time, including the preparation and treatment of bodies, types of burial goods, and mortuary facilities. These changes correlate with increasing population and indicate social differentiation (Pollard 2003a:236). For example, finely decorated pottery and metal ornaments in distinctive shapes and designs are common in the burial sites of elites. Burial sites are also segregated within settlements, with elites and commoners having their own mortuary zones. In burial sites of elites, skeletal remains

Figure 13.6   Yácatas in Tzintzuntzan.

show the modification of teeth and skull deformation, both common markers of elite identification throughout ancient Mesoamerica.

A notable shift in mortuary practices takes place with the consolidation of state power during the 1400s. Before this period, mortuary objects in elite burials such as finished jewelry, shells, and metal objects were imported from other distant powerful political and social centers, such as central Mexico. Later, the objects come from areas under Tarascan control. Archaeologists interpret this shift as indicating the consolidation of a distinctly Tarascan identity among elites, an identification that supported the consolidation of Tarascan state power (Pollard 2003b).

Thinking Like an Anthropologist

Deciphering How Monuments Were Erected

ANTHROPOLOGISTS BEGIN THEIR research by asking questions. In this box, we want you to learn how to ask questions as an anthropological researcher. Part 1 describes a situation and follows up with questions we would ask. Part 2 asks you to do the same thing with a different situation.

PART 1: ERECTING THE PYRAMIDS AT GIZA

Of the seven wonders of the ancient world, only the pyramids of Giza near the modern city of Cairo, Egypt, survive to the present. The largest of these was built as a burial chamber for and monument to the Fourth Dynasty pharaoh Khufu. It stands 481 feet above the desert sands and contains about two million stone blocks, each block weighing about 1.5 tons. What is especially striking is that the pyramid was built in just over twenty years from about 2547–2524 BCE. How could the early Egyptians have built such a massive structure? What can we learn about social complexity by studying such monuments?

The Greek historian Herodotus, writing in the fifth century BCE (2,000 years after construction), asserted that Egyptians had used "machines" to raise the blocks, a comment scholars interpreted as use of cranes. Diodorus of Sicily wrote 300 years later that "construction was effected by mounds," which many took to mean ramps. These two theories, cranes or ramps, were the most favored theories until very recently, when the French architect Jean Pierre Houdin developed what is called the internal ramp theory, which involves both ramps and cranes (Brier 2007).

Both of the traditional theories seem fundamentally flawed. Construction of a ramp that would reach more than 450 feet would require much more material than the entire pyramid and, in any event, its slope would be too steep. The crane theory suggests vast rows of cranes at several levels that would sequentially raise the heavy stones from level to level. It is hard to imagine where Egyptians could have acquired sufficient wood for the cranes. From tomb paintings we know they had cranes, but it is unclear how cranes might have been used or where they might sit on the structure as the monument rose above 200 feet (Brier 2007).

In 2007 Houdin used 3D software (Houdin 2007) to show how a series of internal ramps running around the perimeter of the pyramid could have been installed to facilitate moving the stones from one level to another. The lowest third of the structure would have used a long straight external ramp that was raised slightly as each layer was complete. More than half the stones would then have been in place. From there on the stones could have been pulled up gradual ramps along the sides of the pyramid. Houdin envisions these ramps were inside passageways near the outer surface of the structure. Later the passageways were filled in with stone blocks. Groups of ten men could pull stones on wooden sledges up these ramps. At each corner of the pyramid the passageway would have opened onto a corner platform open to the air that would allow workmen to rotate the sledge a quarter turn before proceeding up the next ramp.

Support for this internal ramp theory comes from a **microgravimetry survey** of the site in the 1980s that measured the gravitational pull of different parts of the pyramid to uncover formerly hollow sections that were filled with less dense stone (see Brier 2007:26). This mapping of the density of the stones inside the pyramid suggests less dense passageways were filled with different stone from the core of the pyramid. Considerably more research is needed to confirm Houdin's hypothesis. These strategies will include infrared photography, more sensitive microgravimetry, and some of the techniques used routinely by archaeologists to resolve different questions.

Houdin's hypothesis for the building of the pyramids raises several important questions for archaeological researchers:

1. Who might have had the specialized engineering and technological knowledge to design the pyramids, and how did they develop this knowledge?

2. How would have workers been identified, trained, and organized to construct the pyramids?

3. What techniques of data collection—whether through old-fashioned excavation or using newer technologies such as infrared light meters—can help us better understand how these pyramids were built?

PART 2: ERECTING RAPA NUI STONE FIGURES (MOAI) ON EASTER ISLAND

Since Europeans encountered Rapa Nui (Easter Island) during the early eighteenth century, they have puzzled over how Polynesian peoples with little evidence of sophisticated technologies could have constructed the famous stone monuments. The scale of the accomplishment suggests a highly organized effort, perhaps a sign of social complexity. What questions about this situation would you ask as an anthropological researcher?

Ceramic, Stone, and Metal Objects

Changes in everyday objects—especially ceramic pottery vessels and figurines, stone tools and weapons, and metal tools, weapons, and ornaments—are also tied to increasing social complexity. By connecting these objects to their sources, archaeologists have demonstrated that expanding trade networks and administrative control brought raw materials from new and distant locales both outside and from within the growing empire. For example, before the period of state consolidation, production of ceramic pots was largely local in scale and unspecialized. With the rise of the state, full-time specialized production facilities, as well as distinctive styles and designs associated with elites, appear. Chemical analysis of clay samples in potsherds also indicates that the number and variability of clay sources increases. In one locality of Tzintzuntzan, the presence of large amounts of non-local ceramic ware, which is similar to materials and styles found among Otomí ethnic group from the empire's northeast border, suggests the importance of ethnic distinctions in the city (Pollard 1993:105).

Changes in production and distribution patterns of obsidian and metals support a similar picture of the empire's social complexity. Obsidian sources increase, and greater quantities of obsidian objects appear in core administrative areas, correlating with the time period of state consolidation. Metal objects are typically associated with elite and ritual deposits. Tracking them to their sources indicates that mining, smelting, and production of metal objects was carried out by full-time specialists who worked under state control (Pollard 2003:234).

The important point about all this evidence is that in isolation none of these findings would automatically suggest the existence of social complexity, but together they create a compelling picture that highlights the rise of state power, social divisions, and social inequality.

Empires, cities, and states do not usually survive for more than a few centuries. So, we may ask why, after mustering the specialization and organization of production, do most complex societies not persist? We address this question in the next section.

- **Microgravimetry survey.** Measuring the gravitational pull of different parts of the stone structure or pyramid to uncover formerly hollow sections that were filled with less dense stone.

THINKING CRITICALLY ABOUT SOCIAL COMPLEXITY

If you were assigned to study some other ancient city or state, could you identify the kinds of archaeological evidence that might indicate greater social complexity? What evidence might suggest greater social and economic inequality?

Why Don't Cities and States Always Survive?

For many of us, nothing evokes romance and adventure more than the discovery of vine-draped ruins of a "lost civilization." Our fascination is fueled by a cottage industry of television documentaries, tourism promoters, and literature devoted to revealing the mysteries and disappearance of once-powerful and sophisticated ancient civilizations. According to this view of history and prehistory, great civilizations rose and eventually fell. But are we misinterpreting or misunderstanding the course of these ancient states?

One popular book, Jared Diamond's *Collapse: How Societies Choose to Fail or Succeed* (2005), has tapped into this fascination and attempts to clear up the mysteries with a moral message: if we understand how and why these ancient societies fell, we can learn important lessons that might prevent our own society's demise, but only if we choose to recognize the lessons and change our ways. Diamond's argument is that the root cause of societal collapse is environmental, resulting when a society overshoots its natural resource base because of population growth and overconsumption of scarce resources, or because some other factor such as climate change undermines a society's ability to feed itself through agriculture.

- **Collapse.** The rapid loss of a social, political, and economic order or complexity.

It is a compelling argument. But attempts such as Diamond's to explain **collapse**—the rapid loss of a social, political, and economic order or complexity—are like viewing a low-resolution digital image: from faraway the image may seem clear, but up close it dissolves into disconnected parts (McAnany and Yoffee 2010:5). In other words, delving deep into the archaeological evidence, most cases for total societal collapse fall apart. In fact, archaeologists mostly agree that collapse is an incredibly rare phenomenon, and that transformation and **resilience**—the ability of a social system to absorb changes and still retain certain basic cultural processes and structures, albeit in altered form—are typical for most human societies (Tainter 2006; McAnany and Yoffee 2010).

- **Resilience.** The ability of a social system to absorb changes and still retain certain basic cultural processes and structures, albeit in altered form.

The classic historical examples of great empires that ended, such as the Roman Empire, the Persian Empire, the empire of Alexander the Great, the early Mesopotamian states, and the many ancient Egyptian dynasties, did not generally end from collapse. Many of these met their political end from internal fragmentation, lack of strong central institutions, or more powerful foreign armies. For example, the Romans developed an imperial economy built on expansion and the conquest of foreign states. As the empire stopped expanding, internal dissention over two centuries led to the inability of Romans to prevent the sacking of Rome by barbarian tribes. And the fall of the Eastern Roman Empire, based at Constantinople, was not a sudden collapse but a gradual decline over nearly a thousand years as the noted historian Edward Gibbon retells in his classic *History of the Decline and Fall of the Roman Empire* (1788). In each of these examples, the original states disappeared or were profoundly transformed, but the people largely survived and became part of new social formations.

In the following discussion, we take two other emblematic examples of apparent collapse—the Four Corners area of the U.S. Southwest and the Classic Maya—and demonstrate that abandoned ruins do not mean that the people themselves did not survive, although they may have undergone substantial social transformation.

Rethinking Abandonment in the U.S. Southwest

During the late thirteenth century CE the Ancestral Pueblo (Anasazi) people who lived in Mesa Verde (now in southern Colorado) and the rest of the Four Corners

Figure 13.7   Mesa Verde.
A city of more than 600
residences.

region picked up and moved away. They left behind well-preserved cliff-dwellings, mesa top pueblos (villages), farming terraces, towers, reservoirs, and irrigation systems (Figure 13.7). Archaeologists and others have long puzzled over why this abandonment occurred, often turning to environmental explanations, among them the "Great Drought" (1276–1299 CE), erosion, soil depletion, dropping water tables, and violence (Lipe 1995; Diamond 2005; Wilcox 2010).

It is not at all clear, however, that environmental stresses are the singular cause of the Four Corners depopulation (Ahlstrom et al. 1995). Soil depletion, for example, is difficult to prove because of the impossibility of identifying exact locations of prehistoric agricultural fields. Furthermore, given the dry environment and the commonality of droughts, the Ancestral Pueblo had developed a wide variety of clever techniques to support dry land agriculture, among them selecting low-moisture crop seeds; farming in high water table areas or areas supplied by floodwater and snow melt; and constructing terraces and irrigation systems with small dams. They also had social networks of trade and exchange to get food and other goods, often from distant locations unaffected by local climate patterns. The likelihood that these social networks, technical adaptations, and the sophisticated knowledge that developed them all failed at once is highly unlikely, and no evidence exists to support such a failure. Furthermore, variability in climate, water levels, and water flow throughout the region mean that, even under long-term drought conditions, some localities would have remained viable.

Unsatisfied with these environmental explanations, many archaeologists have begun to view this region's prehistory through another lens. This lens views abandonment as a social strategy, not of failure, but of resilience so that the people migrated to take advantage of opportunities elsewhere. In fact, the Ancestral Pueblos never "disappeared." Many Pueblo people migrated to the northern Rio Grande region where resources were abundant. Other groups migrated to other areas in the Southwest and formed smaller aggregated pueblo-style villages of several hundred people, a process facilitated by *kachina* (political-religious) authorities (Lekson and Cameron 1995). These migrations created new social groups and ceramic practices, as we explore in "Doing Fieldwork: Studying What Happened After the Migration from the Four Corners with Scott Van Keuren."

Doing Fieldwork

Studying What Happened After the Migration from the Four Corners with Scott Van Keuren

At the end of the thirteenth century, some Ancestral Pueblo groups from the Four Corners area resettled in what is now the Little Colorado River basin in east-central Arizona. There they created and joined a handful of existing large pueblos in which groups from diverse historical backgrounds lived together. Although this resettlement lasted only a century before people moved on again, the social mixing in this area set the stage for fusion and innovation of ceramic traditions, since these groups had brought with them their distinctive ceramic decorative styles and production techniques (Van Keuren 2006). One of the famous results of this dynamic social context is the emergence of a new style of pottery in the 1320s known as Fourmile style pottery. This style of pottery is widely known for its rich imagery of religious icons.

For over a decade, archaeologist Scott Van Keuren has been studying what social life may have been like in these postmigration pueblos of east-central Arizona. His research strategy involves studying changes in ceramic production and the emergence of Fourmile style pottery as a proxy for socioeconomic interactions between groups. Van Keuren has conducted a number of excavations in different pueblos throughout the region that have yielded potsherds and whole bowls decorated in the Fourmile style.

Using these artifacts, as well as collections now in museums, Van Keuren has closely analyzed Fourmile ceramics for deeply embedded clues to social identity and experience. The use of sacred icons suggests that these decorations were intended to communicate religious and esoteric messages. Other messages were unintentional, however, such as those carried by the subtle ways potters painted individual vessels, especially in their paint brushstroke sequences, which Van Keuren has studied under magnification. Reconstructing brushstroke sequences involves studying overlapping strokes of paint and then reconstructing the sequence used to paint the object. Brushstroke sequences reveal

Fourmile Style Pottery.

consistent behaviors and techniques learned by individual potters as members of a community. In an area called Silver Creek, the specific location where the Fourmile style emerged, potters followed the same sequence, indicating that painting pottery was an activity involving certain kinds of standardized knowledge and training. Their use of religious and esoteric iconography also suggests that they were members of a particular community by way of their control of specialized bodies of knowledge.

Within several years of the Fourmile style's appearance in Silver Creek, potters in other pueblos began emulating it. Van Keuren has observed that while the ceramics look similar, the emulators made subtle changes to the esoteric icons and did not follow the same brushstroke sequences as potters in Silver Creek. These subtle differences indicate that potters in other pueblos may not have been allowed to paint these icons and probably did not have access to the esoteric knowledge and specialized training of the Silver Creek potters.

There are several important lessons in Van Keuren's research. One of these is that these potters lived and worked in a broader social and political scene in which craft specialization, social factionalism, and the exclusivity of certain kinds of knowledge and ideological networks characterized the reorganization of postmigration communities. The appearance of religious iconography on pottery doesn't mean everyone had access to the same knowledge, or understood it similarly, or even acted upon it in similar ways. New power relations may have emerged as people competed over valued bodies of knowledge. Sometimes we have to look at the tiniest details, such as paint brushstrokes, to get at these processes.

Questions for Reflection

1. How do you think craft specialization relates to social dynamics like social factionalism and esoteric knowledge?

2. Can you think of physical traces other than brushstroke sequences that might reveal differences in the way knowledge is expressed?

More important, the Ancestral Pueblo and their descendants (among them Hopi, Zuñi, and Rio Grande Pueblo who live in the region today) never truly "abandoned" the Four Corners area (Cameron 1995). They continued to return to the ceremonial centers they had once occupied, viewing them as important cultural, historical, and religious centers. All of this physical movement is supported by a pervasive theme that runs throughout Pueblo legends and cultural thought, even today, which is that movement is necessary for the perpetuation of life (Naranjo 1995).

The Transformation—Not Collapse—of the Classic Maya

The Classic Maya (400–900 CE) of the Mesoamerican lowlands is *the* prototypical ancient complex state society. It was a society of extreme political centralization, rigid social hierarchy, colossal monuments, population centers housing tens of thousands of people, and a hieroglyphic script. During the Late Classic period (the eighth and ninth centuries), royal dynasties disappeared, courts no longer functioned, monumental building projects ended, and important centers were abandoned, mostly without evidence of violence—a prototypical "collapse" (Tainter 2008). Archaeologists and others have advanced dozens of explanations, the most prominent being (McAnany and Negrón 2010:145):

1. *Escalating warfare* between rulers of city-states.
2. *Out-of-control population growth* leading to environmental degradation, erosion, and soil depletion.

3. *Drought*, resulting from climatological change.
4. *Inability of rulers* to adapt to changing economic conditions and social conflict.

Archaeologists continue to debate each of these theories, pulling together new and existing evidence to support their arguments. What we must keep in mind as we evaluate these arguments is that the Maya people never disappeared, the history of the Maya being one of social change and resilience, as the existence of seven million Maya today attests.

Escalating Warfare

- **Stelae.** Carved limestone slabs.

Late Classic period **stelae** (carved limestone slabs) that record the lives and events of Maya royalty have more accounts of warfare than other historic periods, leading some archaeologists (and Mel Gibson's 2006 movie *Apocalypto*) to argue that warfare undermined the whole civilization (Figure 13.8). While martial conflict did exist, there are several reasons to think it didn't cause collapse (McAnany and Negrón 2010). One of these is that we would expect to see widespread evidence of defensive fortifications, but their scale and distribution doesn't support a vision of extensive and constant warfare. Another reason is that Late Classic stelae also record many more accounts of royal activity of all kinds, not just warfare, indicating that more things were being recorded. Furthermore, the Late Classic hieroglyphs are more completely deciphered than other periods of Maya history, so we can't definitively conclude that there was more warfare during the Late Classic period than any other.

Out-of-Control Population Growth and Environmental Degradation

The theory that population growth was out of control depends on the method of estimating population density. The accepted method involves counting the number of structures per square kilometer and assuming about five people for each, then subtracting a fraction of the total for the fact that not every structure was residential. A high estimate for the Classic period Maya lowlands is 150 people per square kilometer, considerably lower than the population density of Los Angeles (2,700 per square mile) (McAnany and Negrón 2010:153). High population is a relative concept. Some have argued that the fragile soils of the region could not sustain large populations. Recent studies of landscape modification during the Classic period indicate that Maya farmers were especially aware of this fact and practiced soil conservation techniques, such as terracing and water management using irrigation across dry slopes (Duning and Beach 2000).

Drought

Based on soil cores taken from the Caribbean region, scientists have argued that the climate during the eighth and ninth centuries was especially dry. Some archaeologists (i.e., Gill 2000) argue that resulting droughts and dropping water tables deprived people of food and even drinking water. There is, however, no evidence to suggest that water shortage was uniform—the Petén lakes never dried up and a number of important centers such as Copán sat near a permanent water source. Yet Copán was one of the first cities to be abandoned (McAnany and Negrón 2010). Furthermore, cities in dry areas of the interior where there are no rivers

Figure 13.8   Maya Stelae. Much of what we know about life in the Maya lowlands of the Classic period is from stelae. Much of what was recorded focused on the activities of members of the royal dynasties.

and water is seasonally in short supply, such as Tikal, Calakmul, and Caracol, survived longer than Copán.

Ineffectiveness of Rulers to Adapt to Change

In his book, Jared Diamond argues that Maya rulers were a lot like contemporary CEOs: so focused on their own short-term interests that they ignored bigger problems, such as social unrest among peasants and ecological problems. There is no doubt that political crises and social conflict eventually rendered these leaders irrelevant, since the royal dynasties dissolved by the end of the Classic period. Economic changes, such as a shift in commercial activities and population from the interior lowlands to the coastal Yucatán peninsula, may have played a role in undermining these leaders.

So what really happened to the Classic Maya? We know that Maya farmers dispersed throughout the countryside and only occasionally congregated to the once occupied centers. Certain social and political structures persisted, including statecraft based on inherited nobility and social hierarchy (observed by the Spaniards several hundred years later). None of this suggests collapse; it does, however, suggest transformation. The important point here is that different polities experienced different histories of transformation (Webster 2002)—some held on longer than others because of their specific political, ecological, historic, and perhaps even climatic conditions. Of course, each of the factors we have considered can reinforce or mitigate the others. A degrading environment can lead to increasing conflict, which in turn can lead to the undermining of political authority, and so on. As we've shown throughout this section, there is no uniform experience or explanation for the depopulation of a city or state.

●●

THINKING CRITICALLY ABOUT THE RISE AND FALL OF CITIES AND STATES

We have argued that while changes in early cities and states are important to understand, although we believe it is more useful to think of these changes as transformations rather than collapse. What difference does it make to think of the southwestern Pueblos at Mesa Verde as belonging to a society that collapsed because of some environmental collapse or as some more complex process of social transformation?

●●

Conclusion

Perhaps because they left behind so many traces—monuments, temples, writing systems, irrigation canals, and burial sites full of artifacts of beauty and artistic sophistication—ancient complex societies can be easily viewed as stories of high human drama and tragedy. Our recent fascination with the idea of the collapse of great societies, cities, and states is likely because we currently face the consequences of global warming, with its prospects of sea levels rising significantly, droughts in some areas, flooding in others, intensifying storm patterns, and mass disruptions around the globe. Rigid social hierarchies, great concentrations of wealth, despotic kings, peasant rebellions, conquest and warfare between competing societies vying for access to resources or trade goods—all of this makes for rich and engaging history, allowing us to look at the past to foresee our global future.

But if we step back from the more dramatic elements of these stories, a focus on complexity is a means by which archaeologists can study the dynamics of social integration and transformation in ancient societies. It can help us focus on the conditions under which societies grew; how people reorganized their economic, political, and social patterns to accommodate such growth; and the contexts in which societies confront political, ecological, and social challenges, not by disappearing into thin air—as many narratives of collapse imply—but by transforming the social order through processes like migration or political reorganization. Viewing situations like Cahokia or the Tarascan empire from this angle, we can better appreciate these stories as human cultural processes, not as media-hyped mysteries.

Archaeologists continue to debate whether these processes of transformation and complexity are more or less uniform, that is, the expression of universal principles such as intensifying conflict and warfare or trade and production. Nevertheless, all archaeologists agree that any explanation of complexity must be rooted in the actual evidence of artifacts and remains themselves. The closer attention we can pay to those objects and their context—whether it's knowing how a monument might have been constructed or identifying the order of brushstrokes on pottery—the greater insight we can gain into how and why states, cities, and other complex societies emerged and, in some cases, declined.

KEY TERMS

Reviewing the Chapter

Chapter Section	What We Know	To Be Resolved
When archaeologists talk about social complexity, what do they mean?	Social complexity—the division of society into groups—exists in all societies. But not all societies are complex societies, that is, societies in which socioeconomic differentiation, large populations, and centralized political control are pervasive and defining features of the society.	Archaeologists continue to debate whether these processes of transformation and complexity are more or less uniform, that is, the expression of universal principles such as intensifying conflict and warfare or trade and production.
How can we identify social complexity from archaeological sites and their artifacts?	Close attention to artifact assemblages, as well as the contexts of their manufacture and distribution, can yield important clues about the rise and decline of ancient cities and states, and of social complexity more generally.	The specific characteristics of states, cities, and city-states sometimes blur because these terms and their definitions do not necessarily capture the actual dynamism of human cultural processes.
Why don't cities and states always survive?	Total societal collapse is extremely rare. Resilience and social transformation are the rule, not the exception.	Anthropologists continue to debate the relative merits of environmental, political, economic, social, and climatic explanations for the abandonment of a city or the disappearance of a particular social or political order. But mostly these debates are specific to the causes for change at a particular site or region rather than as a single global process affecting all states and complex societies.

Readings

Much of the literature on the rise and fall of early cities and states consists of case studies of particular ancient empires. For example, Ian Hodder's *The Leopard's Tale: Revealing the Mysteries of Çatalhöyük* (New York: Thames and Hudson, 2006) focuses on the rise of social complexity in a very early site in southern Turkey. His research at Çatal Höyük is one of the best documented Mesopotamian sites from a very early period.

• •

Two studies of Cahokia along the Mississippi River are Timothy R. Pauketat and Thomas E. Emerson's *Cahokia: Domination and Ideology in the Mississippian World* (Lincoln: University of Nebraska Press, 1997), which emphasizes the rise of social stratification at Cahokia, while Sally A. Kitt Chappell's *Cahokia: Mirror of the Cosmos* (Chicago: University of Chicago Press, 2002) gives somewhat more emphasis on the decline of this important mound-builder site.

• •

David Wengrow's *What Makes Civilization? The Ancient Near East and the Future of the West* (New York: Oxford University Press, 2010) offers a more general overview of the rise of early cities and states in the Fertile Crescent.

• •

A volume edited by Patricia A. McAnany and Norman Yoffee, *Questioning Collapse: Human Resilience, Ecological Vulnerability, and the Aftermath of Empire* (Cambridge: Cambridge University Press, 2010), challenges Jared Diamond's view that the disappearance of great societies in prehistory is generally due to environmental collapse.

• •

Economics

Working, Sharing, and Buying

When the Soviet Union collapsed in 1989, so did the institutions and structures that gave meaning and material sustenance to the lives of millions of Russians. Inflation soared, and massive unemployment replaced the full state-employment that previously fed and clothed most Russians. Most people faced great scarcity, while a handful grew astonishingly wealthy.

So how have people survived in their day-to-day lives? In some respects, people have gotten along as they did under communism (Humphrey 2002). One strategy is what Russians call *blat* [blahtt], which refers to the give and take of favors among personal contacts to obtain hard-to-find goods and services, including food, well-made clothing, help fixing one's car, or assistance at the ministry of trade getting an import permit (Ledeneva 1998). *Blat* is based on long-term trusting relationships among family, friends, and neighbors. Barter, the direct swapping of goods, is another pervasive survivor of the Soviet period in Russia. *Blat* and barter were common during the Soviet era (1917–1989), when shortages and restrictions on consumption were frequent. In post-Soviet Russia, people do use money to buy things, but *blat* has persisted because it is still useful for influencing decision-making and gaining access to all kinds of goods (Ledeneva 1998).

Pains of Privatization. The fall of the Soviet Union in 1989 disrupted people's economic lives, causing widespread difficulties and pain. But people also responded in culturally meaningful ways and mobilized economic practices long used during the Soviet period to get what they needed and wanted.

But the decline of state socialism also created new economic realities and opportunities. For example, many small-scale traders bring goods like blue jeans and household electronics from other countries—a practice that was illegal during the Soviet era. Illicit protection rackets for small business owners have also flourished, permeating nearly all aspects of society in Russia. The Western media have dubbed these rackets "mafias" because of their reputations for brutality. The Russians, however, call them *krysha* [**kree**-shah], which translates as "roof" (Humphrey 2002). *Krysha* demand payments in exchange for providing protection (a "roof") to businesses and individuals from exploitation by criminals or corrupt politicians, as well as other "services" like coupons for rationed goods (Humphrey 2002).

Together, these relationships and practices have helped many people find their way through a complex new world of novel goods, lower wages, and puzzling new regulations to avert the most severe impoverishment. But protection rackets and economic uncertainty have also created widespread anxiety, disillusionment, and mistrust among Russians.

Many Western economists view surviving practices of communism such as *blat* and barter, and the emergence of new actors like protection rackets, as irrational—even corrupt—because they prevent the growth of markets and democracy in post-communist economies. But there are problems. First, markets have existed in these countries for a long time, even during the Soviet period. Second, people in these countries know that to get things done, they have to work within existing social hierarchies and relationships. The fact is, the economy that has taken shape in post-communist Russia does not exist independently of local social relationships, cultures, and moralities. In fact, *all* economies are shaped by these factors.

At the heart of anthropology's interest in economics is the following question: *How do people get what they want and need to live?* Embedded in this larger question are the following problems, around which this chapter is organized:

Is money really the measure of all things?

How does culture shape the value and meaning of money itself?

Why is gift exchange such an important part of many societies?

Why does having some things make you cool?

Are there distinct cultures of capitalism?

Anthropologists who study economies and economic activities are interested in not only how people satisfy their needs but also why they want certain things in the first place. Although we have long debated the exact nature of the relationship between economy and culture, the two clearly interpenetrate each other, and one cannot be fully understood without the other. We begin exploring this relationship by considering the nature of value.

Is Money Really the Measure of All Things?

Many North Americans and Europeans are accustomed, if not also deeply committed, to the idea that money is the measure of all things. We hear all the time that everything has a price and that the price of an object reflects its real value.

But consider these questions. What would be the price in dollars of the original Declaration of Independence of the United States? A favorite blanket you have had since childhood? The Wailing Wall, Jerusalem's most sacred Jewish site? An antique gold wedding band that mothers have passed to their daughters for seven generations?

Somebody could try to set dollar values, or even try to buy or sell them, as when experts on the *Antiques Roadshow* give market values for heirlooms (Figure 14.1). But some objects and relationships carry such sacred or special qualities that they can never really be reduced to a monetary equivalent, even in our own society (Werner and Bell 2004). The awkwardness you might feel thinking about people doing so—as well as the controversies that erupt when someone tries to sell something over the Internet such as human body parts, virginity, Holocaust memorabilia, and so on—suggests that some deep set of processes defines what is an acceptable economic transaction, what is not, and how we establish monetary values for things. Those processes are cultural. Culture—those collective processes that make the artificial seem natural—not only shapes what is acceptable to transact, but also how and why the transaction will take place, and how the objects or services being exchanged are valued.

Figure 14.1 How Much Is Grandmother's Antique Battle-Axe Worth? In the U.S. television show *Antiques Roadshow*, an expert evaluates the market value of household antiques. The popularity of the show, not to mention the motivation people have to go on it with their antiques, is ultimately less about the money than it is about other factors. What do you think those factors are?

Culture, Economics, and Value

- **Value.** The relative worth of an object or service that makes it desirable.

- **Economic anthropology.** The branch of anthropology concerned with how people make, share, and buy things and services.

If money is not the measure of all things, where exactly within the processes of culture does **value**—the relative worth of an object or service—come from? **Economic anthropology**, the subdiscipline concerned with how people make, share, and buy things and services, has considered this question for a century. Economic anthropologists study the decisions people make about earning a living, what they do when they work, the social institutions that affect these activities, and how these three matters relate to the creation of value (Wilk and Cliggett 2007; M. E. Smith 2000).

Although both anthropologists and economists study the origins of value and how economies work, they generally have different goals. Economists typically try to understand and predict economic patterns, often with a practical goal of helping people (usually those with wealth) hold onto and increase their wealth. They may describe the economic lives of less wealthy sectors of society, as one pair of economists recently did in an article entitled "The Economic Lives of the Poor" (Banerjee and Duflo 2006). But such studies tend to describe these communities in terms of economic statistics, and they assume that economic transactions in one country are like transactions in any other.

Anthropologists, on the other hand, do not assume transactions are the same everywhere, recognizing that culture shapes the character of any transaction. Furthermore, we tend to study how people lead their day-to-day economic lives by means of direct, long-term interaction with them. As a result, we tend to focus more than economists do on understanding the world's diversity of **economic systems**, the structured patterns and relationships through which people exchange goods and services, and making sense of how the world's diverse economic systems reflect and shape particular ways of life.

- **Economic systems.** The structured patterns and relationships through which people exchange goods and services.

There are four major theoretical approaches to how economies create value used in anthropology: three of these are traditional approaches within the social sciences—neoclassical economics, substantivism, and Marxism—and a fourth approach, cultural economics, is one developed by anthropologists. Each approach reveals particular dimensions of an economic system, suggesting that no single theory can comprehensively represent the complexity of what an economy is and how it works. These approaches are summarized in outline form in Table 14.1 and discussed in more detail in the text that follows.

The Neoclassical Perspective

- **Division of labor.** The cooperative organization of work into specialized tasks and roles.

Scottish moral philosopher Adam Smith wrote about the creation of value in his influential book *The Wealth of Nations* ([1776]1976). Smith observed that in "primitive" societies individuals did a lot of different kinds of work—growing and preparing food, making their own clothing, building their own homes, and so forth—but in the "civilized" societies of eighteenth-century Europe, such jobs were done increasingly by "the joint labor of a great multitude of workmen" (A. Smith [1776]1976). This change was due to the **division of labor**, the cooperative organization of work into specialized tasks and roles (A. Smith [1776]1976). Citing the example of sewing pins, Smith marveled at how dividing the process of making a sewing pin into distinct actions performed by different specialized laborers—one laborer to draw out the wire, a second to cut it, a third to straighten it, and so on—produced exponential growth in the number of pins that could be made in a day.

This change was revolutionary. Before the division of labor, Smith noted that a pin would take a lot of time and effort for an individual to make, and so the value of the pin lay in the amount of labor it took to make one. But with the division of

TABLE 14.1 THEORIES OF CULTURE, ECONOMY, AND VALUE			
Theoretical Approach	What Is the Economy?	How Does the Economic System Work?	How Is Value Created?
Neoclassical	The economy is a division of labor and the exchange of goods and services in a market.	Workers cooperate in the division of labor to produce goods. The market brings together buyers and sellers to exchange those goods.	Value and wealth are created by competition between buyers and sellers.
Substantivism	The economy is the substance of the actual transactions people engage in to get what they need and want.	Economic processes are embedded in and shaped by non-market social institutions, such as the state, religious beliefs, and kinship relations.	Value is relative, created by particular cultures and social institutions.
Marxism	Capitalism, which is a type of economic system, is a system in which private ownership of the means of production and the division of labor produce wealth for a few and inequality for the masses.	People participate in capitalism by selling their labor. That labor is appropriated by those holding the means of production.	Labor, and especially the exploitation of others' labor, is a major source of value.
Cultural Economics	The economy is a category of culture, not a special arena governed by universal economic rationality.	Economic acts are guided by local beliefs and cultural models, which are closely tied to a community's values.	Value is created by the symbolic associations people make between an activity, good, or service and a community's moral norms.

labor reducing that time and effort, the value of the pin was now established by its **exchange** (the transfer of objects and services between social actors) in a **market**, a social institution in which people come together to buy and sell goods and services.

For Smith and the economists who follow him, market exchange reflects a natural human propensity to (as Smith famously said) "truck, barter, and exchange." It also acts like an "invisible hand" and was the most successful mechanism for determining value and making wealth possible. Within the market, individuals pursue their own self-interest, using their capacity for reason and calculation to maximize their individual satisfaction. The world has finite resources (limited means), but everybody has unlimited desires (unlimited ends), and the result is competition among individuals. Every person's struggle to get the most value theoretically keeps prices, costs of production, profits, and interest rates low while generating great wealth (Wilk and Cliggett 2007). This theory is the foundation of **neoclassical economics**, which studies how people make decisions to allocate resources like time, labor, and money in order to maximize their personal satisfaction (Figure 14.2).

Among anthropologists, this influential theory has provoked a long debate over the nature of the economy. It is, we will see, basically an unresolved debate, but exploring the positions illustrates how anthropologists interested in the relationship between culture, economics, and value have applied—and criticized—neoclassical thought.

The Substantivist–Formalist Debate

In 1944, the Hungarian-American economic historian Karl Polanyi published his book *The Great Transformation* to explain how modern **capitalism**—the economic system based on private ownership of the means of production, in which prices are set and goods distributed through a market—emerged in Europe (Polanyi [1944]1975). In contrast to Smith, who saw the market as emerging naturally from the human

- **Exchange.** The transfer of objects and services between social actors.

- **Market.** A social institution in which people come together to exchange goods and services.

- **Neoclassical economics.** Economic theories and approaches that studies how people make decisions to allocate resources like time, labor, and money in order to maximize their personal benefit.

- **Capitalism.** An economic system based on private ownership of the means of production, in which prices are set and goods distributed through a market.

Figure 14.2   An Invisible Hand?   Neoclassical economists emphasize that the pursuit of self-interest in markets works like an "invisible hand." In reality, modern markets rarely, if ever, operate so freely, since governments impose regulations and enforce actions to keep markets operating smoothly, and in some cases, fairly.

• **Formal economics.** The branch of economics that studies the underlying logic of economic thought and action.

• **Substantive economics.** A branch of economics, inspired by the work of Karl Polanyi, that studies the daily transactions people engage in to get what they need or desire.

• **Redistribution.** The collection of goods in a community and then the further dispersal of those goods among members.

propensity to truck, barter, and exchange, Polanyi insisted that rather than being an expression of an assumed human nature, the rise of the market was a social process that went hand in hand with the creation of the modern state.

In developing that argument, Polanyi proposed that studying economies involves making a distinction between "formal" and "substantive" economics. By **formal economics**, he meant the underlying (formal) logic that shapes people's actions when they participate in an economy, as we see in the apparently self-interested and rational decision-makers of neoclassical economic theory. By **substantive economics**, he referred to the daily transactions people actually engage in to get what they need or desire, or the "substance" of the economy. These transactions are embedded in and inseparable from other social institutions, such as politics, religion, and kinship. Anthropologists found this distinction useful for describing issues they were studying in other societies.

The Substantivist Position

Polanyi's approach to economics was substantivist. Its primary goal was to describe how the production and **redistribution** of goods (collection of goods in a community and then re-division of those goods among members) were embedded in and shaped by non-market social institutions, such as the state, religious beliefs, and kinship relations. Substantivism was *relativistic,* holding that societies have unique social institutions and processes that influence economics like other aspects of culture. From this perspective, the value of goods in an economic system is culturally relative, rooted in particular cultures and social institutions. Second, it was *evolutionary,* recognizing that economies change over time. Third, its *main unit of analysis was a whole society and its institutions,* not individual behaviors and actions. Finally, it was *descriptive,* encouraging researchers to describe social institutions and their underlying principles, something anthropologists already did in a holistic and relativistic way (Wilk and Cliggett 2007).

Substantivists felt that the concept of an "economy" did not do justice to the way making a livelihood is inseparably interwoven with customs and social relations in other societies. They argued that research should focus on a broad field of social relations and institutions that provided people with what they needed to live instead of any predetermined or limited notion of an economy centered on a market. A major proponent of substantivism in anthropology was University of Chicago anthropologist Marshall Sahlins, as we examine in "Classic Contributions: Marshall Sahlins on Exchange in Traditional Economies."

The Formalist Reaction

By the 1960s, some anthropologists began to criticize substantivism's lack of attention to individual action and behavior, shifting their focus to formal economics. To formalists, individuals in all societies are as rational as neoclassical economics says they are. People everywhere confront limited means and unlimited ends (wants), and therefore they make rational decisions that are appropriate to the satisfaction they desire (M. E. Smith 2000). Being anthropologists, the formalists understood that "satisfaction" could be culturally defined and variable but, they asserted, the decision-making processes people used to achieve satisfaction were basically the same

CLASSIC CONTRIBUTIONS

Marshall Sahlins on Exchange in Traditional Economies

SINCE THE 1950s, cultural anthropologist Marshall Sahlins (b. 1930) has been interested in differences and similarities between the economies of small-scale non-Western societies and those of Europe. The following excerpt comes from Sahlins's statement about the nature of the economy in societies with non-industrial technologies, illustrating substantivist economic theory's emphasis on the social nature of economic transactions. To distinguish it from the modern capitalist economy, Sahlins calls this sort of economic system one of "primitive exchange." Although anthropologists no longer use terminology like "primitive," two important elements of Sahlins's explanation are that (1) nearly every transaction involves a social relationship and (2) production is organized by families in what he refers to as the "domestic mode of production."

Marshall Sahlins.

What are [in] the received wisdom "noneconomic" or "exogenous" conditions are in the primitive reality the very organization of economy. A material transaction is usually a momentary episode in a continuous social relation. The social relation exerts governance: the flow of goods is constrained by, is part of, a status etiquette. . . .

Yet the connection between material flow and social flow is reciprocal. A specific social relation may constrain a given movement of goods, but a specific transaction suggests a particular social relation. If friends make gifts, gifts make friends. A great proportion of primitive exchange, much more than our own traffic, has as its decisive function this latter, instrumental one: the material flow underwrites or initiates social relations.

Even on its strictly practical side, exchange in primitive communities has not the same role as the economic flow in modern industrial communities. The place of transaction in the total economy is different: under primitive conditions it is more detached from production, less firmly hinged to production in an organic way. Typically it is less involved than modern exchange in the acquisition of means of production, more involved with the redistribution of finished goods. The bias is that of an economy in which food holds a commanding position, and day-to-day output does not depend on a massive technological complex nor a complex division of labor. It is the bias of a domestic mode of production: of household producing units, division of labor by sex and age. [Sahlins 1965:139–40]

Questions for Reflection

1. How do you think Sahlins was being a substantivist?

2. Why do you think transactions in a "primitive" society are more oriented toward redistribution and less toward the production of goods?

everywhere. Formalists criticized the common argument that the poor and people of non-Western cultures were irrational and unable to efficiently handle resources, which some economists and policymakers used to justify withholding financial aid from such people (Wilk and Cliggett 2007).

By the late 1970s, the debate between substantivists and formalists had fizzled out with no clear winner. The main reason is that the two sides were essentially arguing past each other: one side was talking about societies and their institutions, while the other was talking about individuals, their rationality, and their individual transactions.

The Marxist Perspective

The substantivist–formalist debate also fizzled because a number of anthropologists had begun to adopt Marxism, the political and economic theories associated with German political economist Karl Marx (1818–1883). In his analysis of British capitalism, Marx characterized the English system as pitting the conflicting interests of a wealthy class (who owned factories) against a poorer working class (laborers in the factories) (Marx [1867] 1990). At the heart of this system, Marx argued, was a division of labor that produced inequality and conflict.

From the Marxist point of view, the substantivists and formalists had wasted their time debating the nature of exchange and redistribution, while the neoclassicists misunderstood economic activity as individual choice and decision-making. The real problem is explaining why and how an economy and society based on inequality reproduces itself—in other words, how the production and trade of goods enforces and maintains social inequality.

- **Surplus value.** The difference between what people produce and what they need to survive.

Marxists use the concept of **surplus value**, which is the difference between what people produce and what they need to survive, to address this problem. In a capitalist society, workers create greater output than they get paid, generating surplus value. For example, a worker in a widget factory might make $35 of widgets in an hour from $5 of materials, but gets paid only $10 per hour. What happens to the $20 of surplus value? The owner of the factory, who controls the **means of production**—the machines and infrastructure required to produce the widget—appropriates it, Marxists argue, thus exploiting the worker's productivity. This surplus value is the basis of private wealth, but it also creates permanent conflict between the worker and owner classes. The institution of private property and the state, through its social and economic policies, support this inequality.

- **Means of production.** The machines and infrastructure required to produce goods.

Marxist analysis introduced issues of power, domination, and the unequal distribution of wealth into anthropology's discussions of culture and economy. But not all attempts to apply Marxist analysis to non-Western societies have been entirely satisfying, because non-capitalist economies work so differently. In particular, such studies do not always adequately address the culturally specific symbolic and moral dimensions of economic interaction, to which we turn next.

The Cultural Economics Perspective

- **Cultural economics.** An anthropological approach to economics that focuses on how symbols and morals help shape a community's economy.

The idea that symbols and morals help shape a community's economy lies at the heart of **cultural economics**. Cultural economics views the economy as a category of culture, not a special arena governed by universal utilitarian or practical reason (Sahlins 1972, 1976). The roots of this approach lie in substantivism. The cultural economist's goal is to understand, from the "native's point of view," the local beliefs and cultural models that guide and shape economic activities (Gudeman 1986).

To the cultural economist, a close relationship exists between the words "value" (desirability) and "values" (moral norms). Both refer to the symbolic expression of

Figure 14.3 Members of a Cofradía in Guatemala. Cofradías, which are Catholic civil-religious associations, are a classic example of a prestige economy since members gain social prestige and authority even as they may go deeply into financial debt to participate.

intrinsically desirable principles or qualities. This relationship also implies that moral norms and economic activity influence each other (Sayer 2000).

Anthropologists working in this vein have been especially interested in **prestige economies**, economies in which people seek high social rank, prestige, and power instead of money and material wealth. In indigenous Maya communities of Guatemala and southern Mexico, for example, men have traditionally participated in the Cofradía [ko-fra-**dee**-ah] system, a hierarchical system dating from colonial times that combines civic leadership and Catholic religious authority (M. Nash 1958) (Figure 14.3). As they enter higher offices with greater responsibilities and power, these men also have the obligation to spend more of their personal money and other wealth on community fiestas and infrastructure. Some will go broke or deep into debt doing so. Underlying this system is a moral philosophy (rather than individual self-interest) emphasizing that the path to status and rank requires an individual to share generously with others whatever material wealth he has.

Recent studies in cultural economics have tended to focus on the dynamism of local economies, recognizing that one society may encompass several local economic models simultaneously, perhaps at different levels or among different institutions (Robben 1989; Gudeman 2001). Such a perspective can help us better understand how people in post-Soviet Russia got along, since it is a place where people held distinct and even competing ideas about appropriate ways to get what they need to survive, as we presented at the beginning of the chapter.

Returning to this section's broader focus on how value is created, it should be clear that none of these theoretical approaches—neoclassical economics, formalism, substantivism, Marxism, or cultural economics—accepts that money is the measure of all things. While the specifics of these theories differ—some might even say they are irreconcilable—each nevertheless accepts, at least partially, that cultural processes and social relationships play a central role in establishing value, and that culture and economics are intertwined in complex ways.

• **Prestige economies.** Economies in which people seek high social rank, prestige, and power instead of money and material wealth.

THINKING CRITICALLY ABOUT ECONOMICS

Cultural economics argues that a single society can have multiple local cultural models of appropriate economic action and behavior circulating in it. For example, in the United States, even as dominant cultural models of economic behavior resemble Adam Smith's rational economic actors, some religious communities have certain expectations about appropriate economic behavior, such as saving a certain amount of money, donating a certain percentage to the church, and so on, which make explicit connections between economic behavior and morality. Can you think of other cultural models of economic behavior in the United States?

How Does Culture Shape the Value and Meaning of Money Itself?

If value and its meanings are created through the processes of culture, then it stands to reason that the value and meanings of **money** itself—an object or substance that serves as a payment for a good or service—are also created through culture. Money, which is a type of **currency** (an object used as a medium of exchange), provides a standard measure of value that allows people to compare and trade goods and services. Anything durable and scarce can serve as money. Cowrie (a type of mollusk) shells, rings made of precious metals, brass rods, and even enormous stone disks have been used as money. Money interests anthropologists not simply because it is a medium of economic exchange, but also because it has important cultural dimensions.

Several cultural dimensions of money are of interest to anthropologists, especially the diverse types of money people use and the powerful moral meanings people project onto money and its uses. Together, these dimensions reveal important diversity and subtleties surrounding how people use money and establish its value.

Across the world, money is many things to many people, and not everybody wants it for the same reasons. In market-based economies like that in the United States, people want money because it can be used to buy nearly any good or service. Anthropologists call this **general purpose money** because it is money that is used to buy almost anything. Portability and mobility are important features of general purpose money, as we see in our dollar bills, coins, credit cards, checks, college "smart" identity cards, and electronic transfers. General purpose money has some limits—for instance, most of us will not take a check from just anyone, and you cannot pay for a $50 pair of shoes with a pocketful of pennies—but most Americans are preoccupied with getting money because in order to get almost anything, including the goods necessary for basic subsistence, they need it.

Another type of money is **limited purpose money**, which refers to objects that can be exchanged only for certain things. For example, the pastoral Tiv people of Nigeria traditionally could purchase cattle and pay bride price (things of value a groom gives to his bride's father) only with brass rods. In Tiv society, people traditionally did not use money for basic subsistence, but primarily to gain access to goods that give social

- **Money.** An object or substance that serves as a payment for a good or service.

- **Currency.** An object used as a medium of exchange.

- **General purpose money.** Money that is used to buy nearly any good or service.

- **Limited purpose money.** Objects that can be exchanged only for certain things.

respectability and prestige, such as a marriage partner, cattle, and other livestock (Bohannon and Bohannon 1968).

In the Tiv case, powerful moral rules regulated the ways in which money was used. The Tiv traditionally had three separate **spheres of exchange**, or bounded orders of value in which certain goods can be exchanged only for others: ordinary subsistence goods, prestige goods, and rights in people, especially women and slaves (Bohannon and Bohannon 1968).

The British colonial period in Nigeria (1900–1960) undermined this traditional system, because the British introduced general purpose money. Young Tiv men working as laborers and paid in British currency began using it to pay for prestige goods like cattle and bride price. The acquisition of cash value for prestige goods, Bohannon observed, was not just an economic problem: it was a moral problem since it messed with Tiv notions about what money could be used for.

Even general purpose money, such as the use of dollars and cents, has cultural and moral dimensions beyond its function as a medium of exchange (Parry and Bloch 1989). We all know, for example, that you cannot simply walk into your university's accounting office, pay a large sum of money, and receive a diploma. Our ideas about getting an education involve a moral obligation to work hard and applying oneself before the diploma is awarded. If you tried to buy a diploma outright, your money would have no value for this purpose, and one could even imagine that seeking to buy a diploma could feel "dirty," contaminating the purity and goodness we associate with the process of education. An anthropological explanation for this situation lies in the concept of **transactional orders**, or realms of transactions a community uses, each with its own set of symbolic meanings and moral assumptions (Parry and Bloch 1989). The transactions involved in getting an education, which are steeped in long-term obligations and expectations, are morally distinct from other short-term transactions that have no special moral obligations, such as buying a magazine at your university bookstore.

Although most of us take for granted the existence of money, its use is not universal and people have developed other ways to get what they need and want. Anthropologists have found that non-monetary exchanges are a central economic aspect of all societies, a theme we turn to in the next section.

- **Spheres of exchange.** Bounded orders of value in which certain goods can be exchanged only for others.

- **Transactional orders.** Realms of transactions a community uses, each with its own set of symbolic meanings and moral assumptions.

• •

THINKING CRITICALLY ABOUT ECONOMICS

Do you feel a need to protect certain relationships from money? What relationships? What is the meaning of money for you in these situations?

• •

Why Is Gift Exchange Such an Important Part of All Societies?

Exchange is a practice understood by anthropologists as the transfer of things and gifts between social actors (Carrier 1996a:218). It is a universal feature of human existence and relates to all aspects of life. In many societies, the exchange of gifts is the central defining feature of its economy.

Gift Exchange and Economy: Two Classic Approaches

It may sound strange to think of a gift exchange in economic terms. We tend to think of gifts as personal expressions of **reciprocity**, the give-and-take that builds and confirms relationships. For Americans the problem here is that we distinguish the economy from gift giving, while in the non-industrial societies that anthropologists have traditionally studied, exchanging gifts is at the heart of the local economy. So how are gifts related to economy? Two classic approaches to this question date back to the 1920s.

Malinowski and the Kula

The exchange of gifts is a central feature of life in Melanesian societies of the Southwest Pacific, a fact Malinowski discovered while he was in the Trobriand Islands. He wrote that for Trobrianders "to possess is to give. . . . A man who owns a thing is expected to share it, to distribute it, to be its trustee and dispenser" (1922:97).

He found no better illustration of this phenomenon than the *Kula* [**koo**-la], an extensive inter-island system of exchange in which high-ranking men gave ornamental shell armbands (*mwali*) and necklaces (*soulava*) to lifelong exchange partners on other islands. In the highly structured *Kula*, armbands traveled in one direction and necklaces in the opposite direction (Figure 14.4). For Trobriand Islanders these shell valuables were about the most valuable things one could possess, even though men typically owned them for only a few months before they gave them to other partners (anthropologists call this **delayed reciprocity**—which means a long lag time between giving and receiving). These shell valuables had no real function, as they were rarely worn, and had no other use. Their value came when they were given away because that is when they brought renown to the man who gave them away.

- **Reciprocity.** The give-and-take that builds and confirms relationships.

- **Delayed reciprocity.** A form of reciprocity that features a long lag time between giving and receiving.

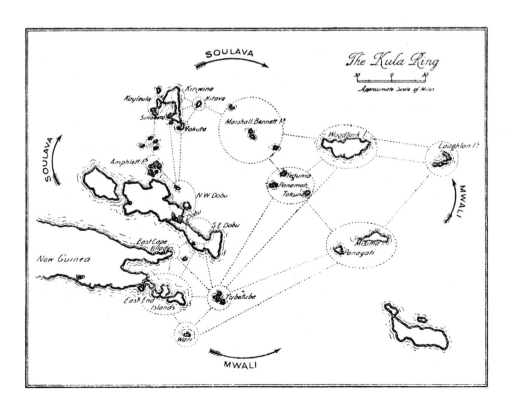

Figure 14.4   The Kula Ring with Mwali (Armbands) and Soulava (Necklaces).

Malinowski did observe that when men sailed to visit their partners on another island, in addition to the armbands and necklaces, they always brought along many utilitarian goods, such as vegetables, fish, or pots to exchange on the side for things they could not get on their own island. Malinowski theorized that these ritualized *Kula* exchanges functioned to enhance the status of individual men and distribute goods that people could not otherwise get on their home islands. *Kula* is such an important dimension of Trobriand society that colonialism did not undermine it. In fact, it has expanded in recent decades, involving more islands and lower ranking individuals.

Although Malinowski did not discuss it, Trobriand women also participated in extensive exchange systems; "Thinking Like an Anthropologist: The Role of Exchange in Managing Social Relationships" explores the significance of women's exchange in the Trobriand Islands.

Mauss and the Spirit of the Gift

Marcel Mauss (1872–1950), nephew and colleague of the French sociologist Emile Durkheim, was the founder of modern French anthropology. In 1924, he published his most influential work, *The Gift* (Mauss 1954, 2000), which compares gift exchange and its functions in a wide range of non-Western societies.

Unlike Malinowski, who viewed gift exchange primarily in terms of how it contributed to an individual's status and identity, Mauss viewed gift exchange in terms of how it builds group solidarity. Gift exchange, Mauss insisted, is based on obligation, which has three dimensions: (1) *the obligation to give,* which establishes the giver as generous and worthy of respect; (2) *the obligation to receive,* which shows respect to the giver; and (3) *the obligation to return the gift in appropriate ways,* which demonstrates honor. It thus creates and maintains bonds of solidarity between people who, Mauss believed, would otherwise pursue their own personal interests. For Mauss, gift giving is steeped in morality and spirituality, so that objects take on the identity of the giver (Figure 14.5).

Later anthropologists have built on Mauss's insights into how gift exchange lies at the heart of human society. One of the most influential of these was Marshall Sahlins (1972), who argued that gift exchanges help manage group boundaries. Sahlins identified three types of reciprocity involved in gift exchange—generalized reciprocity, balanced reciprocity, and negative reciprocity—each of which defines the social relationship between a giver and a receiver.

Generalized reciprocity refers to giving something without the expectation of return, at least not in the near term. It is uninhibited and generous giving, such as that which takes place between parents and children, married couples, or close-knit kin groups.

Balanced reciprocity occurs when a person gives something, expecting the receiver to return an equivalent gift or favor at some point in the future. The *Kula*, *Sagali*, and American birthday presents among good friends are examples.

Finally, **negative reciprocity**, which economists call barter, is the attempt to get something for nothing, to haggle one's way into a favorable personal outcome. It exists between the most distant relations, such as between strangers or adversaries.

Sahlins's typology is useful because it suggests that social relationships shape the kinds of reciprocity people practice. But recent studies of gift giving have focused less on the objective types of reciprocity and more on how people interpret gift exchange. For example, anthropologist Marilyn Strathern (1988) argues that certain Melanesian cultures believe that people acquire their individual identities through gift exchange. These Melanesians do not conceive of people as independent units

- **Generalized reciprocity.** A form of reciprocity in which gifts are given freely without the expectation of return.

- **Balanced reciprocity.** A form of reciprocity in which the giver expects a fair return at some later time.

- **Negative reciprocity.** A form of reciprocity in which the giver attempts to get something for nothing, to haggle one's way into a favorable personal outcome.

Figure 14.5 Marilyn Monroe's Dress. In 1999 this dress sold at auction for $1.5 million. The dress by itself is beautiful, but it is the fact that Marilyn Monroe wore it that makes it so valuable to some collectors.

Thinking Like an Anthropologist

The Role of Exchange in Managing Social Relationships

ANTHROPOLOGISTS BEGIN THEIR research by asking questions. In this box, we want you to learn how to ask questions as an anthropological researcher. Part 1 describes a situation and follows up with questions we would ask. Part 2 asks you to do the same thing with a different situation.

PART 1: MORTUARY EXCHANGE IN THE TROBRIAND ISLANDS

During his field research in the Trobriand Islands, Malinowski paid considerable attention to the inter-island *Kula* exchange. Since then, other scholars have updated Malinowski's picture of the *Kula* and other Melanesian exchange systems. Most notable of these scholars was the American anthropologist Annette Weiner (1933–1997), who conducted fieldwork in the Trobriand Islands during the 1970s and 1980s.

Weiner noted that women rarely participated directly in *Kula*. But she also observed that women participate in their own elaborate exchange system based on delayed reciprocity. This exchange system, called *Sagali*, involves the exchange of grass skirts and bundles made of dried banana leaves and is used almost exclusively in women's exchanges (Weiner 1976, 1988).

Sagali is a mortuary exchange ritual. When someone dies, Trobrianders go through months of mourning during which they shut themselves off from most normal activities. When they eventually emerge from this self-imposed seclusion, their closest relatives give gifts of decorative women's skirts and banana leaf bundles to all the in-laws and other relatives who have helped them during their months of seclusion. Although the fancy skirts can be worn in traditional dances, the banana leaf bundles have no use whatsoever outside the *Sagali*. Women make them all the time, usually while sitting outside their homes with other women discussing village news and gossip. Only women give or receive banana leaf bundles or skirts, and men play no role in the exchange except perhaps to help move the huge baskets of bundles from a house to the village plaza for their wives or sisters.

Weiner nevertheless found important similarities between *Sagali* and *Kula*. For example, they both involve delayed reciprocity. That is, just as a man would not receive any *Kula* valuables between visits to his trading partners on other

⚘ **In Plain Sight.**   Malinowski uncritically accepted certain European preconceptions about women's non-economic status, ignoring almost completely *Sagali* exchanges, even though they were going on all around him. Yet we know that he observed them, because he took photographs like this one of women exchanging banana leaf bundles and skirts that they had made.

islands, a woman who gave away all her bundles would not receive any back until the next *Sagali*. The significance of both kinds of exchange system lay in the prestige that came from giving away the objects involved—bundles and skirts, or armshells and necklaces—not in accumulating them. If a person hoarded *Kula* valuables or skirts and leaf bundles when called on to exchange them, he or she would be subject to ridicule as a stingy and selfish person.

What questions does this situation raise for anthropological researchers?

1. How can a woman guarantee that *Sagali* exchanges will eventually be repaid at some later exchange?

2. In a *Sagali* ritual, the recipients of bundles and skirts see tangible affirmation of their contributions to the family of the deceased. But what does the deceased's family get out of giving away hundreds of bundles and skirts?

3. How do these transactions build social bonds between the family of a dead person and the people who have supported them during the months of mourning?

4. How does giving and receiving bundles enhance an individual's social status?

PART 2: EXCHANGE RELATIONS SURROUNDING AMERICAN FUNERALS AND MARRIAGES

Not all American transactions are about acquiring desired goods and services; some exchanges involve delayed reciprocity much as they do in the Trobriand Islands. Two socially based American transactions are best viewed as ritualized exchanges: giving wedding gifts and giving support to family and friends after a death. If you wanted to understand the ritualized aspects of American wedding gifts or mortuary transactions, what questions would you ask as an anthropological researcher?

who *enter into* gift exchange; instead, they see themselves as *made* into people by gift exchange itself. Strathern's broader point is that culturally different concepts of personhood and relationship lead to different understandings of and motivations for gift exchange.

Our current understandings of the gift clearly owe a great deal to the pioneering work of Malinowski and Mauss, especially the realization that many societies have met people's material and social necessities, not with money, but with highly organized and principled gift exchanges.

Gift Exchange in Market-Based Economies

Although our cultural models dismiss its economic significance, gift exchange is tremendously important in American and European societies for a lot of the same reasons it is in other societies: it establishes social status, reaffirms relationships, and gives people access to the goods and sometimes influence that they want and need. As in any society, important implicit rules guide our gift exchange.

Even the gifts we give for holidays and birthdays follow implicit rules. Gifts between siblings or good friends have to be repaid in equal value every bit as much as the *Kula* valuables do. Ideally, gifts should also be personal and embody the relationship between giver and receiver. Yet such gift exchanges among friends are delicate matters. Most Americans feel these gifts should not be cash, for example, in the form of a $20 bill, because it places a concrete value on the relationship. Somewhat less impersonal are **commodities** (mass-produced and impersonal goods with no meaning or history apart from themselves) bought at a mall (see Chapter 19). As commodities they are equivalent to the money spent to buy them. Somewhat between the two are gift cards, which have the double disadvantage of being the same as money and as impersonal as any commodity in the store. One solution described by anthropologist James Carrier (1995) is to turn impersonal commodities into personal gifts, by wrapping objects as personal presents, or if they are too difficult to wrap, putting bows on them. This simple action symbolically distances the goods from an anonymous retail environment, suggesting that the giver made a greater effort than simply going to a store (Figure 14.6).

Three points stand out here: (1) gift exchanges are deeply embedded in the social relations of every society, including our own; (2) by personalization we can transform impersonal commodities into personal gifts; and (3) we, like everyone else in the world, invest tremendous symbolic meaning in the things we give, receive, and consume. This third point has significant subtleties, which we explore in more detail in the next section.

- **Commodities.** Mass-produced and impersonal goods with no meaning or history apart from themselves.

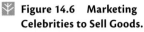 **Figure 14.6   Marketing Celebrities to Sell Goods.** Retailers try to help us overcome the impersonality of commodities by creating marketing campaigns that personalize their products. One strategy is to associate a product with widely recognized celebrities, such as the Argentine soccer star Lionel Messi pictured here. Celebrities can generate positive feelings about a product even if they don't actually say anything about its quality.

THINKING CRITICALLY ABOUT ECONOMICS

The way anthropologists think about it, "reciprocity," "exchange," and "sharing" each have different meanings. In what ways do you think these are different from each other?

Why Does Having Some Things Make You Cool?

In U.S. society, people work hard and spend a great deal of time and money to buy things that make them appear "cool," that is, impressive, trendy, a bit better than other people. "Cool" people understand what is "in" and what is not. Marketing and advertising executives work hard to identify and create an image of coolness in ads and commercials—in the clothing we wear, the music we listen to, the foods we eat, the cars we drive, the smartphones we use, and so on—all to get us to buy more things. But coolness is more than just a tool for selling goods and services. It is also an important way people in a mass society identify who is and is not a member of their "in-crowd"—their social class, rank, lifestyle, ethnic identity, or other particular grouping (Bourdieu 1984).

But neither a Ferrari nor an Abercrombie & Fitch shirt, beloved by many college students, is naturally "cool." Whatever symbolic distinctions or qualities these goods have are culturally constructed. Their meaning results from social and cultural processes that create demand for these objects, such as the fact that everyone is talking about them or important and respected people own them. Less-trendsetting members of a society need and want them because higher status people who set trends have them, and those who do not set the trends can only satisfy their desires through the act of consumption.

Anthropologists define **consumption** as the act of using and assigning meaning to a good, service, or relationship. Through consumption people make cultural meaning, build social relationships, and create identities (Douglas and Isherwood 1978; Appadurai 1986). Every culture distinguishes between what is appropriate and what is inappropriate to consume, providing social avenues to consuming culturally accepted goods and limiting consumption of things considered inappropriate. For example, the noble families of the Mandar people of Sulawesi in Indonesia wear certain patterns of handwoven silk sarongs at weddings and other formal occasions, but have placed restrictions on commoners from wearing certain designs or motifs. This restriction raises the status of nobles, while simultaneously lowering that of commoners (Welsch 1988).

Consumption begins with an act of **appropriation**, which is a process of taking possession of the object (Carrier 1996b; Miller 1987, 1995). Consider, for example, the consumption of a smartphone. The initial act of appropriation takes place as you shop for it. Shopping entails narrowing your choices on the basis of price, size, look, brand, special features, and your sense of how you want to be seen by others until you identify the one you want to buy. After paying for it, you continue the appropriation process by personalizing it—by using it in certain ways, such as programming its memory with your special apps, putting a case with special designs on it, or otherwise customizing it to reflect what you want out of a phone. These customizations, as well as how and when you use your smartphone, in turn reflect and define who you are as a person. An informed techie who loves the latest gadgets, a social butterfly who is always networked, a creative and artistic type, or a serious businessperson. Depending on the brand you purchased or how you customize it, your consumption of this particular smartphone distinguishes your social position in society, as a member of the middle class, or some other grouping based on age, ethnicity, and so on.

In societies where people still make many of the things they consume, people may be just as concerned with wanting cool things—things that identify the owner as worthy of respect—as many Americans are. Of course, other cultures' ideas of what "cool" is may differ greatly from ours. For instance, when people around Aitape on the North Coast of Papua New Guinea exchange food and other subsistence goods with their friends in neighboring villages, they also often give their partners handmade netted string bags with unique designs common to their home villages. String bags are a tangible manifestation of the trader's generosity and commitment to the social and economic relationship between the two exchange partners (Figure 14.7). People are especially proud of the bags that come from very distant villages because they indicate an extensive network of friends.

Changes in consumption patterns are often visible manifestations of broader cultural changes (Miller 1995). For example, let us return to post-Soviet Russia. The shift toward a market economy made it possible for Russians to consume things they could not during the Soviet era. Consumerism itself was not new in Russia; during the Soviet era people were also **consumers**, that is, people who live through objects and images not of their own making (Humphrey 2002:40). But people's consciousness of consumption changed. During the Soviet era, when the state produced and allocated all industrial and agricultural goods, people were encouraged to identify these goods as "their own," because the state presented itself ideologically as an expression of the people.

Now that the state no longer controls consumer goods, and foreign goods pour in, Russians have a bewildering array of choices about how and what to consume. During the Soviet era, consuming foreign goods was viewed positively by many as an act of rebellion and defiance against the state. Today, however, many Russians distrust foreign goods—or even refuse to consume them—because they associate them with the domestic importers and sellers of these goods who are often shady and corrupt

- **Consumption.** The act of using and assigning meaning to a good, service, or relationship.

- **Appropriation.** The process of taking possession of an object, idea, or relationship.

- **Consumers.** People who rely on goods and services not produced by their own labor.

Figure 14.7 Prestige Goods. Although both of these bags are considered prestige goods in their specific cultures, a vast conceptual distance exists between how and why people consume them. String bags represent an individual's wealth in social relationships, while Gucci bags represent an individual's material wealth.

businessmen created by the decline of the state (Humphrey 2002:55). As Russians negotiate who they are through what and how they consume, we can see that the influx of Western consumer goods is not as culturally homogenizing as many commentators have assumed. Instead, the influx is becoming the grounds of creating new cultural meanings and social relationships.

Consumption is a key feature of capitalism, but if consumption varies around the globe, does the capitalist system also vary?

THINKING CRITICALLY ABOUT ECONOMICS

If it is true that changing consumption patterns are visible manifestations of broader cultural changes, what can the massive acquisition of cellular and smartphones by millions of people during the past decade tell us about changes in how people communicate?

Are There Distinct Cultures of Capitalism?

For the better part of the twentieth century, capitalism and socialism existed as opposed forms of economic organization, an opposition that dominated global politics during the Cold War. After the collapse of the Soviet Union and Eastern Bloc regimes in 1989 and communist China's increasing shift toward free markets, many economists and political leaders, especially in the United States, asserted that "capitalism won." But under the influence of local cultures, capitalism can take more varied forms than we might assume. As defined previously, capitalism is an economic system based on private ownership of the means of production, in which prices are set and goods distributed through a market. Beyond this generally accepted definition, theoretical approaches to capitalism vary depending on the researcher's philosophical and political persuasions (Blim 2000). For example, followers of influential sociologist Max Weber study the distinct types of capitalism that have existed in different times and places; formalists study capitalism through the actions of individuals and institutions; and Marxists study the changing nature of industrial production, the conditions of workers, and the connection between small-scale economic activities and broader global economic trends.

In spite of theoretical orientation, however, anthropologists view capitalism as a cultural phenomenon. In fact, its deepest assumptions are cultural: capitalism assumes certain values and ideals to be natural, in the sense that this is the way things really are. It seems inevitable that well-being can be achieved through consuming material things. Anthropologist Richard Robbins (2005:2) suggests that capitalist systems are culturally organized into four distinct social roles. *Capitalists* invest money in real estate, buildings, machinery, and so on to make profit. *Laborers* work for the capitalists; their sole means of support comes from the sale of their labor. The primary role of *consumers* is to purchase and consume quantities of goods and services. Finally, the *state* institutes and enforces policies that structure the relationship between these three other actors, attempting to ensure that capitalists invest, workers work, and consumers consume. These social categories and the cultural ideals associated with them are the basic and universal elements of capitalism.

But anthropologists also recognize that the cultural contexts and meanings of capitalist activities take diverse forms. Let us compare two examples—one drawn from Wall Street, the other from Malaysia—to illustrate how capitalist activities and meanings can vary across cultures.

Culture and Social Relations on Wall Street

Investment banks on Wall Street, site of the New York Stock Exchange and America's financial capital, are popularly seen as a bastion of individual entrepreneurialism and cold rationalism in pursuit of profits (Figure 14.8). If Adam Smith were alive, he'd probably see Wall Street as the epitome of capitalism. But anthropologists have found that social relationships and cultural processes shape transactions on Wall Street in far more complex ways than our image of Wall Street may suggest.

Figure 14.8   The New York Stock Exchange on Wall Street, the Heart of U.S. Capitalism.

What interests anthropologists is how people construct meanings in the context of such social relationships and how those meanings shape social action and individual conduct. For example, anthropologist Karen Ho (2009) studied investment banks and the international banking industry on Wall Street using participant observation and open-ended interviews just as an anthropologist working in a foreign village would. She reports that bankers and traders think of Wall Street as an entity that mediates vast and anonymous flows of capital throughout the world.

But Ho had conducted participant observation within these global networks as an investment banker herself. Throughout her time on Wall Street, Ho also found that strong personal relationships were essential to successful transactions, precisely because the market was so vast and because the risks and strengths of any particular global segment were so difficult to decipher with assurance. As a result, bankers who told their clients they had "global reach" and coverage "everywhere in the world"— which was a central part of the image they promoted to convince investors to do business with them—were not being entirely honest. In reality, Ho found, most firms had minimal coverage in most parts of the world, often maintaining empty or barely staffed offices where they only did occasional business. Their relationships with local banking firms and clients were nearly dormant, only being reactivated when new investment opportunities arose. Ho's point is that without the rich personal relationships and knowledge of local conditions and markets, these banks have almost no reach whatsoever, demonstrating that modern financial markets are every bit as dependent on social relationships and local knowledge as any daily transaction anthropologists might study in a rural village setting.

Entrepreneurial Capitalism Among Malays

The Southeast Asian nation of Malaysia provides an example of a very different culture of capitalism. During the past several decades, Malaysia has aggressively pursued economic growth through industrialization and the creation of investment opportunities. Malaysia is an Islamic country whose majority are Muslim ethnic Malays. During British colonial times (early 1800s to the mid-1900s), the nation's Chinese minority dominated the economy and remained considerably better off than most of the Malay majority. Since the late 1960s, the Malaysian government's goal for economic growth has been to reduce economic inequality between the country's ethnic Chinese and ethnic Malays by giving Malays preferential treatment and greater control over economic resources through set-aside provisions, government subsidies, special investment programs, and preferential opportunities for university education.

Anthropologist Patricia Sloane (1999) studied the impact of these laws on the culture of Malay entrepreneurs in urban Kuala Lumpur, Malaysia's capital. Few Malay capitalists in her study were extremely wealthy but were part of the growing Malaysian middle class. These Malay capitalists' aspirations are not "global" but self-consciously local. The ideology of business was embedded in local values and committed to promoting the economic interests and growth of the Malay ethnic group.

These processes have created a new class of Malay entrepreneurs who think of themselves as the cornerstone of a new, modernized Malaysia. They accept that capitalism is a self-interested enterprise, but they also feel bound by traditional Malay values, insisting on investment and development that serve traditional obligations to family, community, and other Malays. Their idea of capitalism is one in which wealth, social balance, and even salvation are the rewards for those who abide by the moral dictates of social responsibility and obligation. At the heart of these values lie Islamic economic principles—such as the prohibition on charging interest, prohibitions on exploitive or risky activities, and the obligation to share wealth after meeting one's family needs (Sloane 1999:73).

One effect of these ideals is that few enterprises are economically successful, so business failures are common. But Malays do not view these facts with embarrassment, because for many individuals the primary business goal is not to generate huge profits but to extend and deepen their social networks and to cultivate contacts with powerful people. Entrepreneurship is thus not simply about economic action and profit accumulation; it allows people to show how they are both fully engaged in the modern world of global capitalism and respectful of traditional Islamic and Malay obligations and values.

The challenge for Malays, in other words, has been how to pursue a capitalist economy that both improves their material quality of life and conforms to their local cultural values and social practices. This challenge is not unique to Malaysia. In "Anthropologist as Problem Solver: Ashraf Ghani and the Reconstruction of the Afghan Economy," we consider how one anthropologist has sought to create capitalist development that aligns with cultural priorities and social norms in Afghanistan.

THINKING CRITICALLY ABOUT ECONOMICS

If capitalism can vary across cultures, do you think models of capitalist behavior and thought can also differ within a society? Can you think of any examples drawn from what you know about the different kinds of industries and businesses you would find in the American capitalist economic system? How can you explain the variability of capitalism within a single society?

Conclusion

Most North Americans take for granted that the best way to get the things we need and want is to get a job and begin earning a paycheck. But this is definitely not how people do it everywhere in the world. Whether they are Russians gaining access to goods and services through the informal exchange of favors, Trobriand Islanders trading for goods

Anthropologist as Problem Solver

Ashraf Ghani and the Reconstruction of the Afghan Economy

SINCE THE 1970s, the people of Afghanistan have suffered through a Soviet invasion and occupation, a civil war, and the repressive government of the Taliban (a fundamentalist Islamic religious and political group). After the events of 9/11 in 2001, U.S. and NATO troops invaded Afghanistan to overthrow the Taliban who were supporting the 9/11 terrorists. All these events disrupted the country's agricultural economy, and Afghanistan has become a chief supplier of opium for the production of heroin.

After the fall of the Taliban in 2001, Afghan anthropologist Ashraf Ghani, who received his Ph.D. from Columbia University, decided to return to his native country to help with its reconstruction. As a scholar, Ghani had studied social transformation, the role of religion in people's lives, and how states succeed or fail—topics that he taught about in U.S. and Afghan universities for several decades. In the 1990s, he worked at the World Bank on projects related to state reform and later at the United Nations working on the Afghan peace agreement after the U.S. invasion. He was a well-known international expert on state-building and reform (Ghani and Lockhart 2009).

Within several months of his return, Ghani became Afghanistan's finance minister, a position he held between June 2002 and December 2004. As finance minister, Ghani implemented a number of major reforms, including issuing a new currency, creating a national budget, computerizing the operations of the treasury, and sharing treasury reports with the public to provide transparency and accountability in the use of public funds.

As a Marxist anthropologist, Ghani has been a staunch critic of capitalism, insisting that the majority of people in the world experience capitalism mainly through industries that come to extract their countries' resources and wealth, leaving the people with few benefits. But as finance minister, he understood that people in his country could benefit from participation in the global capitalist economy if given the opportunity to do it more or less on their own terms and in

🌱 **Ashraf Ghani**.

partnership with foreign investors. Toward this end, he raised $27.5 billion of international assistance, with the goal of creating new capitalist development programs outside the opium economy.

In spite of his openness to the global economy, Ghani has insisted that elected village-level councils determine the priorities and ways of implementing development plans. Like many other anthropologists, he opposed the idea of having central government and aid officials create and implement development programs, because they have little knowledge of local priorities and social norms. Ghani's approach drew directly and explicitly on Afghan traditions of *Ashar* (community members working together voluntarily to improve community infrastructure); *Jirga* (councils composed of respected members of the community); and Islamic values of unity, equity, and justice (National Solidarity Programme 2014).

As finance minister, Ghani managed all the typical issues—currency, budgets, and treasury functions—but he drew explicitly on his anthropological training when he pressed his government to appreciate the importance of local culture in shaping how economies work. This approach has been tangibly successful from an economic point of view, since Afghan economic growth in recent years has been as high as 30% annually. From a social and political point of view it was also successful. He has become a popular political figure in Afghanistan, and became its president after the 2014 election.

Questions for Reflection

1. What conditions might undermine Ghani's plan to have local communities determine the priorities and ways of implementing development plans?

2. Why might an agent of the World Bank or the U.S. State Department approach rebuilding the Afghan economy differently from Ghani?

on other islands, or Malaysian entrepreneurs building social ties with other entrepreneurs and powerful individuals, people differ in their cultural strategies and ideas about appropriate ways to conduct their economic lives. And, when we step back and look at our own economic lives in a consumer capitalist society, we can see that we too have developed distinctive strategies for exchanging goods and money, such as when we symbolically transform commodities into personalized gifts or possessions.

Economic ideas and behaviors never exist independently of culture, morality, and social relationships. Culture shapes what is acceptable to transact, how and why a transaction occurs, and how the goods and services being exchanged are valued. This point is especially important for understanding the complexities of contemporary global economic changes. In an economically interconnected world, the creation of new markets and economic relationships has an impact on whether and how people in a particular place will be able to acquire certain goods and services. But these processes never occur in a cultural and social vacuum, which is why economic processes continue to play out in distinct ways in communities around the world.

KEY TERMS

Reviewing the Chapter

Chapter Section	What We Know	To Be Resolved
Is money really the measure of all things?	Economies never exist independently of already existing social relationships and culture. Culture shapes what is acceptable to transact, how and why that transaction will take place, and how the goods or services being exchanged are valued.	Still unresolved is the issue of how to define the category "economic." Is it a particular logic and decision-making process? Or is it the substance of the economy, meaning the daily transactions of goods and services?
How does culture shape the value and meaning of money itself?	People's relationships and attitudes toward money depend on factors such as whether their society uses general purpose money and/or limited purpose money; spheres of exchange; and cultural distinctions between transactional orders.	Anthropologists are still working through the diverse cultural meanings of money, especially the ways money circulates and shifts meanings through distinct transactional orders.
Why is gift exchange such an important part of all societies?	The exchange of things is a universal feature of human existence. Many societies have met people's material and social necessities through highly organized and principled gift exchanges, but rich subtleties and cross-cultural variations exist in how, when, what, and why people engage in gift exchange.	Although anthropologists accept the central importance of gift exchange in all societies, they continue to embrace distinct theoretical models concerning reciprocity and gift exchange, and debates persist over whether these models adequately capture the complexity of other cultures' approaches to reciprocity.
Why does having some things make you cool?	The symbolic distinctions and qualities that make objects cool and worthy of respect are always culturally constructed.	People's relationships with objects are more complicated than economic perspectives on consumption suggest. Anthropologists are still documenting and seeking to understand those complexities.
Are there distinct cultures of capitalism?	Capitalism is as much an economic system as it is a cultural phenomenon, whose actual practices and cultural models vary across and within cultures.	The idea that capitalism is not a monolithic economic structure but a variable culturally diverse set of practices is not universally accepted in anthropology, especially by Marxist anthropologists.

Readings

Since Bronislaw Malinowski's classic monograph on the *Kula* exchange among the Trobriand Islanders *Argonauts of the Western Pacific* (London: G. Routledge and Sons, 1922), a considerable amount of anthropological research has focused on gift-giving systems around the world. Marcel Mauss's classic 1924 essay *The Gift: The Form and Reason for Exchange in Archaic Societies* (New York: W. W. Norton, 2000) is a necessary starting point. Marylin Strathern's *The Gender of the Gift: Problems with Women and Problems with Society in Melanesia* (Berkeley: University of California Press, 1988) offers an excellent overview of gift giving in Melanesia—where gift giving plays an especially prominent role in the social lives of many societies—and how

anthropologists should think of those issues.

••••••••••••••••••••

For a useful overview of the field of economic anthropology and its primary theoretical debates and orientations, see Richard R. Wilk and Lisa C. Cliggett's book *Economies and Cultures: Foundations of Economic Anthropology* (Boulder, CO: Westview Press, 2007).

••••••••••••••••••••

When the Soviet Union fell, anthropologists working in Russia and Eastern Europe found themselves in an interesting position trying to document and analyze the dramatic social transformations that were playing out in front of them. Two excellent books on this transformation are Caroline

Humphrey's *The Unmaking of Soviet Life: Everyday Economies After Socialism* (Ithaca, NY: Cornell University Press, 2002) and Katherine Verdery's book *What Was Socialism? What Comes Next?* (Princeton, NJ: Princeton University Press, 1996).

••••••••••••••••••••

The 2008 financial crisis in the United States, which spread to many other countries, revealed to many people the powerful role Wall Street plays in shaping the economic prospects of people who have nothing to do with investment banking. Karen Ho's *Liquidated: An Ethnography of Wall Street* (Durham, NC: Duke University Press, 2009) provides a rich and in-depth ethnographic description of how investment banking culture operates.

••••••••••••••••••••

Sustainability

Environment and Foodways

Once every ten years, people from all over the world attend the World Parks Congress, a conference on formally protected wilderness areas and national parks. During September 2003, several thousand park administrators, policymakers, and scientists from over sixty countries convened in Durban, South Africa. Also in attendance were some 150 leaders of indigenous peoples from around the world. Their clothing of colorful beadwork and headdresses with bright feathers provided a sharp contrast to the dark suits and blazers of the other attendees. Even more dramatic than their clothing, however, was their message of protest: conservationists had to stop abusing indigenous people who traditionally owned and used lands now in conservation areas.

During the Congress, indigenous leaders argued that the dominant model for administering protected areas, which is based on the idea that nature must be kept uninhabited by people, has been a disaster for their communities. They insisted that parks force evictions of indigenous peoples, disrupting their customary livelihoods, ability to feed themselves, and indigenous systems of environmental management.

Indigenous Rights and the Challenge to Conservation. In recent years tensions between indigenous peoples and conservation have intensified over the perception that conservationists do not respect indigenous peoples' rights to land or the validity of their relationships with the environment. Indigenous people, such as the Indians from Brazil pictured here, have become increasingly assertive about protecting those rights in national and international conferences.

395

Parks deny traditional land rights and sometimes lead to repression. In some cases, park administrators have allowed mining and fossil fuel exploration on the very lands formerly inhabited by indigenous groups (Colchester 2003).

The organizers of the conference saw the situation quite differently. They emphasized that parks contribute to economic development and help alleviate poverty. Their approach emphasized the ideals of **sustainable development**, defined as "development that meets the needs of the present without compromising the ability of future generations to meet their own needs" (WCED 1987). For its advocates, sustainable development means that nature protection must address local people's abilities to make a living, involve them in conserving natural resources, and create alternatives to economic activities that deplete natural resources (Wapner 1996:83). Congress organizers wanted to showcase how nature protection will lead to the sustainable development of indigenous and other rural communities.

In theory, it would seem that indigenous people should be strong allies of those who seek sustainable development. Some of the world's most pristine landscapes have had indigenous people living on them for a long time. The late geographer Bernard Nietschmann called this "[t]he Rule of Indigenous Environments: Where there are indigenous peoples with a homeland there are still biologically rich environments" (1992:3). Since the 1970s, environmentalists and indigenous groups have often come together to fight the destruction of some of those landscapes.

But as the Congress protests demonstrate, their interests often clash because they have different relationships to nature and histories of using it, and nature protection agendas often conflict with the agricultural traditions and social agendas of communities who live on or once lived on those landscapes. These issues lead us to the question at the heart of this chapter: *Why do some societies apparently have sustainable relations with the natural world while others seem to be more destructive?* Embedded in this broader question are the following problems, around which this chapter is organized:

- **Sustainable development.** Development that meets the needs of the present without compromising the ability of future generations to meet their own needs (WCED 1987).

Do all people conceive of nature in the same way?

How do people secure an adequate, meaningful, and environmentally sustainable food supply?

How is non-Western knowledge of nature and agriculture similar to and different from science?

How are industrial agriculture and economic globalization linked to increasing environmental and health problems?

Do only industrialized Western societies protect and conserve nature?

Different views of the natural world are closely related to distinct environmental management and food acquisition strategies. The environmental beliefs, knowledge, and practices of different societies, as well as their foodways, have long been major concerns at the heart of cultural anthropology. Although anthropologists traditionally studied these issues in small-scale, non-Western societies, in recent years attention has shifted to the effects of global economic changes on human–nature relations and what sustainability means for different people in all societies. We begin by exploring how a people's environmental values and behaviors emerge from particular ways of thinking about the natural world.

Do All People Conceive of Nature in the Same Way?

What nature means and how people see themselves in relation to it vary greatly around the world. Consider, for example, the relationships between indigenous settlement and natural ecosystems in southern Mexico and Central America (Figure 15.1). Some of these areas, such as the Yucatán Peninsula, the Petén region of Guatemala, and the Miskito Coast of Nicaragua, have been inhabited for many centuries. After the arrival of the Spanish in the 1500s they were safe areas for indigenous people because the Spanish conquerors found the tropical heat and diseases undesirable (Lovgren 2003). Why did the indigenous people not simply cut the forest down for fields, as European settlers did in other parts of the New World?

One reason was their low population density and subsistence economies based on swidden agriculture (see below) in which fields go back to forest to fallow after harvesting. But economic practices alone do not explain good stewardship; for that we need to understand the indigenous views of their environment. As Ken Rapp of the Center for the Support of Native Lands recently observed, "It's part of their belief system. They don't see a division between nature and man" (Lovgren 2003).

The Human–Nature Divide?

A good example of Rapp's statement about beliefs and good stewardship of the environment is the Itzaj, a Maya group that has lived in the Petén tropical lowlands of Guatemala since before Spanish contact. According to Itzaj beliefs, humans and nature do not occupy separate realms; there is both real and spiritual reciprocity and communication between plants, animals, and humans. For example, forest spirits called *arux* (masters of the wind) continually monitor people, and they play tricks on those who cut down too many trees or kill too many animals (Atran 2001:169). It is not accidental that Itzaj agricultural practices respect and preserve the forest.

The Cultural Landscape

Environmental anthropologists—practitioners of the branch of anthropology that studies how different societies understand, interact with, and make changes to nature—have long insisted that it is important to understand the abstract ideas that

- **Environmental anthropologists.** Practitioners of the branch of anthropology that studies how different societies understand, interact with, and make changes to nature and natural ecosystems.

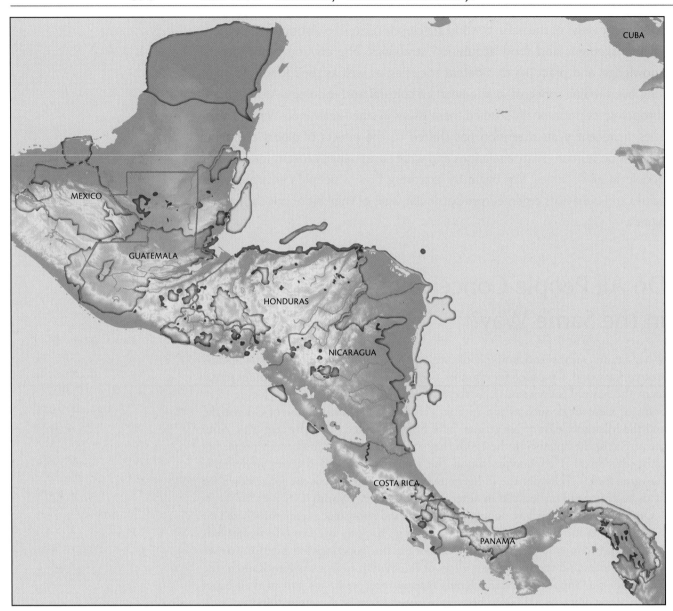

Figure 15.1   Linkages Between Biological and Cultural Diversity.   This map, which is a simplified version of a map produced by the Center for the Support of Native Lands and originally published in *National Geographic,* superimposes the distribution of cultural diversity and the distribution of biological diversity in Central America and southern Mexico. The areas outlined in red mark zones where indigenous populations live and where intact biodiverse ecosystems can be found.

influence people's interactions with landscapes. One way to think of these abstract ideas is through the concept of a **cultural landscape**, which holds that people have images, knowledge, and concepts of the physical landscape that affect how they will actually interact with it (Stoffle, Toupal, and Zedeño 2003:99). For example, the Itzaj consider nature to be an extension of their social world, full of spirits that influence their everyday lives. As a result, they are less likely to wantonly destroy the landscape in which they live because such acts would equate to hurting themselves. Different social groups can also hold distinctly different and conflicting ideas of the same landscape. As we explore in "Classic Contributions: Roy Rappaport's Insider and Outsider Models," understanding how cultural concepts of nature (referred to here as "cognized models") guide behavior has long been a priority of environmental anthropology.

Key to understanding the cultural landscape is the idea that people use metaphors to think about their natural environments, and these metaphors are connected to social behavior, thought, and organization (Bird-David 1993:112). For example, in many hunting-and-gathering societies, people use metaphors of personal relatedness—sexuality, marriage, or family ties—to describe human–nature relations. An illustration

CLASSIC CONTRIBUTIONS

Roy Rappaport's Insider and Outsider Models

THE AMERICAN ANTHROPOLOGIST Roy Rappaport (1926–1997) was a major figure in the field of ecological anthropology, whose specific focus was on the relationship between humans and natural ecosystems. He was a pioneer in the use of systems theory for understanding human populations. In his landmark 1968 study *Pigs for the Ancestors: Ritual in the Ecology of a New Guinea People* (1984), Rappaport distinguished between the insider's mental models of human–nature relations called "cognized models" and "operational models," the ecological dimensions of human–nature relations identified by the observer. He argues that the goal of the anthropologist is to figure out how cognized models guide behavior, and how that behavior helps people adapt to specific environmental conditions:

[T]wo models of the environment are significant in ecological studies, and I have termed these "operational" and "cognized." The operational model is that which the anthropologist constructs through observation and measurement of empirical entities, events, and material relationships. He takes this model to represent, for analytic purposes, the physical world of the group he is studying. . . .

The cognized model is the model of the environment conceived by the people who act in it. The two models are overlapping, but not identical. While many components of the physical world will be represented in both, the operational model is likely to include material elements, such as disease germs and nitrogen-fixing bacteria, *that affect actors but of which they may not be aware. Conversely, the cognized model may include elements that cannot be shown by empirical means to exist, such as spirits and other supernatural beings. . . . [T]he important question concerning the cognized model, since it serves as a guide to action, is not the extent to which it conforms to "reality" (i.e., is identical with or isomorphic with the operational model), but the extent to which it elicits behavior that is appropriate to the material situation of the actors, and it is against this functional and adaptive criterion that we may assess it.* [Rappaport 1984:237–38; emphasis in the original]

Questions for Reflection

1. What are some reasons Rappaport might advocate a balanced approach between "cognized" and "operational" models of human–nature interactions?

2. Can you identify some elements of the insider's view or "cognized model" of our own society?

of this notion is from the Cree who live throughout northern Canada, who describe hunting through sexual metaphors. The hunter "courts" the prey, whether moose, bear, or caribou, using magic and songs to "seduce" it. Hunters describe the kill as sexual intercourse, and its result (the carcass) is believed to be the joint product of hunter and prey. The male hunters, and the women who prepare the carcass to be eaten, are expected to show great respect to the prey (especially by using all parts of the carcass), because they see killing animals as ensuring the reproduction of both humans and animals. In this metaphoric way the Cree think of animals as married to humans.

• **Cultural landscape.** The culturally specific images, knowledge, and concepts of the physical landscape that help shape human relations with the landscape.

Metaphors are always complex, and different people may not understand them in the same ways. Nevertheless, metaphors offer insights into a community's cultural landscapes that symbolize the society's feelings and values about its environment. Yet, whether a society has sustainable relations with nature depends on many factors beyond how they conceptualize human–nature relations, a theme we examine in the next section.

● ●

THINKING CRITICALLY ABOUT SUSTAINABILITY

People's metaphors of human–nature relatedness reflect and communicate what they know about how to work a landscape, and these are important guides to action. Can you think of any metaphors of human–nature relatedness in our society? How do you think those metaphors relate to people's actual interactions with nature?

● ●

How Do People Secure an Adequate, Meaningful, and Environmentally Sustainable Food Supply?

How people think of their landscapes is also intertwined with how they actually get their living from it, specifically, how a community gets and thinks about its food. Anthropologists call the structured beliefs and behaviors surrounding the production, distribution, and consumption of food **foodways**. There are important cross-cultural variations in foodways, which we explore here.

Modes of Subsistence

Cultural anthropologists have long studied **modes of subsistence**, which refers to how people actually procure, produce, and distribute food. There are four major modes:

1. **Foraging**, or the search for edible things.
2. Horticulture, or small-scale subsistence agriculture.
3. Pastoralism, which means the raising of animal herds.
4. Intensive agriculture, or large-scale, often commercial, agriculture.

For the past several thousand years, intensive agriculture has furnished most people with most of their food supplies. But foraging, horticulture, and pastoralism—which we covered in Chapter 12 on the Neolithic Revolution—are still important dimensions in many of the world's diets because societies are rarely committed to a single mode of subsistence, often combining two or more modes.

Foraging

As we explained in Chapter 12, foraging refers to searching for edible plant and animal foods without domesticating them. Hunter-gatherers, who obtain their

- **Foodways.** Structured beliefs and behaviors surrounding the production, distribution, and consumption of food.

- **Modes of subsistence.** The social relationships and practices necessary for procuring, producing, and distributing food.

- **Foraging.** Obtaining food by searching for it, as opposed to growing or raising the plants and animals people eat.

subsistence through a combination of collecting foods and hunting prey, are foragers. Most foragers have mobile lives, traveling to where the food happens to be rather than moving the food to themselves (Bates 1998). Low population densities ensure that their impacts on the environment tend to be minimal.

A common stereotype is that foraging is a brutal struggle for existence. This stereotype is inaccurate, because in reality foragers tend to work less to procure their subsistence than people who pursue horticulture or pastoralism. For example, Richard Lee found that !Kung San (also known as Ju/'hoansi) hunter-gatherers of the Kalahari Desert in Southern Africa spent less than twenty hours per week getting food (Lee 1969). Foragers also tend to view their environments not as harsh but as giving (Figure 15.2). It is easy to view foraging communities as a survival of our Paleolithic past since humans lived this way for 99% of our history. But contemporary foragers tend to inhabit extreme environments where horticulture or pastoralism are not feasible, such as the desert, the Arctic tundra, or certain rain forests, and participate in global and regional economies and political processes.

Horticulture

Horticulture is the cultivation of gardens or small fields to meet the basic needs of a household. It is sometimes referred to as subsistence agriculture, which refers to cultivation for purposes of household provisioning or small-scale trade, but not investment (Bates 1998). Horticulture emerged some 12,000 years ago with domestication, which gave humans selective control over animal and plant reproduction and increased the amount of reliable food energy (Bates 1998:70) (Figure 15.2).

In horticulture, farmers cultivate small plots and employ relatively simple technologies (hand tools like knives, axes, and digging sticks, for example) that have low impacts on the landscape. The most common form of horticulture is **swidden** (slash and burn) **agriculture** in which a farmer cuts forest and burns the vegetation. In some geographic areas, such as the tropics, swidden agriculture is important because burning the vegetation improves the nutrient-poor soils. A farmer can use this plot for several years, usually planting up to a few dozen different crops that mature or ripen at different times, often over a period of two to four years. These gardens often imitate the ecological diversity and structure of the rain forest itself, with some plants living in the understory shade, others in the partly shaded middle level, and others in the sunny top. By the time the

- **Horticulture.** The cultivation of gardens or small fields to meet the basic needs of a household.

- **Swidden agriculture.** A farming method in tropical regions in which the farmer slashes (cuts down trees) and burns small patches of forest to release plant nutrients into the soil. As soil fertility declines, the farmer allows the plot to regenerate the forest over a period of years.

Figure 15.2   !Kung San Hunter-Gatherers in Namibia.

Figure 15.3   Horticulture in Papua New Guinea. Mixed garden in fence in lowland Ningerum area (left). Freshly planted sweet potato mounds in Highland New Guinea (top right). A married couple in their mature Highland sweet potato garden (bottom right).

- **Pastoralist societies.** Groups of people who live by animal husbandry, which is the breeding, care, and use of domesticated herding animals such as cattle, camels, goats, horses, llamas, reindeer, and yaks.

- **Animal husbandry.** The breeding, care, and use of domesticated herding animals such as cattle, camels, goats, horses, llamas, reindeer, and yaks.

crops are all harvested the soil is depleted, and the farmer will move to another plot to repeat the process. Old plots lie fallow, and if there are no other pressures on them, such as population growth or new settlers coming to a rain forest area, a farmer might not return to work one of these fallow plots for several decades (Figure 15.3).

Pastoralism

Pastoralist societies live by **animal husbandry**, which is the breeding, care, and use of domesticated herding animals such as cattle, camels, goats, horses, llamas, reindeer, and yaks (Bates 1998). Rather than raising animals for butchering as food, pastoralists mainly consume their milk and blood and exploit their hair, wool, fur, and the ability of animals to pull or carry heavy loads. This approach allows them to get more out of the animal in the long run. Pastoralists typically occupy the landscapes beyond the reaches of productive agricultural lands, especially arid scrublands where irrigation cannot reach (Figure 15.4).

Because a livestock herd can do quick, even irreparable, damage to vegetation in arid landscapes, this mode of subsistence requires the constant movement of herds through a landscape (Igoe 2004). This movement does not depend on the whims of the animals or the individual herder but is typically coordinated among herd-owning households. At the heart of this system is common ownership of land and social institutions that ensure herders do not sacrifice the fragile environment for short-term individual gains, including livestock exchanges to redistribute and limit herd size, punishments for individuals who diverge from planned movement patterns, and defense of rangeland boundaries to prevent invasions by neighboring pastoral groups (McCabe 1990). When these institutions work successfully, pastoralism is a sustainable mode of subsistence, *providing people with a stable source of nutritious foods* (milk, blood, and meat) without irreversibly destroying the fragile landscape.

Intensive Agriculture

While the goals of horticulture and pastoralism are to feed families, the goal of intensive agriculture is to increase yields to feed a larger community. Approaches to **intensification**, which refers to processes that increase yields (Bates 1998), include:

- *Preparing the soil*, with regular weeding, mulching, mounding, and fertilizers.
- *Technology*, often simple, such as a harness or yoke that allows a farmer to use horses or oxen to plow a field; complex, such as a system of canals, dams, and water pumps that provide irrigation to an arid landscape; or very complex, like a combine harvester, a machine that harvests, threshes, and cleans grain plants like wheat, barley, and corn.
- *Using a larger labor force*, such as in Asian rice farming, which sustains the nutritional and energy needs of large populations and provides many people with employment (although the yield does not always increase enough to feed the additional workers) (Geertz 1963).
- *Water management*, ranging from the practice of adding pebbles to fields to retain soil moisture (as ancient Pueblo dwellers of North America did), to large-scale irrigation systems managed by modern states.
- *Modifying plants and soils*, through selective breeding of plants to produce better yields, reduce the time needed to mature, or create a more edible product, as farmers have done for major grains like maize, rice, and wheat (Bates 1998).

Intensification carries certain trade-offs. On the one hand, it solves an important problem, which is how to provide food for a large number of people, including those who do not work directly in food production. It also provides a relatively steady supply of food, though famines can still happen. On the other hand, intensification can create environmental problems. By rearranging ecosystems to achieve greater control over nature, intensive agriculture is vulnerable to declining environmental conditions. For example, clearing a hillside to plant crops, build terraces, or install water works may increase productivity in the short run, but these can lead to the erosion of topsoils, lowering of water tables, concentration of salts in soils, the silting up of waterworks, and so on.

The most intensive form of agriculture is **industrial agriculture**, which applies industrial principles to farming. Key principles include specialization to produce a single crop, and the obtaining of land, labor, seeds, and water as commodities on the open market. This form of agriculture is characteristic of highly industrialized and postindustrial economies in which only 1 to 5% of the population engages in food production.

Through the use of machines, industrial agriculture harnesses sources of energy such as steam power and petroleum, vastly increasing the scale of productivity. Technology-based farming has also redefined our notion of what agricultural work is (Figure 15.5). On some farms, such as those that produce grains like corn and wheat, farming now means tending to huge machines that provide nearly all the actual farm labor (Bates 1998). As a result of mechanization, a small rural labor force (less than 2% of the total U.S. population) produces so much food that one of industrial agriculture's greatest economic problems is *over*production.

Food, Culture, and Meaning

As the variability in modes of subsistence demonstrates, the human species evolved to be adaptable to many different environments. The human diet also evolved to be

Figure 15.4 Pastoralist in Afghanistan.

- **Intensification.** Processes that increase yields.

- **Industrial agriculture.** The application of industrial principles and methods to farming.

Figure 15.5 Factory Farms in the Twenty-First Century. In the United States, most of the farms that produce meat, eggs, and dairy products are organized on industrial principles. These farms create economies of scale to reduce costs and maximize profits.

flexible, and the range of things the human species can and does eat is tremendous. But our actual everyday diets usually involve a limited range of foods, determined by what is available, dietary restrictions, and by what we have learned to prefer as members of a particular social community. Foodways are always shaped by cultural beliefs and governed by systematic rules and etiquette particular to a social group. These cultural processes have implications for human sustainability because they also shape how people think about and interact with landscapes through foodways.

For example, those of us who get our food from supermarkets tend to think of food as material, impersonal, and dissociated from the producer and the natural environment, reflecting a distinctly urban view of nature as separate from the human domain. In contrast, the Hua, who live in the Eastern Highlands of Papua New Guinea, believe that food possesses mystical dynamism, vitality, and danger (Meigs 1997). For the Hua, the act of eating unites them with the individual who produced or shared food with them and invigorates them with the vital essences of the organisms they are consuming. Because food is so spiritually powerful, humans are susceptible to its influences. To channel and protect these essences, Hua have devised many rules governing who can grow, handle, share, and eat certain foods, as well as how those foods are grown.

Foodways Communicate Symbolic Meaning

In every society, food is a rich source of meaning, and people use it to communicate specific messages. Particular foods and meals can draw people together, especially when they share and consume foods that symbolize concepts like home, family, or conviviality. When you are homesick, the yearning for certain "comfort foods" is not just a desire for a familiar taste. It is also satisfying because it ties you symbolically to home and family. But food can just as easily communicate division and unequal power relations, as with so-called sumptuary laws that limit consumption of certain items along class lines. For example, in Renaissance England the Parliament passed a law that allowed "gentlemen" to eat two courses of meat and fish during a meal, but restricted their servants to only one course of meat during the day, leaving them to eat foods consisting of milk, butter, and cheese the rest of the day.

The use of food as a form of symbolic communication is so pervasive that some anthropologists have suggested that food operates with logic similar to that of language. English anthropologist Mary Douglas, for example, observed that an English formal dinner takes on a certain precise order, just like a sentence: appetizers, soup, fish, and so on to dessert (Anderson 2005:110; Douglas 1966). There is nothing necessary about having sweets at the end of a meal except that we have become used to it. Elsewhere in the world, sweets may be absent or may regularly come earlier in the meal. All of these feel like the "right" order to a meal in particular cultures, and may seem very wrong to others.

Foodways Mark Social Boundaries and Identities

Food preferences, etiquette, and taboos also mark social boundaries and identities. As anthropologist Carole Counihan (1999:8) has observed, "One's place in a social system is revealed by what, how much, and with whom one eats." Eating practices might mark gender differences, as when men and women eat different foods. They might mark ethnic or regional differences, as particular groups identify themselves closely with certain foods. Or they could mark profession or class status, as certain individuals consume certain foods identified with their social station (Lentz 1999). These social markers are closely related to differing notions of **taste** that may exist between or within groups. *Taste* can refer to both the physical sensation on the tongue (as in "this crab cake tastes good") and social distinction and prestige (as in "her consumption of fine wine shows she has good taste") (MacBeth 1997).

- **Taste.** A concept that refers to the sense that gives humans the ability to detect flavors; taste can also refer to the social distinction and prestige associated with certain foodstuffs.

Every society has a notion of the "perfect meal," which typically reflects people's culturally acquired tastes and is closely identified with their social identity and subsistence patterns as a group. For example, German anthropologist Gerd Spittler (1999) found that among the Kel Ewey Tuareg [kell **eh**-way **twar**-egg] nomads who live in the Sahara desert region in northern Mali, West Africa, the perfect meal is simple and is always the same for everybody, regardless of their relative wealth, involving cheese, dates, camel or goat milk, and the grain millet. Spittler theorizes that Tuareg prefer this meal because it identifies them as a people that provides a stable diet for all its members in a precariously dry environment. These Tuareg view variety in the diet— something that many of us take for granted—as a characteristic of people who must be so desperately poor and hungry they are forced to eat anything they can find.

Foodways Are Dynamic

Because foodways are so bound up with people's identities, it is easy to assume that people always hold on to them tightly. In some cases, foodways are remarkably persistent. For example, the diet in the southern Spanish region of Andalucía is about the same as it was during Roman times: crusty bread, olive oil, eggs, pork, wine, cabbage, herbs, onions, and garlic (Anderson 2005:163).

But foodways can also change for many reasons. Environmental changes, like overhunting or overfishing, alter what is available. Or people begin to identify certain foods with good health, such as the reputation beef held among North Americans during the mid-twentieth century, but which in recent decades has given way to new ideas about the healthiness of a diet based on vegetables, whole grains, and so on. Or formerly expensive foods, like white bread and processed sugar, become inexpensive because of new processing techniques. And changes in family dynamics force changes in eating habits, such as in North America, where women's increasing involvement in the workforce (leaving nobody home to cook) has helped fuel the rapid rise of convenience foods such as fast food, frozen dinners, and family restaurants (Anderson 2005:165–68).

Although foodways are dynamic, people have a pretty stable concept of an appropriate diet that reflects their understanding of proper foods, good taste, and nutritional requirements. It is relatively stable because our biological requirements of adequate energy and nutrition and the cultural requirements of meaning and satisfaction are themselves fairly stable. Underlying these facts is a simple logic: if a diet works, if it provides sustenance, meaning, and sustainable ecological relations, then people are unlikely to drop everything when something new comes along. People integrate new foods and cuisines into their existing dietary practices all the time, usually gradually. But since the existing logic of any local foodway is already integrated into the production, preparation, and sharing of food, dramatic change is unlikely. As we will see in the next section, the systematic ways people understand nature and sustainable management of it are also profoundly shaped by culture.

THINKING CRITICALLY ABOUT SUSTAINABILITY

Even though most of us probably get our food from a supermarket, which is one element of the intensive/industrial agriculture mode of subsistence, can you identify examples of other modes of subsistence in our own society? How and why do these multiple modes of subsistence persist? Can you identify situations in which people combine modes of subsistence?

How Is Non-Western Knowledge of Nature and Agriculture Similar to and Different from Science?

Anthropologists try to describe the traditional knowledge that different societies have of their natural environments, recognizing that all knowledge systems about nature, including science, are culturally based. This goal dates back to the beginnings of anthropology as a discipline. For example, during his years among the Trobriand Islanders (1915–1918), Bronislaw Malinowski was keenly interested in people's knowledge of gardening, canoe building, and navigation. From observing these activities, he concluded that "primitive humanity was aware of the scientific laws of natural process" and magical processes, and he went on to add that all people operate within the domains of magic, science, and religion (1948:196).

Do native knowledge systems have scientific validity? Malinowski reasoned that if knowledge is born of experience and reason, and if science is an activity characterized by rationality, then indigenous knowledge is part of humankind's scientific knowledge (Nader 1996:7). Since his time, anthropologists have demonstrated that scientific attitudes and methods of validation—close observation, experimentation, and analysis—are not unique to the West (Nader 1996, 8). One key difference that distinguishes many non-Western knowledge systems from Western sciences, however, is that they are not necessarily viewed as distinct realms of knowledge, being integrated into people's spiritual beliefs and social practices, while in the West people tend to think of science as separate from all these things, as its own special domain of knowledge.

Ethnoscience

Early anthropological interest in knowledge systems of non-Western societies was called **ethnoscience**. During the 1960s, when ethnoscience was at its peak influence, ethnoscientists aimed to describe and understand the conceptual models and rules with which a society operates, following Malinowski's call for anthropologists to see the world from the "native's point of view" (Sturtevant 1964:100). They began by comparing the systems of classification used by the different peoples they studied.

Classification systems are reference systems that group things or ideas with similar features. Examples include plant and animal taxonomies, kinship terminologies, color schemes, and medical diagnoses. Classification systems create a common intellectual framework that people use to work with the natural world, heal the sick, and communicate with each other.

As discussed in Chapter 3, Western scientific disciplines use Linnaean taxonomy to classify all living organisms into species. Brent Berlin, who studied **ethnobiology** (indigenous ways of naming and codifying living things) of the Tzeltal Maya, has argued that the Tzeltal and most societies for whom we have data divide living things into groups based on shared morphological characteristics, as the Linnaen system does (Berlin 1973). Based on these findings, Berlin concluded that all human classification systems reflected a cognitive structure of the human brain that organizes information in systematic ways—in other words, that all human minds more or less think alike.

Numerous challenges to Berlin's conclusions exist, based largely on the observation that some societies use non-morphological characteristics to classify plants and

- **Ethnoscience.** The study of how people classify things in the world, usually by considering some range or set of meanings.

- **Ethnobiology.** The branch of ethnoscience that studies how people in non-Western societies name and codify living things.

animals. For example, the Kalam people of the Papua New Guinea Highlands do not classify the cassowary, a large flightless bird, as a bird. The Kalam classification system gives the cassowary a special taxonomic rank that places them close to humans (Bulmer 1967). Kalam mythology identifies the cassowary as sisters and cousins to Kalam men, and the Kalam place special restrictions on hunting them. The special taxonomic status of these creatures not only results from their unexpected physical characteristics (a bird that cannot fly) but also reflects certain social categories and relationships.

Traditional Ecological Knowledge

Ethnoscience's interests these days continue under the more general label **traditional ecological knowledge**, which studies indigenous ecological knowledge and its relationship with resource management strategies. One of the more important findings of this field is that many ecological relations recognized by indigenous peoples are not known to Western science. One reason is that this knowledge may involve species that are endemic, which means they exist only in one place. Another reason is that knowledge often resides in local languages, songs, or specialized ritual knowledge. Healers and shamans are important repositories of local plant knowledge and lore, and they may even keep their knowledge secret from other people in their own society. In recent years, controversy has erupted because pharmaceutical companies have been trying to gain access to the knowledge of traditional healers to identify plants that might be useful for developing new commercial drugs, sometimes without community consent (Brown 2003).

Because traditional ecological knowledge is customized to particular environments, it can also provide an effective basis for managing resources. For example, in the southern Mexican state of Oaxaca, Zapotec farmers have been growing maize on the same landscape for hundreds of years. Farmers have a systematic understanding of how soil qualities, weather patterns, lunar phases, plant–plant interactions, and plant–insect interactions affect the growing of maize (Gonzalez 2001). Western scientists have discovered that Zapotec practices of intercropping (planting multiple crops together), building soil mounds for planting maize, letting the land lie fallow, and planting and harvesting by the phases of the moon all contribute to creating a highly productive and sustainable agricultural system (Gonzalez 2001).

Some elements of Zapotec science do not correspond to Western science and beliefs about effective resource management, however. For example, ecological knowledge is not separate from other forms of knowledge, such as ideas about morally acceptable behavior. Zapotecs believe that cultivations, especially maize, have a soul that rewards people who share with others. They believe that the success of a harvest is directly related to the farmer's positive social relations with other members of the community.

The Zapotec case demonstrates that traditional ecological knowledge has allowed communities to thrive for a long time on a landscape without destroying it. Unlike Western sciences, which claim to have universal tools for understanding nature, the Zapotec knowledge of nature is rooted in local cultural traditions, beliefs, and landscapes. It is also not viewed as a separate domain of specialized knowledge but is integrated into people's daily lives, spiritual practices, and so on. In the contemporary world, such knowledge and practices are confronting new challenges related to the spread of industrial agriculture and economic globalization. In the next section, we examine how these challenges affect a community's environment and health.

- **Traditional ecological knowledge.** Indigenous ecological knowledge and its relationship with resource management strategies.

● ●

THINKING CRITICALLY ABOUT SUSTAINABILITY

The idea that traditional ecological knowledge provides an effective basis for managing natural resources is often resisted most strongly by Western agricultural scientists, who often dismiss these knowledge systems as not scientific and rigorous. How should environmental anthropologists respond to these kinds of claims?

● ●

How Are Industrial Agriculture and Economic Globalization Linked to Increasing Environmental and Health Problems?

Industrial agriculture and economic globalization are fueling change around the world, creating environmental problems and challenging health and sustainability. In analyzing these problems, anthropologists have found that environmental degradation results from a complex interplay of social, cultural, natural, and political-economic factors that relate to two important questions: How do people consume natural resources in their lifestyles and foodways? And who pays the cost of that consumption? In addressing these questions it is important to examine one of the most common—yet simplistic—explanations for environmental problems, which is population growth.

Population and Environment

Eighteenth-century theologian Thomas Malthus argued that human population grows exponentially, quickly overwhelming a limited resource base and leading to famine. Some modern environmentalists, such as Paul Ehrlich who in 1968 wrote a book with the alarming title *The Population Bomb*, have argued that the same is happening on a global scale in the world today. The problem seems self-evident: a small planet cannot indefinitely support a quickly expanding human population (now over seven billion), and ecological ruin awaits us.

There are several problems with this view. One is that social scientists have yet to identify any confirmed case of environmental and social collapse because of overpopulation or mass consumption (Tainter 2006) (see Chapter 12). Another is that humans have tended to adapt to the land's **carrying capacity**, which is the population an area can support, by developing new technologies and intensifying agriculture, as discussed earlier. Sustainable social systems also often respond by adopting new cultural practices to cope with rapid ecological deterioration. In other words, they are resilient, able to absorb change by changing social practices. For example, anthropologist Clifford Geertz (1963) was one of the first to document how Indonesians on different large islands had increased the carrying capacity through intensification. As populations rose, people began planting wet rice that produced higher yields than dry rice, and later with irrigation produced two or even three crops a year.

● **Carrying capacity.** The population an area can support.

Another example is in the floodplain of the Brazilian Amazon, where attempts to make commercial fisheries more sustainable have focused on how communities can themselves regulate fisheries (de Castro and McGrath 2003). To ensure that overfishing does not take place, communities sign formal fishing accords that regulate who has access to fisheries and the amounts they are allowed to keep. These accords have had some success in controlling commercial fishing, and they show that one of the keys to sustainability is to create innovative social institutions that help people collectively deal with changing environmental circumstances, in this case declining fisheries.

Anthropologists have also shown that the environmental disruptions that lead to famines are the result of a complex interplay of natural conditions and existing patterns of social inequality. For example, during the 1985 Ethiopian famine, Western aid and relief agencies like the World Food Program and the U.S. Agency for International Development argued that Ethiopia's population was too large, resulting in the overconsumption of natural resources, environmental collapse, and famine. Their solution was to implement programs of food relief and land reclamation projects to improve agricultural yield.

But these programs failed because the experts who conceived them misunderstood the complex causes of the famine. The experts based their models on exaggerated data about land degradation and ignored other data, particularly the disastrous effects of the country's civil war and socialist government, which disrupted food distribution channels. Insecure access to land also discouraged farmers from investing in traditional soil-conservation measures (Hoben 1995). This famine was not a consequence of overpopulation but the result of these other interrelated factors. No one of these factors by itself would have produced the famine and the environmental problems associated with it.

Ecological Footprint

None of these situations negate the fact that the planet's resources and ecological systems are enduring great stress. In the Malthusian view, sustainability is a matter of controlling population where it seems to be growing most. But it does not address a simple fact: different societies, as well as people within those societies, consume differing amounts of resources. If we want to think critically about global environmental problems, it is useful to start with this fact. The concept of an **ecological footprint** addresses this issue by measuring what people consume and the waste they produce. It then calculates the amount of biologically productive land and water area needed to support them. As Figure 15.6 demonstrates, people in industrialized countries consume much more than people in non-industrialized countries (Wackernagel et al. 1997). Of course, these are just averages; some individuals consume more and others less, usually related to their relative wealth or poverty.

The distinction between the average Indian and the average North American as shown in the image is the latter's involvement in consumer capitalism. Consumer capitalism promotes the cultural ideal that people will never fully satisfy their needs, so they continually buy more things in their pursuit of happiness. This cultural ideal has enormous consequences for sustainability. We see these consequences in the production of goods (the extraction of non-renewable raw materials to make consumer products); the distribution of goods (the reliance on fossil fuels to transport goods to market); and the consumption of goods (the landfills that get filled with non-organic trash). As a result, while Americans make up only 5% of the world's population, they consume 25% of its resources.

• **Ecological footprint.** A quantitative tool that measures what people consume and the waste they produce. It also calculates the amount of biologically productive land and water area needed to support those people.

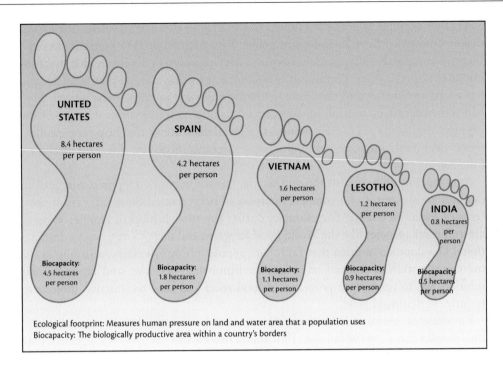

Ecological footprint: Measures human pressure on land and water area that a population uses
Biocapacity: The biologically productive area within a country's borders

Figure 15.6   The Ecological Footprints of Five Countries.

- **Green Revolution.** The transformation of agriculture in the Developing World that began in the 1940s, through agricultural research, technology transfer, and infrastructure development.

Most Americans do not understand the destructiveness of consumer lifestyles, although signs of it are everywhere: urban sprawl, polluted air and waterways, acid rain, unhealthy forests, climate change, and environmental health problems linked to contamination. In "Thinking Like an Anthropologist: Identifying Hidden Costs," we explore how the simple act of eating a hamburger relates to environmental degradation.

As the case of the hamburger demonstrates, industrial agriculture has important impacts on a landscape. In recent decades, thanks to the **Green Revolution**—the transformation of agriculture in the developing world through agricultural research, technology transfer, and infrastructure development—rural communities throughout the world have seen pressures to shift from traditional modes of subsistence and agriculture to industrialized agriculture. Important global institutions such as the World Bank have encouraged many countries in Latin America and Africa to produce non-traditional agricultural exports, commodities like houseplants, flowers, and melons. The goal is to generate foreign revenue by exporting items that other countries do not have, so that the countries can make investments in domestic development and pay back loans to those international institutions.

For small-scale subsistence farmers in Honduras studied by anthropologist Susan Stonich (1993), these pressures have generated dilemmas. Since the 1950s, large commercial cotton plantations and cattle ranches have encroached on small farmers, pushing them into less productive land on mountain slopes. As commercial farms have gotten larger, the size of small farms has declined, causing many farmers to give up and migrate to the cities. Those who remain on the farm have shifted from subsistence agriculture to growing cash crops for export. The pressure to produce high yields has led them to deforest hillsides and abandon soil conservation measures that take more work because they are on steep land, both of which undermine the long-term fertility of their lands. Eventually farmers find themselves in a desperate situation in which they are aware, as the title of Stonich's book suggests, that "I am destroying the land!"

Analyses that focus on the linkages between political-economic power, social inequality, and ecological destruction are typical of the approach called **political ecology**.

- **Political ecology.** The field of study that focuses on the linkages between political-economic power, social inequality, and ecological destruction.

Thinking Like an Anthropologist

Identifying Hidden Costs

ANTHROPOLOGISTS BEGIN THEIR research by asking questions. In this box, we want you to learn how to ask questions as an anthropological researcher. Part 1 describes a situation and follows up with questions we would ask. Part 2 asks you to do the same thing with a different situation.

PART 1: IDENTIFYING THE HIDDEN COSTS OF A HAMBURGER

In his book *Fast Food Nation*, Eric Schlosser points out that the typical American eats three hamburgers and four orders of french fries every week (2001:6). This meal epitomizes American tastes, but its desirability is also due to its low cost to the consumer—this meal comes in at around $4 or $5, perhaps even including a soda, at most fast-food restaurants. Why is the price so low? Traditional economists would answer that it is the fast food industry's technological efficiency and economy of scale that keep costs down. But these facts alone do not explain the low cost, because neither the consumer nor the industry actually pays the real costs for each of the ingredients that go into the meal. Revealing the hidden costs shows who and what bears the actual costs of fast food.

Each ingredient deserves analysis, but in the interest of space, let us consider only the beef that goes into the hamburger. Beef is a notoriously inefficient source of energy and protein. It takes about 2,700 pounds of grain or a couple of acres of pasture to produce a typical 1,050 pound steer (Robbins 2005). The amount of land and water it takes to raise beef cattle is much higher than that required for other forms of agriculture. In fact, our "waving fields of grain" are largely destined for livestock, not human, consumption: 80% of grain production in the United States is for livestock forage (Robbins 2005).

Ranchers do not pay the real costs of beef production but transfer those costs to taxpayers and the environment. Because most grazing land lies in the arid West, a steer needs as many as 200 to 300 acres to support it. To make so much land available to ranchers, Congress passed the Taylor Grazing Act in 1934, which transferred millions of acres of public land to ranchers if they took responsibility for improving them (Robbins 2005:224). These "improvements" are generally minor and self-interested (such as

🌱 **A Hamburger with All the Trimmings.**

barbed-wire fences), so taxpayers assume the greater costs of predator control, drought relief, disease control, and the costly reservoir and irrigation projects required to support cattle in arid lands. One fairly recent estimate calculates that the government subsidizes public land grazing as much as $500 million per year. If the government charged ranchers fees that reflected the real costs of supporting cattle in the arid West, it would annually charge ranchers $175 per steer (Wuerthner 2003).

But most beef cattle are fed grains and cereals. Grains quickly fatten the steer and have become inexpensive to buy because of chemical fertilizers, herbicides, and pesticides, which keep production costs down and enhance the productivity of grain farmers. To keep grain costs low, the government offers reduced tax rates on agricultural lands and pays farmers direct subsidies to protect them from market variations. And approximately half the water we as a nation consume is used to grow the grain needed to feed cattle (Robbins 2005:217). The amount of water used to produce ten pounds of steak equals the household water consumption of a family for an entire year (Robbins 2005)! It is taxpayers, not grain farmers, who assume the costs of building and maintaining expensive water reclamation and irrigation projects.

Water reclamation projects also have enormous ecological impacts, including flooding to create dams, silting of waterways, diversion of waterways, and effects on fish

(continued)

Thinking Like an Anthropologist (continued)

populations. Use of so many chemical fertilizers, pesticides, and herbicides also carries high ecological costs, damaging soil and groundwater throughout grain-producing areas. Finally, beef has to travel over subsidized highways with subsidized gasoline from where it is produced to where it is eaten.

These costs are not borne exclusively by the people of the United States alone, because Americans produce about 9% of beef in the world but consume about 28% of the world's beef production (Robbins 2005:226). Clearly, our analysis of beef's hidden costs would also have to take into account the ecological and social costs of raising beef in other countries.

What questions does the hidden cost of a burger raise for anthropological researchers?

1. What are the different steps involved in the production, distribution, and consumption of beef, and who is involved in this chain of relationships?
2. Who and what assumes the actual costs of production at each of these steps?
3. Why do some actors in this chain pay the costs more than others?
4. Why are the ecological costs of producing beef not paid by agricultural producers?

PART 2: FILLING YOUR TANK
The analysis of hidden costs on people and environments can be applied to virtually any part of a consumer lifestyle, even the most mundane. Consider developing some questions about the hidden costs of filling an automobile gas tank. What questions would you pose as an anthropological researcher in order to explore the hidden environmental and social costs of pumping gasoline?

Many anthropologists who study environmental problems align themselves closely with political ecology, which rejects single-factor explanations, like overpopulation, ignorance, or poor land use, as explanations for environmental degradation, and focuses instead on the socioenvironmental impacts of industrial economies.

Industrial Foods and Food Security

The industrialization of agriculture around the world is putting new pressures on foodways, with important dietary consequences for many people. These dynamics have contributed to certain health problems, such as obesity and overweight for some and hunger and malnutrition for others. Cash crops, tenant farming, and wage labor often undermine local **food security**, which refers to access to sufficient nutritious food to sustain an active and healthy life. As we see in "Anthropologist as Problem Solver: Migrant Farmworker Food Security in Vermont with Teresa Mares," what happens to rural people's food security when their foodways industrialize have become an important area of anthropological research and its application.

• **Food security.** Access to sufficient nutritious food to sustain an active and healthy life.

Because small-scale farms, which produce locally grown and nutrient-rich food, can rarely compete with the low-cost foods of transnational agribusinesses, many small-scale farms shut down their operations. With fewer farms to support rural livelihoods, people then migrate to urban areas where they occupy more sedentary and less physically active lives.

Anthropologist as Problem Solver

Migrant Farmworker Food Security in Vermont with Teresa Mares

KNOWN FOR ITS high-quality cheeses and as the home of the iconic ice cream brand Ben and Jerry's, the New England state of Vermont has long enjoyed a reputation as an idyllic agrarian landscape full of milking cows. But dairy farming is a difficult year-round job with unreliable financial returns due to fluctuations in the price of milk. The activity has shifted in the past sixty years from being managed primarily as small-scale family-run operations to what is now a highly mechanized industry consolidated into a small number of large farms. Unable to rely on locals, who no longer want to work on these farms, the Vermont dairy industry has increasingly staked its survival on the employment of low-wage migrant farmworkers, most of them undocumented laborers from southern Mexican states like Chiapas, Veracruz, and Oaxaca.

University of Vermont food anthropologist Teresa Mares, who studies how the diets and foodways of Latino/a immigrants change as a result of migration (Mares 2014), set out to research ethnographically what the lives of these farmworkers are like and how their dietary patterns have changed now that they work on dairy farms. She quickly found out through interviews with farmworkers and immigrants' rights advocates that working on a dairy farm in rural Vermont is a stressful and isolating experience. These farmworkers rarely get away from their places of work because they are afraid of being deported, a not-insignificant concern being so close to the Canadian border where federal immigration enforcement agents are common. Moreover, they have limited transportation to travel the long distances from the farms to the nearest towns.

Mares conducted a Community Food Security Assessment of farmworkers, which is a U.S. Department of Agriculture survey that measures household access to food, food availability and affordability, and community food production resources. The results showed that something most of us take for granted—the ability to go to a supermarket to get nutritious food—is almost impossible for these farmworkers, and they have to rely on others to do shopping for them, usually their employer or someone else who lives on or near the farm. These trips are often irregular, and miscommunication between Spanish and English speakers is a common problem, which results in hunger due to inconsistent access to food and food that is culturally unfamiliar or unaffordable.

There are multiple ironies to this situation, the most obvious one being that the very people producing Vermont's most iconic food product suffer from food insecurity and hunger. Another irony is that most of these people left their homes in rural Mexico in the first place because of food insecurity brought on by the kinds of globalizing factors now opening jobs for them in Vermont's dairy industry. Among these factors is the 1994 North American Free Trade Agreement (NAFTA), which displaced southern Mexican farmers who could not compete with cheaper American imports of midwestern corn and milk from various dairy states, including Vermont.

Teresa Mares.

A Pastoral Vermont?

(continued)

Anthropologist as Problem Solver (continued)

Recognizing an opportunity to address an acute problem and to create new opportunities for collaborative research with colleagues in other fields like agriculture and health, Mares worked with her university's extension office and community volunteers to create a program that would make seeds, tools, and technical guidance available to farmworkers so that they could plant their own vegetable and herb gardens on the dairy farms. Mares met regularly with farmworkers participating in the program, interviewing them at length about issues such as their knowledge about gardening techniques, what kinds of foods they liked to eat, cooking and household spending patterns. She also worked alongside them in gardens and kitchens—hoeing soils, transplanting seedlings, making meals, and so on—which are useful vantage points from which to observe their actual food practices.

This research has produced rich ethnographic insights into how farmworkers cope with food insecurity and struggle to maintain food practices that are meaningful to them, as well as the successes the program has made in improving farmworker food security. It has also been useful to the people who run the program, who have used Mares's data to assess the effectiveness of the program and to improve its delivery as they begin to address other issues of food insecurity in rural Vermont.

Questions for Reflection

1. Go to the USDA's Community Food Security Assessment Toolkit website (http://www.ers.usda.gov/media/327699/efan02013_1_.pdf) and review the kinds of data it seeks to collect. How do the data this toolkit elicits differ from the data one might gather from participant observation? In what ways do the two complement each other?

2. What kinds of ethical dilemmas accompany research in a community of undocumented farmworkers?

THINKING CRITICALLY ABOUT SUSTAINABILITY

There is perhaps no more consequential issue for the future of human environmental and bodily health than the changing foodways in the contemporary world. What role do you think anthropologists of food should play in the issues of changing foodways? What specific kinds of knowledge or interventions do you think are most appropriate for anthropologists?

Do Only Industrialized Western Societies Protect and Conserve Nature?

The World Parks Congress, described at the beginning of this chapter, is one aspect of a remarkable global phenomenon that began with the founding of the first national park at Yellowstone in 1872. Formal nature protection as we know it—national parks, wilderness areas, and so on—originated in the West, although it is spreading rapidly around the globe as one important solution to problems of environmental degradation and sustainability. Anthropologists have studied these processes closely, especially the social consequences of conservation for local communities.

In exploring whether non-Western societies have had similar intentions to conserve and protect, it is necessary to overcome a powerful stereotype that native peoples are "natural environmentalists" always in tune with the natural world (Figure 15.7).

Anthropologists have documented many examples of destructive indigenous relationships with nature, among them "aboriginal overkill" that led to human-caused extinctions toward the end of the Pleistocene era (Ice Age) (Krech 1999). The key to answering this section's question is to consider, first, how indigenous societies have created landscapes that either deliberately or unintentionally have the effect of protecting natural ecosystems and wildlife and, second, the ways in which Western societies approach the same objective.

Artifactual Landscapes

Upon close examination, many landscapes that appear "natural" to Westerners—sometimes the very landscapes that Westerners want to conserve without people on them—are actually the result of indigenous involvement and manipulation. In other words, they are **artifactual landscapes**, or products of human shaping.

An important example of an artifactual landscape is the East African savannas of northern Tanzania and southern Kenya. The Maasai, who live there as pastoralists, have extensively modified their environment to support their cattle. They burn scrub brush to encourage the growth of nutritious pasture grass, an act that helps support wildlife biodiversity because these are the same nutritious pastures that the savanna's world-famous wildlife populations of zebras, wildebeest, and other large animals also eat (Igoe 2004). But today, some of these fragile scrublands are in crisis because of overgrazing by Maasai cattle. To understand why they now overgraze, we must look at the clash between Western and Maasai notions of managing and conserving nature.

Figure 15.7   Stereotypes of Green Indians. In 1971 the "Keep America Beautiful" campaign developed by the U.S. government aired an antipollution television ad featuring an American Indian (actually an Italian American actor with the stage name of Iron Eyes Cody) who sheds a tear because of pollution. There is usually a large gap between such romantic stereotypes and the real conditions in which indigenous groups relate to their environments.

• **Artifactual landscapes.** The idea that landscapes are the product of human shaping.

The Culture of Modern Nature Conservation

To prevent overgrazing and to conserve resources for themselves and wildlife populations, Maasai traditionally practiced a form of pastoralism called *transhumant pastoralism*, in which they range over large territories of commonly held property on regular paths and cycles. During drought years, when pastures are most susceptible to overgrazing, the Maasai would traditionally bring cattle to swamp areas and permanent waterholes. But during the twentieth century, national parks and nature reserves were formed around these permanent wet areas (since a lot of wild animals congregate there, too), preventing Maasai access to them. Park administrators and scientists did not understand the delicate balance between people and wildlife that was sustained by the constant movement of people, their herds, and the wild animals. The result is that the Maasai were forced to overgraze areas outside the park during drought periods, creating great resentment among the Maasai, which has generated conflicts with park officials (Igoe 2004).

These park officials practice what anthropologist Dan Brockington (2002) calls "Fortress Conservation," an approach to conservation that assumes that local people threaten nature, and that for nature to be pristine the people who live there must be evicted. This approach was undergirded by the philosophical divide that Western cultures imposed between people and nature, and was enabled by European and American colonial expansion, which commonly instituted controls on native people's use of natural resources. The main reason was to eliminate native competition against the European businesses exploiting raw materials in the colonies (Grove 1995). This approach to conservation is precisely what indigenous leaders were protesting at the World Parks Congress because it has persisted beyond the colonial era.

Environmentalism's Alternative Paradigms

Anthropologists recognize that the displacement of local people for the purposes of conserving nature can be counterproductive, producing exclusion, resistance, and social tension. But we also recognize that environmentalism has multiple expressions.

During the past several decades there have been a number of experiments in "co-management" between international conservation groups and indigenous people. In places like Nepal, Alaska, Canada, Panama, Brazil, and Australia, indigenous people have been allowed to continue living in protected areas and have some say in park management. This collaborative approach creates new kinds of opportunities for dialogue, power sharing, and relationship building between conservationists and indigenous communities (Natcher, Hickey, and Hickey 2005). Nevertheless, national and international conservation groups can still exercise considerable control, especially over funding, and government scientists often disrespect indigenous knowledge about wildlife and landscape dynamics even though they are supposed to be "co-managing" the resources with the indigenous community (Igoe 2004:158; Nadasdy 2005).

At the heart of co-management is a move toward recognizing and redressing how social inequalities and injustices affect possibilities for conservation and environmental sustainability. An even stronger approach along these lines is the **environmental justice** movement, a social movement that addresses the linkages between racial discrimination and injustice, social equity, and environmental quality (Figure 15.8).

Environmental justice is now a global movement, and unlike environmentalism oriented toward creating nature preserves that tend to focus on scenic landscapes and biodiversity, environmental justice tends to be organized around the defense of a people's livelihood and social justice concerns (Guha 2000:105). A good international example of this kind of activism is Kenya's Green Belt Movement, which has involved poor rural women in planting trees. Between its founding in 1977 and 2005, Kenyan women have planted 30 million trees, creating over 600 community networks that care for 6,000 tree nurseries (Green Belt Movement 2005). The goal is to address the sources of social problems directly, specifically poor land use and bad governance, by promoting environmental projects that enhance community self-determination. In 2004, Wangari Maathai, the founder of the Green Belt Movement, received the Nobel Peace Prize, suggesting that environmental justice activism is gaining recognition among important global institutions.

Figure 15.8   The Birth of Environmental Justice. Environmental justice was born in the early 1980s, when a toxic waste dump was proposed in Warren County, North Carolina, the poorest county in the state and where 84% of residents were African American. Civil rights leaders organized a protest, arguing that these facts, not the ecological suitability of the site to store toxic waste, motivated the decision to build the waste dump in their county.

• **Environmental justice.** A social movement addressing the linkages between racial discrimination and injustice, social equity, and environmental quality.

THINKING CRITICALLY ABOUT ENVIRONMENTAL ANTHROPOLOGY

Americans often assume that people interested in conserving nature tend to be middle-class people who give money to environmental groups because they have met their other basic requirements, such as access to food, shelter, clothing, and other necessities. In other words, protecting nature is a luxury, and poor people cannot do it because they need to feed themselves. Based on what we have discussed in this section, why is this view skewed?

Conclusion

Anthropologists agree that we must pay close attention to the social practices and structures that shape the way communities relate to their natural environments. We can see that non-industrialized people often have a deep understanding of their environments, and they routinely understand the behaviors of animals and plants as well as, if not better than, scientists from other regions. In such communities, the cultural landscape envisions nature differently than do people in the West, using metaphors that often express people's reciprocal ties to the land.

If we want to understand why indigenous leaders showed up in Durban, South Africa, at the World Parks Congress in protest—as related in the story that opens this chapter—it was at least partially because Westerners, with their cultural landscape of human–nature separation, have not appreciated these facts. Instead, they have designed conservation programs that tend to expel indigenous peoples from landscapes they may have lived on sustainably for many years, even living in ways that support the biodiversity of other species, as is the case of the Maasai. Congress attendees apparently agreed, at least to some extent. In the consensus document published at the end of the Congress, "The Durban Accord," the participants accepted the necessity of a new paradigm for protected areas. Although over a decade later that new paradigm is still not yet worked out, this accord was widely viewed as a major victory for indigenous rights (Colchester 2003:21).

Anthropologists also agree that careful use of natural resources is the basis of a sustainable society. As a result, it is important to look critically at the current causes of the world's ecological crisis, which many prominent scholars and leaders claim is caused by recent, unchecked population growth. However, the causes of today's global ecological crisis—as was the case in past ecological crises—cannot be reduced to any single cause. We have to consider factors like elite mismanagement of resources, government policy choices, inflexible responses to change, and consumption patterns that extract key resources and create waste. We also have to consider who pays the cost of these patterns and realize that questions of unequal access to resources and social patterns of injustice are often at the heart of the world's key ecological crises.

KEY TERMS

Animal husbandry   p. 402

Artifactual landscapes
   p. 415

Carrying capacity   p. 408

Cultural landscape   p. 398

Ecological footprint
   p. 409

Environmental
   anthropologists   p. 397

Environmental
   justice   p. 416

Ethnobiology   p. 406

Ethnoscience   p. 406

Food security   p. 412

Foodways   p. 400

Foraging   p. 400

Green Revolution   p. 410

Horticulture   p. 401

Industrial agriculture
   p. 403

Intensification   p. 403

Modes of subsistence
   p. 400

Pastoralist societies   p. 402

Political ecology   p. 410

Sustainable development
   p. 396

Swidden agriculture
   p. 401

Taste   p. 404

Traditional ecological
   knowledge   p. 407

Reviewing the Chapter

Chapter Section	What We Know	To Be Resolved
Do all people conceive of nature in the same way?	Different cultures have different ways of conceptualizing the boundaries between humans and the natural world. Metaphors often play a major role in these conceptualizations.	Anthropologists continue to debate the extent to which general conceptual models and metaphors, or the material forces of nature itself, shape human relations with the environment.
How do people secure an adequate, meaningful, and environmentally sustainable food supply?	Humans have developed four general modes of subsistence—foraging, horticulture, pastoralism, and intensive agriculture—each of which carries certain social and environmental trade-offs and opportunities. Cultural meanings also play a central role in shaping how people acquire, share, and consume foods.	Although they are under great pressure in a world increasingly dominated by industrial and other forms of intensive agriculture, foragers, horticulturists, and pastoralists still persist. Anthropologists are working to understand how and why they persist, as well as the pressures on these modes of subsistence. In addition, anthropologists continue to work through how cultural attitudes and social practices surrounding food relate to social categories and dynamics such as class, race, ethnicity, and gender.
How is non-Western knowledge of nature and agriculture similar to and different from science?	Different societies have developed highly systematic and sophisticated knowledge systems for classifying the natural world, some of which resemble closely Western science. Unlike Western science, however, which views its methods and findings as universally applicable, these knowledge systems are often highly localized and customized to particular ecosystems and rooted in local moralities.	Anthropologists are still working to understand the specific ways in which traditional ecological knowledge shapes practices of ecological and agricultural management.
How are industrial agriculture and economic globalization linked to increasing environmental and health problems?	The ecological impact of a society depends on its ecological footprint, or the amount of natural resources people require to live their lifestyles. Industrial agriculture's rapid expansion around the globe is related closely to unequal political-economic relationships, and creates new environmental and health risks.	Anthropologists are still identifying the conditions under which social groups can adopt new cultural ideas and practices that promote resilience and sustainability. Anthropologists are also relatively new to public health policy discussions about critical issues, like food security and obesity, and have just begun to define the anthropological dimensions of these issues.
Do only industrialized Western societies protect and conserve nature?	While Western conservation practice is based on the separation of humans and nature, the stewardship traditions of non-Western societies often start from principles that view humans as important actors in nature. Western nature conservation practices have often disrupted and marginalized local cultures, many of which have had highly successful adaptations to their environments.	As some conservationists have realized new opportunities of co-managing natural resources with indigenous communities, anthropologists are divided over whether these approaches actually benefit indigenous communities.

Readings

There are several good general overviews of the field of environmental anthropology, among them Patricia Townsend's *Environmental Anthropology: From Pigs to Policies*, 2nd ed. (Long Grove, IL: Waveland Press, 2008) and Nora Haenn and Richard Wilk's edited reader *The Environment in Anthropology: A Reader in Ecology, Culture, and Sustainable Living* (New York: New York University Press, 2005).

• • • • • • • • • • • • • • • • • • •

Two books that explore dimensions of indigenous ways of knowing and interacting with natural environment include Roberto Gonzalez's study of farming in southern Mexico, *Zapotec Science: Farming and Food in the Northern Sierra of Oaxaca* (Austin: University of Texas Press, 2001) and ethnobotanist Gary Paul Nabhan's, *Cultures of Habitat: On Nature, Culture, and Story* (Washington, DC: Counterpoint, 1997).

• • • • • • • • • • • • • • • • • • •

To explore how differences between insider and outsider understandings of landscapes generate conflicts over conservation, read James Fairhead and Melissa Leach's 1996 book *Misreading the African Landscape: Society and Ecology in a Forest-Savanna Mosaic* (Cambridge: Cambridge University Press, 1996) and James Igoe's book *Conservation and Globalization: A Study of National Parks and Indigenous Communities from East Africa to South Dakota* (Belmont, CA: Wadsworth, 2004).

• • • • • • • • • • • • • • • • • • •

An excellent overview of the relationship between food and culture can be found in Eugene Anderson's *Everyone Eats: Understanding Food and Culture* (New York: New York University Press, 2005). It pairs well with Raj Patel's book *Stuffed and Starved: The Hidden Battle for the World Food System* (Brooklyn: Melville House Press, 2008) or Carole Counihan and Penny Van Esterik's 1997 edited volume *Food and Culture: A Reader* (New York: Routledge, 1997).

• • • • • • • • • • • • • • • • • • •

Power

Politics and Social Control

If you follow the news, you'll know that reporting on politics is a major focus of any newspaper or news website. Stories about what the president recently said, conflicts between political parties, or scandals involving local political figures tend to dominate the headlines. But even as these kinds of stories are the lifeblood of public discourse in any country, they offer a fairly narrow view of what politics actually is. Why do we not find stories like the following?

• In Papua New Guinea, a young woman commits suicide to protest being abused by a man in order to motivate her male relatives to seek justice and reparations.

• In a village in the Venezuelan Amazon, a Yanomamo headman scrapes the ground with a machete to shame others to join him in cleaning the village before a feast.

• In 1930s Italy, government officials concerned with the problem of declining fertility among the Italian people introduced a census, social insurance programs, housing projects, and social work to support an increase in the size, growth rate, and "vitality" of the population.

• In seventeenth-century colonial Virginia, leaders divided European and African settlers into groups based on "white" and "black" skin color to control the colony.

• In Hawai'i, a community leader guides disputing adversaries and family members through a healing process in which everyone is expected to share their feelings and grievances openly.

❦ **Revenge Suicide as Politics**   This painting (detail) represents a suicide perfomed as a revenge against wrongdoing in Papua New Guinea, by native artist Apa Hugo. See page 428 for a discussion of the complete image.

- **Politics.** Those relationships and processes of cooperation, conflict, and power that are fundamental aspects of human life.

Of course, one reason we do not find such reporting about politics in U.S. news is that these events have little or no immediate bearing on our lives. But it is easy to come to the conclusion that politics is simply what politicians or political parties said and did in the latest news cycle. Anthropologists take a wider view of **politics**, understanding it to be those relationships and processes of cooperation, conflict, social control, and power that are fundamental aspects of human life.

The preceding brief list also suggests that people exert power in diverse ways. Some of these are formal and fairly stable, through institutions and procedures—government offices, armies, codified laws, rituals, or legal proceedings—that are easily identifiable elements of most societies. Others are less formal and more fleeting, such as the creation of alliances, or acts of protest, accusation, sorcery, and shame. Techniques range from coercion and oppression to persuasion and influence, as well as truth-seeking, the collection and sharing of information, and the desire to know intimate details about people's lives.

This approach to politics moves beyond the idea that modern states, which function through elections, bureaucracies, and so on, should be the sole focus of anthropological interest. Just as important is the diversity in how people around the world manage power relations at all levels of social life, from the interpersonal to the national and transnational. We can hardly begin to understand this diversity if we focus exclusively on the formal institutions of modern states, because that approach misses the fact that cooperation, conflict, social control, and power are rooted in and emerge from people's everyday social interactions, belief systems, and cultural practices.

At the heart of anthropology's approach to politics is a key question: *How is power acquired and transmitted in a society?* Embedded in this broader question are the following problems, around which this chapter is organized:

Does every society have a government?

What is political power?

How is social inequality constructed and upheld?

Why do some societies seem more violent than others?

How do people avoid cycles of aggression, brutality, and war?

For anthropologists, politics is about how people manage their everyday social relationships through force, influence, persuasion, and control over resources. We begin here by examining the opportunities and pitfalls of thinking about politics solely in terms of how formal political systems work.

Does Every Society Have a Government?

This question might seem strange because the answer seems obvious. Our society has **government** (a separate legal and constitutional domain that is the source of law, order, and legitimate force) from federal to local levels. We may assume other societies must have something similar. Otherwise, wouldn't they be in the throes of anarchy?

Not necessarily. Consider the !Kung San (also known as Ju/'hoansi), a hunter-gatherer society in the Kalahari Desert of southern Africa. !Kung have historically lived in egalitarian bands of fifteen to twenty people, and are an **acephalous society**, that is, they have no governmental head or hierarchical structure. Until they were brought under the control of the Namibian and South African governments, !Kung had no notion of a distinct political sphere, and important band decisions were made by group consensus. Leadership was informal, life was organized around sharing food, and those who did not share were taunted and shamed, even pushed out of the band (Figure 16.1). The emphasis on sharing and egalitarianism kept people more or less in line without the need for government or **laws**, or rules established by some formal authority.

If governments are not a universal feature of human existence, why do we tend to think of politics primarily in terms of how formal governments work? Part of the reason is historical, the other part philosophical.

The Idea of "Politics" and the Problem of Order

Our modern notion of politics emerged during the Enlightenment (1650–1800), a period of social upheaval in Western Europe in which the rise of industrial capitalism and revolutionary democracies challenged the existing social and political order. Two of the major figures concerned with the problem of disorder caused by these changes were the English philosophers Thomas Hobbes (1588–1679) and John Locke (1632–1704). Hobbes believed that humans are naturally selfish, competitive,

- **Government.** A separate legal and constitutional domain that is the source of law, order, and legitimate force.

- **Acephalous society.** A society without a governing head, generally with no hierarchial leadership.

- **Laws.** Sets of rules established by some formal authority.

Figure 16.1   The Power of Sharing.   In many hunter-gatherer societies, such as the !Kung San pictured here, individuals are obligated to share their goods, especially food. This obligation represents a powerful force for ensuring social stability.

- **Structural-functionalism.** An anthropological theory that the different structures or institutions of a society (religion, politics, kinship, etc.) functioned to maintain social order and equilibrium.

- **Age-grades.** Groupings of age-mates, who are initiated into adulthood together.

- **Band.** A small, nomadic, and self-sufficient group of anywhere from 25 to 150 individuals with face-to-face social relationships, usually egalitarian.

- **Tribe.** A type of pastoral or horticultural society with populations usually numbering in the hundreds or thousands in which leadership is more stable than that of a band, but usually egalitarian, with social relations based on reciprocal exchange.

- **Chiefdom.** A political system with a hereditary leader who holds central authority, typically supported by a class of high-ranking elites, informal laws, and a simple judicial system, often numbering in the tens of thousands with the beginnings of intensive agriculture and soma specialization.

- **State.** The most complex form of political organization, associated with societies that have intensive agriculture, high levels of social stratification, and centralized authority.

- **Non-centralized political system.** A political system, such as a band or a tribe, in which power and control over resources are dispersed among members of the society.

and warlike, leading to violence and a chaotic free-for-all as people pursue their own personal interests, a condition avoided only by the absolute rule of a monarch (Hobbes 1909). Locke argued that chaos was avoidable by creating a more limited government based on a "social contract" in which certain basic individual rights are recognized (Locke 2003). This is our modern idea—and justification—for democratic government, and it is what modern politicians refer to when they talk about the "rule of law."

Structural-Functionalist Models of Political Stability

By the 1920s, the global expansion of British colonialism over the previous century meant that colonial administrators had to govern hundreds of diverse indigenous societies in Africa, Asia, the Pacific and the Caribbean. Colonial authorities often turned to anthropologists to help them make sense of these foreign societies, which gave rise to the discipline of anthropology in the United Kingdom. This situation presented British anthropologists with important opportunities for studying the maintenance of order in societies without formal governments and political leaders. The theory they developed was **structural-functionalism**, which held that the different structures of a society (such as religion, politics, kinship, etc.) functioned in an integrated way to maintain social order and control.

In Africa, structural-functionalists identified numerous ways societies maintained order and social control without formal political institutions (Radcliffe-Brown 1952). For example, kinship could work, as it did among the Nuer pastoralists of Sudan, to organize men into lineages that would normally live separately but would come together to meet external threats. The division of men from different families into associations like **age-grades**, which are groupings of age-mates who are initiated into adulthood together, such as among the Maasai of Kenya and Tanzania, could work as a rudimentary political system (Kurtz 2001). Throughout Africa, for example, beliefs in witchcraft or sorcery can also promote order. People who do not behave according to community norms are identified and punished as witches, a practice that maintained the social norms. Without formal courts, structural-functionalists insisted, such practices maintained social control and operated as a simple criminal justice system (Gledhill 2000).

Neo-Evolutionary Models of Political Organization: Bands, Tribes, Chiefdoms, and States

In the 1940s and 1950s, as political anthropology was taking shape in the United States, American anthropologists called *neo-evolutionists* sought to classify the world's diversity of political systems and explain how complex political systems, especially states, had evolved from simpler forms of social and political organization.

Anthropologist Elman Service (1962) suggested a typology of societies with different forms of political and economic organization. By considering who controls food and other resources in any given society, they defined four types of society: **bands**, **tribes**, **chiefdoms**, and **states**. Bands and tribes in this scheme were examples of **non-centralized political systems**, in which power and control over resources are dispersed among members of the society. Chiefdoms and states were examples of **centralized political systems**, in which certain individuals and institutions hold power and control over resources. Table 16.1 outlines how this classification incorporates politics, economy, size, and population density.

TABLE 16.1 A NEO-EVOLUTIONARY TYPOLOGY OF POLITICAL ORGANIZATION			
	NON-CENTRALIZED		CENTRALIZED	
	Band	Tribe	Chiefdom	State
Type of subsistence	Foraging	Horticulture and pastoralism	Extensive agriculture, intensive fishing	Intensive agriculture
Population density	Low	Low to medium	Medium	High
Type of economic exchange	Reciprocity	Reciprocity and trade	Redistribution through chief, reciprocity at lower levels	Markets and trade; redistribution through state based on taxation
Social stratification	Egalitarian	Egalitarian	Ranked	Social classes
Ownership of property	Little or no sense of personal ownership	Lineage or clan ownership of land and livestock	Lineage or clan ownership of land, but with strong sense of personal ownership	Private and state ownership of land
Type of leadership	Informal and situational; headman	Charismatic headman with some authority in group decision-making	Charismatic chief with limited power, usually based on giving benefits to followers	Sovereign leader supported by aristocratic bureaucracy
Law and legitimate control of force	No formal laws or punishments; right to use force is communal	No formal laws or punishments; right to use force is held by lineage, clan, or association	May have informal laws and specified punishments; chief has limited access to coercion	Formal laws and punishments; state holds all access to use of physical force
Some examples	!Kung San (southern Africa); Inuit (Canada, Alaska); Batek (Malaysia)	Yanomamo (South America); Nuer (Sudan); Cheyenne (United States)	Kwakiutl (Canada, Alaska); precolonial Hawai'i	Aztec (Mexico); Inca (Peru); Euro-American monarchies and representative democracies

Source: Adapted from Lewellen 1983:20–21.

Challenges to Traditional Political Anthropology

Political anthropology's early focus on political systems was valuable for describing the diverse ways in which humans create and maintain social order, with or without formal governments. But reality hardly ever corresponds to simple theoretical models. A major problem, for instance, with the bands-tribes-chiefdoms-states typology is that many cases blur the boundaries between types. Societies like the Nuer and Dinka of South Sudan might have tribe-like qualities—no central authority—but because they have a population of 1.8 million people, they do not have the same kinds of social relations as a "tribe" of 500 people. For example, recent fighting between Nuer and Dinka people resembles the small-scale tribal fighting observed by anthropologist E. E. Evans-Pritchard (1940) before World War II, except that Nuer and Dinka tribesmen are now using modern weapons of war with devastating results (see, e.g., Pendle 2014; Verini 2014).

In addition, the emphasis on static political systems and order came at the expense of understanding the dynamic nature of political processes, characterized by conflict, intrigue, manipulation, and other techniques. As the British anthropologist Lucy Mair (1969) pointed out, political structures only provide individuals with roles. Within a role, individuals make choices and decisions, manipulate others, and strategize, all in the pursuit of power. From this point of view, the proper focus of political anthropology is political power, an issue we turn to next.

• **Centralized political system.** A political system such as a chiefdom or a state, in which certain individuals and institutions hold power and control over resources.

THINKING CRITICALLY ABOUT POWER

A complex institution like a college or university has many ways of governing the faculty, staff, and student body. These include formal institutions, such as a faculty senate, president's office, and disciplinary committees of various kinds, as well as less formal associations and belief structures that help maintain order. What are some of these less formal forms of governance, and how do they contribute to the maintenance of order on campus?

What Is Political Power?

The shift from viewing politics as a problem of order to the problem of how people gain and wield power began to flourish in the 1960s and continues to the present. Power is the ability to make people think or act in certain ways, through physical coercion or through more symbolic means, such as persuasion (Kingsolver 1996). Beyond this very general definition, however, there are many nuances to political power.

Defining Political Power

- **Political power.** The process by which people create, compete, and use power to attain goals that are presumed to be for the good of a community.

Whether it is an exchange of goods, a religious ceremony, or a conversation between a man and a woman, practically all aspects of human existence are imbued with power. But not all power is *political.* For anthropologists, **political power** refers to how power is created and enacted to attain goals that are presumed to be for the good of a community, the common good (Kurtz 2001:21).

The exercise of political power requires legitimacy. Legitimacy can come from an independent source—a source outside the individuals that make up a community—such as gods or ancestors, inheritance, high office, the ability to cure an illness, or the outcome of some legal process, such as an election. Or it can come from a dependent source, that is, power given by other social actors: *granted* from one leader to another, *delegated* from a leader to a follower for a specific purpose, or *allocated* by the community to a leader (Kurtz 2001:26).

In addition, political power is tied to control over material resources (territory, money, or other culturally defined goods); human resources (willing followers and supporters); and symbolic resources (flags, uniforms, badges of rank, or other objects that give meaning to political action) (see also Chapter 13). There are other important dimensions to political power.

Political Power Is Action Oriented

- **Action theory.** An approach in the anthropological study of politics that closely follows the daily activities and decision-making processes of individual political leaders emphasizing that politics is a dynamic and competitive field of social relations in which people are constantly managing their ability to exercise power over others.

People everywhere gain and manage political power through a combination of decision-making, cooperation, opportunism, compromise, collusion, charm, gamesmanship, strategic alliance, factionalism, resistance, conflict, and other processes. A focus on these processes was central to **action theory**, an approach that emerged in the 1960s. Action theorists closely followed the daily activities and decision-making processes of individual political leaders like chiefs in African villages or headmen in Amazonian settlements. They argue that politics is a dynamic and competitive field of social relations in which people are constantly managing their ability to exercise power over others (Vincent 1978). In other words, it is not enough to *be* president of the United States. One has to *act* as the president.

To follow political action, one must be familiar with a society's specific rules and codes about who gets to exercise power and under what conditions. Anthropologist F. G. Bailey (1969) compared these codes to those of playing a game. In politics, as in a game, there are *normative rules*, stable and explicit ethical norms by which players must abide, such as honesty, fairness, and so on. There are also *pragmatic rules*, which are the creative manipulations necessary to win the game itself. For example, in U.S. politics, normative rules require political actors to be open, fair, and honest. But we know, based on reading the political news in the newspaper, that there are also the pragmatic rules of gaining and holding onto power, which often involve favoritism and even outright lying (Lewellen 2003).

Political Power Is Structural

It became clear to political anthropologists by the 1980s and 1990s that certain power relationships transcend any individual. Political anthropologists began to refer to such power as **structural power**, which is power that not only operates within settings but that also organizes and orchestrates the settings in which social and individual action take place (Wolf 2001:384). "Structure" here means something very different from how the early structural-functionalists understood it. They were interested in social institutions ("structures," as a noun), while this newer perspective focuses on the processes and relationships that shape or "structure" (as a verb) social action and relationships.

In this view, power does not lie in a group or individual's exercise of will over others through domination or manipulation but is dispersed in many shapes and forms, produced and reproduced through the combined actions of social institutions, science, and other knowledge producers, and people living their everyday lives (Foucault 1978). Anthropologist David Horn (1994) used this approach to study how and why Italians of today accept state intervention in their lives. He traces their acceptance to the rise of social thought, planning, and research around the reproductive health of Italian families after World War I. During this period, the Italian government instituted a census and other programs to measure statistically the population's size, growth rate, and health conditions. Using this information, they instituted new policies of hygiene and family management, including (among others) a 1927 tax on bachelorhood and efforts to eliminate contraception and abortion. Although many of these policies failed, Horn observes that these changes had an important effect on Italians, in that they came to accept the idea that the body is not simply the domain of a private individual but a social problem that requires scientific and state intervention. As a result, they began to willingly accept that they should share intimate details about their reproductive lives with the state and that the state has the right to issue directives intended to manage citizens' lives—all of which are ideas that Italians take for granted today.

- **Structural power.** Power that not only operates within settings, but that also organizes and orchestrates the settings in which social and individual actions take place.

Political Power Is Gendered

During the past thirty years, feminist anthropologists have observed that while men tend to dominate formal political processes in most societies, relationships between

Figure 16.2   Revenge Suicide in New Guinea.   This painting by contemporary Papua New Guinea artist Apa Hugo from 2003 illustrates how suicide can be used as a weapon of the weak. The caption in Pidgin English written on the canvas means: "A man fights with his wife and the wife commits suicide. Her parents are distraught and cry in mourning" (Man krosim meri na—meri i wari na i go sua sait. Na papa mama i wari na karai i stap).

men and women intersect with political power in complex ways. In a number of societies, women exercise formal leadership and political power. In other settings, women may have very little formal power, but they can mobilize to assert power in response to events.

In many societies, women may be so disempowered that their ability to take direct action lies only in the most dramatic action of all, taking one's own life. For example, on the island of New Britain in Papua New Guinea, "revenge suicide" occurs when a woman takes her own life in response to abuse or shame by a man (Figure 16.2). Here young women are powerless figures. But a woman's act of suicide shifts the burden of shame to her tormentor (often a husband) and can mobilize her male relatives and other community members to acknowledge the injustice and seek accountability from the offending party (Counts 1980). Although taking such actions may be difficult for many Westerners to comprehend, this situation suggests that we must consider forms of political power that are available to those we do not conventionally understand to be "powerful."

Political Power in Non-State Societies

To some extent, the exercise of political power differs between state and non-state societies. For example, in non-state societies such as tribal societies of South America and Melanesia, power tends to be temporary and episodic, emerging from personal charisma, not elections or inheritance. The Amazon headman, for example, is "a first among equals." He assumes his status as leader by being able to persuade followers, not because he controls power or resources on his own. Such leaders, who are sometimes called Big Men, cannot transfer their status and power through inheritance when they die.

A Big Man cannot force others to do anything but gains influence and authority by giving away wealth and shrewdly persuading others, through a combination of smooth talk and peer pressure, to produce goods they will provide him, which he can then redistribute. In their 1970 documentary film *The Feast*, filmmaker Timothy Asch and anthropologist Napoleon Chagnon (1997) show how a Yanomamo headman in southern Venezuela sponsors a feast aimed at building an alliance with another community with which his own community had recently been at war. As headman, he could not force anyone to help clear the plaza or cook the plantain soup that would be the centerpiece of the feast. His loud haranguing did little to motivate his fellow clan members, but he led by example and his clansmen started helping and made it a successful feast, forming a new alliance. Persuasion was his most valuable tool.

In contrast to the status leadership of a Big Man, the kind of political power your hometown mayor has is a quintessential expression of how political power works in a state society. Your mayor is an officeholder, a person who gets power from his or her elected or appointed office. In state societies and chiefdoms, power and authority reside in offices and institutions. Formal rules dictate who can gain an office and the conditions under which it can be gained. Officeholders usually have greater access to resources, such as money from taxes and a bureaucracy that can exercise social control over a community. Like Big Men, however, mayors and other U.S. officials do draw on their personal connections to achieve things, as we suggest in "Thinking Like an Anthropologist: The Power of Personal Connections."

The Political Power of the Contemporary Nation-State

Modern states are typically called **nation-states**, independent states recognized by other states and composed of people who share a single national identity. A nation is a population who thinks of itself as "a people" based on sharing—or imagining that they share—a common culture, language, heritage, identity, or commitment to particular political institutions (Robbins 2001:82). Although states are an old phenomenon (see Chapter 13), the political form of the nation-state originated in Europe several hundred years ago. But it has become so common that now all the world's territory falls under the control of one or another nation-state.

Contrary to Locke's idealizations of the "social contract," membership in a nation-state is not typically voluntary. For many of the world's peoples, conquest and colonialism forced them into nation-states. Leaders of nation-states exercise various forms of political power to assert coercion and social control over non-state societies and to ensure the conformity of all their citizens.

These forms of social control and coercion include promoting a sense of unity by drawing symbolic lines between those who are included—often it is some version of the "chosen people"—and those who are excluded. Excluded groups may be defined as enemies (citizens of competing nation-states, or non-state actors such as "terrorists") or as inferior because of racial or ethnic differences. They exercise power over their citizens by creating and managing information about them using institutionalized surveillance, national identity cards, censuses, monitoring social media, wiretapping, and computer hacking. Surveillance secures and expands leaders' power and authority, by identifying potential opposition or non-conformism threatening their authority. Many nation-states also use prisons, torture, and violence against citizens who do not conform to dominant values or identities.

- **Nation-states.** Independent states recognized by other states, composed of people who share a single national identity.

Thinking Like an Anthropologist

The Power of Personal Connections

ANTHROPOLOGISTS BEGIN THEIR research by asking questions. In this box, we want you to learn how to ask questions as an anthropological researcher. Part 1 describes a situation and follows up with questions we would ask. Part 2 asks you to do the same thing with a different situation.

PART 1: PERSONAL CONNECTIONS IN THE PERSIAN-SPEAKING WORLD

While working for the U.S. State Department in Iran during the 1970s, diplomat Whitney Azoy first encountered the concept of *waaseta*, which in Persian refers to "the power of personal connections." *Waaseta* is based on the cultivation of personal relationships by giving and receiving favors. Individuals at all levels of the government use it, from the local village level to the president's office. The more extensive one's network of personal connections, the greater one's ability to ask for, offer, and call in favors, all of which translates directly to political power. As a diplomat, Azoy found that cultivating *waaseta* helped him pursue the interests of the United States.

When he later became an anthropologist conducting research among Persian speakers in Afghanistan, Azoy once again encountered *waaseta*. He observed that among Afghans, "[y]our family core group was a given; what really mattered were your personal connections beyond home and hearth. You were defined by it: enabled by knowing some people, limited by not knowing others. 'Name' or reputation—the currency of old-time, hinterland politics among both [traditional rulers] and small peasants was ultimately reckoned by whom you knew . . . and whom you could get to do favors for you" (Azoy 2002:A9). Afghans assumed that Azoy, as an American and a former official in the State Department, had extraordinary personal connections, and they asked him for many favors even long after he left Afghanistan. For instance, after the United States invaded Afghanistan to overthrow the Taliban in 2001 and began developing reconstruction projects, Azoy received a phone call from an Afghan acquaintance with whom he had not spoken in over twenty years. After they caught up on each other's lives, the Afghan asked if Azoy could draw on his *waaseta* in the U.S. government to get money for a reconstruction project. What questions does this situation raise for anthropological researchers?

1. If *waaseta* encompasses all political relationships in Afghanistan, do Afghans view *waaseta*

as corruption, as many Americans are likely to do?
2. What limitations does *waaseta* place on developing a modern-style democracy?
3. Is a Western-style democracy, with its ideological commitment to transparency and avoidance of corruption, the only way to have a democracy?

PART 2: PERSONAL CONNECTIONS IN U.S. POLITICS

Azoy notes that *waaseta*'s "you-rub-my-back-and-I'll-rub-yours" quality has all the trappings of what we call "corruption." He contrasts it with the rule of law, balance of powers, transparency, and accountability that people in the United States expect of their politicians. But when Azoy made this point to an Afghan acquaintance, the Afghan insisted that American politics is also suffused with *waaseta*. He pointed to the fact that election campaigns are based on the give-and-take of favors between large donors and politicians.

Personal connections are critical to the U.S. government's operations, a fact that very few politicians and bureaucrats hide. The symbol of a successful, well-connected politician is a smartphone full of phone numbers of other powerful people inside and outside the government with whom he or she has personal connections. If you wanted to understand the role of personal connections in American politics, what questions would you ask as an anthropological researcher?

❦ **Afghan Elders Engaging in *Waaseta* with a British Politician.**

Anthropologist as Problem Solver

Maxwell Owusu and Democracy in Ghana

SINCE ITS INDEPENDENCE from Britain in 1957, the West African country of Ghana has alternated between civilian- and military-controlled national governments. When the most recent military government (1981–1992) allowed elections in 1992, the Fourth Republic of Ghana emerged, based on a new constitution with a foundation in democratic principles.

An influential actor in that process was Ghanaian-born political anthropologist Maxwell Owusu of the University of Michigan. Owusu served as a consulting member of the Constitutional Experts Committee, which drafted the 1992 constitution proposals. Owusu has been a staunch critic of autocratic and repressive leadership in post-independence Ghana and other African nation-states. He is an advocate of popular participatory democracy. But as an anthropologist he understood the problems of imposing foreign political models—such as Western-style democracy with competing political parties—on African societies with different

Maxwell Owusu.

histories and indigenous political traditions. As he has written (Owusu 1992:384), "African democracy may require the integration of indigenous methods of village co-operation with innovative forms of government, combining the power of universal rights with the uniqueness of each district's or nation's own customs and respected traditions."

A viable solution, Owusu insisted, is to create a decentralized state in which local authorities, primarily chiefs, headmen, and lineage heads, participate directly in state processes and decision-making. The advantage is that local leaders can better identify the needs and priorities of villagers, while being more accountable to their members and communities than are bureaucrats in a state apparatus. The 1992 constitution put this insight to work, creating "District Assemblies" as the basic unit of national government, two-thirds of which are elected and one-third appointed, the latter being mostly traditional leaders or their representatives (Owusu 1992). Owusu observed that far from making chiefs and other non-state political leaders obsolete, these changes have put traditional leaders at the forefront of political change in the nation-state as a whole (Owusu 1996).

Questions for Reflection

1. How does Owusu's notion of participatory democracy, which relies upon decentralization of power toward local traditional leaders, differ from the way local governments at the city, town, or county level work in the United States?

2. Is it likely to be true that local traditional leaders are better able to identify local priorities than national leaders?

Leaders of nation-states also often co-opt local political actors and their power to serve their own or the nation-state's ends. In post-independence Ghana, for example, where chiefs, headmen, and extended family lineages control village-level resources and political processes, centralized governments have co-opted traditional non-state leaders by rewarding some with high-level positions in the state bureaucracy. Such an appointment to a governmental position makes a local leader responsible for enforcing national laws and mobilizing support for state-led development programs (Owusu 1996). For several decades, anthropologist Maxwell Owusu has researched how this kind of political power works in post-independence Ghana. He has advocated formally incorporating non-state political leaders into nation-state functions. In "Anthropologist as Problem Solver: Maxwell Owusu and Democracy in Ghana," we examine how his ideas have been put to work.

We have so far discussed the exercise of political power in terms of the cultivation of relationships, persuasion, the collection of information, or the strategic manipulation of others. Political power often also involves the production and maintenance of social inequalities, a theme we examine in the next section.

THINKING CRITICALLY ABOUT POWER

As this section shows, different anthropologists have approached political power in different ways. Do you think each of these approaches creates a fundamentally different picture of how political power works? Why or why not?

How Is Social Inequality Constructed and Upheld?

Most Americans assume that social inequalities are a natural and inevitable aspect of human society. Those social inequalities may be based on categories like race, class, ethnicity, gender, caste, and so on. Although they may feel real, powerful, and unchangeable, there is nothing fixed or inevitable about them. All social hierarchies—as well as the political power that shapes and benefits from them—appeal to a natural order to justify the rankings and categories assigned to different groups. To understand why some people are deemed inferior and others superior, we must explore how belief systems and the dynamics of political power perpetuate prejudice, discrimination, and privilege, rather than searching for any preexisting natural or moral imperatives. Here we build on our discussion in Chapter 10 to examine how the race concept organizes people into groups based on specific physical traits that are thought to reflect fundamental and innate differences—and how it reinforces widespread patterns of social inequality.

Race, Biology, and the "Natural" Order of Things

For several centuries, European and American scientists have sought to naturalize race, that is, to categorize humans into racial groups and explain why nature organizes people into those groups. But as we covered in Chapter 10, many anthropologists have long argued that these efforts are scientifically futile. As we explained, because of historical movements and genetic intermingling, human biological variations occur in a "clinal" fashion, which means that change is gradual across groups and that traits shade and blend into each other (Marks 1995). As a result, something like skin tone can be highly variable within any human population, and there are no clear lines between actual skin tones.

We also know that there is no single gene that codes race or is unique to any group of people conventionally thought of as a race (Long 2003). Genetically speaking, humans are a homogeneous species: there is far greater variation *within* human groups than there is *between* them (Long 2003). In the face of such evidence, anthropologists argue that race is culturally constructed. But how does that happen?

The Cultural Construction of Race

Anthropologists, sociologists, and historians refer to the social, economic, and political processes of transforming populations into races and creating racial meanings as **racialization** (Gregory and Sanjek 1994; Omi and Winant 1996). Racialization always occurs under a particular set of cultural and historical circumstances.

- **Racialization.** The social, economic, and political processes of transforming populations into races and creating racial meanings.

A powerful illustration of these processes is the creation of racial groups in colonial Virginia. After the English settled Jamestown in 1607, settlers began to raise tobacco as a cash crop. Because of labor shortages, they brought indentured servants, among them English-speaking Africans living in England (Parent 2003; Smedley 2007a, 2007b). Some of these Africans worked off their debts and became freedmen, even prosperous traders and plantation owners with rights to vote and serve in the Virginia Assembly. Marriages between Africans and non-Africans were not uncommon and carried no stigma. The English considered Africans to be equals because of their success at growing food in tropical conditions, their discipline, and their ability to work cooperatively in groups (Smedley 2007a). In the early 1600s, Africans and their descendants were considered, like any other settlers, as members of the community, interacting with other settlers on an equal footing (Morgan 1975).

By the mid-1600s the Virginia colony was in crisis (Smedley 2007a). A few powerful men had taken most of the fertile land and poor freedmen had difficulty finding land of their own. In 1676 thousands of poor freedmen and indentured servants rebelled (Figure 16.3). Most were Europeans, but among them were several hundred of African origin. To prevent future unrest, the leaders began passing laws aimed at controlling laborers. A number of these laws separated out Africans and their descendants, restricting African rights and mobility including, among others, the ability to vote, own property, and marry Europeans (Parent 2003; Smedley 2007a). These laws took away basic rights that African settlers had previously held, and they opened the door to outright slavery, which followed several years later when the English began bringing slaves directly from Africa.

English colonial leaders also promoted a shift in thinking about Africans and their descendants. They began portraying Africans as uncivilized heathens, intellectually incapable of civilization, which justified African enslavement. They also began to homogenize all Europeans, regardless of ethnicity, class, or social status. In early public records, the word "Christian" commonly appeared next to the names of Europeans but was later replaced by "white." Poor whites received land as a way to encourage their identification with the colony's elites, preventing them from siding with Africans. By the end of the seventeenth century, the terms "black" and "white" came to symbolize the differences between the two groups, and the use of this racialized language helped uphold the artificial lines of difference. Skin color became the chief way of marking status and difference; as Governor William Gooch of Virginia

🌱 **Figure 16.3   Bacon's Rebellion, Virginia Colony, 1676.**

described it, skin color was a "perpetual Brand upon Free Negroes and Mulattos" (Allen 1997:242).

For the next several centuries, the biologizing of race became extreme, particularly after the Civil War. Although most African Americans are of mixed ancestry, biological traits like skin tone and ideologies like the "one-drop rule" (individuals were defined as "black" if they were believed to have just "one drop" of African blood, meaning a single African ancestor) have been used to justify oppression and inequality as the "natural" order of things (Figure 16.4). These sharp racial lines have upheld a particular social and political order and, more important, have served certain economic interests, especially of those who benefited from cheap African and African American labor.

Saying Race Is Culturally Constructed Is Not Enough

It is not enough to say that race is culturally constructed, because it might give the impression that race is not "real" (Hartigan 2006). As we also explored in Chapter 10, race is very real as a social force and by *becoming* biology, that is, by shaping people's biological outcomes due to disparities in access to certain kinds of healthcare and diets, exposure to certain kinds of diseases, and other factors that can make people either sick or healthy (Gravlee 2009).

In addition to its embodied consequences, racial discrimination is a form of social control that can express itself explicitly—through laws and bureaucracies that manage and enforce policies of institutionalized coercion and exploitation—or in disguised ways such as racial profiling. The point here is not that different racial groups cannot have differences in biology, but that these differences in biology are the product of socio-economic, cultural, and political processes that construct and maintain racial inequalities.

Prejudice—preformed, usually unfavorable opinions that people hold about people from groups who are different from their own—also plays an important role in upholding this unequal social order. Prejudice is based on taking arbitrary features and assigning qualities of social superiority and inferiority to them. Worldwide, there is a mind-boggling variety of markers on which prejudices are based. We are most familiar with skin color and hair texture, but other markers include occupation, family lineage, religious affiliation, and gender behavior that suggests sexual orientation.

Most of us learn prejudices at a young age from people whom we regard as authorities, such as parents and other relatives, community leaders, and teachers. Anthropologist Hortense Powdermaker also wrote that prejudices are judgments about a whole group of people based on poor reasoning and insufficient evidence. In "Classic Contributions: Hortense Powdermaker on Prejudice," we examine her point in more detail.

Where they exist, prejudices may feel deep, innate, and natural, but they are not static. As attitudes toward groups change, so do accompanying prejudices. There is no better illustration of this than the fact that a majority of Americans elected an African American president in 2008, which would have been unimaginable only forty years before because of widespread antiblack prejudice. Prejudices tend to express themselves through concrete processes of social rewards and unfair treatment, but they do not always lead to discrimination. In his classic study of prejudice from the 1950s, for example, Gordon Allport (1958) observed that prejudice expresses itself in a continuum from avoidance and non-contact to more aggressive actions, including exclusion, physical attack, and killing. This last point raises a new question about the relationship between cultural attitudes and violence, which we explore next.

Figure 16.4   The One-Drop Rule.   Mark Twain's classic 1894 novel *The Tragedy of Pudd'nhead Wilson* depicts the one-drop rule as a farcical tragedy. In it Roxy (pictured here), a slave who is 1/16 black, switches her baby son, who is 1/32 black, with a white baby, knowing her son will grow up with privileges he would never enjoy if people knew he had even "one drop" of black blood.

- **Prejudice.** Preformed, usually unfavorable opinions that people hold about people from groups, who are different from their own.

CLASSIC CONTRIBUTIONS

Hortense Powdermaker on Prejudice

ANTHROPOLOGIST HORTENSE POWDERMAKER (1896–1970) began studying race relations in Mississippi during the 1930s, making her the first professional anthropologist to conduct ethnographic research in a contemporary American setting. Always interested in issues of social justice (before her Ph.D. at the London School of Economics in the 1920s she was a labor organizer), Powdermaker sought to understand how blacks and whites interacted with each other and the psychological costs of racism.

During the 1940s, she took insights gained from that research to produce the short book *Probing Our Prejudices: A Unit for High School Students*, which was required reading in New York City schools for several decades. In this excerpt from that book, Powdermaker explains how poor reasoning leads to prejudice.

Bill plays marbles with a group of boys in his neighborhood, and one of them, John, a Polish boy, cheats. Bill then concludes that all Poles cheat, and he carries this idea with him throughout his life. . . .

When he is older, Bill reads in the paper that two Italians who were drunk got into a fight and one stabbed the other. Bill has never known any Italians but he swiftly jumps to the conclusion that all Italians are drunkards and stab each other in the back.

Or he hears of a Mexican who stole some money from his boss, and so, forever after, he thinks of all Mexicans as thieves.

In all three cases Bill concluded that because one member of a group acted in a certain way, all members of that group will act the same way. This type of poor reasoning is called false generalization. To generalize is to come to a general conclusion as a result of learning particular facts or ideas. For example, if you are a member of a club that functions well at every meeting

and lives up to its standards, you may justifiably say, "We have a good club." This is a true generalization based on observation. If, however, you observe another club during only one of its meetings when nothing is accomplished, and you say, "That club is no good," you are making a false generalization, because you have not based your conclusion on sufficient evidence.

We all suffer from this unfortunate habit of making false generalizations, especially about racial or religious groups or nationalities other than our own. We do not make them as frequently about our own group. If we are white Protestants and a member of our group cheats, we do not condemn all white Protestants. If we are Catholics and one of our members lies, we do not say "All Catholics are liars." In order to be clear-thinking individuals we must realize this inconsistency and avoid making false generalizations. [Powdermaker 1944:29–30]

Questions for Reflection

1. Can you think of other social or political issues beyond race and nationality where people make false generalizations?

2. Why do people accept the logical inconsistencies and poor reasoning that lead to prejudice?

THINKING CRITICALLY ABOUT POWER

Racialization is not something that happened a long time ago; it is an ongoing process even in the United States today. Can you think of some examples of how it might still be taking place? Can you identify any conditions today that might shape dynamics of racialization differently from, say, during the period of the Virginia Colony?

Why Do Some Societies Seem More Violent Than Others?

By the 1960s, a number of the societies that anthropologists studied were experiencing intense post-independence violence, disruption, and warfare related to the end of European colonialism. This situation prompted an urgent concern to understand the relationship between political power and violence, and why political conflicts in some societies seemed to break out in violence more than conflicts did in other societies. What might be done to end and prevent future violence?

In pursuing answers to these questions, anthropologists have learned that violence is a form of power relations rooted in cultural processes and meanings, just as other strategies of political power, such as persuasion, manipulation, and prejudice, are.

What Is Violence?

Violence is typically defined as the use of force to harm someone or something. It is a highly visible and concrete assertion of power, and a very efficient way to transform a social environment and communicate an ideological message (Riches 1986).

Yet specifying what violence consists of is not always so straightforward, because violence is different things to different people (Eller 2006). The same person might acknowledge that shoving a person into a vat of boiling water is violent, yet may not view placing a lobster, much less a handful of spinach, in that same boiling water as violent. Another factor in assessing what is violent is intention. Did the perpetrator mean to do it (violent), or was it an accident (probably not violent)? And rationality: Did the perpetrator have control over his or her actions (violent), or was it a case of "losing one's mind" (probably not violent, or at least justified)? And legitimacy: Was it a legitimate act, such as a boxer beating on another boxer (sports, not violence), or deviant, such as a man beating his wife (violent)? Even the nature of force: Was the force personal, as in one person punching another (violent), or structural, as in economic conditions depriving a child of food (open to debate)? And depending on whether you are a victim, perpetrator, or witness, you are likely to have a different perspective on whether or not an act is violent.

Even though we might all agree that violence involves some element of harm and an assertion of power over others, people nevertheless have differing opinions on what constitutes violence. To victims violence is almost always meaningful, while it may or may not be as meaningful or obvious to the perpetrators. This distinction is partly why violence is so powerful in enforcing the rules of the powerful. Some of these

• **Violence.** The use of force to harm someone or something.

opinions about violence are individually held, but some are related to differences in how we as members of a particular culture define violence and give meaning to it. Culture shapes not only how people think about violence but also how, why, and when they use it as a form of power over others.

Violence and Culture

Since Hobbes, Europeans and Americans have seen violence and warfare as a natural condition of humans. But anthropologists offer two major challenges to this view: (1) neither violence nor its opposite, non-violence, is an inevitable condition of humanity; both are learned behaviors that express themselves in particular social and historic circumstances; and (2) violence and warfare are generally not chaotic and arbitrary but tend to follow explicit cultural patterns, rules, and ethical codes.

Neither Violence Nor Non-Violence Is Inevitable in Human Societies

In recent years, it has become fashionable to think of aggression and violence as genetically determined. But no animal or human carries genes for dominance, aggression, or passivity. These complex social and psychological conditions and states involve biological processes, such as the production of certain hormones, but they are not fixed properties or traits carried by genes.

So how should we deal with claims—some even made by anthropologists—that some societies are fierce and warlike and others peaceful? The answer, of course, is by demonstrating that neither violence nor non-violence is universal (Fry 2006). Two famous examples—the Yanomamo and the Semai—illustrate our point.

The Yanomamo and the Semai

Anthropologist Napoleon Chagnon (1968) described the Yanomamo Indians of southern Venezuela with whom he has worked since the early 1960s as the "fierce people." According to Chagnon, the Yanomamo have an aggressive style about nearly everything they do. They stage brutal raids against enemy settlements, and they routinely have violent responses to their fellow clansmen (Figure 16.5).

But other anthropologists, including Brian Ferguson (1995) and Jacques Lizot (1985), have seen the Yanomamo in a different light, as warm and caring people, who from time to time had to defend themselves against enemies. Ferguson's research suggests that Yanomamo "fierceness" was not the traditional behavior of these Amazonian Indians but the result of contact with foreigners: missionaries, prospectors, government officials, and anthropologists such as Chagnon, who has come under fire by Yanomami themselves for disrupting their society (Tierney 2002).

A similar point can be made about a very different case, the Semai, egalitarian swidden farmers who live in the Malaysian rain forest. Anthropologist Robert Dentan (1968) characterized the Semai as peaceful and non-violent because they committed little or no interpersonal violence during his field research. The Semai view themselves as peaceful and reject the idea that violence is a natural condition of human life. At the heart of Semai commitment to non-violence is the concept of *persusah*, referring to the value of not causing trouble for others. But the Semai are not completely non-violent either. During the communist insurrection in Malaysia from 1948 to 1960, some Semai became soldiers and a few were renowned fighters. Although Dentan had consistently described the ethos of the Semai as non-violent and

Figure 16.5   The "Fierce People."   In the ethnographic film *The Ax Fight*, from which this image is drawn, the filmmakers represent Yanomamo lives as filled with aggression and near-constant violence. But is it really so?

peaceful, he quoted one former soldier who described himself and his comrades in the counterinsurgency as "drunk with blood" (1968:58–59). Robarchek and Dentan (1987) argue that the Semai are indeed socialized to be non-violent, but when they were brought into the counterinsurgency they were socialized as soldiers and were trained to kill.

The point of this example is that, as with the Yanomamo, violence and non-violence are not absolute or static conditions. They are the result of cultural attitudes and particular social and historical conditions (Fry 2006).

Explaining the Rise of Violence in Our Contemporary World

Anthropologists have long observed that violence and the threat of violence, far from implying chaos, can actually encourage social order because they reflect culturally specific patterns, rules, and ethical codes. These patterns define when and why violence is acceptable, what forms of violence are appropriate, and who can engage in violent acts.

In news reports, pundits routinely explain the rise of violence around the globe as a chaotic outburst of meaningless "tribal" and "ethnic" tensions (Whitehead 2004). Such accounts appear to offer a tidy narrative that seems to explain so much of what is going on in our contemporary world. But they are based on a fundamental misunderstanding of the relationship between violence and culture.

It Is Not Inevitable That Different Ethnic Groups Will Fight

The countries that made up the former Yugoslavia in southeastern Europe, in a region known as the Balkans, share the stereotype of ethnic and religious tribalism. We even have a word for it—"balkanization"—which refers to the fragmentation of society into hostile factions. During the Bosnian civil war in the 1990s, foreign journalists tended to describe acts of violence by Serbs, Croats, and Muslims as "ethnic violence" based on centuries-old hatred between these ethnic groups.

But this explanation is largely wrong and ignores long histories of coexistence, cultural interchange, and peaceful relations that anthropologists had observed in the region (Lockwood 1975; Bringa 2005). A more complex understanding of the conflict sees violence as a byproduct of a struggle over political power among nationalist leaders after the fall of communism. Seeking to consolidate their hold over political power and state institutions, nationalists on all sides used the media to broadcast daily doses of fear, hatred, and dehumanizing images of people from the other "ethnic" group (Bringa 2005). Their public comments asserted that one group or another had targeted violence on people of other ethnic backgrounds. The constant public discourse about ethnic violence generated fear and a sense of powerlessness among ordinary people. When nationalist leaders eventually called on people to attack their neighbors of different backgrounds, some did just that, leading to now well-known incidents of brutality and horror in places such as Srebenica, site of a mass killing of Bosnian Muslims by Bosnian Serbs (Oberschall 2000).

But while the Western media presented these divisions as age-old ethnic tensions, all three spoke the same language, Serbo-Croatian, with slight differences in dialect, and people did not initially see these labels as "ethnic" differences but more as religious ones: the Serbs were Eastern Orthodox, the Croats were Roman Catholic, and Bosnians were Muslim. For many decades these groups intermingled in the same apartment buildings and intermarried. Centuries of generally harmonious relations were on display when the Winter Olympics were held in Sarajevo (Figure 16.6).

Even during the most violent periods, many people found ways to protect their neighbors of different ethnic backgrounds from being attacked. In other words, even in a period of intense, artificially created ethnic conflict, not everybody participated in the violence, and many did not give in to "ethnic" hatred. Both points undermine any simplistic story of seething tribalism. Ethnic conflict is not an inevitable condition, and in this case it was manufactured to serve the political and ideological interests of certain leaders.

Figure 16.6   A Peaceful Balkans. At the time of the 1984 Olympic Games in the Bosnian capital city of Sarajevo, commentators celebrated long-standing peaceful relations between Serbs, Croats, and Muslims in the modern city, challenging any notion of "ancient seething hatreds" portrayed in later years.

Violence Is a Meaningful Political Strategy

In the United States we sometimes hear in the media about events like suicide bombings in Iraqi markets and cafés; machete attacks on innocent people in Liberia, Rwanda, and Sierra Leone in Africa; or plane hijackings by some militant group. Commentators often call these shocking acts "meaningless" and "barbaric." But such acts are never meaningless. They are meaningful—to both victims and perpetrators—although the different sides interpret the violence very differently (Whitehead 2004). For one side the message is threat and hostility, and for the other it is a message of martyrdom and devotion to a cause.

When people refer to such acts as meaningless and barbaric, they interpret violence as emotional, beyond reason. In fact, violence and the threat of violence are often used as strategic tools for pursuing particular political ends. Consider, for example, the civil war in Sierra Leone (1991–2001), in which at least 50,000 people died. This conflict, waged between the government and a "people's army" called the Revolutionary United Front (RUF), gained widespread notoriety as a barbaric and brutal conflict.

According to British anthropologist Paul Richards (1996), the violence was anything but wanton and mindless. He explained that machete attacks, rape, throat slitting, and other acts of terror were "rational ways of achieving intended strategic outcomes" (Richards 1996:58). For example, during 1995 the RUF frequently cut off the hands of village women. This practice was strategically calculated to communicate a political message to the RUF's own soldiers and to prevent defections. RUF leaders reasoned that they could stop defections by stopping the harvest. To stop the harvest, they ordered the hand amputation of women who participated in harvesting grain. As news spread, the harvests stopped, and defections ended because soldiers did not want the same thing to happen to their mothers and sisters. Richards does not justify these repulsive acts. Rather, his point is that violence is not "meaningless" but is highly organized in a systematic, though brutal, fashion.

Not every conflict leads inevitably to violence. We explore this theme in more detail in our final section.

THINKING CRITICALLY ABOUT POWER

Since the early years of structural-functionalism, anthropologists have recognized that violence or the threat of violence, far from implying chaos, can encourage social integration and social order. How? Why?

How Do People Avoid Cycles of Aggression, Brutality, and War?

Although millions of people around the world rarely if ever have direct experiences of aggression, brutality, and war in their daily lives, disputes and conflicts do arise, everywhere, all the time. But, as we discussed, violence is not an inevitable human response to conflict. People always have creative and peaceful ways to manage or settle their disputes. Working out the problems that arise from those conflicting accounts inevitably touches on who has access to power and what allows them to hold it (Rasmussen 1991).

What Disputes Are "About"

Some disputes are explicitly about who can hold political power. But most disputes are also about other matters that are central to the political life of any community (Caplan 1995). Disputes are about property, who gets to make decisions, rules of social interaction, and about dividing or joining people in new ways, because when arguments happen, people take sides.

Most North Americans assume that disputes are about winning and losing. We approach a lawsuit pretty much the same way we approach a sporting event, the point being to vanquish the other side. But for many peoples around the world, disputes are not "about" winning and losing but are intended to repair a strained relationship.

When Trobriand Islanders play the game cricket, for example, the goal of the game is to end with a tie, not to win or lose (Kildea and Leach 1975). Sure, the players play hard and even get hurt in the process, but the game is really "about" reaffirming the social relationships that exist among the players and with their communities. When we look at how people manage disputes around the world, keep in mind that when presented with a dispute, most people prefer to restore harmony by settling the matter to the satisfaction of all parties.

How People Manage Disputes

Legal anthropology, the branch of political anthropology interested in such matters, has identified a number of ways that people manage disputes (Nader and Todd 1978). Some strategies are informal, including avoidance, competition, ritual, and play. Others are formal, involving specialists or specialized institutions.

One of the easiest and most informal ways that people handle their disputes is to avoid the matter altogether, which allows tensions to subside. In small-scale communities, avoiding certain subjects is often the best way of keeping the peace. People often turn to other informal strategies to handle tensions, such as telling jokes, laughter, gossip, song, duels, sporting contests and other forms of competitive play, ridicule, public humiliation, and even witchcraft accusations (Gulliver 1979; Watson-Gegeo and White 1990; Caplan 1995) (Figure 16.7).

When informal strategies do not work, people usually have more formal means of settling disputes. **Adjudication**, which is the legal process by which an individual or council with socially recognized authority intervenes in a dispute and unilaterally makes a decision, is one possibility. The image of a courtroom with a judge in a robe,

• **Adjudication.** The legal process by which an individual or council with socially recognized authority intervenes in a dispute and unilaterally makes a decision.

Figure 16.7   Breakdancing as Dispute Settlement? Breakdancing got its start in New York City in the 1970s. In its early days, street gangs in the South Bronx would battle each other—over turf, because of an affront, or simply to gain respect—through dance.

- **Negotiation.** A form of dispute management in which parties themselves reach a decision jointly.

- **Mediation.** The use of a third party who intervenes in a dispute to help the parties reach an agreement and restore harmony.

a jury, and lawyers comes to mind. Not all societies do it this way, including the Kpelle [keh-**pay**-lay], rice cultivators of central Liberia. Anthropologist James Gibbs (1963) reported that while Kpelle could take their disputes to government courts, they viewed them as arbitrary and coercive (Gibbs 1963). Kpelle often turned to their own "moot courts," which are hearings presided over by respected kin, elders, and neighbors. Kpelle moot courts provided a thorough airing of grievances and a quick treatment of the problem before attitudes hardened. Instead of winner take all, their goal was to restore harmony.

In a **negotiation**, the parties themselves reach a decision jointly. British legal anthropologist Phillip Gulliver (1979) observed that in a dispute between two close neighbors over land and water rights that took place in a small district in northern Tanzania in 1957, many factors influenced the ability and willingness of each side to negotiate a settlement. For example, one disputant was more popular and better connected in the community, and thus had more allies to push his own agenda. But he was willing to negotiate because, like his rival, he was equally worried that the colonial court could intervene and impose a decision. He also worried that if the dispute was not settled, the other side might use witchcraft and further intensify the dispute.

Mediation entails a third party who intervenes in a dispute to aid the parties in reaching an agreement. Native Hawaiians commonly practice a kind of mediation called *ho'oponopono* (**hoh**-oh-poh-no-poh-no], or "setting to right" (Boggs and Chun 1990). This practice is intended to resolve interpersonal and family problems or to prevent them from worsening. It is based on the belief that disputes involve negative entanglements and that setting things right spiritually will lead directly to physical and interpersonal healing (Boggs and Chun 1990). *Ho'oponopono* usually begins when a leader of high status—a family elder, a leader of a community church, or a professional family therapist—intervenes in a dispute, calling the adversaries and all immediate family members to engage in the process. After opening with prayers, the leader instructs participants in the process and guides a discussion in which all participants are expected to air their grievances and feelings openly and honestly. They direct them to the leader, not to one another, to avoid possible confrontation. At the end, the leader asks all sides to offer forgiveness and release themselves and each other from the negative entanglements.

Is Restoring Harmony Always the Best Way?

It is easy to romanticize dispute settlement traditions whose goal is to restore harmony. Legal anthropologist Laura Nader (1990) observed that harmony and reconciliation are cultural ideologies, and like other ideologies they uphold a particular social order and way of doing things, usually protecting the already powerful.

Nader observed that Zapotec Indians in the southern Mexican village of Talea [tah-**lay**-ah] whom she studied have a "harmony ideology." Taleans believe "a bad compromise is better than a good fight." They emphasize that people need to work hard to maintain balance and evenhandedness in their relationships with others. They go to local courts frequently, even for very minor disputes, to avoid escalation.

But peace and reconciliation have their price. Nader has seen how these ideologies can prevent a full airing of problems, can delay justice, or can be used as a form of social control. Harmony ideology sustains a particular power structure, serving the interests of some but not necessarily all.

Since the 1970s, restoring harmony has been a popular strategy in Western countries for conflict resolution studies and practice. Mediation and negotiated settlements deal with disputes from family and work-related problems to complex international clashes, including civil wars and wars between countries (Davidheiser 2007). These techniques are often called "alternative dispute management."

While some anthropologists welcome the rise of alternative dispute management (Avruch 1998), Nader (1995, 2001) questions its implicit harmony ideology. She observes that many people involved in civil wars and other large-scale conflicts do not necessarily want harmony. They want justice, fairness, and the rule of law. This is a sentiment expressed by many Mozambicans, for example, whose civil war ended in a mediated settlement in 1992. Many Mozambicans believe that the settlement, which brought with it the introduction of foreign aid institutions and International Monetary Fund stabilization policies, actually deepened their woes by generating more poverty and inequality than before the war (Hanlon 1996).

There is not necessarily a "best way" to solve a dispute. If there were, there would be no more disputes! But dispute settlement is never a neutral act. In handling their disputes, people make ideological assumptions and enact social relationships that uphold particular power structures or, as Laura Nader suggests, even challenge those power structures.

THINKING CRITICALLY ABOUT POWER

Think about the last time you had a non-violent dispute in your life. How did you handle it? Was one or more of the strategies we discussed—avoidance, adjudication, negotiation, or mediation—involved? How might the outcome have been different if you had pursued a different strategy than the one you did?

Conclusion

If you pay much attention to political news on television or the Internet, you may have the impression that politics is mainly about politicians and their political parties, laws, and bureaucratic institutions. This impression offers only part of the story. Politics often involves some element of state power and bureaucratic processes. Every society has individuals who act a lot like North American politicians. From status leaders such as Big Men and councils of elders who settle disputes, to leaders of armed movements organizing violent acts, leaders everywhere use strategy, manipulation, persuasion, control over resources, and sometimes violence to obtain and maintain power over others.

Yet this view of politics is too narrow to appreciate the diverse forms that political power takes around the world. Not all societies train their young to deal with their problems through violence, and even those that accept violence place limits on its use, encouraging more peaceful ways of handling disputes. People not considered conventionally powerful have ways of challenging the power structure in their societies.

Politics is about relationships of cooperation, conflict, social control, and power that exist in any community and at all levels of social life, from the interpersonal and community levels to the national and transnational. The reason people around the world have so many ways of managing and thinking about those relationships is the same reason that cultural diversity persists in the world today: social processes like those involved in politics are always rooted in and emerge from people's everyday social interactions, belief systems, and cultural practices.

KEY TERMS

Acephalous society
  p. 423

Action theory   p. 426

Adjudication   p. 441

Age-grades   p. 424

Band   p. 424

Centralized political
  system   p. 424

Chiefdom   p. 424

Government   p. 423

Laws   p. 423

Mediation   p. 442

Nation-states   p. 429

Negotiation   p. 442

Non-centralized political
  system   p. 424

Political power   p. 426

Politics   p. 422

Prejudice   p. 435

Racialization   p. 433

State   p. 424

Structural power   p. 427

Structural-functionalism
  p. 424

Tribe   p. 424

Violence   p. 437

Reviewing the Chapter

Chapter Section	What We know	To Be Resolved
Does every society have a government?	Not every society has a government as we know it or makes a distinction between those who govern and those who are governed. Such societies organize their political lives on the basis of principles such as egalitarian social relations, reciprocity, and kinship.	Although classical anthropological studies identified many political processes in non-state societies, anthropologists continue to study and debate how successful these processes have been in confronting the transnational forces that affect almost every society today.
What is political power?	Political power operates in multidimensional ways: it is action oriented, it is structural, and it is gendered. It also tends to operate in particular ways in non-state contexts and in modern nation-states.	Anthropologists debate the relative importance of political power wielded by individuals and structural power shaping fields of social action.
How is social inequality constructed and upheld?	All social hierarchies appeal to a natural order to justify themselves. This natural order may feel inevitable, even morally necessary, but like all other cultural phenomena, it is constructed and dynamic. Races are socially, not biologically or genetically, determined. But due to racism, discrimination, and prejudice, race does have consequences for certain people's biological outcomes.	Anthropologists are still working to understand the ways the social dynamics of inequality, race, and racism express themselves through disparate biological outcomes.
Why do some societies seem more violent than others?	Neither violence nor non-violence is an inevitable condition. Both are learned behaviors expressed in particular social and historic circumstances.	Most peoples who have been characterized either as peaceful or violent are not uniformly peaceful or violent, yet it is not always clear what conditions might have transformed an otherwise peaceful people into a violent one or vice versa.
How do people avoid cycles of aggression, brutality, and war?	Disputes arise in all societies, but they do not necessarily result in aggression, brutality, and war because people everywhere have many peaceful strategies for settling disputes.	Anthropologists continue to debate the effectiveness of the new field of alternative dispute management, especially in cross-cultural and international settings.

Readings

A classic approach to politics is E. E. Evans-Pritchard's 1940 ethnography, *The Nuer: A Description of the Modes of Livelihood and Political Institutions of a Nilotic People* (Oxford: Clarendon Press, 1967). John Gledhill's book *Power and Its Disguises: Anthropological Perspectives on Politics* (Sterling, VA: Pluto Press, 2000) offers a comprehensive overview of this history and current approaches.

• • • • • • • • • • • • • • • • • • •

Two books offer a useful overview of how to think anthropologically about violence, including David Riches's edited book *The Anthropology of Violence* (Oxford: Basil Blackwell, 1986), and Douglas P. Fry's book *The Human Potential for Peace: An Anthropological Challenge to Assumptions About War and Violence* (New York: Oxford University Press, 2006).

• • • • • • • • • • • • • • • • • • •

In recent years, the American Anthropological Association has encouraged national dialogue on race and racism by sharing anthropological perspectives and research on the connections between race, biology, and culture. *Race: Are We So Different?* (http://www.understandingrace .com/home .html) is a website covering the latest anthropological thinking in about race.

• • • • • • • • • • • • • • • • • • •

Understanding Disputes: The Politics of Argument (Oxford: Berg, 1995), edited by Pat Caplan, offers a useful introduction to legal anthropology and includes essays by some of the leading figures in the field.

• •

Laura Nader's book *Harmony Ideology: Justice and Control in a Zapotec Mountain Village* (Stanford, CA: Stanford University Press, 1990) describes how one community manages disputes to maintain social harmony but not always to everyone's liking. It pairs well with the film *Little Injustices: Laura Nader Looks at the Law* (Washington, DC: PBS Video, 1981). Though dated, it offers relevant comparative insights into how two societies—Zapotec and U.S.—handle everyday disputes.

• •

Part IV

Constructing Meaningful Social Worlds

Throughout this book we have argued that meaning is culturally constructed by diverse social processes that touch on the political, economic, environmental, and biocultural aspects of who we are as humans. In this part we focus on three traditional aspects of culture that have long been the hallmark and, for some, the special domain of anthropology. These three are the role that kinship, religion, and material culture play in constructing meaningful social worlds in any community. The emphasis on these three domains does not mean that the prehistoric, economic, political, and other aspects of human social relations covered in Part III are not culturally constructed. They certainly are. But the goal of the chapters in this last part is to examine in closer detail the complex interactions between the creation of meaning, social order, and social change.

In the first of these chapters on kinship and gender, we consider one of the earliest domains studied by anthropologists. For a century from 1870 onward, most anthropologists were forced to tackle the complexities of how people related to one another as men and women in tribal- and village-based societies. There are only half a dozen different ways to organize and classify relatives, and yet within these six patterns humans construct all sorts of meaningful ways for people to live together as kin. These distinctive traditions create the most important and meaningful patterns that are in turn projected onto everything else in the environment. The chapter on religion returns to the next oldest topic anthropologists have studied since the 1870s, namely, how humans construct meaningful worlds that involve the moral, the ethical, and the philosophical. While many people assume that religion is about the supernatural, we argue that it is a meaning system that makes certain actions seem reasonable. Finally, in the last chapter on materiality we draw on cultural and archaeological anthropologies to explore how the most tangible objects in our worlds—everyday "stuff"—blend cultural conventions and individual experiences to create the most meaning of all. We take seriously the idea that human experience is rooted in the intertwining of people and things. We see this final chapter as capturing the essence of the cultural construction of meaning of all the chapters in this book, and yet this view is present to one degree or another in every other chapter.

Kinship and Gender

Sex, Power, and Control

of Men and Women

Soap operas like *General Hospital, Days of Our Lives*, and *The Young and the Restless* are one of the world's most popular and enduring television genres. Every day, hundreds of millions of people around the globe tune into one or more of them. Although some of these American soaps have enjoyed international popularity, it is Latin American shows—produced and exported by Mexicans, Venezuelans, Argentines, and Brazilians in particular—that have ruled screens worldwide during the past two decades.

One of the most popular Latin American exports of all time is the Mexican *telenovela* [tay-**lay**-noh-**vell**-ah] (as such shows are called in Spanish) *También los Ricos Lloran (The Rich Also Cry)*. Produced in 1979, it has enjoyed popularity and rebroadcasts in dozens of countries throughout the Americas, Europe, Asia, and Africa to the present day. *Telenovelas* usually run for only a few months and have a clear ending, unlike U.S. soaps, which are long running and open-ended.

The basic plot of *También los Ricos Lloran*, which many subsequent *telenovelas* have imitated, is as follows. A beautiful and poor young woman named Mariana becomes a maid for a rich and powerful family. She and the youngest son in the family, Luis Alberto, have a scandalous love affair and eventually get married. She has a baby son, Beto, but in a fit of temporary madness she gives him away to an old woman on the street.

Kinship and the Latin American *Telenovela* Latin American soap operas called *telenovelas* such as the Mexican show pictured here, *Ni Contigo Ni Sin Ti (Neither With You Nor Without You)*, have captivated global audiences for decades because of complicated, if perhaps unlikely, kin relations they present.

IN THIS CHAPTER

What Are Families, and How Are They Structured in Different Societies?
- Families, Ideal and Real
- Nuclear and Extended Families
- Kinship Terminologies
- How Families Control Power and Wealth

Why Do People Get Married?
- Why People Get Married
- Forms of Marriage
- Sex, Love, and the Power of Families over Young Couples

In What Ways Are Males and Females Different?
- Toward a Biocultural Perspective on Male and Female Differences
- Rethinking the Male–Female Dichotomy
- Explaining Gender/Sex Inequality

What Does It Mean to Be Neither Male Nor Female?
- Navajo *Nádleehé*
- Indian *Hijras*

Is Human Sexuality Just a Matter of Being Straight or Queer?
- Cultural Perspectives on Same-Sex Sexuality
- Controlling Sexuality

During the next eighteen years, Mariana searches desperately for Beto and miraculously finds him when he begins dating Marisabel, who is Mariana and Luis Alberto's adopted daughter (though she doesn't know she's adopted). Mariana tells Marisabel who Beto really is. Marisabel becomes hysterical at the thought of incest with her brother. Mariana does not, however, tell Luis Alberto, fearing he will get angry with her. He gets angry anyway because she spends so much time with Beto that Luis Alberto suspects the two are having an affair. In the final episode Luis Alberto confronts Beto and Mariana with a gun. In the program's final moments, Mariana screams "Son!" Luis Alberto goes ballistic. Beto screams, "Father, let me embrace you!" and the family is, against all odds, reunited at long last.

Dark family secrets, suspicious spouses, unruly children, irresponsible parents, and possible incest make for gripping television! But to an anthropologist—if not also for many viewers around the world—the fascination this show holds is not due simply to its unlikely storyline but rather to its presentation of the complexities of love, sex, and power that involve men, women, and children anywhere in the world.

Also noteworthy is the show's assumption that blood relations are the central defining relationships in people's lives—after all, Luis Alberto's anger disappears when he realizes Beto is his son, and Marisabel would probably not be so hysterical if she knew Beto wasn't her biological brother. For anthropologists, it is a noteworthy assumption mainly because it reflects one particular culture's way of defining family relationships. Around the world not all cultures give the same weight to biological relatedness for defining a family.

Indeed, the biological facts of procreation are only one aspect of what it means to have a family, or for that matter, to be male or female. What is more important is how these biological facts are interpreted and the special rights, obligations, and identities these facts confer on individuals. At the heart of anthropology's interest in kinship and gender is the question: *Why and how are relationships of kinship and gender more than simply a reflection of biological processes?* Embedded within this larger question are the following questions, around which this chapter is organized.

What are families, and how are they structured in different societies?

Why do people get married?

In what ways are males and females different?

What does it mean to be neither male nor female?

Is human sexuality just a matter of being straight or queer?

Family, sex, and gender are core features of people's lives and identities everywhere. The kinds of influence and control that people can exert on their relatives and individuals as men or women vary widely from one society to another. So let us begin by considering what makes a group of relatives a family.

What Are Families, and How Are They Structured in Different Societies?

Families are important in nearly every society. They give members a sense of comfort and belonging and provide them part of their identity, values, and ideals. They control wealth and the material necessities of life. And, importantly, they assign individuals with basic roles, rights, and responsibilities in relation to other relatives. **Kinship**—the social system that organizes people in families based on descent and marriage—is patterned in culturally specific and dynamic ways.

Families, Ideal and Real

In every society a gap exists between that society's ideal family and the real families that exist, because all families are dynamic. For example, as individuals grow older, they move out of their **natal family**—the family into which they were born and raised—to marry and start their own families. In addition, broader social and economic conditions change the composition, size, and character of ties between family members, as the example of the American family illustrates.

"Traditional" American Families

American politicians and religious leaders frequently extol the virtues of the "traditional" family. Just what family do these people have in mind? Most likely, it is some version of the family in the television show *The Adventures of Ozzie and Harriet* (which aired 1952–1966), with a working husband/father who is the head of the household, a loving stay-at-home wife/mother, and two or three children living in a spic-and-span suburban home.

This ideal is not a "traditional" family, but a new pattern—the independent American suburban family—that emerged in the 1950s and lasted for less than twenty years. During the Great Depression of the 1930s, American birth rates had fallen sharply because of limited incomes. The birth rate remained low throughout World War II. But once the millions of men serving in the military returned, they began to marry and start families. The 1950s were a time of unprecedented economic growth, and the baby boom—77 million babies in 15 years—encouraged expansion of new subdivisions filled with these young families. By the late 1950s around 60% of all Americans lived in such families.

During the late 1960s and 1970s these young families had grown up, children moved out, and some couples divorced. Women began to join the workforce in larger numbers, lowering wages for entry-level jobs. By the 1980s it was hard for young American families to get by on one salary. Two-income households brought in more wages but put stress on couples, who still needed someone to cook their meals, clean up, and look after their children. Divorce became more common than ever before, and today only half of American households are headed by a married couple. When divorced couples with kids get remarried, the composition of a family (with multiple sets of step-parents and step-siblings)—and especially the obligations that individuals in the family have to each other—can get quite complicated.

- **Kinship.** The social system that organizes people in families based on descent and marriage.

- **Natal family.** The family into which a person is born and (usually) raised.

Nuclear and Extended Families

- **Nuclear family.** The family formed by a married couple and their children.

- **Kinship chart.** A visual representation of family relationships.

- **Corporate groups.** Groups of real people who work together toward common ends, much like a corporation does.

- **Extended families.** Larger groups of relatives beyond the nuclear family, often living in the same household.

Still, the **nuclear family**—the family formed by a married couple and their children—is the most important family structure in the United States. Ours is not the only society with nuclear families—nuclear family units occur in and are important to nearly every society around the world. Indeed, for many decades anthropologists wrote of the nuclear family as the most basic unit of kinship (Radcliffe-Brown 1941:2).

Using a basic **kinship chart** (a visual representation of family relationships), we can graph a man's nuclear family easily enough, and we can add another nuclear family for his wife's natal family, and add children (Figure 17.1). Such charts only describe the biological connections, such as mother-daughter or father-daughter—without expressing the content of these different relationships. For example, when the child is young, the relationship between parent and child may involve teaching and training, while later that individual may care for the parent.

One important feature of nuclear and natal families is that they usually function as **corporate groups,** which are groups of real people who work together toward common ends, much like a corporation does. The family's goals are not just the goals of one family member, but of the group as a whole. In every society around the world, families are supposed to look after the needs of all members of the family—parents, children, and any other members who happen to be in residence.

Family groups may also consist of larger groups of relatives beyond the nuclear family, which anthropologists call **extended families**. Extended families may live together and function as a corporate group, or they may merely acknowledge ties with one another. In nineteenth-century America, for example, it was common for households to include a nuclear family at its core, as well as some mix of elderly parents, a single brother or sister, the orphaned children of the wife's sister, and so on (Figure 17.2).

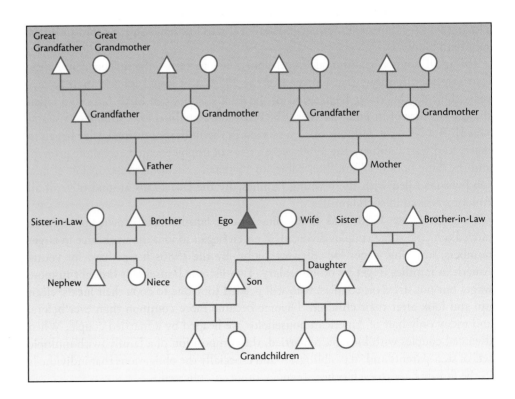

Figure 17.1   A Kinship Chart Plots All Sorts of Kin Relations.   Here the chart shows members of the extended family from a husband/father's perspective. Of course, the chart could be drawn from the wife/mother's perspective as well.

A **clan** is a type of extended family, a special group of relatives who are all descended from a single ancestor. In many societies, links to these ancestors can be quite vague, and in a number of societies these ancestors are animals or humans with distinctive non-human characteristics. Clans are so important in many societies that in the 1940s French anthropologist Claude Lévi-Strauss (1969) argued that the clan, not nuclear family, was the basic unit of kinship. Clans typically control land and other resources, as well as any individual member's access to those resources. They are also usually **exogamous**, which means that members of the clan must marry someone from another clan, effectively building political, economic, and social ties with other clans. **Lineages** are very similar to clans, but lineages tend to be composed of people who are directly descended from known ancestors, while clan membership is often vague and assumed rather than empirically known. Clans and lineages come in three types, as explored in Table 17.1.

Kinship Terminologies

Another way to think about the structure of families is to explore terms that people in different societies use to refer to their relatives. Beginning in the 1860s, with American anthropologist Lewis Henry Morgan (1871), anthropologists have collected thousands of different kinship terminologies. It happens that all of them can be grouped into six basic patterns Morgan identified long ago, as we show in Figure 17.3.

Anthropologists have also realized that kinship terminologies do not just provide descriptive names that indicate relationships between individuals but can also indicate the specific nature of the relationship, rights, and responsibilities that exist between related people. For example, in many American Indian societies, an individual will use the term *father* to

Figure 17.2   Extended Families in North America. (Top) An Indian family from the Kainai tribe in the Canadian plains about 1900. (Bottom) An American extended family gathers for a reunion in Mt. Carmel, Illinois, 1904. Everyone in the photo is descended from one deceased couple, parents of seven of the senior women pictured.

- **Clan.** A group of relatives who claim to be descended from a single ancestor.

TABLE 17.1		TYPES OF CLANS AND LINEAGES		
Type of Clan or Lineage	Definition	Features		Examples
Patrilineal	Membership based on descent from a common male ancestor.	Inheritance of property, rights, names, or titles come through an individual's father.		Omaha Indians, Nuer of South Sudan, many groups in Central Highlands of Papua New Guinea. Most Americans inherit last names patrilineally.
Matrilineal	Membership based on descent from a common female ancestor.	Every man and woman is a member of his or her mother's clan, which is also the clan of their mother's mother. It is not the same as matriarchy, in which women hold political power; it is only about identity and group membership. Land is usually owned by the clan or lineage. While women may have some say in who uses clan land, it is usually the men in the clan who have control over resources.		Trobriand Islanders
Cognatic (also known as "bilateral")	Descent comes through both mother and father.	Membership in multiple clans is possible or even typical.		Samoans of Central Polynesia

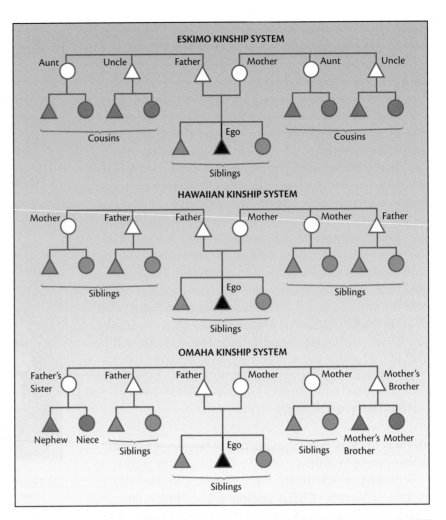

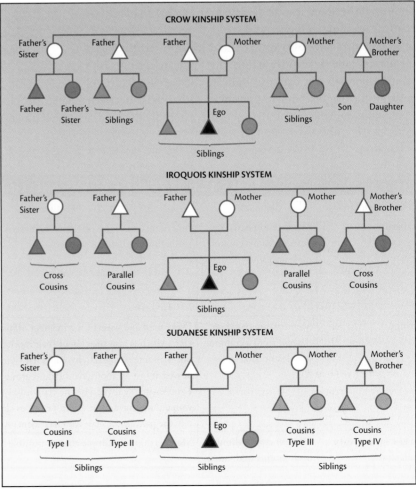

✿ **Figure 17.3 The Six Basic Systems of Kinship.** Anthropologists have identified six different basic kinship systems. The differences can be understood by how people refer to the different cousins.

refer not just to his biological father, but to his father's brothers or even other men of his father's generation with no direct biological ties. The "father" is expected to interact with his "son" in certain culturally accepted ways, such as providing food or assistance.

The Problem of Genealogical Amnesia

Kinship terminologies also help people keep track of their many relatives by assigning categorical terms. But nobody can keep track of everybody. Each society has kinspeople who are vital to keep track of, while others, usually more distant relatives, are forgotten. Anthropologists refer to this structural process of forgetting whole groups of relatives as **genealogical amnesia**. We explore this phenomenon in more detail in "Thinking Like an Anthropologist: Genealogical Amnesia in Bali, Indonesia, and the United States."

How Families Control Power and Wealth

Whatever form of family we might find in a society, one of its key functions is controlling and managing its members' wealth. The most obvious way for a family, lineage, or clan group to control its wealth is by defining rights over the productive and reproductive abilities of its women and children, as well as defining the inheritance rights of family members when someone dies. These dynamics of control involve issues like:

- *Claiming a Bride.* In non-industrial societies in which women provide much of the labor needed to plant, weed, and harvest food from their fields and gardens, when a young woman marries, her family loses that labor. To compensate her clan, the groom's family gives valuables to the bride's family in what has been called bridewealth, or simply **bride price.** Types of valuables given can range from cattle (Zulu tribes of southern Africa) or wild game (some Amazonian communities), to pigs and shell valuables (many Papua New Guinea societies) and cash. In some societies, a young man has to work for his wife's family for a year or more, performing what can be called "bride service."

- *Recruiting the Kids.* Child price payments are another kind of payment to a woman's family, intended to buy rights in the woman's children. Such payments compensate the woman's family for a child who belongs to a different clan and allow the father to recruit the child to his clan. This sort of transaction over children is most typical in societies with patrilineal clans, rather than in those with matrilineal clans, where the children belong to their mother's clan and typically live with her. In some societies, child price payments can be paid all at once, but the power of these transactions can best be understood in societies like the Daribi of the Highlands of Papua New Guinea, where payments may take place over many years. Anthropologist Roy Wagner (1967, 1969), who studied the Daribi, observed that because transactions between clans are about creating alliances, the ongoing series of payments preserve and perpetuate the relationship between the child's father and the uncle who come from different clans.

- *Ensuring a Daughter's Welfare.* Another form of marriage payment occurs in the highly stratified communities of India. Here, high caste families traditionally gave a **dowry** consisting of a large sum of money—or in-kind gifts of livestock, furniture, or even electronics—to a daughter to ensure her well-being in her husband's family. Sometimes the dowry was given, at least in part, to the

- **Exogamous.** A social pattern in which members of a clan must marry someone from another clan, which has the effect of building political, economic, and social ties with other clans.

- **Lineage.** A group composed of relatives who are directly descended from known ancestors.

- **Genealogical amnesia.** Structural process of forgetting whole groups of relatives, usually because they are not currently significant in social life.

- **Bride price.** Exchange of gifts or money to compensate another clan or family for the loss of one of its women along with her productive and reproductive abilities in marriage. Sometimes known as "bride wealth."

- **Dowry.** A large sum of money or in-kind gifts given to a daughter to ensure her well-being in her husband's family.

Thinking Like an Anthropologist

Genealogical Amnesia in Bali, Indonesia, and the United States

ANTHROPOLOGISTS BEGIN THEIR research by asking questions. In this box, we want you to learn how to ask questions as an anthropological researcher. Part 1 describes a situation and follows up with questions we would ask. Part 2 asks you to do the same thing with a different situation.

PART 1: GENEALOGICAL AMNESIA AND NAMING PATTERNS ON THE ISLAND OF BALI

In the late 1950s American anthropologists Hildred and Clifford Geertz (1964, 1975) studied Balinese kinship patterns on the lush, tropical island of Bali in Indonesia. The Balinese have a bilateral kinship system, which means that an individual is related equally to relatives in his or her mother's and father's family (much as Americans are). People are more or less "closely" related, at least in theory, to everyone who is descended from any one of their sixteen great-great-grandparents.

How do the Balinese keep track of them all? The Geertzes found that people don't. While Balinese lived in large extended family groups, the number of relatives they actually interacted with was limited to a few dozen members. Most informants were aware of only a couple hundred kinsmen rather than the thousands that were theoretically possible. The Geertzes referred to this forgetting of relatives as "genealogical amnesia."

Genealogical amnesia was not about how particular individuals literally forgot some of their relatives, but how features of normal social life encourage people to focus on some relatives so that other relatives gradually drift off their radar screen. It is also not random, but quite systematic. In Bali it is the result of a particular naming system. All Balinese have personal names, and as in the United States and other countries, parents often name their children after grandparents, aunts and uncles, and great-grandparents. But after Balinese men and women marry they are no longer called by their personal names; they are referred to as "father of so-and-so" or "mother of so-and-so." As their children get older and marry, they will begin to be referred to as grandfather or grandmother of so-and-so. (Anthropologists call this naming practice **teknonymy**, a system of naming parents by the names of their children.)

In Bali the teknonyms assigned to individuals kept changing over time as people got older, and so the younger people

🌱 **A Modern Balinese Family Attending a Ceremony.** Most members of this extended family live together in several households inside the same house yard.

often never heard the personal names of their grandparents and great-grandparents. The effect of this rather simple naming system was that everyone knew they were related to everyone who was a descendant of a great-grandparent—who would be known as great-grandparent of so-and-so. But the pattern also obscured the precise relationship to living relatives, since all the personal names several generations back were no longer used in conversation. Earlier generations were only known by the names of their first-born grandchildren or great-grandchildren, and even these identifications became difficult to pick out of daily conversation after people in those generations had died.

What questions does this situation raise for anthropological researchers?

1. How does being a grandchild of someone with a particular teknonym help you identify other close relatives?
2. What happens to people's knowledge of their common kin ties once their great-grandparents die?
3. How might people be able to identify kin relations more easily if everyone used personal names rather than teknonyms?

PART 2: GENEALOGICAL AMNESIA IN AMERICAN FAMILIES

In the United States, naming practices also produce a systematic pattern of genealogical amnesia that encourages us to forget large groups of family members because we lose track of their surnames. One of the most obvious effects of genealogical amnesia comes from women dropping their maiden names when they marry. Until the 1970s taking the husband's surname was the most typical pattern. What questions would you ask about this situation as an anthropological researcher?

groom as a way of attracting a prosperous and hard-working husband. The Indian government outlawed the practice of dowry in 1961, though it has continued in many parts of the country. Like many social practices that are changing, dowry can sometimes encourage poor treatment of wives and even the death of a wife as a way of gaining access to the wife's dowry, as we read periodically of dowry deaths in the news.

- *Rules of Inheritance.* Families also control wealth, property, and power through inheritance rules. These rules ensure an orderly process after someone dies and for wealth and property to stay in the family. In Western countries, such rules have been codified in law for a long time. For example, centuries ago Great Britain acknowledged the right of primogeniture, in which the eldest son inherited a man's lands and other wealth. Its goal was to preserve large landed estates and the wealth needed to maintain them. Small-scale non-industrial societies typically have inheritance rules as well, even though many of them lack a formal legal code. When people die in these societies, land and some forms of durable personal property, often controlled by clans, are the most important things to be inherited.

In any society, inheritance goes to legitimate heirs—typically the children of a socially recognized married couple. But marriage is such a complicated social institution that we should consider what motivates people to get married in the first place.

- **Teknonymy.** A system of naming parents by the names of their children.

THINKING CRITICALLY ABOUT KINSHIP, MARRIAGE, AND THE FAMILY

Consider the most recent wedding you may have attended, or ask a friend or relative about a wedding they attended as a guest. Who paid for different parts of the celebration (reception, officiant, wedding license, flowers, bridesmaids' dresses, groomsmen's tuxes, gifts to bridesmaids and groomsmen, rehearsal dinner, etc.)? Who should give gifts and to whom should these gifts should be given? How do the dollars and cents of a wedding outline the structure of American families and kin groups?

Why Do People Get Married?

For at least two centuries American religious leaders have preached that sex is reserved for marriage; it is primarily for procreation. The study *Sex in America* (Michael et al. 1994) found that, on average, married couples (together with unmarried couples who live together) have sex more often and more regularly than single people. But while marriage does indeed involve procreation, it is about a lot more than sex. In this section we explain why and the diverse forms that marriage can take.

Why People Get Married

For the most part, Americans take for granted our individual right to choose a marriage partner, and it is usually rooted in feelings of love. Our ideology of individualism emphasizes that we alone make the decision about who to marry. But in most societies around the world, marriage is about cultivating political and economic relations between families. In such contexts, marriage is considered too important to be left to the whims of an individual, and so family members choose an individual's marriage partner.

Marriage also provides public social recognition of the ties between the couples, their families, and social legitimacy of the children. The importance of public recognition at least partially helps explain why gay and lesbian marriage has become a key issue in the past decade in many societies, including the United States, Canada, Mexico, and Argentina; it also has to do with gaining rights for couples, such as inheritance.

Forms of Marriage

- **Polygamy.** Any form of plural marriage.

- **Polygyny.** When a man is simultaneously married to more than one woman.

- **Polyandry.** When a woman has two or more husbands at one time.

Just as we have seen the definition of marriage widening in some states and countries to include same-sex marriages, the tendency around the world has increasingly been to limit the number of partners to a couple. In many traditional societies in Africa, Asia, the Americas, and the Pacific, **polygamy** (or plural marriage) was far more common previously than it is today. The most common form of plural marriage was **polygyny**, in which one man is married simultaneously to two or more women. In Africa and Melanesia, having more than one wife indicates an important man with wealth and high status. From a woman's point of view, being in a polygynous marriage can mean that other wives provide support in conducting household duties, such as raising children, cooking, and so on. But as these indigenous economies have been drawn into the global system, the number of men with two or more wives has declined, as it is increasingly considered too costly and too old-fashioned (Figure 17.4).

The other form of plural marriage is **polyandry**, in which one woman has two or more husbands at one time. Few societies around the world are known to have allowed polyandry. The best known are the Toda, one of the hill tribes in India (Dakowski 1990; Rivers 1906), and the Sherpas of Nepal, who formerly used polyandry to keep large estates from being divided into tiny estates (Ortner 1989). Among both the Todas and the Sherpas, a group of brothers marries the same woman, a practice known as fraternal polyandry, which limits the tensions among co-husbands.

Sex, Love, and the Power of Families over Young Couples

All societies around the world have rules about who one can have sex and who can get married to whom. Parents and other family members may reject certain possible partners, who come from the "wrong" socioeconomic, religious, educational, or ethnic background. There are also prohibitions against marriage with people who are too closely related.

The Incest Taboo

The prohibition on sexual relations between close family members is generally called the **incest taboo**. It is as close to a universal feature of human societies as anything. There are two well-known exceptions to the incest taboo, both of which prove its generality: in ancient Egypt, during the reigns of the pharaohs, and in Hawai'i, before Europeans encountered the islands for the first time in 1778. In both societies, ruling monarchs could engage in incest because they were considered living gods, who could only preserve the divine essence of their being by marrying a sibling.

For relationships beyond the nuclear family—such as marriage of cousins—societies vary in what they allow. In Africa, Southeast Asia, South America, Australia, and New Guinea, the incest taboo also includes prohibitions on marriage with some kinds of cousins, particularly in societies with a unilineal clan system. And in most clan-based societies the prohibition on marriage within the clan suggests that this extension of the incest taboo defines the boundaries of the clan, just as the boundaries of incest define the boundaries of the nuclear family.

Why Is There an Incest Taboo?

Social scientists have suggested two general explanations for the incest taboo. The most common is that the taboo prevents birth defects caused by inbreeding. The main problem with this explanation is that within a community as small as 300 to 500 individuals, where people are already interrelated, the odds of harmful gene combinations are effectively the same for marriage with a first cousin as for random pairings.

A second explanation, called the "Westermarck Effect," explains the incest taboo as a natural psychological revulsion toward marriage (or sex) with close relatives. Recently, evolutionary psychologists like Steven Pinker (1997) have adopted this explanation, arguing that evolution has selected genes that cause us to feel little sexual attraction for people we have grown up with. But no gene (or combination of genes) has been identified for the proposed revulsion, and the range of relatives prohibited by the incest taboo varies too widely from society to society to be explained by selection. Further, there is no reason to assume that the revulsion is the cause of the taboo, when it is equally probable that the incest taboo itself generates the psychological revulsion.

Many anthropologists reject the idea altogether that the incest taboo emerges out of biology, emphasizing its origins in culture and ordinary life. They point to the research of Melford Spiro (1958), an anthropologist who studied life in an Israeli kibbutz in the 1950s. Spiro found that the adolescents who lived together in large communal settings avoided marrying or even dating members of their communal group. There was no rule against marriage or sex within the group, but there simply was no sexual attraction because they thought of other members as siblings. This situation is not at all unlike what happens in American college coed dorms, where there is similar avoidance of sexual liaisons such as the "hallway hookup" or "dormcest" that can produce social complications for both parties (Sivo 2005).

Figure 17.4 Polygamy Is Largely in Decline Around the World. (Top) An image of a polygamous family in Ramallah in the early twentieth century; most Palestinian men have one wife today. (Bottom) The so-called Jack-Mormons of Utah, Colorado, and Texas, who have broken away from the Mormon Church based in Salt Lake City, are the main exception in the United States and still practice polygyny.

- **Incest taboo.** The prohibition on sexual relations between close family members.

As we have shown here, culture shapes how people handle the biological relationships associated with kinship. In the next section, we shift gears and examine how culture also contributes to how people think about what it means to be male or female.

· ·

THINKING CRITICALLY ABOUT KINSHIP, MARRIAGE, AND THE FAMILY

Americans often think that marriage is about "love." But marriage is also about economics. Being married and having a family cost money. Recent studies have determined that the average age at marriage in the United States has been rising for several decades as middle-class incomes have declined. Discuss how the economics of modern American life help shape the decision to get married.

· ·

In What Ways Are Males and Females Different?

Walk into any kids' clothing store in a North American mall and the message is clear: boys and girls are fundamentally different. The boys' section is stocked with T-shirts in blue and other dark colors emblazoned with images of trucks, guns, or sports equipment. The girls' collection is full of frilly dresses and lace-lined shirts and pants in pastel colors like pink and purple, featuring images of butterflies, flowers, and so on. Judging by these articles, boys are adventuresome, active, and aggressive, while girls are nurturing, domestic, and sentimental (Figure 17.5).

These clothes convey powerful stereotypes about supposed differences in temperament and personality between males and females. In recent decades these stereotypes have become topics of intense debate in the United States, as our culture struggles over issues like why women are excluded from certain kinds of jobs in the military and positions of institutional leadership, and why men dominate certain professions like math and sciences. The issue is not whether our culture distinguishes males and females. The real issue is to explain why our culture constructs these differences in the specific ways it does (Brettell and Sargent 2001).

Toward a Biocultural Perspective on Male and Female Differences

The primary explanation our culture gives for differences between males and females is that they are "hardwired" differently. Differences in **sex**, the reproductive forms and functions of the body, are even thought to produce differences in attitudes, temperaments, intelligences, aptitudes, and achievements between males and females. Some studies have suggested that in all human societies boys tend to engage in more rough-and-tumble play, while girls tend to be more engaged in infant contact and care, suggesting that such behaviors are determined at a species level (Edwards 1993). Recent studies also indicate that male and female brains do in certain senses function

· **Sex.** The reproductive forms and functions of the body.

Figure 17.5   Clothing and Sexual Difference. North American ideas about gender differences are powerfully expressed through the colors and characteristics of the clothing they are assigned from the earliest ages.

differently: women's left-brained tendencies provide them with superior verbal skills, while men's right-brained tendencies give them superior visual and spatial skills (McIntyre and Edwards 2009).

But any conclusions about hardwired sex differences are muddied by evidence that culture also shapes male and female preferences and behaviors. Anthropologists refer to the cultural expectations of how males and females should behave as **gender**. For example, the North American association of girls with pink and boys with blue feels natural and obvious. But it is thoroughly artificial: relatively few cultures associate a color with a particular gender, and a century ago in the United States, the colors were reversed, boys wearing pink and girls blue (Kidwell and Steele 1989). American attitudes toward boys and girls did not shift; what changed was the gender association of each color, which had consequences for children's clothing preferences. Anthropologists have long argued for the importance of gender in understanding males and females, as "Classic Contributions: Margaret Mead and the Sex/Gender Distinction" explores.

The distinction Mead made between sex (biology) and gender (cultural expectations) was influential among anthropologists for decades. But in recent years it has been breaking down because it is difficult to tease apart just how much differences in male and female behavior are caused by "sex," that is, shaped by biology, and how much they are caused by "gender," or cultural expectations (Collier and Yanagisako 1987). We do know that sex-specific biological influences on temperament are strongest during infancy and early childhood (McIntyre and Edwards 2009). But as children get older, cultural influences on behavior become much stronger. Furthermore, "sex" is not simply a product of nature; it is also mediated and produced in the context of a specific culture. In light of this complexity, anthropologists increasingly reject an either-or perspective—that it's *either* biology *or* culture, *either* sex *or* gender—and accept that male–female differences are shaped by a mix of biology, environmental conditions, and sociocultural processes (Worthman 1995).

Reflecting these intellectual shifts, anthropologists are changing their terminology, and commonly refer to the ideas and social patterns a society uses to organize males, females, and those who do not fit either category as **gender/sex systems** (Morris 1995; Nanda 2000). As these older oppositions between culture/gender and biology/sex melt away, more sophisticated biocultural perspectives on male and female differences are emerging, including ones that challenge a simplistic perspective on the male–female dichotomy (McIntyre and Edwards 2009).

Rethinking the Male–Female Dichotomy

In the idealized world of science textbooks, human beings are a **sexually dimorphic** species, which means that males and females have a different sexual form. You already know that, as a rule, nature divides humans into two sexes for the purposes of reproduction. You can probably name some minor exceptions to the rule—men with high voices, women with facial hair—but this is not enough to challenge certainties about the fact of male and female difference. On more systematic inspection, however, the dichotomy between males and females breaks down as variations in chromosomes, gonads, internal reproductive structures, hormones, and external genitalia become apparent (Fausto-Sterling 2000). Individuals who diverge from the male–female norm are called **intersex**, meaning they exhibit sexual organs and functions somewhere between, or including, male and female elements. Some individuals have both ovaries and testes; some have gonad development with separate but not fully developed male and female organs; and some have ovaries and testes growing in the same organ. Many intersex individuals are infertile, but not infrequently at least one of the gonads produces either sperm or eggs.

- **Gender.** Cultural expectations of how males and females should behave.

- **Gender/sex systems.** The ideas and social patterns a society uses to organize males, females, and those who do not fit either category.

- **Sexually dimorphic.** A characteristic of a species, in which males and females have different sexual forms.

- **Intersex.** Individuals who exhibit sexual organs and functions somewhere between male and female elements, often including elements of both.

CLASSIC CONTRIBUTIONS

Margaret Mead and the Sex/Gender Distinction

SINCE THE BEGINNING of her career in the 1920s, anthropologist Margaret Mead (1901–1978) was interested in the differences between males and females, the cultural roles assigned to each, and how sexual differences shaped an individual's life experiences and personality. Mead was possibly the first social scientist to distinguish between biological sex and culturally distinct gender roles (Viswesaran 1997), which she did in her 1935 book *Sex and Temperament in Three Primitive Societies*. This book, which analyzes sex differences in three Papua New Guinea societies (the Arapesh, the Mundugumor, and the Tchambuli), ends with this influential theoretical reflection on the cultural influences on male and female difference.

▼ **Margaret Mead.**

The material suggests that we may say that many, if not all, of the personality traits which we have called masculine or feminine are as lightly linked to sex as are the clothing, manners, and the form of head-dress that a society at a given period assigns to either sex. When we consider the behavior of the typical Arapesh man or woman as contrasted with the typical Mundugumor man or woman, the evidence is overwhelmingly in favour of the strength of social conditioning. In no other way can we account for the almost complete uniformity with which Arapesh children develop into contented, passive, secure persons, while Mundugumor children develop as characteristically into violent, aggressive, insecure persons. Only to the impact of the whole of the integrated culture upon the growing child can we lay the formation of the contrasting types. There is no other explanation of race, or diet, or selection that can be adduced to explain them. We are forced to conclude that human nature is almost unbelievably malleable, responding accurately and contrastingly to contrasting cultural conditions. The differences between individuals who are members of different cultures, like the differences between individuals within a culture, are almost entirely to be laid to differences in conditioning, especially in early childhood, and the form of this conditioning is culturally determined. Standardized personality differences between sexes are of this order, cultural creations to which each generation, male and female, is trained to conform. [Mead 1963:280–81, orig. 1935]

Questions for Reflection

1. Why would an anthropologist study three different societies in New Guinea to demonstrate that gender roles are culturally constructed rather than innately biological?

2. Some scholars have claimed that Mead's New Guinea examples are cultural stereotypes from within the three cultures she studied. If true, would these stereotypes undermine or support her claim that gender roles are cultural rather than biological?

One reputable estimate puts the frequency of intersex in the United States at 1.7% of all live births (Fausto-Sterling 2000). At 1.7 births per 100, intersex is much more common than an unusual but highly recognizable condition like albinism, which is 1 per 20,000 births. This figure of 1.7% is not universal; rates of intersex vary between populations. Yup'ik Eskimos in Alaska, for example, have a higher rate of intersex births: 3.5% of births have congenital adrenal hyperplasia, a condition produced by a genetic mutation that produces masculine genitalia in girls.

Different societies deal with intersex differently. Many cultures do not make anatomical features, such as genitalia, the dominant factors in constructing gender/sex identities, and some cultures recognize biological sex as a continuum. But European and North American societies—which construct sex as *either* male *or* female and focus on genitalia as markers of sex—have considered intersexuality abnormal, sometimes immoral, most recently turning it into a medical problem. In the United States, most intersex children are treated shortly after birth with "sex-assignment surgery," in which a doctor eliminates any genital ambiguity through surgery, and doctors counsel the parents to raise the child to correspond with that sexual assignment.

The decisions involved in sex-assignment surgery are rarely medical; they derive from culturally accepted notions about how a boy or girl should look. Surgeons create realistic-looking genitalia by removing body parts and using plastic surgery to construct "appropriate" genitalia. But there is no biological norm for penis or clitoris size or shape, and in fact, many boys are born with very small penises that get larger at puberty, and girls are born with much larger than average clitorises that present no clinical problems (Fausto-Sterling 2000). The goal of these surgeries is for the genitals' size and shape to convince others—parents, caretakers, other children, and future spouses—that the person is a male or a female.

But sex-assignment surgery shows that "sex" is not simply a biological phenomenon, but is—*quite literally*—constructed upon cultural assumptions: the assumption that sex is a dichotomy, as well as assumptions about what an ideal male or female should look like. These cultural assumptions stand in contrast to the evidence that human sex is not dichotomous and that natural variations occur in the shape and size of genitalia. These surgeries have become controversial, especially among many intersexuals, who during the past several decades have spoken out against their treatment, sometimes describing it as mutilation (Figure 17.6).

Explaining Gender/Sex Inequality

In nearly all societies with any degree of social stratification, more men are in leadership roles than women, not only in political roles, but in economic and social roles involving trade, exchange, kinship relations, ritual participation, and dispute resolution (Ortner 1996:176) (Figure 17.7). In the United States today, only

Figure 17.6 "Human Rights for Hermaphrodites, Too!" So says the man's T-shirt from a 2009 rally urging the International Olympic Committee in Lausanne, Switzerland to reject discrimination against athletes "suspected" of being intersex (the more common term these days for a hermaphrodite) who participate in international sporting competitions. The IOC has been criticized for supporting forced sexual identification tests and sexual reassignment surgery to "clarify" athletes' sex.

Figure 17.7 Batek Headwoman. The few exceptions to systematic male dominance are generally found in small hunter-gatherer societies, like the Batek of the Malay Peninsula in Southeast Asia. This small community lives in bands that anthropologists Kirk and Karen Endicott (2008) report are generally egalitarian in their gender roles, to the extent that the band they lived with during their fieldwork had this woman, Tanyogn, as its headwoman (1976).

Figure 17.8   **Feminism's First and Second Waves.**
The first wave (late 1800s, early 1900s) in Britain and the
United States focused on obstacles to sexual equality, such
as voting and property rights. Here the second wave
(1960s–1970s) focused on issues like unofficial inequalities
and reproductive rights. Both had a major influence on
anthropology.

18% of congressional seats are held by women; in the workplace women earn on average 81% of what their male counterparts earn; and sex discrimination persists in social expectations, such as the notion that women should do housework. Very few of the privileges men have over women are predicated on physical strength. So why is gender/sex inequality such a common feature of many societies?

Debating "the Second Sex"

In 1949, French existentialist philosopher Simone de Beauvoir published an influential book titled *The Second Sex* in which she argued that throughout history women have been considered "the second sex," inferior in status and subordinate to men (2010). Even before the publication of this book, during the Victorian era, a handful of women anthropologists had studied women's status and roles in other societies. A few of these anthropologists, animated by so-called first wave feminism that was beginning to challenge male domination and win the right to vote, wanted to understand if all societies treated women as unequally as Euro-American societies did. Nevertheless, until de Beauvoir's work inspired the emergence of a "second wave" of feminist anthropologists beginning in the 1950s and then again in the 1970s, anthropology as a discipline had largely ignored the issue of gender/sex inequality (Figure 17.8).

Most feminist anthropologists rejected the idea that biological differences are the source of women's subordination. Instead, they argued that cultural ideologies and social relations impose lower status, prestige, and power on women than men. But here the agreement ends, and during the 1970s and 1980s a major debate took place over whether gender inequality is universal and what causes it.

On one side were those who argued that women's lower status is universal. Influential feminist anthropologist Sherry Ortner observed that female subordination resulted from the distinction all societies make between "nature" and "culture" (Ortner 1974). Across many cultures, women are assigned symbolically to nature because of their role in childbearing and thus are viewed as uncultured and uncivilized. Men, on the other hand, are associated symbolically with culture and thus viewed as civilized and superior.

On the other side were feminist anthropologists who argued that egalitarian male–female relations have existed throughout human history. For example, many foraging societies exhibit gender complementarity and relative equality. Where gender/sex inequality does form, they observed, it has been the result of particular historical processes, especially the imposition of European capitalism and colonization on native peoples who were once egalitarian. For example, Eleanor Leacock (1981) argued that among the Montagnais-Naskapi [mohn-tan-**yay** nahs-**kah**-pee] of the Labrador Peninsula in Canada, women enjoyed equal status with men, held formal political power, exercised spiritual leadership, and controlled important economic activities before the arrival of Europeans. By the 1700s, however, dependence on the fur trade with Europeans undercut the traditional political system and economy, and Jesuit missionaries imposed compulsory Catholic schooling, which was hostile to women's independence and power. Eventually, the Montagnais-Naskapi developed a cultural view of women as inferior and subordinate.

Taking Stock of the Debate

On all sides of the feminist anthropology debate, participants recognized that gender/sex inequality is, if not universal, at least pervasive. More important, the debate brought the study of what women say and do to the mainstream of the discipline. The emergence of this so-called anthropology of women successfully challenged the discipline's historical bias toward studying males and closed a gap in the ethnographic record by producing studies of women's experiences and perspectives (Viswesaran 1997).

But the debate came to an impasse. There were differences of interpretation over the evidence, and participants shifted their positions. Ortner, for example, came to recognize that egalitarian relations between men and women can exist but also concluded that these relations are fragile and inconsistent (Ortner 1996). Critics of the debate, some of them calling for a "third wave" of feminism, asserted that second-wave feminism, although well intentioned in its concern for women around the world, made ethnocentric assumptions (Mohanty 1991). The critics challenge the idea that all women view the fight for political equality as a singular global priority. In many other countries, women's movements are more local and oriented toward fighting militarism, challenging foreign ideals about beauty and ways of being a woman, or gaining access to local political processes or economic opportunities (Basu 2010).

Reproducing Gender/Sex Inequalities

The impasse in the debate also accompanied a shift in how anthropologists studied relations between men and women. A number of anthropologists began to emphasize a focus on women *and* men, especially the dynamic relationships between them in everyday life.

From this vantage point, gender/sex inequality is not something static that people "possess"; it is something that they "do." For example, patterns of gender/sex inequality are reproduced in basic things like everyday language. What American men and women may say may include the same words but mean something different to each gender. As we explored in Chapter 5, such miscommunications happen because our culture has different expectations about how men and women should communicate.

Another influence of focusing on what men and women actually do has involved a rethinking of men. Until recently very few anthropologists had closely examined men *as men*, that is, how men and women collectively view and shape what "being a man" means, and how men actually perform, or act out, manhood (Gutmann 1997). The anthropological study of **masculinity**, the ideas and practices of manhood, has not just opened new avenues of research for understanding how gender/sex identities are constructed, it has also generated new perspectives on the issue of gender/sex inequality, including the notion that ideals of masculinity are dynamic and do not in themselves necessarily assume male dominance (Figure 17.9).

By focusing on the dynamic nature of gender/sex inequalities, anthropologists have come to understand that male domination and female subordination are reproduced and performed in complex ways in everyday life. But anthropologists have not only studied "men" and "women," they have also studied people who are not considered, or do not consider themselves, to be either men or women, an issue we address in the next section.

• **Masculinity.** The ideas and practices of manhood.

🌱 **Figure 17.9 Masculinity in Transition.** Broader social transformations—greater numbers of women working outside the home, boys and girls in schools given equal status, and the feminist movement—contribute to changing perceptions of manhood, including a new role in parenting.

●●

THINKING CRITICALLY ABOUT GENDER, SEX, AND SEXUALITY

Gender/sex inequalities are reproduced and performed in many different ways in daily life. Can you identify examples in the following: Advertising? Sports? Language? Cooking? Shopping at a mall? At the same time, these inequalities are often challenged by both men and women. Can you find examples of such challenges in the same contexts?

●●

What Does It Mean to Be Neither Male Nor Female?

Although they feel natural, the dichotomies we take for granted—male and female, man and woman—are as artificial and constructed as any society's gender/sex system. Many gender/sex systems around the world are less rigid or constraining than our own.

In many societies, some people live their lives as neither male nor female. They have a culturally accepted, and in some cases prestigious, symbolic niche and social pathway distinct from the cultural life plan of males and females (Herdt 1994). Anthropologists call this third gender, or **gender variance**, which refers to expressions of sex and gender that diverge from the male and female norms that dominate in most societies.

Third gender has often been entangled in debates about **sexuality**, which encompasses sexual preferences, desires, and practices. It has been viewed as a form of homosexuality, since some third-gender individuals engage in what appear to be same-sex sexual activities (Herdt 1994). But sexual preferences intersect in complex ways with gender variance. People everywhere establish their gender/sex identities, including normative categories like "man" or "woman," not by sexual practices but through social performance: wearing certain clothes, speaking and moving in certain ways, and performing certain social roles and occupations. To illustrate these points, we consider two examples of gender variance drawn from different cultures.

Navajo *Nádleehé*

Gender variance has been historically documented in over 150 American Indian societies, although it remains important in only a few societies. Today, where it exists, American Indian gender variance is often called "two-spirit," meaning that an individual has both male and female spirit. The phenomenon has been greatly misunderstood, largely because Western culture lacks the conceptual categories to translate the specific beliefs and customs related to gender variance in these societies (Roscoe 1994). For decades white Americans have used the term *berdache* [burr-**dash**], a derogatory Arabic term that refers to the younger partner in a male homosexual relationship, to refer to gender variance among American Indians. This term assumes that gender-variant individuals are homosexual, which is sometimes but not always the case (Figure 17.10). Western moral thought also categorized them as deviants, although in a number of Indian societies third-gender individuals are not deviant but held high social status.

- **Gender variance.** Expressions of sex and gender that diverge from the male and female norms that dominate in most societies.

- **Sexuality.** Sexual preferences, desires, and practices.

Figure 17.10   Two Spirit Singers at a Gathering. Unlike traditional gender variants in American Indian societies, many contemporary two spirit individuals are gay. Due to antigay sentiment, they often experience hostility and discrimination in their home communities. They also feel alienated from white gay and lesbian society and political activism, which does not acknowledge their unique cultural heritage and the issues of poverty and racism they face as Indians.

The Navajo, who live in the Four Corners area of the Southwest, present an especially subtle example of gender variance. In Navajo society, *nádleehé* [nahk-**hlay**] are individuals held in high esteem who combine male and female roles and characteristics. They perform both male roles (such as hauling wood and participating in hunts and warfare) and female roles (such as weaving, cooking, sheepherding, and washing clothes). Some, but not all, *nádleehé* cross-dress. Navajo families have traditionally treated *nádleehé* respectfully, even giving them control over family property. The *nádleehé* participate in important religious ceremonies, serve as spiritual healers, and act as go-betweens in arranging marriages and mediating conflicts.

Navajo recognize five genders, two of them being male and female. The term *nádleehé* (in English, "one who changes continuously") refers to intersex individuals whom they consider a third gender. The fourth and fifth genders are also called *nádleehé* but are distinct from intersex individuals. The fourth gender is the masculine-female, female-bodied individuals who do not get involved in reproduction and who work in traditional male occupations (hunting and raiding). Today they often serve as firefighters or auto mechanics. The fifth gender is the feminine-male, male-bodied individuals who participate in women's activities of cooking, tending to children, and weaving. Feminine-males may engage in sexual relations with males, although Navajo do not consider these "homosexual" relationships.

The high social status of *nádleehé* became especially pronounced after the 1890s. The U.S. military forced Navajos onto reservations, undermining men's traditional economic activity of raiding (Roscoe 1994). These changes did not affect women's traditional economic pursuits, especially weaving and sheepherding, in which *nádleehé* also engaged. *Nádleehé* who took advantage of the opportunities presented by these social changes often became wealthy as shepherds and weavers.

Around the same time, however, Christian missionaries tried to eliminate the *nádleehé*. Prominent *nádleehé* began to be more discrete about exposing their identities to the outside world, a situation that continues today (W. Thomas 1997). Although *nádleehé* continue to exist, many young Navajos, especially those raised off reservation, might not identify themselves as *nádleehé* but as "gay" or "lesbian," adopting Western forms of identification that have little to do with traditional Navajo gender notions.

Indian *Hijras*

In India, *hijras* (*hee*-drahs) are a third gender who have special social status by virtue of their devotion to Bahuchara Mata, one of many versions of the Mother Goddess worshiped throughout India (Nanda 1994). *Hijras* are defined as males who are sexually impotent, either because they were born intersex or because they underwent castration. Because they lack male genitals, *hijras* are viewed as "man minus man." They are also seen as "male plus female" because they dress and talk like women, take on women's occupations, and act like women in other ways—although they act as women in an exaggerated, comic, and burlesque fashion (Figure 17.11).

Individuals become *hijras* from many religious backgrounds—Hindu, Christian, and Muslim—but their special status emerges from the positive meanings that Hinduism attributes to individuals who embody male and female characteristics and to individuals who renounce normal social conventions. In Hindu thought, males and females exist in complementary opposition. The important Hindu deities—Shiva, Vishnu, and Krishna—have dual gender manifestations. The female principle is active, both life-giving and destructive, while the male principle is inert and latent. By becoming *hijras* men can tap into the beneficent and destructive powers of the female principle, as vehicles for the Mother Goddess, giving them the ability to both bless and issue curses.

Hijras live in communes of up to twenty people, led by a *guru* (teacher). They live outside normal social bounds, having renounced their caste position and kinship obligations. Their primary social role is to provide blessings when a boy is born (a major cause of celebration in India) or bless a couple's fertility at a wedding. *Hijras* are typically a raucous presence at these events, making crude and inappropriate jokes, performing burlesque dances, and demanding payment for their services. Although it is stigmatized within *hijra* communities, *hijras* also work as prostitutes, engaging in sex acts with men for pay. *Hijra* prostitutes are not necessarily considered "homosexuals"; Indian society does not consider human sexuality as a dichotomy between homosexuality and heterosexuality as ours does, and *hijras* are not considered males anyway.

Although British colonialism tried to outlaw *hijras*, they continued to exist largely by conducting their initiation rites (including castration of willing males) in secret. In recent decades they have had to adapt to a changing Indian society. Government

Figure 17.11   *Hijras* in India.

family-planning programs have reduced birth rates, and urban families increasingly live in apartment buildings with security guards who prevent the entrance of *hijras* when they arrive to bless a baby. In response, *hijras* have exploited new economic opportunities, asking for alms from shopowners and expanding prostitution (Nanda 1994:415). They continue to exist mainly because the Indian gender/sex system still considers the combination of male and female as valid and meaningful.

THINKING CRITICALLY ABOUT GENDER, SEX, AND SEXUALITY

Societies in which gender variance is common tend to also be tolerant toward ambiguity and complexity in other areas of life, such as religious beliefs. How and why might a society develop an acceptance of ambiguity and complexity? Beyond gender and religious beliefs, in what other aspects of social life might one expect to see a tolerance for ambiguity?

Is Human Sexuality Just a Matter of Being Straight or Queer?

Most of us assume that sexuality (sexual preferences, desires, and practices) is an either/or issue, that people are *either* heterosexual *or* homosexual. We also assume that most humans are heterosexual. The term we use to indicate heterosexuality—"straight"—implies that it is normal and morally correct, while anything else is deviant, bent, or "queer," a term that once had derogatory connotations but in recent years has been given positive connotation in gay and lesbian communities.

But human sexuality is far more complex and subtle, something that social scientists began to realize after Indiana University biologist Dr. Alfred Kinsey conducted a series of sexuality studies during the 1940s. Kinsey and his colleagues surveyed the sexual lives and desires of American men and women, discovering that sexuality exists along a continuum. They found, for example, that 37% of the male population surveyed had had some homosexual experience, most of which occurred during adolescence, and at least 25% of adult males had had more than incidental homosexual experiences for at least three years of their lives (Kinsey 1948; Fausto-Sterling 1992). Many of these men did not think of themselves or lead their lives as "homosexuals"; this suggests quite clearly that, in practice, people's sexuality does not fall into absolute categories. More important, Kinsey's research challenged views of homosexuality that considered it a pathological and deviant condition, indicating that psychologically "normal" people may express their sexuality in many ways (Figure 17.12).

Anthropologists today emphasize that human sexuality is a flexible phenomenon ranging along a continuum from asexual (non-sexuality) to polyamorous (love of many). They reject the notion that sexuality is an essence buried deep in a person's psychological self or genetic makeup (Lancaster 2004) or the notion that sexuality is just a matter of personal preference or individual orientation. Instead, they argue that, like other forms of social conduct, sexuality is learned, patterned, and shaped by culture and the political-economic system in which one lives (Weston 1993).

Figure 17.12   Controversial Knowledge. Kinsey's work was highly controversial during a period in American history when homosexuality and heterosexual promiscuity were considered unacceptable.

Cultural Perspectives on Same-Sex Sexuality

Although some anthropologists wrote about sexual desires and practices in certain non-industrialized societies in the 1920s (Lyons and Lyons 2004), it was not until the 1960s and 1970s—when a gay movement emerged in the United States—that anthropologists began paying more consistent attention to same-sex sexuality (Weston 1993). More recently the global HIV/AIDS pandemic, the visibility of openly gay celebrities, and the push for legal rights for gays have encouraged even more anthropological attention (Lewin and Leap 2009; Parker 2009). A number of ethnographers have also written about how their own experience as gay affects their work as anthropologists (Lewin and Leap 1996), a theme we explore in "Doing Fieldwork: Don Kulick and 'Coming Out' in the Field."

One of the difficulties of studying homosexuality in other societies is the problem of adequately naming it (Weston 1993). Most North Americans hold the view that sexuality is a fixed and stable condition and identity. This notion originated in the late nineteenth century, when medical science and psychology turned what people had previously considered "perverse" *behaviors* into biopsychological *conditions* requiring medical intervention. Anthropologists have found in other cultures that same-sex behaviors can exist alongside heterosexual behaviors, suggesting that the assumptions we make about the term "homosexuality"—especially that it is an either/or condition—do not necessarily apply in other cultures.

One example comes from the work of anthropologist Gilbert Herdt, who studied the male initiation rituals of the Sambia people of Papua New Guinea. Boys undergo six elaborate stages of initiation that involve behavior he calls "insemination." To be a

Doing Fieldwork

Don Kulick and "Coming Out" in the Field

IN BRAZIL'S THIRD-LARGEST city of Salvador live nearly 200 *travestis* [trah-vest-tees], men who cross-dress and work as prostitutes. *Travestis* adopt female names, clothing styles, hairstyles, makeup, and linguistic pronouns (like "her"). They also ingest hormones and use silicone to acquire feminine bodily features, such as breasts, wide hips, large thighs, and expansive buttocks (Kulick 1998). But *travestis* do not self-identify as women, nor do they desire to remove their penises surgically. They consider themselves men—gay men—who desire to have sex with other men—non-gay men—and fashion themselves as an object of desire for those men.

Brazilians are fascinated by *travestis*, several of whom have become national celebrities. But the reality for most *travestis* is that they are discriminated against and poor, living a hand-to-mouth existence, and often dying young from violence, drug abuse, and health problems, particularly AIDS. During the late 1990s, Swedish anthropologist Don Kulick spent a year living among Salvador's *travestis* to understand the day-to-day realities of their lives.

Kulick believes that several factors helped him gain acceptance in the insular community. One of these was that *travestis* were open to his involvement in their lives because they viewed Europeans as more liberal and cultivated than Brazilians, and he would not have the same prejudices against their lives that Brazilians would. Another is that when Kulick started his fieldwork he spoke very little Portuguese, and so could not communicate very well. *Travestis* came to see him as a non-threatening presence, someone who would not condemn them.

Kulick believes a third factor played an especially crucial role in his gaining acceptance: he is a gay man. The *travestis* asked about his sexual orientation right away, if he was a *viado* (a "fag"). Kulick observes, "Upon receiving an affirmative answer, *travestis* often nodded and relaxed considerably. My status as a self-acknowledged *viado* implied to the *travestis* that I was, in effect, one of the girls, and that I probably was not interested in them as sexual partners. My behavior quickly confirmed that I was not, and after such preliminaries were out of the way, *travestis* realized that they could continue conversing about the topics—boyfriends, clients, big penises, hormone, and silicone—that occupy their time, without having to worry that I might find such topics uninteresting or offensive" (1998:15).

Previous research on *travestis* had been conducted by heterosexual women and a Brazilian male researcher who had presented himself as a potential client. These studies focused on their work as prostitutes, but these researchers had not gained access to the *travestis'* private worlds. Kulick believes that "coming out" to the *travestis* as an openly gay man facilitated access to confidences and discussions that may not have been granted as easily to other researchers.

Questions for Reflection

1. Kulick argues that an anthropologist's access to this community was benefited by being gay and seen as "one of them." Would this extend to other identities? For example, should women study women's lives and men study men's lives?

2. Although Kulick reports his coming out as positive, it was also risky. What kinds of risks might his coming out have had?

strong, powerful warrior requires *jerungdu* (the essence of masculine strength), a substance a boy can only acquire from ingesting the semen of a man. Before insemination the boys must purge harmful feminine essences with a rite that mimics female menstruation: sharp grasses are shoved up the noses of the boys to make them bleed off the lingering essences of their mother's milk. Finally, they perform fellatio on young married men, receiving *jerungdu*. During the early stages of the initiation the boys are inseminated orally by young married men at the height of their sexual and physical powers. When the initiates reach later stages of initiation—after marriage but before they become fathers—younger initiates will perform oral sex on them. The final stage of initiation occurs after the birth of their first child. Now in their twenties or thirties, the men have sex only with women.

Herdt (1981) referred to these initiation activities as "ritualized homosexuality," a term that highlights the homoerotic nature of these rites. But this is more complicated because after marriage Sambia men shift their erotic focus to women. Furthermore, the term implies that these acts are intended for erotic pleasure, while for the Sambia these ritual acts are intended to develop masculine strength. Herdt and others who study similar rites now refer to them as "semen transactions" or "boy-inseminating rites."

Anthropologists have also learned that concepts of same-sex sexuality differ across cultures. In Latin American countries like Mexico (Carrier 1976), Nicaragua (Lancaster 1992, 1997), and Brazil (Parker 1989, 2009), a man who engages in same-sex practices is not necessarily identified as (nor would he consider himself) a "homosexual." For example, in numerous Latin American countries, sexual culture distinguishes between being active and being passive participants in sexual intercourse, typically considering the active agent masculine and the passive agent feminine. The result is that a man who penetrates another man would not consider himself—nor would he be considered by others—a homosexual, yet the man being penetrated would be considered homosexual.

Controlling Sexuality

Long ago, anthropologists observed that every society places limits on people's sexuality by constructing rules about who can sleep with whom. But in the modern world, governments have asserted unprecedented levels of control over sexuality, routinely implementing and enforcing laws that limit the kinds of sexual relations their citizens can have. For example, in dozens of countries around the world, and even in twenty-one U.S. states, adultery is considered "injurious to public morals and a mistreatment of the marriage relationship" (Adultery 2009) and is treated by authorities as a civil offense (subject to fines) or even a crime (subject to jail time). Until the U.S. Supreme Court overturned such laws in 2003, fifteen states still outlawed "sodomy," or same-sex intercourse. In our country, the most contentious public issues—including the abortion debate, gays in the military, and the right of gays to marry—involve questions over whether and how the government should control the sexuality of its citizens. Family-planning programs can also be viewed as another manifestation of government control over sexuality—especially women's sexuality, since such programs tend to focus on women's bodies (Dwyer 2000).

• •

THINKING CRITICALLY ABOUT GENDER, SEX, AND SEXUALITY

Many queer activists in the United States and Europe have accepted and promote the idea that they were "born" homosexual and that they have no choice in the matter. How do you think anthropologists, who view sexuality as culturally patterned, socially conditioned, and not inborn, should respond to this idea?

• •

Conclusion

The concept of sexuality—who can sleep with whom and the sexual relationships and practices in which people engage—is a key dimension of the larger themes around which this chapter is organized, namely kinship and gender. What unites all of these concepts is that they touch on an issue of central importance to human existence, which is our capacity for procreation. Yet these concepts are intertwined in complex ways, shaping the ideas and social patterns a society uses to organize and control males and females, as well as those who do not fit these categories.

It is important to remember that how we think of these matters, as natural as they feel to us, are not as universal as we may assume. Although the tendency in our own culture—if not also the Mexican *telenovela* that opens this chapter—emphasizes that kinship, family, and gender are primarily matters of blood relationships, anthropologists view the matter rather differently, having seen the great variety of ways different societies construct families and gender relations. It is also good to remember that matters of kinship and gender are not necessarily as stable as they feel to us. The ongoing transformations of the "traditional" American family are but one illustration of that dynamism. But the reason these things feel so stable to us in our everyday experience is that culture—those processes through which the artificial comes to feel natural—is central to defining kinship and gender.

KEY TERMS

Bride price   p. 455

Clan   p. 453

Corporate groups   p. 452

Dowry   p. 455

Exogamous   p. 453

Extended families   p. 452

Gender   p. 461

Gender variance   p. 466

Gender/sex systems   p. 461

Genealogical amnesia p. 455

Incest taboo   p. 459

Intersex   p. 461

Kinship   p. 451

Kinship chart   p. 452

Lineage   p. 453

Masculinity   p. 465

Natal family   p. 451

Nuclear family   p. 452

Polyandry   p. 458

Polygamy   p. 458

Polygyny   p. 458

Sex   p. 460

Sexuality p. 466

Sexually dimorphic   p. 461

Teknonymy   p. 456

Reviewing the Chapter

Chapter Section	What We Know	To Be Resolved
What are families, and how are they structured in different societies?	Families in all societies are dynamic. Kin relationships are about social ties between individuals as much as they are about biological ties. All societies have developed ways of ensuring that the family group has some control over collective resources or the labor of its members.	It is impossible to predict how any society's system of kinship, marriage, and the family will change without understanding the other social, economic, environmental, and political changes in that society.
Why do people get married?	Marriage can take on many diverse forms, and our own cultural model of basing marriage on love and sex is not important to all societies, especially those in which marriage is about creating social, economic, and political ties with other groups.	Although economics has an impact on who gets married and who does not, it is not clear what the long-term impact of delayed marriage or the growing number of unmarried couples with children will be.
In what ways are males and females different?	Every society makes a distinction between "male" and "female" but not all attach the same meanings to apparent biological differences or think they are important for explaining differences between males and females. Biological differences are not the source of women's subordination. Rather, cultural ideologies and social relations impose on women lower status, prestige, and power than men.	Anthropologists continue to work out the relative influences of biological, environmental, and cultural factors on shaping gender/sex.
What does it mean to be neither male nor female?	Many gender/sex systems around the world allow for gender variance. Gender variants generally establish their unique identities through social performance: wearing certain clothes, speaking and moving in certain ways, and performing certain social roles and occupations.	Western terminology and concepts are not always able to capture the subtlety of other cultures' concepts of sex, gender, and sexuality, which raises questions about how to best represent such phenomena.
Is human sexuality just a matter of being straight or queer?	Human sexuality is variable and patterned by cultural ideologies and social relations. It is also not a fixed or exclusive condition.	Anthropologists continue to work through the complex and subtle ways sexuality interacts with gender and sex, as well as other identities like class, race, and ethnicity.

Readings

For a discussion of the origins of kinship studies in U.S. anthropology, see Thomas Trautmann's *Lewis Henry Morgan and the Invention of Kinship* (Lincoln: University of Nebraska Press, 2008). In British anthropology, see the classic volume edited by A. R. Radcliffe-Brown and Daryl Forde, *African Systems of Kinship and Marriage* (London: Oxford University Press, 1950).

American cultural anthropology's argument that kinship is never exclusively about biology is well appreciated in two classics: David Schneider's book *American Kinship: A Cultural Account* (Englewood Cliffs, NJ: Prentice-Hall, 1968), and Carol Stack's, *All Our Kin* (New York: Basic Books, 1997), which explores the dynamism and fluidity of "family" relations among urban African Americans.

Biologist Anne Fausto-Sterling's book *Sexing the Body: Gender Politics and the Construction of Sexuality* (New York: Basic Books, 2000) offers powerful perspectives on the construction of sex, gender, sexuality, and intersex. Caroline Brettell and Carolyn Fishel Sargent's edited reader *Gender in Cross-Cultural Perspective*, 3rd. ed. (Englewood Cliffs, NJ: Prentice Hall, 2001) offers a range of anthropological arguments and case studies about these issues.

● ● ● ● ● ● ● ● ● ● ● ● ● ● ● ● ● ● ●

For an overview of feminist anthropology and debates over male/female inequality, see Sherry Ortner's book *Making Gender: The Politics and Erotics of Culture* (Boston: Beacon Press, 1996). Amitra Basu's 2010 edited volume *Women's Movements in the Global Era: The Power of Local Feminisms* (Boulder, CO: Westview Press, 2010) offers a recent assessment of the diversity of feminisms that exist in the world.

● ● ● ● ● ● ● ● ● ● ● ● ● ● ● ● ● ● ●

Gilbert Herdt's edited book *Third Sex, Third Gender: Beyond Sexual Dimorphism in Culture and History* (New York: Zone Books, 1994) explores gender variance across many cultures. Serena Nanda's book *Neither Man nor Woman: The Hijras of India*, 2nd. ed. (Boston: Cengage, 1999) is a classic ethnographic study of gender variance in India.

● ● ● ● ● ● ● ● ● ● ● ● ● ● ● ● ● ● ●

Andrew P. and Harriet D. Lyons's book *Irregular Connections: A History of Anthropology and Sexuality* (Lincoln: University of Nebraska Press, 2004) examines anthropology's history with the study of sexuality. It pairs well with Don Kulick's ethnography of sexuality among transgender prostitutes in Brazil, *Travesti: Sex, Gender, and Culture Among Brazilian Transgendered Prostitutes* (Chicago: University of Chicago Press, 1998).

● ● ● ● ● ● ● ● ● ● ● ● ● ● ● ● ● ● ●

Religion

Ritual and Belief

It was the South, in the summer of 1965, the darkest days of the civil rights movement in America. The previous year, Ku Klux Klansmen, members of a white supremacist group, had murdered three voting-rights activists in Mississippi. In March the black Baptist civil rights leader Reverend Dr. Martin Luther King, Jr. had called on "clergy of all faiths . . . to join me in Selma for a ministers' march to Montgomery." Hundreds marched, but Alabama State Troopers launched an unprovoked attack on protesters. Two weeks later a white Alabama man slew another civil rights worker. During the summer President Lyndon Johnson signed into law the Voting Rights Act of 1965, but officials in Lowndes County, Alabama, situated between Selma and Montgomery, refused to register any of their nonwhite citizens to vote, as did those in many other Southern counties with large black majorities,

Into this cauldron of politics, fear, and religion came twenty-six-year-old white seminary student Jonathan Daniels of Keene, New Hampshire. Jon had marched through Lowndes County with Dr. King in March 1965, and he spent the summer in Lowndes County protesting racial discrimination and trying to register black voters. In August he participated in a demonstration with Father Richard Morrisroe, a young, white Catholic priest from Chicago, and twenty-seven other activists. All of them were arrested and held for a week in the Lowndes County Jail in the quiet little town of Hayneville. After six days, the entire group was released on their own recognizance.

Selma to Montgomery March The Reverend Dr. Martin Luther King, Jr., drew heavily on religious symbols from the biblical Book of Exodus in his civil rights struggles in 1965. Alabama State Troopers, who attacked protestors during the march, also felt religious conviction in their actions.

Outside, it was hot and dusty, so Jon and Father Morrisroe set off down the street with two young black women working with the Student Nonviolent Coordinating Committee (SNCC), Ruby Sales and Joyce Bailey, to buy soft drinks at the only store in town that regularly served black customers. As Jon opened the screen door, Special Deputy Sheriff Tom Coleman confronted him, holding a 12-guage shotgun. Coleman shouted, "This store is closed. Get off this goddam property before I blow your goddam brains out, you black bastards." With that he aimed his gun at Ruby Sales. Seeing what was happening, Jon pushed Ruby to the ground and moved between her and the gun. Coleman fired at point-blank range. The blast threw Jon out the door and into the street, killing him instantly. Morrisroe grabbed Joyce's hand and ran down the street with her, as Coleman shot him in the back, wounding him critically. Left behind on the ground, Ruby now caught up with Joyce, grabbed her by the hand, and ran for cover. News accounts reported that a few minutes after the shooting, Coleman called the Alabama Director of Public Safety to say, "I just shot two preachers. Get on down here."

This incident arose because of a set of conflicting beliefs—those that motivated Tom Coleman versus those that motivated Jon Daniels. Today, we may find Coleman's prejudicial belief in the so-called racial inferiority of blacks even more difficult to understand than Daniels's religiously inspired altruism. Nevertheless, the bigger issue here is how we make sense of the existence of such different beliefs. It leads us to focus on the phenomenon of beliefs and behaviors, which can vary so radically.

At the heart of anthropology's approach to belief and religion is the question: *Why do people believe things that others consider wrong?* Embedded in this broader question are the following problems, around which this chapter is organized:

How should we understand religion and religious beliefs?

What forms does religion take?

How do rituals work?

How is religion linked to political and social action?

Over the past century anthropologists have come to realize that religious beliefs offer people a roadmap for their behavior: how they should live and how they should understand other people's behaviors, actions, and ideas. At their very heart, religious beliefs create meaning for people through the use of powerful rituals and religious symbols, all of which we discuss in greater depth in this chapter.

How Should We Understand Religion and Religious Beliefs?

Western intellectuals and social scientists have historically found the subject of religion problematic. When scholars in the nineteenth century confronted peoples around the world with mystical views, most considered these ideas to be non-scientific mumbo-jumbo and their adherents to be people of limited intellectual capacity. But by the 1870s, when anthropology was emerging as an academic discipline, scholars began to look systematically for theories that would help them understand the cultural importance of religious beliefs. In this section we consider four different versions or definitions of religion suggested by anthropologists, several of which are still common today. Among these is our own approach to religion that builds on all the others. In our view, the most effective way to think of religion is that it is a symbolic system that is socially enacted through rituals and other aspects of social life.

Understanding Religion version 1.0: Edward B. Tylor and Belief in Spirits

To make sense of the exotic religious beliefs of non-Western cultures, the British anthropologist Sir Edward B. Tylor (1871) suggested that religion had to do with belief in spiritual beings. For him, primitive religions were based on a fundamental error in thinking. He reasoned that people in all societies had dreams, but the so-called primitive peoples had misinterpreted their dreams as reality, transforming the characters in their dreams into souls or spirits. Tylor called such beliefs in spirits **animism**, which refers to the belief that inanimate objects such as trees, rocks, cliffs, hills, and rivers were animated by spiritual forces or beings. For him the idea that trees and rocks might have souls or that carved images contained spirits were just other examples of this same "primitive" misunderstanding. Tylor also reasoned that as societies evolved and became more complex, the supernatural beings they believed in became more complex as well: spirits gave way to demigods and mythical heroes, which gave way to the gods and goddesses of the ancient Greeks and Romans. Finally, these many gods gave way to a single, all-powerful God—which would eventually, in his secular mind, yield to science.

- **Animism.** An early theory that primitive peoples believed which holds that inanimate objects such as trees, rocks, cliffs, hills, and rivers were animated by spiritual forces or beings.

Although many anthropologists later rejected Tylor's evolutionary theories, his basic approach remained influential in anthropology for many decades. Some influential scholars, like Sir James Fraser, suggested that ideas about magic had predated the idea of souls and spirits, but there was no more evidence for magic as the origin of religious ideas than for dreams. By the Second World War, anthropologists in Great Britain were combining the two theories, writing of "magico-religious" ideas.

Understanding Religion version 2.0: Anthony F. C. Wallace on Supernatural Beings, Powers, and Forces

By the 1950s anthropologists in the United States had long abandoned the idea that American Indians and other non-Western peoples were "primitive." Paul Radin, for example, had published *Primitive Man as Philosopher* (1927) in which he argued that there was nothing simple-minded in the myths, legends, and religious practices of tribal peoples. When American anthropologists began to look at how Indian religions

Figure 18.1   The Ghost Dance.   The Ghost Dance among the Sioux in 1891 was an innovative religious movement among various tribes in the Great Plains. It was the Sioux's attempt to recover self-respect and control over traditional resources through ritual, but it led to disastrous consequences at Wounded Knee when U.S. Army soldiers misinterpreted the ritual and killed 150 Lakota Sioux.

• **Rituals.** Stylized performances involving symbols that are associated with social, political, and religious activities.

• *Mana.* A belief that sacred power inheres in certain high-ranking people, sacred spaces, and objects.

were changing in the context of white expansion and domination, they saw systematic shifts in Indian thinking to make sense of changing times (Figure 18.1).

One of the major figures of this period was Anthony F. C. Wallace, who had studied religious change among the Seneca, one of the Iroquois tribes in upstate New York (1956, 1970). For Wallace, religious change could be observed most easily in the changing religious ceremonies and **rituals** (stylized performances involving symbols that are associated with social, political, and religious activities). But he recognized that rituals only made sense in terms of religious beliefs. His definition of religion became standard in anthropology because it linked beliefs with rituals: "beliefs and rituals concerned with supernatural beings, powers, and forces" (Wallace 1966:5).

This approach bounded the field of religion in ways that fit comfortably with traditional European and American views, which also emphasized the supernatural (Figure 18.2). But Wallace's definition is static, offering little or no direction for understanding how or why religious ideas and practices are changing. If a society practices some tribal religion but converted to Christianity, Islam, or Buddhism, Wallace's definition could help us document what had changed, but little else. It also could not tell us what difference these changed beliefs make for real people's lives and tended to depict religious people as intellectually limited. The biggest failing in Wallace's definition is that it does not explain why people hold onto their religious beliefs and practices with such passion, a limitation that was overcome when anthropologists began understanding religion as based on symbols.

Understanding Religion version 3.0: Religion as a System of Symbols

Unsatisfied with Wallace's notion of religion as simply belief in the supernatural, the American cultural anthropologist Clifford Geertz (1966) proposed another kind of

Figure 18.2   One of Anthony Wallace's Supernatural Forces: Hawaiian Temple Complex (Heiau) at Kealakekua Bay on Hawai'i's Big Island.   This religious center possessed *mana* (supernatural power). *Mana* attached to all sacred sites, to persons of noble descent, to ritual carvings of the gods, and to anything the king or nobles touched. For commoners it was dangerous, even deadly, to violate a taboo, touch something with *mana*, or even walk on sacred ground.

definition that could help explain why beliefs are deeply held and motivational, even to the point of negating one's own personal interest as we saw with the example of Jonathan Daniels and Tom Coleman. Geertz argued that religion was a cultural system, or as he put it a "system of symbols" consisting of five elements:

> Religion is (1) a system of symbols which act to (2) establish powerful, pervasive, and long-lasting moods and motivations in men by (3) formulating conceptions of a general order of existence and (4) clothing these conceptions with such an aura of factuality that (5) the moods and motivations seem uniquely realistic. (1966:4)

The most important feature of this definition is that it centers on symbols that seem intensely real and factual. For example, the central symbol in Christianity generally is the most improbable, the notion that after his execution Christ rose from the dead (called the resurrection). Likely or not, hundreds of millions of people around the world accept the resurrection as a historical fact.

Furthermore, the systems of meaning that these symbols generate can create a sense of moral purpose or meaning in people's lives and move them to action. These conceptualizations of the world offer a set of unquestioned assumptions about the world and how it works, called a **worldview**. The notion of culture adopted in this textbook ultimately derives from this understanding of religion as a cultural system. So when we suggest that culture is about symbolic processes that make the artificial and humanly constructed seem natural, we are arguing that culture consists of symbols that are created and given meaning by social life, not just in religious contexts. People's understandings of the world provided by these symbols, like Geertz's religion, seem uniquely realistic and cloaked in an aura of factuality; the world seems uniquely natural. The symbols describe a "model of" how the world is, as they simultaneously depict a "model for" how the world (morally) should be.

- **Worldview.** A general approach to or set of shared unquestioned assumptions about the world and how it works.

Most anthropologists continue to find Geertz's approach to religion useful. Following Geertz, they have tried to understand the worldview and ethos of a religion, adopting what is often called an **interpretive approach**, a style of analysis that looks at the underlying symbolic and cultural interconnections within a society.

In spite of its strengths, Geertz's explanation does have limitations. Some scholars, for example, have argued that Geertz's definition of religion as a cultural system assumes that people have a basic need for meaning and for making sense of the world, which may or may not be the case (Frankenberry and Penner 1999). Furthermore, anthropologist Talal Asad (1993) has argued that Geertz's definition of religion as a cultural system does not adequately distinguish religion from the domains of science, aesthetics, common sense, or law. Asad also questions whether we can ever fully understand the emotions people feel during religious experiences, whether rituals, prayers, or social action (Asad 1993). Still others have charged that it does not pay adequate attention to how institutions and power relations within a society create religious meaning (Eickelman and Piscatori 1996; Foucault 1999).

- **Interpretive approach.** A kind of analysis that interprets the underlying symbolic and cultural interconnections within a society.

Perhaps the most significant limitation of Geertz's strategy for understanding religious phenomena is that his definition of religion reads as if he is describing a lone believer sitting quietly surrounded only by his own moods and thoughts as company. But a key feature of religious beliefs and behavior is that they are rooted in social behavior and social action (Figure 18.3). Beliefs get most of their power from being socially enacted. By acting together, the community of believers begins to accept the group's symbolic interpretations of the world as if they were tangible, authentic, and real rather than merely interpretation.

Figure 18.3   Expressing Religiosity. Many religious rituals around the world are energetic and boisterous rather than somber, sedate, and pensive as Americans sometimes assume. At the top is a West African ritual performance that brings the gods into contact with the community, and on the bottom a modern megachurch in America in which participants take on a vibrant role in the service.

● **Religion.** A symbolic system that is socially enacted through rituals and other aspects of social life.

Understanding Religion version 4.0: Religion as a System of Social Action

In July 2013 three million Brazilians turned out to celebrate mass with Pope Francis, the first Roman Catholic Pope from Latin America. In this public ritual we can see that religion for these millions is important, but it is also an intensely exciting and social experience. It is a very different experience from a single nun on retreat praying quietly by herself for days at a time, eating at a communal meal with other nuns, with no one speaking. Both experiences are "religious" in that they deal with worshipers' understandings of the world and how important the supernatural power of God is in people's lives. But both religious experiences draw power from the social context—being among three million worshipers in Rio on the one hand and mainly by oneself and one's own thoughts on the other.

Thus, when we speak of religion in this book, we feel that **religion** is a symbolic system that is socially enacted through rituals and other aspects of social life. This definition implies several elements that earlier scholars have emphasized:

1. The existence of things more powerful than human beings. Although in many societies it takes the form of some supernatural force, we prefer to think of it as a worldview or cosmology that situates the place of human beings in the universe.
2. Beliefs and behaviors surround, support, and promote the acceptance that those things more powerful than humans actually exist.
3. Symbols that make these beliefs and behaviors seem both intense and genuine.
4. Social settings, usually involving important rituals, that people share while experiencing the power of these symbols of belief.

Armed with this sense of religion, let us apply this understanding of religion to one of the great problems of meaning of our time, suicidal bomber attacks: Why do people strap on bombs or board airplanes intending to kill themselves along with many other people?

Understanding Suicide Bomber Attacks

The recent rise of suicide bombings in Iraq, Israel, Afghanistan, and other countries in the Middle East poses a special problem of meaning for many of us: How can people willingly kill themselves, especially in the name of religion? Such ideas are unthinkable to most Americans. Christian and Jewish Americans have long seen suicide as a mortal sin, sometimes even refusing to bury anyone who has committed suicide in consecrated cemeteries. Nowadays, nearly all Americans tend to interpret suicide as evidence that an individual has severe psychological problems. But as anthropologists, we strive to make sense of how a particular cultural context and belief system make such actions meaningful to the persons involved.

Reframing 9/11

A similar problem of meaning was brought home to Americans on September 11, 2001, when nineteen Arab hijackers commandeered four airplanes and crashed them into the World Trade Center, the Pentagon, and a field in Pennsylvania, killing more than 3,000 people as well as themselves (Figure 18.4). President George W. Bush's first official words about the terrorist attack helped define the event for the nation: "Freedom itself was attacked this morning by a faceless coward." Later the same evening, in an address to the nation, the president redefined the event using a different moral language: "Thousands of lives were suddenly ended by evil, despicable acts of terror." In the weeks following the attacks, Bush repeatedly referred to the hijackers

Figure 18.4   A Problem of Meaning. The terrorist attacks on the United States of September 11, 2001, posed a problem of meaning for Americans: How could anyone kill themselves, just to cause others harm, in the name of religion?

as "the evil ones" or "evildoers," using a moral language that pitted good against evil. The president's use of such phrasing was guaranteed to rally public support across the United States, and it worked.

But referring to the 9/11 hijackers as "evildoers" does not help us understand why they did what they did. One doubts that any of these hijackers thought of themselves as doing evil, and, as we have suggested throughout this book, to understand cultural behavior requires a culturally relative approach. "Evil" acts are essentially irrational acts; they make no sense. "Cowardly" acts can only be explained through fear, which is also irrational. The hijackers' actions were carefully planned and deftly coordinated; the attacks do not look like wild and irrational acts. And the fact that the hijackers were willing to die for their beliefs hardly seems cowardly, no matter how wrong the authors of this book and other Americans may feel these acts were. Nevertheless, we have to reframe 9/11 by seeking to understand the specific beliefs and social contexts that produced it.

Situating Al Qaeda in Its Cultural and Religious Context

The key to understanding these acts is that the nineteen terrorists were part of a larger social group, called Al-Qaeda (al-**kay**-dah), whose members shared a certain model for how the world should be, which was based on religious meanings, values, and actions. They trained under the leadership of Osama bin Laden, a Saudi Arabian who had set up the Al-Qaeda network to wage a **holy struggle** (or *jihad,* in Arabic) against those perceived as oppressing Muslims. Bin Laden's version of Islam is called Wahhabism [wah-**hawb**ism], a conservative reading of Muslim texts and values. Wahhabism is critical of the Saudi royal family for its perceived materialism, corruption, and close ties to the West, especially the United States.

Al-Qaeda developed a strident and radical Islamic ideology, attracting thousands of unemployed Muslim men to training camps in Afghanistan. In these camps Al-Qaeda took on its social character, as individuals from across the Arab world trained, ate, and exercised together (Figure 18.5). Although bin Laden had inherited great wealth from his industrialist father, he lived the simple life of an ascetic, a symbolically loaded image that stood in stark contrast to the luxury of the Saudi royal family.

In Islam, jihad means "struggle," such as the personal struggles anyone confronts trying to follow Islam's rules for proper, moral living. For example, during the holy month

- **Holy struggle.** A conflict—often political or social—that believers see as justified by doing God's work.

Figure 18.5 Creating Meaning Through Social Action.   Osama bin Laden with recruits at an Al-Qaeda terrorist camp in Afghanistan. Religious movements get power from the social support, friendship, and comradeship of their members.

of Ramadan many Muslims "struggle" to fast (not eating or smoking) from before sunrise until sunset. But jihad can also mean struggle against non-believers. Images of the Prophet Muhammad's struggle in the Quran against non-believers trying to kill him mimicked bin Laden's own personal struggle against Saudi royals and provided each (bin Laden and the Saudi princes) with a model of how the world actually was.

Drawing upon such religious imagery in a context where young men spent months in training and talking about little else, bin Laden created a community in which these values and ideas made sense. This community offered a *model of* the world as well as a *model for* how the world should be, and then rooted those beliefs in social action involving guerilla attacks on their enemies. By creating a social world in which sacrifice strengthened good and righteous acts, bin Laden was able to construct a world where political, religious, and social action were one, a topic we turn to later.

But before considering how religious beliefs and behaviors are linked to social action in the world, it is necessary to turn to another major preoccupation of anthropology of religion, the different forms that religion takes around the world.

• •

THINKING CRITICALLY ABOUT RELIGION

Consider how each of the four definitions or understandings of religion would explain why a religious cult like the Jim Jones cult in Guyana or the early Mormons in Nauvoo—where they were attacked by non-Mormons—emerged. Alternatively, use these four explanations or definitions to interpret local reaction in your own community toward people with widely different religions.

• •

What Forms Does Religion Take?

Early anthropologists like Edward B. Tylor largely saw all "primitive" societies as having a "primitive" religion. While anthropologists today reject the notion that some peoples are more "primitive" and others more civilized, it is clear that societies with simple technologies and small populations traditionally had very different religions from those that have formed states with centralized governments and more sophisticated technologies. But there is no evidence that one form inevitably evolves into another as the early anthropologists believed.

The variety of human religions that exists seems to correspond to the kinds of social orders that exist in different scales of society. Societies with small populations, for example, developed few governmental institutions larger than the family, clan, or village, and their religious institutions were typically focused on these same primary institutions. Let us begin by considering clan-based religions and totemism common in small-scale societies and then turn to religions in larger scale and socially stratified societies, like polytheism, monotheism, and world religions.

Clan Spirits and Clan Identities in New Guinea

Nearly all New Guinea societies are organized around families and groups of families that belong to the same clan, and these clans are typically associated with particular kinds of spirits. The Ningerum of Papua New Guinea, for example, who have a very

Figure 18.6   Eharo Mask From Karama Village, Gulf Province, Collected About 1885.   The design features the face of a gecko on the body of the mask, and the body and tail extend upward above the face. A pair of "arms" and "legs" are on the left and right of the body, while the tale extends to the top of the mask. Rattan covered with bark cloth, painted with traditional pigments in red, black, and white. The gecko was a totemic emblem for one of the clans in the village, and this mask would have been worn along with ten or more other masks in the same design by men from the gecko clan. (Hood Museum of Art, Dartmouth College, Hanover, New Hampshire)

● **Totemism.** A system of thought that associates particular social groups with specific animal or plant species called "totems" as an emblem.

low population density of seven to fifteen people per square mile, are concerned with various clan spirits that inhabit their traditional clan lands. These clan spirits have a full range of human emotions, but they become dangerous when they get jealous or angry, whereupon they can cause sickness or even death to people from other clans or even among the children and elders of their own clans. When they are happy and well attended to by the living with gifts of food, especially pork, they bring good harvest in the gardens, success in hunting, and healthy, prosperous families. All of their rituals, aside from a few specific healing rites, emphasize dealing with all of these clan-based spirits, and at major feasts pigs are sacrificed to these spirits to honor them with a bit of pork and other gifts made to them.

Among the Elema and Purari tribes of the Papuan Gulf, population densities are much higher. Each village had several large longhouses, where men lived with their brothers and sons in rooms belonging to particular clans or subclans. These clan and subclan groups had various dances at initiation rituals, and the dance costumes depicted various animals that were associated with the particular clan such as crocodiles and the small lizard known as a gecko (Figure 18.6). These systems of totems are absent among the Ningerum but are clearly present in a very simple but obvious way among the Elema and Purari tribes.

Totemism in North America

Early anthropologists studying American Indian societies observed that people identified with particular animals, often claiming to be descended from them. These symbols indicated their clans, lineages, tribes, or other social groups with emblems, usually animals, plants, places, and geographic or meteorological features (Figure 18.7). Anthropologists usually refer to these emblems as totems, and **totemism** as the system of thought that associates particular social groups with specific animal or plant species. Totems help create social cohesiveness by stressing group identity, focusing group and private rituals on totems. Some Native American societies simultaneously employed color symbolism, directional symbols, and species as totems. Until the 1920s anthropologists interpreted totemism as evidence of a group's limited intellectual capacity, since people could not possibly be descended from eagles, wolves, or pythons.

Anthropologist Ralph Linton (1924) reported that Americans in the military during the First World War adopted a similar reverential attitude toward emblems like the rainbow (for the 42nd or Rainbow Division) without indicating any psychological problems. Of course, in American culture, this phenomenon is widespread, especially with sports teams named after animals or a particular social group. Fans and players alike typically identify with these totemic emblems, sometimes enacting behaviors that everyone understands as symbolic of the animal or social category of the team emblem, such as the Atlanta Braves tomahawk chop. These are examples of American totemism, all of which cultivate a sense of belonging to a social order larger than oneself.

Unlike American totemism, however, which is largely secular in orientation, traditional tribal societies usually understood their relation to a totemic animal in a supernatural way. Along the Northwest Coast of North America, for example, the Native society is divided into two halves (anthropologists call these halves "moieties"). One belongs to the eagle totem, while the other belongs to the raven totem (Figure 18.7). Within these moieties, each clan is identified with other totems, such as the salmon, the frog, the brown bear, and so on. These animals were also thought to have a special spiritual connection to the members of their social groups and appeared prominently in the origin myths of each clan. Native peoples carved these totems on memorial totem poles, painted them on clan houses, and decorated their blankets with them. In this way, the totems not only marked the sociopolitical order of clans within a village, but through ceremonies and myths they also linked people with the supernatural realm.

Figure 18.7 Chiefly Totems. Totemic images identified with the clan and social position of a Kwakiutl chief on Vancouver Island, British Columbia. The main images on the two poles are eagles; other elements associated with the eagle moiety are grizzly bears. The figure at the bottom of the left pole holds a ceremonial copper plaque, suggesting the importance of the chief. These poles capture the social identity, the social position of the chief, and his great accomplishments, all expressed through the carved memorial pole.

Shamanism and Ecstatic Religious Experiences

As early as the sixteenth century, European travelers from Russia and central Europe encountered tribes in Siberia whose religious rituals consisted of spiritual leaders called **shamans,** religious leaders who communicate the needs of the living with the spirit world, usually through some form of ritual trance or other altered state of consciousness. These specialists were not political leaders but focused on healing and ensuring the health and prosperity of the community using drum rituals to connect with the spirits. Anthropologists have observed the role of **trance** (a semiconscious state typically brought on by hypnosis, ritual drumming and singing, or hallucinogenic drugs like mescaline or peyote) as a key element of shamanic practice. The shaman's trance appears to allow them to do difficult feats that would be impossible in normal circumstances, such as chewing glass or possessing great strength.

Shamanism is found in one form or another on all continents but especially in North and South America, Africa, and Asia. The details of these shamanic traditions vary widely, but they are often associated with small-scale societies with more or less egalitarian political structures. Anthropologist Napoleon Chagnon and Timothy Asch's 1973 film *Magical Death* is one of the best known examples of shamanic healing. In this film the Yanomamo shaman heals his family by ingesting hallucinogenic snuff made from a local plant. As in many shamanic traditions, this shaman is assisted by his **spirit familiar** (a spirit that has developed a close bond with the shaman), who helps him see other spirits and heal his children.

The importance of such altered states of consciousness was also explored by anthropologist Barbara G. Myerhoff's (1974) study of the peyote religion of the Huichol [**wee**-choal] Indians of northern Mexico. Myerhoff's key finding is that the rituals of Huichol shamans, including the ritualized hunt for peyote in the Mexican desert, give meaning to the social order of these people. In societies more familiar to Americans, such as some Pentecostal and charismatic Christian traditions, the ecstatic religious experience that has long been associated with shamans is encouraged by members of the congregation through witnessing, singing, and **speaking in tongues** (the phenomenon of speaking in an apparently unknown language, often in an energetic and fast-paced way). Anthropologists have noted that these vocalizations do not correspond to any human language, but symbolically they connect people with God via the Holy Spirit. These individual connections between each participant and the

- **Shaman.** A religious leader who communicates the needs of the living with the spirit world, usually through some form of ritual trance or other altered state of consciousness.

- **Trance.** A semi-conscious state typically brought on by hypnosis, ritual drumming, and singing, or hallucinogenic drugs like mescaline or peyote.

- **Spirit familiar.** A spirit that has developed a close bond with a shaman.

- **Speaking in tongues.** The phenomenon of speaking in an apparently unknown language, often in an energetic and fast-paced way.

Figure 18.8   Symbols of Royal Authority in the Benin Kingdom.   Bronze figures and reliefs represented royal connections to the gods. The focus of all power in the kingdom was in the center of the palace in the person of the oba. (Hood Museum of Art, Dartmouth College, Hanover, New Hampshire)

• **Polytheism.** A type of religion with many gods.

Holy Spirit parallel the egalitarian society they are ritually constructing in their congregations.

Whether it is religions like those of the Ningerum or Elema or totemism among Native American groups, or Shamanism, each of these religious systems draws on a mix of the same sorts of elements. All stress group identities and link these identities to various religious symbols. Symbols are also used in the religions of stratified societies, but the groups they highlight are larger entities or social categories that extend beyond the local, face-to-face community.

Ritual Symbols That Reinforce a Hierarchical Social Order

Ritual symbols tend to reinforce the social hierarchy and the political order at the same time they interact with divine beings and powers. In the former kingdom of Benin in what is now Nigeria in West Africa, for example, the Oba (king) was believed to be divine. The fiercest animal in the region, the leopard, became a symbol of royal power, projecting an image of the Oba's power over his people. The Oba's palace was a model for the structure of the cosmos and the social order. One feature of Benin religious practice was the Igwe Festival, which was a cleansing ritual expelling evil from the entire kingdom led by the Oba. This ritual sequence served to strengthen and renew the Oba's divine powers. Benin bronze sculptures and reliefs from Benin often depict members of the royal family, offering another way for the Benin to venerate their Oba (Figure 18.8). By strengthening the Oba, the community felt it was maintaining the well-being of the kingdom. Their rituals, the palaces, and the royal art together provided a model of the divine nature of the ruler, supporting a social order in which they dominated over all others (Bradbury 1957; Dark 1962, 1982; Eboreime 2003).

Polytheism and Monotheism in Ancient Societies

The kingdoms and dynasties of ancient Egypt provided a similar model of the social order replicated in many of its most important rituals. The Pharaoh was a king ruling over a vast empire of people along the Nile and Mediterranean coast and extending into what is now Israel and the Arabian Peninsula. Everything about Egyptian ritual—as well as the construction of great pyramids and structures like the sphinx—celebrated a complex hierarchy of officials and priests with the Pharaoh as a divine figure at the head of the state and its religious organizations. But the Pharaoh was not the only divine figure; Egyptians held that there were a host of other, more powerful deities, making their religion **polytheistic** (a religion with many gods). All of these gods demanded the attention of humans or, it was thought, they might harm the human world with droughts, plagues, locusts, and floods of the Nile River.

Nearly all the ancient societies in the Middle East and Mediterranean were polytheistic with complex state rituals that promoted an image of the state and its human leaders as superior to ordinary men. The main exception to polytheism in the ancient world was the ancient Hebrews, whose religion focused on a single god called Yaweh. In all likelihood, Yaweh began as a local deity belonging to one of the tribes of Israel, which was worshiped and venerated by one of these groups that became the ancient Hebrews. It seems likely that Yaweh was the deity of Moses's tribe and after the exodus from Egypt under Ramses the Great of the nineteenth dynasty; his clan or tribal deity gradually pushed out Baal and other gods (Armstrong 1994). When the Hebrews established Yaweh as the God of Israel, they began a long-term shift to **monotheism**—the belief in a single god. Monotheism set the Hebrews as distinctive in their neighborhood. The key feature of monotheism was that it symbolized a single universal faith because the single God was presented as the deity of all, whereas polytheism encouraged different groups to identify with different local gods in much the way that totemism works.

- **Monotheism.** The belief in a single god.

World Religions and Universal Understandings of the World

Most of us are more familiar with the universal monotheistic **world religions**—or religions that claim to be universally significant to all people—of Judaism, Christianity, and Islam than the small-scale religions discussed previously. All three of these monotheistic world religions provided a general message that was applicable to all people, not just the members of a small clan or social group. For the most part, all three provided a positive, uplifting message for adherents, and all three became identified with the ruling governments. All three also became state religions, whose religious message and ritual supported the government of the state.

- **World religions.** Religions that claim to be universally significant to all people.

Christianity and Islam illustrate the ways a local monotheistic religion can become universalized through a set of beliefs and social order. Christianity began in what is now Israel but spread to communities in Asia Minor and Greece when the apostle Paul began evangelizing. Expanding membership was possible only after the Jewish requirement of circumcision was abolished for new converts. Monotheism encouraged a universal, pan-human approach to faith, and there were many people in the eastern Mediterranean who wanted a religion that made them part of a new, universal, and growing community.

Five centuries later, Islam emerged in the Arabian Peninsula when the Prophet Muhammad received holy scripture in the form of poetry from a single, universal God—called Allah in classical Arabic. Most Americans are startled to learn that the Prophet had one Christian wife and lived peaceably among a mix of Muslims, Jews, and Christians in Medina, until members of one of the Jewish tribes attempted to assassinate him. Jesus, Mary, John the Baptist, Moses, Abraham, and Adam, among others, are discussed at some length in the Quran and all are considered prophets. From a Muslim point of view, Muslims, Christians, and Jews are all "people of the book," meaning that each of these has scripture received through prophets from God. But followers of Islam, being the newest of these three religions, feel that God's message was most accurately received by the Prophet Muhammad. Thus, they feel that Christians and Jews didn't get the entire message from God, in much the same way that many Christian faiths believe that Jews were not given the full faith until Jesus arrived.

Asia has also produced important world religions that reflect particular histories of social stratification and universalistic belief. Hinduism was a polytheistic religion that emerged in India thousands of years ago. Like the polytheistic religions of the Middle East, Hinduism supported the authority of local princes and kings. Most Hindu ritual was focused on achieving good relations between people and various gods. Sometime in the fourth to sixth centuries BCE, a man named Siddhartha Gutama emerged as a founder of a new faith called Buddhism in reaction to Hindusim. According to Buddhist traditions, having been selfishly pursuing his own pleasure through licentious living, he was mysteriously awakened to his misdeeds and promoted a life of reflection and active commitment to the Buddhist path, accepting the Buddha, the *Dharma* (his teachings), and the *Sangha* (the Buddhist community). Unlike most other religions, Buddhism encourages its members to strive toward greater enlightenment. In this sense Buddhism is neither monotheistic nor polytheistic, but as much a moral code of conduct as anything. The rituals often involve meditation and devotional rituals aimed at turning people from this-worldly desires (wealth, sex, power, etc.) to concern for other people and all other creatures, and a state of enlightenment called *Nirvana*.

How Does Atheism Fit in the Discussion?

Finally, we must ask if atheists, agnostics, and non-believers have a religion. This question has been a worrisome issue for anthropologists, because traditionally anthropologists have defined religion in terms of a belief in the supernatural, which means that these beliefs have little basis in empirical fact.

But taking a step back, if all humans have some sort of worldview, then everyone has some sort of perspective on life analogous to religion. Secular people must also have symbolic systems that give meaning and purpose to their lives. For some, secular rituals that celebrate the state or nation, particular occupations, or other identities may achieve many of the same ends as religious rituals. For others, practicing scientific research may construct a worldview similar to that of people with more traditional religious beliefs. Geertz's definition of religion was specifically designed to be as useful for secular worldviews with a rich array of secular symbols as it is for more traditional religions.

• •

THINKING CRITICALLY ABOUT RELIGION

Consider any three different societies we have discussed in this book. Discuss the extent to which scale of society—measured in terms of population or number of people within the same administrative or governing body—is reflected in complexity of technology and complexity of religious concepts. How do these three measures of complexity—population size, technological complexity, and sophistication of religious ideas—match up? What does this kind of comparison tell us about evolutionary models of society?

• •

How Do Rituals Work?

All rituals have certain key features, including that they are repetitive (happening at set times or before or after certain events) and stylized (following a set order of words or actions). What distinguishes religious ritual from daily habits such as brushing one's teeth (which some of you might think of as a "ritual") is that nobody invests special significance in tooth brushing. Some rituals, such as rites of passage (discussed later) are especially significant in a person's life. But, before we explain why and how they work, it is important to note that anthropologists have long understood that at the heart of all ritual action exists a particular mode of thought that we call "magical." What do we mean?

Magical Thought in Non-Western Cultures

When Americans think of magic, Harry Potter may come to mind. But when anthropologists talk of magic, only rarely are they speaking about conjuring tricks. Instead, anthropologists discuss **magic** as an explanatory system of causation that does not follow naturalistic explanations—such as being struck by a weapon or infected by some virus—often working at a distance without direct physical contact. Informants nearly always accept these explanations as real, and they often believe deeply that they are frightening or dangerous.

   Magic can have many goals, usually goals that are out of reach through an individual taking direct action. The practitioner may want his or her gardens to flourish or his hunt to be successful. She may want the food at her feast to go further than it normally would or to attract the affections of a handsome young man in a neighboring hamlet. Jealous over another man's abundant successes, a man may want to cause his rival to become ill, or—even more maliciously—he may want his enemy to die. Techniques may involve incantations, spells, unusual behaviors, and the manipulation of any number of special objects, all in an effort to cause some desired event to occur. The point is not whether magical practices actually bring about their desired ends or not. It is usually enough to understand that members of a community accept that these processes occur. But why do these puzzling practices make any sense to the people who practice magic?

- **Magic.** An explanatory system of causation that does not follow naturalistic explanations, often working at a distance without direct physical contact.

Sympathetic Magic: The Law of Similarity and the Law of Contagion

The English anthropologist Sir James G. Frazer coined the term **sympathetic magic** to refer to any magical rite that relied on supernatural powers to produce its outcome without working through a specific supernatural being such as a spirit, demon, or deity (see "Classic Contributions: Sir James G. Frazer on Sympathetic Magic"). Drawing on dozens of examples from around the world, Frazer showed that sympathetic magic works on two principles that he called the law of similarity and the law of contagion. Both involved sympathetic magic because the person or object acted upon did so in sympathy with the magical actions.

- **Sympathetic magic.** Any magical rite that relied on the supernatural to produce its outcome without working through some supernatural being such as a spirit, demon, or deity.

The Laws of Magic: Similarities and Contagion

Frazer identified the law of similarities as some point of similarity between an aspect of the magical rite and the desired goal. A good illustration is a so-called voodoo doll, in which people make a doll or image of their enemy. By poking or stabbing the image they hoped to produce pain in the same part of the victim's body. This principle also works on charms or fishhooks representing a seal that allows fishermen or hunters to catch fish as easily as a seal does. Today, anthropologists often speak of these similarities as metaphors, since the fishhook carved as a seal is, of course, not really a seal but merely a hook that resembles a seal (Figure 18.9). Nevertheless, seals are good at catching fish, and this charm on the hook will attract fish.

CLASSIC CONTRIBUTIONS

Sir James G. Frazer on Sympathetic Magic

THE SCOTSMAN JAMES G. FRAZER (1854–1941) was one of the earliest anthropologists in Great Britain. He spent his career studying religion in so-called primitive and archaic societies as an armchair anthropologist. He is best known for his multivolume work *The Golden Bough: A Study in Comparative Religion*, first published in two volumes in 1890 and later expanded (Frazer 1911–1915). Although anthropologists draw on very little of Frazer's work today, they still appreciate his insights about magic. Frazer was the first to offer an explanation of the logic that all magic was based upon—the principle of sympathetic magic—which he discusses here.

Sir James G. Frazer, the Classic Armchair Anthropologist.

One of the principles of sympathetic magic is that any effect may be produced by imitating it. To take a few instances. If it is wished to kill a person an image of him is made and then destroyed; and it is believed that through a certain physical sympathy between the person and his image, the man feels the injuries done to the image as if they were done to his own body, and that when it is destroyed he must simultaneously perish. . . .

Magic sympathy is supposed to exist between a man and any severed portion of his body, as his hair or nails; so that whoever gets possession of hair or nails may work his will, at any distance, upon the person from whom they were cut. This [belief] is worldwide. . . .

Thus we see that in sympathetic magic one event is supposed to be followed necessarily and invariably by another, without the intervention of any spiritual or personal agency. This is, in fact, the modern conception of physical causation; the conception, indeed, is misapplied, but it is there none the less. [Frazer 1890:9–10]

Questions for Reflection

1. Which aspect of sympathetic magic is involved when an athlete wears his or her lucky socks to play a game?

2. Which aspect of sympathetic magic is involved when a boyfriend or girlfriend gives his partner something to keep with him or her during a trip?

Alternatively, a magical rite could follow the law of contagion, in which things that had once been in physical contact with one another could have an effect even when they were no longer in contact. According to the law of contact, mundane objects we've touched or produced as individuals, such as a cigarette butt, a scrap of partly eaten food, hair, nail clippings, sweat, urine, and feces, carry part of our essence, and harmful things done to them by an ill-intentioned magician can by extension hurt us (Figure 18.10).

Applying These Principles to Religious Activities

Although Frazer depicted magical principles as occurring in separate situations, they often occur together, drawing simultaneously on the similarities and previous contact, or contagion. While Frazer saw magic as distinct and separate from

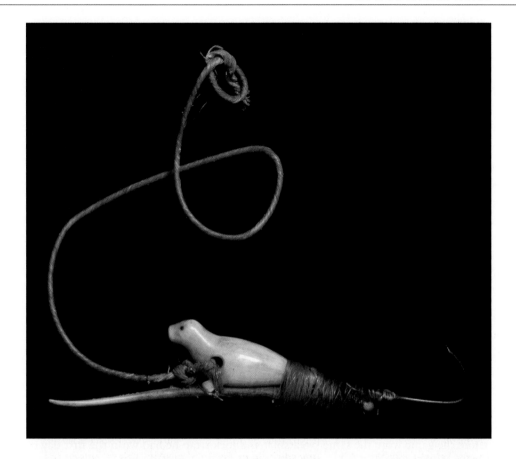

Figure 18.9 Homeopathic Magic Among the Inuit. This fishhook in the collection of the Hood Museum of Art at Dartmouth College is carved of ivory in the shape of a seal so that the hook will be successful in catching fish like a seal is successful in catching fish. (Hood Museum of Art, Dartmouth College, Hanover, New Hampshire)

Figure 18.10 Contagious Magic in Papua New Guinea. A Ningerum man in Papua New Guinea prepares for a pig feast by anointing a pig lengthwise with sago flour in the belief that this rite will make the food go further. When their guests eat just a little of the pork, they will quickly feel full. Anointing the pig uses contagious magic.

religion, most anthropologists now recognize that magical principles are often used in religious rituals.

For example, the Christian ritual of communion embodies both principles of magic simultaneously. The elements used in the rite—the bread and the wine—are consecrated by the priest or pastor with the intention of being consumed by the congregation. This ritual imitates the Last Supper when Jesus shared bread and wine with his

Figure 18.11   The Christian Eucharist or Communion. The similarity of red wine to blood and wafers to flesh establishes the similarities between the ritual objects and their meaning. Consuming them during the ritual spreads the blessings of God among all the people, which is an example of the law of contagion.

most devoted followers. The Last Supper was held at the start of the Jewish feast of Passover, which reenacts the story of the Jewish exodus from Egypt. Because the meal was part of the Passover, the bread was unleavened and flat like the unleavened matzoh bread that is produced as large flat wafers rather than loaves. Jesus himself is using a metaphor when he holds up the bread while announcing "this is my body" and the wine "is my blood." The wine is an appropriate element because it resembles blood in color—law of similarity. The wafer resembles the unleavened bread of the Passover meal, which in turn is a symbol for Jesus's flesh. When congregants eat a consecrated wafer and drink a sip of wine, they are linked together as a congregation because they have shared the same wafers and wine—law of contact or contagion (Figure 18.11).

Magic in Western Societies

Americans tend to believe that modernization has eliminated magical thought in our culture. Yet many of the elements observed in non-Western societies also occur in contemporary America. In his study of baseball players, for example, anthropologist George Gmelch (1978) noted that players often have lucky jerseys, good luck fetishes, or other objects that become charms. For these players, ordinary objects acquire power by being connected to exceptionally hot batting or pitching streaks. These charms follow the law of similarity. For three months during a winning season, one pitcher Gmelch interviewed followed the exact same routine: at lunch he went to the same restaurant, had two glasses of iced tea and a tuna fish sandwich, and for an hour before the game wore the same sweatshirt and jock strap he had worn the first day of the streak. He was afraid that changing anything he had done before the first winning game might produce a bad result.

Rites of Passage and the Ritual Process

- **Rite of passage.** Any life cycle rite that marks a person's or group's transition from one social state to another.

The most important type of ritual is a **rite of passage**, a life-cycle ritual that marks a person's (or group of persons') transition from one social state to another. In 1909 the French sociologist Arnold van Gennep (1960) outlined the structure of rituals that marked that passage of individuals from one status to another. Rites of passage include marriage rituals, in which individuals change status from being single to married, and ones that mark the transition from childhood to adulthood. Initiations are common around the world, even in industrial societies such as ours that carry out such rituals in "sweet sixteen parties" for young women, school graduations, and the like. Funerals represent another rite of passage that ostensibly focuses on the deceased, but they are largely about the transition survivors will experience. In "Thinking Like an Anthropologist: Examining Rites of Passage," we explore the link between symbols and the construction of meaning in two American rituals: funerals and graduations.

For anthropologist Victor Turner (1967, 1969), all rituals invoke symbols that can convey the underlying meanings of the ritual. Ritual symbols can consist of objects, colors, actions, events, or words. Often symbols point to, suggest, or take meaning from myths or sacred texts known to participants, such as the Cross or the wine and wafers in Christian church services. When American brides wear white, they are symbolically expressing their purity, whereas when Chinese wear white at a funeral, they are expressing their grief. What is common throughout these examples is that rituals create solidarity and meaning for participants and represent tradition for a group of people.

Thinking Like an Anthropologist

Examining Rites of Passage

ANTHROPOLOGISTS BEGIN THEIR research by asking questions. In this box, we want you to learn how to ask questions as an anthropological researcher. Part 1 describes a situation and follows up with questions we would ask. Part 2 asks you to do the same thing with a different situation.

PART 1: STATE FUNERAL FOR PRESIDENT RONALD REAGAN

When former President Ronald Reagan died on June 5, 2004, America began a week of national mourning and state ritual that dominated television and radio. State funerals, like inaugurations, are rites of passage that create a model of the state and become a model for how the state should be. Such secular rituals support and help create a sense of nationalism, American pride, a feeling of belonging to the nation, and a way of linking all Americans to state institutions. All funerals, of course, also have an important personal function: disposing of a dead body, and helping the deceased's friends and relatives adjust to the loss. It was no different when President Reagan passed away. Distant relatives and close friends had paid their respects to the president's widow and children. But because of his former role as president of the United States, his death became a rite of passage and transition for all Americans.

The president died in southern California, and the family decided that he would be buried at the Ronald Reagan Presidential Library in Simi Valley, California. The most efficient way to conduct a funeral would be to hold it in California. But most of the ritual occurred in Washington, DC, the center of the government that he led.

Flown to Andrews Air Force base, the flag-draped coffin was brought to the Washington Monument, where it was transferred to a horse-drawn caisson, on which it proceeded slowly up Constitution Avenue to the Capitol. The procession was led by a riderless horse with boots pointed backwards, symbolic of the dead (former) commander in chief. Three pairs of horses pulled the caisson, with riders only on the three left horses. When the procession reached 4th Street, 21 F-15 planes made a flyover, and the coffin was carried the rest of the way to the Capitol by eight-man teams representing each branch of the military. At this point, there was a 21-gun salute, and a band played "Hail to the Chief"

A Public Funerary Ritual.   Mourners file in to view President Ronald Reagan's flag-draped casket as he lies in state in the Rotunda of the U.S. Capitol in Washington, DC, on June 10, 2004.

and "The Battle Hymn of the Republic." Mrs. Reagan was waiting inside the Capitol to meet the coffin.

After a short ceremony the president's body was to lie in state in the Rotunda, which is at the center of the Capitol building. The flag-draped casket rested on a simple pine frame covered with black cloth that had first held the coffin of Abraham Lincoln in 1865. Present were important politicians who had served in the Reagan administration or in the Bush administration. Only the Reagan family was provided seats for the ceremony. After the ceremony, Mrs. Reagan and the dignitaries left, but the public was allowed to walk past and around the casket throughout the night. Thousands filed past President Reagan's coffin to pay their respects in solemnity and silence until 7:00 the next morning.

Afterward, a motorcade took the body to the National Cathedral for the national funeral service, with eulogies from President George W. Bush, former President George H. W. Bush, former British Prime Minister Margaret Thatcher, and former Canadian Prime Minister Brian Mulroney. After the funeral, a motorcade brought the body back to Andrews, whereupon it was flown to California for a private interment ceremony attended only by the Reagan family and close family friends.

What questions does this situation raise for anthropological researchers?

1.   How do the ritual symbols, such as the use of a caisson, riderless horse, 21-plane flyover, 21-gun salute, and so on add meaning to the ritual?

Thinking Like an Anthropologist (continued)

2.   What added meaning was given to the event by holding it in Washington, DC, that could not have been accomplished at the Reagan Library in California?

3.   What meaning was created by the particular dignitaries who attended the Rotunda ceremony?

4.   What model of social order was conveyed by the particular order in which people viewed the flag-draped casket? What difference did it make that viewing went on for thirty-six hours that would not have been accomplished if it had only lasted for three hours?

PART 2: YOUR OWN HIGH SCHOOL GRADUATION

Reflect on your own high school graduation, which was likely marked by special costumes, processions, music, speeches, and some special action (such as shifting the tassel to one side of the hat) that acknowledged your shift from one status to another. Viewing this graduation as a rite of passage, what questions would you ask about this situation as an anthropological researcher?

THINKING CRITICALLY ABOUT RELIGION

Compare the ritual symbols in a Sunday morning television or cable broadcast of a Protestant televangelist with a televised Sunday morning Roman Catholic mass. Although both services are religious rituals for Christian sects, they look very different. How do the different structures in the two services suggest different meanings derived from the same scripture?

How Is Religion Linked to Political and Social Action?

• **Secular worldview.** A worldview that does not accept the supernatural as influencing current people's lives.

Time magazine's cover for April 8, 1966, asked the provocative question, "Is God Dead?" Playing off the nineteenth-century German philosopher Friedrich Nietzsche's famous claim that "God is dead"—suggesting that the **secular worldview,** or a worldview that does not accept the supernatural as influencing current people's lives, had finally overtaken the religious one in Europe—*Time* was asking whether the same secularizing trend was at work in America. Formal church membership in Europe had declined sharply, to fewer than 10% of the population in some countries, and *Time* was suggesting that religion would no longer play a role in political actions, as it had in the abolitionist movement and was then playing in the civil rights movement. *Time* was so wrong. More than fifty years later, we can see the persistent power of religion in the United States, in politics, in social discourse, in civil rights, and on TV. American church membership has risen gradually since the late 1940s to about 75% of American adults today. So, why was *Time* magazine so wrong?

The main reason is the magazine's false assumption that as a society "modernizes" it begins to value scientific knowledge and reason over religious values and practices.

The *Time* authors assumed that secularization would continue to grow, but American churches responded to social change not by ignoring it, but by challenging it. Churches and other religious organizations became increasingly political, often supporting one political party or the other. In nearly every society, political and religious institutions are not only engaged with one another, but they are frequently also the same institutions.

The broader point is that religious values, symbols, and beliefs typically either challenge or uphold a particular social order. We illustrate this point by considering the forceful rise of religious fundamentalisms around the world.

The Rise of Fundamentalism

Since the 1960s, the most significant change in U.S. religion has been how much more active religious organizations have become in public life, particularly among the conservative churches that call themselves **fundamentalist**, people belonging to conservative religious movements that advocate a return to fundamental or traditional principles. Fundamentalist TV preachers have expanded their broadcasting since the early 1980s, and conservative religious groups and religious organizations have been as deeply involved in elections and politics as ever. The rise of fundamentalism is not unique to the United States, either. Across the world, conservative groups have turned to fundamentalism to make sense of and to confront changes happening all around them. As in most other societies, fundamentalist religion and politics are deeply engaged with one another (Berger 1999).

Understanding Fundamentalism

Scholars have had difficulty agreeing to the definition of *fundamentalism*. Traditionally, **fundamentalism** in America has been associated with an extremely literal interpretation of scripture, particularly prophetic books in the Bible. Recently the American media has often associated fundamentalism with Islam, violence, extremism, and terrorism, but both views are far too narrow and biased because most of the world's religions have their own conservative, "back to fundamentals" branches, and most are not so outwardly violent.

To correct these biases, in the 1990s a team of researchers working on the Fundamentalism Project at the University of Chicago studied conservative religious movements within Christianity, Islam, Zionist Judaism, Buddhism, Hinduism, Confucianism, and Sikhism (Marty and Appleby 1991; Almond, Appleby, and Sivan 2003). Not all of these diverse movements rely on literal readings of scripture, and for some groups sacred writings are of little consequence. Nor do fundamentalist groups necessarily reject everything modern. Most have embraced television, computers, the Internet, and other digital technologies to get the word out. And conservative Arab Muslims celebrate the medieval Islamic origins of modern science and technology.

The Fundamentalism Project (Marty and Appleby 1991:viii–x) found several key themes common to all of these conservative religious movements. These include:

- They see themselves as fighting back against the corrosive effects of secular life on what they envision as a purer way of life. They fight for a worldview that prescribes "proper" gender roles, sexualities, and educational patterns. Their interpretation of the purer past becomes the model for building a purer, godlier future.

Figure 18.12   Presenting the Secularization Hypothesis. *Time* magazine's cover on April 8, 1966, wrongly assumed that the power of religion both in America and around the world was on the decline.

- **Fundamentalist.** A person belonging to a religious movement that advocates a return to fundamental or traditional principles.

- **Fundamentalism.** Conservative religious movements that advocate a return to fundamental or traditional principles.

- They are willing to engage in political, even military, battles to defend their ideas about life and death, including issues that emerge in hospitals and clinics dealing with pregnancy, abortion, and the terminally ill.
- They work against others, whether infidels, modernizers, or moderate insiders, reinforcing in the process their identity and building solidarity within their community.
- They have passion, and the most passionate are those who "are convinced that they are called to carry out God's or Allah's purposes against challengers" (Marty and Appleby 1991:x).

Political action among fundamentalists has sometimes taken a more violent course, as suicide bombings and 9/11 suggest, but in India another minority group with a distinctive religion, the Sikhs, have pushed for fundamentalist values through armed combat and insurrection against the Indian government. We explore this case further in "Doing Fieldwork: Studying the Sikh Militants."

The broader point here is that fundamentalists are not isolated from the world of politics, but are actively engaged in it. Unlike religion in most small-scale societies, fundamentalism does not typically support the existing political order but fights against it. We have seen this in the United States, when the evangelical pastor Jerry Falwell founded a political organization called the Moral Majority in 1979. Members of the Moral Majority were fundamentalists, but they became active in the presidential elections throughout the 1980s, supporting conservative candidates. In recent decades, fundamentalist Christians have stood in vocal opposition to non-conservative candidates.

What we do see in fundamentalism is that membership and a sense of belonging to a community is an important feature of religious organizations in industrial societies where it is easy for individuals to feel anonymous. Indeed, part of the power of any religious organizations (churches, synagogues, mosques, and other religious centers) is that they bring people together, provide them social support, and give them an identity within a broader secular world. Anthropologists have long understood that this process of belonging and the social action associated with group membership is bolstered by important symbols.

THINKING CRITICALLY ABOUT RELIGION

Consider a secular ritual, like the 4th of July with its parades and fireworks displays in your hometown. How do the parades and the speeches and fireworks build symbolic support for the state and federal governments and for the U.S. military? How do the symbols support the existing government?

Conclusion

A month after Tom Coleman shot Jonathan Daniels in Hayneville, Alabama, an all-white jury found Coleman not guilty of manslaughter. This was a cause of disbelief for many who sympathized with Jon Daniel's worldview. For example, Jon Daniels's hometown newspaper, the *Keene Sentinel,* editorialized, "White Southerners and Northerners who hold [similar] views . . . do not, and apparently cannot, understand

Doing Fieldwork

Studying the Sikh Militants

ANTHROPOLOGIST CYNTHIA KEPPLEY MAHMOOD, now at the University of Notre Dame, had been studying religion and conflict in the Indian subcontinent for more than a decade, making frequent visits to India, when she became interested in a fundamentalist movement among members of the Sikh religion. From 1980, a militant group of ethnic Sikhs in the northwestern Indian state of Punjab had been engaged in an armed insurgency aimed at forming a sovereign nation called Khalistan (Land of the Pure). This insurgency was built on a fundamentalist religious ideology. Khalistanis identify themselves through both their religious and their ethnic identities. This movement, however, does not represent all or even the majority of Sikh people living in Punjab. Other Sikhs support the idea of independence but reject the violence entailed in winning it.

Wanting to study religion and violence, Mahmood turned her attention to the separatist tensions in Punjab, which were as religious as they were political. Studying a violent religious group presented special problems for the anthropologist, because it was impossible for her to live in a community with the militants, targeted as they were by the Indian government they wanted to overthrow. So Mahmood adopted an innovative strategy by conducting research about militant Sikhs and their movement overseas rather than in India.

Over a period of three years in the early 1990s, Mahmood met intermittently with militant Sikhs in various parts of the United States and Canada to understand the motives, rationale, and ideology of this fundamentalist group. Mahmood's interactions with the Sikhs occurred in restaurants, homes, Sikh temples, and even in prisons. Many of her informants had come to North America as a way of reinvigorating their movement, which was being suppressed by the Indian government in Punjab. Many informants felt that violent acts were reasonable and acceptable responses to the violence that the Indian government had perpetrated against their people. Even though these Sikhs lived overseas, they remained deeply involved in their homeland's affairs. From interviews, Mahmood was able to construct a compelling image of the complex political and religious movement and how participation in it gave meaning to activists based in North America.

Mahmood's interviews posed a variety of ethical issues not present in most kinds of ethnographic research. To protect her informants she had to conceal their identities at every stage in the research, including any identifiers in her fieldnotes. Even though she conducted her study before the terrorist attacks of 9/11, the tapes of her interviews would have posed a danger for her informants if they had fallen into the hands of various law enforcement agencies because, unlike journalists, anthropologists have no First Amendment rights to protect their sources. Of course, she changed the names of her informants and concealed their identities when she published her book *Fighting for Faith and Nation: Dialogs with Sikh Militants* (1997).

Questions for Reflection

1. What is lost by conducting research almost entirely through interviews rather than through participant observation?

2. What ethical complications are involved in studying a militant antigovernment religious group?

3. How would these complications be different if one conducted research in the Methodist Church?

A Sikh Temple in India. The vast majority of Sikhs are not militant or violent, just as most Christians, Jews, Muslims, Hindus, and Buddhists are non-violent.

why a white man would risk his life to help a Negro register to vote or teach Negro children to read. They simply do not understand that, to men like Jonathan Daniels, all men are brothers, and skin color means nothing. . . . In dying, not only was Jonathan Daniels minding his own business, but he was attending to His business."

When Jon first went to Alabama, he did so with a moral and religious commitment to what he understood as social justice. His actions were driven by a worldview that called him to help create a world suggested by his reading of scripture and his understanding of God. But at the same time, Tom Coleman acted out of his own worldview, one clearly shared by the jury. At that time in America, many people were proud of their prejudices and found many justifications for them, even in their religions. As much as people today may disapprove of Coleman's actions and of those on the jury, these actions were motivated by a shared set of assumptions about what the world should be like. Coleman acted in defense of that ideal world. Just as Jon's actions made sense in terms of his belief system, Coleman's beliefs and understandings about the world made sense to a large part of his community. Fifty years later, racial attitudes in America have changed from where they were in Hayneville in 1965.
Whether or not we agree with someone else's perspective, we can never understand the actions of others without understanding a community's worldview and the powerful moods and motivations it creates. These are the benefits of approaching conflicting beliefs from the "native's point of view."

KEY TERMS

Animism   p. 479

Fundamentalism   p. 497

Fundamentalist   p. 497

Holy struggle   p. 484

Interpretive approach
   p. 481

Magic   p. 491

Mana   p. 480

Monotheism   p. 489

Polytheism   p. 488

Religion   p. 482

Rite of passage   p. 494

Rituals   p. 480

Shaman   p. 487

Secular worldview
   p. 496

Speaking in tongues
   p. 487

Spirit familiar   p. 487

Sympathetic magic   p. 491

Totemism   p. 486

Trance   p. 487

World religions   p. 489

Worldview   p. 481

Reviewing the Chapter

Chapter Section	What We Know	To Be Resolved
How should we understand religion and religious beliefs?	Anthropologists have long considered the reasons people have religion and how religions work. While some classic approaches emphasized that religion is about the supernatural, more recent approaches emphasize the symbolic and action-oriented character of religious beliefs.	Many anthropologists accept that we can learn a great deal about the worldviews of the peoples we study, but not all anthropologists believe that we can fully understand how any individual sees and feels about his or her world.
What forms does religion take?	Traditional societies with limited social stratification tend to have simpler religions than the religions of complex societies, but this correlation is not inevitable.	We don't really know what environmental, political, or social conditions produce more complex forms of religious ideas.
How do rituals work?	Rituals use symbols that convey deep meanings about the world and how it should be. All rituals rely on some version of magical thinking. Ritual symbols themselves rely heavily on metaphor and other kinds of resemblances for conveying meaning.	It is not entirely clear why humans in all societies so readily accept ideas and beliefs that can be so easily shown to be incomplete, if not wrong.
How is religion linked to political and social action?	Religions have always been linked to political organizations and the social order. Anthropologists reject the idea that as the world modernized it would become more secular, drawing on the widespread rise of fundamentalism to demonstrate the continuing social and political importance of religion.	There is no real consensus as to how much political institutions can shape religious symbols, rituals, and worldviews, even though it is obvious that groups in power often try to.

Readings

One of the most important early studies of a traditional, non-Western religion is E. E. Evans-Pritchard's 1937 classic ethnography *Witchcraft, Oracles, and Magic Among the Azande*, abridged edition ([1976] Oxford: Clarendon Press), in which ideas about witchcraft, diviners called oracles, and magic are described and discussed in their natural context in what is now South Sudan.

• • • • • • • • • • • • • • • • • • • •

Two important studies provide examples of symbolic studies of religion. Clifford Geertz's 1966 article "Religion as a Cultural System" (in Michael Banton, ed., *Anthropological Approaches to the Study of Religion,* pp. 1–46. ASA Monograph 3. London: Tavistock) explores a symbolic definition of religion that sees religion as a "system of symbols." Victor Turner's book *The Forest of Symbols: Aspects of Ndembu Ritual* (Ithaca, NY: Cornell University Press, 1967) offers a series of explorations of just how such a system of symbols might work in a functioning society in southern Africa.

• • • • • • • • • • • • • • • • • • • •

For an anthropological perspective on the interactions between Islam and politics, see Dale F. Eickelman and James P. Piscatori's book *Muslim Politics* (Princeton, NJ: Princeton University Press, 1996). Even though it was written before the post-9/11 world, it offers useful analytical tools to understand the complex intersections of religion and political action in the Muslim world.

• • • • • • • • • • • • • • • • • • • •

If you want to understand the rise of religious fundamentalisms in recent decades, see Martin Marty and R. Scott Appleby's edited volume *Fundamentalisms Observed* (The Fundamentalism Project, Volume 1, Chicago: University of Chicago Press, 1991).

• • • • • • • • • • • • • • • • • • • •

Materiality

Constructing Social Relationships and Meanings with Things

Along old U.S. Highway 77 about eight miles south of the town of Brookings, South Dakota, near the intersection with 220th Road is a roadside historical marker that reads:

> *You Are About to Enter*
> BROOKINGS COUNTY
> *home of roving Indians until 1862. The exploring party of Nicollet,*
> *scientist, and Fremont, "Pathfinder of the West," visited*
> *Oakwood Lakes,*
> *July 1838, leaving the first reliable record.*

This marker further explains that the Santee Sioux—the "roving Indians"—"ceded" the eastern part of the county to the U.S. government in 1858 and offers highlights of early white settlement in the years following.

Most people would simply drive by, vaguely registering the marker's presence. But for someone interested in the real history of this place, this marker likely raises more questions than it answers. Just who were these "roving Indians"? Had they always been "roving" or had something happened to make them so? How and why did they "cede" this territory to whites? Here's what we know. Originally, the Santee Sioux had lived in the region around Mille Lacs Lake in what is now east central Minnesota. There they were a sedentary tribe raising corn, squash, and other woodland crops. By 1700 the expansion of British settlers in New York, southern Canada, and New England displaced

Sioux Indians Performing in a Modern Pow Wow.

many eastern tribes, who moved westward, forcing the Santee further westward into the Great Plains of what is now South Dakota. There they adopted a nomadic lifestyle with the benefit of horses that had gone feral and spread out from Spanish settlements in New Mexico and Arizona. They were "roving" only in the sense that they followed the buffalo and other game on horseback as all of the other Plains Indians were doing at this time. After brutal military repression by the U.S. Army that brought the Santee Sioux to the brink of extinction as a people, white people claimed the land as their own, although the Santee still exist (Figure 19.1).

Historical markers are tangible objects that present an image of history. Simple as they are, they produce a kind of petrified history, fixed and unchangeable. But how can an object so simple ignore so much? Our landscapes and cities are full of similar markers, monuments, and memorials that systematically omit or misrepresent the facts of American history (Loewen 1999). They frequently ignore unpleasant aspects of the past, such as forcing American Indians off their land. Such public treatment of history is not about uncovering the historical facts of what happened or exploring how different people might view these events differently. In fact, such markers and memorials are generally intended as celebrations of those in power (Loewen 1999:130–32).

Many of us take for granted historical markers and monuments as a natural, obvious, or somewhat uninteresting background to our daily lives. It is only

Figure 19.1   Brookings County Historic Marker. On the roadside as one enters Brookings County, South Dakota, this marker describes the Santee Sioux people, who were the inhabitants of the county when Whites arrived, as "roving Indians." Everything else about them including their tribal name and the fact that they still live a few miles from this marker is erased from the record.

when we make a concerted effort to look closely at them as objects—asking who made them, and with what purpose—that we can begin to appreciate how objects carry subtle social and political messages, and how objects can tell us a lot about social relationships between groups of people. Further, the physical presence of an object gives it a concreteness that the same text read over the radio might not. We call this concrete, physical presence its **materiality** (having the quality of being physical or material)**,** the theme we will explore in this final chapter. At the heart of anthropological interest in materiality is this question: *What is the role of objects and material culture in constructing social relationships and cultural meanings?* Embedded within this larger question are several more focused questions around which this chapter is organized.

- **Materiality.** Having the quality of being physical or material.

Why is the ownership of artifacts from another culture a contentious issue?

How should we look at objects anthropologically?

Why and how do the meanings of things change over time?

What role does material culture play in constructing the meaning of a community's past?

This chapter examines **material culture**, the objects made and used in any society, which is of special interest to both cultural and archaeological anthropologies. Traditionally the term referred to technologically simple objects made in preindustrial societies, but material culture may refer to all the objects or commodities of modern life as well. In previous chapters we have reflected on the many ways that objects and material culture are important to the material existence of human societies. In this chapter we look at objects in a different way, how they shape meaning for people and allow us to communicate meaning. When we take objects seriously, all the ways people use objects to communicate with others, define themselves through objects, and control others using objects, anthropology is not "simply" about people but about the intertwining of people and material things.

- **Material culture.** The objects made and used in any society, traditionally the term referred to technologically simple objects made in preindustrial societies, but material culture may refer to all of the objects or commodities of modern life as well.

Why Is the Ownership of Artifacts from Another Culture a Contentious Issue?

In the United States, the discipline of anthropology began in museums, arising amidst the scramble for collections of cultural, archaeological, linguistic, and biological data to document the human story. At first, most of the material culture was from Native Americans in the western states. From 1850 on, many of these objects were held in the Smithsonian Institution in Washington, DC.

By the time of the Chicago World's Fair of 1893, the Smithsonian's curators had assembled impressive anthropological exhibits. But rather than rely exclusively on the national collection, the Chicago organizers of the World's Fair appointed Professor Frederic Ward Putnam of Harvard's Peabody Museum of Archaeology and Ethnology (established 1866) to organize its own anthropological exhibits. Putnam competed with the Smithsonian researchers to present the cultures and prehistory of the New World, sending out teams of researchers to acquire new collections from dozens of Indian tribes and excavate Indian mounds in Ohio, Pueblos like Mesa Verde in the Southwest, and ancient sites in Peru. At the end of the Fair, Marshall Field, the wealthy department store merchant, donated a million dollars for a new museum, now known as The Field Museum—on the site of the Fair Grounds—which purchased the artifacts and exhibits (Figure 19.2).

The World's Fair motivated the American Museum of Natural History in New York City to hire a young Franz Boas, who immediately began building its collections. He organized a series of collecting expeditions to the Northwest Coast that brought back many objects for display as well as many volumes of myths and field-notes about local customs to help interpret these collections. What followed during the early twentieth century was an international scramble for collections from societies around the world that Western scholars thought of as "primitive" (Cole 1985; Shildkrout and Kelm 1998) These objects documented the lives, economic activities,

Figure 19.2   Kwakiutl Indians with Totem Poles. Collected for F. W. Putnam and displayed at the World's Columbian Exposition in Chicago in 1893, now in the collections of The Field Museum. From *Vistas of the Fair in Color: A Portfolio of Familiar Views* (Chicago: Poole Brothers, 1894). © The Field Museum. #GN85650c.

and rituals of peoples around the globe, and the possession of more of these exotic objects set one museum apart from the others. These objects clearly meant something different to the museums than they did to the native peoples who had used them.

The picture that emerges from all this is that the major American museums actively competed with one another for objects, in the process employing a lot of anthropologists. For a long time, nobody was concerned about who owned all of these objects, since in a legal sense they belonged to the individual museums. But in recent decades, questions of ownership and control over these objects have become a contentious issue. Shouldn't the people whose direct ancestors made or used these objects have some rights over these collections? Who has the right to sell them to museums? Who has the moral right to display and interpret them? These are complex questions that may be easiest to answer if we begin by asking who owns the archaeological and skeletal material found at an archaeological site.

Archaeological Excavation and Questions of Ownership

For many years the United States had only a few basic laws to protect archaeological sites, mostly on government lands. Among these was the Antiquities Act of 1906, requiring permission for excavations on government lands; and the National Historic Preservation Act of 1966, requiring government agencies to consider the effects of development projects on historical or archaeological sites. But an incident in Kentucky in 1987 led to new state and federal laws that make it a felony to disturb archaeological sites on both government and private lands everywhere.

The Problem of Looting and the "Tragedy of Slack Farm"

Setting this legislation in motion was what archaeologist Brian Fagan has called the "Tragedy of Slack Farm." In Uniontown, Kentucky, on a farm owned by the Slack family, there was an important late Mississippian site with 1,000 graves that seemed to date to the period 1450–1650 CE, an important period before people in this area had direct contact with European settlers. The Slacks had not disturbed the site, but they sold the property in 1987. For $10,000, the new owner sold rights to "excavate" the site, and ten men started plundering it with a tractor in search of anything they could sell on the black market (pots, pipes, etc.), scattering human bones across the site (Fagan 1988, 2000).

Residents complained to the state police, who arrested the looters on the misdemeanor charge of desecrating a venerated object, a charge used primarily when gravestones and cemeteries are damaged. Negative publicity put pressure on lawmakers to do something about looting (Fagan 1988; Arden 1989). The Kentucky legislature passed a bill making it a felony to disturb any and all burial sites. This incident was so offensive to American Indian groups that it gave them further impetus to lobby the federal government, which the following year passed the Native American Graves Protection and Repatriation Act (NAGPRA). **NAGPRA** is the 1990 law that established the ownership of human remains, grave goods, and important cultural objects as belonging to descendants of the native communities they came from.

Such problems—and efforts to address them—are not limited to the United States. Many countries have implemented legislation and programs of their own, and most governments support UNESCO's **World Heritage Site program**, which provides financial support to maintain sites of importance to humanity. The majority of these 802 currently recognized cultural sites have played a key role in human history. Five of them are sites where early fossil hominids have been found in Africa, China, and Australia. Others are key archaeological sites such as the pyramids of Giza, Thebes, and Luxor in Egypt; Ankor Wat in Cambodia; Chichén Itzá in Mexico; Mesa Verde

- **NAGPRA (Native American Graves and Repatriation Act).** The 1990 law that established the ownership of human remains, grave goods, and important cultural objects as belonging to the Native Americans, whose ancestors once owned them.

- **World Heritage Site program.** Which provides financial support to maintain sites of importance to humanity.

in Colorado; and the Moai statues on Rapa Nui (Easter Island), all of which are typical of what we often think of as ancient historic and prehistoric sites. UNESCO cannot force countries to protect these sites, but it can formally delist a site if the host country fails to protect it from destruction (UNESCO 2015c). Internationally, there is agreement that such archaeological and historical sites belong to all peoples, not just to the governments that happen to control them at any particular moment.

Indian Reactions to Archaeological Excavations of Human Remains

In the United States, "The Tragedy of Slack Farm" aggravated long-brewing tension over who has a moral right to examine, study, and possess the artifacts and bones recovered from archaeological sites. On the one hand, many archaeologists felt that as scientists they had the moral right to excavate, while pot hunters had no rights because they were simply out to make money. Where they excavated, archaeologists also felt that they and their institutions owned the bones because of their labor and research grants. But the laws governing excavations of human remains were highly discriminatory, treating Native Americans differently than Euro-Americans.

A notorious example of this took place in Glenwood, Iowa, in 1971, where archaeologists excavated twenty-seven skeletal remains. Of these skeletons, twenty-six belonged to Euro-American pioneers, and one was that of an Indian woman. Reflecting the same sort of dismissive attitudes that we saw in the Brookings, South Dakota, historical marker, existing Iowa state policy required the Euro-American remains to be reburied, while the Indian skeleton was sent to a local museum for "study." Local Indians protested this disrespectful treatment, and eventually the Indian remains were also reburied (Ubelaker and Grant 1989:253).

The Road to NAGPRA

- **AIM (American Indian movement).** The most prominent and one of the earliest Native American activist groups, founded in 1968.

- **Repatriation.** The return of human remains or cultural artifacts to the communities of descendants of the people to whom they originally belonged.

During the 1970s, activists associated with the **American Indian movement (AIM),** a prominent Native American rights group founded in 1968, began to protest how national, state, and local officials treated Indian remains. AIM activists asserted that the treatment of Indian remains was an element of a larger pattern of disrespect for Indian cultures. They pointed to histories of forced settlement on reservations; punishment for speaking their native languages in government schools; and pressures on reservations after the Dawes Act of 1887, which allowed reservations to be broken up into individually owned lots that could be sold to white Americans. Calls for **repatriation**, or the return of human remains and artifacts to the communities of descendants of the people to whom they originally belonged, came to stand for something much more important than the objects themselves. Repatriating artifacts became a material symbol of Indian identity itself.

These concerns grew throughout the 1980s. Archaeologists have always held a range of views on whether prehistoric bones should be studied scientifically, reburied after examination, reburied without being studied, or never excavated at all. A number of Indian groups took more radical positions, asserting their right to rebury all Indian bones found in any museum, regardless of whether the bones had a connection to their own tribe (Council for Museum Anthropology 1983). The professor of American Indian Studies James Riding In, who is Pawnee, succinctly expressed his opposition to "scientific grave looting" arguing that excavation of burial sites is and always has been a sacrilege, and all Indian remains should be reburied (Riding In 1996).

Some archaeologists and anthropologists worried that information about the prehistory of Native Americans, an important part of the heritage of all humans, would be lost if reburial became commonplace (Buikstra 1983). Moreover, some archaeologists and biological anthropologists feel that scientists have a moral and professional obligation to the archaeological data with which they work as well as to the broader public good that can benefit from such studies (Meighan 1992). Others rejected the Indian position altogether; as one prominent archaeologist was once heard to say, the Indians would "get my bones over my dead body."

But after the Slack Farm Tragedy, Congress was mobilized to action and passed two acts: the National Museum of the American Indian Act of 1989, which established a new museum for preservation and display of American Indian artifacts; and in 1990 NAGPRA, the Native American Graves Protection and Repatriation Act. NAGPRA mandated that museums notify tribes about the cultural objects they hold in their collections—particularly human remains, grave goods, and religious objects. It also gives tribes the right to request repatriation from any public museum collection. The legislation also created new jobs for anthropologists, archaeologists, and museum professionals to help process NAGPRA requests.

Assessing NAGPRA

In the years since its passage, repatriation has proceeded reasonably well (McKeown 2002; McManamon 2002). Most museums have notified tribes about their holdings, and Indian tribes have become empowered to make claims that in the past would have fallen on deaf ears (Figure 19.3). Nevertheless, some museums have taken too long to comply with these mandates, and the regulations weren't always clear about which objects are covered by NAGPRA and which groups can submit repatriation requests—which is only federally recognized tribes. Moreover, some museum skeletal collections are so poorly documented, nobody knows which tribe the remains belonged to originally. Consequently, it's not always clear which native group has legal authority to manage repatriation of the remains.

As "Anthropologist as Problem Solver: John Terrell, Repatriation, and the Maori House at The Field Museum" suggests, the issues of rights of indigenous peoples to their cultural resources is an ongoing topic for discussion at the international level as well.

Put another way, NAGPRA has helped clarify that American Indians own the bones of their ancestors and any grave goods found with these remains, but each new excavation or older museum collection presents new dimensions to the question of ownership that needs to be negotiated through ongoing dialogue.

Cultural Resource Management

In response to all the new legislation, archaeologists in the United States have taken a leading role in managing and preserving prehistoric and historic heritage. These efforts are often referred to as **cultural resource management (CRM)**, which is a form of applied archaeology. CRM's goal is to protect and manage the cultural resources of every community, especially important prehistoric sites and structures. The vast majority of archaeological work in the Americas and around the world is done by contract archaeologists, and CRM has become a major focus for those seeking careers in archaeology. Many projects are done under the supervision of the National Park Service or state department of historic resources.

Although many Indian groups historically criticized archaeologists as doing little to help their communities and disturbing the bones of their ancestors (Deloria 1969), an

• **Cultural resource management (CRM).** Research and planning aimed at identificating, interpretating, and protecting sites and artifacts of historic or prehistoric significance.

Figure 19.3   Repatriating a Chilkat Blanket to the Tlingit at a Memorial Potlatch in Sitka, Alaska, Fall 2002.

Above, Tlingit elders who organized the memorial potlatch wearing Chilkat blankets or button blankets: Edwell John (Killer Whale Clan), Joe Murray (representing Killer Whale Clan), a man from Wolf Clan (Kaagwaantaan), Dan Brown (Brown Bear or Teikweidee Clan), and Randy Gamble (Kaagwaantaan Clan). They wear headdresses from their respective clans.
Below, on the right Kellen Haak (Registrar of the Hood Museum of Art at Dartmouth College) presents the Museum's Chilkat blanket being returned to the Deisheetaan Clan in the Raven Moiety. To the left is Nell Murphy (from the American Museum of Natural History in New York), anthropologist Sergei Kan (Dartmouth College) speaking for the group, and Terri Snowball (National Museum of the American Indian in Washington, DC). Tlingit leader in this photo include: Alan Zuboff (Dog Salmon Clan) and Garfield George (Deisheetaan Clan).

increasing number of Indians have earned postgraduate degrees in archaeology and use the techniques of CRM to preserve their tribe's cultural heritage. Nearly all tribes that use CRM view heritage management differently than most federal government agencies (Anyon, Ferguson, and Welch 2000:132). One key difference is that non-Indian agencies nearly always see heritage resources as tangible places and things, and scientific study as a way of finding a middle ground between the heritage resource and some other use. Emphasizing their spiritual connections to the past, tribes tend to prefer avoiding the disturbance of the heritage resource altogether, including scientific investigation (Dongoske et al. 1995).

As this section has demonstrated, the social conflicts around objects are complex, suggesting that the meanings and uses of objects are not straightforward matters. In the next section we expand on this point by pulling back and reviewing how we can look at objects anthropologically.

The Anthropologist as Problem Solver

John Terrell, Repatriation, and the Maori Meeting House at the Field Museum

At the heart of any Maori community in New Zealand is a meeting house where rituals, business, and other important community processes take place. Meeting houses have elaborately carved images in the posts and ridge poles, which not only symbolize a Maori family's ancestry but embody the spirits of these ancestors as well.

In 1905 The Field Museum of Chicago purchased a nearly complete meeting house named Ruatepapuke [roo-ah-tay-pah-**poo**-kay] that originally came from Tokomaru Bay, New Zealand. The museum bought it from a European curio dealer who had convinced one member of the family to sell this house. The structure had been quietly and quickly dismantled and shipped overseas. For the Maori family, this was a shameful act that amounted to selling off their ancestors carved in the boards.

When archaeologist John Terrell became The Field Museum's Curator of Oceanic Archaeology and Ethnology in 1971, he began researching this Maori meeting house. He brought specialists to the museum to examine the carvings, including Hirini (Sidney) Moko Mead, one of the leading Maori anthropologists. Terrell also visited Tokomaru Bay to confirm what he and other specialists had suspected—that this was indeed their meeting house that had been sold and packed off around 1900.

Terrell then began working with elders at Tokomaru Bay, discussing the future of the structure. Some of the young people wanted their house and their ancestors to come back to the community. But after talking over the matter with Terrell, the elders agreed to keep the house in Chicago, so long as The Field Museum would work with the community to restore the structure. Terrell, in collaboration with Tokomaru elders, chose Maori curators, conservators, and artists to help with the restoration (Hakiwai and Terrell 1994).

The house went on display for the public in 1986 as part of an exhibition called *Te Maori*, and Maori elders were invited to help with the opening. Later, more than twenty elders, both men and women, came to Chicago to perform the rituals that would bring their ancestral spirits from the museum's lower level, where the house had been for many decades, to the second floor, where the house would be reassembled. Elders have been involved with planning and executing all important decisions about Ruatepapuke ever since. They selected their own Maori curator and conservator, as well as a Maori artist who was tasked with carving new pieces missing from the front of the structure. Maori curator Arapata Hakiwai discovered several boards from this meeting house in Te Papa, the National Museum of New Zealand, and Tokomaru elders requested that these carved boards join the house in Chicago where they belonged, and the museum complied with the request. One carved house board was found in the collections of the Peabody-Essex Museum in Salem, Massachusetts. It too has been reunited with the other boards from Te Papa in Chicago. The people of Tokomaru Bay are now well known by Maori across New Zealand because their meeting house is so prominently displayed overseas. By working with Terrell and The Field Museum, the people of Tokomaru Bay

John Terrell at the Maori Meeting House at The Field Museum in Chicago. John Terrell speaking at a workshop held in the meeting house. #GN91326_119d by John Weinstein. (below) The restored meeting house. #A112518c by Diane Alexander White and Linda Dorman. Both courtesy of The Field Museum.

(continued)

Anthropologist as Problem Solver (continued)

transformed an embarrassing situation into an object of national pride.

By April 2007 a number of the elders who had been involved with The Field Museum passed away. The younger generation had not been as involved with the museum, and some were talking about bringing Ruatepapuke back to Tokomaru Bay. The Field Museum invited some fifty Maori from Tokomaru Bay, both elders and younger members of the community, to celebrate the meeting house and Maori culture for a week. After this experience, many of those young people recognized that if they want a place for their cultural traditions on the world stage, they can be more successful by working with The Field Museum than they ever could be on their own. As in the 1980s, John Terrell has worked hard to engage with indigenous communities who made and formerly owned the artifacts his museum now holds. Together, the curator and the Maori community

have found alternative solutions to the question of repatriation of cultural objects that for Maori are the embodiment of their ancestors.

Questions for Reflection

1. What does this example illustrate about the role archaeologists and anthropologists can play in explaining and promoting a community's culture around the world?

2. Many archaeologists have assumed there is a natural tension between them and indigenous peoples. To what extent do you feel this tension is inevitable?

3. Archaeologists and anthropologists have always been the outsiders who most understand the native cultures they study. Why have indigenous peoples so often wanted to challenge their ownership of artifacts?

THINKING CRITICALLY ABOUT MATERIALITY

How do the meanings of museum collections of Native American material culture change depending on who is thinking about them? How would these meanings be different if the objects were historical artifacts from a white community in the National Museum of American History, another museum in the Smithsonian Institution?

How Should We Look at Objects Anthropologically?

Until the 1980s anthropologists tended to look at the study of objects as evidence of cultural distinctiveness. They approached cultural and artistic objects as expressions of a society's environmental adaptation, aesthetic sensibilities, or as markers of ethnic identity. Viewed in this way, arts and craftwares were considered an expression of a particular tradition, time, or place, but even more so, an expression of the individual creativity of the artist or craftperson. This way of looking at objects may seem reasonable, but in the mid-1980s anthropologists began to look at objects in a new way. In particular they started to recognize that objects were capable of conveying meaning in many different ways simultaneously.

The Many Dimensions of Objects

The historian of anthropology George W. Stocking, Jr. edited an influential book called *Objects and Others: Essays on Museums and Material Culture* (1985). Stocking's introduction to this book explained that anthropology's history began with the study of objects in museums decades before anthropologists even began conducting their own field research. Using these collections, they developed crude analyses of how civilized, barbaric, or primitive a society was from the kinds of objects they had or did not have. Later, when anthropologists started conducting fieldwork, they noticed firsthand the importance of objects in rituals, social exchanges, and political activities. Anthropologists began to look at objects to understand the meaning of rituals, the interconnections between people who exchanged particular objects, or the social stratification within a society that could be seen in the presence or absence of objects in a particular household or community. In its most basic sense, this approach has endured until the present.

But the importance of Stocking's work is his argument that objects are multidimensional, and if we really want to understand them, we have to recognize and try to understand not just their three basic physical dimensions—height, width, depth—but four others as well, among them time (history), power, wealth, and aesthetics, making a total of seven dimensions that he recognized.

The dimension of *time* or *history* refers to the fact that objects in museums came from somewhere and each had an individual history. In part this asks when, by whom, and how were they produced; how did they get to the museum or their current location; and how have interpretations of the object changed over time? The dimension of *power* reveals the relations of inequality reflected in objects, especially why the objects of non-Western people sit in ethnographic museums, while very few non-Western peoples have museums or repositories where local people can view Western objects. During the heyday of colonialism, European and American anthropologists collected thousands of objects from the peoples they studied. Rarely could a community know enough about how these objects might be displayed or studied to be able to give informed consent. *Wealth* reflects the fact that people use objects to establish and demonstrate who has wealth and social status. We have seen how the American museum directors saw showy and impressive objects as being quite valuable for their museums and the museums' reputations. The dimension of *aesthetics* is reflected in the fact that each culture brings with it its own system or patterns of recognizing what is pleasing or attractive, which configurations of colors and textures are appealing, and which are not.

What intrigued Stocking most about objects, especially those now found in museums, was that these things were a historical archive in multiple dimensions that can tell us a great deal about the cultures that made and used these objects as well as the relationships between the collectors' societies and the communities who originally used them. Furthermore, objects could offer a window for understanding local symbolic systems of meaning. This point was more expansive than just being focused on the objects found in art and ethnographic museums. His insights can actually be applied to any everyday object. Consider, for example, a shiny new bicycle.

A Shiny New Bicycle in Multiple Dimensions

Picture a shiny new bicycle chained to a bicycle rack on your campus (Figure 19.4). Made of a strong yet lightweight alloy, it is fast, sleek, and an exquisite example of modern technology applied to an object that has been around for more than a century. Like all objects, this bicycle has the physical properties of height, length, and

Figure 19.4   The Bicycle, Like Anything, Is a Multidimensional Object.

width, dimensions that are quite important for any individual mounting one: think of how difficult it is to ride a bicycle that is too big or too small.

Objects are defined by more than their physical traits, however. Objects also embody a temporal dimension of having a past, present, and future. The shape and form of this particular object have emerged from improvements on the functions of generations of bicycles, used by generations of cyclists as a childhood toy, as an inexpensive mode of transport, for racing, or for casual weekend riding. If we think of a bicycle in the abstract, we can choose from among all of these meanings and uses of a bicycle. The particular owner of this bicycle has certain associations that come to mind when he or she thinks of a bicycle, and these associations may be quite different from cyclists who race, from mothers who pedal around the neighborhood with their children, or from the bike messenger in a city who spends the day cycling through busy urban traffic. The owner's view of his or her bicycle may be shaped by previous bicycles he or she may have owned; it may be influenced by feelings that the owner is being ecologically "green" and better for the environment than other modes of getting around campus or the city. And such images shape how the owner views himself or herself today or how he or she imagines the future (Vivanco 2013).

This bicycle—like practically every other object North American consumers purchase—is also a commodity that has parts and as a finished product has circulated through a complex economic system, supported by an equally complex set of regulatory rules. As deeply personal as the selection and purchase of an object like a bicycle may be for us as individuals, it was made on an assembly line by dozens of workers, each contributing a small part to the finished effort. This happened overseas, and the bicycle has traveled through a worldwide network of economic linkages, not to mention the complex set of domestic warehouses and shippers, to reach to its owner.

In that process, the manufacturer and the mainstream culture generally have carefully cultivated the current owner's desire to own and use this object. The owner has purchased this particular bicycle and not a more expensive one and not a beaten-up second-hand one. The owner may even have replaced an older bike with this newer and more efficient one, imagining himself as more of a racer than he really is, or thinking of herself as more environmentally conscious than she might actually be. And our impressions of particular bicycles may be shaped by the images we have seen of them in films, TV programs, ads, and shiny brochures advertising one brand of bicycle (Vivanco 2013).

Finally, this bicycle, like every other object we own, is a useful object, not only for where or how far it can take us, not just in how much it can help keep us healthy because of the exercise it provides, and not simply from the fuel it saves us, but also from the impressions of us that it creates in others as they see us ride.

The point of our bicycle example is that *any* mundane object can help us imagine ourselves, our past, and where we are headed. We may use objects to attract the attention and admiration of others. And our objects may be used by others to classify and stereotype us. Although Stocking's seven dimensions do not cover all the aspects or dimensions suggested about the shiny bicycle, they do offer a simple first glance at how we feel we should look at objects anthropologically.

The Power of Symbols

Now we have you thinking about objects in multiple dimensions, we can turn to the aesthetic. By studying the art traditions and objects of non-Western peoples, anthropologists have learned that the complex ideas and understandings about the gods, ghosts, spirits, and other supernatural beings who inhabit their cosmologies are embodied in the physical representations we see in carvings. The African carving in Figure 19.5 is a good case in point. The African carver of that sculpture was not trying to depict the human form, but was displaying the distinctive characteristics of supernatural beings by symbolically representing them as anatomical features.

There is every reason to believe that carvers and other people alike imagined that their spirits and demons looked like the carvings. But when one grows up and the only depiction of a particular spirit is the mask or carving that represents the spirit, one will likely understand the spirit to look just like the carvings. Similarly, although nobody knows what the ancient Hebrew prophet Moses may have looked like, when we hear a discussion of Moses, most of us will immediately imagine Charlton Heston, who starred as Moses in the classic 1956 film *The Ten Commandments* (de Mille 1956), because this is the way Moses appears in nearly all popular images of this ancient figure. As the "Classic Contributions: Nancy Munn on Graphic Signs of the Walbiri of the Australian Desert" box shows, anthropologists have long considered the relationship between aesthetics, symbolism, and the meaning of objects.

The Symbols of Power

Just as the aesthetic dimensions of objects shape an object's meaning, powerful people use aesthetics in ways to demonstrate and legitimate their social, political, or religious power. In many traditional African kingdoms, such as those whose artworks now get displayed in museums in places like New York, the kings and chiefs who ruled these communities distinguished themselves from ordinary people with symbols of rank and authority—staffs, chairs, thrones, clothing, and so forth—artfully carved or woven in a particular local style or aesthetic. Similarly, in many religions authorities employ aesthetics to indicate that the holder of an item possesses divine power as well as power here on earth.

What sets these objects of power apart is, in part, their aesthetic style that establishes the objects, and by extension their owners, as important and special. But it is also true that the aesthetic settings and ways in which such objects are used and displayed can also symbolically communicate the power of their owners. An interesting illustration comes from the island of Walis

Figure 19.5   Rethinking African Art. When Western audiences were first introduced to objects like the Nkisi figure from the Democratic Republic of Congo pictured here, they often responded dismissively and ethnocentrically. They misunderstood African notions of aesthetics. In this Nkisi figure at the Hood Museum of Art at Dartmouth College, each additional element adds meaning and power to the object—the most important here are nails. Each nail pounded into the carving requested some favor from the spirit in this figure, and it also strengthened the spirit. (Hood Museum of Art, Dartmouth College, Hanover, New Hampshire)

along the north coast of Papua New Guinea, as witnessed by Rob Welsch, one of the authors of this textbook, in 1993. A century earlier, a religious cult leader named Barjani had foretold the coming of Europeans and was believed to be a prophet. After his death, his family's clansmen had erected a shrine to him, where people in need of supernatural assistance could leave a small amount of money or tobacco to ensure Barjani's assistance. When Welsch and his colleague, John Terrell, went to see the shrine, they were mostly interested in the building's historically important architectural style.

But the real surprise came when they climbed the small ladder to peer into Barjani's shrine. The interior of the small shrine held a single object in a place of honor on a simple but small platform of palm leaves: an old and well-worn bowler hat, much like the one Charlie Chaplin wore in some of his movies. This was Barjani's hat, an object that possessed its power from Barjani's having worn it but also from being the only object in the shrine. The meaning of this hat, standing out starkly in such an unexpected place, came partly from its association with Barjani and partly from his association with the foreigners he had predicted would come. In addition, the fact that it

CLASSIC CONTRIBUTIONS

Nancy Munn on Graphic Signs Among the Walbiri of the Australian Desert

ABORIGINAL PEOPLES OF central and northern Australia use a great deal of symbolism in their religious ceremonies. These ceremonies typically refer to ancestral or mythic times—known as the **dreaming or the dreamtime**—when the ancestors created the natural features of their world as well as the plants and animals that inhabit it. The purpose of their rituals is to insure and maintain for the present generation what the ancestors had set in motion during the dreaming.

In the 1950s, American anthropologist Nancy Munn conducted fieldwork among an Aboriginal group in central Australia called the Walbiri, focusing on how men and women use and understand the meanings of symbols and graphic imagery. She was especially interested in how ritual performances used art objects, such as sand paintings, to depict dream time stories of ancestors making their way across the countryside. For example, a line in the sand simultaneously represented a kangaroo's tail and a spear, because both are long and straight. But the image also metaphorically represents a boy's penis and becomes part of a larger pattern of culturally standardized metaphoric usages (Munn 1962:978; Munn 1973).

The following brief quotation from her classic 1962 essay in the *American Anthropologist* emphasizes that the repetitive use of graphic signs in many rituals creates their meaning for participants.

I have suggested that Walbiri Dreaming designs are not isolated or unique forms, but specializations of a more general system or "language" of graphic signs. In the narrative contexts of sand drawing, the use of graphic signs is interlocked with verbal communication, and regular associations between standard graphic forms and certain meaning situations can readily be observed.

An important feature of this usage is that it is part of the repetitive, informal patterns of daily behavior. While particular designs and meanings are secret, the basic core of the graphic system is common knowledge.

We may phrase this in terms of a more general theoretical issue. Complex religious symbols such as Walbiri guruwari designs are the end products of social processes through which meaning is "built into" the signs. In this respect, Malinowski's concept of "context of situation" is as relevant for non-verbal as for verbal sign systems. One important anthropological question is not simply what these end products signify, but how in terms of ongoing sociocultural processes they come to acquire the signification at all. In the Walbiri case a consideration of this problem leads ultimately to an examination of storytelling behavior and the use of graphs in general communication.

Although the Walbiri graphic system is obviously not a code for language morphemes (i.e., a form of writing), it does operate as a visual code for verbally conveyed narrative sequences. That the Dreaming designs have a mnemonic function is apparent. [Munn 1962:981]

Questions for Reflection

1. Can you think of an example of a symbol from a religious tradition you're more familiar with, maybe one that you practice, that is "part of repetitive, informal patterns of daily behavior"? What does that symbol communicate?

2. Munn's theoretical insights are applicable beyond religious contexts and arts. If you wanted to study the social processes through which meaning is "built into" the signs of modern fast-food advertising, such as the McDonald's sign, how would you do it?

was a foreign object that few if any other Walis Islanders could have owned must have made it both exotic and valuable as a relic of this local prophet (Figure 19.6).

Although Barjani's hat for Walis Islanders is a statement about relations between themselves and powerful outsiders, it is also a window into the historical context of both their society and the changing meaning that this bowler hat has had over its century of existence. To pursue this issue further, let us consider the next question around which this chapter is organized, which is why objects change meaning over time. Although Barjani's hat is for Walis Islanders a statement about relations between themselves and powerful outsiders, it is also a window into the historical context of both their society and the changing meaning that this bowler hat has had over its century of existence.

Figure 19.6   Barjani's Shrine on Walis Island in Papua New Guinea.   Inside, the room was empty except for Barjani's bowler hat and offerings or gifts that had been left in exchange for Barjani's help.

THINKING CRITICALLY ABOUT MATERIALITY

Most people take the objects around them at face value, but anthropologists think about things in more multidimensional ways. Consider some object, statue, artwork, building, or other physical feature on your campus and outline its different dimensions as an anthropologist might. What new insights about your campus, your school's history, or the school's distinctive local culture do you get from this analysis?

- **Dreaming or the dreamtime.** The mythological period when the ancestors created the natural features of their world as well as the plants and animals that inhabit it.

Why and How Do the Meanings of Things Change over Time?

Anthropologists today study some of the very same museum collections that anthropologists studied over a century ago. But we often come to very different conclusions about the people who made and used the objects in those collections. What has changed? Maybe one change is that the objects in the collection have deteriorated over time, but that doesn't really explain the difference. More important is the change in interpretation that we give to the object. This is a key aspect of what Stocking was getting at when he indicated that objects have a temporal dimension: all objects change over time, *if not in their physical characteristics, then in the significance we give to them.*

Around the same time that Stocking was laying out his framework for understanding objects in seven dimensions, another group of anthropologists was developing a set of complementary theories and techniques for analyzing in depth this issue of how objects change over time. Declaring that "things have social lives," they published a book called *The Social Life of Things: Commodities in Cultural Perspective* (Appadurai 1986) in which they laid out some useful concepts and approaches for thinking anthropologically about objects. So how can an *inanimate* object have a *social* life?

The Social Life of Things

The idea that inanimate things have social lives is based on the assumption that things have forms, uses, and trajectories that are intertwined in complex ways with people's lives. Just as people pass through different socially recognized phases of life, objects have "careers" (in the sense of course or progression) with recognizable phases, from their creation, exchange, and uses, to their eventual discard. Along the way, it is possible to identify social relationships and cultural ideologies that influence each period in this career. Across cultures, these relationships and ideologies can vary drastically.

Consider a pair of running sneakers sold at a mall. This pair of sneakers may start as cotton fabric and rubber in a Chinese factory. But the shoes mean something quite different there from what they mean to the mall salesperson who rings up your purchase or from what they mean to you when you wear them to some social event. The shoes may have aged only a few weeks from the time they were made until you wear them; the change in significance comes not from aging, but from moving from one person to another, some of whom see it as a way to make a living, while others see it as a way to look cool at the party next Friday. That pair of shoes has a complicated life, taking on meanings from the contexts it passes through and, to the sensitive observer, revealing a whole range of complex social relations in the process. And throughout it all, the same pair of shoes has changed.

Three Ways Objects Change over Time

All objects change over time, but they can do so in different ways. Most objects age and weather with time, of course, usually becoming less significant because they get old and worn out. But for the purposes of understanding the social life of things, there are three major ways that objects change over time:

1. The form, shape, color, material, and use may change from generation to generation.
2. An object changes significance and meaning as its social and physical contexts change.
3. A single object changes significance and meaning as it changes hands.

Let us consider a few examples of each of these kinds of changes to illustrate how the social meanings of an object can change over time.

Changing Form from Generation to Generation

Nearly every manufactured product has changed over time as styles and social preferences have changed. While we usually understand these changes as gradual improvements in form or technology, they are just as often due to introducing innovations or differences in style, simply to be different. One of the best examples came from an anthropological study of ladies' fashion.

Just before World War II, anthropologists Jane Richardson and Alfred Kroeber (Richardson and Kroeber 1940) published an analysis of skirt length in women's dresses over the previous 300 years (Figure 19.7). Studying all sorts of pattern books, sketches, and photographs of women's dresses, they documented how styles of dresses had changed over this period. They found that skirt length had risen and fallen in ways that most women were unaware of. In a more or less predictable way, hem length fluctuated from extremes of long to short over a fifty-year period or cycle. Subsequent studies since 1940 have suggested that this cycle has now shortened to about twenty or twenty-five years (Bernard 2011:355).

What is the cause of these cyclical changes? There are actually at least two causes. First, fashionable women want to wear the latest fashion, and this desire encourages

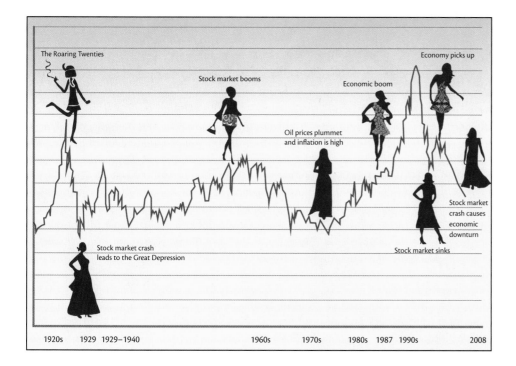

The Roaring Twenties

Economy picks up

Stock market booms

Economic boom

Oil prices plummet
and inflation is high

Stock market crash
leads to the Great Depression

Stock market
crash causes
economic
downturn

Stock market sinks

1920s   1929 1929–1940   1960s   1970s   1980s 1987 1990s   2008

Figure 19.7 Shifting Dress Styles. Although dress styles in Europe and America have changed in many ways from period to period, they reflect cyclical trends and stylistic and aesthetic innovations.

many others to follow their lead. Second, the factories and seamstresses that have been making women's dresses for 300 years have a vested interest in these objects changing, even if hems will eventually return to their original length. They want to sell new dresses, and the best way to sell new dresses is if the styles change so much that everyone's closet is filled with "old-fashioned" dresses. But there is more to it than simply encouraging new sales, because the symbolism of being fashionable relies on constantly changing preferences. And all aspects of the fashion industry are involved in creating long-term changes that involve thousands and thousands of people in the fashion industry as a whole, from the high-end designers to the most inexpensive stores and even the consignment shops, who all rely on—and help produce—those changing preferences.

Changing Meaning with Changing Contexts

Contexts often change as environments and technologies change as well. Tahitians, like other Polynesians, had no knowledge of iron until Europeans first visited their islands (Figure 19.8). On June 18, 1767, the British Captain Samuel Wallis was the first Westerner to reach Tahiti, and that day Tahitians learned about the powerful abilities of iron tools for cutting, chopping, and carving. But after learning about iron tools, Tahitian men started plotting ways they could get access to Wallis's iron. The traditionally stodgy and sexually restrained Tahitian society became transformed almost overnight as men sent their wives, daughters, and sisters out to Wallis's ship, the HMS *Dauphin*, to engage in sex in exchange for any sort of iron tools: knives, axes, or even nails that could be fashioned into cutting tools. The following year the French Captain Bougainville arrived at Tahiti, and a year later Captain Cook first reached Tahitian shores; they both found Tahitian women to be so sexually promiscuous that the crew nearly dismantled their small lifeboats in a quest for much desired nails. On his second voyage Cook brought along quantities of nails and hoop iron to satisfy the local desire for iron. Of course, these interactions with Tahitian women created the stereotype that Polynesians were traditionally very promiscuous, when in fact it was the horny sailors combined with the Tahitian desire for iron that transformed Tahitian society and introduced sexual license to these islands (Howe 1984). Something as simple as a new technology can have profound impacts on local communities.

Figure 19.8   Queen Oberea Welcomes Capt. Samuel Wallis at Tahiti. The queen and the captain exchanged gifts that included some small iron-cutting tools that transformed Tahitian society almost immediately.

Changing Meaning from Changing Hands

The most powerful examples of objects that change meaning when they pass into different hands come from the situation where an anthropologist or collector buys objects from exotic villagers for a museum. Until steel axes replace stone axes, the collector is buying objects that people feel are useful. But for the collector, the objects are not going to be used, except as examples of a traditional society's technology and way of life. Once the object reaches a museum its meaning changes profoundly; it no longer has a useful function but becomes a rare example of something from an exotic culture far away in time and space. Being in a museum is, of course, not the only force that can change the meaning of an object with the changing of hands, as we explore in "Thinking Like an Anthropologist: Looking at Objects from Multiple Perspectives."

Geographical movements of objects mean that objects also move across differences in both cultural and individual perspective. Commodities, as we suggested previously, are examples of the changing significance of objects as these objects change hands. But rather than focus too directly on how commodities create meaning, let us consider how objects represent and even help us create who we are.

THINKING CRITICALLY ABOUT MATERIALITY

The meaning of an object clearly depends on the context from which its owner views it. Over centuries the change in meaning is often obvious, but what about changes in meaning over a single lifetime? Consider some possession that excited you some years ago when you bought it or were given it as a gift. How do you think about this object today, what has changed to make it more or less valuable? Is it valuable in a different way today, or has it lost its value altogether?

Thinking Like an Anthropologist

Looking at Objects from Multiple Perspectives

ANTHROPOLOGISTS BEGIN THEIR research by asking questions. In this box, we want you to learn how to ask questions as an anthropological researcher. Part 1 describes a situation and follows up with questions we would ask. Part 2 asks you to do the same thing with a different situation.

PART 1: NICHOLAS THOMAS
ON ENTANGLED OBJECTS IN FIJI

Anthropologist Nicholas Thomas (1989) was studying British museum collections from Fiji that were acquired in the 1870s around the time that the British government was annexing the Fijian Islands as a colony. He noticed that there was an extraordinarily large number of weapons brought back by sailors, traders, and people with business interests in the islands. The clubs and the so-called cannibal forks were sought after by wealthy collectors—nearly all of whom were male—probably because such weapons fed their image of tribal societies as vicious and bloodthirsty savages.

Thomas did not see these objects as evidence of savagery, as early collectors had. He knew that these wooden forks were used by high-ranking chiefs who were prohibited by taboos from touching food with their fingers because their personal power would in effect poison the food for others. Rarely would these have been used for human flesh. Fijian men could be violent, but they also carried clubs mostly in ceremonial situations as a symbol of their strength and masculine power. But for early collectors in England, who had never visited these tropical islands, clubs presented tangible evidence of an aggressive primitive society they imagined living halfway around the world from Victorian England.

In his research, however, Thomas also found that not everybody interested in these objects bought into the idea that Fijians were bloodthirsty savages. For example, he studied how when the Austrian-Scottish traveler and later collector Anatole von Hügel arrived in Fiji in 1874, von Hügel was surprised to find that nobody had attempted to assemble a systematic collection of objects from the islands. Von Hügel was dismissive of the hodge-podge of personal collections he found among the traders and planters in Fiji. For each of them every object had a personal story, "every dish was a cannibal dish, every club had been the instrument of some atrocious murder, and every stain on either was caused by blood" (quoted in Thomas 1989:45). Von Hügel

Breastplate, Civavonovono, of Whale Ivory, Pearl Shell, and Vegetable Fiber. This breastplate was collected by Sir Arthur Gordon, first governor of Fiji between 1875 and 1880. It previously belonged to Ratu Seru Cakobau, Vunivalu (war chief) of Bau, who inherited it from his father, Ratu Tanoa Visawaqa. This breastplate is at the Museum of Archaeology and Anthropology at the University of Cambridge.

went on to assemble a large personal collection representative of all aspects of Fijian culture. For him these objects as a collection suggested a complex, socially stratified society with a rich culture. He understood his collection not in personal terms but as scientific data.

Thomas also learned that there was yet another set of perspectives on these objects. It happens that von Hügel arrived in Fiji about the same time as the newly appointed colonial governor Arthur H. Gordon. As the first British governor of what became the Crown Colony of Fiji, he viewed Fijian objects very differently from either the traders and planters on the one hand and von Hügel on the other. As representative of Queen Victoria and as head of the Fijian government, Fijian chiefs gave him gifts in nearly every village he visited. He reciprocated with gifts, usually of British manufacture. As a "chief" himself, Gordon negotiated the political relations with other chiefs using Fijian objects, especially the whale tooth ornaments called *tabua*. *Tabua* were much admired by Fijians, and their possession marked high social status, which was always on the minds of Fijians. For Gordon, Fijian objects were not scientific specimens, as von Hügel viewed them, or evidence of Fijian savagery, as traders and planters viewed them, but tools for promoting government control of the islands and its people.

Thomas concluded that these Fijian objects were "entangled," that is, taken up in complex ways across cultural boundaries based on differing views about the objects. To understand how different parties viewed Fijian objects differently, Thomas began with a set of anthropological questions:

1. How did Fijians view different kinds of objects differently from white people in Fiji?
2. Why did white planters and traders emphasize the bloodthirsty images of Fijians?
3. Why did von Hügel emphasize these objects as scientific specimens rather than as souvenirs?
4. How would the exchange of *tabua* with Governor Gordon enhance his position in the islands?

PART 2: ENTANGLED OBJECTS IN YOUR ROOMMATE'S LIFE

Consider an object of importance to your roommate (or to one of your friends on campus). Explore how and why your roommate places a different significance on this object than you do or other friends of your roommate might. What questions would you pursue to understand how you, your roommate, and perhaps other friends view an object that your roommate thinks of as significant?

What Role Does Material Culture Play in Constructing the Meaning of a Community's Past?

The objects found in archaeological sites are not just data for scientific analysis; they contribute to public discourse on social and political issues relevant to our present-day concerns, especially how people view their own past. Americans, for example, like to think of our country as one built on equality and opportunity. Historical markers, like the one in Brookings County, may help us sweep harsh historical realities under the rug, allowing us to think of ourselves as a people who have always treated others fairly. To suggest otherwise, some believe, challenges our right to tell our history, to own our past as a nation.

The fact is that no one can own the past, but many will claim it because it fits their ideas of what the past was supposed to be like. The effect for archaeologists is that their interpretations of the past may provoke public controversy, thus drawing them into political battles, many of which are not of their own making, although some are.

In this final section, we examine the complicated politics of contemporary archaeological research.

Claiming the Past

Archaeologists encounter situations that challenge the images we have come to accept about strands in our nation's history. One of these challenges came in 1991 during the construction of a new federal office building in lower Manhattan in New York City. An archaeological assessment of the site using test pits revealed human skeletal remains; they uncovered a long-forgotten burial ground for African slaves used from the late 1600s until 1796 (Blakey 1998). Now known as the African Burial Ground, eventually more than 400 sets of remains—many of them children—were uncovered, showing evidence of harsh conditions, beatings, and other brutal treatment (Blakey 1998; NPR 2007) (Figures 19.9 and 19.10)

Figure 19.9   Biological Anthropologist Michael Blakey.   In his laboratory at Howard University where he supervised analysis of skeletal remains from the African Burial Ground.

Construction teams pressured the archaeologists to excavate the graves as quickly as possible, so they could complete the office building on time and within budget. Because of the forced rapid excavation, archaeologists lost considerable contextual data. Outrage arose in the African American community, and by 1992, black community leaders were demanding that the remains be reinterred and a landmark established.

African Americans also wanted some control over how the site was interpreted and the kind of history it told. New Yorkers had long liked to think of their city and state as free from the evils of slavery. In fact, in the 1700s New York was the state with the second-largest number of slaves and important slave rebellions took place there with brutal consequences for the slaves (NPR 2007). Black leaders wanted to use such facts—as well as this physical site—to help Americans understand the experience of their African slave ancestors and to publicize the contributions of Africans to the city and its history (Katz 2006). Based on their pressure, in 2003 the remains were reburied at one end of the site, and in 2007 President George W. Bush established the African Burial Ground National Monument.

Figure 19.10   Dedication of the African Burial Ground National Monument.   In 2003, New York City officials stand behind four coffins containing the remains of free and enslaved African-Americans. The remains were reburied in a ceremony at a site known as the African Burial Ground Memorial some 300 years after they were first laid to rest.

As this situation demonstrates, uncovering the past can challenge our understandings of the world in unexpected ways and provoke social controversy in which different groups lay claim to the past.

The Politics of Archaeology

Archaeology plays a role in politics, and politics plays a role in archaeology. We may want to think of archaeology as just about the facts, and nothing but the facts, but what is considered a fact has to do with the concerns and agendas of the times in which we live. Ultimately these factors affect the conditions under which archaeological knowledge about the past is produced. We can find an illustration of this phenomenon in the World Heritage Site of the ancient Maya city of Chichén Itzá.

The ruins of the ancient Maya city of Chichén Itzá are situated halfway between Cancún and Mérida on the Yucatán Peninsula of southern Mexico. The city, which was originally established as early as 415–455 CE and built up over the next several centuries, has a number of dramatic pyramids, temples, and a ball court, all in the Maya-Yucatec architectural style (ICOMOS 1987).

American cultural anthropologist Quetzil Castañeda has studied how diverse interested parties—explorers, archaeologists, tourists, New Age pilgrims, and government officials—have used this archaeological site to construct various images of the ancient Maya, each supporting particular political, economic, and cultural agendas. The story begins in the 1840s, when a U.S. diplomat named John Lloyd Stephens (1843) "rediscovered" the ruins of Chichén Itzá, setting into motion the first of many reinterpretations of these monuments and the people who made them. Stephens's book, *Incidents of Travel in Yucatan,* provided a romanticized vision of Chichén Itzá as a "lost city" for American readers (Castañeda 1996).

But Castañeda notes that it was not just Americans who warmed to these images. Yucatec intellectuals also used them to establish a Mayan cultural heritage "that would legitimize the goal of a politically independent state" (1996:5). The Yucatán of the mid-nineteenth century declared its independence from Mexico. For such nationalist purposes, imposing ruins and monuments from an indigenous past have important symbolic power.

In 1923, the Carnegie Institution of Washington organized a long-term multidisciplinary study of the Maya. With huge financial investments from both the Carnegie Institution and the Mexican government, American researchers transformed Chichén Itzá from an archaeological site to a factory of knowledge. That research strengthened Mexico's legitimacy as a country with an ancient heritage. At the same time this knowledge became the basis for transforming the site into a tourist attraction that could support both the project and the local Maya people. As a tourist attraction the site had two goals: (1) to showcase—and help create—an indigenous Maya ethnic consciousness, and (2) to showcase the modern science of archaeology (Figure 19.11).

Since then, Chichén Itzá has become one of the most important tourist attractions in the Yucatán, listed as a World Heritage Site in 1988. In addition to Americans and Europeans, who visit the site while vacationing in Cancún, New Age pilgrims go there to celebrate the spring equinox (Castañeda 1996; Himpele and Castañeda 2004). Many of these New Age pilgrims have read archaeological accounts but interpret the site in their own, sometime idiosyncratic, theological terms.

Since Chichén Itzá's "rediscovery" archaeologists have played a central role in explaining its ancient past and using the site to promote their scientific credentials. But this work has always existed alongside and been influenced by others using Chichén Itzá to legitimize their own national and ethnic identities, economic interests, and

Figure 19.11 **Chichén Itzá.** New Age Pilgrims visiting at the time of the vernal equinox in March.

religious perspectives. The important point here is that all anthropologists—not just those working over the years in Chichén Itzá—are immersed in such political and social realities.

THINKING CRITICALLY ABOUT MATERIALITY

What are the ways that activists or even archaeologists and historians can try to shape the meaning of an artifact, an historic site, or even some other unique object for others?

Conclusion

Driving along a highway in rural South Dakota—and many others across the United States—it is easy to speed past historical markers like the one announcing Brookings County. For those who stop to read such markers, the facts of history are presented in a clear and straightforward manner. But as we know, those facts can focus on certain themes that a dominant social group wants to present, while other more unsettling or complicated stories go unrecognized.

The issues raised by this simple material object—a historical marker—is but one example of a broader dynamic that also affects the social and cultural construction of meaning. Control over the past is a highly contentious issue, but control of the meaning of objects from the present, such as a smartphone, is equally contentious. This dynamic has two dimensions. One of these dimensions lies in who has control over access to the resources, both historical and archaeological, from which we can document and uncover the story of how things came to be. Archaeologists have become actively involved in protecting and managing archaeological and historic sites precisely because they recognize that powerful forces, such as development and looting, threaten their access to those resources.

The other dimension is that interpretations of the material world, whether from the past or our very modern present, differ according to social interests. So the interpretation of objects, artifacts, archaeological sites, and human remains always has a wide variety of legal, moral, and political implications. These implications are constructed by many different people, each with a different set of personal and social agendas. We call this the cultural construction of meaning, whether applied to objects, bodies, practices, or human experiences, and it is this that defines what anthropology is all about.

KEY TERMS

AIM (American Indian movement)   p. 508

Cultural resource management (CRM)   p. 509

Dreaming or the dreamtime   p. 516

Material culture   p. 505

Materiality   p. 505

NAGPRA (Native American Graves and Repatriation Act)   p. 507

Repatriation   p. 508

World Heritage Site program   p. 507

Reviewing the Chapter

Chapter Section	What We Know	Unresolved Issues
Why is the ownership of artifacts from another culture a contentious issue?	Ownership of artifacts raises difficult moral, social, and political questions about who has the right to control and display objects. In the U.S., NAGPRA legislation has clarified who should control the bones and artifacts of Indians that archaeologists uncover in their excavations.	NAGPRA does not completely resolve conflicts over who should control archaeological objects, because some museum skeletal collections are poorly documented, so nobody now knows which tribe the remains may have belonged to originally. Archaeologists, museums, and American Indians continue to have to negotiate what happens to the objects.
How should we look at objects anthropologically?	All objects, old and new, from the most special to the most mundane, have multiple dimensions.	Stocking's original notion of seven dimensions to objects is a useful starting point for analyzing objects. But there is debate over whether these are always the most useful dimensions for analyzing all objects, as well as which dimensions he may have missed.
Why and how do the meanings of things change over time?	All objects change over time, if not in their physical characteristics, then in the significance people give to them. Meanings change because of generational change, changes in social and technological context, and as objects change hands.	Anthropologists have not yet systematically explored whether the importance of objects changes and has always changed in the same ways, or if different kinds of societies (literate vs. preliterate; stratified vs. egalitarian, etc.) change the meanings of things in precisely the same ways.
What role does material culture play in constructing the meaning of a community's past?	No community can truly "own its past," but all interpretations can be understood as cultural constructions and these are subject to biases that come from factors such as that dominant social groups have more control on how to interpret everyone's past.	While nobody owns their own past, anthropologists are still debating how to interpret the objects in ways that simultaneously reflect the empirical evidence and the interests and concerns of both dominant and minority communities.

Readings

Regna Darnell's *And Along Came Boas: Continuity and Revolution in Americanist Anthropology* (Amsterdam: John Benjamins, 2000) offers an overview of the early development of anthropology in museums. Stocking's *Objects and Others* (Madison: University of Wisconsin Press, 1985) remains a classic on the topic. David J. Meltzer's essay "North American Archaeology and Archaeologists, 1879–1934" (*American Antiquity* 50(2):249–60, 1985) offers a complementary view from an archaeological perspective.

Two histories of archaeology are Brian M. Fagan's *A Brief History of Archaeology: Classical Times to the Twenty-First Century* (Upper Saddle River, NJ: Pearson Prentice Hall, 2005) and Bruce G. Trigger's *A History of Archaeological Thought*, 2nd ed. (Cambridge: Cambridge University Press, 2006). For an account focused more specifically on American archaeology, one should see Gordon R. Willey and Jeremy A. Sabaloff's *A History of American Archaeology*, 3rd ed. (New York: W. H. Freeman, 1993). Joan Gero and Margaret Conkey's edited volume

Engendering Archaeology: Women and Prehistory (Oxford: Blackwell, 1991) explores the increasingly important role of women in archaeology.

● ● ● ● ● ● ● ● ● ● ● ● ● ● ● ● ● ● ● ●

For a general survey of NAGPRA and its wider implications, see the volume, edited by Devon A. Mihesuah, *Repatriation Reader: Who Owns American Indian Remains* (Lincoln: University of Nebraska Press, 2000). David Hurst Thomas's *The Skull Wars: Kennewick Man, Archaeology, and the Battle for Native American*

Identity (New York: Basic Books, 2000) offers a case study of a particularly controversial set of remains. For a more general view of CRM, see F. O. McManamon and A. Hatton, eds., *Cultural Resource Management in Contemporary Society: Perspectives on Managing and Presenting the Past* (London: Routledge, 2000).

● ●

For treatment of objects in cultural anthropology, see Arjun Appadurai's collection of essays *The Social Life of Things: Commodities in Cultural Perspective* (New York: Cambridge University Press, 1986) and Daniel Miller's *Material Cultures: Why Some Things Matter* (Chicago: University of Chicago Press, 1998). Luis Vivanco, a coauthor of this book, has applied the social-life-of-things approach to the bicycle in his 2013 book *Reconsidering the Bicycle: An Anthropological Perspective on a New (Old) Thing* (New York: Routledge)

Glossary

Absolute dating (or chronometric dating). Any dating method that determines an age of a fossil, rock, artifact, or archaeological feature on some specified time scale.

Acephalous society. A society without a governing head, generally with no hierarchial leadership.

Acheulian tools. A more complex and diverse stone-tool kit than earlier Olduwan tools. The main characteristic was bifacial flaking, a process that produced strong, sharp edges.

Action theory. An approach in the anthropological study of politics that closely follows the daily activities and decision-making processes of individual political leaders emphasizing that politics is a dynamic and competitive field of social relations in which people are constantly managing their ability to exercise power over others.

Adaptation. The development of a trait that plays a functional role in the ability of a life form to survive and reproduce.

Adjudication. The legal process by which an individual or council with socially recognized authority intervenes in a dispute and unilaterally makes a decision.

Affiliation. A relationship between individuals who are frequently in close association based on tolerance, even friendliness.

Age-grades. Groupings of age-mates, who are initiated into adulthood together.

AIM (American Indian Movement). The most prominent and one of the earliest Native American activist groups, founded in 1968.

Alleles. The variants in the DNA sequences for a given gene.

Alluvial soil. Rich, fine-grained soils deposited by rivers and streams.

Altruism. Seemingly "selfless" acts that have a net loss of energy to the actor but a net gain in energy to the receiver.

Analogous. Similar in appearance or function, not the same due to shared ancestry.

Animal husbandry. The breeding, care, and use of domesticated herding animals such as cattle, camels, goats, horses, llamas, reindeer, and yaks.

Animism. An early anthropological theory that primitive peoples believed which holds that inanimate objects such as trees, rocks, cliffs, hills, and rivers were animated by spiritual forces or beings.

Anthropocene. Refers to the geological epoch defined by substantial human influence over ecosystems.

Anthropoid. A primate superfamily that includes monkeys, apes, and humans.

Anthropological linguistics. The branch of anthropology that studies human beings through their languages.

Anthropology. The study of human beings, their biology, their prehistory and histories, and their changing languages, cultures, and social institutions.

Anthropology of development. The field of study within anthropology concerned with understanding the cultural conditions for proper development or, alternatively, the negative impacts of development projects.

Anthropometry. The measurement of body parameters that assess physical variation and the relative contributions of particular body parts to overall body shape.

Applied anthropology. Anthropological research commissioned to serve an organization's needs.

Appropriation. The process of taking possession of an object, idea, or relationship.

Arboreal. Living in the trees.

Archaeology. The study of past cultures, by excavating sites where people lived, worked, farmed, or conducted some other activity.

Artifactual landscapes. The idea that landscapes are the product of human shaping.

Assemblage. A group or collection of objects found together at an excavation or site.

Australopithecines. A word that refers to the genus *Australopithecus*.

Balanced reciprocity. A form of reciprocity in which the giver expects a fair return at some later time.

Band. A small, nomadic, and self-sufficient group of anywhere from 25 to 150 individuals with face-to-face social relationships, usually egalitarian.

Behavioral ecology. The study of behavior from ecological and evolutionary perspectives.

Behavioral system of inheritance. The types of patterned behaviors that parents and adults pass to young members of their group by way of learning and imitation.

Biocultural. A phenomenon that intertwines dynamics of human biology with processes of culture

Biocultural evolution. The interaction of cultural capacity and biology to meet selective demands.

Biological anthropology. The study of the biological and biocultural aspects of the human species, past and present, along with those of our closest relatives, the non-human primates.

Biological determinism. The idea that human behaviors and beliefs are primarily, if not solely, the result of biological characteristics and processes.

Bipedal locomotion. The use of two legs rather than four for movement.

Blood types. Sets of proteins that coat the red blood cells, which serve a variety of functions in the human body, including delivering oxygen to tissues and producing antibodies as an immune response.

Breccia. A rock composed of broken fragments or minerals cemented together by a fine-grained matrix.

Bride price. Exchange of gifts or money to compensate another clan or family for the loss of one of its women along with her productive and reproductive abilities in marriage. Sometimes known as "bride wealth."

Call systems. Patterned sounds or utterances that express meaning.

Canine/Premolar-3 shearing complex. A condition in which the lower first premolar tooth is somewhat sharpened or flattened from rubbing against the upper canine as the mouth closes.

Capitalism. An economic system based on private ownership of the means of production, in which prices are set and goods distributed through a market.

Carbon-14 dating. A dating method that establishes the date or period of an organic artifact or feature from the relative proportions of radioactive carbon to non-radioactive isotopes.

Carrying capacity. The population an area can support.

Centralized political systems. A political system, such as a chiefdom or a state, in which certain individuals and institutions hold power and control over resources.

Chiefdom. A political system with a hereditary leader who holds central authority, typically supported by a class of high-ranking elites, informal laws, and a simple judicial system, often numbering in the tens of thousands with the beginnings of intensive agriculture and some specialization.

Chronometric dating. Any dating method that determines an age of a fossil, rock, artifact, or archaeological feature on some specified time scale.

Cities. Relatively large and permanent settlements, usually with populations of at least several thousand inhabitants.

City-state. An autonomous political entity that consisted of a city and its surrounding countryside.

Clan. A group of relatives who claim to be descended from a single ancestor.

Clinal. A type of variation in which change is gradual across groups and that traits shade and blend into each other.

Clinical therapeutic process. The healing process in which medicines have some active ingredient that is assumed to address either the cause or the symptom of a disorder.

Cognate words. Words in two languages that show the same systematic sound shifts as other words in the two languages, usually interpreted by linguists as evidence for a common linguistic ancestry.

Collapse. The rapid loss of a social, political, and economic order or complexity.

Colonialism. The historical practice of more powerful countries claiming possession of less powerful ones.

Commodities. Mass-produced and impersonal goods with no meaning or history apart from themselves.

Comparative method. A research method that derives insights from careful comparisons of aspects of two or more cultures or societies.

Complex societies. Societies in which socioeconomic differentiation, large populations, and centralized political control, are pervasive and defining features of the society.

Constructivist approach. Emphasizes that a core dynamic of human biology and culture is processes of construction: the construction of meanings, social relationships, ecological niches, and developing bodies.

Consumers. People who rely on goods and services not produced by their own labor.

Consumption. The act of using and assigning meaning to a good, service, or relationship.

Cormic index. Standing height divided by sitting height.

Corporate groups. Groups of real people who work together toward common ends, much like a corporation does.

Costs and benefits. An analytical approach that considers the caloric cost of obtaining food and the calories obtained.

Creole language. A language of mixed origin that has developed from a complex blending of two parent languages that exists as a mother tongue for some part of the population.

Cross-cultural perspective. Analyzing human social phenomenon by comparing that phenomenon in different cultures.

Cultigen. Any plant that is intentionally grown for human use.

Cultural anthropology. The study of the social lives of living communities.

Cultural appropriation. The unilateral decision of one social group to take control over the symbols, practices, or objects of another.

Cultural construction. The meanings, concepts, and practices that people build out of their shared and collective experiences.

Cultural determinism. The idea that all human actions are the product of culture, which denies the influence of other factors like physical environment and human biology on human behavior.

Cultural economics. An anthropological approach to economics that focuses on how symbols and morals help shape a community's economy.

Cultural imperialism. The promotion of one culture over others, through formal policy or less formal means, like the spread of technology and material culture.

Cultural landscape. The culturally specific images, knowledge, and concepts of the physical landscape that help shape human relations with the landscape.

Cultural relativism. The moral and intellectual principle that one should withhold judgment about seemingly strange or exotic beliefs and practices.

Cultural resource management. Research and planning aimed at identifying, interpreting, and protecting sites and artifacts of historic or prehistoric significance.

Culturally constructed concept of race. A set of cultural or ethnic factors combined with easily perceived morphological traits (e.g., skin reflectance, body shape, cranial structure) in an artificial "biologized" category.

Culture-bound syndrome. A mental illness unique to a culture.

Currency. An object used as a medium of exchange.

Customs. Long-established norms that have a codified and law-like aspect.

Delayed reciprocity. A form of reciprocity that features a long lag time between giving and receiving.

Deoxyribonucleic acid (DNA). Spiral-shaped molecule strands that contains the biological information for the cell.

Descriptive linguistics. The systematic analysis and description of a language's sound system and grammar.

Development anthropology. The application of anthropological knowledge and research methods to the practical aspects of shaping and implementing development projects.

Developmental bias. The idea that not all variations are random, but a function of the developmental processes organisms undergo during their lives that tend to generate certain forms more readily than others.

Developmental systems theory (DST). An approach that combines multiple dimensions and interactants toward understanding the development of organisms and systems and their evolutionary impact.

Diffusionists. Early twentieth-century Boasian anthropologists who held that cultural characteristics result from either internal historical dynamism or a spread (diffusion) of cultural attributes from other societies.

Discrimination. The negative or unfair treatment of an individual because of his or her membership in a particular social group or category.

Disease. The purely physiological condition of being sick, usually determined by a physician.

Dispersal. A pattern of one sex leaving the group they were born into about the time of reproductive maturity.

Diversity. The sheer variety of ways of being human around the world.

Division of labor. The cooperative organization of work into specialized tasks and roles.

Domestication. The converting of wild plants and animals to human uses by taming animals or turning them into herds that can be raised for meat or milk or making plants able to be grown for food or other uses.

Dominance hierarchy. The ranking of access to desired resources by different individuals relative to one another.

Dowry. A large sum of money or in-kind gifts given to a daughter to ensure her well-being in her husband's family.

Dreaming or the dreamtime. The mythological period when the ancestors created the natural features of their world as well as the plants and animals that inhabit it.

Dual-inheritance theory (DIT). The perspective that culture is evolutionarily important, that culture evolves in a Darwinian fashion, and that understanding gene-culture coevolution is the key to understanding human behavior.

Ecological footprint. A quantitative tool that measures what people consume and the waste they produce. It also calculates the amount of biologically productive land and water area needed to support those people.

Economic anthropology. The branch of anthropology concerned with how people make, share, and buy things and services.

Economic system. The structured patterns and relationships through which people exchange goods and services.

Embodiment. A concept that refers to how people literally incorporate, biologically, the material and social worlds in which they live, from conception to death.

Emergence. Refers to important processes and events that arise from interactions of wholes that are not explainable by the action of their parts.

Empirical. Verifiable through observation rather than through logic or theory.

Enculturation. The process of learning the social rules and cultural logic of a society.

Environmental anthropologists. Practitioners of the branch of anthropology that studies how different societies understand, interact with, and make changes to nature and natural ecosystems.

Environmental justice. A social movement addressing the linkages between racial discrimination and injustice, social equity, and environmental quality.

Epigenetic system of inheritance. The biological aspects of bodies that work in combination with the genes and their protein products, such as the machinery of the cells, the chemical interactions between cells, and reactions between types of tissue and organs in the body.

Essentialism. The philosophical position that dictates that each organism has a true, ideal form, and that all living representatives of that organism are slight deviations from the ideal type.

Ethics. Moral questions about right and wrong and standards of appropriate behavior.

Ethnobiology. The branch of ethnoscience that studies how people in non-Western societies name and codify living things.

Ethnocentrism. The assumption that one's own way of doing things is correct, while dismissing other people's practices or views as wrong or ignorant.

Ethnographic method. A prolonged and intensive observation of and participation in the life of a community.

Ethnography of speaking. An anthropological approach to language that distinguished the ways that people actually speak from the ideal ways that people in any culture are supposed to speak.

Ethnopoetics. A method of recording oral poetry, stories, ritual language, and nearly any narrative speech act, as verses and stanzas rather than as prose paragraphs in order to capture the format and other performative elements that might be lost in written texts.

Ethnoprimatology. The study of the interface between human and ape communities.

Ethnoscience. The study of how people classify things in the world, usually by considering some range or set of meanings.

Eugenics. The study of genetics with the notion of improving human biology and biological potential; often associated with simplistic, erroneous assumptions about the relationship of behavior or cultural traits with simple genetic systems.

Evolution. The adaptive changes in populations of organisms across generations.

Evolutionary psychology (EP). A perspective focused on understanding the evolution of psychological mechanisms resulting in human behavior.

Exchange. The transfer of objects and services between social actors.

Exiles. People who are expelled by the authorities of their home countries.

Exogamous. A social pattern in which members of a clan must marry someone from another clan, which has the effect of building political, economic, and social ties with other clans.

Explanatory model of illness. An explanation of what is happening to a patient's body, by the patient, by his family, or by a healthcare practitioner, each of which may have a different model of what is happening.

Extended evolutionary synthesis. The view of evolution that accepts the existence of not just genetically based, but also non-genetically based, processes of evolution: developmental bias, plasticity, niche construction, and extra-genetic inheritance.

Extended families. Larger groups of relatives beyond the nuclear family, often living in the same household.

Extra-genetic inheritance. The socially transmitted and epigenetic factors that can aid in the adaptive success of organisms.

Fieldnotes. Any information that the anthropologist writes down or transcribes during fieldwork.

Fieldwork. Long-term immersion in a community, normally involving firsthand research in a specific study community or research setting where people's behavior can be observed and the researcher can have conversations or interviews with members of the community.

Food security. Access to sufficient nutritious food to sustain an active and healthy life.

Foodways. Structured beliefs and behaviors surrounding the production, distribution, and consumption of food.

Foraging. Obtaining food by searching for it, as opposed to growing or raising the plants and animals people eat.

Foramen magnum. The opening at the base of the skull (cranium) where the spinal column enters and connects to the brain

Forensic analysis. The identification and description of dead people.

Formal economics. The branch of economics that studies the underlying logic of economic thought and action.

Fossilization. The process by which hard tissues like bone and teeth slowly turn to stone as molecule by molecule the hard tissues turn to rock keeping the shape of the original bone.

Founder effect. A form of genetic drift that is the result of a dramatic reduction in population numbers so that descendent populations are descended from a small number of "founders."

Functionalism. A perspective that assumes that cultural practices and beliefs serve social purposes in any society.

Fundamentalism. Conservative religious movements that advocate a return to fundamental or traditional principles.

Fundamentalist. A person belonging to a religious movement that advocates a return to fundamental or traditional principles.

Gender. Cultural expectations of how males and females should behave.

Gender/sex systems. The ideas and social patterns a society uses to organize males, females, and those who do not fit either category.

Gender variance. Expressions of sex and gender that diverge from the male and female norms that dominate in most societies.

Gene. A segment of DNA that contains the code for a protein.

Gene flow. The movement of genetic material within and between populations.

Genealogical amnesia. Structural process of forgetting whole groups of relatives, usually because they are not currently significant in social life.

General purpose money. Money that is used to buy nearly any good or service.

Generalized foraging model. A model which asserts that hunter-gatherer societies have five basic characteristics.

Generalized reciprocity. A form of reciprocity in which gifts are given freely without the expectation of return.

Genetic drift. A change in genetic variation across generations due to random factors.

Geneticization. The use of genetics to explain health and social problems rather than other possible causes.

Genome. The complete set of an organism's DNA.

Genotype. An organism's genetic component.

Geographical information system (GIS). A computerized methodology that brings together data from several sources and integrates them with a geographic reference map.

Geomorphologists. Geologists who study the formation and structure of the earth's surface.

Glaciation. A condition when the land surface is covered with sheets of glacial ice.

Globalization. The widening scale of cross-cultural interactions caused by the rapid movement of money, people, goods, images, and ideas within nations and across national boundaries.

Government. A separate legal and constitutional domain that is the source of law, order, and legitimate force.

Gracile. A body of slender build.

Green Revolution. The transformation of agriculture in the developing world that began in the 1940s, through agricultural research, technology transfer, and infrastructure development.

Grooming. Touching another individual to remove dirt, insects, and debris, usually as a way for individuals to bond.

Habitation sites. Places where people lived at some time in the past.

Haplogroups. Lineages that share certain haplotypes.

Haplorrhini. The infrorder of primates including monkeys, apes, and humans.

Haplotype. A group of distinctive inherited genes.

Headnotes. The mental notes an anthropologist makes while in the field, which may or may not end up in formal fieldnotes or journals.

Holism. Efforts to synthesize distinct approaches and findings into a single comprehensive interpretation.

Holistic perspective. A perspective that aims to identify and understand the whole—that is, the systematic connections between individual cultural beliefs and practices—rather than the individual parts.

Holy struggle. A conflict—often political or social—that believers see as justified by doing God's work.

Hominidae. A family of primates that includes the Hominids, namely humans and their ancestors.

Homininae. The African subfamily of the Family Hominidae, which includes humans, chimpanzees and gorillas.

Hominine. The division (called a tribe) in the superfamily Hominoidea that includes humans and our recent ancestors.

Hominini. The tribe to which humans and our direct human ancestors belong, who are referred to as hominins.

Hominoid. The primate superfamily Hominoidea that includes all the apes and the humans.

Homologous. Similar due to shared ancestry.

Horticulture. The cultivation of gardens or small fields to meet the basic needs of a household.

Human behavioral ecology (HBE). A perspective that focuses on how ecological and social factors affect behavior through natural selection.

Human biodiversity. The similarities and differences within and across human groups that have biological dimensions.

Human Genome Project. An international scientific research project between 1990 and 2003 whose goal was to identify all the genetic material in humans.

Human leukocyte antigen system (HLA). A series of proteins on the surface of white blood cells that recognize foreign particles or infectious agents.

Hybridization. Persistent cultural mixing that has no predetermined direction or end-point.

Hydraulic despotism. Denotes empires built around the control of water resources by despotic, or all-powerful, leaders.

Illness. The psychological and social experience a patient has of a disease.

Immigrants. People who enter a foreign country with no expectation of ever returning to their home country.

Incest taboo. The prohibition on sexual relations between close family members.

Industrial agriculture. The application of industrial principles and methods to farming.

Industrialization. The economic process of shifting from an agricultural economy to a factory-based one.

Informant. Any person an anthropologist gets data from in the study community, especially people interviewed or who provide information about what he or she has observed or heard.

Intensification. Processes that increase yields.

Interglacials. Warm periods between ice ages, usually referring to warm periods during the Pleistocene.

Intermembral index. The ratio of arm length to leg length.

Interpretive approach. A kind of analysis that interprets the underlying symbolic and cultural interconnections within a society.

Interpretive theory of culture. A theory that culture is embodied and transmitted through symbols.

Intersex. Individuals who exhibit sexual organs and functions somewhere between male and female elements, often including elements of both.

Intersubjectivity. The realization that knowledge about other people emerges out of relationships and perceptions individuals have with each other.

Interview. Any systematic conversation with an informant to collect field research data, ranging from a highly structured set of questions to the most open-ended ones.

Kin selection. The behavioral favoring of your close genetic relatives

Kinship chart. A visual representation of family relationships.

Kinship. The social system that organizes people in families based on descent and marriage.

Language. A system of communication consisting of sounds, words, and grammar.

Language ideology. Widespread assumptions that people make about the relative sophistication and status of particular dialects and languages.

Laws. Sets of rules established by some formal authority.

Levallois technique. Stone tool-making technique that involves complex preparation of the stone and provides a higher quality toolkit than previous types with more uses.

Limited purpose money. Objects that can be exchanged only for certain things.

Lineage. A group composed of relatives who are directly descended from known ancestors.

Linguistic anthropology. The study of how people communicate with one another through language and how language use shapes group membership and identity.

Linguistic relativity. The idea that people speaking different languages perceive or interpret the world differently because of differences in their languages.

Localization. The creation and assertion of highly particular, often place-based, identities and communities.

Macaca. The genus of macaque monkeys.

Magic. An explanatory system of causation that does not follow naturalistic explanations, often working at a distance without direct physical contact.

Maize. The indigenous species of corn that was first domesticated in Mexico—the term is often used for any variety of corn, since all current varieties are thought to have been derived from this early version of so-called Indian corn.

Mana. A belief that sacred power inheres in certain high-ranking people, sacred spaces, and objects.

Market. A social institution in which people come together to exchange goods and services.

Masculinity. The ideas and practices of manhood.

Material culture. The objects made and used in any society; traditionally the term referred to technologically simple objects made in preindustrial societies, but material culture may refer to all of the objects or commodities of modern life as well.

Materiality. Having the quality of being physical or material.

Matrifocal unit. A cluster of individuals generally made up of related females.

Means of production. The machines and infrastructure required to produce goods.

Mediation. The use of a third party who intervenes in a dispute to help the parties reach an agreement and restore harmony.

Medicalization. The process of viewing or treating as a medical concern conditions that were not previously understood as medical problems.

Megadontia. The characteristic of having large molar teeth relative to body size.

Meiosis. The process of gamete production.

Melanin. A complex polymer that is the main pigment in human skin, occurring in two colors, black and brown.

Mesolithic. The period from the end of the last ice age until the beginning of agriculture, when a number of hunter-gatherer-forager groups established lakeside or seaside settlements that seem to have been year-round sites during this period.

Microgravimetry survey. Measuring the gravitational pull of different parts of the stone structure or pyramid to uncover formerly hollow sections that were filled with less dense stone.

Migrants. People who leave their homes to work for a time in other regions or countries.

Mind. Emergent qualities of consciousness and intellect that manifest themselves through thought, emotion, perception, will, and imagination.

Mitosis. The process of cell division and replication.

Modern synthesis. The view of evolution that accepts the existence of four genetically based processes of evolution: mutation, natural selection, gene flow, and genetic drift.

Modes of subsistence. The social relationships and practices necessary for procuring, producing, and distributing food.

Money. An object or substance that serves as a payment for a good or service.

Monotheism. The belief in a single god.

Morphology. The structure of words and word formation in a language.

Mousterian industry. A disk-core technique of stone tool making that allowed the tool makers to produce many good flakes with little effort and then turn those flakes into a wide variety of fine tools. Associated with the Neanderthals.

Multiple dispersals model (MD). Incorporates complexities in genetic datasets to argue that humans left Africa in multiple waves.

Multiregional evolution model (MRE). Modern humans are only the most recent version of a single species, *Homo sapiens*, that had been in Africa, Asia, and Europe for nearly two million years.

Multisited ethnography. An ethnographic research strategy of following connections, associations, and putative relationships from place to place.

Mutation. Change at the level of the DNA (deoxyribonucleic acid).

Mya. Abbreviation for million years ago.

NAGPRA (Native American Graves and Repatriation Act). In the United States, the 1990 law that established the ownership of human remains, grave goods, and important cultural objects as belonging to the Native Americans, whose ancestors once owned them.

Natal family. The family into which a person is born and (usually) raised.

Nation-states. Independent states recognized by other states, composed of people who share a single national identity.

Natural selection. The process through which certain heritable traits become more or less common in a population related to the reproductive success of organisms interacting with their environments.

Naturalized. Made part of the natural order of things through the production of scientific theories, schemes, and typologies.

Negative reciprocity. A form of reciprocity in which the giver attempts to get something for nothing, to haggle one's way into a favorable personal outcome.

Negotiation. A form of dispute management in which parties themselves reach a decision jointly.

Neoclassical economics. Economic theories and approaches that studies how people make decisions to allocate resources like time, labor, and money in order to maximize their personal benefit.

Neolithic. The "new" stone age when humans had begun growing crops and raising animals for food, using a stone-tool technology.

Niche construction. When organisms play an active role in their evolution by reshaping the environment to suit their own needs.

Nocturnal. Active during the nighttime.

Non-centralized political systems. A political system, such as a band or a tribe, in which power and control over resources are dispersed among members of the society.

Norms. Typical patterns of actual behavior as well as the rules about how things should be done.

Nuclear family. The family formed by a married couple and their children.

Olduwan tools. Rocks that were modified to produce sharp flakes and edged choppers.

Optical stimulated luminescence (OSL). A dating method that measures electrons trapped within the crystalline structure found in quartz and feldspar after being buried in the earth. Crystals in these grains absorb energy from trace amounts of radioactive material in the soil and rock. When exposed to light, the electrons are released and can be measured to estimate the date they were buried.

Paleoanthropologists. Physical anthropologists and archaeologists who study the fossilized remains of ancient primates and humans to understand their biological and behavioral evolution.

Paleoethnobotany. The study of ancient plant remains in order to reconstruct a picture of prehistoric environments and human–plant interactions.

Paleolithic. Literally "old stone," refers to a long epoch in human prehistory from about 2.5 mya to 10,000 years ago, and roughly corresponds with the Pleistocene geological epoch.

Pan. The genus of chimpanzees.

Participant observation. The standard research method used by sociocultural anthropologists that requires the researcher to live in the community he or she is studying to observe and participate in day-to-day activities.

Pastoralism. The practice of animal husbandry, which is the breeding, care, and use of domesticated herding animals such as cattle, camels, goats, horses, llamas, reindeer, and yaks.

Pastoralist societies. Groups of people who live by animal husbandry, which is the breeding, care, and use of domesticated herding animals such as cattle, camels, goats, horses, llamas, reindeer, and yaks.

Patrilocal bands. Small groups where men controlled resources and hunting territories.

Phenotype. The observable and measurable traits of an organism.

Philology. Comparative study of ancient texts and documents.

Phonology. The systematic pattern of sounds in a language, also known as the language's sound system.

Phylogeny. A graphic representation that traces the evolutionary relationships and identifies points when an evolutionary event or change occurred, such as the creation of a new species.

Pidgin language. A mixed language with a simplified grammar, typically borrowing its vocabulary from one language but its grammar from another.

Placebo effect. A healing process that works on persuading a patient he or she has been given a powerful medicine, even though the "medicine" has no active medical ingredient.

Plasticity. A particular form of developmental bias in which an organism responds to its environment by changing during its lifetime.

Pleistocene. A geologic period in which much of the land in the Northern Hemisphere was covered by glaciers. These ice sheets retreated about 12,000 years ago.

Political ecology. The field of study that focuses on the linkages between political-economic power, social inequality, and ecological destruction.

Political power. The process by which people create, compete, and use power to attain goals that are presumed to be for the good of a community.

Politics. Those relationships and processes of cooperation, conflict, and power that are fundamental aspects of human life.

Polyandry. When a woman has two or more husbands at one time.

Polygamy. Any form of plural marriage.

Polygyny. When a man is simultaneously married to more than one woman.

Polytheism. A type of religion with many gods.

Ponginae. The Asian derived subfamily of Hominidae to which the Orangutan belongs

Population. A cluster of individuals of the same species who shares a common geographical area and find their mates more often in their own cluster than in others.

Postcolonialism. The field that studies the cultural legacies of colonialism and imperialism.

Postorbital constriction. An indention of the sides of the cranium behind the eyes.

Potassium-argon dating. A dating method that measures the decay of an isotope of potassium into argon, used to date minerals, clays, and sediments over 100,000 years old in igneous rock that was laid down as volcanic ash.

Potlatches. Opulent ceremonial feasts intended to display wealth and social status by giving away or destroying valuable possessions like carved copper plates, button blankets, and baskets of food. These were characteristic of the communities on the northwestern coast of North America.

Practicing anthropology. Anthropological work involving research as well as involvement in the design, implementation, and management of some organization, process, or product.

Prehensile. The ability to grasp things, usually referring to hands or tails.

Prejudice. Preformed, usually unfavorable opinions that people hold about people from groups, who are different from their own.

Prestige economies. Economies in which people seek high social rank, prestige, and power instead of money and material wealth.

Protein synthesis. How DNA assists in the creation of the molecules that make up organisms (proteins).

Proto-language. A hypothetical common ancestral language of two or more living languages.

Psychological modules. Adaptive clusters of cognitive function or information-processing mechanisms situated in human minds.

Qualitative method. A research strategy producing an in-depth and detailed description of social activities and beliefs.

Quantitative method. A methodology that classifies features of a phenomenon, counting or measuring them, and constructing mathematical and statistical models to explain what is observed.

Race. A system that organizes people into hierarchical groups based on specific physical traits that are thought to reflect fundamental and innate differences that are rooted in genetic and biological differences.

Racialization. The social, economic, and political processes of transforming populations into races and creating racial meanings.

Racism. The repressive practices, structures, beliefs, and representations that uphold racial categories and social inequality.

Recent African origin model (RAO). Modern humans arose as a new species in Africa about 150,000 years ago, during the late Pleistocene.

Reciprocity. The give and take that builds and confirms relationships.

Redistribution. The collection of goods in a community and then the further dispersal of those goods among members.

Refugees. People who migrate because of political oppression or war, usually with legal permission to stay in a different country.

Relative dating. Any dating techniques provide us with rough assessments of the age of a fossil, artifact, or archaeological feature relative to other fossils, rocks, artifacts, or features.

Religion. A symbolic system that is socially enacted through rituals and other aspects of social life.

Repatriation. The return of human remains or cultural artifacts to the communities of descendants of the people to whom they originally belonged.

Replication. The process by which DNA makes copies of itself.

Reproductive success. How many surviving offspring an organism has.

Residue analysis. Microscopic analysis of the residues of plant and animal foods, especially starches, on pottery or tools.

Resilience. The ability of a social system to absorb changes and still retain certain basic cultural processes and structures, albeit in altered form.

Rite of passage. Any life-cycle rite that marks a person's or group's transition from one social state to another.

Rituals. Stylized performances involving symbols that are associated with social, political, and religious activities.

Ruralization. Process in which the countryside was configured as a contested no-man's land lying between competing city-states.

Sagittal crest. A ridge running along the top of the cranium, usually representing increased bone area for the attachment of chewing muscles.

Sagittal keel. A raised area in the midcranium.

Salvage paradigm. The paradigm which held that it was important to observe indigenous ways of life, interview elders, and assemble collections of objects made and used by indigenous peoples.

Scientific concept of race. A population or group of populations within a species that has measurable, defining biological characteristics and low statistical measures of similarity.

Scientific method. The standard methodology of science that begins from observable facts, generates hypotheses from these facts, and then tests these hypotheses.

Secular worldview. A worldview that does not accept the supernatural as influencing current people's lives.

Sedentism. Year-round settlement in a particular place.

Seriation. A relative dating method that analyzes changing styles of pottery or other artifacts over time to situate any particular assemblage of artifacts into a time series of styles and designs.

Sex. The reproductive forms and functions of the body.

Sexual dimorphism. A difference between the sexes of a species in body size or shape.

Sexuality. Sexual preferences, desires, and practices.

Sexually dimorphic. A characteristic of a species, in which males and females have different sexual forms.

Shaman. A religious leader who communicates the needs of the living with the spirit world, usually through some form of ritual trance or other altered state of consciousness.

Sick role. The culturally defined agreement between patients and family members to acknowledge that a patient is legitimately sick.

Sites. Any location that shows evidence of human activity including those with monuments and buildings.

Social complexity. A society that have many different parts organized into a single social system.

Social institutions. Organized sets of social relationships that link individuals to each other in a structured way in a particular society.

Social sanction. A reaction or measure intended to enforce norms and punish their violation.

Social support therapeutic process. A healing process that involves a patient's social networks, especially close family members and friends, who typically surround the patient during an illness.

Sociobiology. An approach that uses principles drawn from the biological sciences to explain human social behavior and social institutions.

Sociolinguistics. The study of how sociocultural context and norms shape language use and the effects of language use on society.

Speaking in tongues. The phenomenon of speaking in an apparently unknown language, often in an energetic and fast-paced way.

Speciation. The process by which new species arise.

Spheres of exchange. Bounded orders of value in which certain goods can be exchanged only for others.

Spirit familiar. A spirit that has developed a close bond with a shaman.

State. The most complex form of political organization, associated with societies that have intensive agriculture, high levels of social stratification, and centralized authority.

States. Societies with forms of political and economic control over a particular territory and the inhabitants of that territory.

Stelae. Carved limestone slabs.

Stops. Sounds that are formed by closing off and reopening the oral cavity so that it stops the flow of air through the mouth, such as the consonants *p*, *b*, *t*, *d*, *k*, and *g*.

Strategy. A set of behaviors that has become prominent in a population as a result of natural selection

Stratigraphy. The study of layers of soil or rock and how they were deposited.

Strepsirrhini. The infraorder of primates including lemurs, galagos, and lorises.

Structural power. Power that not only operates within settings, but that also organizes those and orchestrates the settings in which social and individual actions take place.

Structural-functionalism. An anthropological theory that the different structures or institutions of a society (religion, politics, kinship, etc.) function to maintain social order and equilibrium.

Subspecies. A population that meets the criteria defined within the scientific concept of race.

Substantive economics. A branch of economics, inspired by the work of Karl Polanyi, that studies the daily transactions people engage in to get what they need or desire.

Surface collection. A collection of pottery and stone artifacts made from the surface of the soil around a possible site.

Surplus value. The difference between what people produce and what they need to survive.

Sustainable development. Development that meets the needs of the present without compromising the ability of future generations to meet their own needs (WCED 1987).

Swidden agriculture. A farming method in tropical regions in which the farmer slashes (cuts down trees) and burns small patches of forest to release plant nutrients into the soil. As soil fertility declines, the farmer allows the plot to regenerate the forest over a period of years.

Symbol. Something—an object, idea, image, figure, or character—that represents something else.

Symbolic system of inheritance. The linguistic system through which humans store and communicate their knowledge and conventional understandings using symbols.

Symbolic therapeutic process. A healing process that restructures the meanings of the symbols surrounding the illness, particularly during a ritual.

Sympathetic magic. Any magical rite that relied on the supernatural to produce its outcome without working through some supernatural being such as a spirit, demon, or deity.

Syntax. Pattern of word order used to form sentences and longer utterances in a language.

Taste. A concept that refers to the sense that give humans the ability to detect flavors; taste can also refer to the social distinction and prestige associated with certain foodstuffs.

Taxonomy. A system of naming and classifying organisms.

Teknonymy. A system of naming parents by the names of their children.

Terrestrial. Living on the ground.

Test pit. A preliminary excavation, usually of a single 1 meter by 1 meter square (or half meter square) to see if artifactual material exists at the site and to assess the character of the stratigraphy.

Theory. A tested and repeatedly supported hypothesis.

Thermoluminescence dating. A dating method for estimating dates of pottery that has been fired.

Totemism. A system of thought that associates particular social groups with specific animal or plant species called "totems" as an emblem.

Trace fossils. Soft tissues such as organs, skin, and feathers that do not fossilize, but sometimes leave impressions, or traces on the sedimentary rock that forms around them.

Tradition. Practices and customs that have become most ritualized and enduring.

Traditional ecological knowledge. Indigenous ecological knowledge and its relationship with resource management strategies.

Trance. A semiconscious state typically brought on by hypnosis, ritual drumming, and singing, or hallucinogenic drugs like mescaline or peyote.

Transactional orders. Realms of transactions a community uses, each with its own set of symbolic meanings and moral assumptions.

Transhumance. The practice of moving herds to different fields or pastures with the changing seasons.

Transnational. Relationships that extend beyond nation-state boundaries without assuming they cover the whole world.

Tree-ring dating (or dendrochronology). A dating technique that counts years by establishing a standard pattern of thick and thin tree rings and matching the ring pattern in a wooden artifact to a point on this sequence.

Tribe. A type of pastoral or horticultural society with populations usually numbering in the hundreds or thousands in which leadership is more stable than that of a band, but usually egalitarian, with social relations based on reciprocal exchange.

Urbanization. Process by which towns grew as residential centers as opposed to being trading centers.

Use-wear. Patterns of wear and tear on an artifact that is presumed to be due to use.

Value. The relative worth of an object or service that makes it desirable.

Values. Symbolic expressions of intrinsically desirable principles or qualities.

Violence. The use of force to harm someone or something.

World culture. Norms and values that extend across national boundaries.

World Heritage Site program. Provides financial support to maintain sites of importance to humanity.

World religions. Religions that claim to be universally significant to all people.

World systems theory. The theory that capitalism has expanded on the basis of unequal exchange throughout the world, creating a global market and global division of labor, dividing the world between a dominant "core" and a dependent "periphery."

Worldview. A general approach to or set of shared unquestioned assumptions about the world and how it works.

References

Adultery. 2009. "Adultery: Criminal Laws, Enforcement of Statutes, as a Defense, Divorce, Cross-Reference." Accessed 8/18/09: http://law.jrank.org/pages/4112/Adultery.html.

Agar, Michael, and James MacDonald. 1995. Focus Groups and Ethnography. *Human Organization* 54(1):78–86.

Ahlstrom, Richard V. N., Carla R. Van West, and Jeffrey S. Dean. 1995. Environmental and Chronological Factors in the Mesa Verde-Northern Rio Grande Migration. *Journal of Anthropological Archaeology* 14:125–42.

Ahr, Steven W., Lee C. Nordt, and Steven L. Forman. 2013. Soil Genesis, Optical Dating, and Geoarchaeological Evaluation of Two Upland, Alfisol Pedons within the Tertiary Gulf Coastal Plain. *Geoderma* 192:211–26.

Aiello, L. C. and J. C. K. Wells. 2002. Energetics and the Evolution of the Genus *Homo. Annual Review of Anthropology* 31:323–38.

Aitken, M. J. 1985. *Thermoluminescence Dating.* New York: Academic Press.

Allen, Theodore W. 1997. *The Invention of the White Race.* Vol. 2. London: Verso.

Allport, Gordon. 1958. *The Nature of Prejudice.* Abridged edition. New York: Doubleday Anchor Books.

Almond, Gabriel, A., R. Scott Appleby, and Emmanuel Sivan. 2003. *Strong Religion: The Rise of Fundamentalisms Around the World.* Chicago: University of Chicago Press.

American Anthropological Association. 2015. Race: Are We So Different? Accessed 12/21/ 2015: http://www.understandingrace.org/home.html.

American Psychological Association. 1994. *Diagnostic and Statistical Manual of Mental Disorders: DSM-IV.* Washington, DC: American Psychological Association.

Ames, Michael. 1999. How to Decorate a House: The Re-negotiation of Cultural Representations at the University of British Columbia Museum of Anthropology. *Museum Anthropology* 22(3):41–51.

Amuyunzu-Nyamongo, Mary. 2006. "Challenges and Prospects for Applied Anthropology in Kenya." In Mwenda Ntarangwi, David Mills, and Mustafa Babiker, eds., *African Anthropologies: History, Critique and Practice*, pp. 237–49. Dakar: CODESRIA.

Anderson, Eugene N. 2005. *Everyone Eats: Understanding Food and Culture.* New York: NewYork University Press.

Anton, Susan C., Richard Potts, and Leslie C. Aiello. 2014. Evolution of early *Homo*: An integrated biological perspective. *Science* 345 (6192): 1236828.

Anyon, Roger, T. J. Ferguson, and John R. Welch. 2000. Heritage Management by American Indian Tribes in the Southwestern United States. In F. O. McManamon and A. Hatton, eds., *Cultural Resource Management in Contemporary Society: Perspectives on Managing and Presenting the Past*, pp. 142–59. London: Routledge.

Appadurai, Arjun, ed. 1986. *The Social Life of Things: Commodities in Cultural Perspective.* Cambridge: Cambridge University Press.

Appadurai, Arjun. 1996. *Modernity at Large: Cultural Dimensions of Globalization.* Minneapolis: University of Minnesota Press.

Arden, Harvey. 1989. An Indian Cemetery Desecrated: Who Owns Our Past. *National Geographic* 175:376–92.

Armstrong, Karen. 1994. *A History of God: The 4,000-Year Quest of Judaism, Christianity and Islam.* New York: Ballantine Books.

Arnold, Jeanne. 1996. The Archaeology of Complex Hunter-Gatherers. *Journal of Archaeological Method and Theory* 3(1):77–126.

Arnold, Kate and Filippo Aurelli. 2007. Postconflict Reconciliation. In Christina J. Campbell, Agustín Fuentes, Katherine C. MacKinnon, Melissa Panger, and Simon K. Bearder, eds., *Primates in Perspective*, pp. 592–608. New York: Oxford University Press.

Arsuaga, J. L., J. M. Bermudez de Castro, and E. Carbonell, eds. 1997. The Sima de los Huesos Hominid Site. *Journal of Human Evolution* 33:105–421.

Arthur, Wallace. 2004. *Biased Embryos and Evolution.* Cambridge: Cambridge University Press.

Asad, Talal. 1993. *Genealogies of Religion: Discipline and Reasons of Power in Christianity and Islam.* Baltimore: John Hopkins University Press.

Asch, Timothy, and Napoleon Chagnon. 1997. *The Feast.* Videocassette. Watertown, MA: Documentary Educational Resources. [Released as 16 mm film, 1970.]

Asfaw, B., T. White, O. Lovejoy, B. Latimer, S. Simpson, and G. Suwa. 1999. *Australopithecus garhi*: A New Species of Early Hominid from Ethiopia. *Science* 284:629–35.

Atran, Scott. 2001. "The Vanishing Landscape of the Petén Maya Lowlands: People, Plants, Animals, Places, Words, and Spirits." In Lisa Maffi, ed., *On Biocultural Diversity: Linking Language, Knowledge, and the Environment*, pp. 157–76. Washington, DC: Smithsonian Institution Press.

Avruch, Kevin. 1998. *Culture and Conflict Resolution.* Washington, DC: United States Institute of Peace.

Azoy, Whitney. 2002. "Waaseta (Personal Connections)." *Bangor Daily News,* Feb. 9–10, A9–10.

Bahuchet, Serge. 1988. Food Supply Uncertainty among the Aka Pygmies. In I. de Garine and G. A. Harrison, eds., *Coping with Uncertainty in Food Supply*, pp. 118–49. Oxford: Clarendon Press.

Bailey, Edward. 1962. *Charles Lyell.* London: Nelson.

Bailey, F. G. 1969. *Stratagems and Spoils: A Social Anthropology of Politics.* London: Basil Blackwell.

Balter, Michael. 2010. Candidate Human Ancestor from South Africa Sparks Praise and Debate. *Science* 328(5975):154–55.

Balter, Michael. 2014a. Bones from a Watery "Black Hole" Confirm First American Origins. *Science* 344(6185):680–81.

Balter, Michael. 2014b. World's Oldest Stone Tools Discovered in Kenya. *Science.* April 20. Accessed 5/8/15: http://news.sciencemag.org/africa/2015/04/world-s-oldest-stone-tools-discovered-kenya.

Banerjee, Abhijit V., and Esther Duflo. 2006. *The Economic Lives of the Poor.* MIT Department of Economics Working Paper No. 06–29. Cambridge, MA.

Bannister, Bryant and William J. Robinson. 1975. Tree-Ring Dating in Archaeology. *World Archaeology* 7(2):210–25.

Barkow, Jerome H, Leda Cosmides, and John Tooby, eds. 1992. *The Adapted Mind: Evolutionary Psychology and the Generation of Culture.* New York: Oxford University Press.

Bartlett, Robert. 1982. *Gerald of Wales, 1146–1223.* Oxford: Oxford University Press.

Basch, Linda, Nina Glick Schiller, and Cristina Szanton Blanc. 1993. *Nations Unbound: Transnational Projects, Postcolonial Predicaments, and Deterritorialized Nation-States.* Basel: Gordon and Breach.

Basu, Amitra, ed. 2010. *Women's Movements in the Global Era: The Power of Local Feminisms.* Boulder, CO: Westview Press.

Bates, Daniel G. 1998. *Human Adaptive Strategies: Ecology, Culture, and Politics.* Boston: Allyn and Bacon.

Bates, Daniel G. 2005. *Human Adaptive Strategies: Ecology, Culture, and Politics.* 3rd Edition. Boston: Pearson Allyn and Bacon.

Bauman, Richard and Joel Sherzer, ed. 1974. *Explorations in the Ethnography of Speaking.* London: Cambridge University Press.

Bearak, Barry. 2001. Over World Protests, Taliban Are Destroying Ancient Buddhas. *New York Times*, Mar. 4, p. 10.

Bearder, Simon. K., Paul E. Honess, and Lesley Ambrose. 1995. Species Diversity Among Galagos with Special Reference to Mate Recognition. In L. Alterman, Gerald A. Doyle, M. Kay Izard, eds. *Creatures of the Dark: The Nocturnal Prosimians,* pp. 331–52. New York: Plenum Press.

Beebe, James. 1995. Basic Concepts and Techniques of Rapid Appraisal. *Human Organization* 54(1):42–51.

Begun, David R. 1999. "Hominid Family Values: Morphological and Molecular Data on the Relations Among the Great Apes and Humans." In Sue Taylor Parker, Robert W. Mitchell, and H. Lyn Miles, eds. *The Mentalities of Gorillas and Orangutans: Comparative Perspectives,* pp. 3–42. Cambridge: Cambridge University Press.

Bellwood, Peter. 2005. *First Farmers: The Origins of Agricultural Societies.* Malden, MA: Blackwell.

Bender, Barbara. 1978. Gatherer-hunter to Farmer: A Social Perspective. *World Archaeology* 10(2):204–22.

Benedict, Ruth. 1946. *The Chrysanthemum and the Sword: Patterns of Japanese Culture.* Boston: Houghton Mifflin.

Benefit, Brenda R., and Monte L. McCrossin. 1995. Miocene Hominoids and Hominid Origins. *Annual Review of Anthropology* 24:237–56.

Berger, Lee, Darryl de Ruiter, Steven Churchill, Peter Schmid, Kristan Carlson, Paul Dirks, Job Kibii. 2010. *Australopithecus sediba:* A New Species of *Homo*-like Australopith from South Africa. *Science* 328(2010):195–204.

Berger, Peter L., ed. 1999. *The Desecularization of the World: Resurgent Religion and World Politics.* Washington, DC: Ethics and Public Policy Center.

Bergmann, J. F., O. Chassany, J. Gandiol, P. Deblois, J. A. Kanis, J. M. Segresta, C. Caulin, R. Dahan. 1994. A Randomized Clinical Trial of the Effect of Informed Consent on the Analgesic Activity of Placebo and Naproxen in Cancer Pain. *Clinical Trials Meta-Analysis* 29:41–47.

Beriss, David. 2005. Review of Reckoning with Homelessness. *American Anthropologist* 107(4):729–30.

Berlin, Brent. 1973. Folk Systematics in Relation to Biological Classification and Nomenclature. *Annual Review of Systematics and Ecology* 4:259–71.

Berlin, Brent, and Paul Kay. 1969. *Basic Color Terms: Their Universality and Evolution.* Berkeley: University of California Press.

Bermudez de Castro, J. M., J. L. Arsuaga, E. Carbonell, A. Rosas, I. Martinez, and M. Mosquera. 1997. A Hominid from the Lower Pleistocene of Atapuerca, Spain: Possible Ancestor to Neanderthals and Modern Humans. *Science* 276:1392–95.

Bernard, Russell H. 2011. *Research Methods in Anthropology: Qualitative and Quantitative Approaches.* Lanham, MD: AltaMira Press.

Berwick, Robert C., Angela D. Friederici, Noam Chomsky, and Johan J. Bolhuis. 2013. Evolution, Brain, and the Nature of Language. *Trends in Cognitive Science* 17(2):89–98.

Binford, Lewis. 1968. "Post-Pleistocene Adaptations." In S. R. Binford and L. Binford, eds., *New Perspectives in Archaeology,* pp. 313–41. Chicago: Aldine.

Bird-David, Nurit. 1992. Beyond the "Original Affluent Society": A Culturalist Reformulation. *Current Anthropology* 33(1):25–47.

Bird-David, Nurit. 1993. "Tribal Metaphorization of Human-Nature Relatedness: A Comparative Analysis." In K. Milton, ed., *Environmentalism: The View from Anthropology,* pp. 112–25. London: Routledge.

Black, Davidson. 1933. On the Endocranial Cast of the Adolescent Sinanthropus Skull. *Proceedings of the Royal Society of London, Series B, Containing Papers of a Biological Character* 112(776): 263–76.

Blake, Michael. 2015. *Maize for the Gods: Unearthing the 9,000-Year History of Corn.* Berkeley: University of California Press.

Blakey, Michael L. 1998. The New York African Burial Ground Project: An Examination of Enslaved Lives, a Construction of Ancestral Ties. *Transforming Anthropology* 7(1):53–58.

Blim, Michael. 2000. Capitalisms in Late Modernity. *Annual Reviews of Anthropology* 29:25–38.

Boas, Franz. 1889. Die Ziele der Ethnologie. *Gemeinverständliche Vorträge gehalten im Deutsche Gesellig-Wissenschaftlichen Verein* 16:3–30. New York: Herman Bartsch.

Boas, Franz, ed. 1911. *Handbook of North American Indian Languages.* Bulletin of the Bureau of American Ethnology, No. 40. Washington, DC: Government Printing Office for the Smithsonian Institution.

Boas, Franz. 1940. *Race, Language, and Culture.* New York: Macmillan.

Bodley, John. 1999. *Victims of Progress.* 4th Edition. New York: McGraw-Hill.

Boggs, Stephen T., and Malcolm Naea Chun. 1990. "Ho'oponopono: A Hawaiian Method of Solving Interpersonal Problems." In Karen Ann Watson-Gegeo and Geoffrey White, eds., *Disentangling: Conflict Discourse in Pacific Societies,* pp. 123–53. Stanford, CA: Stanford University Press.

Bohannon, Paul, and Laura Bohannon. 1968. *Tiv Economy.* Evanston, IL: Northwestern University Press.

Boserup, Ester. 1965. *The Conditions of Agricultural Growth: The Economics of Agrarian Change Under Population Pressure.* London: G. Allen and Unwin.

Bourdieu, Pierre. 1984. *Distinction: A Social Critique of the Judgement of Taste.* Cambridge, MA: Harvard University Press.

Boxberger, Daniel L. 2003. History, Ethnohistory, and Oral History: The Ethnographer's Dilemma. Park Ethnography Program, National Park Service, U.S. Department of the Interior. Accessed 11/22/2015: http://www.nps.gov/ethnography/training/TAPS/history.htm.

Boyd, Robert and Peter, J. Richerson. 2005. *The Origin and Evolution of Cultures.* New York: Oxford University Press.

Bradbury, R. E. 1957. *The Benin Kingdom and the Edo-speaking Peoples of South-Western Nigeria.* London: International African Institute.

Braidwood, Robert. 1952. *The Near East and the Foundations for Civilization: An Essay in Appraisal of the General Evidence.* Eugene: Oregon State System of Higher Education.

Brakefield, P. M. 2006. Eco-devo and Constraints on Selection. *Trends in Ecology and Evolution* 21(7):362–68.

Bramble, Dennis and Daniel Lieberman. 2004. Endurance Running and the Evolution of *Homo. Nature* 432:345–52.

Brettell, Caroline B., and Carolyn F. Sargent, eds. 2001. *Gender in Cross-Cultural Perspective.* 3rd Edition. Upper Saddle River, NJ: Prentice Hall.

Brewis, Alexandra. 2011. *Obesity: Cultural and Biocultural Perspectives.* New Brunswick, NJ: Rutgers University Press.

Brier, Bob. 2007. How to Build a Pyramid: Hidden Ramps May Solve the Mystery of the Great Pyramid's Construction. *Archaeology* 60(3):22–27

Bringa, Tone. 2005. "Haunted by Imaginations of the Past: Robert Kaplan's Balkan Ghosts." In Katherine Besteman and Hugh Gusterson, eds., *Why America's Top Pundits Are Wrong: Anthropologists Talk Back,* pp. 60–82. Berkeley: University of California Press.

British Association for the Advancement of Science. 1899. *Notes and Queries on Anthropology.* 3rd Edition. London: Anthropological Institute.

Brockington, Dan. 2002. *Fortress Conservation: The Preservation of the Mkomazi Game Reserve.* Bloomington: Indiana University Press.

Brody, Howard, and Linda Hunt. 2006. BiDil: Assessing and Race-Based Pharmaceutical. *Annals of Family Medicine* 4(6):556–60.

Brookfield, Harold C. and J. Peter White. 1968. Revolution or Evolution in the Prehistory of the New Guinea Highlands: A Seminar Report. *Ethnology* 7(1):43–52.

Brown, Michael. 2003. *Who Owns Native Culture?* Cambridge, MA: Harvard University Press.

Brown, P., T. Sutikna, M. J. Morwood, R. P. Soejono, Jatmiko, E. Wayhu Saptomo, Rokus Awe Due. 2004. A New Small-bodied Hominin from the Late Pleistocene of Flores, Indonesia. *Nature* 431(7012):1055–1061.

Brown, Peter J. 1991. Culture and the Evolution of Obesity. *Human Nature* 2(1):31–57.

Brownell, K. D. 2002. "The Environment and Obesity." In C. G. Fairburn and K. D. Brownell, eds., *Eating Disorders and Obesity: A Comprehensive Handbook*. 2nd Edition, pp. 433–38. New York: Guilford Press.

Brunet, Michael, Guy Frank, David Pilbeam, et al. 2002. A New Hominid from the Upper Miocene of Chad, Central Africa. *Nature* 418(6894):145–51.

Buikstra, Jane. 1983. Reburial: How We All Lose—An Archaeologist's Opinion. *Council for Museum Anthropology Newsletter* 7(2):2–5.

Bullard, Robert. 1994. *Dumping in Dixie: Race, Class, and Environmental Quality*. 2nd Edition. Boulder, CO: Westview Press.

Bulmer, Ralph. 1967. Why Is the Cassowary Not a Bird? *Man* 2:5–25.

Burks, Jarrod. 2014. Junction Group: Magnetic Re-Survey of Junction Group Archaeological Preserve. Archaeological Conservancy Blog, Nov. 12. http://www.archaeologicalconservancy.org/tag/junction-group/.

Burling, Robbins. 1971. *Man's Many Voices: Language in Its Cultural Context*. New York: Holt, Rinehart and Winston.

Bygren, L. O., P. Tinghög, J. Carstensen, S. Edvinsson, G. Kaati, M. E. Pembrey, and M. Sjöström. 2014. Change in paternal grandmothers' early food supply influenced cardiovascular mortality of the female grandchildren. *BMC Genetics* 2014(15):12.

Caldwell, Christine A. and Andew Whiten. 2011. "Social Learning in Monkeys and Apes: Cultural Animals?" In Christina J. Campbell, Agustín Fuentes, Katherine C. MacKinnon, Melissa Panger, and Simon K. Bearder, eds., *Primates in Perspective*, pp. 652–62. New York: Oxford University Press.

Cameron, Catherine M. 1995. Migration and the Movement of Southwestern Peoples. *Journal of Anthropological Archaeology* 14(2):104–24.

Campbell, Christina J., Agustín Fuentes, Katherine C. MacKinnon, Simon K. Bearder, and Rebecca M. Stumpf. 2011. *Primates in Perspective*. 2nd edition. New York: Oxford University Press.

Cann, Rebecca L., Mark Stoneking, and Allan C. Wilson. 1987. Mitochondrial DNA and Human Evolution. *Nature* 325:31–36.

Caplan, Pat, ed. 1995. *Understanding Disputes: The Politics of Argument*. Oxford: Berg.

Carey, Benedict. 2007. Brainy Parrot Dies, Emotive to the End. *New York Times*, Sept. 11, 2007. Accessed 7/20/2010: http:// www.nytimes.com/2007/09/11/science/11parrot.html?_r=1.

Carneiro, Robert L. 1974. "Slash-and-Burn Cultivation Among the Kuikuru and Its Implications for Cultural Development." In Patricia J. Lyon, ed., *Native South Americans*, pp. 73–91. Boston, MA: Little, Brown.

Carrier, James. 1995. *Gifts and Commodities: Exchange and Western Capitalism Since 1700*. London: Routledge.

Carrier, James. 1996a. "Exchange." In Alan Barnard and Jonathan Spencer, eds., *Encyclopedia of Social and Cultural Anthropology*, pp. 218–21. London: Routledge.

Carrier, James. 1996b. "Consumption." In Alan Barnard and Jonathan Spencer, eds., *Encyclopedia of Social and Cultural Anthropology*, pp. 128–29. London: Routledge.

Carrier, Joseph M. 1976. Family Attitudes and Mexican Male Homosexuality. *Urban Life* 5(3):359–75.

Carroll, John B., ed. 1956. *Language, Thought, and Reality: Selected Writings of Benjamin Lee Whorf*. Cambridge, MA: Technology Press of MIT.

Carsten, Janet. 1989. "Cooking Money: Gender and the Symbolic Transformation of Means of Exchange in a Malay Fishing Community." In J. Parry and M. Bloch, eds., *Money and the Morality of Exchange*, pp. 117–41. Cambridge: Cambridge University Press.

Castañeda, Quetzil E. 1996. *In the Museum of Maya Culture: Touring Chichén Itzá*. Minneapolis: University of Minnesota Press.

Castrì, Loredana, Flory Otárola, Mwenza Blell, Ernesto Ruiz, Ramiro Barrantes, Donata Luiselli, Davide Pettener, and Lorena Madrigal. 2007. Indentured Migration and Differential Gender Gene Flow: The Origin and Evolution of the East-Indian Community of Limón, Costa Rica. *American Journal of Physical Anthropology* 134 (2): 175–89.

Centers for Disease Control and Prevention (CDC). 2013. Antibiotic Resistance Threats in the U.S. Accessed 3/18/15: http://www.cdc.gov/drugresistance/threat-report-2013/.

Chagnon, Napoleon. 1968. *Yanomamö: The Fierce People*. New York: Holt, Rinehart and Winston.

Chagnon, Napoleon and Timothy Asch. 2007. *Magical Death*. DVD. Watertown, MA: Documentary Educational Resources. (Originally produced 1973.)

Chambers, Robert. 1997. *Whose Reality Counts? Putting the Last First*. 2nd Edition. London: Intermediate Technology.

Chappell, Sally A. Kitt. 2002. *Cahokia: Mirror of the Cosmos*. Chicago: University of Chicago Press.

Chatters, James C., Douglas J. Kennett, Yemane Asmerom, et al. 2014. Late Pleistocene Human Skeleton and mtDNA Link Paleoamericans and Modern Native Americans. *Science* 344(6185):750–54.

Childe, V. Gordon. 1936. *Man Makes Himself*. London: Watts.

Childe, V. Gordon. 1950. The Urban Revolution. *Town Planning Review* 21:3–17.

Choquet, Hélène and David Meyre. 2011. Genetics of Obesity: What Have We Learned? *Current Genomics* 12(3):169–79.

Chossudovsky, Michel. 1997. *The Globalization of Poverty: Impacts of IMF and World Bank Reforms*. Atlantic Highlands, NJ: Zed Books.

CNN. 2015. ISIS Destroys Arch of Triumph in Syria's Palmyra Ruins. Accessed 11/26/ 2015: http://www.cnn.com/2015/10/05/middleeast/syria-isis-palmyra-arch-of-triumph/.

Codere, Helen. 1950. *Fighting with Property: A Study of Kwakiutl Potlatching and Warfare*. New York: J. J. Augustin.

Cohen, Mark Nathan. 1977. *The Food Crisis in Prehistory: Overpopulation and the Origins of Agriculture*. New Haven, CT: Yale University Press.

Cohen, Mark Nathan. 1998. *Culture of Intolerance: Chauvinism, Class, and Racism in the United States*. New Haven, CT: Yale University Press.

Cohen, Mark Nathan and Gillian M. M. Crane-Kramer. 2007. *Ancient Health: Skeletal Indicators of Agricultural and Economic Intensification*. Gainesville: University of Florida Press.

Colchester, Marcus. 2003. "The Vth World Parks Congress: Parks for People or Parks for Business?" *World Rainforest Movement Bulletin No. 75*, October. Accessed 2/15/2005: http:// www.wrm.org.uy/bulletin/75/parks.html.

Cole, Douglas. 1985. *Captured Heritage: The Scramble for Northwest Coast Artifacts*. Seattle: University of Washington Press.

Collier, Jane, and Sylvia Yanagisako, eds. 1987. *Gender and Kinship: Essays Toward a Unified Analysis*. Stanford, CA: Stanford University Press.

Conkey, Margaret W. 1999. "Mobilizing Ideologies: Paleolithic "Art," Gender Trouble, and Thinking about Alternatives." In Lori D. Hager, ed., *Women in Human Evolution*, pp.172–207. New York: Routledge University Press.

Connor, Linda. 1982. Ships of Fools and Vessels of the Divine: Mental Hospitals and Madness, A Case Study. *Social Science and Medicine* 16:783–94.

Conroy, Glenn C. 1997. *Reconstructing Human Origins: A Modern Synthesis*. New York: W. W. Norton.

Coon, C. S., S. M. Garn, and J. B. Birdsell. 1950. *Races*. Springfield, IL: Thomas.

Council for Museum Anthropology. 1983. "You Shall Dig No More Forever!": Editorial. *Council for Museum Anthropology Newsletter* 7(3):1–3.

Counihan, Carole. 1999. *The Anthropology of Food and Body: Gender, Meaning, and Power*. New York: Routledge.

Counts, Dorothy A. 1980. Fighting Back Is Not the Way: Suicide and the Women of Kaliai. *American Ethnologist* 7:332–51.

Crossette, Barbara. 2001. Taliban Explains Buddha Destruction. *New York Times*, Mar. 19. Accessed 11/26/2015: http://www.nytimes.com/2001/03/19/world/19TALI.html.

Csordas, Thomas, and Arthur Kleinman 1996. "The Therapeutic Process." In Carolyn F. Sargent and Thomas M. Johnson, eds., *Medical Anthropology: Contemporary Theory and Method*, pp. 3–20. Revised Edition. Westport, CT: Praeger.

Curtis, Garniss H. 1975. Improvements in Potassium-Argon Dating: 1962–1975. *World Archaeology* 7(2):198–209.

Dakowski, Bruce. 1990. "Everything Is Relatives: W. H. R. Rivers." In *Pioneers of Social Anthropology: Strangers Abroad* (Documentary Film Series). Videorecording. Princeton, NJ: Films for the Humanities and Sciences.

Dalan, Rinita A., George R. Holley, William I. Woods, Harold W. Watters, Jr., and John A. Koepke. 2003. *Envisioning Cahokia: A Landscape Perspective*. DeKalb: Northern Illinois University Press.

Daltabuit, Magalí, and Thomas Leatherman. 1998. "The Biocultural Impact of Tourism of Mayan Communities." In Alan Goodman and Thomas Leatherman, eds., *Building a New Biocultural Synthesis: Political-Economic Perspectives on Human Biology,* pp. 317–38. Ann Arbor: University of Michigan Press.

Dark, Philip J. C. 1962. *The Art of Benin: A Catalogue of an Exhibition of the A. W. F. Fuller and Chicago Natural History Museum Collections of Antiquities from Benin, Nigeria.* Chicago: Chicago Natural History Museum.

Darwin, Charles. 1859. *On the Origin of Species by Means of Natural Selection: Or, The Preservation of Favoured Races in the Struggle for Life.* London: J. Murray.

Darwin, Charles. 1871. *The Descent of Man, and Selection in Relation to Sex.* London: J. Murray.

Darwin, Charles. 2003. *The Origin of Species.* 150th Anniversary Edition. New York: Signet.

Darwin, Erasmus. 1796. *Zoonomia, or, The Laws of Organic Life.* New York: T. and J. Swords.

Davidheiser, Mark. 2007. Overview of Peace and Conflict Resolution Study and Practice. *Anthropology News,* Oct. 11–12.

Dávila, Arlene. 2001. *Latinos, Inc.: The Marketing and Making of a People.* Berkeley: University of California Press.

de Beauvoir, Simone. 2010. *The Second Sex.* Trans. Constance Borde and Sheila Malvany-Chevallier. New York: Alfred A. Knopf.

de Castro, Fabio, and David McGrath. 2003. Moving Toward Sustainability in the Local Management of Floodplain Lake Fisheries in the Brazilian Amazon. *Human Organization* 62(2):123–33.

de Heinzelin, J, J. Desmond Clark, T. White, W. Hart, P. Renne, G. WoldeGabriel, et al. 1999. Environment and Behavior of 2.5 Million Year Old Bouri Hominids. *Science* 284:625–29.

de Mille, Cecil B., director. 1956. *The Ten Commandments.* Hollywood, CA: Paramount Pictures.

deWaal, Frans. 2001. *The Ape and the Sushi Master: Cultural Reflections of a Primatologist.* New York: Basic Books.

deWaal, Frans. 2013. *The Bonobo and the Atheist: In Search of Humanism Among the Primates.* New York: W. W. Norton.

Delaney, Carol. 1988. Participant Observation: The Razor's Edge. *Dialectical Anthropology* 13(3):291–300.

Deloria, Vine, Jr.. 1969. *Custer Died for Your Sins: An Indian Manifesto.* New York: Macmillan.

Dennell, R. 1997. The World's Oldest Spears. *Nature* 385:767–69.

Dentan, Robert Knox. 1968. *The Semai: A Non-Violent People of Malaya.* New York: Holt, Rinehart, and Winston.

Dettwyler, Katherine A. 2013. *Dancing Skeletons: Life and Death in West Africa.* 2nd Edition. Prospect Heights, IL: Waveland.

Diamond, Jared. 2002. Evolution, Consequences and Future of Plant and Animal Domestication. *Nature* 418(6898):700–7.

Diamond, Jared. 2005. *Collapse: How Societies Choose to Fail or Succeed.* New York: Viking Books.

Dietrich, Oliver, Manfred Heun, Jens Notroff, Klaus Schmidt, and Martin Zamkow. 2012. The Role of Cult and Feasting in the Emergence of Neolithic Communities: New Evidence from Göblekli Tepe, South-eastern Turkey. *Antiquity* 86(333):674–95.

Dongoske, K., M. Yeatts, T. Ferguson, and L. Jenkins. 1995. Historic Preservation and Native American Sites. *SAA Bulletin* 13(4):13, 39.

Douglas, A. E. 1919. *Climatic Cycles and Tree Growth.* Vol. 1. Washington, DC: Carnegie Institution of Washington.

Douglas, Mary. 1966. *Purity and Danger: An Analysis of the Concepts of Pollution and Taboo.* New York: Praeger.

Douglas, Mary, and Baron Isherwood. 1978. *The World of Goods.* Harmondsworth: Penguin.

Dressler, William. 2005. What's Cultural About Biocultural Research? *Ethos* 31 (1): 20–45.

Dreyer, Edward L. 2007. *Zheng He: China and the Oceans in the Early Ming Dynasty, 1405–1433.* New York: Pearson Longman.

Drucker, Philip and Robert F. Heizer. 1967. *To Make My Name Good: A Reexamination of the Southern Kwakiutl Potlatch.* Berkeley: University of California Press.

Dunning, Nicholas and Timothy Beach. 2000. "Stability and Instability in Prehispanic Maya Landscapes." In David L. Lentz, ed. *Imperfect Balance: Landscape Transformations in the Pre-Columbian Americas,* pp. 179–202. New York: Columbia University Press.

Dwyer, Leslie. 2000. "Spectacular Sexualities: Nationalism, Development, and the Politics of Family Planning in Indonesia." In Tamar Mayer, ed., *Gender Ironies of Nationalism: Sexing the Nation,* pp. 25–62. New York: Routledge.

Eboreime, Joseph. 2003. *The Installation of a Benin Monarch: Rite de Passage in the Expression of Ethnic Identity in Nigeria.* Paper from the ICOMOS 14th General Assembly. Accessed 3/3/2005: http://www.international.icomos.org/victoriafalls2003/papers/ B3–1%20-%20Eboreime.pdf.

Edgar, Heather and Keith Hunley. 2009. Race Reconciled?: How Biological Anthropologists View Human Variation. *American Journal of Physical Anthropology* 139(1):1–4.

Edwards, Carolyn P. 1993. "Behavioral Sex Differences in Children of Diverse Cultures: The Case of Nurturance to Infants." In Michael E. Pereira and Lynn A. Fairbanks, eds., *Juvenile Primates: Life History, Development, and Behavior,* pp. 327–28. New York: Oxford University Press.

Ehrlich, Paul R. 1968. *Population Bomb.* New York: Balantine Books.

Eickelman, Dale F., and James Piscatori. 1996. *Muslim Politics.* Princeton, NJ: Princeton University Press.

Eisenberg, Leon. 1977. Disease and Illness: Distinctions Between Professional and Popular Ideas of Sickness. *Culture, Medicine and Psychiatry* 1(1):9–23.

Eller, Jack David. 2006. *Violence and Culture: A Cross-Cultural and Interdisciplinary Approach.* Belmont, CA: Thomson Wadsworth.

Ellwanger, Nicholas. 2011. Primatology as Anthropology. Anthropologies: A Collaborative Online Project. Accessed 4/10/15: http://www.anthropologiesproject.org/2011/08/primatology-as-anthropology.html.

Endicott, Kirk, and Karen Endicott. 2008. *The Headman Was a Woman: The Gender Egalitarian Batek of Malaysia.* Long Grove, IL: Waveland Press.

Erasmus, Charles John. 1952. Changing Folk Beliefs and the Relativity of Empirical Knowledge. *Southwestern Journal of Anthropology* 8(4):411–28.

Erickson, Clark. 2000. An Artificial Landscape-scale Fishery in the Bolivian Amazon. *Nature* 408:190–93.

Escobar, Arturo. 1991. Anthropology and the Development Encounter: The Making and Marketing of Development Anthropology. *American Ethnologist* 18:658–82.

Escobar, Arturo. 1995. *Encountering Development: The Making and Unmaking of the Third World.* Princeton, NJ: Princeton University Press.

Escobar, Arturo, Sonia Alvarez, Adusta E. Dagnino. 1998. "Introduction: The Cultural and the Political in Latin American Social Movements." In Arturo Escobar, Sonia Alvarez, and E. Dagnino, eds., *Cultures of Politics/Politics of Culture: Revisioning Latin American Social Movements,* pp. 1–32. Boulder, CO: Westview Press.

Eshed, Vered, Avi Gopher, Ron Pinhasi, and Israel Hershkovitz. 2010. Paleopathology and the Origin of Agriculture in the Levant. *American Journal of Physical Anthropology* 143(1):121–33.

Esteva, Gustavo. 1992. "Development." In Wolfgang Sachs, ed., *The Development Dictionary,* pp. 6–25. London: Zed Books.

Evans-Pritchard, E. E. 1940. *The Nuer: A Description of the Modes of Livelihood and Political Institutions of a Nilotic People.* Oxford: Oxford University Press.

Evans-Pritchard, E. E. 1961. *Anthropology and History: A Lecture Delivered at the University of Manchester with Support of the Simon Fund for the Social Sciences.* Manchester: Manchester University Press.

Evans-Pritchard, E. E. 1976. *Witchcraft, Oracles, and Magic Among the Azande.* Abridged edition. Oxford: Clarendon Press. (Orig. published 1937.)

Eyer, Diane. 1993. *Mother-Infant Bonding: A Scientific Fiction.* New Haven, CT: Yale University Press.

Fabian, Johannes. 1971. On Professional Ethics and Epistemological Foundations. *Current Anthropology* 12(2):230–2.

Fabian, Johannes. 2001. *Anthropology with an Attitude: Critical Essays.* Palo Alto, CA: Stanford University Press.

Fadiman, Anne. 1997. *The Spirit Catches You and You Fall Down: A Hmong Child, Her American Doctors, and the Collision of Two Cultures.* New York: Farrar, Strauss and Giroux.

Fagan, Brian M. 1988. Black Day at Slack Farm. *Archaeology* 41(4):15–73.

Fairhead, James, and Melissa Leach. 1996. *Misreading the African Landscape: Society and Ecology in a Forest-Savanna Mosaic.* Cambridge: Cambridge University Press

Farmer, Paul. 1992. *AIDS and Accusation: Haiti and the Geography of Blame.* Berkeley: University of California Press.

Fausto-Sterling, Anne. 1992. Why Do We Know So Little About Human Sex? *Discover Magazine.* June. Accessed 8/19/09: http://discovermagazine.com/1992/jun/whydoweknowsolit64.

Fausto-Sterling, Anne. 2000. *Sexing the Body: Gender Politics and the Construction of Sexuality.* New York: Basic Books.

Fazioli, K. Patrick. 2014. The Erasure of the Middle Ages from Anthropology's Intellectual Genealogy. *History and Anthropology* 25(3):336–55.

Ferguson, James. 1994. *The Anti-Politics Machine: "Development," Depoliticization, and Bureaucratic Power in Lesotho.* Minneapolis: University of Minnesota Press.

Ferguson, R. Brian. 1995. *Yanomami Warfare: A Political History.* Santa Fe: School of American Research Press.

Fernandez-Duque, Eduardo. 2014. "Of Monkeys, Moonlight, and Monogamy in the Argentinian Chaco." In Karen B. Strier, ed. *Primate Ethnographies,* pp. 81–91. Boston: Pearson.

Field, Les, and Richard G. Fox. 2007. "Introduction: How Does Anthropology Work Today?" In Les Field and Richard G. Fox, eds., *Anthropology Put to Work,* pp. 1–19. Oxford: Berg.

Finney, Ben R. 1973. *Big Men and Business: Entrepreneurship and Economic Growth in the New Guinea Highlands.* Honolulu: University of Hawaii Press.

Fisher, Christoper T. et. al. 2003. A Reexamination of Human-Induced Environmental Change Within the Lake Pátzcuaro Basin, Michoacán, Mexico. *PNAS* 100(8):4957–62.

Flannery, Kent. 1969. "Origins and Ecological Effects of Early Domestication in Iran and the Near East." In P. Ucko and G. W. Dimbleby, eds., *The Domestication and Exploitation of Plants and Animals,* pp. 73–100. London: Duckworth.

Fletcher, Robert V., Terry L. Cameron, Bradley T. Lepper, Dee Anne Wymer, and William Pickard. 1996. Serpent Mound: A Fort Ancient Icon? *Midcontinental Journal of Archaeology* 21(1):105–43.

Fluehr-Lobban, Carolyn. 2003. *Ethics and the Profession of Anthropology: Dialogue for Ethically Conscious Practice.* Walnut Creek, CA: AltaMira Press.

Foley, William. 1997. *Anthropological Linguistics: An Introduction.* Malden, MA: Blackwell.

Foster, George M. 1952. Relationships Between Theoretical and Applied Anthropology: A Public Health Program Analysis. *Human Organization* 11 (3): 5–16.

Foster, Robert J. 2008. *Coca-Globalization: Following Soft Drinks from New York to New Guinea.* New York: Palgrave Macmillan.

Foucault, Michel. 1978. *The History of Sexuality:* Vol. 1. *An Introduction.* Trans. Robert Hurley. New York: Vintage Books.

Foucault, Michel. 1999. *Religion and Culture.* Selected and edited by Jeremy R. Carrette. New York: Routledge.

Frankel, David, director. 2006.*The Devil Wears Prada.* DVD. Beverly Hills, CA: 20th Century Fox Home Entertainment.

Frankenberry, Nancy, and Hans H. Penner. 1999. Clifford Geertz's Long-Lasting Moods, Motivations, and Metaphysical Conceptions. *Journal of Religion* 79(4):617–40.

Frazer, James G. 1890. *The Golden Bough: A Study in Comparative Religion.* 1st Edition. 2 Vols. London: Macmillan.

Frazer, James G. 1911–1915. *The Golden Bough: A Study in Magic and Religion.* 3rd Edition. 12 Vols. London: Macmillan.

Freidson, Eliot. 1970. *Profession of Medicine: A Study of the Sociology of Applied Knowledge.* New York: Dodd, Mead.

Friedman, Jonathan. 1994. *Cultural Identity and Global Process.* London: Sage.

Friedman, Jonathan. 1999. "The Hybridization of Roots and the Abhorrence of the Bush." In Michael Featherstone and Scott Lash, eds., *Spaces of Culture: City-Nation-World,* pp. 230–55. London: Sage.

Fry, Douglas. 2006. *The Human Potential for Peace: An Anthropological Challenge to Assumptions About War and Violence.* New York: Oxford University Press.

Fuentes, Agustín. 2004. It's Not All Sex and Violence: Integrated Anthropology and the Role of Cooperation and Social Complexity in Human Evolution. *American Anthropologist* 106(4):710–18.

Fuentes, Agustín. 2007. Core Concepts in Biological Anthropology. 1st edition. New York: McGraw-Hill.

Fuentes, Agustín. 2009a. A New Synthesis. Resituating Approaches to the Evolution of Human Behavior. *Anthropology Today* 25(3):12–17.

Fuentes, Agustín. 2009b. *Evolution of Human Behavior.* New York: Oxford University Press.

Fuentes, Agustín. 2012. Ethnoprimatology and the Anthropology of the Human-Primate Interface. *Annual Reviews of Anthropology* 41:101–17.

Fuentes, Agustín. 2014a. Human Evolution, Niche Complexity, and the Emergence of a Distinctively Human Imagination. *Time and Mind* 7(3):241-257.

Fuentes, Agustín. 2014b. "There's a Monkey in My Kitchen (and I Like It): Fieldwork with Macaques in Bali and Beyond." In Karen B. Strier, ed. *Primate Ethnographies,* pp. 151–62. Boston: Pearson.

Fuentes, Agustín. 2014c. The Troublesome Ignorance of Nicholas Wade. Huffington Post. Accessed 5/19/2014: http://www.huffingtonpost.com/agustin-fuentes/the-troublesome-ignorance-of-nicholas-wade_b_5344248.html.

Fuentes, Agustín. 2015. *Race, Monogamy, and Other Lies They Told You: Busting Myths About Human Nature.* Berkeley: University of California Press.

Fuentes, Agustín, Matthew Wyczalkowski, and Katherine MacKinnon. 2010. A Nonlinear Dynamics Contribution to Modeling Facets of the Evolutionary History in the Genus *Homo.* *Current Anthropology* 51(3):435–44.

Fullagar, Richard. 2005. "Residues and Usewear." In J. Balme and A. Patterson, eds., *Archaeology in Practice: A Student Guide to Archaeological Analyses,* pp. 207–34. Malden, MA: Blackwell.

Galbraith, John Kenneth. 1958. *The Affluent Society.* Boston: Houghton Mifflin.

Gallagher, Nancy L. 1999. *Breeding Better Vermonters: The Eugenics Project in the Green Mountain State.* Hanover, NH: University Press of New England.

Garber, Paul A. and Robert W. Sussman. 2007. "Cooperation and Competition in Primate Social Interactions." In Christina J. Campbell, Agustín Fuentes, Katherine C. MacKinnon, Melissa Panger, and Simon K. Bearder, eds., *Primates in Perspective,* pp. 636–51. New York: Oxford University Press.

García-Canclini, Nestor. 1995. *Hybrid Cultures: Strategies for Entering and Leaving Modernity.* Minneapolis: University of Minnesota Press.

Gardner, R. Allen, Beatrix T. Gardner, and Thomas E. van Cantfort, eds. 1989. *Teaching Sign Language to Chimpanzees.* Albany: State University of New York Press.

Gardner, Robert. 2004. *Dead Birds.* DVD. Cambrige, MA: Harvard University, Peabody Museum of Archaeology and Ethnology, Film Study Center.

Gardner, Robert and Karl G. Heider. 1969. *Gardens of War: Life and Death in the New Guinea Stone Age.* New York: Random House.

Garn, Stanley. 1961. *Human Races.* Springfield, IL: C. C. Thomas.

Geertz, Clifford. 1963. *Agricultural Involution: The Processes of Ecological Change in Indonesia.* Berkeley: University of California Press.

Geertz, Clifford. 1966. "Religion as a Cultural System." In Michael Banton, ed., *Anthropological Approaches to the Study of Religion,* pp. 1–46. ASA Monograph 3. London: Tavistock.

Geertz, Clifford. 1973. *The Interpretation of Cultures: Selected Essays.* New York: Basic Books.

Geertz, Hildred, and Clifford Geertz. 1964. Teknonymy in Bali: Parenthood, Age-Grading, and Genealogical Amnesia. *Journal of the Royal Anthropological Institute of Great Britain and Ireland* 94 (2): 94–108.

Geertz, Hildred, and Clifford Geertz. 1975. *Kinship in Bali.* Chicago: University of Chicago Press.

Gellner, Ernest. 1983. *Nations and Nationalism.* Ithaca, NY: Cornell University Press.

Gennep, Arnold van. 1960. *The Rites of Passage.* Trans. Monica B. Vizedom and Gabrielle L. Caffee. Chicago: University of Chicago Press. (Orig. published 1909 in French.)

Ghani, Ashraf, and Clare Lockhart, eds. 2009. *Fixing Failed States: A Framework for Rebuilding a Fractured World.* New York: Oxford University Press.

Gibbs, James L., Jr. 1963. The Kpelle Moot. *Africa* 33(1):1–11.

Gill, Richardson B. 2000. *The Great Maya Droughts: Water, Life, and Death.* Albuquerque: University of New Mexico Press.

Glaskin, Katie, and Richard Chenhall, eds. 2013. *Sleep Around the World: Anthropological Perspectives.* New York: Palgrave MacMillan.

Gledhill, John. 2000. *Power and Its Disguises: Anthropological Perspectives on Politics.* London: Pluto Press.

Gmelch, George. 1978. Baseball Magic. *Human Nature* 1(8):32–39.

Goldschmidt, Walter. 2000. A Perspective on Anthropology. *American Anthropologist* 102(4):789–807.

Golson, J., R. J. Lampert, J. M. Wheeler, and W. R. Ambrose. 1967. A Note on Carbon Dates for Horticulture in the New Guinea Highlands. *Journal of the Polynesian Society* 76:369–71.

Gonzalez, Roberto. 2001. *Zapotec Science: Farming and Food in the Northern Sierra of Oaxaca.* Austin: University of Texas Press.

Goode, Mary-Jo Delvecchio, Paul E. Brodwin, Byron J. Good, and Arthur Kleinman. 1992. *Pain as Human Experience: An Anthropological Perspective.* Berkeley: University of California Press.

Goodman, Alan H. and Thomas L. Leatherman, eds. 1998. *Building a New Biocultural Synthesis: Political-Economic Perspectives on Human Biology.* Ann Arbor: University of Michigan Press.

Gould, Stephen Jay. 1983. *Hens Teeth and Horse's Toes: Further Reflections on Natural History.* New York: W. W. Norton.

Gould, Stephen Jay. 1996. *The Mismeasure of Man.* New York: W. W. Norton.

Gow, David. 1993. Doubly Damned: Dealing with Power and Praxis in Development Anthropology. *Human Organization* 52(4):380–97.

Grant, Bob. 2007. Do Chimps Have Culture? *The Scientist.* Accessed 4/12/15: http://www.the-scientist.com/?articles.view/articleNo/25249/title/Do-Chimps-Have-Culture-/.

Gravlee, Clarence. 2009. How Race Becomes Biology: Embodiment of Social Inequality. *American Journal of Physical Anthropology* 139(1):47–57.

Green Belt Movement. 2005. Achievements. Accessed 3/20/2005: http://www.greenbeltmovement.org/achievements.php.

Gregory, Steven, and Roger Sanjek, eds. 1994. *Race.* New Brunswick, NJ: Rutgers University Press.

Grimm, Jakob. 1822. *Deutsche Grammatik.* Göttingen: Dieterichsche Buchhandlung.

Grove, Richard. 1995. *Green Imperialism: Colonial Expansion, Tropical Island Edens and the Origins of Environmentalism, 1600–1860.* Cambridge: Cambridge University Press.

Grün, Rainier. 2008. Electron Spin Resonance Dating. In Deborah Pearsall, ed. *Encyclopaedia of Archaeology,* pp. 153–99. Oxford: Elsevier Science and Technology.

Gudeman, Stephen. 1986. *Economics as Culture: Models and Metaphors of Livelihood.* London: Routledge and Kegan Paul.

Gudeman, Stephen. 2001. *The Anthropology of Economy: Community, Market, and Culture.* Oxford: Blackwell.

Guha, Ramachandra. 2000. *Environmentalism: A Global History.* New York: Longman.

Gulliver, Phillip H. 1979. *Disputes and Negotiations: A Cross-Cultural Perspective.* New York: Academic Press.

Gutmann, Matthew C. 1997. Trafficking in Men: The Anthropology of Masculinity. *Annual Review of Anthropology* 26:385–409.

Haas, Jonathan. 1990. *The Anthropology of War.* Cambridge: Cambridge University Press.

Haenn, Nora, and Richard Wilk. 2005. *The Environment in Anthropology: A Reader in Ecology, Culture, and Sustainable Living* New York: New York University Press.

Haeri, Niloofar. 1997. The Reproduction of Symbolic Capital: Language, State, and Class in Egypt. *Current Anthropology* 38(5): 795–805, 811–16.

Haeri, Niloofar. 2003. *Sacred Language, Ordinary People: Dilemmas of Culture and Politics in Egypt.* New York: Palgrave Macmillan.

Haile-Selassie, Yohannes. 2001. Late Miocene Hominids from the Middle Awash, Ethiopia. *Nature* 412:178–81.

Haile-Selassie, Yohannes, Luis Gibert, Stephanie M. Melillo, Timothy M. Ryan, Mulugeta Alene, Alan Deino, Naomi E. Levin, Gary Scott, and Beverly Z. Saylor. 2015. New Species from Ethiopia Further Expands Middle Pliocene Hominin Diversity. *Nature* 512:483–88.

Hakiwai, Arapata, and John Terrell. 1994. *Ruatepupuke: A Maori Meeting House.* The Field Museum Centennial Collection. Chicago: The Field Museum.

Hale, Kenneth L. 1992. On Endangered Languages and the Safeguarding of Diversity. *Language* 68(1):1–3.

Hamilton, W. D. 1964. The Genetical Evolution of Social Behavior, I and II. *Journal of Theoretical Biology* 7:1–52.

Hanlon, Joseph. 1996. Strangling Mozambique: International Monetary Fund "Stabilization" in the World's Poorest Country. *Multinational Monitor* 17 (7–8) July/August: 17–21.

Hannerz, Ulf. 1992. "The Global Ecumene." In *Cultural Complexity: Studies in the Social Organization of Meaning,* pp. 217–67. New York: Columbia University Press.

Hansen, Karen Tranberg. 2000. *Salaula: The World of Secondhand Clothing and Zambia.* Chicago: University of Chicago Press.

Haraway, Donna. 1989. *Primate Visions: Gender, Race, and Nature in the World of Modern Science.* New York: Routledge.

Harris, Marvin. 1979. *Cultural Materialism.* New York: Random House.

Harrison, Faye V. 1998. Introduction: Expanding the Discourse on "Race." *American Anthropologist* 100(3):609–31.

Hart, Donna, and Robert W. Sussman. 2005. *Man the Hunted: Primate Predators and Human Evolution.* New York: Westview Books.

Hartigan, John, Jr. 2005. *Odd Tribes: Towards a Cultural Analysis of White People.* Durham, NC: Duke University Press.

Hartigan, John, Jr. 2006. Saying "Socially Constructed" Is Not Enough. *Anthropology News,* Feb., p. 8.

Harvard University Skeletal Biology Lab. 2015. Biomechanics of Footstikes and Applications of Running Barefoot or in Minimal Footwear. Accessed 4/20/15: http://www.barefootrunning.fas.harvard.edu/.

Harvey, L. P. 2007. *Ibn Batuta.* London: I. B. Tauris and Oxford Centre for Islamic Studies.

Hastorf, Christine. 1988. "The Use of Paleoethnobotanic Data in Prehistoric Studies of Crop Production, Processing, and Consumption." In Christine Hastorf and Virginia Popper, eds. *Current Paleoethnobotany: Analytical Methods and Cultural Interpretations of Archaeological Plant Remains,* pp. 119–144. Chicago: University of Chicago Press.

Hastrup, Kirsten, and Peter Elass. 1990. Anthropological Advocacy: A Contradiction in Terms. *Current Anthropology* 31(3):301–11.

Hawks, John. 2013. Significance of Neandertal and Denisovan Genomes in Human Evolution. *Annual Review of Anthropology* 42:433–49.

Hawks, John, Keith Hunley, Sang-Hee Lee, and Milford Wolpoff. 2000. Population Bottlenecks and Pleistocene Human Evolution. *Molecular Biology and Evolution* 17(1):2–22.

Hayden, Brian. 2003. Were Luxury Foods the First Domesticates? Ethnoarchaeological Perspectives from Southeast Asia. *World Archaeology* 34(3):458–69.

Heckenberger, Michael J. 2005. *Ecology of Power: Culture, Place, and Personhood in the Southern Amazon, A.D. 1000–2000.* New York: Routledge.

Heckenberger, Michael J., Afukaka Kuikuro, Urissapá Tabata Kuikuro, I. Christian Russell, Morgan Schmidt, Carlos Fausto, and Bruna Franchetto. 2003. Amazonia 1492: Pristine Forest or Cultural Parkland? *Science* 301(5640):1701–14.

Herdt, Gilbert H. 1981. *Guardians of the Flutes: Idioms of Masculinity.* New York: Mcgraw-Hill.

Herdt, Gilbert H. 1994. "Introduction: Third Sexes and Third Genders." In Gilbert Herdt, ed., *Third Sex, Third Gender: Beyond Sexual Dimorphism in Culture and History,* pp. 21–81. New York: Zone Books.

Herdt, Gilbert H., ed. 1994. *Third Sex, Third Gender: Beyond Sexual Dimorphism in Culture and History.* New York: Zone Books.

Herrmann, Edward W., G. William Monaghan, William F. Romain, Timothy M. Schilling, Jarrod Burks, Karen L. Leone, Matthew P. Purtill, and Alan C. Tonetti. 2014. A New Multistage Construction Chronology for the Great Serpent Mound, USA. *Journal of Archaeological Science* 50:117–25.

Hildebrand, Elisabeth. 2003. Motives and Opportunities for Domestication: An Ethnoarchaeological Study in Southwest Ethiopia. *Journal of Anthropological Archaeology* 22(4):358–75.

Hill, Jane H. 1978. Apes and Language. *Annual Review of Anthropology* 7:89–112.

Hill, Jane H. 1993. Hasta la vista, baby: Anglo Spanish in the American Southwest. *Critique of Anthropology* 13(2):145–76.

Hill, Jane H. 1998. Language, Race, and White Public Space. *American Anthropologist* 100:680–9.

Himpele, Jeffrey D. and Quetzil E. Castañeda. 2004. *Incidents of Travel in Chichén Itzá.* Videorecording. Watertown, MA: Documentary Educational Resources.

Ho, Karen. 2009. *Liquidated: An Ethnography of Wall Street.* Durham, NC: Duke University Press.

Hobbes, Thomas. 1909. *Leviathan.* Oxford: Clarendon Press. [Orig. published 1651.]

Hoben, Alan. 1995. Paradigms and Politics: The Cultural Construction of Environmental Policy in Ethiopia. *World Development* 23(6):1007–1021.

Hobsbawn, Eric, and Terence Ranger, eds. 1983. *The Invention of Tradition.* Cambridge: Cambridge University Press.

Hodder, Ian. 2006. *The Leopard's Tale: Revealing the Mysteries of Çaltalhöyük.* New York: Thames and Hudson.

Hoffman, Carl L. 1984. "Punan Foragers in the Trading Networks of Southeast Asia." In C. Shrire, ed., *Past and Present in Hunter Gatherer Studies,* pp. 123–149. Orlando: Academic Press.

Hoijer, Harry. 1961. "Anthropological Linguistics." In Christine Mohrmann, Alf Sommerfelt, and Joshua Whatmough, eds., *Trends in European and American Linguistics 1930–1960,* pp. 110–127. Utrecht and Antwerp: Spectrum.

Hopper, Kim. 1988. More Than Passing Strange: Homelessness and Mental Illness in New York City. *American Ethnologist* 15(1):155–67.

Hopper, Kim. 2002. When (Working) in Rome: Applying Anthropology in Caesar's Realm. *Human Organization* 61(3):196–209.

Horn, David. 1994. *Social Bodies: Science, Reproduction, and Italian Modernity.* Princeton, NJ: Princeton University Press.

Houdin, Jean Pierre. 2007. Khufu Revealed. 3-D Web program. Accessed 4/2007. http://khufu.3ds.com/introduction/revealed/.

Howe, K. R. 1984. *Where the Waves Fall: A New South Sea Islands History from Its First Settlement to Colonial Rule.* Honolulu: University of Hawaii Press.

Human Terrain Systems (HTS). 2010. Overview. Accessed 7/31/10: http://humanterrainsystem.army.mil/overview.html.

Humphrey, Caroline. 2002. *The Unmaking of Soviet Life: Everyday Economies After Socialism.* Ithaca, NY: Cornell University Press.

Huntington, Samuel. 1996. *The Clash of Civilizations and the Remaking of World Order.* New York: Simon and Schuster.

Hymes, Dell H. 1962. "The Ethnography of Speaking." In Thomas Gladwin and William C. Sturtevant, eds., *Anthropology and Human Behavior,* pp. 13–53. Washington, DC: Anthropological Society of Washington.

Hymes, Dell H. 1972. "Toward Ethnographies of Communication." In Pier Paolo Giglioli, ed., *Language and Social Context,* pp. 21–44. Baltimore, MD: Penguin Books.

Hymes, Dell H. 1973. *Toward Linguistic Competence.* Texas Working Papers in Sociolinguistics, No. 16. [Later translated as *Vers la competence de communication,* Paris: Hatier, 1991.]

ICOMOS (International Council on Monuments and Sites). 1987. Recommendation on Chichén Itzà. Accessed 12/21/2015: http://whc.unesco.org/archive/advisory_body_evaluation/483.pdf.

Igoe, James. 2004. *Conservation and Globalization: A Study of National Parks and Indigenous Communities from East Africa to South Dakota.* Belmont, CA: Wadsworth.

Inda, Jonathan Xavier. 2014. *Racial Prescriptions: Pharmaceuticals, Difference, and the Politics of Life.* Burlington, VT: Ashgate.

Inda, Jonathan, and Renato Rosaldo, eds. 2002. *The Anthropology of Globalization: A Reader.* Malden, MA: Blackwell.

Inglis, Meera. 2015. Chimps and Gorillas Desperately Need Ebola Vaccine too—Virus Has Wiped Out a Third of Them. The Conversation. Accessed 4/10/15: http://theconversation.com/chimps-and-gorillas-desperately-need-ebola-vaccine-too-virus-has-wiped-out-a-third-of-them-35503.

Jablonka, Eva and Marion Lamb. 2005. *Evolution in Four Dimensions: Genetic, Epigenetic, Behavioral, and Symbolic Variation in the History of Life.* Cambridge, MA: MIT Press.

Jablonski, Nina G. 2004. The Evolution of Human Skin and Skin Color. *Annual Review of Anthropology* 33:585–623.

Jablonski, Nina G. 2006. *Skin: A Natural History.* Berkeley: University of California Press.

Jablonski, Nina, and George Chaplin. 2000. The Evolution of Human Skin Color. *Journal of Human Evolution* 39:57–106.

Jantz, Richard L., and L. Meadows Jantz. 2000. Secular Change in Craniofacial Morphology. *American Journal of Human Biology* 12:327–38.

Johnston, Francis E. 2004. "Race and Biology: Changing Currents in Muddy Waters." Paper presented at the conference "Race and Human Variation: Setting an Agenda for Future Research and Education." September 12–14, Alexandria, Virginia. http://www.understandingrace.com/resources/ papers_activity.html.

Kalipeni, Ezekiel. 2004. *HIV and AIDS in Africa: Beyond Epidemiology.* Malden, MA: Blackwell.

Kan, Sergei. 1989. *Symbolic Immortality: The Tlingit Potlatch of the Nineteenth Century.* Washington: Smithsonian Institution Press.

Kaplan, David, and Robert A. Manners. 1972. *Culture Theory.* Prospect Heights, IL: Waveland Press.

Kaptchuk, Ted J. 2001. The Double-blind, Randomized, Placebo-controlled Trial: Gold Standard or Golden Calf? *Journal of Clinical Epidemiology* 54:541–49.

Katz, Sarah R. 2006. *Redesigning Civic Memory: The African Burial Ground in Lower Manhattan.* Master's Thesis, University of Pennsylvania.

Kearney, Michael. 1995. The Local and the Global: The Anthropology of Globalization and Transnationalism. *Annual Review of Anthropology* 24:547–65.

Kelly, Robert L. 1995. *The Foraging Spectrum: Diversity in Hunter-Gatherer Lifeways.* Washington, DC: Smithsonian Institution Press.

Kelly, Robert L. 2013. *The Lifeways of Hunter Gatherers: The Foraging Spectrum.* Cambridge: Cambridge University Press.

Khanmohamadi, S. 2008. The Look of Medieval Ethnography: William of Rubruck's Mission to Mongolia. *New Medieval Literatures* 10(1):87–114.

Kidder, Alfred V. 1927. Southwestern Archaeological Conference. *Science* 66(1716):489–91.

Kidder, Alfred V. 1931. *The Pottery of the Pecos*. Vol. 1. Andover, MA: Phillips Academy.

Kidwell, Claudia Brush, and Valerie Steele, eds. 1989. *Men and Women: Dressing the Part*. Washington, DC: Smithsonian Institution Press.

Kildea, Gary, and Jerry Leach. 1975. *Trobriand Cricket: An Ingenious Response to Colonialism*. DVD. Berkeley, CA: Berkeley Media.

Kingsolver, Ann. 1996. "Power." In Alan Barnard and Jonathan Spencer, eds., *Encyclopedia of Social and Cultural Anthropology*, pp. 445–48. London: Routledge.

Kinsey, Alfred. 1948. *Sexual Behavior in the Human Male*. Philadelphia: W. B. Saunders.

Kittles, Rick A., and Kenneth M. Weiss. 2003. Race, Genes and Ancestry: Implications for Defining Disease Risk. *Annual Review of Genomics and Humans Genetics* 4:33–67.

Kleinman, Arthur. 1975. "Social, Cultural and Historical Themes in the Study of Medicine in Chinese Societies: Problems and Prospects for the Comparative Study of Medicine and Psychiatry." In A. Kleinman et al., eds. *Medicine in Chinese Cultures: Comparative Studies of Health Care in Chinese and Other Societies. Papers and Discussions from a Conference Held in Seattle, Washington, U.S.A., February 1974*, pp. 589–657. Washington, DC: U.S. Department of Health, Education, and Welfare.

Kleinman, Arthur. 1980. *Patients and Healers in the Context of Culture: An Exploration of the Borderland Between Anthropology, Medicine, and Psychology*. Berkeley: University of California Press.

Kluckhohn, Clyde. 1959. "The Role of Evolutionary Thought in Anthropology." In Betty J. Meggers, ed., *Evolution and Anthropology: A Centennial Appraisal*, pp. 144–57. Washington, DC: Anthropological Society of Washington.

Konnor, Melvin. 2011. *Evolution of Childhood: Relationships, Emotion, Mind*. Cambridge, MA: Harvard University Press.

Koos, Earl Lomon. 1954. *The Health of Regionville*. New York: Columbia University Press.

Kopytoff, Igor. 1986. "The Cultural Biography of Things: Commoditization as Process." In Arjun Appadurai, ed., *The Social Life of Things: Commodities in Cultural Perspective*, pp. 64–91. New York: Cambridge University Press.

Korten, David. 1995. *When Corporations Rule the World*. West Hartford, CT: Kumarian Press.

Kowaleski, Stephen A. 1990. The Evolution of Complexity in the Valley of Oaxaca. *Annual Review of Anthropology* 19:39–58.

Kramer, S. N. 1963. *The Sumerians*. Chicago: University of Chicago Press.

Krech, Shepard. 1999. *The Ecological Indian: Myth and History*. New York: W. W. Norton.

Krieger Nancy. 2005. Embodiment: A Conceptual Glossary for Epidemiology. *Journal of Epidemiology and Community Health* 59:350–55.

Kroeber, A. L. 1923. *Anthropology*. New York: Harcourt, Brace.

Kuklick, Henrika, ed. 2007. *A New History of Anthropology*. Malden, MA: Wiley-Blackwell.

Kulick, Don. 1998. *Travesti: Sex, Gender, and Culture Among Brazilian Transgendered Prostitutes*. Chicago: University of Chicago Press.

Kuper, Adam. 2000. *Culture: The Anthropologists' Account*. Cambridge, MA: Harvard University Press,

Kurtz, Donald V. 2001. *Political Anthropology: Paradigms and Power*. Boulder, CO: Westview Press.

Labov, William. 1990. "Intersection of Sex and Social Class in the Course of Linguistic Change." *Language Variation and Change* 2(2):205–54.

Labov, William, Sharon Ash, and Charles Boberg. 2006. *The Atlas of North American English: Phonetics, Phonology, and Sound Change: A Multimedia Reference Tool*. Berlin: Mouton de Gruyter.

Lakoff, George. 1980. *The Metaphors We Live By*. Chicago: University of Chicago Press.

Lakoff, Robin. 1975. *Language and Woman's Place*. New York: Harper and Row.

Laland, K. N., T. Uller, M. W. Feldman, K. Sterelny, G. B. Muller, A. Moczek, E. Jablonka, and F. J. Odling-Smee. 2014. Does Evolutionary Theory Need a Rethink? *Nature* 514:161–64.

Lancaster, Roger. 1992. *Life Is Hard: Machismo, Danger, and the Intimacy of Power in Nicaragua*. Berkeley: University of California Press.

Lancaster, Roger. 1997. On Homosexualities in Latin America (and Other Places). *American Ethnologist* 24(1):193–202.

Lancaster, Roger. 2004. The Place of Anthropology in a Public Culture Shaped by Bioreductivism. *Anthropology News* 45(3):4–5.

Larner, John. 1999. *Marco Polo and the Discovery of the World*. New Haven, CT: Yale University Press.

Latinis, D. Kyle. 2000. The Development of Subsistence System Models for Island Southeast Asia and Near Oceania: The Nature and Role of Arboriculture and Arboreal-based Economies. *World Archaeology* 32(1):41–67.

Leacock, Eleanor. 1981. *Myths of Male Dominance*. New York: Monthly Review.

Leakey, M. G., C. S. Feibal, I. McDougall, C. Ward, and A. Walker. 1998. New Specimens and Confirmation of an Early Age for *Australopithecus anamensis*. *Nature* 393:62–67.

Leakey, Richard, and Roger Lewin. 1977. *Origins: What New Discoveries Reveal About the Emergence of Our Species and Its Possible Future*. New York: E. P. Dutton.

Leakey, M. G., F. Spoor, F. H. Brown, P. N. Gathogo, C. Kiarie, L. N. Leakey, and I. McDougall. 2001. New Hominin Genus from Eastern Africa Shows Diverse Middle Pliocene Lineages. *Nature* 410:433–40.

Leary, John. 1995. *Violence and the Dream People: The Orang Asli and the Malaysian Emergency, 1948–1960*. Athens, OH: University Center for International Studies.

Lechner, Frank, and Boli, John. 2005. *World Culture: Origins and Consequences*. Malden, MA: Blackwell.

Ledeneva, Alena V. 1998. *Russia's Economy of Favors: Blat, Networking and Informal Exchange*. Cambridge: Cambridge University Press.

Lederman, Rena. 1990. "Pretexts for Ethnography: On Reading Field Notes." In Roger Sanjek, ed., *Field Notes: The Making of Anthropology*, pp. 71–91. Ithaca, NY: Cornell University Press.

Lee, Richard B. 1968. "What Hunters Do for a Living or How to Make Out on Scarce Resources." In R. B. Lee and I. DeVore, eds., *Man the Hunter*, pp. 30–43. Chicago: Aldine.

Lee, Richard. 1969. "!Kung Bushmen Subsistence: An Input-Output Analysis." In Andrew P. Vayda, ed., *Environment and Cultural Behavior*, pp. 47–79. Garden City, NY: Natural History Press.

Lee, Richard B. and Irven DeVore, eds. 1968. *Man the Hunter*. Chicago: Aldine.

Lekson, Stephen H. and Catherine M. Cameron. 1995. The Abandonment of Chaco Canyon, the Mesa Verde Migrations, and the Reorganization of the Pueblo World. *Journal of Anthropological Archaeology* 14:184–202.

Lende, Daniel. 2008. "Successful Weight Loss." Neuroanthropology Blog. Accessed 5/18/15: http://neuroanthropology.net/2008/04/05/successful-weight-loss/.

Lentz, Carola. 1999. "Changing Food Habits: An Introduction." In Carola Lentz, ed., *Changing Food Habits: Case Studies from Africa, South America, and Europe*, pp. 1–25. Newark, NJ: Harwood Academic.

Leonard, William R. 2002. Food for Thought: Dietary Change was a Driving Force in Human Evolution. *Scientific American*, Dec., pp. 106–115.

Lepper, Bradley T. 2013. Who Built Serpent Mound? Ohio History Connection Archaeology Blog, Nov 17. http://apps.ohiohistory.org/ohioarchaeology/who-built-serpent-mound/.

Lepper, Bradley T. 2015. Amazing Discoveries Just Waiting to Be Made. Ohio History Connection Archaeology Blog, Jan. 11. http://apps.ohiohistory.org/ohioarchaeology/amazing-discoveries-just-waiting-to-be-made/.

Lévi-Strauss, Claude. 1961. "The Effectiveness of Symbols." In *Structural Anthropology*, pp. 186–205. New York: Basic Books.

Lévi-Strauss, Claude. 1969. *The Elementary Structures of Kinship.* Boston: Beacon Press.

Lewellen, Ted C. 1983. *Political Anthropology: An Introduction.* 1st Edition. South Hadley, MA: Bergin and Garvey.

Lewellen, Ted C. 2003. *Political Anthropology: An Introduction.* 3rd Edition. Westport, CT: Praeger.

Lewin, Ellen, and William L. Leap, eds. 1996. *Out in the Field: Reflections of Lesbian and Gay Anthropologists.* Urbana: University of Illinois Press.

Lewin, Ellen, and William L. Leap, eds. 2009. *Out in Public: Reinventing Lesbian/Gay Anthropology in a Globalizing World.* Malden, MA: Wiley-Blackwell.

Lewontin, R.C. 1972. The Apportionment of Human Diversity. *Evolutionary Biology* 6:381–98.

Lifton, Robert Jay. 1986. *The Nazi Doctors: Medical Killing and the Psychology of Genocide.* New York: Basic Books

Linton, Ralph. 1924. Totemism and the A. E. F. *American Anthropologist* 26:296–300.

Lipe, William D. 1995. The Depopulation of the Northern San Juan: Conditions in the Turbulent 1200s. *Journal of Anthropological Archaeology* 14:143–69.

Lippman, Abby. 2001. The Power of Naming Things Genetic. Review of "Sociological Perspectives on the New Genetics." *Second Opinion* 7:99–100.

Little, Peter, and Michael Painter. 1995. Discourse, Politics, and the Development Process: Reflections on Escobar's "Anthropology and the Development Encounter." *American Ethnologist* 22(3):602–9.

Lizot, Jacques. 1985. *Tales of the Yanomami: Daily Life in the Venezuelan Forest.* Trans. Ernest Simon. Cambridge: Cambridge University Press.

Lock, Margaret. 2005. Eclipse of the Gene and the Return of Divination. *Current Anthropology* 46(S5):S47-S70.

Locke, John. 2003. *Two Treatises on Government: And a Letter Concerning Toleration.* New Haven, CT: Yale University Press. [Orig. published 1690.]

Lockwood, William G. 1975. *European Moslems: Economy and Ethnicity in Western Bosnia.* New York: Academic.

Loewen, James. 1995. *Lies My Teacher Told Me: Everything Your American History Textbook Got Wrong.* New York: Simon and Schuster.

Loewen, James. 1999. *Lies Across America: What Our Historic Sites Get Wrong.* New York: New Press.

Long, J. C., J. Li, and M. E. Healy. 2009. Human DNA Sequences: More Variation and Less Race. *American Journal of Physical Anthropology* 139(1):23–34.

Long, Jeffrey. 2003. *Human Genetic Variation: The Mechanisms and Results of Microevolution.* Paper presented at the American Anthropological Association 2003 annual meeting, November 21, Chicago. Accessed 5/24/07: http://www .understandingrace.com/resources /papers_author.html.

Love, Michael. 1999. "Ideology, Material Culture, and Daily Practice in Pre-Classic Mesoamerica: A Pacific Coast Perspective." In David C. Grove and Rosemary A. Joyce, eds. *Social Patterns in Pre-Classic Mesoamerica*, pp. 127–53. Washington, DC: Dumbarton Oaks Research Library and Collection.

Lovgren, Sven. 2003. "Map Links Healthier Ecosystems, Indigenous Peoples." *National Geographic News,* Feb. 27. Accessed 5/15/2005: http://news.nationalgeographic.com/news/ 2003/02/0227 _030227_indigenousmap.html.

Luntz, Frank I. 2007. *Words That Work: It's Not What You Say, It's What People Hear.* New York: Hyperion.

Lurie, Nancy Oestreich. 1961. Ethnohistory: An Ethnological Point of View. *Ethnohistory* 8(1):78–92.

Lyell, Charles. 1830. *Principles of Geology.* London: John Murray.

Lyons, Andrew P., and Harriet D. Lyons. 2004. *Irregular Connections: A History of Anthropology and Sexuality.* Lincoln: University of Nebraska Press.

MacBeth, Helen. 1997. *Food Preferences and Taste: Continuity and Change.* New York: Berghahn Books.

MacNeish, Richard S. 1967. A Summary of Subsistence. In D. S. Byers, ed., *The Prehistory of the Tehuacan Valley,* vol. 1, pp. 290–310. Austin: University of Texas Press.

Mahmood, Cynthia Keppley. 1997. *Fighting for Faith and Nation: Dialogues with Sikh Militants.* Philadelphia: University of Pennsylvania Press.

Mair, Lucy. 1969. *Anthropology and Social Change.* New York: Humanities Press.

Malinowski, Bronislaw. 1922. *Argonauts of the Western Pacific: An Account of Native Enterprise and Adventure in the Archipelagoes of Melanesian New Guinea.* London: Routledge and Kegan Paul.

Malinowski, Bronislaw. 1948. *Magic, Science and Religion and Other Essays.* Boston: Beacon Press.

Malotki, Ekkehardt. 1983. *Hopi Time: A Linguistic Analysis of the Temporal Concepts of the Hopi Language.* Berlin: Mouton.

Malthus, Robert, 1798. *An Essay on the Principle of Population, as it Affects the Future Improvement of Society.* London: J. Johnson.

Mamdani, Mahmood. 1972. *The Myth of Population Control: Family, Caste, and Class in an Indian Village.* New York: Monthly Review Press.

Marcus, George. 1995. Ethnography in/of the World System: The Emergence of Multi-Sited Ethnography. *Annual Review of Anthropology* 24:95–117.

Mares, Teresa. 2014. "Another Time of Hunger." In Women Redefining the Experience of Food Insecurity: Life off the Edge of the Table: Janet Page-Reeves, ed, pp. 45-64. Lexington Books.

Marks, Jonathan. 1995. *Human Biodiversity: Genes, Race, and History.* New York: Aldine de Gruyter.

Marks, Jonathan. 2015. *Tales of the Ex-Apes: How We Think About Human Evolution.* Berkeley: University of California Press.

Marshall, John, and Adrienne Miesmer. 2007. *N!ai, Story of a !Kung Woman.* DVD. Watertown: Documentary Educational Resources. [Orig. published 1980.]

Marty, Martin E., and R. Scott Appleby, eds. 1991. *Fundamentalisms Observed.* The Fundamentalism Project, vol. 1. Chicago: University of Chicago Press.

Mauss, Marcel. 1973. Techniques of the Body. *Economy and Society* 2 (1):70–88. [Orig. published 1934.]

Marx, Karl. 1990. *Capital: A Critique of Political Economy.* New York: Penguin. [Orig. published 1867.]

Mauss, Marcel. 1954. *The Gift: The Form and Reason for Exchange in Archaic Societies.* Trans. Ian Cunnison, with introduction by E. E. Evans-Pritchard. Glencoe, IL: Free Press.

Mayr, Ernst. 2002. *What Evolution Is.* New York: Basic Books.

McAnany, Patricia A., and Tomás Gallareta Negrón. 2010. "Bellicose Rulers and Climatological Peril? Retrofitting Twenty-First Century Woes on Eighth-Century Maya Society." In Patricia A. McAnany and Norman Yoffee, eds., *Questioning Collapse: Human Resilience, Ecological Vulnerability, and the Aftermath of Empire,* pp. 142–75. Cambridge: Cambridge University Press.

McAnany, Patricia A., and Norman Yoffee. 2010. "Why We Question Collapse and Study Human Resilience, Ecological Vulnerability, and the Aftermath of Empire." In Patricia McAnany and Norman Yoffee, eds., *Questioning Collapse: Human Resilience, Ecological Vulnerability, and the Aftermath of Empire,* pp. 1–20. Cambridge: Cambridge University Press.

McCabe, Terrence. 1990. Turkana Pastoralism: A Case Against the Tragedy of the Commons. *Human Ecology* 18(1):81–103.

McDade, Thomas. 2001. Lifestyle Incongruity, Social Integration, and Immune Function in Samoan Adolescents. *Social Science and Medicine* 53(10):1351–62.

McDade, Thomas, J. Stallings, and Carol Worthman. 2000. Culture Change and Stress in Western Samoan Youth: Methodological Issues in the Cross-cultural Study of Stress and Immune Function. *American Journal of Human Biology* 12(6):792–802.

McDougall, Christopher. 2011. *Born to Run: A Hidden Tribe, Superathletes, and the Greatest Race the World Has Never Known.* New York: Vintage Books.

McGrath, J. W., C. B. Rwabukwali, D. A. Schumann, J. Pearson-Marks, R. Mukasa, B. Namande, S. Nakayiwa, and L. Nakyobe. 1992. Cultural Determinants of Sexual Risk Behavior Among Baganda Women. *Medical Anthropology Quarterly* 6(2):153–61.

McHenry, Henry M. and Katherine Coffing. 2000. Australopithicus to Homo: Transformations in Body and Mind. *Annual Review of Anthropology* 29:125–46.

McIntyre, Matthew H., and Carolyn Pope Edwards. 2009. The Early Development of Gender Differences. *Annual Review of Anthropology* 38:83–97.

McKenna, James. 1993. An Evolutionary Analysis of Infant Sleep. *Sleep* 16(3):264–69.

McKenna, James J. 1996. Sudden Infant Death Syndrome in Cross-Cultural Perspective: Is Infant-Parent Cosleeping Protective? *Annual Review of Anthropology* 25:201–16.

McKenna, James, Helen Ball, Lee Gettler. 2007. Mother–Infant Cosleeping, Breastfeeding and Sudden Infant Death Syndrome: What Biological Anthropology Has Discovered About Normal Infant Sleep and Pediatric Sleep Medicine. *Yearbook of Physical Anthropology* 50:133–61.

McKeown, C. Timothy. 2002. "Implementing a 'True Compromise': The Native American Graves Protection and Repatriation Act After Ten Years." In C. Fforde, J. Hubert, and P. Turnbull, eds., *The Dead and Their Possessions: Repatriation in Principle, Policy and Practice*, pp. 108–32. London: Routledge.

McKinnon, Susan, and Sydel Silverman. 2005. "Introduction." In Susan McKinnon and Sydel Silverman, eds., *Complexities: Beyond Nature and Nurture*, pp. 1–22. Chicago: University of Chicago Press.

McManamon, Francis P. 2002. "Repatriation in the USA: A Decade of Federal Agency Activities under NAGPRA." In C. Fforde, J. Hubert, and P. Turnbull, eds., *The Dead and Their Possessions: Repatriation in Principle, Policy and Practice*, pp. 133–148. London: Routledge.

McNeil, William. 1976. *Plagues and People*. Garden City, NY: Anchor Books.

Mead, Margaret. 1928. *Coming of Age in Samoa: A Psychological Study of Primitive Youth for Western Civilization*. New York: William Morrow.

Mead, Margaret. 1963. *Sex and Temperament in Three Primitive Societies*. New York: William Morrow. [Orig. published 1935.}

Meggers, Betty J. 1971. *Amazonia: Man and Culture in a Counterfeit Paradise*. Chicago: Aldine, Atherton.

Meighan, Clement W. 1992. Some Scholars' Views on Reburial. *American Antiquity* 57(4):704–10.

Meigs, Anna. 1997. "Food as a Cultural Construction." In Carole Counihan and Penny Van Esterik, eds., *Food and Culture: A Reader*, pp. 95–106. New York: Routledge.

Menzies, Gavin. 2002. *1421: The Year China Discovered America*. London: Transworld.

Merry, Sally Engle. 2003. Human Rights Law and the Demonization of Culture. *Anthropology News* 44(2):4–5.

Michael, Robert T., John H. Gagnon, Edward O. Lauman, and Gina Kolata. 1994. *Sex in America: A Definitive Survey*. Boston: Little Brown.

Michaels, Eric. 1994. *Bad Anthropological Art: Tradition, Media, and Technological Horizons*. Sydney: Allen and Unwin.

Miller, Daniel. 1987. *Material Culture and Mass Consumption*. Oxford: Basil Blackwell.

Miller, Daniel, ed. 1995. *Acknowledging Consumption: A Review of New Studies*. London: Routledge.

Mithen, Steven. 2007. Did Farming Arise from a Misapplication of Social Intelligence? *Philosophical Transactions of the Royal Society B: Biological Sciences* 362(1480):705–18.

Mohanty, Chandra Talpade. 1991. "Under Western Eyes: Feminist Scholarship and Colonial Discourses." In Chandra Talpade Mohanty, Ann Russo, and Lourdes Torres, eds., *Third World Women and the Politics of Feminism*, pp. 333–58. Indianapolis: Indiana University Press.

Money, John. 1985. *Destroying Angel: Sex, Fitness, and Food in the Legacy of Degeneracy Theory, Graham Crackers, Kellogg's Corn Flakes, and American Health History*. Buffalo, NY: Prometheus Books.

Montagu, Ashley. 1997. *Man's Most Dangerous Myth: The Fallacy of Race*. 6th Edition. Walnut Creek, CA: AltaMira. [Orig. published 1942.]

Morgan, Edmund. 1975. *American Slavery, American Freedom*. New York: W. W. Norton.

Morgan, Lewis Henry. 1871. *Systems of Consanguinity and Affinity of the Human Family*. Washington, DC: Smithsonian Institution.

Morris, Rosalind C. 1995. All Made Up: Performance Theory and the New Anthropology of Sex and Gender. *Annual Review of Anthropology* 24:567–92.

Munn, Nancy D. 1962. Walbiri Graphic Signs: An Analysis. *American Anthropologist* 64(5, pt. 1):972–84.

Munn, Nancy D. 1973. *Walbiri Iconography: Graphic Representation and Cultural Symbolism in a Central Australian Society*. Ithaca, NY: Cornell University Press.

Munson, Barbara. 1999. Not for Sport. *Teaching Tolerance Magazine*. Accessed 7/31/10: http://www.tolerance.org/magazine/number-15-spring-1999/not-sport.

Murray, Gerald. 1987. "The Domestication of Wood in Haiti: A Case Study in Applied Evolution." In R. M. Wulff and S. J. Fiske, eds., *Anthropological Praxis: Translating Knowledge into Action*, pp. 223–40. Boulder, CO: Westview Press.

Myerhoff, Barbara G. 1974. *Peyote Hunt: The Sacred Journey of the Huichol Indians*. Ithaca, NY: Cornell University Press.

Myers, P. Z. 2014. Developmental Plasticity Is Not Lamarckism. Accessed 3/24/15: http://scienceblogs.com/pharyngula/2014/08/28/developmental-plasticity-is-not-lamarckism/.

Nabhan, Gary Paul. 1997. *Cultures of Habitat: On Nature, Culture, and Story*. Washington, DC: Counterpoint.

Nabhan, Gary Paul, and Amadeo Rea. 1987. Plant Domestication and Folk-Biological Change: The Upper Piman/Devil's Claw Example. *American Anthropologist* 89:57–73.

Nadasdy, Paul. 2005. The Anti-Politics of TEK: The Institutionalizaton of Co-Management Discourse and Practice. *Anthropologica* 47 (2): 215–32.

Nader, Laura. 1990. *Harmony Ideology: Justice and Control in a Zapotec Mountain Village*. Stanford, CA: Stanford University Press.

Nader, Laura. 1995. "Civilization and Its Negotiators." In Pat Caplan, ed., *Understanding Disputes: The Politics of Argument*, pp. 39–63. Oxford: Berg.

Nader, Laura, ed. 1996. *Naked Science: Anthropological Inquiry into Boundaries, Power, and Knowledge*. New York: Routledge.

Nader, Laura. 2001. "The Underside of Conflict Management—in Africa and Elsewhere." *IDS Bulletin* 32(1):19–27.

Nader, Laura, and Terry Kay Rockefeller. 1981. *Little Injustices: Laura Nader Looks at the Law*. Odessey Series. Washington, DC: PBS Video.

Nader, Laura, and Harry F. Todd, eds. 1978. *The Disputing Process—Law in Ten Societies*. New York: Columbia University Press.

Nanda, Serena. 1994. "Hijras: An Alternative Sex and Gender Role in India." In Gilbert Herdt, ed., *Third Sex, Third Gender: Beyond Sexual Dimorphism in Culture and History*, pp. 373–417. New York: Zone Books.

Nanda, Serena. 1999. *Neither Man nor Woman: The Hijras of India*. 2nd Edition. Boston: Cengage.

Nanda, Serena. 2000. *Gender Diversity: Crosscultural Variations*. Prospect Heights, IL: Waveland Press.

Naranjo, Tessie. 1995. Thoughts on Migration by Santa Clara Pueblo. *Journal of Anthropological Archaeology* 14:247–50.

Nash, June. 1981. Ethnographic Aspects of the World Capitalist System. *Annual Review of Anthropology* 10:393–423.

Nash, June. 2007. Consuming Interests: Water, Rum, and Coca-Cola from Ritual Propitiation to Corporate Expropriation in Highland Chiapas. *Cultural Anthropology* 22(4):621–39.

Nash, Manning. 1958. *Machine Age Maya*. Glencoe, IL: Free Press.

Natcher, David C., Susan Hickey, and Clifford G. Hickey. 2005. Co-Management: Managing Relationships, Not Resources. *Human Organization* 64(3):240–50.

National Anthropology Archives. 2015. National Anthropology Archives Home. Smithsonian, National Museum of Natural History. Accessed 11/23/ 2015: http://anthropology.si.edu/naa/home/naahome.html.

National Collegiate Athletic Association (NCAA). 2005. "NCAA Executive Committee Issues Guidelines for Use of Native American Mascots at Championship Events." (Released August 5). NCAA Press Release Archive. Accessed 8/2014: http://fs.ncaa.org/Docs/PressArchive/2005/Announcements/NCAA%2BExecutive%2BCommittee%2BIssues%2BGuidelines%2Bfor%2BUse%2Bof%2BNative%2BAmerican%2BMascots%2Bat%2BChampionship%2BEvents.html.

National Public Radio (NPR). 2007. Unearthing New York's Forgotten Slavery Era. Broadcast on NPR, October 11. Accessed 12/4/2015: http://www.npr.org/templates/story/story.php?storyId=15187759.

National Solidarity Programme. 2014. "NSP Basic Introduction." Accessed 6/1/2014: http://www.nspafghanistan.org/default.aspx?sel=109.

Nederveen Pieterse, J. 2004. *Globalization and Culture: Global Mélange*. Lanham, MD: Rowman and Littlefield.

Neel, James. 1962. Diabetes Mellitus: A 'Thrifty' Genotype Rendered Detrimental by Progress? *American Journal of Human Genetics* 14:3535–62.

Nietschmann, Bernard. 1992. *The Interdependence of Biological and Cultural Diversity*. Occasional Paper No. 21. Center for World Indigenous Studies, December.

Norberg, Johan. 2006. "How Globalization Conquers Poverty." Accessed 11/19/06: http://www.cato.org/special/symposium/ essays/norberg.html.

Nordstrum, Carolyn R. 1988. Exploring Pluralism: The Many Faces of Ayurveda. *Social Science and Medicine* 27(5):479–89.

Nyamwaya, D. O., 1993. Anthropology and HIV/AIDS Prevention in Kenya: New Ways of Cooperation. *AIDS and Society* 4(4):4, 8.

Oakley, Kenneth. 1964. *Frameworks for Dating Fossils*. New Brunswick, NJ: Aldine Transaction.

O'Connell, J. F., K. Hawkes, K. D. Lupo, and N. G. Blurton-Jones. 2002. Male Strategies and Plio-Pleistocene Archeology. *Journal of Human Evolution* 43:831–72.

Oberschall, Anthony. 2000. The Manipulation of Ethnicity: From Ethnic Cooperation to Violence and War in Yugoslavia. *Ethnic and Racial Studies* 23(6):982–1001.

Odling-Smee, F. John, Kevin N. Laland, and Marcus W. Feldman. 2003. *Niche Construction: The Neglected Process in Evolution*. Monographs in Population Biology 37. Princeton, NJ: Princeton University Press.

Omi, Michael, and Howard Winant, eds. 1996. *Racial Formation in the United States*. 2nd Edition. New York: Routledge.

Ong, Aihwa. 1988. The Production of Possession: Spirits and the Multinational Corporation in Malaysia. *American Ethnologist* 15(1):28–42.

Ortner, Sherry B. 1971. On Key Symbols. *American Anthropologist* 75:1338–46.

Ortner, Sherry B. 1974. "Is Female to Male as Nature is to Culture?" In Michelle Rosaldo and Louise Lamphere, eds., *Woman, Culture, and Society*, pp. 67–88. Stanford, CA: Stanford University Press.

Ortner, Sherry B. 1989. *High Religion: A Cultural and Political History of Sherpa Buddhism*. Princeton, NJ: Princeton University Press.

Ortner, Sherry B. 1996. *Making Gender: The Politics and Erotics of Culture*. Boston: Beacon Press.

Owusu, Maxwell. 1992. "Democracy and Africa: A View from the Village. *Journal of Modern African Studies* 30(3):369–96.

Owusu, Maxwell. 1996. Tradition and Transformation: Democracy and the Politics of Popular Power in Ghana. *Journal of Modern African Studies* 34(2):307–43.

Oyama, Susan, Paul E. Griffiths, and Russell D. Gray. 2001. "Introduction: What Is Developmental Systems Theory?" In Susan Oyama, Paul E. Griffiths, and Russell D. Gray, eds., *Cycles of Contingency: Developmental Systems and Evolution*, pp. 1–12. Cambridge, MA: MIT Press.

Paramount Pictures. 1999. *Grass: A Nation's Battle for Life*. DVD. New York: Milestone Film and Video.

Parent, Anthony S., Jr. 2003. *Foul Means: The Formation of Slave Society in Virginia, 1660–1740*. Chapel Hill: University of North Carolina Press.

Park, Michael. 2003. *Introducing Anthropology: An Integrated Approach*. New York: McGraw-Hill.

Parker, Richard. 1989. Acquired Immunodeficiency Syndrome in Urban Brazil. *Medical Anthropology Quarterly* 1 (2): 155–75.

Parker, R. G. 2009. *Bodies, Pleasures, and Passions: Sexual Culture in Contemporary Brazil*. 2nd Edition. Nashville, TN: Vanderbilt University Press.

Parkin, David, and Stanley Ulijaszek, eds. 2007. *Holistic Anthropology: Emergence and Convergence*. New York: Berghahn Books.

Parry, Jonathan, and Maurice Bloch, eds. 1989. *Money and the Morality of Exchange*. Cambridge: Cambridge University Press.

Parsons, Talcott. 1951. *The Social System*. Glencoe, IL: Free Press.

Partners in Health. 2010. Home page. http://www.pih.org/.

Patel, Raj. 2007. *Stuffed and Starved: The Hidden Battle for the World Food System*. London: Melville House.

Patterson, Penny, Director. 2003. *Koko and Friends*. Videorecording, produced by the Gorilla Foundation, distributed by Dave West, Utah Film and Video.

Pauketat, Timothy R. 1994. *The Ascent of Chiefs: Cahokia Mississippian Politics in Native North America*. Tuscaloosa: University of Alabama Press.

Pauketat, Timothy R., and Thomas E. Emerson. 1997. *Cahokia: Domination and Ideology in the Mississippian World*. Lincoln: University of Nebraska Press.

Perris, Joseph S. M., Yuen Kwok Y, Albert Osterhaus, and Klaus Stöhr. 2003. The Severe Acute Respiratory Syndrome. *New England Journal of Medicine* 349:2431–41.

Peterson, Jane. 2002. *Sexual Revolutions: Gender and Labor at the Dawn of Agriculture*. Gender and Archaeology Series. Walnut Creek, CA: AltaMira Press.

Peet, Richard, and Michael Watts, eds. 2004. *Liberation Ecologies: Environment, Development, Social Movements*. 2nd Edition. London: Routledge.

Pendle, Naomi. 2014. Interrupting the Balance: Reconsidering the Complexities of Conflict in South Sudan. *Disasters* 38(2): 227–48.

Peregrine, Peter N., Carol R. Ember, and Melvin Ember. 2003. Cross-cultural Evaluation of Predicted Associations Between Race and Behavior. *Evolution and Human Behavior* 24(5):357–64.

Peters, William, producer. 1970. *Eye of the Storm*. Human Relations Film Series. Videocassette. New York: Insight Media.

Petrie, William Flinders. 1891. *Tell el Hesy (Lachish)*. London: Watt (for Palestine Exploration Fund).

Petrie, William Flinders. 1899. Sequences in Prehistoric Remains. *Journal of the Anthropological Institute* 29:295–301.

Petryna, Adriana. 2002. *Life Exposed: Biological Citizenship After Chernobyl*. Princeton, NJ: Princeton University Press.

Pinker, Steven. 1994. *The Language Instinct*. New York: W. Morrow.

Pinker, Steven. 1997. *How the Mind Works*. New York: W. W. Norton.

Piot, Charles. 1999. *Remotely Global: Village Modernity in West Africa*. Chicago: University of Chicago Press.

Piperno, D. R. and K. V. Flannery. 2001. The Earliest Archaeological Maize (*Zea mays* L.) from Highland Mexico: New Accelerator Mass Spectrometry Dates and Their Implications. *Proceedings of the National Academy of Science* 98(4):2101–3.

Polanyi, Karl. 1975. *The Great Transformation*. New York: Octagon Books. [Orig. published 1944.]

Pollard, Helen Perlstein. 1993. *Tariacuri's Legacy: The Prehispanic Tarascan State*. Norman: University of Oklahoma Press.

Pollard, Helen Perlstein. 2003a. "Development of a Tarascan Core: The Lake Patzcuaro Basin." In Michael E. Smith and Frances F. Berdan, *The Post-Classic Mesoamerican World*, pp. 227–37. Salt Lake City: University of Utah Press.

Pollard, Helen Perlstein. 2003b. "The Tarascan Empire." In Michael E. Smith and Frances F. Berdan, *The Post-Classic Mesoamerican World,* pp. 78–86. Salt Lake City: University of Utah Press.

Post, Lennart von. 1946. The Prospect for Pollen Analysis in the Study of the Earth's Climatic History. *New Phytologist* 45(2):193–217.

Powdermaker, Hortense. 1944. *Probing Our Prejudices: A Unit for High School Students.* New York: Harper and Brothers.

Putnam, F. W. 1890. The Serpent Mound of Ohio. *Century Magazine* 39:871–88.

Radcliffe-Brown, Alfred R. 1941. The Study of Kinship Systems. *Journal of the Royal Anthropological Institute of Great Britain and Ireland* 71(1/2):1–18.

Radcliffe-Brown, Alfred R. 1950. *African Systems of Kinship and Marriage.* London: Oxford University Press.

Radcliffe-Brown, Alfred R. 1952. *Structure and Function in Primitive Society: Essays and Addresses.* Glencoe, IL: Free Press.

Radin, Paul. 1927. *Primitive Man as Philosopher.* New York: D. Appleton.

Radovčić, Davorka, Ankica Oros Sršen, Jakov Radovčić, David W. Frayer. 2015. Evidence for Neandertal Jewelry: Modified White-Tailed Eagle Claws at Krapina. *PLoS ONE* 10(3): e0119802.

Rahnema, Majid, and Victoria Bawtree. 1997. *The Post-Development Reader.* London: Zed Press.

Rappaport, Roy. 1984. *Pigs for the Ancestors: Ritual in the Ecology of a New Guinea People.* 2nd Edition. Prospect Heights, IL: Waveland Press.

Rasmussen, Susan. 1991. Modes of Persuasion: Gossip, Song, and Divination in Tuareg Conflict Resolution. *Anthropological Quarterly* 64(1):30–46.

Reeves, Dache M. 1936. Aerial Photography and Archaeology. *American Antiquity* 2(2):102–7.

Relethford, J. H. 1997. Hemispheric Differences in Human Skin Color. *American Journal of Physical Anthropology* 104(4):449–57.

Relethford, John H. 2002. Apportionment of Global Human Genetic Diversity Based on Craniometrics and Skin Color. *American Journal of Physical Anthropology* 118(4):393–98.

Relethford, John H. 2009. Race and Global Patterns of Phenotypic Variation. *American Journal of Physical Anthropology* 139(1):16–22.

Renfrew, Colin, and Paul Bahn. 2004. *Archaeology: Theory, Methods, and Practice.* 4th Edition. London: Thames and Hudson.

Research Advisory Committee on Gulf War Veterans' Illnesses. 2008. http://www1.va.gov/rac-gwvi/.

Richards, Paul. 1996. *Fighting for the Rainforest.* London: James Currey.

Richardson, Jane, and Alfred L. Kroeber. 1940. Three Centuries of Women's Dress Fashions: A Quantitative Analysis. *University of California Anthropological Records* 5(2):i–iv, 100–53.

Riches, David. 1986. "The Phenomenon of Violence." In David Riches, ed., *The Anthropology of Violence,* pp. 1–27. Oxford: Basil Blackwell.

Riding In, James. 1996. Repatriation: A Pawnee's Perspective. *American Indian Quarterly* 20(2):238–50.

Riley, Erin P., Linda D. Wolfe, and Agustín Fuentes. 2011. "Ethnoprimatology: Contextualizing Human and Nonhuman Primate Interactions." In Christina J. Campbell, Agustín Fuentes, Katherine C. MacKinnon, Melissa Panger, and Simon K. Bearder, eds., *Primates in Perspective,* pp. 676–86. New York: Oxford University Press.

Rindos, David. 1984. *The Origins of Agriculture: An Evolutionary Perspective.* Orlando, FL: Academic Press.

Ritzer, George. 1996. *The McDonaldization of Society: An Investigation into the Changing Character of Contemporary Social Life.* Thousand Oaks, CA: Pine Forge Press.

Rivers, William H. R. 1906. *The Todas.* London: Macmillan.

Rivers, W. H. R. 1910. The Genealogical Method of Anthropological Inquiry. *Sociological Review* 3(1):1–12.

Rivoli, Pietra. 2005. *The Travels of a T-Shirt in the Global Economy: An Economist Examines the Markets, Power, and Politics of World Trade.* Hoboken, NJ: John Wiley and Sons.

Robarchek, Clayton A., and Robert Knox Dentan. 1987. Blood Drunkenness and the Bloodthirsty Semai: Unmaking Another Anthropological Myth. *American Anthropologist* 89 (2): 356–65.

Robben, Antonius. 1989. *Sons of the Sea Goddess: Economic Practice and Discursive Conflict in Brazil.* New York: Columbia University Press.

Robbins, Richard. 2001. *Cultural Anthropology: A Problem-Based Approach.* 3rd Edition. Itasca, IL: F. E. Peacock.

Robbins, Richard. 2005. *Global Problems and the Culture of Capitalism.* 3rd Edition. Boston: Pearson/Allyn and Bacon.

Roberts, D. F. 1968. Genetic Fitness in a Colonizing Human Population. *Human Biology* 40:494–507.

Roosevelt, Anna C. 1999. The Development of Prehistoric Complex Societies: Amazonia, A Tropical Forest. *Archaeological Papers of the American Anthropological Association* 9(1):13–33.

Rosaldo, Renato. 1989. *Culture and Truth: The Remaking of Social Analysis.* Boston: Beacon Press.

Roscoe, Will. 1994. "How to Become a Berdache: Toward a Unified Analysis of Gender Diversity." In Gilbert Herdt, ed., *Third Sex, Third Gender: Beyond Sexual Dimorphism in Culture and History,* pp. 329–72. New York: Zone Books.

Rowe, Noel. 1996. *The Pictorial Guide to the Living Primates.* East Hampton, NY: Pogonias Press.

Rowe, Noel. 2015. How and Why All the World's Primates Project Began. Accessed 6/16/2015: http://www.alltheworldsprimates.org/About.aspx.

Rue, Loyal. 2007. A Guide to Thinking about Emergence. *Zygon* 42(4):829–35.

Ruff, Christopher. 2002. Variation in Human Body Size and Shape. *Annual Review of Anthropology* 31:211–32.

Sahlins, Marshall. 1965. "On the Sociology of Primitive Exchange." In M. Banton, ed., *The Relevance of Models for Social Anthropology,* pp. 123–236. ASA Monographs, 1. London: Tavistock.

Sahlins, Marshall. 1968. "Notes on the Original Affluent Society." In R. B. Lee and I. DeVore, eds., *Man the Hunter,* pp. 85–89. Chicago: Aldine.

Sahlins, Marshall. 1972. *Stone Age Economics.* Chicago: Aldine-Atherton.

Sahlins, Marshall. 1976. *Culture and Practical Reason.* Chicago: University of Chicago Press.

Sahlins, Marshall. 1999. Two or Three Things That I Know About Culture. *Journal of the Royal Anthropological Institute* 5(3):399–421.

Sakiestewa Gilbert, Matthew. 2010. *Education Beyond the Mesas: Hopi Students at Sherman Institute, 1902–1929.* Lincoln: University of Nebraska Press.

Sanjek, Roger. 1990. "Vocabulary for Fieldnotes." In Roger Sanjek, ed., *Fieldnotes: The Making of Anthropology,* pp. 71–91. Ithaca, NY: Cornell University Press.

Sankararaman Sriram, Nick Patterson, Heng Li, Svante Pääbo, and David Reich. 2012. The Date of Interbreeding Between Neandertals and Modern Humans. *PLoS Genetics* 8(10): e1002947.

Sapir, Edward. 1929. The Status of Linguistics as a Science. *Language* 5 (4): 207–14.

Sapir, Edward. 2004. *Language: An Introduction.* New York: Dover.

Sapolsky, Robert M. 2004. *Why Zebras Don't Get Ulcers.* 3rd Edition. New York: Owl Book/Henry Holt.

Saussure, F. de. 1916. *Cours de linguistique générale.* Paris: Payot.

Saussure, F. de. 1986. *Course in General Linguistics.* LaSalle, IL: Open Court.

Sayer, Andrew. 2000. Moral Economy and Political Economy. *Studies in Political Economy* (Spring):79–103.

Scally, Aylwyn, and Richard Durbin. 2012. Revising the Human Mutation Rate: Implications for Understanding Human Evolution. *Nature Reviews* 13(10):745–53.

Scheper-Hughes, Nancy. 1995. The Primacy of the Ethical: Propositions for a Militant Anthropology. *Current Anthropology* 15:227–83.

Schildkrout, Enid, and Curtis A. Kelm. 1998. *The Scramble for Art in Central Africa*. Cambridge: Cambridge University Press.

Schlosser, Eric. 2001. *Fast Food Nation: The Dark Side of the All-American Meal*. Boston: Houghton Mifflin Company.

Schneider, David M. 1968. *American Kinship: A Cultural Account*. Englewood Cliffs, NJ: Prentice-Hall.

Segal, Charles M., and David C. Stineback. 1977. *Puritans, Indians, and Manifest Destiny*. New York: Putnam.

Segal, Daniel A., and Sylvia J. Yanagisako, eds. 2005. *Unwrapping the Sacred Bundle: Reflections on the Disciplining of Anthropology*. Durham, NC: Duke University Press.

Seligman, Rebecca. 2005. Distress, Dissociation, and Embodied Experience: Reconsidering the Pathways to Mediumship and Mental Health. *Ethos* 33(1):71–99.

Senut, B. et al. 2001. First Hominid from the Miocene (Lukeio Formation, Kenya). *C.R. Academy of Science Paris* 332:137–44.

Service, Elman. 1962. *Primitive Social Organization: An Evolutionary Perspective*. New York: Random House.

Sheridan, Michael. 2006. "Linguistic Models in Anthropology 101: Give Me the Cup." In P. Rice and D. McCurdy, eds. *Strategies in Teaching Anthropology*, pp. 54–56. 4th Edition. Upper Saddle River, NJ: Prentice Hall Professional.

Shieffelin, Bambi B., Katharyn A. Woolard, and Paul V. Kroskrity, eds., *Language Ideologies: Practice and Theory*. New York: Oxford University Press.

Shore, Bradd. 1996. *Culture in Mind: Cognition, Culture, and the Problem of Meaning*. New York: Oxford University Press.

Shorris, Earl. 1992. *Latinos: A Biography of the People*. New York: W. W. Norton.

Silverblatt, Irene. 1988. "Political Memories and Colonizing Symbols: Santiago and the Mountain Gods of Colonial Peru." In Jonathan Hill, ed., *Rethinking History and Myth: Indigenous South American Perspectives on the Past*, pp. 174–94. Urbana: University of Illinois Press.

Simmons, Ozzie G. 1955. Popular and Modern Medicine in Mestizo Communities of Coastal Peru and Chile. *Journal of American Folklore* 68(1):57–71.

Simpson, Scott W. 2002. "*Australopithecus afarensis* and Human Evolution." In P. N. Peregrine, C. R. Ember, and M. Ember, eds., *Physical Anthropology: Original Readings in Method and Practice*, pp.103–23. Saddle River, NJ: Prentice-Hall.

Sivo, Ellen. 2005. The DOs and DON'Ts of College Romance. *The Vermont Cynic* Nov. 29. http://media.www.vermontcynic.com/media/storage/paper308/news/2005/11/29/LifeAndStyle/The-Dos.And.Donts.Of.College.Romance-1115738.shtml.

Skipper, Robert, 2004. The Heuristic Role of Sewall Wright's 1932 Adaptive Landscape Diagram. *Philosophy of Science* 71:1176–88.

Sloane, Patricia. 1999. *Islam, Modernity, and Entrepreneurship Among the Malays*. New York: St. Martin's Press.

Small, Meredith. 1998. *Our Babies, Ourselves: How Biology and Culture Shape How We Parent*. New York: Anchor Books.

Smedley, Audrey. 2007a. *The History of the Idea of Race . . . And Why It Matters*. Paper presented at the conference "Race, Human Variation and Disease: Consensus and Frontiers," Warrenton, Virginia, March 14–17: http://www.understandingrace .com/resources/papers_author.html.

Smedley, Audrey. 2007b. *Race in North America: Origin and Evolution of a Worldview*. 3rd Edition. Boulder, CO: Westview Press.

Smith, Adam. 1976. *An Inquiry into the Nature and Causes of The Wealth of Nations*. Chicago: University of Chicago Press. [Orig. published 1776]

Smith, M. Estellie. 2000. *Trade and Tradeoffs: Using Resources, Making Choices, and Taking Risks*. Long Grove, IL: Waveland Press.

Smith, Michael E. 2009. V. Gordon Childe and the Urban Revolution: A Historical Perspective on a Revolution in Urban Studies. *Town Planning Review* 80(1):3–29.

Smithsonian Institution. 2015. Our History: James Smithson and the Founding of the Smithsonian. Accessed 11/27/2015: http://www .si.edu/About/History.

Society for Medical Anthropology. 2014. What Is Medical Anthropology? Accessed 6/1/14: http://www.medanthro.net/9/comment-page-1/#comment-36.

Spiro, Melford E. 1958. *Children of the Kibbutz*. Cambridge, MA: Harvard University Press.

Spittler, Gerd. 1999. "In Praise of the Simple Meal: African and European Food Culture Compared." In Carola Lentz, ed., *Changing Food Habits: Case Studies from Africa, South America, and Europe*, pp. 27–42. Newark, NJ: Harwood Academic.

Spitulnik, Debra. 1998. "Mediating Unity and Diversity: The Production of Language Ideologies in Zambian Broadcasting." In Bambi B. Shieffelin, Katharyn A. Woolard, and Paul V. Kroskrity, eds., *Language Ideologies: Practice and Theory*, pp. 163–88. New York: Oxford University Press.

Spurlock, Morgan, dir. 2004. *Supersize Me*. DVD video. New York: Hart Sharp Video.

Squier, Ephraim G., and Edward H. Davis. 1848. *Ancient Monuments of the Mississippi Valley*. Smithsonian Contributions to Knowledge, vol. 1. Washington, DC: Smithsonian Institution.

Stack, Carol. 1997. *All Our Kin*. New York: Basic Books.

Stapp, Darby C., ed., 2012. *Action Anthropology and Sol Tax in 2012: The Final Word?* Society for Applied Anthropology Annual Meeting. Journal of Northwest Anthropology, Memoir No. 8. Richland, WA: Journal of Northwest Anthropology.

Starr, Paul. 1982. *The Social Transformation of American Medicine*. New York: Basic Books.

Steele, D. Gentry, and Joseph F. Powell. 1999. "Peopling of the Americas: A Historical and Comparative Perspective." In Robson Bonnichsen, ed., *Who Were the First Americans?: Proceedings of the 58th Annual Biology Colloquium, Oregon State University*, pp. 91–120. Corvallis, OR: Center for the Study of First Americans.

Stephens, John L. 1843. *Incidents of Travel in Yucatan*. New York: Harper and Brothers.

Stern, Jack T. 2000. Climbing to the Top: A Personal Memoir of *Australopithecus afarensis*. *Evolutionary Anthropology* 9:113–33.

Stocking, George W., Jr. 1968. *Race, Culture, and Evolution: Essays in the History of Anthropology*. Chicago: University of Chicago Press.

Stocking, George W., Jr., ed. 1985. *History of Anthropology*. Vol. 3. *Objects and Others: Essays on Museums and Material Culture*. Madison: University of Wisconsin Press.

Stoffle, Richard, Rebecca Toupal, and Nieves Zedeño. 2003. "Landscape, Nature, and Culture: A Diachronic Model of Human-Nature Adaptations." In H. Selin, ed., *Nature Across Cultures: Views of Nature and the Environment in Non-Western Cultures*, pp. 97–114. London: Kluwer Academic.

Stonich, Susan. 1993. *I Am Destroying the Land!: The Political Ecology of Poverty and Environmental Destruction in Honduras*. Boulder, CO: Westview Press.

Strathern, Marylin. 1988. *The Gender of the Gift: Problems with Women and Problems with Society in Melanesia*. Berkeley: University of California Press.

Strier, Karen B. 2003. *Primate Behavioral Ecology*. 2nd Edition. Boston: Allyn and Bacon.

Strier, Karen B., ed. 2014. *Primate Ethnographies*. Boston: Pearson.

Strier, Karen B., Jean P. Boubli, Francisco B. Pontual, and Sérgio L. Mendes. 2006. Human Dimensions of Northern Muriqui Conservation Efforts. *Ecological and Environmental Anthropology* 2(2):44–53.

Stringer, Chris. 2002. Modern Human Origins: Progress and Prospects. *Philosophical Transactions of the Royal Society of London*, Series B. 357(1420):563–79.

Strong, Pauline. 1996. Animated Indians: Critique and Contradiction in Commodified Children's Culture. *Cultural Anthropology* 11(3):405–24.

Stumpf, Rebecca M. 2011. "Chimpanzees and Bonobos: Inter- and Intraspecies Diversity." In Christina J. Campbell, Agustín Fuentes, Katherine C. MacKinnon, Simon K. Bearder, and Rebecca M. Stumpf, *Primates in Perspective*. 2nd edition, pp. 340–56. New York: Oxford University Press.

Sturtevant, William. 1964. "Studies in Ethnoscience." In A. Kimball Romney and Roy G. D'Andrade, eds., *Transcultural Studies of Cognition,* pp. 99–131. Menasha, WI: AAA.

Sussman, Robert W. 2011. "A Brief History of Primate Field Studies." In Christina J. Campbell, Agustín Fuentes, Katherine C. MacKinnon, Simon K. Bearder, and Rebecca M. Stumpf, *Primates in Perspective.* 2nd edition, pp. 6–11. New York: Oxford University Press.

Sussman, Robert W. 2014. "The Lure of Lemurs to an Anthropologist." In Karen B. Strier, ed. *Primate Ethnographies,* pp. 34–45. Boston: Pearson.

Tainter, Joseph. 2006. Archaeology of Overshoot and Collapse. *Annual Review of Anthropology* 35:59–74.

Tainter, Joseph. 2008. Collapse, Sustainability, and the Environment: How Authors Choose to Fail or Succeed. *Reviews in Anthropology* 37:342–71.

Tannen, Deborah. 1990. *You Just Don't Understand: Men and Women in Conversation.* New York: Morrow.

Tannen, Deborah. 1994. *Talking from 9 to 5: How Women's and Men's Conversational Styles Affect Who Gets Hired, Who Gets Credit, and What Gets Done at Work.* New York: W. Morrow.

Tattersall, Ian. 2012. *Masters of the Planet: Seeking the Origins of Human Singularity.* New York: Palgrave Macmillan.

Tax, Sol. 1975. Action Anthropology. *Current Anthropology* 16(4):514–17.

Taylor, R. E. 1975. Fluorine Diffusion: A New Dating Method for Chipped Lithic Materials. *World Archaeology* 7(2):125–35.

Tedlock, Dennis. 1972. "Pueblo Literature: Style and Verisimilitude." In Alfonso Ortiz, ed., *New Perspectives on the Pueblos,* pp. 219–42. Albuquerque: University of New Mexico Press.

Tedlock, Dennis. 1988. "Ethnography as Interaction: The Storyteller, the Audience, the Fieldworker, and the Machine." In Regna Darnell and Michael K. Foster, eds., *Native North American Patterns,* pp. 80–94. Papers of the Canadian Ethnology Service 112. Hull, Quebec: Canadian Museum of Civilization.

Tedlock, Dennis. 1993. *Breath on the Mirror: Mythic Voices and Visions of the Living Maya.* San Francisco, CA: HarperSanFrancisco.

Tedlock, Dennis. 1999. *Finding the Center: Art of the Zuni Storyteller.* 2nd Edition, Revised and Expanded. Lincoln: University of Nebraska Press.

Teeter, Karl V. 1964. "Anthropological Linguistics" and Linguistic Anthropology. *American Anthropologist* 66 (4), Part 1:878–79.

Templeton, Alan R. 1998. Human Races: A Genetic and Evolutionary Perspective. *American Anthropologist* 100(3):632–50.

Templeton, Alan. 2002. Out of Africa Again and Again. *Nature* 416:45–51.

Templeton, Alan R. 2013. Biological Races in Humans. *Studies in History and Philosophy of Biological and Biomedical Sciences* 44(3):262–71.

Terrell, John, and Robert L. Welsch. 1990. Trade Networks, Areal Integration, and Diversity along the North Coast of New Guinea. *Asian Perspectives* 29:156–65.

Thierry, Bernard. 2007. "The Macaques: A Double Layered Social Organization." In Christina J. Campbell, Agustín Fuentes, Katherine C. MacKinnon, Melissa Panger, and Simon K. Bearder, eds., *Primates in Perspective,* pp. 224–39. New York: Oxford University Press.

Thomas, Mark. 2008. *Belching Out the Devil: Global Adventures with Coca-Cola.* London: Ebury.

Thomas, Nicholas. 1989. Material Culture and Colonial Power: Ethnological Collecting and the Establishment of Colonial Rule in Fiji. *Man* 24(1):41–56.

Thomas, Wesley. 1997. "Navajo Cultural Constructions of Gender and Sexuality." In Sue-Ellen Jacobs, Wesley Thomas, and Sabine Lang, eds., *Two-Spirit People: Native American Gender Identity, Sexuality, and Spirituality,* pp. 156–73. Urbana: University of Illinois Press.

Thompson, Edward Herbert. 1932. *People of the Serpent: Life and Adventure among the Maya.* Boston: Houghton Mifflin.

Thomson, Rob, Tamar Murachver, and James Green. 2001. Where Is the Gender in Gendered Language? *Psychological Science* 12:171–5.

Thorne, A. G., and M. H. Wolpoff. 1992. The Multiregional Evolution of Humans. *Scientific American* 266(4):76–83.

Tierney, Patrick. 2002. *Darkness in El Dorado: How Scientists and Journalists Devastated the Amazon.* New York: W. W. Norton.

Toren, Christina. 1996. "Psychological Anthropology." In Alan Barnard and Jonathan Spencer, eds., *Encyclopedia of Social and Cultural Anthropology,* pp. 456–61. London: Routledge.

Townsend, Patricia. 2008. *Environmental Anthropology: From Pigs to Policies.* 2nd edition. Long Grove, IL: Waveland Press.

Trevor-Roper, Hugh R. 1983. "The Invention of Tradition: The Highland Tradition of Scotland." In Eric Hobsbawn and Terence Ranger, eds., *The Invention of Tradition,* pp. 15–41. Cambridge: Cambridge University Press.

Trubek, Amy. 2008. *The Taste of Place: A Cultural Journey Into Terroir.* Berkeley: University of California Press.

Truman, Harry S. 1949. Inaugural Address, January 20. Accessed 6/3/14: http://www.bartleby.com/124/pres53.html.

Trut, Lyudmila D. 1999. Early Canid Domestication: The Farm-fox Experiment. *American Scientist* 87:160–8.

Tsing, Anna Lowehaupt. 2000. The Global Situation. *Cultural Anthropology* 15(3):327–60.

Tsing, Anna Lowehaupt. 2005. *Friction: An Ethnography of Global Connection.* Princeton, NJ: Princeton University Press.

Turner, Victor. 1967. *The Forest of Symbols: Aspects of Ndembu Ritual.* Ithaca, NY: Cornell University Press.

Turner, Victor. 1969. *The Ritual Process: Structure and Anti-Structure.* Chicago: Aldine.

Two Bears, Davina R. 2006. Navajo Archaeologist Is Not an Oxymoron: A Tribal Archaeologist's Experience. *American Indian Quarterly* 30(3–4):381–87.

Tylor, E. B. 1871. *Primitive Culture: Researches into the Development of Mythology, Philosophy, Religion, Art, and Custom.* London: John Murray.

Ubelaker, Douglas H. and Lauryn Guttenplan Grant. 1989. Human Skeletal Remains: Preservation or Reburial? *Yearbook of Physical Anthropology* 32:249–87.

Ulanowicz, Robert E. 2007. Emergence, Naturally! *Zygon* 42(4):945–60.

Ulijaszek, Stanley. 2007. "Bioculturalism." In David Parkin and Stanley Ulijaszek, eds., *Holistic Anthropology: Emergence and Convergence,* pp. 21–51. New York: Berghahn Books.

Ulijaszek, Stanley J., and Hayley Lofink. 2006. Obesity in Biocultural Perspective. *Annual Review of Anthropology* 35:337–60.

Underhill, Paco. 2005. *Call of the Mall: A Walking Tour Through the Crossroads of Our Shopping Culture.* New York: Simon and Schuster.

UNESCO. 2015a. Cultural Landscape and Archaeological Remains of the Bamiyan Valley. World Heritage List, No. 208. Accessed 11/26/2015: http://whc.unesco.org/en/list/208.

UNESCO. 2015b. Site of Palmyra. World Heritage List, No. 23. Accessed 11/26/2015: http://whc.unesco.org/en/list/23.

UNESCO. 2015c. World Heritage List, Delisted Sites. Accessed 11/26/2015: http://whc.unesco.org/en/list/?&&&delisted=1.

Ungar, Peter S., Frederick E. Grine, and Mark F. Teaford. 2006. Diet in Early Homo: A Review of the Evidence and a New Model of Adaptive Versatility. *Annual Review of Anthropology* 35:209–88.

Urry, James. 1972. "*Notes and Queries on Anthropology* and the Development of Field Methods in British Anthropology, 1870–1920." In *Proceedings of the Royal Anthropological Institute of Great Britain and Ireland* for *1972,* pp. 45–57. London: The Royal Anthropological Institute.

U.S. Census Office, J. D. B. DeBow, Superintendent. 1853. *The Seventh Census of the United States: 1850.* Washington, DC: Robert Armstrong, Public Printer.

Van Keuren, Scott. 2006. Decorating Glaze-Painted Pottery in East-Central Arizona. *In* Judith Habicht-Mauche, Suzanne Eckert, and Deborah Huntley, eds., *The Social Life of Pots: Glaze Wares and Cultural Dynamics in the Southwest, AD 1250-1680,* pp. 87–104. Tucson: University of Arizona Press.

van Schaik, C. P. 1989. "The Ecology of Social Relationships Among Females." In V. Standee, and R. A. Foley, eds., *Comparative Socio-ecological: The Behavioral Ecology of Humans and Other Mammals*, pp. 195–218. Oxford: Blackwell Scientific Press.

Verdery, Katherine. 1996. *What Was Socialism?: What Comes Next?* Princeton, NJ: Princeton University Press.

Vergano, Dan. 2014. Cave Paintings in Indonesia Redraw Picture of Earliest Art. *National Geographic*, Oct. 8. Accessed 5/26/15: http://news.nationalgeographic.com/news/2014/10/141008-cave-art-sulawesi-hand-science/.

Verini, James. 2014. How the World's Youngest Nation Descended into Bloody Civil War: Fighting Between Its Two Main Tribal Groups Threatens to Tear South Sudan Apart. *National Geographic*, Special Feature. Accessed 12/20/2015: http://news.nationalgeographic.com/news/special-features/2014/10/141001-south-sudan-dinka-nuer-ethiopia-juba-khartoum/.

Veseth, Michael. 2005. *Globaloney: Unraveling the Myths of Globalization*. Lanham, MD: Rowman and Littlefield.

Vincent, Joan. 1978. Political Anthropology: Manipulative Strategies. *Annual Review of Anthropology* 7:175–94.

Viswesaran, Kamala. 1997. Histories of Feminist Ethnography. *Annual Review Anthropology* 26:591–621.

Vivanco, Luis. 2013. *Reconsidering the Bicycle: An Anthropological Perspective on a New (Old) Thing*. New York: Routledge.

Voegelin, C. F. 1965. Sociolinguistics, Ethnolinguistics, and Anthropological Linguistics. *American Anthropologist* 67(2):484–5.

Wackernagel, Mathis, Larry Onisto, Alejandro Callejas Linares, Ina Susana López Falfán, Jesús Méndez García, Ana Isabel Suárez Guerrero, et. al. 1997. *The Ecological Footprints of Nations: How Much Nature Do They Use? How Much Nature Do They Have?* Report manuscript. Toronto: International Council for Local Environmental Initiatives.

Wade, Edwin L. 1985. "The Ethnic Art Market in the American Southwest, 1880–1980." In Richard Handler (series ed.) and George W. Stocking, Jr. (volume ed.), *History of Anthropology: Vol. 3. Objects and Others: Essays on Museums and Material Culture*, pp.167–91. Madison: University of Wisconsin Press.

Wagner, Roy. 1967. *The Curse of Souw: Principles of Daribi Clan Definition and Alliance*. Chicago: University of Chicago Press.

Wagner, Roy. 1969. "Marriage Among the Daribi." In R. M. Glasse and M. J. Meggitt, eds., *Pigs, Pearlshells, and Women: Marriage in the New Guinea Highlands*, pp. 56–76. Englewood Cliffs, NJ: Prentice Hall.

Wagner, G. A. and P. Van den Haute. 1992. *Fission Track-Dating*. Dordrecht: Kluwer Academic.

Wallace, Anthony F. C. 1956. Revitalization Movements: Some Theoretical Considerations for Their Comparative Study. *American Anthropologist* 58:264–81.

Wallace, Anthony F. C. 1966. *Religion: An Anthropological View*. New York: Random House.

Wallace, Anthony F. C. 1970. *The Death and Rebirth of the Seneca*. New York: Knopf.

Wallman, Joel. 1992. *Aping Language*. Cambridge: Cambridge University Press.

Walsh, Peter D., Kate A. Abernathy, Magdalena Bermejo, et. al. 2003. Catastrophic Ape Decline in Western Equatorial Africa. *Nature* 422:611–14.

Wapner, Paul. 1996. *Environmental Activism and World Civic Politics*. Albany: State University of New York Press.

Ward, C. V., M. G. Leakey, and A. Walker. 2001. Morphology of *Australopithecus anamensis* from Kanapoi and Allia Bay. *Journal of Human Evolution* 41(4):255–368.

Warren, Kay. 1998. *Indigenous Movements and Their Critics: Pan-Maya Activism in Guatemala*. Princeton, NJ: Princeton University Press.

Washburn, Sherwood L. 1951. The New Physical Anthropology. *Transactions of the New York Academy of Sciences*, Series III, 13(7): 298–304.

Washburn, Sherwood L. 1961. *The Social Life of Early Man*. Chicago: Aldine.

Watahomigie, Lucille, and Akira Yamamoto. 1992. Local Reactions to Perceived Language Decline. *Language* 68(1):10–17.

Watson, James B. 1965. From Hunting to Horticulture in the New Guinea Highlands. *Ethnology* 4(3):295–309.

Watson, James B. 1977. Pigs, Fodder, and the Jones Effect in Postipomoean New Guinea. *Ethnology* 16:57–70.

Watson-Gegeo, Karen Ann, and Geoffrey White, eds. 1990. *Disentangling: Conflict Discourse in Pacific Societies*. Stanford, CA: Stanford University Press.

Watters, Ethan. 2011. *Crazy Like Us: The Globalization of the American Psyche*. New York: Free Press.

Wax, Murray, and Felix Moos. 2004. Anthropology: Vital or Irrelevant. *Human Organization* 63(2):246–7.

Webster, D. 2002. *The Fall of the Ancient Maya: Solving the Mystery of the Maya Collapse*. London: Thames and Hudson.

Weiner, Annette B. 1976. *Women of Value, Men of Renown: New Perspectives in Trobriand Exchange*. Austin: University of Texas Press.

Weiner, Annette B. 1988. *The Trobrianders of Papua New Guinea*. Fort Worth, TX: Harcourt Brace Jovanovich College.

Welsch, Robert L. 1983. "Traditional Medicine and Western Medical Options Among the Ningerum of Papua New Guinea." In Lola Romanucci-Ross, Daniel E. Moerman, and Laurence R. Tancredi, eds., *The Anthropology of Medicine: From Culture Toward Medicine*, pp. 32–53. New York: Praeger.

Welsch, Robert L. 2006. "Coaxing the Spirits to Dance." In Robert L. Welsch, Virginia-Lee Webb, and Sebastine Haraha, eds., *Coaxing the Spirits to Dance: Art and Society in the Papuan Gulf of New Guinea*, pp. 4–44. Hanover, NH: Hood Museum of Art.

Welsch, Robert L. 1988. Traditional Silk Sarongs of Mandar, South Sulawesi, Indonesia. *Field Museum of Natural History Bulletin* 59 (4):13–22.

Welsch, Robert L. and John Terrell. 1998. "Material Culture, Social Fields, and Social Boundaries on the Sepik Coast of New Guinea." In Miriam Stark, ed., *The Archaeology of Social Boundaries*, pp. 50–77. Washington, DC: Smithsonian Institution Press.

Wengrow, David. 2010. *What Makes Civilization?: The Ancient Near East and the Future of the West*. New York: Oxford University Press.

Werner, Cynthia, and Duran Bell, eds. 2004. *Values and Valuables: From the Sacred to the Symbolic*. Lanham, MD: Rowman Altamira.

West-Eberhard, M. J. 2003. *Developmental Plasticity and Evolution*. Oxford: Oxford University Press.

Westermark, George D. 1998. History, Opposition, and Salvation in Agarabi Adventism. *Pacific Studies* 21(3):51–71.

Weston, Kath. 1993. Lesbian/Gay Studies in the House of Anthropology. *Annual Review of Anthropology* 22:339–67.

Wheatley, Bruce P. 1999. *The Sacred Monkeys of Bali*. Long Grove, IL: Waveland Press.

White, D. Steven. 2010. "The Top 175 Global Economic Entities, 2010." Accessed 1/24/14: http://dstevenwhite.com/2011/08/14/the-top-175-global-economic-entities-2010/.

White, Leslie. 1949. *The Science of Culture: A Study of Man and Culture*. New York: Farrar, Strauss.

Whitehead, Neil L. 2004. "Cultures, Conflicts, and the Poetics of Violent Practice." In Neil Whitehead, ed., *Violence*, pp. 3–24. Santa Fe: School of American Research.

Whiten, A., J. Goodall, W. C. Mcgrew, T. Nishida, V. Reynolds, Y. Sugiyama, C. E. G. Tutin, R. W. Wrangham, and C. Boesch. 1999. Cultures in Chimpanzees. *Nature* 399:682–85.

Wilcox, Michael. 2010. "Marketing Conquest and the Vanishing Indian: An Indigenous Response to Jared Diamond's Archaeology of the American Southwest." In Patricia A. McAnany and Norman Yoffee, eds., *Questioning Collapse: Human Resilience, Ecological Vulnerability, and the Aftermath of Empire*, pp. 113–141. Cambridge: Cambridge University Press.

Wiley, Andrea. 2004. "Drink Milk for Fitness": The Cultural Politics of Human Biological Variation and Milk Consumption in the United States. *American Anthropologist* 106(3):506–17.

Wiley, Andrea. 2011. *Reimagining Milk: Cultural and Biological Perspectives.* New York: Routledge.

Wilk, Richard, and Lisa Cliggett. 2007. *Economies and Cultures: Foundations of Economic Anthropology.* 2nd Edition. Boulder, CO: Westview Press.

Willey, Gordon. 1953. Prehistoric Settlement Pattern in the Virú Valley, Peru. *Bureau of American Ethnology,* Bulletin 155. Washington: Bureau of American Ethnology.

Wilson, Edmund O. 1975. *Sociobiology: The New Synthesis.* Cambridge, MA: Belknap Press at Harvard University Press.

Winterhalder, Bruce. 1993. Work, Resources and Population in Foraging Societies. *Man* 28(2):321–40.

Winterhalder, Bruce, and Eric A. Smith, eds. 1981. *Hunter-Gatherer Foraging Strategies.* Chicago: University of Chicago Press.

Wolf, Eric. 1984. *Europe and the People without History.* Berkeley: University of California Press.

Wolf, Eric. 2001. *Pathways of Power: Building an Anthropology of the Modern World.* Berkeley: University of California Press.

Wood, Bernard. 2010. Reconstructing Human Evolution: Achievements, Challenges, and Opportunities. *Proceedings of the National Academy of Sciences* 107 (Suppl. 2):8902–9.

Wood, Bernard, and Mark Collard. 1999. The Changing Face of the Genus Homo. *Evolutionary Anthropology* 8:195–207.

Woolard, Kathryn A. 1998. "Introduction: Language Ideology as a Field of Inquiry." In Bambi B. Shieffelin, Kathryn A. Woolard, and Paul V. Kroskrity, eds., *Language Ideologies: Practice and Theory,* pp. 3–47. New York: Oxford University Press.

World Commission on Environment and Development (WCED). 1987. *Our Common Future.* Report. Oxford: Oxford University Press.

World Health Organization (WHO). 2012. The 10 Leading Causes of Death by Country Income Group (2012). Accessed 5/20/15: http://www.who.int/mediacentre/factsheets/fs310/en/index1.html.

Worthman, Carol M. 1995. "Hormones, Sex, and Gender." *Annual Review of Anthropology* 24:593–616.

Worthman, Carol. 2007. After Dark: Evolutionary Ecology of Human Sleep. *In* Wenda Travathan, E. O. Smith, and James McKenna, eds., *Evolutionary Medicine and Health: New Perspectives,* pp. 291–313. New York: Oxford University Press.

Worthman, Carol. 2012. "Anthropology of Sleep." In Dierdre Barrett and Patrick McNamara, eds., *Encyclopedia of Sleep and Dreaming: The Evolution, Function, Nature, and Mysteries of Slumber,* pp. 45–49. Santa Barbara, CA: Greenwood.

Wrangham, Richard. 2009. *Catching Fire: How Cooking Made Us Human.* New York: Basic Books.

Wright, Lawrence. 1994. One Drop of Blood. *New Yorker,* July 25, pp. 46–55.

Wright, Sewell. 1932. The Roles of Mutation, Inbreeding, Crossbreeding and Selection in Evolution. *Proceedings of the Sixth International Congress of Genetics* 1:356–66.

Wuerthner, George. 2003. Welfare Ranching: Assessing the Real Cost of a Hamburger. *Vegetarian Voice.* Accessed 3/15/2005: http://www.navs-online.org/environment/cattle_ranching/welfare_ranching.php.

Yardley, Jim. 2012. Malnutrition Widespread in Indian Children, Report Finds. *New York Times,* Jan. 10. Accessed 8/12/13: http://www.nytimes.com/2012/01/11/world/asia/ malnutrition-in-india-is-widespread-report-finds.html.

Yoffee, Norman. 1995. Political Economy in Early Mesopotamian States. *Annual Review of Anthropology* 24:281–311.

Young, Michael W. 1998. *Malinowski's Kiriwina: Fieldwork Photography 1915–1918.* Chicago: University of Chicago Press.

Zimmer, Carl. 2015. The Human Family Tree Bristles with New Branches. *New York Times,* May 27, http://www.nytimes.com/2015/06/02/science/adding-branches-to-the-human-family-tree.html?_r=0.

Zvelebil, Marek and Peter Rowley-Conwy. 1984. Transition to Farming in Northern Europe: A Hunter-Gatherer Perspective. *Norwegian Archaeological Review* 17(2):104–128.

Zohary, Daniel, and Maria Hopf. 2000. *Domestication of Plants in the Old World.* 3rd Edition. Oxford: Oxford University Press.

Photo Credits

(p. 105): Courtesy of Library of the London School of Economics and Political Science, MALINOWSKI/3/ARG/1; **Figure 4.13 (p. 106):** Courtesy of Library of the London School of Economics and Political Science, MALINOWSKI/3/B/18/1; **Figure 4.14 (p. 109):** Anna Luisa Daigneault

CHAPTER 5

Chapter opening (p. 114): © Image Source/Alamy Stock Photo; **Figure 5.1 (p. 118):** Ron Cohn/Gorilla Foundation/koko.org; **Figure 5.2 (p. 119):** OUP; **Figure 5.3 (p. 120):** OUP; **Figure 5.4 (p. 123):** Tsuji/Getty Images; **Figure 5.5 (p. 124):** © Jake Warga/Corbis; **Figure 5.6 (p. 125):** AP Photo/Pablo Martinez Monsivais; **Figure 5.7 (p. 125):** Zoe Cormack; **Classic Contributions (p. 127):** Ruth Benedict Papers, Archives & Special Collections Library, Vassar College; **Figure 5.8 (p. 128):** © Stapleton Collection/Corbis; **Figure 5.9 (p. 129):** Source: http://www.icsi.berkeley.edu/wcs/data.html; **Figure 5.10 (p. 131):** Courtesy of Robert L. Welsch; **Figure 5.11 (p. 131):** John Mahoney/The Gazette; **Thinking Like an Anthropologist (p. 134, left):** © NoDerog/iStockphoto; **Thinking Like an Anthropologist (p. 134, right):** Ellen Roberts; **Doing Fieldwork (p. 136):** © gulfimages/Alamy Stock Photo

CHAPTER 6

Chapter opening (p. 140): Paw Media; **Figure 6.1 (p. 144):** public domain via Wikimedia Commons; **Figure 6.2 (p. 145):** RAJESH JANTILAL/AFP/Getty Images; **Figure 6.3 (p. 146):** Redrawn from Segal, A. (1993) *An Atlas of International Migration.* London: Hans Zell Publishers. Copyright remains with the estate of Aaron Segal; **Thinking Like an Anthropologist (p. 147):** Lynsey Addario/Getty Images Reportage; **Classic Contributions (p. 150):** Courtesy of Sydel Silverman; **Figure 6.4 (p. 152):** © Per-Anders Pettersson/Corbis; **Figure 6.5 (p. 154):** © Paul Jeffrey; **Figure 6.6 (p. 157):** KIRILL KUDRYAVTSEV/AFP/Getty Images; **Figure 6.7 (p. 158):** Krannert Center; **Doing Fieldwork (p. 160):** AP Photo/Igor Kostin

CHAPTER 7

Chapter opening (p. 166): © Minden Pictures/Corbis; **Figure 7.1 (p. 169):** public domain via Wikimedia Commons (originally published in *The Hornet* magazine); **Figure 7.2 (p. 170):** Agustín Fuentes, *Core Concepts in Biological Anthropology*, McGraw Hill 2007: 126, Figure 5.2; **Figure 7.3a–d (p. 171):** © imageBROKER/Alamy Stock Photo; © Ariadne Van Zandbergen/Alamy Stock Photo; Berendje Photography/Shutterstock; Paul Maguire/Shutterstock; **Figure 7.4a–e (p. 172):** Erni/Shutterstock; apple2499/Shutterstock; Alan Jeffery/Shutterstock; Dmitri Gomon/Shutterstock; Ksenia Ragozina/Shutterstock; **Figure 7.5a–c (p. 173):** nikolay100/Shutterstock; Mees Kuiper/Shutterstock; Sergey Uryadnikov/Shutterstock; **Figure 7.6 (p. 174):** Agustín Fuentes, *Core Concepts in Biological Anthropology*, McGraw Hill 2007: 190, Figure 6.16; **Doing Fieldwork (p. 175):** Eduardo Fernandez-Duque; **Figure 7.7 (p. 178):** Agustín Fuentes, *Core Concepts in Biological Anthropology*, McGraw Hill 2007: 143, Figure 5.16; **Figure 7.8 (p. 178):** © robertharding/Alamy Stock Photo; **Figure 7.9 (p. 179):** Copyright © Gibson, Mickey/Animals Animals—All rights reserved; **Thinking Like an Anthropologist (p. 181):** © Photoshot License Ltd/Alamy Stock Photo; **Figure 7.10 (p. 183):** Devi Snively; **Figure 7.11a–c (p. 185):** Dean Pennala/Shutterstock; Steve Meese/Shutterstock; Reprinted courtesy of the Jane Goodall Institute of Canada. www.janegoodall.ca; **Figure 7.12 (p. 186):** USO/iStockphoto; **Figure 7.13 (p. 187):** © Steve Bloom Images/Alamy Stock Photo; **Classic Contributions (p. 190):** © Ted Streshinsky/CORBIS

CHAPTER 8

Chapter opening (p. 194): Brent Stirton/Getty Images Reportage; **Figure 8.1 (p. 198):** Agustín Fuentes, *Core Concepts in Biological Anthropology*, McGraw Hill 2007: 199, Figure 7.3; **Figure 8.2 (p. 198):** OUP; **Figure 8.3 (p. 208):** © The Natural History Museum/Alamy Stock Photo; **Figure 8.4 (p. 210):** OUP; **Anthropologist as Problem Solver (p.212):** FCG/Shutterstock; **Figure 8.5 (p. 215, top):** © Bone Clones, www.boneclones.com; **Figure 8.5 (p. 215, bottom):** © The Natural History Museum/Alamy Stock Photo; **Classic Contributions (p. 222):** Wellcome Library, London; **Figure 8.6 (p. 224):** Photo © 2001 David L. Brill, humanoriginsphotos.com; **Figure 8.7 (p. 226):** © Heritage Image Partnership Ltd/Alamy Stock Photo; **Figure 8.8 (p. 228):** Agustín Fuentes, *Core Concepts in*

Biological Anthropology, McGraw Hill 2007: 279, Figure 9.10; **Figure 8.8 (p. 229):** Javier Trueba/MSF/ Science Source; **Figure 8.9 (p. 229):** based on: Bordes, Francois, *The Old Stone Age.* Copyright © 1969 by Francois Bordes, McGraw-Hill; **Figure 8.10 (p. 230):** © Hercules Milas/Alamy Stock Photo; **Thinking Like an Anthropologist (p. 231):** Memo Angeles/Shutterstock

The Evolution of Humans 8.1 (pp. 200–201): (1) Didier Descouens/Wikipedia; **(2)** Muséum national d'histoire naturelle; **(3)** © 1999 David L. Brill, humanoriginsphotos.com

The Evolution of Humans 8.2 (pp. 202–207): (1) © Exploratorium, www.exploratorium.edu; **(2)** © Exploratorium, www.exploratorium.edu; **(3)** Copyright © 2015, Rights Managed by Nature Publishing Group; **(4)** © 1999 David L. Brill, humanoriginsphotos.com; **(5)** © Bone Clones, www .boneclones.com; **(6)** © Exploratorium, www.exploratorium.edu; **(7)** Smithsonian Institute; **(8)** © Exploratorium, www.exploratorium.edu; **(9)** Bjørn Christian Tørrissen/Wikipedia; **(10)** Collection of the Transvaal Museum, Northern Flagship Institute, Pretoria South Africa; **(11)** © Exploratorium, www.exploratorium.edu; **(12)** © Exploratorium, www.exploratorium.edu; **(13)** Photo by Brett Eloff courtesy of Lee Berger and the University of the Witwatersrand, Johannesburg; **(14)** John Hawks

The Evolution of Humans 8.3 (pp. 216–221): (1) © Exploratorium, www.exploratorium.edu; **(2)** © Exploratorium, www.exploratorium.edu; **(3)** Xvazquez/Wikipedia; **(4)** © Exploratorium, www.exploratorium.edu; **(5)** © Exploratorium, www.exploratorium.edu; **(6)** Bence Viola. Used with permission; **(7)** Carl Bento, Australian Museum; **(8)** © Exploratorium, www.exploratorium.edu

CHAPTER 9

Chapter opening (p. 236): Air Images/Shutterstock; **Figure 9.1 (p. 240):** OUP; **Figure 9.2 (p. 243):** Copyright © Smith, Scott W./Animals Animals—All rights reserved; **Classic Contributions (p. 244):** AMERICAN PHILOSOPHICAL SOCIETY/SCIENCE PHOTO LIBRARY; **Figure 9.3 (p. 246):** © John Warburton-Lee Photography/Alamy Stock Photo; **Figure 9.4 (p. 250):** © Xinhua/XINHUA/ Corbis; **Figure 9.5 (p. 251):** Centers for Disease Control and Prevention. *CDC Health Information for International Travel 2012.* New York: Oxford University Press, 2012; **Figure 9.6 (p. 252, left):** © robertharding/Alamy Stock Photo; **Figure 9.6 (p. 252, right):** kevinruss/iStockphoto; **Anthropologist as Problem Solver (p. 253):** Tish1/Shutterstock; **Figure 9.7 (p. 255):** © Maximilian Norz/dpa/Corbis; **Figure 9.8 (p. 255, left):** © Paul Almasy/Corbis; **Figure 9.8 (p. 255, right):** © Alex Segre/Alamy Stock Photo; **Figure 9.9 (p. 258):** Agustín Fuentes, *Core Concepts in Biological Anthropology*, McGraw Hill 2007: 361, Figure 11.14

CHAPTER 10

Chapter opening (p. 262): AP Photo/Chitose Suzuki; **Figure 10.1 (p. 266):** © Archive Farms Inc/ Alamy Stock Photo; **Figure 10.2 (p. 269):** Agustín Fuentes, *Core Concepts in Biological Anthropology*, McGraw Hill 2007: 321, Figure 10.11; **Figure 10.3 (p. 271):** Agustín Fuentes, *Core Concepts in Biological Anthropology*, McGraw Hill 2007: 310, Figure 10.4; **Figure 10.4 (p. 272):** Agustín Fuentes, *Core Concepts in Biological Anthropology*, McGraw Hill 2007: 312, Figure 10.5; **Figure 10.5 (p. 273, left):** Photo by Eliot Elisofon/The LIFE Picture Collection/Getty Images; **Figure 10.5 (p. 273, right):** MJ Photography/Alamy Stock Photo; **Figure 10.6 (p. 274):** Agustín Fuentes, *Core Concepts in Biological Anthropology*, McGraw Hill 2007: 317, Figure 10.9; **Figure 10.7 (p. 275):** OUP; **Figure 10.8 (p. 276):** public domain, originally published in *Harper's Weekly*; **Figure 10.9 (p. 277):** public domain via archive.org; **Thinking Like an Anthropologist (p. 279):** public domain; **Classic Contributions (p. 281):** AP Photo; **Figure 10.10 (p. 282):** Agustín Fuentes, *Core Concepts in Biological Anthropology*, McGraw Hill 2007: 65, Figure 2.18; **Doing Fieldwork (p. 286):** Thomas McDade

CHAPTER 11

Chapter opening (p. 290): Photo by Joe Raedle/Getty Images; **Anthropologist as Problem Solver (p. 295):** Photo by Nancy Travers, 2009, courtesy of Kim Hopper; **Figure 11.1 (p. 296):** Used by permission of Documentary Educational Resources, Inc.; **Figure 11.2 (p. 296):** YASUYOSHI CHIBA/AFP/Getty Images; **Figure 11.3 (p. 298):** AP Photo/Jerome Delay; **Figure 11.4a (p. 300):** George Grantham Bain Collection (Library of Congress); **Figure 11.4b (p. 300):** public domain; **Figure 11.4c (p. 300):** Library of Congress Prints and Photographs Division Washington, D.C.;

CHAPTER 16

Chapter opening (p. 421): by Apa Hugo, courtesy of Robert L. Welsch; **Figure 16.1 (p. 423):** © Anthony Bannister/Gallo Images/Corbis; **Figure 16.2 (p. 428):** by Apa Hugo, courtesy of Robert L. Welsch; **Thinking Like an Anthropologist (p. 430):** AP Photo/Murad Sezer; **Anthropologist as Problem Solver (p. 431):** Maxwell Owusu/Shafica Ahmed; **Figure 16.3 (p. 434):** *The Burning of Jamestown* by Howard Pyle; **Figure 16.4 (p. 435):** from *Pudd'nhead Wilson and Those Extraordinary Twins* by Mark Twain (1894), via HathiTrust; **Figure 16.5 (p. 438):** Used by permission of Documentary Educational Resources, Inc.; **Figure 16.6 (p. 440):** AP Photo; **Figure 16.7 (p. 442):** Daily Mail/Rex/Alamy Stock Photo

CHAPTER 17

Chapter opening (p. 448): Photo by Edgar Negrete/Clasos.com/LatinContent/Getty Images; **Figure 17.1 (p. 452):** OUP; **Figure 17.2 (p. 453, top):** James Willard Schultz, Photographer. Merrill G. Burlingame Special Collections at Montana State University Libraries; **Figure 17.2 (p. 453, bottom):** Courtesy of Robert L. Welsch; **Figure 17.3 (p. 454):** OUP; **Thinking Like an Anthropologist (p. 456):** © Trevor Thompson/Alamy Stock Photo; **Figure 17.4 (p. 459, top):** Library of Congress Prints and Photographs Division Washington, D.C. 20540 USA; **Figure 17.4 (p. 459, bottom):** GEORGE FREY/AFP/Getty Images; **Figure 17.5 (p. 460):** © Iris Images/Corbis; **Classic Contributions (p. 462):** Photo by George Rose/Getty Images; **Figure 17.6 (p. 463):** FABRICE COFFRINI/AFP/Getty Images; **Figure 17.7 (p. 463):** Photo courtesy of Kirk and Karen Endicott; **Figure 17.8 (p. 464, top):** Photo by Keystone/Getty Images; **Figure 17.8 (p. 464, bottom):** Photo by David Fenton/Getty Images; **Figure 17.9 (p. 465):** Jonatan Fernstrom/Getty Images; **Figure 17.10 (p. 467):** Photo by David Victor; **Figure 17.11 (p. 468):** INDRANIL MUKHERJEE/AFP/Getty Images; **Figure 17.12 (p. 470):** Photo by Arthur Siegel/The LIFE Images Collection/Getty Images

CHAPTER 18

Chapter opening (p. 476): AP Photo/BH; **Figure 18.1 (p. 480):** National Archives American West Photographs; **Figure 18.2 (p. 480):** Photo by SSPL/Getty Images; **Figure 18.3 (p. 482, top):** Photo by Dan Kitwood/Getty Images; **Figure 18.3 (p. 482, bottom):** AP Photo/Jessica Kourkounis; **Figure 184 (p. 483):** Photo by 2001 The Record (Bergen Co. NJ)/Getty Images; **Figure 18.5 (p. 484):** press handout; **Figure 18.6 (p. 486):** 53.65.13194/probably Elema People/Eastern Papuan Gulf; Papua New Guinea; Melanesia; Oceania/*Barkcloth Mask (Eharo)*, collected 1885/Bark cloth, rattan, plant fiber and pith, natural pigment (black, white, and red)/Overall: 29 1/2 × 14 1/2 × 4 15/16 in. (75 × 36.8 × 12.5 cm)/Hood Museum of Art, Dartmouth College, Hanover, New Hampshire; **Figure 18.7 (p. 487):** Edward S. Curtis Collection (Library of Congress); **Figure 18.8 (p. 488):** 2001.51.34345/Yoruba people/Nigeria/Guinea Coast/Africa/Scepter, 19th century/Bronze with leather bound handle/Overall: 14 3/8 × 4 3/16 × 2 3/16 in. (36.5 × 10.7 × 5.5 cm)/Hood Museum of Art, Dartmouth College, Hanover, New Hampshire; gift of Peter H. Voulkos; photography by Jeffrey Nintzel; **Classic Contributions (p. 492):** © National Portrait Gallery, London; **Figure 18.9 (p. 493):** 29.58.7934/Inuit/Canada/Arctic/North America/*Fishhook Decorated with an Ivory Seal*, late 19th or early 20th century/Brass, copper, ivory, and sinew/Hood Museum of Art, Dartmouth College; photography by Jeffrey Nintzel; **Figure 18.10 (p. 493):** Courtesy of Robert L. Welsch; **Figure 18.11 (p. 494):** AP Photo/Chris Clark; **Thinking Like an Anthropologist (p. 495):** Photo by Mario Tama/Getty Images; **Figure 18.12 (p. 497):** © 1966 Time Inc. All rights reserved. Licensed from TIME and published with permission of Time Inc. Reproduction in any manner in any language in whole or in part without written permission is prohibited; **Doing Fieldwork (p. 499):** Photo by Frank Bienewald/LightRocket via Getty Images

CHAPTER 19

Chapter opening (p. 502): © Ermanno Iselle | Dreamstime.com; **Figure 19.1 (p. 504):** Ruth Van Steenwyk; **Figure 19.2 (p. 506):** Photo by Diane Alexander White and Linda Dorman, courtesy of The Field Museum, GN85650c; **Figure 19.3 (p. 510):** Courtesy of Kellen Haak/the Hood Museum of Art; **The Anthropologist as Problem Solver (p. 511):** © The Field Museum. GN91326_119d. Photo by John Weinstein (top); © The Field Museum. A112518c, Catalog No. 143961 (bottom); **Figure 19.4 (p. 513):** Courtesy of Luis A. Vivanco; **Figure 19.5 (p. 515):** 996.22.30233/Solongo style/Kongo people/Angola/

Democratic Republic of Congo/Central Africa/Africa/Nkisi Nkondi, Power Figure, 19th century/Wood and mixed medium/Overall: 23 in. (58.42 cm)/Overall: 23 1/16 in. (58.5 cm)/Hood Museum of Art, Dartmouth College: purchased through the Mrs. Harvey P. Hood W'18 Fund, the William B. Jaffe and Evelyn A. Jaffe Hall Fund, the William B. Jaffe Memorial Fund, the William S. Rubin Fund, the Julia L. Whittier Fund and through gifts, by exchange; photography by Jeffrey Nintzel; **Figure 19.6 (p. 517):** Courtesy of Robert L. Welsch; **Figure 19.7 (p. 519):** Courtesy of Paradigm PR; **Figure 19.8 (p. 520):** Private Collection/The Stapleton Collection/Bridgeman Images; **Thinking Like an Anthropologist (p. 521, top):** Museum of Archaeology and Anthropology, University of Cambridge; **Thinking Like an Anthropologist (p. 521, bottom):** David Rumsey Map Collection via Wikipedia (public domain); **Figure 19.9 (p. 523):** AP Photo/Bebeto Matthews; **Figure 19.10 (p. 523):** STAN HONDA/AFP/Getty Images; **Figure 19.11 (p. 525):** BornaMir/iStockphoto

Text Credits

INSIDE FRONT COVER

American Anthropological Association. 2012. *Statement on Ethics: Principles of Professional Responsibilities.* Arlington, VA: American Anthropological Association. Available at: http://www .aaanet.org/profdev/ethics/upload/Statement-on-Ethics-Principles-of-Professional-Responsibility.pdf

CHAPTER 1

Classic Contributions (p. 11): Tylor, E. B. 1871. *Primitive Culture: Researches into the Development of Mythology, Philosophy, Religion, Art, and Custom.* London: John Murray. (p. 1)

CHAPTER 2

Classic Contributions (p. 38): Boas, Franz. 1940. *Race, Language, and Culture.* New York: Macmillan. (p. 636)

CHAPTER 3

Classic Contributions (p. 65): Kluckhohn, Clyde. 1959. "The Role of Evolutionary Thought in Anthropology." In Betty J. Meggers, ed. *Evolution and Anthropology: A Centennial Appraisal.* Washington, D.C.: The Anthropological Society of Washington, p. 154.

CHAPTER 4

Classic Contributions (p. 87): Leakey, Richard and Roger Lewin. 1977. *Origins: What New Discoveries Reveal About the Emergence of our Species and Its Possible Future.* New York: E.P. Dutton, pp. 84–5.

CHAPTER 5

Classic Contributions (p. 127): Sapir, Edward. 1929. "The Status of Linguistics as a Science." *Language* 5(4): 207–14. (pp. 209–210)

CHAPTER 6

Classic Contributions (p. 150): Wolf, Eric. 1984. *Europe and the People without History.* Berkeley: University of California Press. (pp. 17–18)

CHAPTER 7

Classic Contributions (p. 190): Washburn, S.L. (1951) "The New Physical Anthropology." *Transactions of the New York Academy of Sciences.* Vol. 13, Issue 7, Series II: 298–304.

CHAPTER 8

Classic Contributions (p. 222): Black, Davidson. 1933. "On the Endocranial Cast of the Adolescent Sinanthropus Skull." *Proceedings of the Royal Society of London, Series B, Containing Papers of a Biological Character* 112(776):263–276 (Jan 2, 1933).

CHAPTER 9

Classic Contributions (p. 244): Wright, Sewall. 1932. "The Roles of Mutation, Inbreeding, Crossbreeding and Selection in Evolution." *Proceedings of the Sixth International Congress of Genetics*, Vol. 1:356–366.

CHAPTER 10

Classic Contributions (p. 281): Montagu, Ashley. 1997. *Man's Most Dangerous Myth: The Fallacy of Race*. Sixth edition. Walnut Creek, CA: AltaMira Press, pp. 41–2. [Originally published 1942.]

CHAPTER 11

Classic Contributions (p. 302): Kleinman, Arthur. 1975. "Social, Cultural and Historical Themes in the Study of Medicine in Chinese Societies: Problems and Prospects for the Comparative Study of Medicine and Psychiatry." In A. Kleinman et al., eds. *Medicine in Chinese Cultures: Comparative Studies of Health Care in Chinese and Other Societies*. Papers and Discussions from a Conference Held in Seattle, Washington, U.S.A., February 1974, pp. 589–657. Washington, DC: U.S. Department of Health, Education, and Welfare. (pp. 652–653)

CHAPTER 12

Classic Contributions (p. 328): Childe, V. Gordon. 1936. *Man Makes Himself*. London: Watts & Co.

CHAPTER 13

Classic Contributions (p. 351): Carneiro, Robert L. 1974. "Slash-and-Burn Cultivation Among the Kuikuru and Its Implications for Cultural Development." In Patricia J. Lyon, ed., *Native South Americans*, pp. 73–91. Boston, MA: Little, Brown and Company.

CHAPTER 14

Classic Contributions (p. 377): Sahlins, Marshall. 1965. "On the Sociology of Primitive Exchange." In M. Banton, ed., *The Relevance of Models for Social Anthropology*, pp. 123–236. ASA Monographs, 1. London: Tavistock. (pp. 139–140)

CHAPTER 15

Classic Contributions (p. 399): Rappaport, Roy. 1984. *Pigs for the Ancestors: Ritual in the Ecology of a New Guinea People*. 2nd Edition. Prospect Heights, IL: Waveland Press. (pp. 237–238)

CHAPTER 16

Classic Contributions (p. 436): Powdermaker, Hortense. 1944. *Probing Our Prejudices: A Unit for High School Students*. New York: Harper and Brothers Publishers. (pp. 29–30)

CHAPTER 17

Classic Contributions (p. 462): Mead, Margaret. 1935/1963. *Sex and Temperament in Three Primitive Societies*. New York: William Morrow. (pp. 280–281)

CHAPTER 18

Classic Contributions (p. 492): Frazer, James G. 1890. *The Golden Bough: A Study in Comparative Religion*. 1st Edition. 2 Vols. London: Macmillan. (pp. 9–10)

CHAPTER 19

Classic Contributions (p. 516): Munn, Nancy D. 1962. "Walbiri Graphic Signs: An Analysis." *American Anthropologist* 64(5, pt. 1): 972–84. (p. 981)

Index